THE HISTORY OF JAZZ

SECOND EDITION

Ted Gioia

OXFORD
UNIVERSITY PRESS

OXFORD
UNIVERSITY PRESS

Oxford University Press, Inc., publishes works that further
Oxford University's objective of excellence
in research, scholarship, and education.

Oxford New York
Auckland Cape Town Dar es Salaam Hong Kong Karachi
Kuala Lumpur Madrid Melbourne Mexico City Nairobi
New Delhi Shanghai Taipei Toronto

With offices in
Argentina Austria Brazil Chile Czech Republic France Greece
Guatemala Hungary Italy Japan Poland Portugal Singapore
South Korea Switzerland Thailand Turkey Ukraine Vietnam

Published by Oxford University Press, Inc.
198 Madison Avenue, New York, New York 10016

www.oup.com

Oxford is a registered trademark of Oxford University Press.

Library of Congress Cataloging-in-Publication Data
Gioia, Ted.
The history of jazz / Ted Gioia. — 2nd ed.
p. cm.
Includes bibliographical references and index.
ISBN 978-0-19-539970-7
1. Jazz—History and criticism. I. Title.
ML3506.G54 2011
781.6509—dc22   2010023182

All photographs in this book are courtesy of The Frank Driggs Collection.

15 17 19 18 16 14
Printed in the United States of America
on acid-free paper

for my wife, Tara

Contents

3   1. The Prehistory of Jazz

27   2. New Orleans Jazz

53   3. The Jazz Age

89   4. Harlem

127   5. The Swing Era

185   6. Modern Jazz

253   7. The Fragmentation of Jazz Styles

309   8. Freedom and Fusion

345   9. Traditionalists and Postmodernists

369   10. Jazz in the New Millennium

389   Notes

399   Further Reading

403   Recommended Listening

419   Acknowledgments

421   Index

The History of Jazz

1 The Prehistory of Jazz

THE AFRICANIZATION OF AMERICAN MUSIC

An elderly black man sits astride a large cylindrical drum. Using his fingers and the edge of his hand, he jabs repeatedly at the drumhead—which is around a foot in diameter and probably made from an animal skin—evoking a throbbing pulsation with rapid, sharp strokes. A second drummer, holding his instrument between his knees, joins in, playing with the same staccato attack. A third black man, seated on the ground, plucks at a stringed instrument, the body of which is roughly fashioned from a calabash. Another calabash has been made into a drum, and a woman beats at it with two short sticks. One voice, then other voices join in. A dance of seeming contradictions accompanies this musical give-and-take, a moving hieroglyph that appears, on the one hand, informal and spontaneous yet, on closer inspection, ritualized and precise. It is a dance of massive proportions. A dense crowd of dark bodies forms into circular groups—perhaps five or six hundred individuals moving in time to the pulsations of the music, some swaying gently, others aggressively stomping their feet. A number of women in the group begin chanting.

The scene could be Africa. In fact, it is nineteenth-century New Orleans. Scattered firsthand accounts provide us with tantalizing details of the slave dances that took place in the open area then known as Congo Square—today Louis Armstrong Park stands on roughly the same ground—and there are perhaps no more intriguing documents in the history of African American music. Benjamin Latrobe, the noted architect, witnessed one of these collective dances on February 21, 1819, and not only left us a vivid written account of the event but made several sketches of the instruments used. These drawings confirm that the musicians of Congo Square, circa 1819, were playing percussion and stringed instruments virtually identical to those characteristic of indigenous African music.

Later documents add to our knowledge of the public slave dances in New Orleans but still leave us with many open questions—some of which, in time, historical research may be able to elucidate, while others might never be answered. One thing, however, is clear. Although we are inclined these days to view the intersection of black and white musical currents as a theoretical, almost symbolic issue, these storied accounts of the Congo Square dances provide us with a real time and place, an actual transfer of totally African ritual to the native soil of the New World. "Congo Square may have looked like it was nothing but a party," music historian Ned Sublette has written, "but to play a hand drum in 1819 in the United States, where overt manifestations of Africanness had elsewhere been so thoroughly, deliberately erased, was a tremendous act of will, memory and resistance."[1]

The dances in Congo Square were a nexus where opposites collided. The ingrained Western division between performer and audience was eradicated—a distinction so fundamental to us, but of such little importance in traditional African cultures. The separation of song from dance, also pervasive among Western thinkers who deal with the arts, was equally nullified, replaced with a more intrinsically African congruence of sound and movement. These gatherings, a mixture of the ceremonial and social, further broke down barriers between secular and spiritual impulses—a firsthand account from 1808 even uses the word *worship* to describe them.

The dances themselves, marked by clusters of individuals moving in a circular pattern—the largest less than ten feet in diameter—harken back to one of the most pervasive ritual ceremonies of Africa. This rotating, counterclockwise movement has been noted by ethnographers under many guises in various parts of the continent. In the Americas, the dance became known as the ring shout, a ritual that, in the words of scholar Sterling Stuckey, served as "the main context in which Africans recognized values common to them."[2] The appearance of this African carryover in New Orleans is only one of many documented instances in the New World. This tradition persisted well into the twentieth century: John and Alan Lomax recorded a ring shout in Louisiana for the Library of Congress in 1934 and attended others in Texas, Georgia, and the Bahamas. As late as the 1950s, jazz scholar Marshall Stearns witnessed unmistakable examples of the ring shout in South Carolina.

The Congo Square dances were hardly so long-lived. Traditional accounts indicate that they continued, except for an interruption during the Civil War, until around 1885. Such a chronology implies that their disappearance almost coincided with the emergence of the first jazz bands in New Orleans. More recent research argues convincingly for an earlier cutoff date for the practice, probably before 1870, although the dances may have continued for some time in private settings.[3] But even after the public gatherings came to halt, the tradition of the ring shout lived on in many ways. Samuel Floyd has gone so far as to contend that the ring later "straightened itself to become the Second Line of jazz funerals." Here, he writes, "the movements of the participants were identical to those of the participants in the ring—even to the point of individual counterclockwise movements by Second Line participants." Only the ring itself was missing, since the participants had a set destination, and needed to direct their movements back to town from the cemetery.[4]

Above all, this transplanted African ritual loomed large in the collective memory and oral history of the city's black community, even among those too young to have participated in it. These memories shaped, in turn, the jazz performers' self-image, their sense of what it meant to be an African American musician. "My grandfather, that's about the furthest I can remember back," wrote the renowned New Orleans reed player Sidney Bechet in his autobiography, *Treat It Gentle*. "Sundays when the slaves would meet— that was their free day—he beat out rhythms on the drums at the square—Congo Square they called it. . . . He was a musician. No one had to explain notes or feeling or rhythm to him. It was all there inside him, something he was always sure of."[5]

Within eyesight of Congo Square, Buddy Bolden—who legend and scattered first-person accounts credit as the earliest jazz musician—performed with his pioneering band at Globe Hall. The geographical proximity is misleading. The cultural gap between these two types of music is dauntingly wide. By the time Bolden and Bechet began playing jazz, the Americanization of African music had already begun, and with it came the Africanization of American music—a synergistic process that we will study repeatedly and at close quarters in the pages that follow. Anthropologists call this process *syncretism*—the blending together of cultural elements that previously existed separately. This dynamic, so essential to the history of jazz, remains powerful even in the present day, when African American styles of performance blend seamlessly with other musics of other cultures, European, Asian, Latin, and, coming full circle, African.

The mixture of African and European culture began, of course, long before the slave dances in Congo Square—in fact, at least one thousand years prior to the founding of New Orleans in 1718. The question of African influence on ancient Western culture has become a matter of heated debate in recent years—with much of the dispute centering on arcane methodological and theoretical issues. But once again, careful students of history need not rely on abstract analysis to discover early cultural mergings of African and European currents. The North African conquest of the Iberian peninsula in the eighth century left a tangible impact on Europe—evident even today in the distinctive qualities of Spanish architecture, painting, and music. Had not Charles Martel repelled the Moorish forces in the south of France at the Battle of Tours in 732 A.D., this stylized cultural syncretism might have become a pan-European force. If not for "the genius and fortune" of this one man, historian Gibbon would declare in *The Decline and Fall of the Roman Empire*, the Moorish fleet "might have sailed without a naval combat into the mouth of the Thames" and "the Koran would now be taught in the schools of Oxford."[6]

As it turned out, the spread of African currents into the broader streams of Western culture took far longer to unfold, spurred in large part by defeat rather than conquest—not by triumphant naval fleets toppling the continental powers, but by the dismal commerce of slave ships headed for the New World. Yet the traces of the early Moorish incursion may have laid the groundwork for the blossoming of African American jazz more than a millennium later. Can it be mere coincidence that this same commingling of Spanish, French, and African influences was present in New Orleans at the birth of jazz? Perhaps because of this marked Moorish legacy, Latin cultures have always seemed receptive to fresh influences from Africa. Indeed, in the area of music alone, the number of successful African and Latin hybrids (including salsa, calypso, samba, tango, and cumbia, to name only a few) is so great that one can only speculate that these two cultures retain a residual magnetic attraction, a lingering affinity due to this original cross-fertilization. Perhaps this convoluted chapter of Western history also provides us with the key for unlocking that enigmatic claim by Jelly Roll Morton, the pioneering New Orleans jazz musician, who asserted, "if you can't manage to put tinges of Spanish in your tunes, you will never be able to get the right seasoning, I call it, for jazz."[7]

The Latin tinge was already a long-established fact of New Orleans music well before the arrival of jazz on the scene—perhaps not surprising for a city that was still only around one-eighth Anglo-American in the years following the Louisiana Purchase. Around the time of Morton's birth, a massive Mexican cavalry band performed daily in free concerts at the Mexican Pavilion as part of the 1884–85 World's Cotton Centennial Exposition in New Orleans. A little-known and undated work, titled "Los Campanillas," by black New Orleans composer Basile Barès (1845–1902), effectively employs a Cuban habanera rhythm long before W. C. Handy relied on it to make "St. Louis Blues" into a hit, or Morton himself adopted it for his composition "The Crave." Even earlier, Louis Moreau Gottschalk enjoyed a transatlantic success with his composition *Bamboula*. As these examples attest, the "tinge" entered the parlors of the city's many amateur pianists long before the appearance of jazz music. Responding to this demand, Hart's music store on Canal Street published over eighty Mexican compositions during the late nineteenth century, influencing local instrumentalists and providing one more link in the complex history of interlocking Latin and African American musical styles.

Beyond its purely musicological impact, the Latin-Catholic culture, whose influence permeated nineteenth-century New Orleans, benignly fostered the development of jazz music. This culture, which bore its own scars of discrimination, was far more tolerant in accepting unorthodox social hybrids than the English-Protestant ethos that prevailed in other parts of the New World. Under Spanish law, slaves could be set free without official permission, could own property, and had the right of *coartación*, which allowed them to purchase their own freedom based on an adjudicated contract. This comparatively less rigid atmosphere helped shape attitudes and behavior patterns in New Orleans; indeed, it is hard to imagine the dances of Congo Square taking place in the more Anglicized colonies of the Americas.

Less than half a century after the city's founding, in 1764, New Orleans was ceded by France to Spain. In 1800, Napoleon succeeded in forcing its return from Spain, but this renewed French control lasted only three years before possession passed to the United States as part of the Louisiana Purchase. As a result, French and Spanish settlers played a decisive role in shaping the distinctive ambiance of New Orleans during the early nineteenth century, yet immigrants from Germany, Italy, England, Ireland, and Scotland also made substantial contributions to the local culture. The city's black inhabitants were equally diverse: many had been transported directly from various parts of Africa, especially from Senegambia, in the early years of French settlement;[8] some were native-born Americans; still others came to the United States via the Caribbean. Civil unrest in Hispaniola was especially influential in bringing new immigrants, both black and white, to New Orleans: in 1808 alone, as many as six thousand refugees fleeing the Haitian revolution arrived in the city, after being forced to leave Cuba. The resulting amalgam—an unprecedented mixture of European, Caribbean, African, and American elements—made Louisiana into perhaps the most seething ethnic melting pot that the nineteenth-century world could produce.

This cultural gumbo would serve as breeding ground for many of the great hybrid musics of modern times. Not just jazz, but also cajun, zydeco, blues, and other new styles flourished as a result of this laissez-faire environment. In New Orleans warm, moist atmosphere, sharp delineations between groups and customs gradually softened and ultimately gave way. Today, the city's residents of Irish descent celebrate St Patrick's Day by parading in a Second Line of their own. At Mardi Gras time, black celebrants still dress up as Native Americans, sometimes adopting costumes that cost thousands of dollars—a practice that dates back to the nineteenth century. Consider, as well, the distinctive culinary arts of the region, with their creative mixture of French, Spanish, African, Choctaw, German, and other traditions. Locals here are hardly surprised by fluid rituals that refuse to be limited by racial or ethnic categories. Indeed, the masquerades of Mardi Gras are a fitting symbol for this city, where the most familiar cultural artifacts appear in the strangest garb.

Yet the decisive creative currents in this society came from the African American underclass. Should this surprise us? The reputation of musicians, and other performing artists, as outsiders or pariahs, as practitioners who exist at the limits of the socially acceptable, has a long tradition dating back to ancient times. Just a few decades ago, many cultures still retained religious prohibitions asserting the "uncleanliness" of believers eating at the same table as musicians. And long before music became a consumer product, one more form of idle entertainment for the masses, it was the domain of mystics and magicians, the excluded and ostracized. The story of jazz moving into the center of society from a starting point at the fringes is but one more chapter in this ongoing saga.

Even so, the role of slave labor in the production of African American song makes for an especially sad interlude in this melancholy history. The presence of Africans in the New World, the first documented instance of which occurred in Jamestown in 1619, predated the arrival of the Pilgrims by one year. By 1807, some 400,000 native-born Africans had been brought to America,[9] most of them transported from West Africa. Forcibly taken away from their homeland, deprived of their freedom, and torn from the social fabric that had given structure to their lives, these unwilling immigrants clung with even greater fervor to those elements of their culture that they could carry with them. Music and folktales were among the most resilient of these. Even after family, home, and possessions were taken away, they remained.

In this context, the decision of the New Orleans City Council, in 1817, to establish an official site for slave dances stands out as an exemplary degree of tolerance. In other locales, African elements in the slaves' music were discouraged or explicitly suppressed. During the Stono Rebellion of 1739, drums had been used to signal an attack on the white population. Anxious to prevent further uprisings, South Carolina banned any use of drums by slaves. The Georgia code went even further in prohibiting not only drums, but also horns or other loud instruments. Religious organizations assisted in the efforts to control the African elements of the slaves' music. The *Hymns and Spiritual*

Songs of Dr. Isaac Watts, published in various colonial editions beginning in the early 1700s, was frequently used as a way of "converting" African Americans through more edifying examples of Western music.

We are fortunate that these attempts bore little success. Indeed, in many cases, the reverse of the intended effect took place: European idioms were transformed and enriched by the African tradition onto which they were grafted. Alan Lomax, the pioneering scholar and preserver of African American music, writes:

Blacks had Africanized the psalms to such an extent that many observers described black lining hymns as a mysterious African music. In the first place, they so prolonged and quavered the texts of the hymns that only a recording angel could make out what was being sung. Instead of performing in an individualized sort of unison or heterophony, however, they blended their voices in great unified streams of tone. There emerged a remarkable kind of harmony, in which every singer was performing variations on the melody at his or her pitch, yet all these ornaments contributed to a polyphony of many ever changing strands—surging altogether like seaweed swinging with the waves or a leafy tree responding to a strong wind. Experts have tried and failed to transcribe this river-like style of polyphony. It rises from a group in which all singers can improvise together, each one contributing something personal to an ongoing collective effect—a practice common in African and African-American tradition. The outcome is music as powerful and original as jazz, but profoundly melancholy, for it was sung into being by hard-pressed people.[10]

This ability of African performance arts to transform the European tradition of composition while assimilating some of its elements is perhaps the most striking and powerful evolutionary force in the history of modern music. The genres of music that bear the marks of this influence are legion. Let's name a few: gospel, spirituals, soul, rap, minstrel songs, Broadway musicals, ragtime, jazz, blues, R&B, rock, samba, reggae, funk, salsa, calypso, even some contemporary operatic and symphonic music.

The history of jazz is closely intertwined with many of these other hybrid genres, and tracing the various genealogies can prove dauntingly complex. For example, minstrel shows, which developed in the decades before the Civil War, found white performers in blackface mimicking, and most often ridiculing, the music, dance, and culture of the slave population. Frequently the writer of minstrel songs worked with little actual knowledge of southern black music. A surprising number of these composers hailed from the Northeast, and the most celebrated writer of minstrel-inflected songs, Stephen Foster, created a powerful, romanticized image of southern folk life despite the most limited firsthand contact—his travels in the Deep South were restricted to a single trip down the Mississippi to New Orleans.[11] Later generations of black entertainers, influenced by the popularity of these secondhand evocations of their own culture, imitated in turn the white stereotypes of African American behavior. Thus, in its impact on early jazz, minstrel music presents a rather convoluted lineage: a black imitation of a white caricature of black music exerts its influence on another hybrid form of African and European music.

The work song, another frequently cited predecessor to jazz, is more purely African in nature—so much so that some examples recorded in the southern United States in the last century show almost no European or American influence. Here, for once, brute economics served to preserve rather than eradicate African traditions, with even the most callous overseers encouraging music making when it contributed to the productivity of the laborer. This ritualized vocalizing of black American workers, with its proud disregard for Western systems of notation and scales, came in many variants: field hollers, levee camp hollers, prison work songs, street cries, and the like. This entire category of singing has all but disappeared in our day, yet the few surviving recordings documenting this time-honored tradition reveal a powerful, evocative, and comparatively undiluted form of African music in the Americas.[12]

Generalizations about African music are tricky at best. Many commentators have treated the culture of West Africa as though it were a homogenous and unified body of practices. In fact, many different elements contribute to the traditions of West Africa. Even so, a few shared characteristics stand out, amid this plurality, in any study of African music—with many of these same ingredients reappearing, in a somewhat different guise, in jazz. For example, call-and-response forms that predominate in African music figure as well in the work song, the blues, jazz, and other Americanized strains of African music; yet, in its original African form, call-and-response is as much a matter of social integration as a method of performing music. It reflects a culture in which the fundamental Western separation of audience from artists is transcended. This brings us to a second unifying element of African musical traditions: the integration of performance into the social fabric. In this light, African music takes on an aura of functionality, one that defies any "pure" aesthetic attempting to separate art from social needs. Yet, since these functions are often tied to rituals and other liminal experiences, music never falls into the mundane type of functionality— background music in the dentist's office, accompaniment to a television commercial, and so on—that one sees increasingly in the West. Integrated into ritual occasions, music retains its otherworldliness for the African, its ability to rise above the here and now. The cross-fertilization between music and dance is a third unifying theme in traditional African cultures—so deeply ingrained that scholar John Miller Chernoff remarks that, for an African, "understanding" a certain type of music means, in its most fundamental sense, knowing what dance it accompanies.[13] A fourth predominant feature of African music is the focus on sounds in instances where Western composers would rely on notes—one of the results of this profound shift in perspective is the use of instruments to emulate the subtle modulations of the human voice. This technique, which also plays a key role in early jazz music, even extends to percussion instruments, most notably in the *kalangu*, the remarkable talking drum of West Africa. An emphasis on improvisation and spontaneity is a further shared trait of different African musical cultures, and these too have figured prominently in—and, to some extent, have come to define—the later jazz tradition.

However, the most distinctive characteristic, the core element of African music, is its extraordinary richness of rhythmic content. It is here one discovers the essence of the African musical heritage, as well as the key to unlocking the mystery of its tremendous influence on so many disparate schools of twentieth-century music. The first Western scholars who attempted to come to grips with this rhythmic vitality, whether in its African or Americanized form, struggled merely to find a vocabulary and notational method to encompass it. Henry Edward Krehbiel, author of an early study of African American folk songs, conveys the frustration of these endeavors in describing the African musicians he encountered at the World's Columbian Exposition, held in Chicago in 1893:

The players showed the most remarkable rhythmical sense and skill that ever came under my notice. Berlioz in his supremest effort with his army of drummers produced nothing to compare in artistic interest with the harmonious drumming of these savages. The fundamental effect was a combination of double and triple time, the former kept by the singers, the latter by the drummers, but it is impossible to convey the idea of the wealth of detail achieved by the drummers by means of the exchange of the rhythms, syncopations of both simultaneously, and dynamic devices.[14]

Krehbiel engaged the services of John Comfort Fillmore, an expert in Native American music, in an attempt to notate the playing of these musicians, but eventually they gave up in despair. "I was forced to the conclusion," Krehbiel later recalled, in an account in which irritation and awe are present in equal doses, "that in their command of the [rhythmic] element, which in the musical art of the ancient Greeks stood higher than either melody or harmony, the best composers of today were the veriest tyros compared with these black savages."

The vocabularies of certain Eskimo tribes, we are told, possess dozens of words for *snow*—where other cultures see only an undifferentiated substance, they perceive subtle differences and a plethora of significations. Similarly, for the African, virtually every object of day-to-day life could be a source of rhythm, an instrument of percussion, and an inspiration for the dance. The tools and implements with which the African subdued the often hostile surrounding environment may well have been the first sources of instrumental music on our planet. Here we perhaps come to realize the hidden truth in the double meaning of the word *instrument*, which signifies both a mechanism for altering the natural world and a device for creating sound. We begin with the given: shells, flints, animal hides, trees, stones, sticks. And we end up with a dazzling array of instruments, both implements used in day-to-day life—weapons, tools, wheels, building devices—and in music making—drums, rattles, scrapers, gongs, clappers, friction instruments, percussion boards, and the like. But even earlier, the human body itself must have served as a rich source of musical sound. "Despite the non-African's conception of African music in terms of drums," historian John Storm Roberts has pointed out, "the African instruments most often used by the greatest number of people in the greatest variety of societies are the human voice and the human hands, used for clapping."[15] Both approaches to music—one that reached out and found it in the external world, the second that drew it from the physiological characteristics of the human form—came with the African to America.

In the 1930s, researchers working for the Federal Writers' Project undertook a comprehensive program of recording the memoirs of former slaves. This collection, housed today at the Archive of Folksong at the Library of Congress, provides telling insight into this distinctive African American ability—strikingly similar to native African practices—to extract music from the detritus of day-to-day life. "There wasn't no music instruments," reads the oral history of former slave Wash Wilson. Drums were fashioned out of a variety of discarded items: "pieces of sheep's rib or cow's jaw or a piece of iron, with an old kettle, or a hollow gourd and some horsehairs."

Sometimes they'd get a piece of tree trunk and hollow it out and stretch a goat's or sheep's skin over it for the drum. They'd be one to four foot high and a foot up to six foot across. . . . They'd take the buffalo horn and scrape it out to make the flute. That sho' be heard a long ways off. Then they'd take a mule's jawbone and rattle the stick across its teeth. They'd take a barrel and stretch an ox's hide across one end and a man sat astride the barrel and beat on that hide with his hands and his feet and if he got to feel the music in his bones, he'd beat on that barrel with his head. Another man beat on wooden sides with sticks.[16]

This ingenuity in creating percussion instruments was accompanied by a corresponding richness of rhythmic impulses. In African music, in both its original and its various Americanized forms, different pulses are frequently superimposed, creating powerful polyrhythms that are perhaps the most striking and characteristic aspect of these traditions. In the same way that Bach might intermingle different but interrelated melodies in creating a fugue, an African ensemble would construct layer upon layer of rhythmic patterns, forging a counterpoint of implied time signatures, a polyphony of percussion. We will encounter this multiplicity of rhythms again and again in our study of African American music, from the lilting syncopations of ragtime to the diverse offbeat accents of the bebop drummer, to the jarring cross-rhythms of the jazz avant-garde.

Theorists of rhythm often dwell on its liberating and Dionysian element, but the history of rhythm as a source of social control and power has yet to be written. The historian Johan Huizinga hypothesized that the introduction of drums into the ranks of soldiers marked the end of the feudal age of chivalry and signaled the beginning of modern warfare, with its coordinated regiments and precise military discipline.[17] Perhaps the unobtrusive and steady rhythms of modern office music—and is not Muzak the work song of our own age?—serve today to exert a subtle control over the white-collar worker of postindustrialized society. In any event, both aspects of rhythm—on the one hand, as a source of liberation and, on the other, as a force of discipline and control— make their presence felt in African American music. The work song was the melody of disciplined labor, and even here its source could be traced back to Africa. "The African tradition, like the European peasant tradition, stressed hard work and derided laziness in any form," writes historian Eugene D. Genovese in his seminal study of slave society *Roll, Jordan, Roll.*[18] The celebration of labor, inherent in the African American work song, must otherwise seem strangely out of place coming from an oppressed race consigned to the indignities of slavery. But as soon as one sees the song of work as part of an inherently African approach to day-to-day life, one that integrates music into the occupations of here and now, this paradox disappears entirely.

If the work song reflects rhythm as a source of discipline, the blues represents the other side of African rhythms, the Dionysian side that offered release. More than any of the other forms of early African American music, the blues allowed the performer to present an individual statement of pain, oppression, poverty, longing, and desire. Yet it achieved all this without falling into self-pity and recriminations. Instead the blues offered a catharsis, an idealization of the individual's plight, and, in some strange way, an uplifting sense of mastery over the dire circumstances typically recounted in the context of these songs. In this regard, the blues offers us a psychological enigma as profound as any posed by classical tragedy. How art finds fulfillment—for both artist and audience—by dwelling on the oppressive and the tragic has been an issue for speculation at least since the time of Aristotle. Simply substitute the word *blues* for *tragedy* in most of these discussions, and we find ourselves addressing the same questions, only now in the context of African American music.

COUNTRY BLUES AND CLASSIC BLUES

Long before the blues became recognized as a distinct style of music, it lived a subterranean existence in African American communities. The blues would not emerge as a major force in the recording industry until the 1920s, but persistent scholars have uncovered earlier traces and hints of the music throughout the former slave states going back to the nineteenth century, especially in geographic settings with a high proportion of black sharecroppers and farmworkers. Unlike jazz, which first came to the fore in New Orleans and flourished in other large cities, early blues found its most fertile breeding ground in rural areas and the most impoverished parts of the country. This humble lineage is all the more ironic when one considers how much the financial well-being of the later entertainment industry in New York, Chicago, Los Angeles, London, and elsewhere would depend on this rustic music and its many offshoots in rock, R&B, funk, and other assorted urban genres.

Blues songs began appearing in sheet music form as early as 1912, none with more staying power than W. C. Handy's "St. Louis Blues" (1914), which would rank as the second most recorded song of the first half of the twentieth century, surpassed only by "Silent Night." The term *blues*—often misused to refer to any sad or mournful tune—is more properly linked, as we see in Handy's composition, to a precise structure that has come to be known as blues form. This repeating twelve-bar pattern is typically built on three chords—tonic, dominant, and subdominant—and would later serve as the foundation for countless jazz and popular songs, as well as take on a second life in the 1950s as a widely used recipe for rock-and-roll and R&B music. When sung, as it usually was in its earliest variants, the blues also employs a specific stanza form for its lyrics in which an initial line is stated, repeated, and then followed with a rhyming line. For example, Handy's "St. Louis Blues" begins:

> I hate to see that evenin' sun go down
> I hate to see that evenin' sun go down
> 'Cause my baby, he done lef' this town.

Yet this type of lyric and chord pattern are not sufficient to convey the essence of the blues. The most characteristic component of this music is found in its distinctive melodic lines, which emphasize the so-called blue notes: often described as the use of both the major and minor third in the vocal line, along with the flatted seventh; the flatted fifth was a later addition, but would in time become equally prominent as a blue note. In truth, this stock description is also somewhat misleading. In early blues, the major and minor thirds were not used interchangeably; instead the musician might employ a "bent" note that would slide between these two tonal centers, or create a tension by emphasizing the minor third in a context in which the harmony implied a major tone. Sometimes this effect was achieved by means of a melismatic shift in the voice of the blues singer, but even instrumentalists made use of this approach—most strikingly in the slide guitar techniques that relied on moving a bottle, knife, or other object across the fretboard to stretch the individual pitches. After the arrival of the blues, notes were no longer just notes, but flexible sounds that could change in ways unforeseen by the most renowned nineteenth-century composers.

Much speculation has been offered as to the historical origin of this powerful and unique melodic device; some commentators, for example, have suggested that this tonal ambiguity originated when the newly arrived slaves tried to reconcile an African pentatonic scale with the Western diatonic scale. This musical mash-up resulted in two areas of aural potency, situated around the third and seventh intervals—sounds that evolved into the modern blue notes. In any event, this effect, which is impossible to convey in traditional notation, is one of the most gut-wrenching ingredients in twentieth-century music. Given its visceral impact, this approach to singing and instrumental performance inevitably spread beyond the blues idiom into jazz and a host of other commercial performance styles.

The most traditional style of blues typically relies on just a vocal line with guitar accompaniment. Handy was inspired by just such a performance back in the Mississippi Delta, when he heard a raggedy musician playing a guitar with a knife at a train station in Tutwiler, circa 1903. But this minimalist style of performance, often referred to as "country blues," was slow in finding its way onto recordings. Not until the late 1920s, with the commercial success of Blind Lemon Jefferson, would this music demonstrate its clout in the marketplace. Jefferson, born near Wortham, Texas, in the closing years of the nineteenth century, employed a spare, riff-oriented guitar style behind his droning and resonant vocalizing. Although he was capable of raspy low tones, his voice was perhaps most admired for its thin, high tones—a stylistic device that, for many listeners, stands out as the most distinctive characteristic of the early Texas blues sound. Jefferson recorded around one hundred tracks for the Paramount label from 1926 through 1929, and his performances of songs such as "Long Lonesome Blues," "Matchbox Blues," and "See That My Grave Is Kept Clean" continue to delight fans today. Despite the efforts of various researchers, this artist's life remains clouded in mystery, and even the circumstances of his death are a matter of contentious speculation. Yet Jefferson appears to have traveled and performed widely before his demise in December 1929, and his fame and example paved the way for many later traditional blues artists.

Paramount was anxious to build upon this success, and brought two now-legendary Mississippi blues artists to their recording studio in Grafton, Wisconsin, with hopes of making them into stars as well. Charley Patton's powerful vocals and free-flowing guitar work captured the raw energy of the Delta tradition, but were combined with a slick showmanship that revealed how easily this often dark and introspective music could take on the trappings of commercial entertainment. Long before Jimi Hendrix and Stevie Ray Vaughan rose to fame on similar exhibitionist antics, Patton would play the guitar behind his back or between his legs, spin it round, or slap it like a drum. His "Pony Blues," recorded in June 1929, was a hit for Paramount, and at a follow-up session for the label Patton brought along Eddie "Son" House, recently released from Parchman Prison, who would later inspire many important blues artists, most notably Robert Johnson and Muddy Waters. House's music was more foreboding than Patton's, and at times almost apocalyptic in tone. His performances on recordings such as "Preachin' the Blues" and "Dry Spell Blues," with their quasi-biblical language and stark guitar accompaniment, may not have sold well at the time, but they eventually contributed to the now-pervasive image of the Delta blues as a haunted music sung by troubled souls.

This mythology of the blues as the music of salvation and damnation reached its highest pitch in the figure of Robert Johnson. Even people who know little about blues music have usually heard the story of Johnson selling his soul to the devil at midnight at a crossroads, in exchange for a preternatural ability to play the guitar. In recent years, blues scholars such as Elijah Wald, Barry Lee Pearson, and Bill McCulloch have tried to defuse this legend as an embarrassing example of the mythologizing tendency of overly zealous fans. Yet one cannot excuse Johnson himself of complicity in the diffusion of this oft-told tale. Some of his best-known recordings, such as "Hellhound on My Trail," "Cross Road Blues," or "Me and the Devil Blues" helped propel the attention-getting rumor, although this artist also left behind songs dealing with other time-honored blues themes: romantic love and its more carnal manifestations, revelries, infidelities, and especially rambling and life on the road.

Johnson's travels started soon after he was born, the eleventh child of Julia Major Dodds, probably on May 8, 1911. As an infant he lived in various migrant labor camps with his mother and sister Carrie, or in Memphis under the same roof as Julia's husband, Charles Dodds, or with her later spouse Dusty Willis back in the Delta. When he started performing as a guitarist, Johnson wandered even farther, throughout Mississippi, and around the South and up north as far as Canada, if various accounts can be believed. He may have used a half dozen or more aliases in these various settings, further complicating the task of any biographer but adding to the mystique of an artist who often seemed on the run rather than merely on the road.

But of the power of his music, as documented at two sessions in 1936 and 1937, there can be no dispute. More than any other artist, Robert Johnson codified the disparate strains of the blues guitar tradition into a coherent musical vision that could be assimilated and adapted by the broader stream of American popular music. Johnson had listened widely—not just to other guitarists in the Delta, but also to many recordings of artists from other parts of the country—and learned deeply, mastering a host of techniques later imitated by generations of followers: turn-arounds, passing chords, boogie patterns, fills, vamps, licks, and the like. Moreover, Johnson forged these building blocks into compositions that sound more like crafted tunes than the hand-me-down blues favored by so many of his predecessors and contemporaries—as testified to by the success of frequently covered Johnson songs such as "Come on in My Kitchen," "Sweet Home Chicago," and "I Believe I'll Dust My Broom." Less often noted, but equally important to the success of this artist, was the intimacy and flexibility of his voice. Johnson was known to use his singing to seduce women, and apparently some of that seductive power lingers on in recordings that have found a surprising crossover audience. Not only have rock icons such as the Rolling Stones and Eric Clapton turned to Robert Johnson for inspiration, but their fans have also followed suit, so much so that *The Complete Recordings*, issued in 1990, which label execs only expected to sell a few tens of thousands of copies, eventually found an audience of millions. Johnson, for his part, never lived to enjoy the rewards of this success. He died on August 13, 1938, at age twenty-seven, apparently poisoned by a jealous husband.[19]

Many scholars have tried to link the blues convention of a singer accompanied by solo guitar back to earlier African traditions, envisioning the blues as a New World continuation of the West African performance practices associated with the griots, the musical bards of their aural-oral societies. Certainly some similarities can be seen in the two musical idioms. For example, the stringed accompaniment of the kora, a West African harp-lute characteristic of griot music, is somewhat reminiscent of the role of the guitar in early blues styles, especially in the use of the plucked string to continue and comment on the melody line of the singer. However, in traditional West African society the griot's songs figured not as an outpouring of personal expression—something that is so essential to the blues—but as a way of preserving historical and folkloric stories for the larger tribal unit. Hence, in terms of function, the griot is perhaps closer to the singing bards who shaped epic poetry in Western cultures than to a Robert Johnson or Charley Patton, whose recorded performances reflect distinctly individualistic perspectives on the subjects addressed in their songs. Blues expert Samuel Charters undertook field research in West Africa in 1974, where he tried to document the connections between these musical currents of two continents, while other scholars have proposed linkages between American blues and the bardic tradition of East Africa, or the music of Yoruban priests or even the Islamic call to prayer. Despite these efforts, many key aspects of blues music—its distinctive bent thirds, its chord patterns, and its heady mixture of bravado and alienation—resist reduction into African antecedents. As Charters himself eventually concluded: "Things in the blues had come from the tribal musicians of the old kingdoms, but as a style the blues represented something else. It was essentially a new kind of song that had begun with the new life in the American South."[20]

If the country blues tradition, with its emphasis on a solo singer, usually male, accompanying himself on guitar, shows the closest ties to these African precedents, a more acculturated variant of this music relying primarily on female vocalists would exert greater influence on early jazz. The songs of the great women blues singers of the 1920s and 1930s—sometimes referred to as "classic blues"—would find a commercial market several years before Blind Lemon Jefferson or Charley Patton made their first recordings. While the country blues singer would take liberties with the bar lines, the classic blues vocalist would strictly follow the twelve-bar form. While the Delta blues player would accompany himself on guitar, the classic blues singer would typically front a band. The classic blues came to draw more readily and obviously on other forms of music—from Tin Pan Alley and the jazz world (with many musicians performing in both the blues and jazz genres) as well as from minstrel shows, circuses, vaudeville, and other sources of traveling music in the South. As part of this process, the structural underpinnings of the music—arrangements, solos, introductions, the use of call-and-response—became more formulaic, and thus more easy for outsiders to assimilate.

Still other aspects of the blues were transformed under the influence of the classic blues singers. As Sandra Lieb, biographer of Ma Rainey, explains: "The Classic Blues revealed a specifically female awareness, especially about the nature of love."[21] Unrequited love, salacious love, abused love—these now emerged even more prominently as central aspects of the blues ethos, both amplifying and sometimes countering the more general spirit of alienation, loneliness, and desolation that permeated the country blues idiom. At the same time, blues performance was now moving from the happenstance surroundings of the street corner, train station, and juke house to formally designated locations—including theaters, tents, barns, and assembly halls—where paying customers came specifically seeking name acts and their well-known songs. In essence, the blues had evolved from a folk art to a form of mass entertainment.

This transformation was fueled in part by a tremendous growth in the market for blues recordings by black female vocalists. In 1920, the General Phonograph Company achieved an unexpected hit with a recording of "Crazy Blues" sung by Mamie Smith. In its first month of release, Smith's debut sold 75,000 copies, and within a year sales had surpassed one million. This surprising success prompted several other companies to enter this nascent market. "One of the phonograph companies made over four million dollars on the Blues," a writer proclaimed in *Metronome* magazine. "Now every phonograph company has a colored girl recording."[22] The "race records," as these releases were labeled, encompassed a wide range of black musical forms, with both secular and religious material finding an enthusiastic audience. In 1926 alone, more than three hundred blues and gospel recordings were released in the United States, most of them featuring African American women vocalists. Priced at fifty or seventy-five cents, these records sold well, and by the following year the number of releases increased to five hundred. To meet the growing demand, companies sent talent scouts on field trips to find and record promising black musicians. No fewer than seventeen field trips, for example, were made by record industry representatives to Atlanta during the late 1920s, while Memphis, Dallas, and New Orleans were also frequent stopping points for these song-seeking expeditions.[23]

Gertrude "Ma" Rainey, who was born in Columbus, Georgia, on April 26, 1886, typified the first generation of blues divas. Together with her husband Will—or "Pa Rainey" as he was sometimes called—this immensely popular artist toured the South as part of a traveling minstrel show. She recorded extensively in the mid-1920s, and her throbbing contralto voice graced over one hundred records during a five-year period. In stark contrast to the country blues singers, who usually accompanied themselves, Rainey recorded with some of the finest jazz musicians of her day, including Louis Armstrong and Coleman Hawkins. Her career also reflected the sharp difference between the informal blues stylings of the Delta and other rural areas and the polished stage presentations that marked the classic blues as commercial fare for a mass audience. The Delta musician often traveled with little more than a guitar in hand; in contrast, Rainey brought four trunks of props, backdrops, lighting, and other show business trappings, as well as a lavish array of costumes and fashion accessories. Rainey's performances served to entertain, indeed to dazzle; they incorporated humor as a characteristic element; and they revealed a more overt connection to the popular music, minstrel shows, and jazz of the day. But a deep artistry coexisted with the theatrical aspects of Rainey's work. In a piece such as "Yonder Come the Blues," recorded in 1926, the virtues of her singing are readily apparent: her straightforward declarative manner of presenting a lyric, her succulent held notes, which hang in the air like ripe fruit from the tree, and her sure sense of time, which propels the rest of the band. Rainey's recordings span a scant half-decade. Like many musicians of her generation, Rainey's career was irreparably hurt by the barren economic prospects of the 1930s. In 1935, Rainey retired from performing and returned to her native Georgia, where she became active in the Baptist Church. She died in Rome, Georgia, on December 22, 1939.

Bessie Smith, a protégée of Rainey's, stands out as the greatest of the classic blues singers. Born in Chattanooga, Tennessee, probably on April 15, 1894 (although the 1900 census gives an 1892 date), Smith began singing and dancing on street corners for spare change around the age of nine. In her midteens, Smith went on the road as a member of Ma Rainey's touring show, and though Rainey has often been credited as a mentor and teacher to the younger singer, the exact extent of this education is a matter of conjecture. Smith's deeply resonant voice was probably evident from the start and may have been the key factor in getting her the job with the Rainey troupe. On the other hand, Rainey's skills as a performer, as well as her mastery of the blues repertoire, must have been an inspiration to this teenage newcomer to the world of traveling shows.

Smith soon came to surpass her teacher in the variety of her melodic inventions, her impressive pitch control, and the expressive depth of her music. Inevitably the younger vocalist decided to leave Rainey to further her own career, and was initially employed as a singer for Milton Starr's theater circuit, the infamous TOBA—which stood ostensibly for Theatre Owner's Booking Agency, but which was often referred to by black performers, with grim humor, as Tough on Black Artists (or sometimes as Tough on Black Asses). In Smith's case, the caustic acronym was well deserved: as a TOBA artist she joined Pete Werley's Minstrel Show, where her pay, at least initially, was as little as $2.50 per week. However, in 1923, Smith's recording "Down Hearted Blues" boosted her to widespread fame; the record reportedly sold over a half million in copies in a few months, and soon Smith was recording regularly and performing for as much as $2,000 per week. She toured extensively, entertaining capacity audiences in large venues—tents set up on the outskirts of town as well as in downtown theaters—in the South and along the eastern seaboard.

Smith, like the blues itself, had risen from the streets to the most spacious performance halls, a setting for which her talents were admirably suited. Her powerful voice could reach to the back row of the largest theater without the need for amplification, and her sure skills as a comedienne and entertainer, as well as her dominating stage presence, enabled Smith to captivate audiences who would have been put off by the troubled, introspective blues of a Robert Johnson or Son House. The poignant aspects of the blues here became tempered with humor and the use of sexual double entendre. Songs such as "Empty Bed Blues," "Need a Little Sugar in My Bowl," "You've Got to Give Me Some," and "Kitchen Man" expounded on, with varying degrees of subtlety, the subject of copulation. This openness to sexual themes helped, on the one hand, to sell records, while on the other, it led to the condemnation of Smith in particular and the blues in general among many social and religious groups, including much of the black middle class.

Although Smith played a prominent role in the merging of blues and popular music, her ambitions could hardly have been realized without the complementary efforts of a host of songwriters, publishers, musicians, and record producers. This evolutionary process, still making its impact felt today, exerted an especially transformative influence on American music in the years between 1910 and 1930. Even before the first blues recordings were made, the blues idiom began filtering into the mainstream of American parlor sheet music, under the influence of Tin Pan Alley songwriters such as W. C. Handy. Alabama-born Handy drew on his experiences as a bandleader in Mississippi and his early apprenticeship with a touring minstrel troupe in his visionary efforts to expand the vocabulary of American popular song. His success in this regard is amply documented in milestone compositions such as "Memphis Blues" (1912), "St. Louis Blues" (1914), and "Beale Street Blues" (1916). Although his fame as "father of the blues"—as some have designated this composer—is an overstatement, Handy's impact as an innovator and popularizer of this new genre justifies his prominent place in the annals of American music. After moving to New York in 1917, Handy was well positioned to champion African American popular music not only as a performer and songwriter, but also as a music publisher and owner of a record company. Many of the songs written by Handy and other blues-influenced songwriters became core components of Smith's repertoire—a mutually beneficial collaboration in which Smith tapped the songwriting skills of the New York professionals and in which Tin Pan Alley profited in turn from the power and authenticity of Smith's interpretations. At the same time, Smith's work betrayed strong jazz ties, as demonstrated by her recordings with Louis Armstrong, Benny Goodman, Coleman Hawkins, James P. Johnson, Jack Teagarden, Fletcher Henderson, and others. These various links characterized an important evolution in the blues, from the idiosyncratic music of the Mississippi Delta to the syncretic music of the recording studios. This ability to evolve in tandem with changes in other spheres of popular music would continue to characterize the blues in ensuing decades.

Yet the blues has also retained a primal core that has resisted assimilation and change. When we listen to Smith in her 1925 collaborations with Armstrong on "St. Louis Blues" and "Reckless Blues," we can already hear the different aesthetic sensibilities that, even at this early date, were beginning to distinguish the jazz and blues idioms. Armstrong favors ornamentation and elaboration; Smith tends toward unadorned emotional directness. In contrast to Armstrong's baroque accompaniment, Smith's singing is built around drawn-out tones, sometimes bellowed with authority, occasionally betraying a tremulous vulnerability. Smith preferred languorous tempos, while jazz music of this period increasingly relied on faster, dance-oriented rhythms. On "St. Louis Blues," the tempo lingers around sixty beats per minute. Compare this with Armstrong's recording of the same piece from December 1929, which jumps along at well over twice this pace. Even a comparatively fast Smith performance, such as her "Gimme a Pigfoot" from November 1933, barely breaks above one hundred beats per minute. In the final analysis, Smith's music celebrated an intensity of feeling, rather than demonstrations of technique. The blues idiom, as it has developed, has mostly stayed true to this inspiring vision, while the jazz world has evinced a more fickle temperament, with its methods and vocabulary constantly changing, sometimes mutating into surprising new forms. Yet the two styles, blues and jazz, have remained intimate bedfellows over the years, despite these many fluctuations—an intimacy so close that, at times, it is hard to determine where the one ends and the other begins.

The most enduring myth of the blues culture is its fatalistic celebration of "dues paying," of each musician's need to internalize a blues ethos through the acceptance of—and ultimately the transcendence of—personal tragedy and disappointment. The details of Bessie Smith's life fit in with this attitude, perhaps all too well; yet commentators have not been above embellishing the facts to accentuate its tragic dimensions. At the same time, the feisty, independent side of the singer's personality is often minimized or ignored—this was, remember, a woman who flung society matron Fania Marinoff Van Vechten to the floor at a posh gathering, slugged pianist Clarence Williams in a dispute over cash, and, according to legend, stared down and ultimately intimidated the Ku Klux Klan when they tried to disrupt a performance.

Yet ultimately Smith can be rightly viewed as, at least in part, the victim of the lifestyle excesses that she celebrated in her music. Alcohol and smoking coarsened her voice; her drinking binges led to violent outbursts, which made many in the industry wary of this temperamental star; her marriage to policeman Jack Gee developed into the type of exploitive personal relationship so often the subject of blues songs. While her career was in bloom, and the money was coming in, Smith was able to rise above these troubles, but the collapse in the recording industry during the early 1930s occurred at the same time that urban black audiences were turning to the faster-paced and slicker music of the larger jazz ensembles. Even so, a star of this magnitude can sometimes resist forces that would bring down a lesser artist, and in 1937 Smith seemed on the verge of a comeback. Recording and performing opportunities were on the rise, and even appearances in films—Smith had already been involved in a short movie in the late 1920s—were being discussed.

These plans never came to fruition. During a tour in the Deep South, Smith was killed in a car accident on September 26, 1937. She was forty-three years old. Two years later, Ma Rainey would die from a heart attack at age fifty-three. The record industry would eventually recover from its troubles and enjoy unprecedented success in the 1940s and later decades, but the era of classic blues had ended with the passing of these two seminal figures. Their influence, however, continues to echo in the work of countless later singers, whose note bending and stage strutting could hardly be envisioned without the pioneering efforts of these grand divas of secular African American music.

Ragtime music rivals the blues in importance—and perhaps surpasses it in influence—as a predecessor to early jazz. Indeed, in the early days of New Orleans jazz, the line between ragtime and jazz was so fine that the two terms were often used interchangeably. With the benefit of hindsight, we can draw sharp distinctions between these two genres, but in the context of African American music in turn-of-the-century New Orleans, the grounds for such subtle delineations were hardly so clear.

In his Library of Congress recordings, Jelly Roll Morton demonstrated an illuminating comparison of two ways of playing Scott Joplin's "Maple Leaf Rag"—one reflecting the Missouri ragtime tradition and the second showing a New Orleans jazz–inflected approach to the composition. But even with Morton, the dividing line between these two styles could be elusive: in this same series of interviews, Morton asserted that the celebrated jazz pianists of the 1930s, such as Fats Waller and Art Tatum, were simply "ragtime pianists in a very fine form." Few jazz historians would agree with this latter categorization, but statements such as these reveal how fluid the borderline between ragtime and jazz could seem to educated listeners, and not just at the turn of the century, but well into the era of swing music and big bands.

Perhaps the best way of understanding the differences and similarities between these two musical idioms is to distinguish between ragtime as a manner of composition and ragtime as a style of instrumental (primarily piano) performance. The similarities Morton perceived between ragtime and 1930s jazz relate primarily to keyboard techniques, most notably the striding on-the-beat bass employed by the left hand and the riveting right-hand syncopations. The latter were often so predominant in ragtime that entire melody lines might be constructed out of repeated syncopated figures. The result, at its worst, was a melody so convoluted and inherently pianistic that few vocalists could sing it, and fewer would want to. But even the second-rate rag pieces compensated for this lack of melodic integrity through the manic rhythmic intensity of their two-handed assault of the keys.

In ragtime's finer moments, especially in the mid and late career efforts of Scott Joplin, these devices were subtly incorporated into his supremely memorable melodies, the syncopations employed in the same way a master chef adds spice to a recipe, for shades of flavor, not overpowering effect. The left-hand structures of ragtime were equally influential, with a whole generation of jazz pianists adopting its use of a resounding low bass note or octave (sometimes a fifth or tenth) on beats one and three, followed by a middle register chord on beats two and four. The resulting combination of the pounding four-to-the-bar foundation of the left hand and the rhythmic acrobatics of the right hand was a full-bodied piano sound that required no other accompaniment. This style of performance became known as "ragging" or "ragged time" at some point in the nineteenth century, a term that likely served as the source for the generic title ragtime.

Ragtime rhythms appeared in print as early as the first half of the nineteenth century, but the first published ragtime piece is generally acknowledged to be "Mississippi Rag" (1897), composed by William Krell. Later that same year, Tom Turpin became the first black composer to publish a ragtime composition with his work "Harlem Rag." Both are well crafted and suggest that the ragtime style had been in incubation for some time prior to their appearance. Before the year was out, Ben Harney had published his method book *Rag Time Instructor*, the first of many pedagogical works that built on, and fueled, the public's appetite for this intoxicating new music. By the turn of the century, the ragtime craze was in full swing, so much so that highbrow critics felt compelled to attack it. "Ragtime's days are numbered," declared *Metronome* magazine in 1901. "We are sorry to think that anyone should imagine that ragtime was of the least musical importance. It was a popular wave in the wrong direction."[24] That same year, the American Federation of Musicians ordered its members to desist from playing ragtime, declaring "the musicians know what is good, and if the people don't, we will have to teach them."

In the midst of this rapid dissemination of a new musical style, the term *rag* invariably became both overused and misapplied, often employed indiscriminately to denote a wide range of African American musical idioms. As a result, published compositions from this period may use the word *rag* in their title while bearing little resemblance to what has come to be known as classic rag style, just as many so-called blues compositions strayed, sometimes considerably, from the standard twelve-bar form. But as the style evolved, ragtime coalesced into a structured four-theme form, with each melody typically encompassing sixteen bars. The most common form for these classic rag pieces was AABBACCDD, with a modulation to a different key typically employed for the C theme.

Although the published ragtime compositions came to include vocal works and band arrangements, this style reached its highest pitch as a form of solo piano music. Nor should this be surprising. In many ways, the spread of this jubilant new music went hand in hand with the growing popularity of pianos in turn-of-the-century American households. Between 1890 and 1909, total piano production in the United States grew from under 100,000 instruments per year to over 350,000—and it is worth noting that 1909 marked the peak level not only in American piano production but also in the number of ragtime pieces published.[25] By 1911, a staggering 295 separate companies engaged in the manufacture of pianos had set up operations in the United States—by comparison there are only three local producers remaining today—while another 69 businesses served the market for piano supplies. During this same period, player pianos increasingly made their way into homes and gathering places. In 1897, the same year that witnessed the publication of the first ragtime piece, the Angelus cabinet player piano, the first such instrument to use a pneumatic push-up device to depress the keys, was released to an enthusiastic marketplace, and by 1919 player pianos constituted over half the output of the U.S. piano industry. These two powerful trends—the spread of pianos into American households and the growing popularity of mechanical player pianos—helped spur the enormous public appetite for ragtime music during the early years of the twentieth century.

This unprecedented outpouring of ragtime artistry was centered, to a striking degree, in a fairly small geographical area. Just as the rural blues blossomed in the hothouse atmosphere of the Mississippi Delta, and as early jazz would later flourish in the environs of New Orleans, so early ragtime reached its zenith in turn-of-the-century Missouri. The cities of Sedalia, Carthage, and St. Louis, among others, served as home base for a who's who of rag composers, as well as an ambitious group of music publishers who recognized the extraordinary body of talent at hand. In Sedalia, a booming railroad town that almost became the state capital, Scott Joplin gathered a cadre of promising rag composers around him, including his students Scott Hayden and Arthur Marshall, while Sedalia music publisher John Stark, a major advocate for ragtime in general and Joplin in particular, proved to be an important catalyst in bringing the work of these local composers to the attention of the broader public. Stark, Joplin, and Hayden eventually moved to St. Louis, another major center of rag activity during these glory years. The local composers there also included Louis Chauvin, an exceptionally talented native of the city who left behind all too few compositions, as well as Tom Turpin and Artie Matthews. In Carthage, Missouri, James Scott created a number of outstanding ragtime pieces, many of which were published by the local Dumars music store where Scott worked—initially washing windows and sweeping floors, and later serving as composer-in-residence. Eventually Scott also benefited from a fruitful partnership with Stark, one that produced a body of compositions second only to Joplin's as exemplars of the ragtime style. With the exception of Joseph Lamb, a white composer from Montclair, New Jersey, virtually all the leading exponents of the classic rag style made their home, at one point or another, in Missouri.

Scott Joplin stands out as the greatest of these composers. In fact, the resurgence of interest in ragtime that began in the 1970s would be hard to imagine if not for the timeless appeal of Joplin's music. While others may have written rags that were more technically demanding or that boasted more striking novelty effects, none could approach the structural elegance, the melodic inventiveness, or the range of expression that characterized Joplin's major works. Nor would any other rag composer match Joplin's ambitions for the music—ambitions that led to the composition of two operas, a ballet, and other works that squarely challenged the lowbrow reputation of the rag idiom. Although his more daring works never gained the acceptance, at least during his lifetime, that Joplin craved, his oeuvre stands out today all the more due to the high standards to which he aspired, as well as to his determined belief in ragtime as a serious form of music—a belief that, more than a half-century after Joplin's death, became validated by his belated enshrinement as a major American composer.

Joplin was born in Texarkana, Texas, probably in 1868. His father, the former slave Jiles Joplin, had played the violin for house parties given by the local slave owner in the days before the Emancipation Proclamation, while his mother, Florence Givens Joplin, sang and played the banjo. The latter instrument may have had an impact on Scott's musical sensibilities: the syncopated rhythms of nineteenth-century African American banjo music are clear predecessors of the later piano rag style. The banjo itself has a fascinating lineage—in America it is considered the plaything of hillbillies and rustics, but its roots are clearly African, where it is prefigured in many variants, and is often associated with bards and nobility. It is all too fitting that Scott Joplin's earliest encounters with music came via this rare American survival of lofty African performance traditions.

While Scott was still in his youth, his father left the family, and his mother was forced to rely on work as a domestic to support her six children. The future composer already exhibited his affinity for the keyboard at this early age. He often accompanied his mother to the houses where she worked and would play and improvise on the piano while she went about her chores. By his teens, Joplin had established himself as a professional pianist, with opportunities to ply his trade at churches, clubs, and social gatherings in the border area of Texas and Arkansas. Later he became involved in teaching music as well as singing with a vocal quintet that performed widely in the region. During this period, Joplin made his first attempts at composition.

At some point in the mid-1880s, Joplin moved to St. Louis, where he supported himself primarily as a pianist, both as a soloist in saloons and other nightspots as well as with a band. The ensemble work gave Joplin an opportunity to develop the skills in arranging that would later reach their pinnacle in orchestrations for his two operas. Joplin made his home in St. Louis for almost a decade, but he traveled widely during these years. His visit to the 1893 World's Columbian Exposition in Chicago, a massive fair that attracted some of the finest musicians of the day, may have been especially influential. Although ragtime music had not yet been published, it was apparently widely played at the Exposition, albeit most often at the outskirts of the fairgrounds, where black musicians performed—while the choicer, more centrally located venues were reserved for white entertainers. At some point in the mid-1890s, Joplin settled down in Sedalia, where he eventually undertook formal study of harmony and composition at the nearby George R. Smith College.

Around 1897, Joplin wrote the "Maple Leaf Rag," a composition that was destined to become the most famous ragtime piece of its day. It wasn't until two years later that John Stark published the work, and over the next twelve months only four hundred copies were sold. But in the fall of 1900, the "Maple Leaf Rag" caught on with the general public, and became the first piece of sheet music to sell more than one million copies—a figure all the more stunning when one realizes that there were fewer than 100,000 professional musicians and music teachers in the United States at the time. Amateur pianists, for their part, must have found it anything but easy to navigate the technical and rhythmic difficulties of Joplin's celebrated rag; however, many no doubt purchased the sheet music and labored over its intricate syncopations.

With the benefit of hindsight, we can see that the "Maple Leaf Rag" only hinted at the full extent of Joplin's talent. It lacks the melodic subtlety, compositional ingenuity, and emotional depth that would eventually separate Joplin from other rag composers. But in rhythmic intensity the "Maple Leaf Rag" stands out even today. Put simply, it is the most intoxicatingly syncopated of any of Joplin's rags. If the essence of ragtime's popularity was, as Irving Berlin later suggested, its ability to capture the "speed and snap" of modern American life, then no piece of music evoked this emerging sensibility better than the "Maple Leaf Rag."

Later Joplin pieces revealed the wide range of compositional techniques that this ambitious African American composer had mastered: the parlor waltz refinement of "Bethena" (1905), the coy interludes that temper the syncopations of "The Ragtime Dance" (1906), the boogie-woogie-inflected third section of "Pine Apple Rag" (1908), the languid habanera rhythms of "Solace" (1909), the almost self-parodying syncopations of "Stoptime Rag" (1910), the moving minor key sections of "Magnetic Rag" (1914). With the Brahmsian darkness of "Scott Joplin's New Rag" (1912) and, especially, his "Magnetic Rag," the last piece he completed, Joplin had pushed his compositions far beyond the boisterous beer hall ambiance that characterized, for many listeners and players, the rag idiom. This was music on a large scale that was now being squeezed into the narrow confines of rag form—so much so that the songs seemed almost consciously designed to defy the commercial expections that Joplin's earlier successes had engendered.

These genre-breaking excursions into other styles were defining qualities of Joplin's music. Accounts that stress his role in uplifting and refining the rag idiom mostly miss the point. True, Joplin set high goals for himself, but his relationship to ragtime was more one of fighting against its constraints and stylistic dead ends rather than battling for its honor and glory. "Joplin's ambition is to shine in other spheres," a 1903 newspaper article about him recounts. "He affirms that it is only a pastime for him to compose syncopated music and he longs for more arduous works."[26] Joplin was also ambivalent, at times even hostile, toward the pyrotechnics of most rag pianists, which emphasized speed and showmanship at the expense of melodic beauty. Hence the well-known admonition that graces many of his published compositions: "NOTE: Do not play this piece fast. It is never right to play Ragtime fast."

The most controversial result of Joplin's high-flung aspirations was his opera *Treemonisha*, often misleadingly referred to as a "ragtime opera," but which has very little ragtime in it. Instead it probes deeply into the pre-rag folk roots of black American music, as well as taps the full range of European operatic devices—the work comes complete with orchestration, overture, recitatives, arias, and ensembles. The last years of Joplin's life found him increasingly preoccupied with this project. It made enormous demands on the composer, not only because of the massive scale of the work, but perhaps even more from the considerable challenge of finding financial and public support for the undertaking. Around 1903, Joplin had written a first opera, now lost, titled *A Guest of Honor*, which apparently kept fairly close to the ragtime style. *Treemonisha* proved to be a far more expansive and consuming musical project.

As early as 1907, Joplin may have discussed the new opera with Eubie Blake, and the following year he played parts of it for Joseph Lamb. John Stark turned down the work, sensing the poor commercial prospects for an African American folk opera, and it was not until 1911 that Joplin, financing the venture himself, was able to publish the 230-page score for piano and eleven voices. His single-minded focus on the opera forced Joplin to ignore more lucrative publishing opportunities—the year before the release of the piano score, only one other Joplin rag appeared in print—causing financial difficulties for the composer and precipitating a break with Stark. Undeterred, Joplin proceeded with the daunting tasks of orchestrating the lengthy work and seeking financial backing for a full-scale production. On completing the orchestration, Joplin began auditioning singers, determined to stage the opera at his own expense to test the public response. A single performance took place, in 1915 in a Harlem hall, with an underrehearsed cast, no scenery or costumes, and without an orchestra—merely the composer playing the piano score. The work, staged in such an austere manner, generated little enthusiasm at the time among a Harlem audience more interested in assimilating established artistic traditions than in celebrating the roots of African American culture.

In the fall of 1916, a year after the disastrous performance of *Treemonisha*, Joplin was committed to the Manhattan State Hospital. On April 1, 1917, Joplin died from "dementia paralytica-cerebral," brought on by syphilis. Although he had not yet reached his fiftieth birthday, Joplin had already outlived his fame. The ragtime craze in America had passed, and Joplin's popularity had waned to such an extent that a number of his unpublished compositions remained hidden away in the Stark company files and were eventually destroyed when the operation moved in 1935. Other compositions—which may have included a piano concerto—came into the hands of Wilbur Sweatman, who was executor of Joplin's widow's estate, but they too have disappeared. The various books on African American music written in the decades following the composer's death devoted little or no space to Joplin, and it was not until Rudi Blesh and Harriet Janis published their seminal work *They All Played Ragtime* in 1950 that Joplin's extraordinary career began to be understood in any degree of perspective. And it took the surprising and unprecedented ragtime resurgence of the 1970s before Joplin's works took the next step and moved beyond the confines of scholars and specialists to reenter the mainstream of American culture. In the mid-1970s, Joplin's popularity, and the sales of recordings of his music, matched rock-star levels; one piece, "The Entertainer," even became the basis for a hit single. But most gratifying to Joplin would have been the eventual success of his opera *Treemonisha*. Some sixty-odd years after its failed debut, the work was successfully revived and recorded, and its composer posthumously awarded a Pulitzer Prize.

Joplin's single-minded determination to merge vernacular African American music with the mainstream traditions of Western composition prefigured, in many regards, the later development of jazz. By straddling the borders of highbrow and lowbrow culture, art music and popular music, African polyrhythm and European formalism, Joplin anticipated the fecund efforts of later artists such as Duke Ellington, James P. Johnson, Benny Goodman, Charles Mingus, Stan Kenton, Art Tatum, and Wynton Marsalis, among others. In his own day, Joplin's audience—both white and black—was ill prepared to understand the nature of such hybrid efforts; we can easily imagine them harboring a preconception that these different traditions were too radically opposed to allow a seamless merging. The idea of a ragtime ballet or opera must have seemed an oxymoron to most of those on both sides of the great racial divide that characterized turn-of-the-century American society. It required the development of a different aesthetic before such works could be appreciated on their own terms.

In our own day, we have embraced just such a new aesthetic, one that allows audiences not only to accept, but often rush to praise, willy-nilly, various transformations of popular styles of entertainment into serious art. This tendency is evident not only—or even primarily—in jazz but in virtually every contemporary genre and style of creative human expression. But even in tolerant, liberal-minded times, the tension between these two streams of activity continues to seethe under the surface. This dynamic interaction, the clash and fusion—of African and European, composition and improvisation, spontaneity and deliberation, the popular and the serious, high and low—will follow us at virtually every turn as we unfold the complex history of jazz music.

2 New Orleans Jazz

THE CELEBRATIONS OF A CITY IN DECLINE

With the lifting of trade restrictions on the Mississippi River following the 1803 Louisiana Purchase, the New Orleans economy entered a period of unprecedented prosperity that would last over half a century. The population of the city had already doubled by the time, less than a decade later, that the first steamboat—aptly named the *New Orleans*—was put into service on the Mississippi, facilitating upstream navigation and further enhancing New Orleans's position as a major hub of commerce. The effect of this shift can be measured by the staggering growth in downriver cargo received at the port: between 1801 and 1807, an average of $5 million worth of goods came downstream each year, but in 1851 alone almost $200 million worth of freight was measured. Shipments of cotton constituted almost half of these receipts, but many other goods—grain, sugar, molasses, tobacco, manufactured items, and much more—as well as people passed through this New Orleans hub, creating a prosperous, cosmopolitan environment that few cities in the New World could match.[1]

This localized economic boom, built on the contingencies of geography, began to subside in the years following the Civil War. The city's position on the wrong side of the Mason-Dixon line was only one small part of the problem. Even more pressing was an inexorable shift in the nation's infrastructure. During the closing decades of the nineteenth century, the railroad gradually replaced the steamboat as the major transportation industry in America. Trading hubs grew up elsewhere, and New Orleans's position at the gateway of the major inland water system waned in importance. Economic woes were further aggravated by chronic political corruption. The result: by 1874, the state of Louisiana was insolvent, unable to pay either principal or the accumulated interest on its $53 million debt.[2] Investment capital, to the extent that it stayed within the region, gravitated to natural resources and oil fields, with attendant wealth moving outside New Orleans to other parts of Louisiana and beyond the state line to Texas. The boisterous histories of New Orleans jazz often obscure this underlying truth: by the time of the birth of jazz, New Orleans was already a city in decline.

The city's population had increased more than fourfold during the half-century from 1825 to 1875, but in 1878, 2 percent of the city's inhabitants perished in a devastating yellow fever epidemic. The risk of pestilence was always present in nineteenth-century New Orleans, especially during the long, hot summer months. The city sits below sea level, and its damp, warm climate combined with dismal local sanitation—the city had no sewage system until 1892, long after most North American cities had adopted modern methods of fluid waste disposal—made the Crescent City an ideal breeding ground for mosquitoes, roaches, and other assorted vermin. New Orleans bassist Pops Foster recalled conditions being so poor that he was required to wear mosquito nets during some performances.[3] After the 1878 epidemic, population growth resumed at a sluggish 1 percent annual rate, but the number of foreign-born members of the population actually declined, as new immigrants sought more flourishing economies and healthier surroundings.

The average life span for a black native of New Orleans in 1880 was only thirty-six years; even white inhabitants lived, on average, a mere forty-six years. Black infant mortality was a staggering 45 percent. During that decade, mortality rates for New Orleans as a whole were 56 percent higher than for an average American city. Seen in the context of the time and place, the New Orleans natives' extreme fascination with celebrations, parades, and parties—an obsession that reaches its highest pitch in the New Orleans parade for the dead, that extraordinary combination of funeral and festival—is reminiscent of the revelers in Edgar Allan Poe's "The Masque of the Red Death," whose merrymaking allowed them to distance themselves from the sufferings and pestilence of the here and now. From one point of view, this exuberance is the utmost decadence; from another, it is a necessary self-defense mechanism of a society living on the brink.

The dictates of commerce made it inevitable that a major city would be established near the base of the Mississippi River. But, in the words of historian Ned Sublette, it was "a terrible place to build a town."[4] New Orleans has the lowest elevation of any major U.S. city, and with 41 percent of the continental United States's runoff flowing down and through the Mississippi, the Crescent City is to America what plumbing pipes are to your home. Tropical storms are frequent visitors, brushing by or making a direct hit once every three or four years on average, and any resident who lives to middle age will likely confront the ravages of the region's hurricanes, marauders that periodically force evacuations and leave behind untold damage. And in a land that is gradually sinking lower and lower below sea level—some foresee a day in which New Orleans will be completely surrounded by the Gulf of Mexico—the risk of flooding is ever present. In short, the city's history of homegrown catastrophes, whether acts of God or merely those of the lower deities known as elected officials, testifies both to the challenges facing the inhabitants as well as to their hardiness and perseverance.

Yet historians of New Orleans jazz have preferred to focus on the city's moral dangers, linking the rise of hot music to sin and licentiousness. One can construct a colorful story here. After all, the city was named after a debauched noble (Philippe Charles d'Orléans, Duke of Orléans), populated with prisoners and prostitutes (Louisiana became a French penal colony in 1719), financed by a charismatic adventurer and swindler (John Law, famous instigator of the Mississippi Bubble), and came of age as the Big Easy, a place where the rest of world flocks for a fast and loose time. Given this quasi-mythic history, who can be surprised that music writers have been tempted to describe the birth of jazz as a product of vice, paying more attention to bordellos, gambling, and liquor than to the contingencies of culture and economics?[5]

The standard accounts focus on Storyville, a red-light district in New Orleans that existed for a scant twenty years—created by the city aldermen on October 1, 1897, and closed by the U.S. Navy on November 12, 1917—as the birthplace of jazz music. Close investigation of the facts casts more than a few doubts on this colorful lineage. Donald Marquis, a leading expert on New Orleans jazz who painstakingly researched the life of Buddy Bolden—commonly credited with being the first jazz musician— was forced to conclude that Bolden "did not play in the brothels. None of the musicians who were interviewed remembered playing with a band in a whorehouse, nor did they know of anyone who had."[6] Even the name Storyville, now enshrined in the jazz lexicon, was largely unknown to jazz musicians at the time. As jazz bassist Pops Foster recalled:

Long after I left New Orleans guys would come around asking me about Storyville down there. I thought it was some kind of little town we played around there that I couldn't remember. When I found they were talking about the Red Light District, I sure was surprised. We always called it the District.[7]

Other sources suggest that piano music was often featured in the bawdy houses— although in many instances player pianos were used—and that only a few locations employed larger ensembles. Certainly prostitution was big business in Storyville: at its peak some 2,000 women and more than 200 brothels were involved in the trade. Yet jazz bands were more commonly found in the cabarets and dance halls in the district, rather than in the bordellos themselves. Hence, even if one agrees with historian Bill Russell's assessment that Storyville was "kind to hot music," the conclusion that jazz music was born in the brothels or had some special relationship with prostitution sacrifices scrupulous accuracy for a tawdry tabloid sensationalism.[8]

Chastized as the devil's music, jazz may have even deeper ties with the house of God. "You heard the pastors in the Baptist churches," explained Paul Barbarin, one of the finest of the early New Orleans jazz drummers, "they were singing rhythm. More so than a jazz band." "Those Baptist rhythms were similar to the jazz rhythms," concurred Crescent City banjoist Johnny St. Cyr, "and the singing was very much on the blues side." Kid Ory, the most famous of the New Orleans trombonists, claimed Bolden drew inspiration from the church, not the nightlife of Storyville: "Bolden got most of his tunes from the Holy Roller Church, the Baptist church on Jackson Avenue and Franklin. I know that he used to go to that church, but not for religion. He went there to get ideas on music."[9]

But sporting houses and Baptist churches, for all their significance, were only a small part of the broad musical panorama of turn-of-the-century New Orleans. String trios of mandolin, guitar, and bass, sometimes joined by banjo and violin, performed at Saturday night fish fries. On Sundays, city residents migrated to Milneburg and the shores of Lake Pontchartrain, where as many as thirty-five or forty bands of varying instrumentation would entertain. On Mondays and Wednesdays, lawn parties—which, like the fish fries, were typically private fund-raising ventures comparable to the Harlem rent parties of a later day—were thrown all over New Orleans. Milk dairy stables provided another common setting for dances, organized by the owner or hired for the night by locals who cleaned the stables and hosted parties from dusk until the predawn hours. Collections of youngsters playing mostly homemade instruments—the so-called spasm bands with their hodgepodge of music-making cigar boxes, pipes, gourds, and other ready-at-hand objects—could be found on the streets, cadging nickels and dimes from the passersby. Lincoln Park and Johnson Park were other favorite locations for crowds to gather and listen to New Orleans bands, and a wide range of other spots—including restaurants, saloons, and assembly halls—commonly featured music, as did virtually every major event, not just rallies and athletic competitions, or the celebrations of Mardi Gras and Easter, but even the solemn occasions of funeral and burial.

The second-line participants who followed the family and friends (the first line), attracted by the music of the the New Orleans funeral procession, have become famous the world over—and so beloved in the Crescent City that no burial is required these days to justify their inclusion in a public event. As such traditions suggest, if you didn't go to the music in New Orleans, it often came to you. Local residents during the early days of jazz frequently encountered performances on the move, in parades and marches and from strolling vendors—a number of sources testify to the importance of wandering rags-bottles-and-bones men who, in the words of Jelly Roll Morton, "would play more low-down dirty blues" on the wooden mouthpieces of their cheap horns "than the rest of the country ever thought of."[10] The Mississippi steamboats also served as important traveling showcases for early African American music, and jazz's journey by river to other locales is often cited and romanticized by historians of jazz. Less celebrated, but also important, were the Sunday train excursions, promoted by the Southern Pacific and other railroads, which featured some of the finest local musicians. Given these precedents, who can doubt that, even from its birth, jazz was destined to spread its joyous sounds far and wide?

One could perhaps imagine jazz developing in New Orleans even without the bawdy houses of Storyville, but the birth of this music would have been unthinkable without the extraordinary local passion for brass bands, an enthusiasm that lay at the core of that city's relationship to the musical arts. Of course, the brass band phenomenon was by no means limited to New Orleans: in the years following the Civil War, similar ensembles were organized in many cities and villages across the United States, with some towns hiring a professional bandmaster to organize and rehearse the group, while in many other instances—especially with black bands— the units were sponsored by fraternal organizations, social clubs, or the musicians themselves. But the role of these groups was especially important in New Orleans, where brass bands played not only for Sunday afternoon concerts in the village square, as happened in many communities, but for almost every type of social event.

The Excelsior Brass Band and the Onward Brass Band, both formed in the 1880s, were the best known of these ensembles, but there were many others, probably dozens, of varying degrees of fame and ability. Drummer Baby Dodds recalled the instrumentation for the marching brass bands:

There was a traditional line-up for the New Orleans parades. The trombones were always first. Behind the trombones would be the heavy instruments, like bass, tubas and baritones. Then behind them were the altos, two or three alto horns, and behind them were the clarinets. It was very good if there were two. Usually it was only one, an E flat. Then behind the clarinets would come the trumpets, always two or three, and they came next. Bringing up the rear would come the drums, only two, a bass drum and a snare drum. That was for balance. For funeral marches the snare drum is muffled by pulling the snares off. When the snares are off it's the same as a tom-tom. But you don't muffle drums with parades, or going back from the cemetery. At most there were eleven or twelve men in the whole brass band.[11]

Sometimes the same instrumentation would be employed for dances, but in many instances a smaller subset of these musicans, often joined by string players, would be used. The repertoire of these bands was remarkably varied. In addition to concert and march music, the ensembles also knew a range of quadrilles, polkas, schottisches, mazurkas, two-steps, and other popular dance styles. As the ragtime craze swept the country around the turn of the century, syncopated pieces became more and more frequently played by these bands, a shift that was accompanied by increased interest in "ragging" more traditional compositions. This blurring of musical genres was, as we shall see, central to the creation of jazz music.

The blossoming of vernacular music took place in tandem with a tremendous outpouring of European concert music, opera, and drama. The opening of the first major theater in New Orleans in 1792 initiated a vibrant tradition of formal musical and theatrical performance. Another major venue, the Théâtre d'Orléans, opened in 1813 and was rebuilt, following a fire, in 1819; the American Theatre followed in 1824; the 4,100-seat St. Charles Theatre, where Jenny Lind sang, opened in 1825, and it too was rebuilt following a fire, in 1843; the Varieties Theatre, established in 1848, was rebuilt on a different site in 1871 and, ten years later, became the Grand Opera House; the Academy of Music opened in 1853; the French Opera House, perhaps the greatest of these, opened on the corner of Bourbon and Toulouse Streets in 1859, and stood out as one of the most elegant performing halls in the United States until it too went up in flames in 1919. In short, music of all types permeated New Orleans social life; whether high or low, imported or indigenous, it found a receptive audience in this cosmopolitan city. Indeed, has any metropolis in history exhibited a greater love affair with the musical arts?

The influence of this highbrow, European musical tradition was especially strong within the local black Creole culture. The role of these New Orleans Creoles in the development of jazz remains one of the least understood and most commonly misrepresented issues in the history of this music. Part of the confusion comes from the term *Creole* itself. In many contexts, the word has been used to denote individuals of French or Spanish descent who were born in the Americas. As such, it was a mark of pride that distinguished descendants of the first settlers of New Orleans from later groups of immigrants. However, many of these early inhabitants had slave mistresses, and the offspring of these relationships and their later progeny constituted a second group of Creoles—the so-called Creoles of color or black Creoles.

Many black Creoles were freed long before the abolition of slavery in the South. The famous Code Noir or Black Code of 1724, which regulated interactions between slaves and masters, allowed for the liberation of slaves with the consent of their owner. Paternal feelings, among other motives, led many slave owners to follow this course with these children of miscegenation. Even after the Civil War, these Creoles of color did not associate with black society; instead they imitated the ways of the continental European settlers, often spoke a French patois, and, in general, clung tenaciously to the privileges of their intermediate social position. Toward the close of the nineteenth century, this separate existence no longer remained possible for many black Creoles. Perhaps the most decisive turning point was the passage of Louisiana Legislative Code No. 111 in 1894, which designated anyone of African ancestry as a Negro. Slowly, but inexorably, these Creoles of color were pushed into closer and closer contact with the black underclass they had strenuously avoided for so long.

This forced association took place not only in the broader social arena, but also in the musical subculture of New Orleans. The Creole musicians were, for the most part, better trained than the black players from uptown; they were steeped in the classics and skilled at reading music. But suddenly these polished Creole ensembles were forced to compete for work against the less schooled, more boisterous black bands that were pursuing a "hotter" style, one that would serve as the foundation for New Orleans jazz. In time, the hotter sound would emerge as the dominant strain— although assimilating many aspects of the Creole tradition in the process. At the close of the nineteenth century, John Robichaux's Creole band, with its studied arrangements and skilled musicianship, represented the best of the older style. The newer, more intense approach was exemplified in the music of cornetist Charles "Buddy" Bolden.

Buddy Bolden, often cited as the first jazz musician, may well be the most mysterious figure in the annals of New Orleans music. No recordings survive of this seminal figure—despite the rumored existence of a cylinder recording from the turn of the century—and no mention of his music appeared in print until 1933, two years after his death, and some three decades after Bolden contributed to the revolutionary birth of a new style of American music. Hence any assessment of his importance must be drawn from scattered and often contradictory accounts, almost all of them documented, sometimes with mixed motives, long after the fact. For years, only the barest sketch of a biography was available—an account that placed Bolden as a barber and editor of a local scandal sheet, both facts ultimately proven to be untrue. However, detailed research conducted by Donald Marquis, which culminated in his 1978 book *In Search of Buddy Bolden, First Man of Jazz*, put to rest the many misconceptions and brings us probably as close as we will ever get to Bolden and his music.[12]

In 1877, the year Bolden was born, President Rutherford Hayes removed the last federal soldiers from Louisiana, signaling an end to the Reconstruction era in New Orleans and its surroundings. The apparent return to normalcy was deceptive: Bolden, the son of a domestic servant, was raised in a society that would never match the prosperity and general well-being of prewar New Orleans. In 1881, four years after Bolden's birth, his sister Lottie, five years of age, died of encephalitis; two years later, Bolden's father died, at age thirty-two, of pneumonia. These personal tragedies reflected a broader, more disturbing social reality. As the mortality statistics cited earlier make clear, the abbreviated life spans of the Bolden clan were, for the most part, typical of black society in late nineteenth-century New Orleans.

Bolden would have been exposed to music not only at various social events, but also at church and in school—in fact, two of John Robichaux's musicians taught at the Fisk School for Boys, which Bolden likely attended. At some point in the mid-1890s, Bolden began playing the cornet, initially taking lessons from a neighbor, and was soon supplementing his income as a plasterer with earnings from performing. At this remove, it is hard to evaluate how much formal training Bolden enjoyed. "[I] don't think he really knew how to blow his horn right," Louis Armstrong has suggested, and members of the Robichaux band dismissed Bolden's group as a bunch of "routineers," by which they meant fakers.[13] Yet Bolden listed himself as a "music teacher" in the local directory. Certainly one would give much to know what pearls of wisdom he passed on to his private students. In any event, the lessons he gave in public, through the example of his own playing, came to exert an even greater influence over the nascent jazz style of his hometown.

Unlike many New Orleans horn players, Bolden's initiation into the public music life of the city came not through the brass bands that figured prominently in the local social life, but instead as a member of the string ensembles that entertained at dances and parties. The personnel and instrumentation of Bolden's band underwent constant shifts, but its general evolution tended to emphasize the wind instruments at the expense of the strings—the only surviving photo of the group reveals an ensemble consisting of cornet, valve trombone, two clarinets, guitar, and bass; drums, although absent in the photograph, also played an important role in the band according to all accounts. The evolution in instrumentation was accompanied by a shift in musical perspectives. By the closing years of the century, Bolden's band was gaining increasing notoriety for its daring move into the syncopated and blues-inflected sounds that would prefigure jazz.

Bolden's single biggest contribution to jazz may have been his focus on the blues. "On those old, slow, lowdown blues, he had a moan in his cornet that went right through you," trombonist Bill Matthews recalled, "just like you were in church or something." Trumpeter Peter Bocage concurred: "He played a lot of blues, slow drags, not too many fast numbers. . . . [B]lues was their standby, slow blues."[14] It is worth recalling that the blues form was little known at the time. W. C. Handy may be lauded by his admirers as the "Father of the Blues," but he never encountered this style of music until around 1903, when Bolden was already twenty-five years old. Yet Jelly Roll Morton describes a blues he heard played by New Orleans resident, Mamie Desdoume, at the turn of the century. Bolden was likely incorporating the blues sensibility and structure into his music around this same time.

Certainly Bolden, even if he did not invent jazz, had mastered the recipe for it, which combined the rhythms of ragtime, the bent notes and chord patterns of the blues, and an instrumentation drawn from New Orleans brass bands and string ensembles. As we have seen, the syncopated rhythms of ragtime spread into the mainstream of American culture before the the blues became well known, and Bolden can hardly take credit for this aspect of African American music, although it certainly served as another key ingredient in his work. Yet his instistence on marrying these syncopations to the blues, in an era when the latter idiom existed only on the fringes of the music world, was a brash move, and no doubt a key reason why he captured the attention of his contemporaries and the later chroniclers of New Orleans jazz.

Bolden's ragged and raucous music stood in stark contrast to the more traditional quadrilles, waltzes, and marches of the New Orleans Creoles. Although the Creole players tried initially to dismiss the new style, its vigor appealed to the local black audience, especially to the younger, more independent generation of African Americans born and raised after the Civil War. This was more than a matter of musical techniques. Bolden's daring lyrics to his signature song, which included biting reference to a local judge and other contemporary figures, can be viewed as symbolic of the more outspoken attitudes of the younger black men of his day. Even so, Bolden pushed the limits as few of his contemporaries dared, no doubt enhancing the allure of his quasi-forbidden music in the process. Referring to the cornetist's trademark piece, known under varying names—"Funky Butt," "Buddy Bolden's Stomp," "Buddy Bolden's Blues," or "I Thought I Heard Buddy Bolden Say"—Sidney Bechet recalls: "The police put you in jail if they heard you singing that song. I was just starting out on clarinet, six or seven years old, Bolden had a tailgate contest with the Imperial Band. Bolden started his theme song, people started singing, policemen began whipping heads."[15]

Bolden's career would span only a few years. By 1906, his playing was already on the decline, aggravated by the cornetist's heavy drinking and increasing mental instability. In March of that year, he was arrested after assaulting his mother-in-law with a water pitcher—an event that led to the only newspaper articles mentioning this jazz icon during his lifetime. A second arrest, in September, and a third one the following March resulted in Bolden's being declared legally insane and committed to an asylum in Jackson. For the next twenty-four years, Bolden remained at this institution, his condition deteriorating into pronounced schizophrenia. On November 4, 1931, Bolden died at the age of fifty-four—according to the death certificate, from cerebral arterial sclerosis—only a few years before growing interest in the early history of jazz would lead researchers back to this seminal figure.

Although Bolden has been typically heralded as the progenitor of jazz, such simplistic lineages ignore the broader musical ferment taking place in turn-of-the-century New Orleans. Many musicians—mostly black, but also Creole and white—were experimenting with the syncopations of ragtime and the blues tonality and applying these rhythmic and melodic devices to a wide range of compositions. At first, improvisational techniques were probably used merely to ornament composed melodies, but at some point these elaborations must have evolved into more free-form solos. What began as experimentation eventually led to formalized practice. Reconstructing these events with any precision is all but impossible—a terminology for describing this music would not exist for quite some time, and the first recordings of this new style would not be made for at least twenty years. Whether Bolden was the decisive figure or merely one among many to spur this transformation remains a matter for speculation. In any event, all our research indicates that sometime around the end of the nineteenth century, a growing body of musicians in New Orleans were playing a type of music that, with benefit of hindsight, can only be described as jazz.

A number of uptown cornetists built on the foundations that Bolden and others had created, including Bunk Johnson, Joe "King" Oliver, Mutt Carey, and later, Louis Armstrong, the greatest of the New Orleans trumpeters. But jazz quickly leaped over the racial barriers that divided New Orleans in the early 1900s. Musicians who were early practitioners of this new idiom also included Creoles Sidney Bechet, Jelly Roll Morton, Kid Ory, and Freddie Keppard, as well as white players Papa Jack Laine, Emmett Hardy, Sharkey Bonano, and Nick LaRocca. By the 1920s, when the first recordings of a wide range of New Orleans jazz ensembles were made, the ethnic mix of the local bands was almost as diverse as the city's population. These recordings featured, in addition to the major black and Creole players, such ensembles as Johnny Bayersdorffer's Jazzola Novelty Orchestra, a solid New Orleans jazz band composed of musicians of central and southern European ancestry; Russ Papalia's orchestra, another jazz unit, this one primarily comprising Italian Americans; and the New Orleans Owls, which included in its ranks, among others, clarinetist Pinky Vidacovich, pianist Sigfre Christensen, trombonist Frank Netto, banjoist Rene Gelpi, and tuba player Dan LeBlanc—a lineup whose lineage spanned much of Europe. Certainly jazz remained primarily an African American contribution to the city's—

and, eventually, the nation's—culture; but like all such contributions, once given, it no longer remained the exclusive property of the giver. Instead, destined to become part of the broader cultural gene pool, it was taken up with enthusiasm by musicians of all colors, all nationalities.

Many of the earliest generation of players never recorded; others—such as Keppard—recorded when past their prime, thus limiting our ability to make a full and accurate assessment of their talent and influence. Still others, such as Jelly Roll Morton and Bunk Johnson, made outstanding recordings, but did so, for the most part, some years after the New Orleans style of performance was perfected, thus raising questions about how accurately these recordings represent turn-of-the-century practices. Our ability to decipher this history is further complicated by the personal mythmaking of important firsthand informants such as Johnson, Morton, and LaRocca—all players whose autobiographical narratives were tainted by a desire to enshrine themselves as major protagonists in the creation of this new music.

As previously mentioned, some twenty years transpired between Bolden's glory days and the release of the first jazz recordings. Nor do these first commercial discs simplify the historian's task. If anything, the opposite is true: the history of recorded jazz was initiated with an event that remains to this day clouded in controversy. And, as with so many of the loaded issues in the story of the music, the question of race lies at the core of the dispute. In an ironic and incongruous twist of fate, the Original Dixieland Jazz Band (ODJB), an ensemble consisting of white musicians, was the first to make commercial recordings of this distinctly African American music. Raised in New Orleans, these five instrumentalists—leader and cornetist Nick LaRocca, clarinetist Larry Shields, trombonist Eddie Edwards, drummer Tony Sbarbaro, and pianist Henry Ragas—joined forces and performed in Chicago in 1916, then opened in New York in January 1917. During an engagement at Reisenweber's Restaurant, the group attracted large audiences with its novel and spirited music, and spurred the interest of East Coast recording companies. Columbia was the first to record the band, but hesitated to release the sides because of the unconventional and ostensibly vulgar nature of the music. Soon after, the Victor label overcame such scruples, and a second session produced a major commercial success in "Livery Stable Blues."

Partisan polemics have made it all the more difficult to assess this band's importance and merits. LaRocca and his apologists have offered a stridently revisionist history that places the ODJB as key contributors to the creation of jazz.[16] In contrast, critics of the band have attacked its playing as stiff and unconvincing, some going so far as to claim that it did not play jazz at all, just a raucous variant of ragtime. Others have looked for earlier examples of recorded jazz in their attempt to dislodge the ODJB from their place in the jazz pantheon, often tendentiously striving to classify the 1913–14 sides by James Europe's Society Orchestra as the true maiden voyage of the new musical style, or else hypothesizing about lost recordings by Bolden and others.

Any fair assessment of this controversial band needs to tread cautiously through the exaggerations made on both sides. On the one hand, no evidence exists to support the claim that the ODJB initiated the jazz tradition—indeed, it is even doubtful that the band was the first white group of New Orleans musicians to play jazz (Papa Jack Laine, a turn-of-the-century bandleader, has stronger claims on that distinction). Yet smug dismissals of the ensemble are equally off the mark. LaRocca's cornet playing stands out as especially supple and often inspired, while Larry Shields's clarinet work, although seldom remembered nowadays, also exerted an influence on other musicians at the time. Sixty years later, Benny Goodman recalled that Shields had been a strong early influence (along with Jimmie Noone and Leon Roppolo) on his music, adding that he could still play Shields's chorus on "St. Louis Blues" note for note. True, the group indulged in novelty effects of questionable taste, but so would a host of later jazz musicians—from Jelly Roll Morton to the Art Ensemble of Chicago—without subverting the underlying virtues of their efforts.

Although not the best of the early jazz bands, the ODJB was certainly one of the most wide ranging. Its recordings encompassed jazz, blues, rag forms, and pop songs, as well as arrangements with an additional horn that anticipated the textured voicings of swing music. In their travels, the band members were among the first global ambassadors for hot music; they moved from New York to England, where they gave a private command performance for the royal family, and also journeyed to France, where they helped celebrate the signing of the Treaty of Versailles. The group disbanded in 1925 but rejoined forces briefly in 1936 to record again for the Victor label and go on tour, but this reunion proved short lived. LaRocca would survive another quarter of a century, and though he no longer performed on the horn, he worked tirelessly as an advocate arguing for the ensemble's historical importance. Inevitably, this zeal in promoting the ODJB as pioneers of the music—no less than the "Creators of Jazz," as their public billings proclaimed—created a fierce backlash within the jazz world, as would their success in securing a recording contract at a time when so many African American artists were ignored. Yet few bands of that period did more to expose the wider public, at home and abroad, to the virtues of this new music from New Orleans.

THE WORLD'S GREATEST HOT TUNE WRITER

Jelly Roll Morton, the greatest of the New Orleans jazz composers, also generated controversy by his claims to have invented the music. Indeed, Morton was known to exaggerate about many things, so much so that he has acquired the persona of a blustering loudmouth in most historical accounts. However, a careful study of Morton's firsthand recollections, preserved by Alan Lomax in a series of taped interviews and performances for the Library of Congress, reveals that this often maligned figure could be, when the occasion warranted, one of the most thoughtful and accurate sources of information on early jazz.

More often than not, later historical research has vindicated Morton's assertions as well as validated his recreations of earlier musical styles. Moreover, few jazz figures of any era have matched him in providing insightful commentary into the aesthetic dimensions of the music. Although Morton did not invent jazz, he was perhaps the first to think about it in abstract terms, and articulate—in both his remarks and his demonstrations—a coherent theoretical approach to its creation. On a wide range of topics—dynamics, vibrato, melodic construction, the use of breaks, the essence of Latin music—Morton's comments continue to provoke thought and demand our attention.

Yet Morton's assertions, for all their musical insight, stand out as paragons of doublespeak and evasion on autobiographical matters. Like his fictional contemporary from the Jazz Age, F. Scott Fitzgerald's Jay Gatsby, Morton had a flair for rewriting his life story to match the dimensions of his ego. He sometimes gave his birthdate as 1885—like many early New Orleans players, adding to his age to strengthen his case for being present at the birth of jazz—and stated that his original name was Ferdinand LaMenthe. In fact, Jelly Roll was born in or around New Orleans in 1890, as Ferdinand Joseph LaMothe, and was raised in a strict Creole environment that strenuously resisted assimilation into New Orleans's black population.

Morton's family all but disowned him when he became involved in the world of jazz, with its low-life connotations and attendant vices. Not that Morton himself was open minded in embracing African American culture. On the contrary, Morton's tendency to rewrite the past was never more apparent than when he dealt with racial issues. In a typically bizarre aside, Morton explained to Lomax that he abandoned the name LaMenthe for racial reasons—because of ethnic hostility directed at the French! As to his own African roots, Morton was in a lifelong state of denial, pointing instead to his European ancestry (*"All* my folks came directly from the shores of France," he told Lomax[17]) and upper-class Creole background, and putting faith in his relatively light complexion and his mastery of white diction and mannerisms. Even by the standards of black Creole society of the turn of the century—many of whose members shared his anxieties about assimilation into black culture—Morton's protestations were extreme. Despite his insatiable ego, Morton would have been nonplussed to see himself lauded by posterity as a major African American musician.

Yet in his actions, if not his words, Morton strived to relinquish all the highbrow trappings of his Creole youth. More than any other major New Orleans jazz artist, Morton's apprenticeship in the music business took place largely in the bordellos of Storyville (although Morton worked mainly in the white bordellos where few other jazz players could follow). Rather than regretting the low-life associations of the District, Morton luxuriated in the company of pimps, prostitutes, murderers, gamblers, pool sharks, and dealers and hustlers of various sorts, and at times could rely on a few of these trades himself. At some point in the early 1900s—Morton claimed 1902, although this seems too early, given his birthdate—he began working as a musician in Storyville. His great-grandmother expelled him from home when she learned of his activities in the District, and before long Morton started on the peripatetic freelancing that would occupy most of his life. His early travels brought him to Memphis, New York, Chicago, St. Louis, Detroit, Tulsa, Houston, and other locales. By 1917, Morton had traveled farther west, visiting California, Canada, Alaska, and Mexico.

Wherever Morton journeyed, he was noticed. How could it have been otherwise? He was a big spender, wore a diamond in his tooth and more on his garters, was known to boast that he kept a trunk full of money back in his hotel room (only the top tray carried the cash, but visitors catching a glimpse walked away believers), and showed off an extensive and expensive wardrobe, often by changing outfits several times a day. His skills as a pianist and composer were no doubt refined during these years, but Morton's income at this time almost certainly relied more on his activities as a procurer and pool shark. However, when he returned to Chicago around 1923, Morton was well prepared to draw on his considerable talents for self-promotion in building a musical career. Certainly the time was ripe. The Jazz Age had begun in earnest, and Morton looked to capitalize on the public's insatiable demand for this new style of music.

Morton's Chicago years, which lasted until 1926, constitute the most prolific musical period of his career. He made over one hundred recordings or piano rolls of his compositions, published a steady stream of pieces, and formed his most famous ensemble, the Red Hot Peppers. This band, which recorded in both Chicago and New York during the remaining years of the decade, achieved a level of collective artistry that few New Orleans groups ever matched, and none surpassed. Nor would Morton's preeminence as a jazz composer—"the world's greatest hot tune writer" was how his business card modestly described it—be seriously challenged until Duke Ellington pushed the limits of creativity even further in the following decade. But, above all, in its mastery of ensemble interaction—so essential to the New Orleans aesthetic—this band remains the paragon to this day.

Morton (again like Ellington) was able to get the most out of his musicians, so much so that his groups could rise above the limitations of individual players. Here Morton's high opinion of his own talents was clearly a decisive factor: by sheer force of will, he prodded his sidemen into sharing his exalted vision of New Orleans jazz. Sometimes Morton used even more dramatic means to keep his musicians on track. A telling anecdote from the 1920s describes a recording session at which trombonist Zue Robertson refused to play the melody of one of Morton's pieces the way the composer wanted. Morton took a large pistol from his pocket and placed it on top of the piano. On the next take, Robertson played the melody note for note.[18]

Morton's 1926 recording of his "Sidewalk Blues" testifies to the results achieved by this single-mindedness. The piece begins with a roll call, a ten-bar introduction in which each major instrument is summoned to order: piano, trombone, cornet, and clarinet. This leads directly into a twelve-bar cornet melody statement over blues harmonies supported by a stop-time vamp. Stop-time techniques such as this—here the band propels the soloist with sharp accents on beats two and four—were a trademark of Morton's music, invariably used for a brief spell to add variety to the accompaniment. A second twelve-bar melody follows, this time employing the interlocking trombone-cornet-clarinet counterpoint style, which is the calling card of classic New Orleans jazz. The piece then returns to the opening twelve-bar melody, but with the clarinet taking the lead this time. A four-bar interlude segues into a new thirty-two-bar melody played by cornet, trombone, and clarinet (interrupted briefly at bar sixteen by a car horn, a typical Morton novelty twist) that abandons the blues form and sensibility in favor of a plaintive parlor song style. This thirty-two-bar melody is repeated, but now played in an arrangement for three clarinets. In the context of the New Orleans style, this was a startling device. Morton brought two extra clarinetists to the session, letting them sit idly by most of the day, merely requiring their presence at certain key junctures of the performances such as this interlude. This change of instrumentation in midsong, so rare in other jazz recordings of the period, is representative of Morton's penchant to pull out some surprising sound at unexpected places in his music. This understated clarinet section changes direction dramatically in the final eight bars, with the return of the energetic New Orleans–style counterpoint. A five-bar tag closes this whirlwind three-and-a-half-minute performance. In a compact form, Morton has covered a world of sounds.

When lecturing on Morton's music, I have always been struck by how long it takes to describe in words what is happening in any one of his pieces. For a three-minute recording, it requires ten times as much time to provide even a cursory explanation of the various shifts in instrumentation, harmonic structure, and rhythmic support that characterize these performances. This structural complexity is not arbitrary, but essential to Morton's maximalist aesthetic. In his September 1926 version of "Black Bottom Stomp," another telling example of this approach, the band disappears midway through the piece, leaving the leader to keep the music flowing with a blistering, two-fisted stomp, which Jelly ardently attacks as though it were the star soloist's cadenza in a classical concerto. But, in a flash, the Red Hot Peppers are back, this time supporting cornetist George Mitchell in a heated stop-time chorus. This leads directly into a Johnny St. Cyr conversation, in syncopated time, with the ensemble. Soon the New Orleans counterpoint of trombone, clarinet, and cornet returns with redoubled energy, the trademark sound—as inevitable as the "happily ever after" at the close of a fairy tale—that indicates a Red Hot Peppers performance has reached its intended conclusion. Here again, three minutes of vinyl are forced to accommodate symphonic aspirations.

Morton was not without his limitations. His harmonies, as in "Finger Buster" or "Froggie Moore," occasionally present clumsy combinations of chromatic and diatonic tendencies, suggesting that the composer was reaching beyond his grasp of theory; his piano playing, for all his assertions to the contrary, was typically less than virtuosic; his claim to have invented jazz hardly merits serious debate. Nonetheless, in terms of overall artistry, Morton's achievements were considerable. These 1926 Victor recordings find Morton at the peak of his creative powers. In performances such as "Sidewalk Blues," "Black Bottom Stomp," "Dead Man Blues," "Grandpa's Spells," "Smokehouse Blues," and "The Chant," he tilled a fertile middle ground between the rigid compositional structures of ragtime and the spontaneous vivacity of jazz improvisation. This style would soon become anachronistic—in fact, it may already have been so by the time these recordings were made—as jazz came to forget its origins in the multithematic ragtime form. In this context, Morton's work represents both the highest pitch and final flowering of this approach.

Although his artistic vision dominates these sides, Morton benefited from the presence of a seasoned group of New Orleans players. Trombonist Kid Ory, a Creole born in LaPlace, Louisiana, at some point between 1886 and 1890, had been a successful bandleader in New Orleans before taking his music on the road. In Los Angeles, in 1922, his band released the first New Orleans jazz recording featuring black musicians, and in 1925 he moved to Chicago where he participated in several of the most important studio dates in jazz history, working not only with Morton on the seminal Red Hot Peppers dates, but also recording with Louis Armstrong and King Oliver, among others. His frequent colleague Johnny St. Cyr, born in New Orleans in 1890, was one of the first jazz string players. St. Cyr was trained as a plasterer, but a musical career beckoned after he taught himself to play a homemade guitar. As a performer with Fate Marable's riverboat band, St. Cyr traveled extensively, finally settling in Chicago in the early 1920s, where he also recorded with Armstrong and Oliver. In these years, St. Cyr often played a hybrid instrument, a six-string guitar-banjo, which combined the guitar's neck and fingerboard with the banjo's body. Other members of the 1926 Red Hot Peppers included cornetist George Mitchell, clarinetist Omer Simeon, bassist John Lindsay, and drummer Andrew Hilaire.

Jelly Roll continued to record frequently during the remainder of the 1920s. The members of his band changed regularly, but, regardless of the sidemen or the evolving musical tastes of the American public, Morton's ensembles were at their best when working within the aesthetic constraints of the classic New Orleans idiom. Noteworthy Morton recordings from the 1920s include an invigorating 1927 trio session with clarinetist Johnny Dodds and drummer Baby Dodds, a tantalizing 1924 duet date with King Oliver, and Morton's 1923 work with the New Orleans Rhythm Kings—a historic event that not only produced fine music but served as a milestone in countering the segregation of black and white jazz players in the recording studio—as well as ongoing performances as a solo pianist. As with so many of the artists from this period, Morton's recording career came to a sudden halt with the Great Depression, but even under happier economic circumstances his music would almost certainly have fallen out of favor. Jazz had become a soloist's music, and the structured, collectivist aesthetic of Morton's finest work was not in keeping with the prevailing tone of the Swing Era.

Morton had his own, somewhat paranoid interpretations of his fall from the limelight after his Victor contract ran out in 1930. At times, he blamed a conspiracy of music industry insiders (led by ASCAP and MCA) for his problems; on other occasions, he asserted that a voodoo curse was the main culprit. In any event, Morton made only one recording during an eight-year stretch during the 1930s. If he maintained any degree of notoriety, it was as the composer of the "King Porter Stomp," a piece popularized through the efforts of big band leaders Fletcher Henderson and Benny Goodman, who adapted it to meet the new tastes of the time. In the mid-1930s, Morton settled in Washington, DC, where he ran an unsuccessful nightclub on U Street—the club changed names every few months in a fruitless attempt to attract a clientele—and continued to hatch schemes for reviving his music career.

In 1938, he succeeded in doing just that, spurring his comeback through an auda-
cious move marked by all the trademark Morton excesses. "It is evidently known,
beyond contradiction, that New Orleans is the cradle of jazz, and I myself happened
to be the creator," opens a celebrated letter Morton sent to *Downbeat* magazine.[19]
The conclusion of this long-winded epistle put everything into perspective, or at
least into a Jelly Roll perspective:

My contributions were many: First clown director, with witty sayings and flashily
dressed, now called master of ceremonies; first glee club in orchestra; the first
washboard was recorded by me; bass fiddle, drums—which was supposed to be impossible to record. I produced the fly swatter (they now call them brushes). Of course many
imitators arose after my being fired or quitting. . . . Lord protect us from more Hitlers
and Mussolinis.

The letter is signed, "Jelly Roll Morton, Originator of Jazz and Stomps, Victor Artist,
World's Greatest Hot Tune Writer."

Similar letters were sent to other parties, and before long Morton had established
his position as, if not the inventor of jazz, at least its most noteworthy cause célèbre.
Further attention came on the heels of the Library of Congress recordings conducted
by Alan Lomax. If the *Downbeat* letter presented Morton as blusterer, the Lomax
interviews offered a more compelling account of his achievements. In his playing,
singing, theorizing, and reminiscing on these sessions, Morton left behind one of the
most spellbinding documents in the history of jazz music. An era comes to life,
revivified under the sure touch of his fingers as they glance over the keyboard and
sketched with oratorical aplomb by Morton's hypnotic voice. Whether as huckster
or historian, Morton was a persuasive talker, and record companies were again
listening, after the long dry spell of the early and mid-1930s. He made the best of
these new opportunities. In particular, a series of intimate recordings, released under
the name "New Orleans Memories," showcased not only his strengths as a composer
(most notably on "The Crave") and pianist, but also his less-known skills as a
vocalist. His singing here, as well as on the Lomax sessions, is deeply moving and
suggests that, under different circumstances, Morton might have made his name in
the music world without touching the keyboard.

Morton enjoyed his new status as an elder statesman of jazz for only a few short
years. Late in 1940, following the death of his godmother, Morton drove across the
country in inclement weather, with his Lincoln and Cadillac chained together. He
was concerned that some diamonds that were in his godmother's possession might
be stolen (as events turned out, his fears were confirmed). He stayed on in California,
working sporadically as a musician, but soon fell ill. On July 10, 1941, he died in the
Los Angeles County General Hospital.

The jazz world still has not come to grips with this complicated figure from its
earliest days. Morton has served as the inspiration for a novel and has been depicted
in a Hollywood movie, excoriated in a Broadway musical, commemorated in modern
dance choreography, and psychoanalyzed in liner notes, essays, and articles. Most of
these efforts, however, latch on to one side of this variegated personality, usually

emphasizing the braggadocio, the gems and flashy wardrobe, or the underworld trappings, painting Morton as some sort of Crescent City Mack the Knife. Too often the music, which is the *real* diamond in this psychological abyss, gets lost in the process. Even the Broadway musical based on Morton's life and times, *Jelly's Last Jam*, conveniently relied on other composers for much of its score—almost as if the Morton persona were sufficient, while the artistry could be safely ignored.

But, in the final analysis, Morton's position in jazz history depends on none of these superfluities, neither the boasting nor the bordello sidelines. Morton's most important legacy lies in his body of compositions, recordings, piano rolls, reminiscences, and lucid commentary on the jazz idiom. It is through these that he earned his place as the most consummate craftsman of the traditional New Orleans style.

THE NEW ORLEANS DIASPORA

One of the supreme ironies of the history of New Orleans jazz is that so much of it took place in Chicago. By the early 1920s, the center of the jazz world had clearly shifted northward. New Orleans musicians continued to dominate the idiom, but they were now operating far afield from their native soil. Well before the middle of the decade, a large cadre of major New Orleans jazz musicians were making their reputations in other locales—Jelly Roll Morton left New Orleans around 1908; Freddie Keppard departed in 1914 (if not earlier); Sidney Bechet in 1916, Jimmie Noone in 1917, King Oliver in 1918, Kid Ory in 1919, Johnny Dodds around that same time, Baby Dodds in 1921, and Louis Armstrong in 1922. These moves may have begun as brief stints on the road, but in the end proved all but permanent. The vast majority of the New Orleans diaspora never returned to their home state except for brief visits.

This exodus was anything but a purely musical phenomenon. Between the years 1916 and 1919, a half-million African Americans left the South for more tolerant communities in the North, with almost one million more following in their wake in the 1920s. This vast population shift, which has since come to be known as the Great Migration, encompassed the whole range of black society, from doctors and lawyers to musicians and ministers, from teachers and merchants to artisans and manual laborers. Musicians moved north for the same reasons that motivated other groups: the search for a better life, for greater opportunities to work, to support a family, to enjoy a modicum of personal freedom—options that were much harder for an African American to pursue in the segregated South. As a result, in a host of major cities—Chicago, New York, Cleveland, Detroit, Philadelphia—the black population more than tripled between 1910 and 1930.

Certainly there were outstanding musicians who stayed behind in New Orleans, and some even had a chance to record in their native city. Hear, for example, the distinguished sides made by Sam Morgan's band in New Orleans during 1927 with their uncanny anticipation of the later four-beats-to-the-bar Kansas City swing style. Yet, for the most part, ambitious players intent on advancing their careers in jazz during the 1920s had little choice but to look beyond their home turf. In retrospect, we can see that only those who departed made major reputations, both for themselves and for the musical riches of their hometown. In this regard, New Orleans was no different than Memphis, Clarksdale, and the other centers of distinctive local and regional performance styles in the South. Nashville has emerged as the only exception, the one city that could build national reputations for its home-grown talent, and serve as a destination rather than a starting point for celebrated music careers. New Orleans, for all its fame as a city built on nightlife and entertainment, never achieved that level of self-sufficiency. Bechet, Oliver, Morton, Armstrong, and others were able to put New Orleans jazz on the musical map of American culture, but only by leaving the Big Easy behind.

White New Orleans jazz musicians also made the move to Chicago during this period, but in their case the motivation was not to escape racial intolerance, but to tap the larger economic base of the northern city. As in the case of the ODJB, these white ensembles also found it easier to interest record companies in their music, and for a while enjoyed a virtual monopoly on the jazz record market—at least until the tremendous popularity of the first race records revealed the commercial potential of African American performers. Within a few months of the initial recordings of black Chicago musicians, racially mixed bands also entered the studio—although the issue of segregation in jazz was anything but resolved by this move, and would continue to be a focal point for conflicts, personal as well as societal, for many years.

The collaboration between Jelly Roll Morton and the New Orleans Rhythm Kings, a Chicago-based unit of white Louisiana instrumentalists, was the occasion for this signal event, the first interracial session in the history of Chicago jazz. The Rhythm Kings had already undertaken recording sessions in August 1922 and March 1923 when, in July 1923, they engaged Morton to serve as pianist and composer for a follow-up date. "We did our best to copy the colored music we'd heard at home," group organizer Paul Mares later recalled. "We did the best we could, but naturally we couldn't play real colored style."[20] In Mares's case, his pungent middle-range cornet solos reflect the influence of his contemporary Joe "King" Oliver, whose band made its first sides in Chicago a few months after the initial Rhythm Kings recordings. Although less rhythmically exciting than King Oliver's Creole Jazz Band, the New Orleans Rhythm Kings featured strong ensemble work, a sure sense of swing, especially at medium tempos, and the impressive clarinet stylings of Leon Roppolo. Roppolo's work, as demonstrated in his solos on "Wolverine Blues" and "Panama," avoids the arpeggio-based approach that imparted a mechanical quality to so many other first-generation New Orleans clarinetists. Instead, he offers a more linear, melodic style that would come to exert a marked influence on numerous later Chicago school reed players.

Yet those seeking the hottest jazz in Chicago, circa 1923, inevitably found their way to Lincoln Gardens, the largest dance hall on the South Side, where King Oliver led a band built primarily on the skills of transplanted New Orleans players. Was Oliver the greatest of the early New Orleans cornetists? On this matter, historical accounts are inconclusive. If anything, the deeper one probes, the more one encounters contradictions and unanswered questions. "Most everybody has heard of Joe Oliver and Louis Armstrong," Preston Jackson has asserted, "but few ever heard of Mutt Carey in his prime. Mutt Carey, in his day, was equal to Joe Oliver." Carey himself had a different story to tell, remarking that "Freddie Keppard had New Orleans all sewed up. He was the King—yes, he wore the crown." Edmund Hall, another of the first-generation players, cast his vote for Buddy Petit: "Buddy is a man they've never written much about. He kind of what you call set a pace around New Orleans. . . . If Buddy had left New Orleans to go to Chicago when a lot of the other men left, I'm positive he would have had a reputation equal to what the others got."[21] Or what about Emmett Hardy, the white New Orleans cornetist who never recorded and died of tuberculosis in 1925 at the age of twenty-two? "Emmett was the greatest musician I ever heard," later wrote Bix Beiderbecke, who had encountered the New Orleans player when Hardy traveled to Iowa to perform in the early 1920s.[22]

Whatever the virtues of these and other neglected figures, Oliver stands out as the New Orleans cornetist who left behind the most impressive body of recordings— recordings that, in many ways, help us understand what the other early figures of New Orleans jazz might have sounded like in their prime. Oliver's band may have lacked the ingenious arrangements of the Red Hot Peppers, or the understated elegance of the New Orleans Rhythm Kings. But its hot, dirty, swinging sound comes closest to the essence of the jazz experience. Its appeal draws from its rawness, its earthiness, its insistence. If Jelly Roll's music has aged like a fine wine, Oliver's still cuts to the quick like a jug of bootleg moonshine.

Oliver, for his part, was neither the most melodically inventive nor the most technically skilled of the New Orleans cornetists. Yet he remains, in many ways, the measuring rod by which we can gauge the work of other New Orleans brass players. His throaty, vocal sound inspired many imitators and represented, both conceptually and historically, a meeting ground of earlier and later jazz styles. Hence, Oliver's playing carried within it a clear link to a long list of underrecorded (or unrecorded) early New Orleans cornetists such as Manuel Perez, Freddie Keppard, Buddy Petit, and Buddy Bolden; it also looked ahead to the work of later players influenced by Oliver, not only the most famous musical son of New Orleans, Louis Armstrong, but also a host of brass players schooled in the Chicago tradition as well as the cadre of growling and moaning soloists in various Ellington bands, all of whom are clear descendants of King Joe. In his summation of the past, Oliver could integrate into his playing both the spontaneous (Bolden) and studied (Perez) traditions of early New Orleans brass playing, and in his anticipation of the future we can draw connecting lines all the way to Wynton Marsalis and beyond. By almost any measure—historical, musical, biographical—Joe "King" Oliver stands out as a seminal figure in the history of the music.

We know little about this performer's earliest years, and contradictory sources make even his date of birth a matter for speculation. It may have been as early as 1881 (according to his World War I draft registration card) or as late as 1885 (based on U.S. Census data). In any event, Oliver came of age in New Orleans during a period in which marching bands played a prominent role in the city's social activities. By his midteens, Oliver was playing with these ensembles, and an early apprenticeship with Perez in the Onward Brass Band was perhaps a crucial step in his musical development. Oliver's work retained the influence of these ensembles to the end, as shown by the marchlike elements in performances such as "High Society" and "Snake Rag." In 1918, Oliver left New Orleans, and over the next several years he performed not only in Chicago but as far away as California. In 1921, Oliver returned to Chicago, where his Creole Jazz Band drew an enthusiastic following, among both musicians and the general public, during an extended stint at Lincoln Gardens, a dance hall on East Thirty-first Street.

For the Lincoln Gardens engagement, Oliver used the same front-line players who had traveled with him to California: Honore Dutrey on trombone and Johnny Dodds on clarinet. But in a surprising move, Oliver now decided to add a second cornet player to the band. This duplication of roles was an oddity at the time—indeed, as it would be in a combo today—but it was an especially peculiar change for Oliver. In California, by contrast, he had relied on violin and saxophone in his attempts to give a richer texture to the group's sound. One might think Oliver would follow a similar path in Chicago or, at a minimum, hesitate to hire another cornetist, if only because of the risk that his own role as star cornetist in the band would be lessened.

In fact, something of this sort soon happened. As fate would have it, Oliver's choice for this new spot in the band, Louis Armstrong, an ascending star then still largely unknown outside New Orleans, would come to outshine not only Oliver, but the whole first generation of jazz musicians. Some have stressed Oliver's appreciation of Armstrong's talent as the motivating factor in this move; others have pointed to Oliver's desire to enhance the musicianship of the Creole Jazz Band. Perhaps Oliver's sense of his own declining skills as a cornetist—gum problems would eventually force him to abandon the horn—spurred him in this direction. Whatever the reason, Oliver acted quickly: within a few weeks of securing the Lincoln Gardens gig, in July 1922, he sent a telegram to Louis Armstrong requesting his immediate presence in Chicago.

KING OLIVER AND LOUIS ARMSTRONG

Even within his own lifetime, the mythic elements in Armstrong's biography began crowding out the facts. This conflation of truth and error begins literally with the details of his birth—usually given, by Armstrong and many later commentators, as the Fourth of July in the year 1900. One could hardly imagine a more fitting birthday for a legendary American figure, combining as it does both a symbolic commemoration of national independence and the dawn of the American century. Reality is less elegant. As Tad Jones and Gary Giddins have convincingly proven, the conventional account is exactly thirteen months out of synch. The baptismal certificate that Jones uncovered at Sacred Heart of Jesus Church in New Orleans states (in Latin) that Armstrong was born on August 4, 1901, the illegitimate son of William Armstrong and Mary Albert, and was baptized three weeks later.[23]

Armstrong's own accounts of his parents' role in his upbringing are not consistent, and statements by others are often equally incoherent. For example, Armstrong's parents, according to some versions, were born into slavery; yet records clearly show that the birthdates for both came after the Emancipation Proclamation. All accounts agree, however, in indicating that both William and Mayann, as Armstrong invariably referred to his mother, were often absentee parents. William was soon living with another woman, and eventually devoted his energies to raising a family with his new lover. Mayann, who appears to have been only fifteen years old at the time of Armstrong's birth, left Louis with his grandmother Josephine and moved to Perdido Street, at a time when that area was the center of prostitution in black Storyville—the implication being that Mayann earned her livelihood by that means.[24] Armstrong did not return to his mother's care until he was five; from that time on, he later recalled, a number of different "stepfathers" shared their living quarters. At the age of seven, Armstrong began working, selling coal to prostitutes in the red-light district.

The next turning point in Armstrong's biography has also taken on the overtones of popular legend in narrative accounts of his life and times. Shortly after midnight on January 1, 1913, Armstrong was arrested for disturbing the peace. His crime: shooting six blanks into the air from his stepfather's .38 revolver. Armstrong was placed in the Colored Waif's Home for Boys, where he remained for eighteen months. This punishment may have been a blessing in disguise: the youngster clearly flourished amidst the military discipline of the Waif's Home. Armstrong had already played cornet before this period—again contrary to the usual accounts[25]—as well as performed in a vocal quartet; nonetheless, the Waif's Home presented a secure, structured environment, where music making in the military tradition was stressed, and where recognition for achievement was provided. In this setting, Armstrong steadily moved up the ranks, first playing tambourine, then alto horn, next bugle, and finally cornet.

At the time of his release, into his father's custody in June 1914, Armstrong was reluctant to leave the Waif's Home. Perhaps with good reason: he was soon employed in backbreaking labor, driving a coal wagon, an occupation he pursued until the close of World War I. But as older, more experienced brass players left New Orleans, opportunities for Armstrong to earn money as a musician were on the rise. Over the next several years, his playing graced a number of celebrated bands, including Kid Ory's group (where he replaced Oliver, after the latter's departure to Chicago), clarinetist Sam Dutrey's Silver Leaf Band, Fate Marable's riverboat ensemble, and Papa Celestin's Tuxedo Brass Band. By the time Oliver sent for the young cornetist, Armstrong may have been unknown to jazz fans in Chicago; however, musicians in New Orleans were already taking note of this up-and-coming player.

The recordings made by Armstrong's new ensemble, King Oliver's Creole Jazz Band, present a number of challenges to the modern-day listener. The most obvious one stems from the poor sound quality of circa 1923 acoustic recordings. This technology, while acceptable in capturing the sound of a single instrument or a human voice, was decidedly weak in presenting the delicate balance between different instruments in a jazz band. And few ensembles were less well suited to this technology than the Creole Jazz Band, with its passionate interplay between contrasting horn lines. But sonic authenticity is perhaps less of a stumbling block to modern ears than is the very unmodern aesthetic vision underpinning early New Orleans jazz music. Unlike later jazz, with its democratic reliance on individual solos, the

New Orleans pioneers created a music in which the group was primary, in which each instrument was expected to play a specific role, not assert its independence. The most characteristic moment in these recordings of early jazz takes place when the lead instruments, usually cornet, clarinet, and trombone, engage in spontaneous counterpoint. The trombone takes over the low register, providing a deep, deliberate bass melody; the clarinet plays more complex figures, often consisting of arpeggios or other rapidly fingered patterns, in a higher register; the cornet moves mostly within the middle register, playing less elaborate melodies than the clarinet, but pushing the ensemble forward with propulsive, swinging lead lines. No early jazz band was better at this ensemble style of playing than Oliver's Creole Jazz Band.

Oliver's melodic vocabulary was primitive, almost simpleminded, by modern standards. His famous solo on "Dipper Mouth Blues" builds off a few notes, a concise melodic fragment played over and over with minor variations. Here, as elsewhere, the virtue of Oliver's playing lies not in linear improvisation but in his seamless blending with the band and, especially, in the haunting vocal quality of his cornet work. King Oliver left behind no interviews with jazz historians, and we can only speculate about the specifics of his artistic vision; however, one comment that has come down to us is especially revealing. Oliver claimed to have spent ten years refining his cornet tone. This obsession with sound gets to the heart of the New Orleans revolution in music, and to the essence of Oliver's contribution to it. Instead of aspiring to classical purity of tone, emulating an otherworldly perfection, the early jazz players strived to make their instruments sound like human voices, with all the variations, imperfections, and colorations that such a model entailed.

This was an approach to music that defied conventional notation and refused to be reduced to a systematic methodology. Richard Hadlock, recalling a music lesson given to him by Sidney Bechet, conveys something of this fastidious New Orleans attention to tone production:

"I'm going to give you one note today," he once told me. "See how many ways you can play that note—growl it, smear it, flat it, sharp it, do anything you want to it. That's how you express your feelings in this music. It's like talking."[26]

This admonition—"growl it, smear it, flat it, sharp it, do anything you want to it"— could very well be a description of the rugged beauty of Oliver's playing. His music is not about scales or passing chords; it is a celebration of color and texture.

From this perspective, King Oliver's Creole Jazz Band provided an odd context for Armstrong to hone his skills as a jazz musician. Herein lies the oddity: Armstrong would soon emerge as the first great soloist in the history of jazz, yet he refined his talents in an ensemble that featured few solos. Oliver conceived of jazz as collective music making in which the instruments were interdependent, and no one horn was allowed to dominate. Armstrong, in particular, was especially constrained: as second cornetist, he was expected to add a supporting line or harmonic fill under Oliver's lead line—and the recordings of the band show that, when so inclined, he was capable of doing this with great skill; nonetheless, Armstrong's more powerful tone and greater technical facility made him a poor choice for such a subservient role.

At times, as on the OKeh recording of "Mabel's Dream" or in his quasi-solo on "Froggie Moore," the second cornetist clearly overpowers the bandleader—in New Orleans jazz, the equivalent of the chief steward's mutiny. On the rare occasions when he was allowed to stand out from the rest of the group, on "Chimes Blues" and "Tears," Armstrong presents poised and fluid lines that contrast markedly with the rest of the band. Even at this early stage, Armstrong was a player of consequence, demonstrating his ability to hear and adapt to the musical flow around him, as well as a rhythmic sensibility that was paradoxically both relaxed and propulsive. On the other hand, Armstrong would never match Oliver's mastery of the mute, or be able to evoke the wide range of growls and moans the latter could elicit from his horn. His wife (and colleague in Oliver's band) Lil Hardin would later recall how Armstrong spent days trying to imitate his boss's famous solo on "Dipper Mouth Blues"—a solo that, despite its melodic simplicity, he could never quite recreate. "I think it kind of discouraged him," she noted, "because Joe was his idol and he wanted to play like Joe."[27]

The sensation of listening to these performances is both exhilarating and disturbing. Armstrong's musicianship was far beyond that of his colleagues—hence the exhilaration. It contrasts in the sharpest degree with Hardin's penchant for muddling the chord changes, trombonist Honore Dutrey's often uninspired melody lines, and Dodds's hesitant approach to his parts (compare the King Oliver sides to Dodds's carefree and superior work with Jelly Roll Morton or his fine performances with the New Orleans Wanderers). Armstrong's mastery can only stand out impressively in such a setting. Yet, at the same time, his individualistic approach also comes across as disturbingly subversive. Is it not a deliberate undermining of a collective aesthetic? In the context of his later recordings, with their emphasis on solo playing, his charismatic and heroic stance is an asset, but in the setting of the Creole Jazz Band it disrupts the seamless blending of instrumental voices that is the crowning glory of the early New Orleans style. Here we encounter one of the grand ironies of jazz history—and a telling reminder of the rapid pace of change in the music's development—namely that, because of Armstrong's presence, the King Oliver recordings from the early 1920s stand out both as a paramount example of the New Orleans collective style and also anticipate its obsolescence, already hinting at the more individualistic ethos that would replace it.

The passing of the baton from Oliver to Armstrong also marks another decisive turning point in the history of American music. Oliver represents a more Africanized sensibility, in which musicians work with sound textures rather than pure and discrete notes. The idea of codified musical structures built on notes and scales is a distinctly Western idea, our legacy from Pythagoras and the Greeks, and quite alien to the traditions of Africa. For Western music to assimilate the jazz sensibility, it required an innovator like Louis Armstrong, a visionary who was more than just a sound painter, but a true master of licks and phrases and all the complicated combinations of notes that appeal to the Western musical mind. We see the same transition in the blues, when we move from the aural ambiguities of Son House to the precise constructions of Robert Johnson. This adaptation is never pure or complete. What an Armstrong or Johnson plays is never just notes. Even so, an important divide has been crossed, and the African heritage has now been schematized in a new manner, transformed through the impact of these masters in a way that allows the alien style to seep into the inner life of American (and eventually global) music.

By mid-1924, the core of Oliver's band had left, primarily because of the sidemen's suspicion that their leader was withholding money due them. By the time Oliver recorded again, with a new group named the Dixie Syncopators, the jazz world had changed as a result of the growing popularity of the big band format. Oliver attempted to adjust his music to this emerging sensibility with the addition of two or three saxophones and the adoption of more tightly arranged pieces. This later phase in Oliver's career is often dismissed by critics for its abandonment of the more spontaneous New Orleans interplay between the horns. Nonetheless, Oliver might have successfully weathered the transition to the big band era with this new approach had not his playing begun to deteriorate in the face of continual embouchure problems. The extent of these and their chronology are a matter of debate, but the broad general trend is unmistakable: as time went on, Oliver played less frequently, and the quality of his work was inconsistent at best. By the mid-1930s, he could no longer play at all.

Various letters written by the cornetist toward the end of his life, and later published, have been rightly called by jazz critic Martin Williams "among the most moving documents which have been preserved from the past in jazz."[28] These, combined with anecdotal accounts of Oliver's later days, serve as a disturbing reminder of not only Oliver's plight, but also the degraded conditions of life for southern blacks during the Great Depression. Having outlived his fame, Oliver worked long hours in menial jobs—pool-room janitor, roadside vendor, and the like—struggling, without success, to raise enough money to purchase a railroad ticket to join his sister in New York. At his death, in April 1938, he was living in near poverty in Savannah, Georgia. His return to New York was posthumous: Oliver's sister used her rent money to bring the cornetist's body to New York, where he was buried at Woodlawn Cemetery in an unmarked grave, since no funds were left to provide a headstone. (A memorial was later put in place, courtesy of the New Jersey Jazz Society.) Louis Armstrong, Clarence Williams, and a few other musicians were in attendance.

By the late 1930s, Oliver's music may have been all but forgotten among the general public, but through his protégé, Louis Armstrong, Oliver would leave a lasting mark on both the jazz idiom and the broader streams of popular culture. By this time, Armstrong's influence was pervasive in the jazz world. But even more remarkable was Armstrong's ability, then becoming increasingly evident, to extend his fame beyond the confines of jazz, to develop an international renown and status, with his visage and demeanor instantly recognizable even to those who paid little attention to jazz music. In this regard, Armstrong ranks with only a handful of figures from the first half of the twentieth century—Charlie Chaplin, Pablo Picasso, Babe Ruth, Al Jolson, Shirley Temple, Winston Churchill—whose fame transcends the realities of time and place and blends into a mythic larger-than-life presence, one in which the border between image and actuality blurs.

Armstrong's status as cultural icon, however, is perhaps a mixed blessing for the student of jazz history. With such celebrities, the image threatens to overshadow the essence, or even to become the essence. To understand Armstrong's role as jazz innovator, and not just as a mass market entertainer, requires us to look past the superficial trappings of his fame, and instead probe deeply into the body of work he left behind. It is here that we will uncover the vital core of Armstrong's achievement as a jazz musician.

3 The Jazz Age

THE AGE OF THE SOLOIST

Revolutions, whether in arts or matters of state, create a new world only by sacrificing the old. With jazz, it is no different. To be sure, Louis Armstrong, who closed the book on the dynastic tradition in New Orleans jazz—putting an end to its colorful lineage of Kings Bolden, Keppard, and Oliver—stands out as an unlikely regicide. Armstrong always spoke with deference, bordering on awe, of his musical roots, and with especial devotion of his mentor Joe Oliver. Yet the evidence of the grooves does not lie: the superiority of Armstrong's musicianship, the unsurpassed linear momentum of his improvised lines, could serve only to make Oliver, Morton, Bolden, and the whole New Orleans ensemble tradition look passé, a horse-and-buggy cantering by Henry Ford's assembly line. The New Orleans pioneers exit stage left; Armstrong on trumpet enters stage right heralding the new Age of the Soloist.

Or so it seems in retrospect. But the ebb and flow of any history seldom match the rigid categories and sharp delineations we apply after the fact. In actuality, the revolution initiated by Armstrong took place in fits and starts, and with little fanfare at the time. After Armstrong's departure from King Oliver's Creole Jazz Band, over a year would pass before he would record as a leader. And even when those famous recordings were planned—the classic "Hot Fives"—the record company considered enlisting a better-known leader to front the band. Most accounts stress that Armstrong's talents may have been neglected by the general public, but were amply recognized by the musical community—"his playing was revered by countless jazz musicians," runs a typical commentary[1]—but even this claim is suspect.

Fletcher Henderson, Armstrong's first major employer after Oliver, made the trumpeter accept a cut in pay to join his band. Many accounts suggest that Henderson, in fact, preferred the playing of cornetist Joe Smith, and that Armstrong was hired only because Smith was unavailable.

Could this be true? The recorded evidence bears out the claim: when Smith rejoined the Henderson band in the spring of 1925, an increasing number of solos went to him, not Armstrong. Smith, to his credit, performed admirably: though he lacked Armstrong's rhythmic drive, his warm sound and ease of execution could hardly be faulted and may have been better received by the average dance hall patron, circa 1925. Henderson was even less enthusiastic about Armstrong's singing, an attitude that greatly frustrated the new band member. Years later he would exclaim: "Fletcher didn't dig me like Joe Oliver. He had a million dollar talent in his band and he never thought to let me sing."[2]

Armstrong may not have taken New York, or even the Henderson band, by storm, but slowly and steadily he exerted his influence on the musical community. Brass players were the first to feel the heat of Armstrong's rising star; but, as with Charlie Parker's innovations twenty years later, Armstrong's contributions eventually spread to every instrument in the band. Don Redman's arrangements, Coleman Hawkins's saxophone work—one by one, the converts were won. Armstrong the sideman? Not really. Armstrong was a leader, if only by example, during his time with the Henderson band. In an eight-bar passage from his solo on "Shanghai Shuffle," he offers a telling lesson in rhythmic ingenuity; here Armstrong stokes the fire merely by repeating— with variations in length, placement, and intensity—a single note. What would have been monotonous in the hands of any other band member comes to life under the sway of Armstrong's sure mastery of syncopation. On "Shanghai Shuffle" and many of his other features with the Henderson band—"Copenhagen" from October 1924, "Mandy Make Up Your Mind" from early December, "I'll See You in My Dreams" recorded a month later—Armstrong was pointing the way to a more modern conception of improvisation. In the end, his impact was decisive—for the Henderson band, for the New York scene, for the jazz world.

Armstrong's stiffest challenge during these months leading up to the Hot Five recordings came in a different setting. As a sideman in the Clarence Williams Blue Five, Armstrong faced off with Sidney Bechet—"the only man who," in the words of critic Gary Giddins, "for a short while, seemed [Armstrong's] equal as an improviser during those transitional years."[3] Bechet, born May 14, 1897, in New Orleans, may have been only four years older than Armstrong, but he already had accumulated a world of experience since first leaving New Orleans in his late teens. In 1919, he had traveled to Europe with Will Marion Cook's Southern Syncopated Orchestra, where he dazzled audiences and won the praise of noted Swiss conductor Ernest Ansermet. In a prescient piece published in *Revue Romande* in 1919, Ansermet declared Bechet to be "an artist of genius" and suggested that his clarinet playing was "perhaps the highway the whole world will swing along tomorrow."[4] Other memorable performances by this early ambassador for hot music included a garden party at Buckingham Palace for the Prince of Wales (the future King Edward VIII) and an Armistice Ball at the Royal Albert Hall. Bechet returned to the United States with an enhanced reputation, but also—and perhaps more importantly—with a soprano saxophone, which he had spotted in a shop window during a stroll through London's West End.

Up until this point, Bechet's work had been restricted to clarinet, an instrument he had learned under the influence of three New Orleans pioneers of the instrument: George Baquet, "Big Eye" Louis Nelson, and Lorenzo Tio. The tradition Bechet inherited from these musicians was anything but primitive; indeed, the clarinet was, in certain respects, the most advanced of the jazz instruments during these early years. Clarinetists in the New Orleans tradition worked assiduously to develop great finger flexibility and, as a result, were often assigned the most intricate parts in performance. This fluid approach to the clarinet grew out of a tradition of melodic embellishment, rather than the freer linear development we associate with later jazz horn players, as demonstrated by the well-known obbligato section in the piece "High Society," which served as a technical showpiece for many New Orleans clarinetists. Melodic complexity, however, was far from the only distinguishing characteristic of the New Orleans clarinet sound. Figured patterns built from arpeggiated chords were often employed as the building blocks for New Orleans clarinet solos; because of this, these players needed to have a reasonably sophisticated understanding of chord structures. Years later, Coleman Hawkins would develop this penchant into a probing, harmonically adept saxophone style, but even with the first generation of jazz reed players, the chordal implications of their playing were prominent.

Yet the clarinet tradition that Bechet inherited was not without its limitations. The figured patterns that served as the foundation for many early clarinet solos soon came to represent a stylistic dead end. Caught up in the static vocabulary, these first-generation players tended to leave the rhythmic potential of their instrument largely untapped. Syncopations played a modest role in their efforts and, when employed, rarely moved beyond restatements of the rhythmic patterns developed years before in the ragtime idiom. And even at its dirtiest, the New Orleans clarinet rarely approached the rawness of the more unbridled cornet improvisations. In this environment, it was mostly left to the brass players—Bolden, Keppard, Oliver, Armstrong—to expand the rhythmic vocabulary and explore the variations of tone possible within the context of the New Orleans style.

Bechet played the most prominent role in developing the clarinet as a mature solo voice in jazz. Other performers, no doubt, also contributed—hear, for instance, Leon Roppolo's underappreciated recordings with the New Orleans Rhythm Kings that gave notice of the instrument's potential as early as 1922—yet Bechet's role was especially influential in pointing the way toward a more melodic, linear conception of the horn, and drawing on a more expansive palette of sounds. Much like King Oliver, Bechet developed a voicelike quality to his playing, and exhibited a rare sensitivity to the potential of timbre and phrasing. These skills allowed him to stand out as a premier soloist, yet—unlike Armstrong—Bechet felt equally at home submerging his melody lines in the larger ensemble.

This difference in temperament between the two great New Orleans players is evident in their December 1924 pairing on "Early Every Morn," where they ostensibly support vocalist Alberta Hunter. Bechet's soprano work, with its mixture of high held notes and diving phrases into the lower register, blends well with the group and provides ample space for Armstrong's countermelodies. Armstrong, in contrast, assumes a more assertive posture and belts out a flamboyant coda to the performance, one that tends to eclipse Hunter and the rest of the band. Such exhibitions of technique were not Bechet's forte. Yet he too could indulge in grandstanding when the situation so warranted. On another collaboration from the period, "Texas Moaner Blues," Armstrong again takes center stage with a brief burst of double time in his feature break, but Bechet is not to be outdone in this encounter. He lets loose a swarming cannonade of angular phrases, less fluid than the cornetist's, but clearly signaling a determination to match any contender note for note, even the great Louis Armstrong. And this time Bechet steals the show with a bluesy coda.

Bechet flirted with big band music, and even served a brief stint with the Ellington orchestra; but, for the most part, he retained his predilection for the New Orleans ensemble style. In the early 1930s, when Armstrong adapted his music to the public's newfound preference for big bands, Bechet kept true to the earlier approach, most notably in his recordings with trumpeter Tommy Ladnier. Their work on "I Found a New Baby" and "Maple Leaf Rag" from 1932 demonstrated, to those willing to listen, that the old style had not lost its charm. Audiences, however, were largely unimpressed—the New Orleans revival was still almost a decade away. After an unsuccessful stint at the Savoy Ballroom, Bechet and Ladnier temporarily left the music business, setting up a tailor shop in Harlem, where the trumpeter shined shoes while Bechet focused mostly on pressing and repairs—when he wasn't busy in the back room cooking Creole food or hosting a jam session.

Bechet was eventually enticed back into performing by an offer from bandleader Noble Sissle. For four years, until 1938, Bechet worked as a sideman for Sissle, before leaving to front his own group and pursue freelance opportunities. During the late 1930s and early 1940s, public interest in the early pioneers of jazz was on the rise, with Bechet being one of the beneficiaries of these changing attitudes. Bechet began recording in traditional jazz settings, for Blue Note and other labels, as well as gigging regularly at Nick's and other New York venues. Unlike some other first-generation players, Bechet's skills had not declined by the time his music had come back into favor with jazz fans. His celebrated 1939 recording of "Summertime" is a case in point. Playing soprano saxophone—an instrument that in the hands of many others has an all too limited expressive range and a disconcerting tendency to veer out of tune—Bechet employs his full arsenal: growls, moans, plaintive calls, luminous high tones, whispered asides, even a sly quote from an opera aria.

Bechet returned to Europe in May 1949, for the first time in almost twenty years, to participate in a Paris jazz festival. The event was a success, and Bechet came back to France in the fall for more performances, followed by a trip to England. In a move that many later American jazz musicians would emulate, Bechet decided to settle permanently overseas; it was not a departure from his roots, he explained, since it brought him "closer to Africa." In the Old World, he received the adulation, financial security, and social acceptance that no black jazz musician could find in the music's native country. Performing and recording dates were abundant, as were a whole range of other artistic opportunities; these years found Bechet entertaining capacity audiences at nightclubs and concert halls, and also involved in ballet and cinema projects. Shortly before his death in 1959 he even turned *litterateur*, completing his autobiography *Treat It Gentle*, a plainspoken work that many of his fans cherish almost as much as his legacy of recordings.

THE HOT FIVES AND HOT SEVENS

Several months before leaving for New York, Armstrong married his colleague in the Oliver band, pianist Lil Hardin. This was the second marriage for both the twenty-three-year-old Armstrong (in his teens he had tied the knot with Daisy Parker, from whom he soon was separated and eventually divorced) and for twenty-six-year-old Hardin. College educated, sophisticated, ambitious: Hardin possessed many of the qualities that Armstrong lacked. Most accounts agree that her aspirations for his career, not Armstrong's, were responsible for his break with Oliver and his decision to join Fletcher Henderson.

Similarly, Hardin served as the reason for Armstrong's return to Chicago in the latter part of 1925. The stint with Henderson in New York and an ensuing tour with the band had meant an enforced separation for the pair. Several motives now drove Hardin to seek his return: like any newlywed, she was appropriately anxious to have her husband closer at hand; in addition, she may have suspected Armstrong's dalliances (which ultimately capsized their marriage); she may have also seen opportunities for advancing Armstrong's career in Chicago; and clearly she could benefit from his presence in her own band, now set for an engagement at Chicago's Dreamland Cafe. With some misgivings, Armstrong left the Henderson ensemble, yet took consolation in the leader's promise to rehire him if he decided to return to New York.

If duties as a husband and opportunities as a sideman brought Armstrong back to Chicago, it was work as a recording star that eventually proved decisive during this period. On November 12, 1925, Armstrong entered a makeshift studio—the OKeh label's portable recording equipment was in Chicago only a few months out of the year—to undertake his first session as a leader. This date initiated a period of fertile music making, one that would establish Armstrong as the dominant jazz instrumentalist of his generation, perhaps of all time. Surely no other body of work in the jazz idiom has been so loved and admired as the results of these celebrated sessions, the immortal Hot Fives and Hot Sevens. In historical importance and sheer visionary grandeur, only a handful of other recordings—the Ellington band work of the early 1940s, the Charlie Parker Savoy and Dial sessions, the Miles Davis recordings of the late 1950s come to mind—can compare with them. Certainly none can surpass them. It was a rare, felicitous instance of an artist facing a defining moment in a career, and in the process of self-discovery also crystallizing a turning point for an entire art form.

What were the elements that constituted this breakthrough in jazz performance? Armstrong's role in transforming the focus of jazz from the ensemble to the soloist has already been mentioned. But how Armstrong effected this change is the real crux of the story. It wasn't that earlier jazz players were incapable of playing solos. But, compared with Armstrong, they lacked the technical resources and, even more, the creative depth to make the solo the compelling centerpiece of jazz music. For all their virtues, none of the other great players of the day—whether Bechet or Beiderbecke, Hawkins or Hines—could match Armstrong's vast range of rhythmic devices, his variegated ways of phrasing, or just the sheer inner momentum and outer logic of his melody lines.

The method book Armstrong inspired during this period, called *50 Hot Choruses for the Cornet*, is far from his greatest artistic achievement, but in its own way it reveals the essence of his contribution to jazz in a way that no single solo can. To compile this volume, the Melrose publishing house recorded numerous Armstrong improvisations, had them transcribed and printed commercially, then sold the sheet music to other aspiring jazz players. The original recordings that led to this tutorial have been lost, but one need go no farther than the transcriptions to see, in page after page, measure after measure, the innovative quality of the trumpeter's work. Many of these advanced melodic ideas simply did not exist in jazz before Armstrong. The individual phrases and ways of incorporating syncopation into a jazz line were no doubt highly original at the time; but over and above these isolated gems of improvisational acumen, an ineffable wholeness to Armstrong's improvisational style must have been a revelation to other players of that era. The unassailable logic of the phrases matched their rhythmic intensity and sense of purpose. As Richard Hadlock describes it, Armstrong "regardless of tempo, always *completed* each phrase and carried each sustained tone out to its fullest value, creating the illusion of unhurried ease, even in the most turbulent arrangement."[5]

It is one of the ironies of jazz history that this fundamental element of Armstrong's contribution is mostly obscured for many modern listeners by the very success of the trumpeter's trailblazing. To uninformed ears, these Armstrong phrases often sound commonplace today, familiar devices used by many players; it is easy to forget that the jazz world originally learned them from Armstrong. To gauge his true impact, one must go back and compare his solo work with what came before. Listen, for example, to King Oliver's stilted attempt to swing the two-bar break on his September 1924 recording of "Construction Gang." Halfway through his break, Oliver loses his way, unable to marry his ambitious double-time phrasing to the ground rhythm. After a brief burst of energy, the horn line fades away abruptly, the beat lost until the piano reenters a moment later. Compare this with any number of Armstrong hot breaks, with their rhythmic vitality and assured execution.

The Hot Five, unlike most previous jazz recording units, was not a regular working band, but was put together solely for these sessions on the OKeh label. At first glance, the band's pretensions were modest. In terms of instrumentation and repertoire, the Hot Five was very much in the mold of earlier New Orleans ensembles. The group's lineup, which overlapped to a great degree with King Oliver's Creole Jazz Band, featured Armstrong with wife Lil Hardin Armstrong on piano, Johnny Dodds on clarinet, Kid Ory on trombone, and Johnny St. Cyr on banjo. But from the opening measures of the first take, "My Heart," something different is in the air. The three horns may be playing New Orleans counterpoint, but here Armstrong's lead line dominates the proceedings from the start in a way King Oliver would never have allowed. Armstrong once claimed that Oliver had asked him to stand far away from the recording horn during the Creole Jazz Band sessions so that his cornet would not overwhelm the ensemble. On these Hot Five sides, the opposite seems true; Armstrong is clearly positioned front and center and, if anything, the other players sound as though they are standing several paces behind him. But this dominance of Armstrong is more than a matter of relative volume. His melody lines ripple with a newfound freedom and confidence that set them apart from the other instrumental sounds. Who dares to complain that, when his bandmates solo on the ensuing take of "Gut Bucket Blues," Armstrong talks over their contributions? He is the clear star here, and the other solos are featured—or drowned out—at his discretion.

Follow-up recording dates for Louis Armstrong and His Hot Five find the bandleader even more in command. The clearest indication of this comes in the February 26 session of the following year, where Armstrong the vocalist takes charge, not only revealing his highly personal manner of interpreting a song, but also inventing—at least according to legend—scat singing in the process. Armstrong later described how, in the middle of recording "Heebie Jeebies," he had dropped the lyric sheet to the tune and was forced to improvise hornlike lines, built on wordless syllables, with his voice. We have good reason to be skeptical of this colorful story. Earlier examples of scat singing (as this technique came to be called) can be found: Al Jolson relied on it repeatedly on his 1911 recording of "That Haunting Melody," to cite one prominent example, and Jelly Roll Morton traced it back another decade, claiming that New Orleans musicians learned scat singing from Mississippi-born Joe Sims, who was performing wordless vocals around the turn of the century. Yet after the Hot Five recording, this practice became closely associated with Armstrong, and it remains, to this day, a trademark of jazz vocalists.

As if this were not enough for a day's work, Armstrong also contributed a number of his finest horn solos to date at this same session. Armstrong always took delight in the use of stop-time choruses, a tried-and-true jazz device in which the band would accompany a lead player with a simple rhythmic pattern—in its most common form, striking a staccato note on the first beat of each bar or every other bar—while remaining silent the rest of the time. Unless the soloist possessed enormous rhythmic ingenuity, these stop-time choruses could sound tense or even clumsy; but with a master of percussive phrasing, such as Armstrong, the stop-time technique could serve as the compelling centerpiece to a performance. On two of the numbers recorded at this February 26, 1926, session, "Oriental Strut" and "Cornet Chop Suey," Armstrong bursts forth with his finest stop-time playing to date, and on the latter he adds a swirling coda that was much imitated by his contemporaries. (The use of Asian-inflected song titles to emphasize the exoticism of early jazz was not uncommon during the period, and makes the later accusations that Armstrong and others of his generation leveled at bebop—deriding it as "Chinese music" or "jujitsu music"—all the more ironic.) By comparison with Armstrong's work from the following year, these solos reveal slight imperfections and moments of tentativeness, but at the time they represented the finest body of jazz improvisation yet recorded. Follow-up sessions from June and November 1926 find Armstrong displaying increasing fluency in the upper register of the horn, and exerting more control over his tone and phrasing.

After the November session, a period of almost six months passed before Armstrong's band returned to the studio, this time in an enlarged format. With the addition of Baby Dodds on drums and Pete Briggs on tuba, the new group—christened the Hot Seven—boasted a more prominent, more driving rhythm section, one better able to provide a hard-swinging foundation to Armstrong's horn lines and vocals. Armstrong's new conception of jazz, with its emphasis on the soloist, demanded just such a change. His choice of instrumentation reinforced this shift, and reflected his need for a more streamlined accompaniment, one that anticipated the future evolution of the rhythm section—in which piano, bass (filling a functional role similar to the tuba in early jazz by supporting the group with low register on-the-beat bass lines), and drums, with the optional addition of guitar, worked together in providing a looser and more fluid underpinning to improvisation.

During the course of several sessions in May 1927, this expanded Armstrong ensemble showed how much the leader's conception—as well as the scope of his musical ambitions—had continued to mature in the intervening months. On "Wild Man Blues" the old New Orleans counterpoint is all but gone, relegated to a few brief bars at the close. Instead, the piece is given over to two long solos, one by Armstrong and another by Johnny Dodds. Dodds's work from the Hot Seven sessions reveals the great strides he had made since his days with Oliver, with his bluesy solos on "Willie the Weeper" and "Alligator Crawl" standing out as especially poised. But no other horn player could outshine Armstrong at this point in the music's history. On "Alligator Crawl," Armstrong follows Dodds with a masterful solo, both in terms of his rhythmic command (hear the skipping syncopations with which he kicks off his solo) and technical acumen, as he moves with ease from register to register. But the crowning glory of these May sessions came in Armstrong's brilliant stop-time work on "Potato Head Blues." This virtuoso improvisation set a new standard, even for Armstrong. The phrasing, the tonal control, the assured sense of time—one is aware of only the slightest hint of hesitation, midway through the chorus, before Armstrong pushes ahead triumphantly—all contributed to making "Potato Head Blues" the most memorable of the Hot Seven recordings. Follow-up efforts with the Hot Five, from later in the year, find Armstrong in equally fine form, contributing bravura performances of "Struttin' with Some Barbecue" and "Hotter Than That."

The Armstrong revolution was clearly announced in these recordings; yet—strange to say—few members of the general public took notice. He continued to work as a sideman even after this extraordinary output with the Hot Five and Hot Seven. Anticipating the Beatles and Glenn Gould, Armstrong apparently felt no need to bring the music of the recording studio out in front of paying audiences, and these two bands, by any measure his most famous, never went on the road or played a nightclub engagement. Armstrong's chief paying gig during these Chicago days was as a member of violinist Carroll Dickerson's ensemble. Yet the Dickerson connection was not without its benefits, if only for its fortuitous pairing of Armstrong with pianist Earl Hines, another rising star laboring in semi-obscurity as a sideman in the band. The intersection of these two careers would produce some of the most exciting jazz of the decade.

The twenty-four-year-old Hines had come to Chicago at the close of his teens. A native of Duquesne, Pennsylvania, where he was born on December 28, 1903, Earl Kenneth Hines grew up in a middle-class black family where, as he later described it, "I was just surrounded by music."[6] Years later, critics would characterize his distinctive approach to the piano as the "trumpet style," linking it to the melody lines of Armstrong, yet the roots of this technique can perhaps be traced back to his childhood, when he began his musical studies learning trumpet from his father, who worked days as a foreman on the coal docks, and piano from his mother. But Hines's stylistic breakthrough went far beyond the use of trumpetlike lines on the piano. As part of his development, he also studied and assimilated elements of the classical repertoire as well as a wide range of popular styles, including the blues, ragtime, and early stride piano. Hines's ability to integrate these sources of inspiration seamlessly into his own vision of keyboard performance remains a crucial part of his legacy. For, more than any other musician, Hines stands out as responsible for pushing jazz piano beyond the limiting horizontal structures of ragtime and into a more versatile and linear approach, one that continues to hold sway to this day.

Hines may have lacked the harmonic sophistication of an Art Tatum or the dulcet-toned piano touch of a Teddy Wilson, but his rhythmic ingenuity—the complex interweavings of his phrases, his gamesmanship with the beat, the percussive quality of his attack—was unsurpassed. At critical moments in the course of a solo, Hines's hands would nervously fly across the keyboard, letting loose with a jagged, off-balance phrase, a flurry of notes as agitated as a swarm of honeybees forced from their hive. In the midst of this chaos, the pulse of the music would disappear. Time stood suspended. Yet almost as unexpectedly as it had erupted, this musical anarchy would suddenly subside, and the measured swing of the composition would reemerge, again solidly locked into the ground beat. Put a metronome to this apparent burst of jazz arrhythmia, and you will find that Hines has kept strict time all along.

By all accounts, Hines developed his mastery of the piano at an early age. Even during his high school years, Hines led his own trio, and by the time he left for Chicago had gigged widely in and around Pittsburgh as a piano soloist, sideman, and accompanist to vocalists. While still in Pittsburgh he heard stride pianists Luckey Roberts and James P. Johnson, and his tenure in Chicago overlapped with Jelly Roll Morton's as well as Teddy Weatherford's—the latter is a fascinating figure, best known for influencing Hines with his intricate two-handed keyboard style, but who deserves equal credit for his pioneering jazz advocacy in South Asia, where he performed from 1937 until his death from cholera in Calcutta in 1945. In Chicago,

Hines worked primarily as a solo pianist before joining Dickerson, in time to participate in a lengthy road trip that took him to California and back. His return to Chicago coincided roughly with Armstrong's, and soon these two dominant forces in the city's jazz life were collaborating regularly, in Dickerson's band and in many other settings. For a while, the two even joined forces in operating their own dance hall—a venture that lasted only a few weeks before they decided that working as sidemen offered a higher (and more predictable) income stream.

Following the closure of their club, Hines entered into a second musical partnership almost as fruitful as his work with Armstrong. Soon after joining New Orleans clarinetist Jimmie Noone at Chicago's Apex Club, Hines participated in a series of recordings that rank among the finest combo sides of the era. Known as the Apex Club recordings, they reflect a combination of melodic fluency and hot rhythms that was rare at the time. Noone had studied with Bechet and apprenticed with Keppard before leaving New Orleans in 1917, and later served a lengthy stint with Doc Cooke. During this period, Noone developed a clarinet style distinguished by its smooth phrasing and assured execution—one that would inspire Benny Goodman and many other players associated with Chicago jazz. Hines was the perfect foil for Noone. Their crisp clarinet-piano dialogues would stand unsurpassed until Benny Goodman and Teddy Wilson initiated a further revolution in small-combo jazz some years later. Indeed, there was only one jazz collaboration of any sort at the time to rival the Apex Club music—and that was the one Hines embarked on in late June 1928, when he joined Armstrong in the studio for follow-up recordings of the latter's Hot Five.

Armstrong leads off "West End Blues" with an unaccompanied introduction that has justly been praised over the years. It lasts a brief twelve seconds, but what an amazing twelve seconds. Armstrong's singular mastery of the horn is packed solidly into these few bars of improvisation. "I felt as if I had stared into the sun's eye," was Max Kaminsky's later description of his first hearing of this recording—a reaction that must have been shared by many other jazz musicians of the time. "All I could think of doing was run away and hide until the blindness left me."[7] Yet Hines's piano solo, also only a few measures in duration, does not suffer by comparison. Midway through his chorus, his right hand accentuates a stuttering phrase in octaves—one of the trumpetlike lines so characteristic of his approach to the keyboard—that both propels the music forward and encapsulates the wide chasm between the jazz sensibility of Hines and the ragtime-based approach of virtually all of his piano contemporaries. On any short list of the defining recordings in the history of jazz, this performance holds a secure position.

"Weather Bird," the duet Hines recorded with Armstrong a few months later, reflects this same assured command of the new musical vocabulary being developed in Chicago at the close of the Jazz Age. Compare the fluid phrasing of Armstrong and Hines on this performance with the duet version of "King Porter Stomp" recorded, four years earlier, by Jelly Roll Morton and King Oliver. On the latter number, Morton keeps close to the "oom-pah, oom-pah" rhythm of ragtime, while Oliver sounds reluctant to move too far afield from the written melody. In contrast, on "Weather Bird," both Armstrong and Hines playfully employ subtle hesitations and anticipations in phrasing and engage in ambitious flights beyond the written score—if, in fact, there was a written score at the session—all with a comfortable command several steps beyond the scope of the early New Orleans pioneers. This was jazz, pure and simple, freed from both the shadow of ragtime and the dictates of dance music.

Yet Armstrong, more than Hines—indeed, more than any jazz player of his day—was just as comfortable working within the narrower confines of popular music. Especially in his singing, which he increasingly featured during the closing years of the decade, Armstrong captured the imagination of both jazz devotees and the general public. Musicians could marvel at his ability to swing the melody with his voice, to recraft a song with the same inventiveness that he brought to his trumpet work, but the irrepressible gusto of Armstrong's delivery and his instantly recognizable style, epitomized in the raspiness that increasingly marked his singing after the early 1930s, appealed to the mass market as well. He could take a dirge and make it into an ode to joy, transform the despair of "(What Did I Do to Be So) Black and Blue" into, in the words of Ralph Ellison, "a beam of lyrical sound." As early as his March 1929 recording of "I Can't Give You Anything but Love," Armstrong was already demonstrating his sure instinct for deconstructing the vocal line, departing radically from the melody, and singing far behind the beat in a performance that ranks among the finest early ballad recordings in the jazz idiom. A few weeks later, Armstrong dazzled the audience of the Broadway musical revue *Hot Chocolates* with his performance of "Ain't Misbehavin'." Although Armstrong merely sang from the orchestra pit between acts, the *New York Times* reviewer heralded this performance by "an unnamed member of the band" as the highlight of the show. The producers, realizing Armstrong's appeal, soon changed the script to bring him on stage to sing.

This shift from the anonymity of the orchestra pit to the acclaim of a Broadway stage is in many ways symbolic of Armstrong's whole career during the period. One month after the *Times* review, Armstrong entered the studio to capitalize on the popularity of his work in *Hot Chocolates*. The approach adopted here—a trumpet melody statement, followed by an Armstrong vocal and then a trumpet solo—would become an oft-repeated recipe for success for Armstrong over the next several years. Although his vocal work takes on greater prominence in these sides, they also include some of the finest trumpet playing of Armstrong's career. One listens with admiration to Armstrong's relaxed control of the rapid tempo on "Shine," the strafing double-time passages of "Sweethearts on Parade," or the fluent mute work on "Between the Devil and Deep Blue Sea." Armstrong's repertoire also changed during this period, with well-crafted popular songs such as "Stardust" and "Body and Soul" developing into outstanding vehicles—a far cry from the instrumental charts and novelty numbers that had been his staple in earlier years. In particular, Armstrong's vocalizing takes on an idiosyncratic splendor at this stage in his rise to fame. His "Stardust" veers so far from Hoagy Carmichael's original that it might as well be a new song. Yet Armstrong's alterations, simplifying and distilling the intervallic gymnastics of Carmichael's melody, underscore the music's emotional essence and serve as a deepening rather than a distraction.

Armstrong's work as a vocalist would exert a tremendous influence on later jazz and popular singers. With good reason, Leslie Gourse gave the title *Louis' Children* to her history of jazz singing. Even among his contemporaries—singers only a few years younger than Armstrong, such as Bing Crosby, Fats Waller, Jack Teagarden, and Mildred Bailey—his impact can be clearly heard. Among the next generation, it is pervasive. Armstrong's music stood out as the most dominant early influence on Billie Holiday, who carefully studied and assimilated aspects of both his singing style and trumpet work. Ella Fitzgerald was equally drawn to this same source of inspiration—her childhood friend Annette Miller recalled her, at an early age, emulating the nuances of Armstrong's 1929 version of "Ain't Misbehavin'"—which helped shape her sense of phrasing, rhythm, delivery, even her choice of songs. Later singers from many different orbits, from Frank Sinatra to Betty Carter, Billy Eckstine to Anita O'Day, Louis Prima to Harry Connick Jr. (names that hint at the diversity of influence; to probe the depth would take a volume) were equally satellites, albeit at varying distances, each feeling the gravitational pull and drawing on the warmth and fire of Armstrong's overarching star.

By the close of the 1920s, a number of other trumpeters were crafting virtuoso styles in the Armstrong mold. Jabbo Smith and Henry "Red" Allen, in particular, deserve recognition for their command and artistry, and their recordings serve as useful reminders that other horn players could find inspiration in Armstrong's work while also establishing their own personal sound and conception of jazz improvisation. Although he may have lacked Armstrong's magisterial phrasing and sense of solo construction, Smith demanded the utmost respect for the speed and range of his playing. And, in many ways, his driving, energetic attack foreshadows the later evolution of jazz trumpet, as represented by Roy Eldridge and Dizzy Gillespie, more clearly than even Armstrong's efforts of the period. While still in his teens, Smith turned down a chance to join Ellington's band, although he made his presence felt in recording "Black and Tan Fantasy" with that group in 1927. In 1929, Smith made a number of sides for the Brunswick label, which include some of the most fervent trumpet playing of the period, but they sold poorly at the time. Henry "Red" Allen also emerged on the scene in 1929 with impressive recordings as leader and sideman on the Victor label. His playing at this stage was akin to Armstrong's in tone and structure—hear, for example, his exultant solos on Luis Russell's "Louisiana Swing" (1930) and Don Redman's "Shakin' the African" (1931)—but, as it evolved in later years, it took on a freer, more undulating sense of time. At its best, Allen's approach to melodic construction captured a sense of spontaneity and free invention that stood out even in an art form built on these values. Such artists were formidable rivals, by any measure.

Armstrong thrived on the competition offered by other luminaries of the horn. He refined a crowd-pleasing bravura style during the 1930s, with many solos serving as elaborate vehicles to demonstrate his mastery, especially his skill at hitting high notes. Armstrong exhibited endless ingenuity in building up to the latter: sometimes they cap a spirited performance ("I Surrender Dear" from 1931; "Thanks a Million" from 1935); elsewhere he might develop repeated descending phrases from Olympian altitudes ("I'm a Ding Dong Daddy" from 1930); or indulge in lazy, sliding tones that may take anywhere from one beat to two bars before they arrive—with a *pop*—at the designated high tone ("Shine" from 1931); or let loose with repeated rhythmic stabs into the stratosphere ("Swing That Music" from 1936).

The commercial orientation of his work became especially pronounced after the trumpeter began his long-term association with manager Joe Glaser in 1935. This relationship brought Armstrong a degree of financial security he had never yet enjoyed. Yet critical opinion about the music of this period is mixed and often contradictory.[8] His performances and even studio dates often relied heavily on material he had mastered in earlier decades—a pattern that would continue for the rest of his career, with Armstrong eventually leaving behind more than forty recordings of "St. Louis Blues" and over fifty of "Basin Street Blues." Although these new versions occasionally repeated older renditions virtually note for note, Armstrong was capable of mounting impressive reconfigurations of his classic songs, as in his 1938 version of "Struttin' with Some Barbecue," which would earn praise from trumpeters as diverse as Bobby Hackett and Maynard Ferguson. Through it all, Armstrong's showboat trumpet style—criticized by some for its formulaic qualities, lauded by others for its sheer bravura—remained a calling card of his work; yet he also well knew the power of understatement, as on his 1940 reunion session with Sidney Bechet, an inspired pairing that anticipated Armstrong's celebrated return to a "trad jazz" working band seven years later.

His vocal work is perhaps less daring—albeit more stylized—on his post-1934 projects, compared with the liberating and quasi-avant-garde efforts of the late 1920s and early 1930s. Yet no matter the setting or audience, Armstrong seemed almost incapable of singing a tune straight. Even the conventional Armstrong vocals had a way of sounding unconventional, and audiences delighted with the liberties he took—for example, at his performance for King George V of England, when he introduced a song with an unusual royal dedication: "This one's for you, Rex." (Adding to the piquancy, the song was "I'll Be Glad When You're Dead, You Rascal You.") In the final analysis, Armstrong's stiffest competition during this period was primarily with his own landmark performances from the past. And if his musical vocabulary now seemed somewhat clichéd, Armstrong was hardly to blame: after all, the jazz world had stolen it from him, not the other way around.

These years also saw Armstrong broaden his audience and build on his gifts as an entertainer. In 1932, during his debut tour of Europe, he both fascinated and dismayed local musicians—one delegation even demanded to examine his horn and mouthpiece, suspecting he had doctored them to facilitate his pyrotechnics. The following year Armstrong returned, visiting England, Denmark, Sweden, Norway, and Holland, and, in 1934, he took an extended vacation in Paris, followed by more concerts and recordings. Soon after returning to the United States, Armstrong initiated his relationship with Glaser, whose savvy sense of career management further advanced the trumpeter's commercial prospects. For example, Armstrong's decision to work in a more traditional, small-combo setting in the late 1940s is often cited as a nostalgic return to the roots, but it was just as much a smart business move, driven in no small part by Glaser's appreciation of the public's renewed interest in earlier jazz styles (discussed later in this book). Above all, it was also the right artistic decision, reuniting Armstrong with Hines, Teagarden, and other sympathetic fellow travelers. Armstrong's prominent role in the 1947 Hollywood film *New Orleans* had paved the way for this shift and contributed to the public's growing perception of him as a historical figure, as did his celebrated February 8, 1947, Carnegie Hall concert, which featured the trumpeter in traditional small combo and more contemporary big band settings. Critics and fans expressed their preference for the former, and though Glaser and Armstrong griped about throwing "eighteen cats out of work," the trumpeter was soon working full time in a downsized ensemble.

In his later career, Armstrong's stage presence, repartee, and globe-roving activities as an unofficial ambassador for jazz almost overshadowed his role as a musician. Yet his playing and singing, when they took center stage, radiated an endearing, carefree ambiance that contrasted greatly with the heroic exhibitions of technique from earlier decades. Armstrong could seemingly fit in effortlessly in almost any musical setting, jazz or popular, as witnessed by memorable collaborations with Ella Fitzgerald, Oscar Peterson, Duke Ellington, Bing Crosby, Johnny Cash, Barbra Streisand, Leonard Bernstein, and others. In an era in which jazz was increasingly hard edged, some lamented the soft contours of Armstrong's music and public persona. But he was not hesitant to confront mainstream America, as when he canceled a 1957 government-sponsored tour of the Soviet Union to protest President Eisenhower's initially tepid response to the exclusion of black students from a high school in Little Rock, Arkansas.

Through it all, Armstrong retained his prominence as a public figure—even more, enlarged it to quasi-mythic status. As a senior citizen, he knocked the Beatles off the charts with his hugely successful recording of "Hello Dolly." The power of his artistry was further confirmed when, almost two decades after his death, his recording of "What a Wonderful World" became a posthumous hit on the strength of its brief appearance in a Hollywood movie. His name was not mentioned in the film, nor was his image featured, yet audiences instantly recognized and responded to his inimitable style. The choice of both singer and song were fitting. For this figure—described by the newspapers at his death in 1971 as the most widely known American of his day—left behind an enduring and endearing artistic legacy, marked by a world-embracing warmth and a universality that transcended musical genres and national boundaries. For Louis Armstrong, it was truly a wonderful world.

BIX BEIDERBECKE AND THE JAZZ AGE

The compact geography of early jazz, as it is commonly told, is deceptively simple. Drawing its ebb and flow on a map, we seem to find ourselves staring at a sharply articulated triangle formed by three urban centers: the starting point is New Orleans, next comes Chicago, finally New York. So much of our history flows along this closed loop that we are tempted to ignore the rest of the map. Yet the Jazz Age was not confined to three cities, or even thirty or three hundred. Probing deeper into the mythology of early jazz, we see the Mississippi River immortalized as the music's lifeline, inspiring the blues roots of the music, and eventually transporting jazz by riverboat to its second home, Chicago. The story is charming. However, the map will not oblige us this time: the Mississippi skirts Chicago by a wide margin. When Louis Armstrong traveled to Chicago to join the King Oliver Creole Jazz Band, he arrived by train. And years before Armstrong's fateful trip, countless other New Orleans jazz musicians had already journeyed, by train and other means, not only to Chicago, but throughout the United States and, in some instances, overseas. A number of early jazz players have left behind memoirs of these years, and their tales of nomadic adventures almost overshadow stories of the music. These various sources do, however, agree on one point: almost from the start, jazz went on the road.

These itinerant jazzmen were not alone in their missionary work for the new music. The phonograph record, even more than the musicians themselves, would play a critical role in disseminating the creative fruits of New Orleans jazz to all who cared to listen. As early as 1909, some $12 million in phonograph records and cylinders (at wholesale prices) were manufactured in the United States; only twelve years later, sales were running at four times this level, reaching $47.8 million.[9] This tremendous growth set the stage for a substantial increase in the recording of jazz music over the next several years. Our knowledge of jazz before the early 1920s is mostly based on hearsay. But from this point on, recordings document the intricate and variegated evolution of the music.

The complex synergism between technologies of dissemination and the growth of African American music can only be hinted at here. But even when it is sketched in broad brushstrokes, one cannot ignore the telling pattern: the growth of ragtime takes place in conjunction with the spread of parlor pianos, mechanical pianos, and mass-produced sheet music; then the blossoming of early jazz and blues occurs in tandem with the nascent market for recordings; still ahead in our story lies the birth of the Swing Era—a history that took place, in large measure, over the airwaves. Record sales had collapsed with the Great Depression, falling almost 40 percent in 1930 alone, with many listeners now turning to broadcasts, not the phonograph, for their music. Previously, the musical celebrities may have made broadcasts, but, by the late 1930s, in a telling flip-flop, the broadcasts now made the celebrities, now created the audience for live music, now set the agenda for the musical tastes of a nation. The medium is the music: a truism as much today as at the dawn of jazz. Who can doubt that downloading and music files are the platform for jazz careers in the new millennium, just as 78s and radio broadcasts were in an earlier day? In truth, the entire history of jazz finds the music periodically adapting and responding to new technologies of distribution and dissemination as they emerge.

It would be hard to conceive of Bix Beiderbecke becoming a jazz musician without the intervention of technology, in this case a Columbia Graphophone that entered the Beiderbecke household circa 1918. Davenport, Iowa—where Leon Bix Beiderbecke was born on March 10, 1903—may have been, as often pointed out, a riverboat stop, albeit some thousand miles distant from New Orleans. But the span in miles was small compared to the even greater gap in culture, demographics, and attitude between the two cities. If New Orleans was a city immersed in music, Davenport was a community steeped in—what else?—cornfields. By Davenport standards, the Beiderbeckes were a musical family—Bix's grandfather had led the Deutsche-Amerikanische choral society before the turn of the century—but brass dance bands, funeral parades, and blues singing played no part in their musical heritage. By almost any measure, the city and household were an unlikely setting for the education of a jazz legend.

Bix's older brother Charles, who returned from service in World War I, owned this phonograph player and a few records, including the popular jazz sides made some months earlier by the Original Dixieland Jazz Band. The playing of Nick LaRocca, the standout cornetist with the ODJB, made an especially strong impression on Bix. Excited by the music, Bix announced to his befuddled parents his aspiration to learn to play jazz on the cornet. Their attempts to discourage this interest failed: Bix purchased a used horn with his allowance money and began teaching himself how to play it. At this point he had already studied the piano; as early as 1910, the *Davenport Chronicle* ran an article about the seven-year-old Beiderbecke who, it claimed, "can play any selection he hears, on the piano, entirely by ear."[10] Soon he was applying this same native talent, with even greater fervor, to his new instrument.

Beiderbecke's noted ear for music would take him far, but—like his idol LaRocca (and many other jazz players)—Bix used it as a crutch, as a way of avoiding the rigors of formal study. His early piano lessons were deemed, despite the youngster's talent, a failure: Beiderbecke never learned to read music fluently, since it was much easier for him to play the lesson by ear. The same mixture of precociousness and studied nonchalance marked his approach to the cornet. Not only did his reading skills fail to improve on the new instrument but, in his attempt to teach himself, Bix adopted an unusual, dry embouchure and fell into a habit of using unconventional fingerings—which he stuck with even after the "proper" method was pointed out to him. No doubt a characteristic streak of obstinacy underlay this chronic disregard of the tried-and-true. Years later, Beiderbecke was equally stubborn in continuing to play the cornet long after most of his contemporaries had switched to the trumpet. In so many aspects of his life, Beiderbecke was determined to do things his way or not at all.

Wary of their child's growing interest in jazz music (perhaps rightly, given Beiderbecke's later fatal adoption of all the worst habits of the jazz lifestyle), Bix's parents decided that firm action was required. The youngster was enrolled in a boarding school where, they hoped, he would pick up a solid education and greater self-discipline. In retrospect, the decision was fated for failure from the start—for their chosen school, Lake Forest Academy, was situated only a short train ride away from Chicago, then rapidly becoming the jazz capital of the world. The worst that Bix could have done in Davenport paled in comparison to the potential for trouble in this new setting. Within a short time of his arrival at the academy, Bix was regularly violating the strict curfew regulations—their disregard would eventually lead to his dismissal—and haunting the various nightspots of Chicago and its environs. At first, Bix went on these midnight expeditions simply to listen and, occasionally, to sit in with various bands; but, as word of his prowess on the cornet spread, he began performing with his own group, composed of a mix of Lake Forest Academy coconspirators and ringers from Chicago. After his expulsion from Lake Forest Academy, Bix must have recognized that his passport to a career would never be reached through an Ivy League degree—although Bix would hatch occasional plans to return to his studies for years—but by means of his cornet and ear for music.

Beiderbecke's first major band, the Wolverines, brought together a group of like-minded instrumentalists. These all but unknown young jazz devotees took their inspiration primarily from the performances of the New Orleans Rhythm Kings. During that band's engagement at Friar's Inn, members of Bix's circle were frequently in attendance: listening, learning, sometimes sitting in with the group. A chance to put this education into practice came in October 1923, when clarinetist Jimmy Hartwell succeeded in obtaining regular employment for the Wolverines at the Stockton Club, located seventeen miles north of Cincinnati. Performances here and at other venues in the area gave the musicians ample opportunity to refine their craft and develop an enthusiastic local following; but greater fame would have been inconceivable this far distant from the major music capitals of America had not the Wolverines secured an opportunity to spend a day recording at the Gennett recording studio in Richmond, Indiana, some 125 miles away from Cincinnati. This was a turning point, not only in documenting the band's progress to date, but also in reinforcing the confidence of this group of novices to the music industry. "No amount of words could adequately describe the excitement and utter amazement of that first recording, played back to us for correction of positions around the recording horns," recalled George Johnson, tenorist with the group. "I doubt if any of us realized until that moment how different in style and how dissimilar in effect our results were from the music of the Friar's band that had thrilled us all so, barely months before."[11]

Beiderbecke's debut recordings with the Wolverines only hint at the potential of the young cornetist. His solos, for all their poise, are melodically simple by comparison with the work he would create over the next several years. Evidence of Beiderbecke's sensitivity to altered tones is apparent—hear his use of flatted fifths and ninths in his work on "Riverboat Shuffle"—but one also notes the relaxed delivery, so characteristic of Bix's phrasing. Above all, the expressive, at times haunting, tone of Beiderbecke's cornet demands our attention. Bix may not have mastered the dirty, rough-edged sound of a King Oliver, a style vastly influential at this stage in the history of jazz; nor do his solos burst forth with the unbridled energy that Armstrong would soon bring to the music. But they sing in a way that was unique in the context of mid-1920s jazz. Not so much played, they sound as though lofted gently from the bell of the horn, left to float in a stream of warm air.

Eddie Condon, a collaborator of Beiderbecke's, also sensed an invitation in Bix's sound: "like a girl saying yes," was his oft-quoted appraisal of his initial encounter with it. "For the first time I realized that music isn't all the same, that some people play so differently from others that it becomes an entirely new set of sounds." Hoagy Carmichael, grabbing for an even odder allusion, saw Bix's music affecting him "in a different way. Can't tell you how—like licorice, you have to eat some. . . . Bix's breaks were not as wild as Armstrong's, but they were hot, and he selected each note with musical care. He showed me that jazz could be musical and beautiful as well as hot." To Mezz Mezzrow, Beiderbecke's tone was "pickled in alcohol. . . . I have never heard a tone like he got before or since. He played mostly open horn, every note full, big, rich and round, standing out like a pearl, loud but never irritating or jangling, with a powerful drive that few white musicians had in those days." Louis Armstrong, recalling a Beiderbecke performance in Chicago in the mid-1920s, said simply: "I'm tellin' you, those pretty notes went right through me."[12]

A pearl or a girl? Liquor or licorice? These poetic comparisons may strike some listeners today as being at odds with the body of work that Beiderbecke left behind. Studio technology of the 1920s did not serve the cornetist well. "Records never quite reproduced his sound," Pee Wee Russell has attested, with many others concurring in the judgment.[13] Acoustic recordings, with their use of a single horn to capture music and translate it mechanically into grooves on a wax disk, present modern-day fans, weaned on the crystal clarity of digital technology, with a flattened, one-dimensional sound. Like shadows in Plato's cave, these artifacts from audio's earliest days are merely indicative, not truly representative, of the absent originals. And electric recordings, launched in the mid-1920s, sound only marginally better—this innovation was slow in demonstrating its advantages, so much so that, at the time, many listeners lamented its introduction as a step backward. For a solo performance, such as a classical piano piece, or for a vocal number in which the singer was situated front center, the early recording devices proved adequate, if just barely, in conveying the essence of live music. But for ensemble music, such as New Orleans and Chicago-style jazz, the clarity of the individual instruments was greatly compromised. Although the rhythm, melody, and harmony are there for the careful listener to hear, or even to notate, the subtleties of tone are all but lost. For an artist like Beiderbecke, for whom quality and texture of sound were almost as important as the actual notes played, the resulting records are little more than a simulacrum of the actual performance. But, like sailors peering into murky waters, we find that, though we may not be able to measure Beiderbecke's genius in precise fathoms, even this indistinct ebb and flow gives little doubt that it is ever so deep and broad.

Between the first and second 1924 sessions for the Wolverines, Beiderbecke celebrated his twenty-first birthday. Strange to say, though Bix was barely out of his teens, the cornetist was poised to enter the middle period of his career. Indeed, the chronology of this celebrated musician is all too compact: his entire recorded oeuvre would span less than seven years, with even this abbreviated history broken down into several distinct stages. By the time of Bix's final recordings with the Wolverines, in late 1924, the band had already traveled to New York (at almost the same time that Armstrong had moved there to join Henderson). Before the close of the year Beiderbecke had left the band to embark on a fertile period of freelancing and experimentation.

These halcyon days, which lasted from the middle of the decade to the stock market crash of 1929, witnessed much of Beiderbecke's greatest work. But this period also encompassed an exceptional flourishing of improvised music on a much wider scale, one that music historians have come to designate simply as Chicago jazz. Beiderbecke's contributions, as great as they are, were just one facet of this new sound, this new style. Like the New Orleans tradition that preceded it, and the Swing Era offerings that followed it, Chicago jazz was not just the music of a time and place, but also a timeless style of performance—and for its exponents, very much a way of life—one that continues to reverberate to this day in the work of countless Dixieland and traditional jazz bands around the world. For many listeners, the Chicago style remains nothing less than the quintessential sound of jazz.

CHICAGO AND NEW YORK

As with much of early jazz, the story of the Chicago school has taken on a larger-than-life quality with the passage of time. Facts and falsehoods, myths and memories have coalesced into a pseudohistory, a romanticized account of glory days with all the authenticity of a maudlin Hollywood script. Here we find gangsters and speakeasys, riverboats and flashy attire, all bundled together in a colorful tapestry. The truth is somewhat more complicated, and often less glamorous. True, jazz traveled to Chicago—albeit by land not river—at an early stage in its development, but it also journeyed to many other parts of the country through the missionary efforts of King Oliver, Freddie Keppard and the Original Creole Orchestra, Jelly Roll Morton, and others. The Chicago nightspots were often makeshift rather than opulent—Lincoln Gardens, the celebrated home base for King Oliver, had chicken wire on the ceiling, and the famous Dreamland Ballroom doubled as a roller rink. And, yes, booze and criminal elements could be found where the music played, but this connection neither started in the Windy City nor ended there.

Further, the association of the so-called Chicago style of music with its leading figure, Bix Beiderbecke, is also rather puzzling: Bix played little in Chicago—if anything, his residencies in New York stand out as the decisive interludes in his musical career. (Then again, when dealing with the topsy-turvy subject of jazz geography, be prepared for the strangest contradictions: just as much of the history of New Orleans jazz took place in Chicago, so did the sounds of Chicago jazz eventually find their most hospitable home in New York.) The further stereotype that associates early Chicago jazz almost solely with white musicians is equally off mark: as we have already seen, the finest African American musicians from New Orleans and elsewhere—Armstrong, Hines, Morton, Oliver, Noone, Dodds—had already gravitated to Chicago by the mid-1920s. William Howland Kenney, in his study of the biographies of fifty-five black musicians associated with Chicago jazz during the 1920s, determined that nearly half came from New Orleans, and a similar percentage arrived during or just following World War I.[14] Black jazz, white jazz, hot jazz, sweet jazz, New Orleans jazz, Dixieland jazz: no matter what you call it or how you define it, it all became part of Chicago jazz during these formative years.

The similarities between the music of the white Chicagoans and their New Orleans models have often been noted—frequently by the Chicagoans themselves. But close listening reveals subtle gradations of difference. A certain restless energy begins to reverberate in the music. Counterpoint lines no longer weave together, as in the earlier New Orleans style, but often battle for supremacy. The specific roles filled by the New Orleans front line are modified. The tailgate trombone tradition, with its use of portamentos (or slurs) to link harmony notes, is less evident among the Chicago players; and, at times, the trombone is totally absent, replaced by the tenor sax, which takes on a more linear and overtly melodic role. The Chicago clarinetists, following the lead of Roppolo, move away from the figured arpeggios of New Orleans, instead adopting mannerisms that, in New Orleans style, were more typical of cornetists. Hear, for instance, Frank Teschemacher's pungent and, at times, raspy lines—a cheeky attitude on the horn that would influence Benny Goodman and other Swing Era players. The Chicago horns often join together for brief written introductions and interludes, a technique closer to the big band idiom than to the New Orleans tradition. A host of stylistic devices, with some precedent in New Orleans jazz, also figure as signposts of the white Chicagoans: the *flare up*, a polyphonic outburst—at its simplest, merely a held chord—initiated by a drum break, placed for best effect at the close of the first chorus; the *explosion*, a forerunner of the bop drummer's bomb, which aimed to light a fire under the soloist or ensemble by accentuating the backbeat in the measure before the start of a new eight-bar section; the *shuffle rhythm*, which conveyed the feel of double time, often used to add variety to the bridge of a thirty-two-bar song form; and the *break*, the time-honored formula, honed in New Orleans, a two- or four-bar interlude during which the band held back while the soloist stepped forward to proclaim a hot phrase.

But we should not neglect the influence of the various nonjazz musical traditions that the multiethnic Chicagoans (as well as the later members of the New York school) brought with them to their jazz making. At times, their minor key melodies conveyed more than a hint of klezmer, as for instance on Goodman's early leader sides "That's a Plenty" and "Clarinetitis." Teschemacher also showed the influence of his early violin training, which occasionally transmits the ambiance of a European street fiddler to his clarinet lines. And who can listen to the string music of Joe Venuti and Eddie Lang without hearing echoes of the Italian lyric tradition? A fascination with contemporary classical music and other experimental currents is also evident among this generation of jazzmen, inspiring their adoption of esoteric harmonies and rhythms—Beiderbecke is the most prominent example, but also note Tesch's use of 6/4 in the intro to "Liza." These tributaries of inspiration flowed together in broadening the vocabulary of jazz during the late 1920s and early 1930s. The music was still a paean to the New Orleans sound, but it also pointed forward to the later Swing Era preferences for tighter arrangements, greater expressive range and variety, and a more pronounced separation of solo and ensemble textures.

Yet it is important to recognize that economic as well as aesthetic considerations contributed to the evolution of this music. Musicians of all styles, all races, all instruments came to Chicago not because of an allegiance to a certain idiom of jazz, but rather to tap the opportunities to perform and earn a livelihood that the setting offered. Sidemen in Chicago bands could earn $40 per week or more during the years following World War I—a far cry from the $1.50 to $2.50 per engagement a

New Orleans player might have commanded during that era.[15] In response, musicians from all regions converged on the city—a process that we have already described with regard to the World's Columbian Exposition, which drew Scott Joplin and many other rag pianists to Chicago in 1893. There were, of course, many outstanding jazz players from this period who were born or raised in Chicago—Benny Goodman, Gene Krupa, Muggsy Spanier, and others; just as many came from the suburbs or, like Beiderbecke, from other parts of the Midwest. But these players remained in Chicago not due to any loyalty to their native soil, but because of the vibrant local jazz scene and the financial security it represented.

As previously mentioned, the conventions of New Orleans jazz began to change in this new setting, but even in this regard economic factors may have exercised a predominant influence. Perhaps the most obvious shift came in the repertoire of the local jazz bands. During the decade of the 1920s, popular songs and thirty-two-bar forms were increasingly used by Chicago jazz musicians, while blues and multitheme ragtime structures, so central to the New Orleans tradition, became less common. This move does not seem to have been driven by aesthetic considerations—it is hardly mentioned by the players themselves in the many memoirs and interviews from the period—but came about gradually as a response to the changing demands of audiences. The blues recording craze of the early 1920s had already subsided by the time Chicago jazz took off in full force, while the ragtime explosion of the turn of the century was only a distant memory. In this new world of mass marketing, jazz as a category of entertainment came to occupy a wider and wider orbit, encompassing a broad spectrum of performance styles. The definition of jazz already emerges as a problem by the middle of the decade, and this too must have contributed to an expansion in the repertoire of jazz performers. Consider, for example, the featured songs from the hit 1927 movie *The Jazz Singer*, the first talking film, which were much closer to popular music than to jazz; or Gershwin's jazz-based classical compositions, which took the country by storm in the mid-1920s; or the success of Paul Whiteman, the ostensible "King of Jazz," whose song choices cut across a dizzying array of musical genres. During the Jazz Age, as the period came to be known, it seems almost anything in fashion would, sooner or later, be classified as jazzy. Who can be surprised that, in this environment, jazz players felt that the popular songs of the day should be under their domain, subject to their interpretation and modification?

The music was now permeated by a mythology, one that romanticized the jazz life, and celebrated its leading practitioners as defiant, rebellious youths determined to go their own way in music, as in other pursuits. Some years later, Hollywood movies glamorized a series of antiheroes—one can see early hints of this figure in the films of Clark Gable and Humphrey Bogart; it found its ideal type in the 1950s with Marlon Brando and James Dean; and lingers as an enduring archetype to the present day—whose quasi-cynical American individualism engages in an uneasy dance with conventional social mores. American novelists, especially Hemingway, had already drawn inspiration from this new character type. But even earlier, the Chicago jazzmen anticipated this powerful current in the popular imagination. They embodied in their lives and attitudes a fascinating series of antihero contradictions:

they were worldly wise yet innocent; hard-edged yet wearing their hearts on their sleeves, especially in their music; self-centered but with a deep sense of camaraderie; flip and cynical, yet deeply committed to their calling.

If the mythology of Chicago jazz has a founding father, it is Eddie Condon. True, if our history dealt only with musical achievement, Condon's role would be a small one, properly fitted to the dimensions of a footnote or an aside. Condon was certainly a capable banjoist with a buoyant front-of-the-beat pulse—hear him, for instance, joyously careening alongside Fats Waller on "Minor Drag"—yet his native talent shone more brightly in other spheres. As an advocate of hot music, a chronicler of his times, an epigrammist, a master of the grand style, and behind-the-scenes doer, Condon demands respect as a central figure in Chicago jazz. Histories, after all, need to celebrate the jesters and jousters and not just those with crowns on their heads.

Condon's efforts led to gainful employment and a more bountiful recording legacy for other, greater players; and he, more than anyone else, created the appealing public image of the Chicago jazzman as bohemian revolutionary. Condon the aphorist was rarely at a loss for words. Complaining about a mediocre bandleader: "He made the clarinet talk and it usually said 'please put me back in my case.'" Describing an equally lamentable vocalist: "He once tried to carry a tune across the street and broke both legs." On his chronic late-night partying: "I began losing sleep [in 1919] and I have never been able since to pay myself any more than the interest on the debt." On the advances of modern jazz: "The boppers flat their fifths. We drink ours." Whether quoted, lambasted, idealized, praised, dismissed—one way or another, this secondary figure managed somehow to become a primary source in the history of jazz.[16]

Born in Goodland, Indiana, on November 16, 1905, Eddie Condon apprenticed in dance bands throughout the Midwest. In Chicago during the mid-1920s, Condon became involved with a number of like-minded players, most notably a group of young instrumentalists who would come to be known as the Austin High School Gang. Like Condon, they displayed an almost obsessive fixation on jazz music and jazz culture. "They talked about jazz as if it were a new religion just come from Jerusalem," was Condon's account of his first meeting with cornetist Jimmy McPartland and tenor saxophonist Bud Freeman, two of the most prominent members of the Austin High School group.[17] But then again, Condon could have been talking about himself. Enthusiasm ran deep with the Chicago school, and even in their musical triumphs they retained much of the wide-eyed ardor of a fan.

Austin, located to the west of downtown Chicago, was an inauspicious setting for a jazz movement. In 1922, a group of students began gathering regularly at a soda parlor located near the nondescript buff brick Austin High School. The parlor featured a windup Victrola and a pile of records. "One day we found a record by the New Orleans Rhythm Kings in the stack, and we put it on, not knowing what kind of band we were about to hear," Freeman later recalled. "Were we excited by it! We were used to hearing commercial dance bands, but this sound was something else."[18] "Right then and there," Jimmy McPartland continues the story, "we decided we would get a band and try to play like these guys. So we all picked out our instruments.

Tesch [Frank Teschemacher] said he was going to buy a clarinet, Freeman plumped for a saxophone, [Jim] Lannigan picked a bass tuba, my brother [Dick McPartland] said he'd play the banjo, and I chose cornet, the loudest instrument."[19] All but Freeman had studied violin before their introduction to the jazz idiom.

Within a short while, the students had formed a working band, the Blue Friars—named after the Friar's Inn, the Chicago nightspot where the New Orleans Rhythm Kings played—in emulation of the new jazz sounds they had discovered. Nonetheless, mastering the transition to improvisation required a practical education, in which study of the Rhythm Kings was supplemented by careful listening to recordings (especially the Wolverines' sides with Bix Beiderbecke), as well as Saturday night visits to performances (including firsthand appreciations of King Oliver's Creole Jazz Band at Chicago's Lincoln Gardens). Before long, other young players fell into the orbit of the Austin High Gang. Drummer Dave Tough, who was dating an Austin girl, became a close associate of the group. Sometime later, when Tough left the band to travel to Europe, his younger friend Gene Krupa stepped in to play drums with the Austin High crew. Clarinetist Benny Goodman, then a freshman at nearby Harrison High, became acquainted with the Austin High musicians when he attended a performance at a boathouse in Columbus Park. Soon he too was playing with various members of the group.

The 1927 recordings by the McKenzie-Condon Chicagoans reveal the ebullient approach of these young jazz players. On "China Boy," Krupa's solidly swinging drum work sets the tone for this more insistent style. "He was into a new concept of drumming on those McKenzie-Condon Chicagoan records," John Hammond recalled many years later. "Gene was rock solid and swinging. . . . I felt he was the best drummer I had heard up to that time."[20] Joe Sullivan, making his recording debut on this session, contributes a driving solo that further stokes the fire. Jimmy McPartland's cornet work here may have been less pathbreaking, but nonetheless confirms his growing reputation as one of the finer Beiderbecke disciples of the period—it is not surprising that, even before this session, he had been asked to replace Bix in the Wolverines. Bud Freeman's tenor work from this period, in contrast, carries a rough-edged, guttural quality. In later years his style would take on a smoother sheen, but what we encounter on these early sides is a bellowing, rumbling growl announcing a ruffian saxophonist, one who gives no shelter and takes no prisoners. Teschemacher, who left behind only a handful of recordings before his death in an automobile accident on his twenty-sixth birthday, is perhaps the most difficult to evaluate of this group. On the McKenzie-Condon rendition of "Sugar," his loping lines, laced with hints of the blues, show a flair for melodic improvisation, free from clichés, and set an example that later Chicago clarinetists would follow. Yet he is often remembered best for his influence on these other players, especially Benny Goodman, rather than for his own achievements. True, Teschemacher may have lacked Goodman's virtuosity, yet his few recordings reveal a daring performer, one willing to delve into the dirtier tones and gutbucket sounds more commonly associated with black clarinetists and make them work in a manner that was never merely imitative.

Pee Wee Russell, two weeks younger than Teschemacher, developed an even more stylized approach. The son of a St. Louis bartender and steward, Pee Wee—his formal name was much more elegant: Charles Ellsworth Russell—studied piano, drums, and violin in his youth, but began focusing on the clarinet in his early teens. Like Beiderbecke, with whom he later performed and shared a close friendship, Russell was expelled from boarding school before embarking on a jazz career. Russell later quipped: "I learned one thing: how to get where you're going on time."[21] The only problem Russell faced after this dismissal was where exactly to go. His travels over the next few years brought him to Mexico, the West Coast, Arizona, Kansas, Iowa, North and South Dakota, Texas (where he encountered Jack Teagarden), back to St. Louis (where he met Beiderbecke), and on to New York—indeed, almost any-where a paying gig materialized. True to form, like several of the other noted "Chicagoans," Russell performed infrequently in that city, but was part of a St. Louis contingent that later developed strong ties to the Condon crew.

Some have suggested that Russell's eccentric style of improvisation defies description. Not true. Jazz writers have had a field day articulating and analyzing its mysterious essence. "Half B flat, half saliva," was Leonard Feather's characterization of the classic Russell tone, which was all part of a manner of phrasing that resembled "the stammering of a woman scared by a ghost." "Much of the time, his sound was astringent," Nat Hentoff has explained, "as if it had taken a long time to find its way out of that long contorted body and was rather exasperated at the rigors of the journey." A number of commentators have looked for different levels of intent in Russell's work, almost as though it were a literary text in which the surface meaning and the symbolic meaning were at odds. "He sounded cranky and querulous," Whitney Balliett has asserted, "but that was camouflage, for he was the most plaintive and lyrical of players." Gunther Schuller goes even further in expostulating this theory of "the two Russells": "At first hearing one of these Russell solos tended to give the impression of a somewhat inept musician, awkward and shy, stumbling and muttering along in a rather directionless fashion. It turns out, however, upon closer inspection that such peculiarities—the unorthodox tone, the halting continuity, the odd note choices—are manifestations of a unique, wondrously self-contained musical personality, which operated almost entirely on its own artistic laws."[22] Bud Freeman offers a far different interpretation of Russell's muse, reducing it to the classic Aristotelian concepts of pity and fear—with a slightly different twist: "He became a world famous figure because people would suffer with him. They'd say 'O my God, I hope he gets through this chorus.'" Yet, whether his music is viewed as a Delphic utterance laden with secret meanings, an expression of eccentricity, or simply a style built around various limitations, Russell ultimately succeeded where it counted most: in attracting a devoted following, one that lived vicariously through his embrace of the unorthodox. For those fans who became part of the cult of Pee Wee, there was no other clarinetist half so grand.

Russell's playing revealed his taste for the bizarre almost from the start. On his 1929 recording of "That Da Da Strain," Russell opens his solo with a halfhearted attempt to imitate the florid and fluid clarinet stylings pioneered by the New Orleans masters. Alas, with meager success. After floundering energetically in this manner for three bars, Russell abandons this attempt at virtuosity, instead tossing out isolated notes and jagged phrases, offering up all the makeshift sounds—growls that end up as whimpers, staccato jabs that shadow box with the rhythm section, notes bent until they scream—that came to characterize this artist's oeuvre. His celebrated solo, recorded that same day, on "Basin Street Blues," relies on a similar knack for raising aberrations to the level of a musical style, only here within the context of the twelve-bar blues. The combination is gripping: blues, the music of pathos, and Pee Wee, the master of the pathological, meet in a surreal halfway land, one where Dixieland and Dada gropingly join hands. Throughout his career, Russell would return to the blues and, in a manner all his own, somehow manage each time to extract the inevitable bloody victory. But though the eccentricities of Russell's style might temporarily mask the fertile muse inspiring his efforts, they could never hide it. His work was especially effective when contrasted with another player who possessed an equally strong sense of style: whether alongside Coleman Hawkins on "Hello Lola" and "One Hour," or decades later matching his wits with Gerry Mulligan or Thelonious Monk (whom he "out-Monked," his fans insisted, with some justification). In a fitting tribute, Bud Freeman lauded Russell's charisma and creativity, and compared his work favorably with the most illustrious clarinetist of the era, predicting that "in another hundred years, if there is another hundred years, people will talk more about Pee Wee's records than about Benny Goodman's."

Adrian Rollini may have boasted a less idiosyncratic improvisational style than Russell, yet he made up for it in other ways. His choice of bass saxophone as his major instrument was in itself unconventional. This horn has made infrequent appearances in jazz bands in later years (although players with a penchant for experimentation, such as Boyd Raeburn, Anthony Braxton, and Roscoe Mitchell, have enjoyed its penetrating sound). Rollini's other horns could be even more peculiar: note his use of the goofus, the celeste, and his own creation, the oddly named "hot fountain pen," a type of dwarf clarinet. He was also an early exponent of the xylophone, marimba, and vibraphone, played the piano, and was a superb, much underrated drummer. This capricious array of instruments has often distracted commentators from the core virtues of Rollini's playing: his solid sense of swing, his uncluttered, probing improvised lines, and the joyous energy of his solos. Many of Rollini's finest efforts from the late 1920s find him working in a sideman role, on "Kickin' the Cat" and "Beatin' the Dog" as a member of Joe Venuti's Blue Four; alongside Bix Beiderbecke and Frank Trumbauer on "Three Blind Mice" and "At the Jazz Band Ball"; and with Miff Mole on "Feelin' No Pain." In the 1930s, Rollini continued to refine his saxophone style, as witnessed by the effective "Bouncin' in Rhythm" from 1935. But his efforts during this period increasingly emphasized his vibraphone playing which, while noteworthy for its mellow tone and smooth phrasing, rarely approached the zest of his sax performances. However, his drum work supporting Freddy Jenkins's band on "Toledo Shuffle" from 1935 is quite impressive, suggesting that Rollini might have enjoyed a substantial career by focusing on that instrument alone.

Although not as outré as the reed players of the era, a number of white brass players were also developing poised, individual approaches to the jazz art during this period. The so-called New York style of Red Nichols—one of the most recorded bandleaders of the day and a capable cornetist in a Bix vein—and trombonist Miff

Mole softened the rough-and-ready urgency of the Chicagoans and other jazz pioneers in crafting a more introspective approach. Their recording of "Davenport Blues" from 1927 provides a good example of their conception of jazz: the melodic lines are infused with a floating quality, resisting the gravitational pull of the rhythm section. One senses an attitude of almost bemused detachment, yet the music retains a bouncy, light swing that keeps the piece rooted in a danceable two-step. Mole's trombone work in such settings revealed a linear conception freed from the New Orleans tailgate tradition and paved the way for the more modern approach of Jack Teagarden and other later trombonists. Chicago native Francis Joseph "Muggsy" Spanier, in contrast, maintained allegiance to the New Orleans roots of the music, with his clipped, incisive middle-register lines and deference to the ensemble sound. New Orleans–born Joseph Matthews "Wingy" Manone, in contrast, adapted comfortably to the stylistic demands of Chicago although his efforts may have been distinguished less by their musical innovations than through his sure sense of the comedic and his talents as an entertainer. When the Dixieland revival took off in the 1940s, these musicians were well positioned to benefit from the newfound interest in the music's roots. With few exceptions (Dave Tough's embrace of more modern styles comes to mind), they remained faithful to the sounds of their youth, whether their personal jazz tradition was in or out of fashion.

Only one other white brass player of the day could approach Beiderbecke in terms of individuality and creativity. Jack Teagarden stands out as the greatest of the traditional jazz players on the trombone, and also left his mark as an important jazz singer. Teagarden had the weakest Chicago ties of the group, with his career beginning in his native Texas while New York served as his home base during most of his glory years. The Teagardens of Vernon, Texas, were raised far afield from the major urban centers of jazz—the city was a former cattle station, a final supply base before a several-hundred-mile journey to the Kansas railhead—but the family compensated by forming a self-contained unit of professional-caliber musicians. In addition to Jack, the family included trumpeter Charlie, drummer Cub, and pianists Norma and Helen. Jack, who was christened Weldon Leo Teagarden (named after a dime-novel hero of the time) was the oldest. He studied piano with his mother during his childhood and later learned baritone horn before settling on the trombone.

Teagarden had few role models to draw on—either on record or in person—during his formative years. The New Orleans tradition, despite its frequent use of the trombone, had done little to develop the instrument's potential as a solo voice. It more often served as a source of countermelodies or rhythmic accents, often linking harmonies with the slurred chromatic glissandi that characterized the tailgate sound, a stock New Orleans device associated most closely with Kid Ory (hear his definitive work on the 1927 Armstrong side "Ory's Creole Trombone") but adopted by many other early players of the instrument. The melodic potential of the horn was first demonstrated in the work of Miff Mole, whose prolific recordings from the late 1920s proved that the trombone need not be relegated to a supportive role, but could stand out in front as a full-fledged solo voice. Mole's influence on Teagarden cannot be denied, yet it is likely that the Texan had already developed the rudiments of his style well before he heard Mole's work. In many ways, Teagarden's playing showed a disregard of formal methods, especially in his reliance on embouchure and alternate positions rather than slide technique. Whatever his sources of inspiration may have been, Teagarden already stood out as a seasoned musician by the time of his first recordings.[23]

In 1921, while still in his midteens, he joined pianist Peck Kelley's band in Houston, which also included Pee Wee Russell. Paul Whiteman heard the group during a road stop in Houston and offered Teagarden a job, but the youngster declined. Some time later, when the twenty-two-year-old Teagarden finally journeyed to New York, he brought along a half-dozen years of professional experience in a fertile jazz environment, albeit somewhat distant from the more visible currents of New Orleans, New York, and Chicago. In this new setting, Teagarden was active in the recording studio—in the late 1920s hardly a week passed without his participation in a session—and joined the Ben Pollack Orchestra. Pollack was an admirable drummer and had once propelled the New Orleans Rhythm Kings, but is best remembered for discovering young talent. His orchestra featured, at one time or another, a host of important future bandleaders, not only Teagarden, but also Benny Goodman, Glenn Miller, and Harry James. Over the next several years, Teagarden's work, with Pollack and in other settings, would establish him as one of the leading jazz soloists of his generation.

Teagarden displayed a sensitivity to the blues that few white players of his generation could match. On his 1929 recording with Louis Armstrong, "Knockin' a Jug," Teagarden initiates the proceedings with two heartfelt blues choruses that transcend the trombone—indeed, his solo lines here are more akin to the vocal work of a Bessie Smith than to either the urbane stylings of Mole or the tailgate tradition of Ory. The rhythm section (guitarist Eddie Lang, pianist Joe Sullivan, drummer Kaiser Marshall) offer admirable assistance, establishing an exemplary slow tempo that is as relaxed and uncluttered as any recorded performance from this period. In various other recordings from the early 1930s—"Basin Street Blues," "I Gotta Right to Sing the Blues," "Beale Street Blues," "Stars Fell on Alabama"—Teagarden showed that his approach to singing was very much akin to his trombone stylings. Although he was capable of virtuosic displays, Teagarden was most at home delivering carefree, behind-the-beat phrases. When he was singing, the lazy, after-hours quality to his delivery—incorporating elements of song, patter, and idle conversation—proved endearing to audiences, especially in the context of a jazz world that was only just discovering the potential of understatement. Teagarden was equally deft in simplifying the written melody as in ornamenting it. In this regard, his work reflected an ongoing evolution in American popular singing. Jack Teagarden, Bing Crosby, Fats Waller, Louis Armstrong—each was distilling, in a somewhat different way, a new, more personalized style of vocalizing. This was music taken out of the concert hall, made more intimate, and adapted to the demands of the new mass-market technologies (microphones, recordings, broadcasts), as well as to the modern sensibility and tastes that these inventions helped to form. Music could now be consumed on an individual basis, one listener at a time, often in the privacy of the home, enabling Teagarden and these other innovators—who offered a down-to-earth, direct, and nontheatrical delivery, wholly purged of the grand style—to rise to fame by responding to the needs of this changed environment.

Red Norvo, who arrived on the New York scene toward the close of this period, presents an especially acute challenge to jazz historians. His various musical associations flew in the face of stylistic categories and conventions—perhaps ultimately to the detriment of his career. How else can we explain why this illustrious jazz veteran remained all but forgotten in the years leading up to his death in 1999, while other survivors of his generation were receiving honorary degrees and various accolades, and were venerated as important elder statesmen of jazz? Certainly one would struggle to find another jazz musician who had made his presence felt in so many different ways as Norvo. During his early New York years he worked with Paul Whiteman and did much to legitimize the role of the xylophone in jazz. His recordings of "In a Mist" and "Dance of the Octopus" from 1933 are shimmering, ethereal performances that reveal his acute comprehension of the harmonic implications of Beiderbecke's legacy. "Blues in E Flat" from 1934 finds Norvo playing at top form in a stellar integrated band under his leadership that also included Teddy Wilson, Gene Krupa, Bunny Berigan, and Chu Berry. Equally praiseworthy are Norvo's recordings from the late 1930s of the sophisticated, albeit unconventional, arrangements of Eddie Sauter, with their foreshadowing of cool jazz techniques.

A number of sides from this period feature Norvo in the company of his wife, vocalist Mildred Bailey, whose lithe phrasing and expressive delivery put her at the forefront of the white female jazz singers of her day. Their collaborations capture a range of emotional stances, from delicate reserve to brash assertiveness, but in general tend toward an exuberance that might serve as a virtual mirror image of the moody introspection found in the Billie Holiday/Lester Young efforts of this same period. Even an ostensibly melancholy song such as Bailey's trademark "Rockin' Chair" conveys a soft fineness of feeling that is more endearing than somber. Bailey's career was all too short. She and Norvo got a divorce in 1945, and soon after the singer cut back her performances due to diabetes and other ailments, aggravated by her excessive weight. Bailey increasingly passed her time on a farm she owned in upstate New York, far away from the entertainment world, before her death from a heart attack in 1951 at the age of forty-four.

In the 1940s, Norvo played both sides of the swing-or-bop controversy, serving as a member of Benny Goodman's sextet, but also hiring Charlie Parker and Dizzy Gillespie for a leader date that produced some of the most influential early bop sides. In the late 1940s, Norvo continued to expand his horizons, working with Woody Herman and Billie Holiday, and in the 1950s blazed ahead with a blistering trio that found him playing vibraphone alongside guitarist Tal Farlow and bassist Charles Mingus. At the close of the decade he joined Frank Sinatra on a tour of Australia, supporting the megastar in the context of a quintet that seemed to elicit some of the singer's jazziest work of the era. In later years, Norvo tended to return to swing settings in the company of Benny Goodman, Benny Carter, and other masters of the genre. Jazz history books have poorly served this master of many idioms; their rigid categorizations apparently incapable of dealing with his chameleon career. Yet Norvo's skill in navigating across artificial stylistic and racial barriers merits both praise and emulation.

For a time in the 1920s, saxophonist Frank Trumbauer enjoyed an influence and reputation that even surpassed that of his frequent collaborator Bix Beiderbecke. Beiderbecke eventually came to take center stage in accounts of this body of music, yet this posthumous transformation should not blind us to Trumbauer's compelling achievements. Two years older than the cornetist, Tram (as he came to be known) was born in Carbondale, Illinois, on May 30, 1901. Musical studies began early for him—like Beiderbecke, he showed signs of being a child prodigy—but his career as a professional saxophonist started late, not taking off in earnest until he completed a stint in the military. After joining forces in 1925, the two musicians became a package deal for bandleaders. They entered the Goldkette band at virtually the same time—Trumbauer later claimed that Beiderbecke's employment was a condition he set for taking the gig—and moved to the Whiteman band in tandem, starting at the same Indianapolis performance. The duo also worked together in a St. Louis-based band, as well as served an overlapping and all-too-brief stint in an exceptional all-star group that also featured Joe Venuti, Eddie Lang, and Adrian Rollini.

But this close companionship belied deep differences. The contrast began with their physical appearance: photos show a Laurel-and-Hardy composite, the lanky Trumbauer, partly of American Indian descent, standing tall with bemused expression next to the cherubic Beiderbecke, with his clean-faced Teutonic bearing. In social settings, the difference was even more pronounced: Trumbauer, taciturn almost to an extreme, was mostly a silent partner to Bix, who enjoyed his status as an articulate commentator on both highbrow and lowbrow culture of the 1920s—with words to spare on everything from Proust ("no good in translation," was his alleged verdict) to P. G. Wodehouse ("he could quote long passages," recalls an associate), with early twentieth-century classical music standing out as an almost obsessive interest. Even in their chosen profession, the two went different ways: Beiderbecke, the unschooled player, was devoted to music, and one can hardly imagine him pursuing any other livelihood; while Trumbauer, although the more formally trained of the two—his proficiency extended to the piano, trombone, cornet, violin, bassoon, and flute, with the saxophone being something of an afterthought—betrayed an ambivalent commitment to the jazz life; he later served as a test pilot in World War II and eventually abandoned music for aeronautics. But perhaps most decisive were their differences not in vocation but in avocation: outside music, Beiderbecke's fatal passion was for alcohol, the forbidden fermented fruit of Prohibition, while Trumbauer drank little, and after a gig promptly returned home to his wife and child—with the result that he outlived his younger collaborator by a full quarter-century.

In their music, though, both players shared an aesthetic—one that, with the benefit of hindsight, we can call cool jazz, but which at the time was uncharted territory. The lyrical strain in jazz, the focus on attaining a clarity of musical expression, the achievement of an Arcadian purity of sound—these milestones in the evolution of jazz can trace their heritage, at least in part, back to such compelling Beiderbecke-Trumbauer collaborations as "Singin' the Blues" and "I'm Comin' Virginia."

Beiderbecke cared little for the taxonomy of tone alteration—the various mutes, vibrato effects, and note-bending acrobatics that were tricks of the trade for most earlier jazz cornetists; Trumbauer, for his part, refined a clean, light tone that was worlds apart from the earthier reed work of Bechet and Hawkins.

Beiderbecke's life story reads like a novel (and later inspired one: Dorothy Baker's 1938 *Young Man with a Horn*, which built on old clichés and created a few new ones) and continues to fascinate with its gripping combination of tragic and romantic elements. Not so Trumbauer's biography. Movie scripts are not written about teetotaling jazz musicians who quit the band to take a day job. Yet, at the time, Tram's virtuosic and expressive saxophone work certainly cast a spell over other musicians. "As to sax players, it was Frankie Trumbauer," writes clarinetist Joe Darensbourg in his memoirs. "When those Bix records came out, that was the greatest thing to hit the music scene. Trumbauer's solo on 'Singin' the Blues' was one of the few tunes I ever copied off anybody."[24] Referring to a different recording, "I'll Never Miss the Sunshine," Michael Brooks recalls that Trumbauer's solo was "as much a yardstick to young reedmen as the Charlie Parker Dials, twenty-five years later." "At that time," Budd Johnson would later tell interviewer Michael Zwerin, "Frankie Trumbauer was the baddest cat around."[25] But the ultimate tribute to Trumbauer came from Lester Young, who adopted Tram's silky phrasing as the foundation for his own moving— and vastly influential—style of saxophone playing. "Trumbauer was my idol," Young explained to Nat Hentoff in a 1956 interview. "When I had just started to play, I used to buy all his records. I imagine I can still play all those solos off the record. He played the C melody saxophone. I tried to get the sound of the C melody on the tenor. That's why I don't sound like other people. Trumbauer always told a little story."[26]

In essence, these "little stories" offered an alternative to the harmonically oriented, arpeggio-based style characteristic of so many earlier jazz reed players. Trumbauer's horn lines were less vertical, less built on spelling chords and inserting predictable patterns; they moved more ethereally, fashioned from an assortment of melodic phrases—some syncopated, others anticipating the velvety, less articulated style of Young—dosed with a leavening of unexpected, almost exotic (given the era) intervals. "I'll Never Miss the Sunshine," recorded only ten weeks after Louis Armstrong and King Oliver's debut session, could be considered the first milestone of cool jazz, and Trumbauer's "San" from nine months later is an impressive display of this artist's ingeniuity and versatility in constructing sax lines. On occasion, Tram's solos (for example, on "Trumbology" from 1927) rely too much on novelty effects reminiscent of vaudeville entertainers such as Rudy Wiedoeft. But his technical mastery of the horn was never in doubt, and his finest efforts rank among the most important jazz recordings of the era.

Beiderbecke and Trumbauer reached their peak on heartfelt performances such as "Singin' the Blues" and "I'm Comin' Virginia," both recorded in 1927, which went a long way toward establishing the ballad tradition in jazz. True, earlier hot musicians had often played slow blues, but the ambiance of such performances was much different from the purer, more fragile melodicism of these inspired Beiderbecke-Trumbauer collaborations. It was almost as if, before these sides, the hot and the sweet were thought to be mutually exclusive, not to be joined, except in some fanciful chimera not found in reality. But far from being opposites, these two currents, the lyric and the intense, blend seamlessly on these late vintages of the Jazz Age. Especially on "I'm Comin' Virginia," the 2/4 bounce so prevalent on most earlier jazz recordings gives way to a smooth 4/4 ballad tempo, helped along admirably by Eddie Lang's subtle guitar textures. Yet the achievements of the rhythm section are overshadowed by the pungent solos by Beiderbecke and Trumbauer, with their artful balance of emotion and logic. Above all, the essence of Beiderbecke's conception of jazz stands out in relief on these performances; the substitution chords implicit in his solos—superimposed diminished chords, augmented chords, dominant ninth chords—are incorporated with such ease that it is easy to overlook the hard harmonic edge to Bix's melodicism. Instead, the technical aspects are submerged in the free play of his musical creativity.

During this same period, both Beiderbecke and Trumbauer worked with a number of other bandleaders, notably Jean Goldkette and Paul Whiteman. Later commentators have sometimes lamented these associations, asserting that the commercial music played by such ensembles compromised the jazz skills of the two soloists. Goldkette, certainly, was anything but a jazz player. Born in France, he studied piano in Greece and Russia before emigrating to the United States. In his new setting, Goldkette embraced the American dream with a vengeance, showing talents as a businessman and booking agent that increasingly eclipsed his reputation as a concert pianist. Yet if Goldkette was a better impresario than player, his bands were all the stronger for these nonmusical skills. In addition to Bix and Tram, the Goldkette group also featured, at one time or another, Joe Venuti, Eddie Lang, the Dorsey Brothers, Red Nichols, Miff Mole, Don Murray, Steve Brown, and arranger Bill Challis—an impressive lineup by any standard. Goldkette's modest ambitions—primarily aimed, it seems, at producing inoffensive commercial music—were what limited his achievements, not any lack of firepower on the bandstand. The Goldkette orchestra was clearly capable of playing at a much higher level than its recordings indicate. How else can we explain Rex Stewart's account of a 1926 battle of the bands between Fletcher Henderson's group (in which Stewart served as cornetist) with Goldkette's orchestra? "This proved to be a most humiliating experience for us, since, after all, we were supposed to be the world's greatest dance orchestra," Stewart later wrote. "The facts were that we simply could not compete with Jean Goldkette's Victor Recording Orchestra. Their arrangements were too imaginative, their rhythm too strong." "Fletcher was the King up there, had Hawk and all them guys and Goldkette's band washed them away," adds Sonny Greer. "Man, that was the sensation of New York. . . . Goldkette's band was something else."[27] The surviving recordings contain only hints—in an occasional choice solo or well-arranged ensemble part—of what Stewart describes as "the first original white swing band in history."

Bix and Tram were far from the only famous jazz buddies recruited into the Goldkette band. Two innovative string soloists, guitarist Eddie Lang and violinist Joe Venuti, were added for recording sessions, and stand out as the premier players on their instruments from the early days of jazz. They had met during their childhood in Philadelphia, even sharing a music stand while performing in the local school orchestra. Both Venuti and Lang, who was born as Salvatore Massaro, began studies on the violin—it was a favored instrument of European immigrants, some have suggested, since it could be easily carried along as families migrated to a new homeland—but Lang later switched to banjo and guitar. The duo played together in Philadelphia and Atlantic City in the early 1920s when both were in their late teens. In 1926, they reunited in New York and embarked on a series of important recordings. Their 1926 duet, "Stringing the Blues," not only showcases their deep rapport and the ease of their playing, but is also a landmark in defining the role of guitar and violin in the jazz idiom (anticipating the celebrated later work of the Quintette of the Hot Club of France). Later collaborations, such as "Running Ragged" from October 1929 and "The Wild Dog" from October 1930, document the pair's progress in expanding the jazz vocabulary on their instruments. These seminal recordings went a long way toward forging a chamber music style of jazz combo playing.

Eventually the core of jazz soloists on the Goldkette roster—Bix, Tram, Lang, Venuti—made the move to the more successful Paul Whiteman orchestra, a group that, if anything, presents later listeners with an enigma even more puzzling than Goldkette's. Whiteman's knack for public relations, which led to his being dubbed the "King of Jazz," may have helped boost his fame in the 1920s but caused an intense backlash in later years. Robert Goffin, whose 1931 work *Aux Frontieres du Jazz* was the first major book on the music, reflected the view of many jazz lovers when, in a pointed jab at Whiteman, he dedicated the work to "Louis Armstrong, the real King of Jazz." Whiteman's music, in his opinion, reflected "a compromise between real jazz and the prejudices of the bourgeois public."[28] Although he had not yet visited America, Goffin was extraordinarily prescient in his early evaluations of Armstrong, Beiderbecke, Ellington, Hawkins, and others. For that matter, his irritation at Whiteman's spurious title was hardly unjustified. Yet Whiteman, like Goldkette, is a far too complex and problematic figure to dismiss with a cursory judgment.

To a great degree, this is because the accepted discourses relating to twentieth-century music are poorly equipped to cope with figures who straddle different idioms. For example, most chronicles of musical activity in the 1920s will draw an implicit delineation between popular music, jazz, and classical composition. Hence, accounts of the evolution of jazz tend to present a polarized landscape in which hot bands (Henderson, Ellington, Goodman, Basie) thrive, develop, and change in complete isolation from other musical currents. Such categorizations may make the narrative structure of a music history book flow more smoothly, but much is lost in the process. This approach is especially maladroit when dealing with an artist such as Whiteman, who operated primarily in the interstices between different types of music. Perhaps this would not be so much of a problem if genres rarely crossed paths, but—for better or worse—the modern age is marked by the tendency for distinct styles to coalesce and cross-fertilize. In music, purity is a myth, albeit a resilient one. The historian who hopes to come to grips with the powerful currents of creativity in modern times must learn to deal with these composite art forms on their own terms or not at all. There is no high road on the postmodern map, just a myriad of intersecting and diverging paths.

Where do we start in assessing Whiteman across his broad spectrum of musical activism? It is Whiteman's equivocal position as a footnote to the history of classical music that most accounts stress: namely, his role in commissioning (although coercing might be a better term for what actually happened) George Gershwin to write his famous *Rhapsody in Blue*. But the jazz credentials of the Whiteman band were also considerable. Borrowing the best of the Goldkette orchestra—Beiderbecke, Trumbauer, Challis, Venuti, Lang, Brown—Whiteman brought them together with a host of other rising young talents, ranging from Bing Crosby to Ferde Grofé. But these artists were often required to perform material with minimal jazz content. The sweet popular music of Whiteman's band was its weakest side—which is all the more unfortunate, given how much Whiteman has come to be evaluated on these pieces. Recordings such as "Whispering" and "Japanese Sandman" sold well at the time, but sound dated to ears weaned on more declamatory musical styles. The same is true of the Victor Herbert works that Whiteman promoted, as well as the pseudo-classical arrangements of pieces such as Lehar's "Merry Widow Waltz" and Liszt's "Liebestraum." There is a reserved daintiness about them that recalls, not without a certain charm, the naiveté of the Jazz Age; but, in the final analysis, they lack the robustness that would have allowed them to weather the passing decades.

But another, jazzier side of Whiteman deserves to be celebrated, one that is too often forgotten or dismissed out of hand these days. Whiteman may not have lived up to his claim to be the King of Jazz, but neither was he a mere commoner in the kingdom of hot music. Even before Beiderbecke joined his band, Whiteman had fine hot players on hand—check out the trumpet solos from Tommy Gott on "I'll Build a Stairway to Paradise" (1922), or Henry Busse on "Hard Hearted Hannah" (1924). By the same token, Bing Crosby's singing from his Whiteman period is often obscured by his later fame as a Hollywood entertainer, yet his early jazz work exerted a powerful and lasting influence. More than any other white singer of his day, Crosby created an intimate style of delivery, perfectly suited for an age in which microphones and recordings had replaced unamplified concert hall performances. Heard alongside Beiderbecke on Whiteman's 1927 recording of "Mary," Crosby clearly demonstrates his allegiance to the same cool jazz aesthetic that Bix and Tram were advocating. Whiteman's chief "composer in residence," Ferde Grofé, for his part, is a major talent who has somehow been forced into a cameo role in music history, as the arranger who scored Gershwin's *Rhapsody in Blue*; yet even before joining Whiteman, in his charts for Art Hickman's band, Grofé played a key role in defining the potential for a sax section in dance music, and his later compositions for Whiteman such as "Mississippi Suite" and "Metropolis" are important contributions to the concert jazz tradition.

The main failing of these latter works is not in what they included—the arrangements themselves are smartly done—but in what they left out. Grofé's focus on emulating Gershwin's *Rhapsody* led him to downplay the role of improvisation; even Beiderbecke's "solo" on "Metropolis" shows up on the surviving chart spelled out note-for-note. If Grofé had left room in these otherwise impressive pieces for hot solos, they would probably be acknowledged today as jazz classics. As it stands, they have simply fallen through the cracks, not jazzy enough for jazz fans and insufficiently highbrow for the symphony halls. And Grofé was far from the only star arranger in Whiteman's corner. Bill Challis's arrangements represent some of the band's most advanced and jazziest material, while Eddie Sharpe, Matty Malneck, and Tom Satterfield were also capable of sophisticated, jazz-oriented writing. One hears, for example, on Challis's "Changes," another unfairly neglected masterpiece of the era, a subtle command of voice leading, one which invites comparisons to Beiderbecke's hypermodern piano piece "In a Mist."

Direct influence is quite likely. Beiderbecke, realizing his poor skills with musical notation, relied on Challis to write down his piano compositions—a painful process since Bix was a perfectionist, and it took six months before Challis could notate "In a Mist" in a way that met with the approval of the composer. Numerous memoirs from the period stress that Beiderbecke's piano music was almost as striking as his cornet work, yet little substantive evidence survives beyond a single recording of Bix at the piano, and Challis's transcriptions. Even the now-famous recording of "In a Mist" has been dismissed by friend Ralph Berton as "feeble, stiff, self-conscious" in comparison to what he had heard the artist do at the keyboard.[29] Nonetheless, this performance stands out for its radical reconfiguration of the jazz piano tradition, and provides a tantalizing hint of the direction Beiderbecke's artistry might have taken had he lived beyond his twenties.

This is a difficult piece to place in Bix's oeuvre. Many commentators have described it as an outgrowth of Beiderbecke's fascination with impressionism and other modern styles of composition (reflected elsewhere, for example, in his use of altered dominants and whole-tone scales). Others have viewed it as an expression of the romantic, plaintive side of his music and personality. Yet there is a cold, diamond-edged hardness to this piano piece, neither impressionist nor romantic in origin. Only probing underneath its steely surface do we see the core emotion, not the warm suggestiveness evoked by Beiderbecke's cornet playing, but a poignant sense of isolation and anomie, perhaps even despair. Those who celebrate Bix, the carefree player of pretty melodies, must struggle to reconcile such a view with this work, a remote, harsh musical landscape out of character with the mythic Beiderbecke persona.

Throughout 1928, Bix's drinking excesses began to take an increasing toll, eventually contributing to a December hospitalization for pneumonia. By the beginning of 1929, Beiderbecke had returned to the Whiteman band, but sporadic problems continued to plague him throughout the year, apparently worsening in the fall. He was a young man in his mid-twenties, yet his walk showed a marked limp, and eventually he needed a cane; he suffered from cramps, shortness of breath, memory lapses, and looked pale and unhealthy. On September 15, 1929, Bix came back to Davenport, to recuperate at the family home. A month later, only a few days before the stock market crash, he entered the Keely Institute in Dwight, Illinois, a well-known rehab facility for the medical treatment of alcoholism. On his release, in November, Bix appeared relatively healthy and ready to return to performing. After a series of local gigs, Beiderbecke began pursuing more far-flung employment opportunities in Chicago, St. Louis, and New York.

This period found Beiderbecke increasingly focused on composing at the piano. Friends and colleagues, hoping for the best, envisioned Beiderbecke embarking on a new stage of his career, in which the inspired spontaneity of his cornet work and the disciplined structure of the classical music he loved would merge in a totally new sound, capturing the best of both worlds. Such hopes proved illusory. Beiderbecke's return to music was soon accompanied by a resumption of the problems that had led to his departure from the Whiteman band. Consumed in a downward spiral of drinking, fatigue, and frailty, Bix seemed intent on pursuing a slow, prolonged process of self-destruction. Few recordings were made during this final period, and his performing opportunities were now mostly at house parties and college dates—a far cry from the theaters, auditoriums, and concert halls of his Whiteman days. The end came in New York on August 6, 1931, when Beiderbecke succumbed to lobar pneumonia, perhaps accompanied by a fit of delirium tremens. He was twenty-eight years old. Five days later, Bix Beiderbecke was buried at Oakdale Cemetery in his native Davenport, Iowa.

4 Harlem

THE TWO HARLEMS

Harlem in the late 1920s was a society precariously balanced between two extremes. The Harlem Renaissance—the name given to the broad-based flowering of black cultural and intellectual life during these years—crystallized the first of these possibilities, reflecting a forward-looking optimism and deeply felt community pride. It was tempting to reach for scriptural imagery in describing this vision of Harlem. Here was a promised land for a downtrodden race, delivered from slavery as in the Old Testament, now answerable to its own needs, and finally free to pursue its own vision of civil society. As such, Harlem in this era symbolized a coming of age for all African Americans—whether living in the North or South, East or West—who participated vicariously, if not in fact, in the formation of a community where they could exist not as a minority culture, dependent on the tolerance or philanthropy of others, but as a self-sufficient body. More than any other aspect of Harlem in the late 1920s, its intellectual currents showed how far things had progressed. Certainly there had been African American intellectuals before, but too often they had labored in isolation, if not in the face of overt oppression. In this new setting, however, an entire cultural elite had come together, drawing confidently on the full range of human expression—in poetry, fiction, visual arts, music, history, sociology, and various other disciplines in which creative thought could flourish.

Only a few years earlier, Harlem had been a white neighborhood, of European immigrants and Lutheran churches, a community where the sound of lieder, not ragtime, was heard coming from the windows of apartment houses. Named after

Haarlem, the Netherlands city, by early Dutch settlers, the neighborhood retained its Old World roots well into the early twentieth century. But the years following the start of World War I witnessed a massive demographic shift, as the African American population boomed, with southern migrants joining refugees from the overcrowded midtown tenements of Manhattan. Here they formed a new society: not just as transients, or even residents, but as proprietors—by the late 1920s, 70 percent of Harlem's real estate was under black control—with all the independence that ownership conveyed.

But another Harlem coexisted alongside this one, reflecting a crueler reality and a less promising future. Historian David Levering Lewis, drawing on "a prism of census tracks, medical data, and socioeconomic studies," reaches the conclusion that, even in the midst of this so-called renaissance, "Harlem was becoming a slum."[1] This second Harlem was one of harsh economics, low salaries, and looming rent payments. A 1927 study showed that 48 percent of Harlem renters spent more than twice as much of their income on rent as similarly situated white city dwellers. In this hand-to-mouth environment, a quarter of Harlem families took in at least one lodger—double the rate for white New Yorkers. Sometimes the same mattress was rented out twice, to tenants on different work shifts. Wages for blacks may well have been higher in the North than in the South, but the earning differential between white and black was still an unbridgeable gulf. Black independence, in this setting, came at a price, one meted out daily in the cost of food and shelter.

Jazz was very much a part of this second Harlem—more at home here than in the "other" Harlem of high culture and higher aspirations. True, the Harlem Renaissance created an ideology, a cultural context for jazz. But the Harlem of rent parties and underground economies created music. Even before the onset of the Great Depression, the rent party had become established as accepted way of paying for the high cost of lodging. Flyers might be circulated up to a month in advance, advertising which entertainers would be performing. Admission on the night of the party might cost anywhere between twenty-five cents and a dollar. The money would pay for both the cost of the party and the next month's rent. "They would crowd a hundred or more people into a seven room railroad flat, and the walls would bulge," recalled Willie "The Lion" Smith, one of the greatest of the Harlem pianists. "Some of the parties spread to the halls and all over the building."[2]

Such activities, for all their vibrancy and social significance, were a dividing point for the two Harlems. Rent parties were "the special passion of the community," writes one historian, yet "their very existence was avoided or barely acknowledged by most Harlem writers."[3] The music of this hidden Harlem was also long ignored in most books on the Renaissance, with even seminal figures such as Duke Ellington and Fats Waller playing only the most modest role in many of the histories.[4] Although their artistry represented the highest pinnacle of African American culture, their affiliation with jazz relegated them to the submerged Harlem, the lowlife world of speakeasies and slumming. Cab Calloway, recalling Harlem during these years, amplifies on the marginal role of jazz in the context of this cultural outpouring: "Those of us in the music and entertainment business were vaguely aware that something exciting was happening, but we weren't directly involved."[5] Benny Carter concurs: "We in music knew there was much going on in literature, for example, but our worlds were far apart. We sensed that the black cultural as well as moral leaders looked down on our music as undignified."[6] In 1936, when stride piano master James P. Johnson, in hopes of winning a Guggenheim Fellowship, enlisted the help of Harlem Renaissance litterateur James Weldon Johnson, the deferential tone of the musician's letter and its acknowledgment that these two respective leaders of their spheres of Harlem had never met personally testified to this still marked separation between their worlds. The Guggenheim judges, for their part, showed their opinion of the hot and swinging side of Harlem culture by turning down Johnson's request and rejecting his second application in 1942.[7]

Attitudes, in some spheres of Harlem society, had changed little since Scott Joplin had tried unsuccessfully to interest local patrons in supporting his opera *Treemonisha* back in 1915, and found no encouragement for his exalted vision of the high art potential of vernacular forms of African American music. Middle-class and upper-class black families were, at best, ambivalent about celebrating the cultural contributions of ragtime, jazz, and blues musicians—and often explicitly hostile to these elements in their community. Recalling that "the average Negro family did not allow the blues or even the raggedy music played in their homes," Willie "The Lion" Smith added that "among those who disliked this form of entertainment the most were the Negroes who had recently come up from the South to seek a better life."[8] And not without reason. "Native or long time Harlemites," W. O. Smith stresses, "looked down on southern blacks."[9] In an attempt to appear sophisticated and gain acceptance, new arrivals from the Deep South were quick to disavow the telltale signs of their origins, whether culinary, sartorial, linguistic, or cultural. Musical imports from the South—Delta blues, New Orleans jazz, Missouri rags—were often tainted with the same brush. In almost every sphere of day-to-day Harlem life, the desire for assimilation into the ways of the Northeast exerted a powerful motivating force. Is it any surprise that, in such an environment, the two Harlems—the Harlem of literary aspirations and the Harlem of jazz and blues—were, if not at war, at least caught up in an uncomfortable truce?

The piano was often the battleground between these two visions of black artistic achievement. It is not going too far to suggest that the piano was to Harlem what brass bands had been to New Orleans. The instrument represented conflicting possibilities—a pathway for assimilating traditional highbrow culture, a calling card of lowbrow nightlife, a symbol of middle-class prosperity, or, quite simply, a means of making a living. But, with the benefit of hindsight, we tend to view the piano in Harlem of the late 1920s and early 1930s as the center of a new type of music. Harlem stride piano, as it has come to be known, stood as a bridge between the ragtime idiom of the turn of the century and the new jazz piano styles that were in the process of evolution. Almost a half-century after his arrival in New York in 1908, James P. Johnson recalled the musical scene of those years: "There weren't any jazz bands like they had in New Orleans or on the Mississippi river boats, but the ragtime piano was played all over, in bars, cabarets and sporting houses."[10]

Between 1900 and 1914, around one hundred New York companies were involved in publishing ragtime sheet music. Yet commercial interests and artistic values coexisted uneasily in Tin Pan Alley, with scores of mediocre rag songs—most of them bearing little resemblance to the classic ragtime music of Scott Joplin, James Scott, and Joseph Lamb—overshadowing the more sophisticated compositions of the masters. Stride piano players were well aware of the gulf between highbrow and lowbrow that Joplin—perhaps foolishly, perhaps wisely—had refused to recognize back in 1915; and though they sometimes tried to bridge it, they never forgot the importance of their roots in popular music. Understanding that music required an audience, preferably a large one, they mastered a wide range of novelty devices and popular effects. At times the superficial glitter could outshine the jazz content— "When I began my work, jazz was a stunt," was Duke Ellington's later critique of some of this music[11]—but the slick professionalism of the Harlem stride style also served to expand the audience for African American music in the face of discrimination from the cultural elite, both within and without the black community, and despite a severe economic downturn. For better or worse, the stride players did not shy away from being entertainers. Indeed, the most famous of them, Fats Waller, displayed a knack for captivating audiences unsurpassed by any jazz musician, past or present, with the possible exception of Louis Armstrong.

But stride piano was more than mass entertainment. In the years following the decline of ragtime, the New York players kept true to the basic ethos of that music, especially its rhythms and syncopations, while incorporating a broad range of other devices, borrowed both from jazz players such as Jelly Roll Morton and Earl Hines, as well as from classical pianists. The result was a virtuosic, orchestral style of performance. James P. Johnson noted the origins of this style in the competitive musical environment of New York:

The other sections of the country never developed the piano as far as the New York boys did. Only lately have they caught up. The reason the New York boys became such high class musicians was because the New York piano was developed by the European method, system and style. The people in New York were used to hearing good piano played in concerts and cafes. The ragtime player had to live up to that standard. They had to get orchestral effects, sound harmonies, chords and all the techniques of European concert pianists who were playing their music all over the city.[12]

Johnson's own music epitomized this approach; it represents a critical link between the ragtime of Joplin and the jazz of Waller and Tatum. His early efforts remain true to the rag style, with his composition "Carolina Shout" gaining particular favor among his peers. The work was widely imitated by other players even before the sheet music was published, and eventually replaced the "Maple Leaf Rag" as the ultimate test piece for aspiring rag pianists. Johnson's works may have lacked the melodic inspiration and compositional balance that characterized Joplin's pieces, but he made up for it in the sheer breadth of his musical aspirations. His popular songs were great successes, with "If I Could Be with You (One Hour Tonight)," "Old Fashioned Love," and "Charleston" reaching a mass audience that was only vaguely familiar with the composer's jazz credentials. Yet Johnson also attacked the citadels of concert music with a determination akin to Joplin's: his legacy includes *Harlem*

Symphony, American Symphonic Suite (based on W. C. Handy's "St. Louis Blues"), *Concerto Jazz a Mine*, a piano rhapsody *Yamekraw* (performed at Carnegie Hall with Fats Waller as soloist), and the opera *De Organizer* (boasting a libretto by Langston Hughes). Johnson received little encouragement during his lifetime for these efforts, and a posthumous search through his personal archives revealed numerous rejection letters from conductors and potential benefactors. Only sporadic performances in the years following Johnson's death in 1955 have saved these works from total obscurity. But Johnson's high aspirations for African American music were a harbinger of later developments. In particular, Duke Ellington's more visionary projects, most notably *Black, Brown and Beige* and *Harlem*, are an outgrowth of—and may have been directly influenced by—the efforts of this ambitious predecessor.

Even when he kept true to the stride idiom, Johnson was an inveterate experimenter who was willing to look outside the jazz and rag idiom for techniques he could apply to his compositions. These devices included classical interpolations (his repertoire included hot versions of the *William Tell Overture* and *Peer Gynt*), counterpoint exercises using national anthems (the final theme of his "Imitators' Rag" mixes "Dixie" in the right hand with the "Star-Spangled Banner" in the left), and much else besides. In later years, Johnson even adapted to the demands of jazz-combo work, recording with the Blue Note Jazzmen and on a number of sides by prominent Chicago players. There may have been greater jazz musicians than James P. Johnson, but few artists of his day sensed so clearly the latent potential of African American music or worked so vigorously to bring it into reality.

Under the inspiration of Johnson and others, the world of stride piano developed a macho, competitive ethos that has since come to permeate the jazz world as a whole. This overlay of artistry and combat remains an important—and often overlooked—tradition in African American culture. Duke Ellington, recalling his own schooling in the Harlem stride piano tradition, explained: "Anybody who had a reputation as a piano player had to prove it right there and then by sitting down to the piano and displaying his artistic wares."[13] In later years, the cutting contest—a jam session in which outplaying the other participants ("cutting" them, in jazz jargon)—became an important part of jazz pedagogy and practice, and the most crucial rite of passage for a young player. Its overtones now hover over even the friendliest of jazz encounters. In an age in which other art forms have come to eschew demonstrations of virtuosity, the jazz world continues to embrace one-upmanship and displays of technique as an integral part of its culture. To a great extent, the hothouse environment of Harlem helped to produce this new image of the jazz musician as half artist, half warrior.

Willie "The Lion" Smith epitomized this new breed of jazz player. His reputation in the jazz world was made not in concert halls or clubs, but in backrooms and private gatherings. Asserting his supremacy among the assembled piano players was the core value of his musicality. Ellington called him "a gladiator at heart." Smith's attitude to lesser talents was anything but tolerant. Ellington describes the Lion's typical response to these ill-suited aspirants to his throne:

Before he got through too many stanzas the Lion was standing over him, cigar blazing. Like if the cat was weak with the left hand, the Lion would say, "What's the matter, are you a cripple?" Or, "When did you break your left arm?" Or, "Get up, I will show you how it's supposed to go."

Smith's swagger was as much a part of his reputation as his playing. "When Willie Smith walked into a place," James P. Johnson explained, "his every move was a picture . . . studied, practiced and developed just like it was a complicated piano piece." Nat Hentoff likened the Lion's stroll to the keyboard to "Don Juan on the way to an assignation."[14]

Smith met formidable competitors in the nightspots and rent parties where Harlem stride evolved. In addition to Johnson, these late-night sessions might feature any one of a number of keyboard protagonists. Taken as a whole, they form a cast of characters worthy of a Damon Runyon novel. Luckey Roberts had worked as a child acrobat before becoming a professional pianist and brought a flair for dramatic pyrotechnics with him to the keyboard. His massive hands could span a fourteenth, and his octaves and tremolos were the envy of his peers. Little is known about stride player Abba Labba, but his powerful left hand and predilection for sophisticated harmonic substitutions may have prefigured the later work of Art Tatum. Another mysterious stride master, known simply as Seminole, was a formidable southpaw—in his autobiography Count Basie recalls losing a cutting contest to him, lamenting "he had a left hand like everybody else had a right hand. . . . And he dethroned me. Took my crown!"[15] Donald Lambert spent only four years in Harlem, but though he was nicknamed the Lamb he was more than ready to match up with the Lion at piano battles. "I believe this performance is technically impossible," Ethan Iverson, a historian of the keyboard as well as a skilled practitioner himself with his trio The Bad Plus, has quipped with regard to Lambert's rendition of "Anitra's Dance"; but a surviving video testifies to Lambert's ability to play it with just his two hands and no assistance from the audience.[16] Eubie Blake, a songwriter and raconteur as well as a noted pianist, was another charismatic exponent of the new style. Earl Hines recalls Blake, during this era, sporting a raccoon coat and derby, and always carrying a cane to enhance his stage presence—even when no stage was in sight; but Blake saved his best effects for the piano, where he would lift his hands high, in theatrical fashion, sometimes conducting with one, while continuing to pound the keys with the other. Blake lived to celebrate his hundredth birthday (although official documents only give him credit for ninety-six years at his death in 1983), but by any measure he spent more than eighty of them earning his living in the music industry, entertaining audiences with a keyboard style that combined a sure sense of ragged syncopation with a sensitivity to the melodic possibilities of popular music.

Yet Thomas "Fats" Waller did more than any of these players to bring the Harlem style to the attention of the broader American public. Born in Harlem on May 21, 1904, Waller honed his skills by drawing on the full range of opportunities that New York City could provide. His teachers included two great local institutions, Juilliard and James P. Johnson, as well as much in between. His early performance venues were equally diverse, reflecting Waller's adaptability to a gamut of settings, from the sacred to the profane. He was heard at religious services (where his father, a Baptist lay preacher, presided); at Harlem's Lincoln Theater, where he accompanied silent movies on the pipe organ; at rent parties and cabarets; literally everywhere and anywhere a keyboard might be at hand. His pristine piano tone and and technical assurance could well have distinguished him even in symphonic settings. Yet these considerable skills as an instrumentalist were eventually overshadowed by Waller's other talents. While still in his teens, Waller initiated his career as a songwriter, and over the next two decades he would produce a number of successful compositions, many of which remain jazz standards, including "Ain't Misbehavin'," "Honcysuckle Rose," "Squeeze Me," and "Jitterbug Waltz." In time, Waller's comedic abilities and engaging stage persona would add further momentum to his career, pointing to a range of further opportunities, only some of which he lived to realize.

Waller's reputation in the jazz world rests primarily on his many boisterous per-formances and recordings—the latter comprising around six hundred tracks made over a twenty-year period. With unflagging exuberance, Waller talked, sang, joked, exhorted band members, and, almost as an afterthought, played the piano on these memorable sides. At times, they sound more like a party veering out of control than a recording session. Indeed, this was the quintessential party music for those who had come of age under Prohibition—a time when the most festive soirees were, by definition, illicit. Waller was skilled at playing Falstaff to this generation, hinting at speakeasy enticements with a wink of the eye, a telling quip, or other intimations of immorality. True, a cavalier aesthetic has always dominated jazz, celebrating the eternal in the most intense aspects of the here and now—do we expect anything less from an art form built on improvisation?—but few artists pushed this attitude to the extremes that Waller did. And audiences loved it. With a winning, warm demeanor, Waller made them feel like they were honored guests at his party, drinking from the best bottle in the house, privy to the wittiest asides, and seated front-row center to hear the band.

Although Waller's small-combo work captured the public's imagination, his solo keyboard performances, documented on a handful of recordings and player piano rolls, remain his most poised statements as a jazz artist. Familiar stride piano elements—an oompah left hand coupled with syncopated right-hand figures—serve as the building blocks of his playing here, but Waller leavens them with a composi-tional ingenuity that raises them above the work of his peers. Waller's solo work reveals his omnivorous musical appetite, drawing on the blues (hear the majestic slow blues in "Numb Fumblin'"), classical music (evoked, for instance, in the high-register figures of "African Ripples"), and boogie-woogie (note its ingenious inter-polation in the opening phrase of "Alligator Crawl"), as well as the ragtime roots of the music (as in "Handful of Keys" and "Smashing Thirds"). On "Viper's Drag," Waller toys with the contrast between an ominous dark opening theme in a minor key and a swinging major mode section—a device Ellington used frequently during this same period in crafting his own version of Harlem jazz. Combining his talents as a pianist and his sense of compositional balance, Waller's solo works stand out as the high point of the Harlem stride tradition.

While most other jazz musicians of his generation gravitated toward the big bands in the 1930s and 1940s, Waller cultivated other ambitions. His activities took him anywhere and everywhere the entertainment industry flourished, from the theaters of Broadway to the motion picture studios of Hollywood. Even when he confined his attentions to music, Waller's restless seeking after new challenges was ever apparent. In a half-dozen areas—as pianist, organist, vocalist, songwriter, band-leader, and sideman—he made a mark that is still felt in the worlds of jazz and popular music. His successes of the prewar years were topped by a well-received 1938 European tour. In Scotland, wearing a Glengarry tartan, he dazzled the audience with a Harlem stride reworking of "Loch Lomond" and was brought back for ten curtain calls. The following year he returned to England, where he worked on a grand scale, composing and recording his "London Suite," comprising six piano sketches. Back in the States, he performed and recorded prolifically and undertook a range of new projects. In 1943, Waller managed to write the music for the stage show *Early to Bed*, tour extensively, and travel to Hollywood to costar in the film *Stormy Weather* (along with Lena Horne, Cab Calloway, and Bill "Bojangles" Robinson). The strain of pursuing these multiple careers may have been too much. On December 15, 1943, Waller died of pneumonia while on a cross-country train trip back to New York. At the time of his passing, he was at the peak of his popularity. Had he lived, Waller would no doubt have built on his early forays into radio and movies and would have been a natural for the medium of television.

Around this same time, another vernacular form of African American keyboard music was making a mark on American popular tastes. Boogie-woogie, as this style was called, first came to the attention of the music industry in the 1920s but achieved its greatest popularity in the early 1940s, when the faddish sound served as the basis for a number of hit records. This musical idiom combined insistent left-hand patterns based on blues chord progressions with syncopated melody lines or block chords in the right hand. The style demanded exceptional hand independence and a sure sense of time from the performer. The term *boogie-woogie* first came into use in the late 1920s—although the roots of this style may date back to the late nineteenth century—and might have originally applied to a dance that was accompanied by this boisterous piano music (implied, for example, in Pine Top Smith's spoken commentary on "Pine Top's Boogie Woogie" from 1928). The style achieved its highest pitch as unaccompanied keyboard music, although it was not uncommon for pianists to perform together in duos and trios, as on "Boogie Woogie Prayer" recorded by Meade Lux Lewis, Albert Ammons, and Pete Johnson. The leading practitioners occasionally tried their dextrous hands at other keyboard styles, but, for the most part, boogie-woogie remained a fringe music, lingering in the interstices between blues and jazz. For a brief spell, mainstream performers embraced it, as demonstrated by Tommy Dorsey in "Boogie Woogie" (1938), Count Basie in "Basie Boogie" (1941), and the Andrews Sisters in "Boogie Woogie Bugle Boy" (1941). More authentic examples of the idiom can be found in such recordings as Meade Lux Lewis's "Honky Tonk Train Blues" and Albert Ammons's "Shout for Joy."

Historians of these and other early twentieth-century piano styles—Harlem stride, boogie-woogie, and other strands of jazz and popular keyboard music—face their greatest challenge in trying to place the genre-crossing and genre-busting artist Art Tatum, whose work from the early 1930s through the mid-1950s seemed to set its own rules and follow its own evolutionary schemas. He stands out as the greatest virtuoso in the Harlem stride piano tradition—and also demonstrated his mastery, on many occasions, of boogie-woogie—yet he also did much more; as such, he remains a complex and controversial figure, one difficult to situate with any real precision in the stylistic pigeonholes commonly used in histories of modern American music. One invariably ends up reaching for the oldest cliché of them all: simply asserting that Tatum was "ahead of his time." Yet it is equally valid to see Tatum as obsessed with the achievements of the past, not just in jazz but also in classical music, given the bravura Lisztian aspects of his playing.

Certainly Tatum's vision of jazz music was initially inspired by the Harlem stride tradition, and though he stayed true to many of its mannerisms and devices until the end of his career, he more often than not subverted these selfsame conventions, tore them apart, and used them piecemeal in building his own grandiloquent conception of jazz piano. For Tatum, Harlem stride served as a foundation on which more complex musical superstructures could be built, just as medieval Christians often constructed cathedrals on the sites of pagan shrines. And though some might suggest that Art Tatum represented the finest flowering of the Harlem stride tradition, in point of fact, he rang its death knell. In developing his mature style, Tatum all but exhausted the possibilities of stride, forcing later piano modernists—Monk, Powell, Tristano, Brubeck, Evans, and others—to veer off into far different directions in an attempt to work their way outside the massive shadow of this imposing figure. Because of this, much of the musical vocabulary developed by Tatum remains unassimilated by later jazz pianists. Long after the phraseology of such later jazz masters as Charlie Parker and John Coltrane has been widely imitated and mastered, Tatum's legacy still sits in probate, waiting for a new generation of pianists to lay claim to its many riches.

Tatum's virtuosity clouds the issue of his role in the history of jazz. Although his music has been, by turns, lauded and attacked for its showmanship and often gratuitous displays of technique, Tatum's importance is as much due to his advanced musical conception as to his agile fingers. True, no other jazz pianist of his generation (or later ones, for that matter) could equal the speed and clarity of his execution. But equally compelling are the structural components of his playing. Employing massive chord voicings as building blocks, Tatum created dazzling harmonic variations and elevated passing chords (often compacted four to a bar, measure after measure) to a level of sophistication that has never been surpassed in either jazz or classical music. And though some of his techniques—abrupt modulations, rhythmic disjunctions, interpolations from concert hall pieces—had been employed by earlier players, none had incorporated them into the jazz idiom with the grace, ease, and creativity of Art Tatum. By the time he had completed his heroic task of recrafting the jazz keyboard vocabulary, he had taken the various hints and ideas that had existed earlier in the African American tradition and mixed them with large doses of European classical music to form a systematic, all-encompassing vision of jazz piano.

Tatum was born in Toledo, Ohio, on October 13, 1909, far afield from Harlem and the other centers of jazz activity. Afflicted with cataracts in both eyes, Tatum underwent thirteen operations in his youth, which eventually restored reasonable sight to one eye. But a blow to the head from an assailant, dating probably from the pianist's early twenties, undid much of the benefit of these procedures. For the rest of his life, Tatum enjoyed only partial sight in his right eye and remained totally blind in his left. But, as seems so often the case with blind musicians, Tatum compensated for his poor vision through a preternatural acuteness of ear. At age three, he amazed his mother by picking out melodies on the piano that he had heard her sing at a choir rehearsal, and before long he was imitating jazz pieces learned from player pianos and radio broadcasts. Tatum's mother, as well as his teacher Overton Rainey, of the Toledo School of Music, attempted to steer the youngster into a career in classical music. But though Tatum showed an extraordinary talent for playing the concert hall repertoire, his attraction to jazz eventually proved decisive. At age sixteen he began working in and around Toledo, and by his late teens he was performing on a local radio station.

Word of mouth had brought news of Tatum's piano prowess to other parts of the jazz world. Still, the Harlem musicians were not prepared for the impact that Tatum made when he traveled to New York as an accompanist to singer Adelaide Hall in 1932. Within days of his arrival, the local piano titans had decided to test the mettle of the newcomer from Toledo. Tatum found himself escorted to a Harlem nightspot where the greatest masters of stride—including Fats Waller, James P. Johnson, and Willie "The Lion" Smith—were ready to do battle. When it came Tatum's time to play, he let loose with a dazzling "Tea for Two" full of dense harmonies and sweeping runs and arpeggios that left the audience speechless. James P. Johnson gamely followed with his "Carolina Shout," and Waller checked in with his "Handful of Keys," but Tatum responded with a virtuoso version of "Tiger Rag," taken at a breakneck tempo, that made comparisons pointless. Johnson returned to the keyboard with a final fiery rendition of Chopin's "Revolutionary Etude," and though Waller later said he had never heard this elder statesman of stride play quite so well, the final verdict was no longer in doubt. "That Tatum, he was just too good," Waller later recollected. "He had too much technique. When that man turns on the powerhouse, don't no one play him down. He sounds like a brass band." James P. Johnson, for his part, later mused, "When Tatum played 'Tea for Two' that night, I guess that was the first time I ever heard it really *played*."[17]

Several months later, Tatum made his first records, which included the two showpieces he had performed at that Harlem cutting contest. In later years, Tatum expanded his range of pianistic devices and became even more daring harmonically, but for the most part these early recordings reveal a style almost fully formed, at least from the standpoint of technique and showmanship. Over the next three decades, Tatum recorded frequently, laying down over six hundred tracks as soloist or bandleader. Despite the many virtues of Tatum's music from the 1930s and 1940s, he remains best known for a massive recording project made under the supervision of producer Norman Granz and completed toward the close of the pianist's career. Between December 1953 and September 1956, Tatum recorded over two hundred numbers for Granz, most done in a single take during marathon sessions. This body of work features Tatum both as a soloist and in collaborations with other jazz masters, including especially successful pairings with Ben Webster and Roy Eldridge. These late recordings reveal a mature, secure artist playing at near peak level. Somewhat less elegant but more viscerally exciting are the handful of live performances that Tatum left behind. Informal sessions recorded in the early 1940s by Jerry Newman, a Columbia University graduate student at the time, showcase Tatum in a looser, uninhibited mood at various Harlem nightspots—playing, accompanying, even singing the blues. These majestic performances, both playful and awe-inspiring, give credence to the view that Tatum was at his best when playing after hours. Also worth noting is Tatum's Shrine Auditorium concert from 1949, where the pianist's astonishing double-time work on "I Know That You Know" (at a tempo well over four hundred beats per minute), his titanic Gershwin medley, and the sly dissonances of "The Kerry Dance" hint at the broad range of his musical imagination. In November 1956, a short while after completing the recording project instigated by Granz, Tatum died in Los Angeles from uremia at age forty-seven.

Tatum's work, for all its virtues, was not above reproach. In some respects, he stands out as one of the most controversial figures in the history of the music, with supporters and detractors much at odds. French critic André Hodeir, in a celebrated attack, lamented the limitations of Tatum's repertoire (built, he asserted, on "sentimental ballads" and "popular hits"), his preference for embellishing the melody of a song rather than constructing original improvisations, as well as Tatum's overreliance on arpeggios, scales, and other keyboard flourishes. Gunther Schuller, in his 1989 study *The Swing Era*, amplifies on Hodeir's points, describing Tatum's work as predictable and highly derivative ("the entire range of Tatum's virtuosic skills, including his lightning fast arpeggios and runs, are set forth in the middle-to-late nineteenth-century piano literature. . . . It is simply untrue that Tatum created his arabesque, virtuoso technique out of the blue").[18]

These criticisms are not without validity, but they need to be placed in context. First, with regard to repertoire, jazz fans are certainly justified in lamenting that Tatum did not focus more attention on original compositions and ambitious large-scale projects. Yet how can one fault Tatum's reliance on the great popular songwriters of his time? Drawing almost entirely on the masterpieces of his contemporaries, which included George Gershwin, Cole Porter, Irving Berlin, Richard Rodgers, Harold Arlen, Duke Ellington, and others, Tatum consistently featured the finest songs of his day—indeed, of his century—oftentimes recognizing them long before they had become standards. (On his first record session, Tatum performed "Sophisticated Lady" although Ellington's own debut recording of the piece was literally only a few weeks old at the time.) As for Tatum's dependence on the virtuoso tricks of nineteenth-century classical music, a similarly equivocal response must be made. True, the superficial piano pyrotechnics may be derivative, but where is the nineteenth-century equivalent of Tatum's inspired passing chord reharmonizations, sometimes seasoned with hints of bitonality and playful dissonances, and executed with rapid-fire precision? Or of his rhythmic explosions in which the ground beat is eclipsed by a dizzying two-handed cannonade of notes? Or of his syncopated stride eruptions, which push the metronome settings to hitherto unknown levels? Within the annals of classical music there is no equivalent, and although jazz historians can trace the roots of some of these techniques to Hines, Waller, and others, Tatum elevates them to a level of brilliance not found in the original sources. As to Tatum's delight in ornamenting the melody of a piece, one is as justified in praising as in critiquing these reworkings of the original songs, given the ingenuity and inexhaustible variety Tatum brings to the task. Finally, the complaint that Tatum did not improvise, but merely played set pieces, must be dismissed by anyone who has listened to his many recordings, especially those made in informal settings where Tatum was often at his best, and invariably at his most daring.

In truth, the closer one gets to the core of Tatum's music, and away from the surface activity, the more original it sounds. The strongest validation of this comes not from jazz critics but from the musicians themselves, who are anything but ambiguous on this account. A survey of musicians conducted in 1956 by Leonard Feather for his *Encyclopedia of Jazz* found a stunning 68 percent of them citing Tatum as the preeminent jazz pianist. A 1985 survey of jazz pianists conducted by Gene Lees again placed Tatum comfortably on top, suggesting that despite the passing of almost three decades, changing tastes, and the emergence of many new masters of the keyboard, Tatum had lost none of his power to astonish and inspire, and often to dismay, other practitioners of the art.

THE BIRTH OF THE BIG BAND

The emergence of the big band idiom, with its subtle interweaving of four sections—saxophone, trumpet, trombone, and rhythm—may seem, with the benefit of hindsight, an inevitable development in the evolution of jazz music. Was it not some law of aesthetic Darwinism that forced the rough-and-ready small combos of early jazz to give way to the more robust and polished orchestras of Ellington and Goodman? Not really. The connecting line between the roots of jazz and the later big band sound is far from direct or clear. During the so-called Jazz Age, most of the music's key exponents focused their creative energy on soloing not bandleading, on improvisation not orchestration, on an interplay between individual instruments not between sections. The move to a more compositionally oriented idiom of dance music, under the rubric of big band jazz, was anything but smooth or obvious at the time. Commercial pressures, rather than artistic prerogatives, stand out as the spur that forced many early jazz players (including Armstrong, Beiderbecke, and Hines) to embrace the big band idiom. But even in the new setting, they remained improvisers, first and foremost, not orchestrators or composers. A different body of individuals, with different talents and inclinations—Don Redman, Fletcher Henderson, Duke Ellington, Ferde Grofé, Benny Carter, Bill Challis, Art Hickman, and others—would be required to decipher the artistic implications in this shift in the public's taste, to comprehend it as a guidepost pointing to a truly revolutionary, rather than evolutionary, change in the sound of American band music.

As in so many other aspects of the history of jazz, the intermingling of musical genres played a critical role in shaping a new idiom, and New York served as the crucible in which this fusion of styles took place. As early as 1915, the Original Creole Orchestra featuring Freddie Keppard performed in New York; its success paved the way for the more celebrated visit of the Original Dixieland Jazz Band in 1917. By the close of World War I, the influence of these jazz ensembles could be heard throughout the city at vaudeville shows, theaters, society dances, restaurants, and cabarets—indeed, almost anywhere live music was performed. The jazz idiom, in this setting, was already revealing its omnivorous diet—a trait we will witness repeatedly in the course of this history—and was foraging now in Tin Pan Alley, Broadway, and wherever else a fertile musical enivronment could be found. It could digest other musical styles, in whole or in part, all the while maintaining its distinctive characteristics. Certainly this quality, more than any other, proved decisive in the development of that distinctively American orchestra: the jazz big band.

The recorded work of James Reese Europe reflects the degree to which syncopation had entered the dance orchestra vocabulary even before the 1920s. In 1912, Europe brought an African American orchestra into Carnegie Hall for a celebrated performance, silencing the naysayers—including Will Marion Cook, who predicted that the concert would be a fiasco that would "set the Negro race back fifty years."[19] But the event proved to be a huge success, and Europe returned for follow-up performances in 1913 and 1914. Europe would exert even more influence through his Society Orchestra's accompaniment of the celebrated dance team of Irene and Vernon Castle, who established the foxtrot as a dance sensation. A short while later, Europe formed a military band that played a key role in popularizing African American music among overseas audiences. Despite these substantial achievements, it would be going too far to see James Reese Europe as the originator of the jazz big band style. With its ponderous sound, which relied heavily on unison voicings, and its lack of improvisational fire, Europe's Society Orchestra stood out as a late flowering of the ragtime idiom, rather than as a harbinger of the Jazz Age. Nonetheless, the role of the Europe ensemble in supporting new popular dance styles was indicative of an important change in American tastes—and one that anticipated the later evolution of big band jazz.

In the years before 1910, mainstream social dancing in America had relied primarily on European-influenced waltzes, galops, polkas, jigs, quadrilles, and the like with only occasional crossover dances, such as the cakewalk, coming from African American culture. But, by 1914, new and different dance steps were gaining widespread popularity—so much so that the Vatican felt compelled that year to publicly denounce the turkey trot and the tango. Building off the musical support of James Reese Europe, the Castles incorporated elements of different vernacular dances into their polished performances, creating a jazzier, less refined style that rapidly gained the favor of East Coast society. Through their exhibitions and their New York school, they served as an important link between African American dance and white society. Histories of jazz often overlook the critical role these shifting currents in social dancing exerted on the music. The changing nature of the jazz orchestra in New York during the years following the Castle-Europe collaboration was, in many ways, dictated from the dance floor as much as from the bandstand.

Fletcher Henderson, who helped define the emerging jazz big band sound in the 1920s, also drew inspiration not just from New Orleans and Chicago jazz, but even more from these currents of popular music and dance that were sweeping New York in those years. Ethel Waters, in a telling anecdote, described how she had to force Henderson to listen to player piano rolls so that he could understand how to accompany her properly on a blues recording. Henderson was a quick study and eventually made extensive use of the blues in his music, but initially it was the ethos of the ballrooms, of Tin Pan Alley, of Broadway and vaudeville, as well as of the rag bands of the Northeast that set the context for his dramatic reconstruction of the American jazz orchestra. In truth, by both temperament and training, Henderson was an unlikely jazz innovator. Born in Cuthbert, Georgia, in 1897, Fletcher Henderson was raised in a middle-class black family where European concert music, not rags and blues, was considered an indispensable part of a youngster's education. He went on to take a degree in chemistry and mathematics at Atlanta University, and his decision to move to New York was ostensibly motivated by his desire to find a job as a chemist. With his reserved and unassuming demeanor, Henderson made little headway in chemistry, and soon found himself demonstrating songs, at $22.50 per week, for the Pace-Handy Music Company, a black-owned publishing house of the day, an involvement that eventually led to Henderson's role organizing studio sessions for Harry Pace's Black Swan record label. Hiring and performing in various studio groups, Henderson had found a way to make a living, but still might never have parlayed this opportunity into a full-time career as a bandleader had his sidemen not talked him into auditioning for an opening for a dance orchestra at the Club Alabam on West Forty-fourth Street. He secured the Alabam gig, which soon led to a more visible engagement at Roseland, then in the process of becoming the most important ballroom in New York, if not the whole country. For the next decade, Henderson used this venue as his home base, as he developed a new, progressive jazz vocabulary in synergistic relationship with the popular dance styles of the day.

Henderson has often been criticized for his supposed inability, whether due to indifference or diffidence, to assume the leadership responsibilities that would have given his orchestra the public success it so richly deserved. In this regard, Henderson is typically compared to Duke Ellington, whose gift as a leader of musicians may have been as great as his instrumental acumen, or to Benny Goodman, who some years later would use Henderson's arrangements as a building block in his own much greater popular acclaim. Yet if Henderson lacked the interpersonal skills necessary to run a band, one could hardly tell it by looking at the roster of musicians he attracted to his orchestra. Even Ellington, despite all his genius for eliciting the most from his eccentric group of players, pales in comparison to Henderson in this arena. Henderson's reed section featured, for greater or lesser stints, Coleman Hawkins, Lester Young, Ben Webster, Chu Berry, and Benny Carter—one could plausibly argue that these were the five greatest saxophonists of their day. His brass players during these years included Louis Armstrong, Roy Eldridge, Henry "Red" Allen, Rex Stewart, Tommy Ladnier, Dickie Wells, J. C. Higginbotham, Joe Smith, Benny Morton, and Jimmy Harrison. Has any other jazz bandleader, of any era—even a Miles Davis, a Count Basie, an Art Blakey, or a Benny Goodman—been able to boast of a more illustrious set of alumni?

Yet the most powerful influence on the band came from none of these sources. More than any of these justly celebrated musicians, Don Redman served as a key force in transforming this working dance band into an influential link between the Jazz Age and the Swing Era. Without Redman, the Henderson orchestra might have remained a finishing school for talented soloists, but under his influence it became something more: the birthplace of a new jazz sound and a repository for an emerging aesthetic. Like Henderson, Redman was a college-educated Southerner who had found steady employment in the burgeoning New York jazz scene. In his native West Virginia, where he was born in 1900, Redman had garnered attention as a child prodigy who easily mastered the rudiments of a wide range of instruments—versatility that held him in good stead when he later undertook the blending of these different textures in his pathbreaking arrangements. In his early twenties, Redman went on the road with Billy Paige's Broadway Syncopators, playing clarinet and saxophones in addition to writing band charts. This affiliation brought Redman to New York, where he met Henderson. Their collaboration began at studio sessions even before the formation of the Henderson orchestra. When the Roseland gig became available, Redman was enlisted to join the band.

Coleman Hawkins, destined to mature into one of the most important soloists in the history of jazz, was also present with the Henderson ensemble virtually from the start. The similarities in background between Hawkins, Redman, and Henderson are striking. Like the others, Hawkins was a newcomer to the Northeast—he was born in St. Joseph, Missouri, on November 21, 1904—and had already pursued a musical education in an academic setting (perhaps informally: his official attendance at Washburn College, where he claimed to have studied harmony and composition, is not substantiated by school records). But the shared personality traits are even more striking than these biographical details. Diffident, professional, soft-spoken, wordly, disciplined, well-trained, fascinated by progressive trends in music—these qualities marked each of the three. Do we see here the emergence of a new type of jazz musician? Beiderbecke, the high school dropout who could barely read music; Armstrong, the juvenile delinquent, who refined his native talent at the Waif's Home—these personality types, so indicative of the pioneers of New Orleans and Chicago, were now to be replaced by a new breed of player, the professional big band instrumentalist. Here was the jazz equivalent of the organization man. And at this point in time, the Henderson orchestra was the consummate organization.

Hawkins learned piano at age five and took up cello two years later. For his ninth birthday he received a saxophone, and by age twelve he was playing at school dances. In 1921, Hawkins went on the road with singer Mamie Smith, who one year earlier had achieved a huge success with "Crazy Blues," a million-selling hit that initiated the craze for race records. Smith provided Hawkins with a number of opportunities: to perform in front of large crowds, to initiate his recording career (in May 1922), and to come to New York. But by the summer of 1923, Hawkins had left Smith and was recording with Henderson. While Redman did much of his work behind the scenes, crafting the band's arrangements, Hawkins stood out on the bandstand as the group's featured soloist, usually on tenor saxophone, but sometimes playing clarinet, C-melody saxophone, baritone saxophone, or bass saxophone.

Today the saxophone is not only an accepted and popular band instrument, but to many listeners represents the quintessential sound of jazz. This was far from the case during the years in which Hawkins mastered his craft. The saxophone family was still in its infancy, virtually unknown in the symphonic world, and relegated primarily to military bands. The Belgian instrument maker Antoine-Joseph "Adolphe" Sax had patented the horn in Paris in 1846. But Sax, despite his zeal for invention (his inspirations also include the saxhorn, saxtuba, saxotromba, and even the saxocannon, his neglected contribution to the Crimean War campaign), gained little financial benefit from his efforts and died in poverty in 1894. But the intrinsic advantages of his most famous instrument—it was easy to learn, forgiving in its tone production, and relatively inexpensive to make with its simple metal body attached to a conventional clarinet-type mouthpiece—proved decisive in the long run. By the early years of the twentieth century, the saxophone had established itself as an important instrumental voice, first in military bands and later in popular and jazz ensembles. The only thing lacking was a tradition and an accepted body of playing techniques.

This was provided, in large part, by Hawkins. Certainly there had been earlier jazz saxophonists; Hawkins himself was quick to give credit to largely forgotten figures such as Stump Evans, Prince Robinson, and Happy Caldwell. And Sidney Bechet, as we have seen, had also made important early contributions to the saxophone tradition in jazz. Even so, at the start of Hawkins's career the saxophone had yet to match the role of the cornet or clarinet as an important jazz solo voice. Years later, many devotees of New Orleans style would grumble that the death knell for "pure" jazz was sounded when the saxophonists took over the music. Blame Mr. Hawkins for that palace coup. In particular, the tenor saxophone held an especially insignificant role in jazz before Hawkins's influential advocacy. Rudy Wiedoeft had recorded on the C melody saxophone as early as 1916, while Frank Trumbauer's later work on that instrument was also very influential in its day. Given these predecessors, as well as the rich clarinet tradition in New Orleans and Chicago bands, few would have predicted, at the time, that the tenor would become the dominant saxophone voice in jazz—indeed, even Hawkins had begun by playing the C melody sax. Without his later championing of the tenor, with its heavier and more dominating presence, the later evolution of the jazz reed tradition might have unfolded far differently.

Yet Hawkins's impact extended even more to the sound and fury of the tenor, not merely its selection as a jazz instrument. This was an important achievement. Prior to Hawkins, the saxophone's versatility and the absence of role models from classical music were as much a curse as a blessing. For better or worse, the tenor sax lacked a correct sound, an accepted way of tone production. Whinnying noises, smears, slap-tonguing, barks, growls, novelty effects—the strangest assortment of sounds were all part of the shared vocabulary of the pre-Hawkins saxophone idiom. In the wake of the first generation of clarinet and C melody sax players, the reed tradition in jazz had favored a lighter sound, with a greater emphasis on ornamentation and patterns than on robust push-the-band improvisation. But by the time Hawkins had finished his redefinition of the instrument, a streamlined jazz tenor sax sound had been forged, one that remained dominant for the next forty years, and retains considerable influence to this day. For good reason he is often lauded as the father of tenor sax.

Even with Redman and Hawkins on board, the earliest recordings of Henderson's band are lackluster. The arrangements are simple, sticking close to the model set by

King Oliver (whose influence looms large on these sides) and the other New Orleans pioneers, while the improvised sections of the music are often repetitive and unimaginative, with only an occasional phrase or hot break to indicate the potential of the band's soloists. But in the months following Henderson's opening at the Club Alabam, a number of changes can be heard: the band adds more players; its sound gets denser and more complex; the performances become tighter and more focused. The group still has not abandoned its allegiance to formulas associated with New Orleans jazz, especially in terms of rhythmic conception and solo construction, but already the barest indications of a different paradigm—more arranged, more harmonically sophisticated—can be heard in incipient form. And even the lingering influence of the New Orleans style was not without its value in this new setting—a perspicacious listener can hear the later battling exchanges of sections in a jazz big band anticipated in the dueling counterpoint of individual horns in the traditional jazz of Oliver and other Crescent City pioneers.

More than any other event, Henderson's hiring of Louis Armstrong in 1924 served as a catalyst in accelerating the band's evolution. Comparisons of Armstrong's solo work with Hawkins's on performances from 1924 and 1925 such as "Money Blues," "Go 'Long Mule," "How Come You Do Me Like You Do?," or "Carolina Stomp" show how much the cornetist had to teach—and, equally, how much the saxophonist still had to learn. In this setting, Hawkins gradually softened the rough edges of his phrasing and smoothed out the rhythmic flow of his playing. By the time of his influential performance on "The Stampede" from the spring of 1926, Hawkins was showing the first glimmerings of the self-assurance and fluidity that would distinguish his mature work. Hawkins was only twenty-one years old at the time, but this recording already served to generate a great deal of interest among his contemporaries. And not only with reed players—trumpeter Roy Eldridge learned this solo note for note and played it at an early audition. However, the finishing touches on Hawkins's musical education would come three years later when the saxophonist heard Art Tatum during a Henderson road trip through Ohio. Inspired by this chance encounter, Hawkins further reconfigured his approach to the horn, incorporating harmonic concepts learned from the pianist.

Don Redman's growth during this period is, if anything, even more remarkable. Yet his was the type of progress marked by continual refinement and steady improvement, rather than overnight breakthroughs. Even before Redman, the more savvy dance bandleaders had drawn on jazz elements in crafting their arrangements. Art Hickman's San Francisco–based dance band, which came to New York in 1919, attracted attention for its use of saxophone section playing, while Paul Whiteman could count on Bill Challis, Matty Malneck, Tom Satterfield, and Ferde Grofé (who had earlier worked for Hickman) to provide forward-looking jazz-oriented charts. Meanwhile, other bandleaders, such as Vincent Lopez and Paul Specht, were tapping into the growing demand for a more polished, high-society type of jazz orchestra.[20] Yet the hotter, more potent style crafted slowly and painstakingly by Redman during these years would come to exert the most direct and decisive influence on the evolution of the jazz big band.

Redman's arrangement of "Dicty Blues" from the summer of 1923 already captures the essential quality of the new style: namely, the grouping of reed and brass instruments into separate sections, and their use as foils for each other. Over the next several years, Redman and Henderson would explore a wider and wider range of techniques that built on this simple principle. Interweaving, dueling, engaging in call-and-response forms, alternating between supporting and dominant roles, sometimes combining in thickly textured block chords—these varied possibilities of section writing are now taken for granted by jazz listeners, and in many instances have become overworked clichés. But in these early days of the Henderson band, they cut through the tired formulas of New Orleans and Chicago jazz, which had relied almost exclusively on contrasting monophonic voices, and presented a new building block for jazz: the section, rather than the instrumentalist. Locking together with the precision and discipline of military regiments on an advance, the combined sections could achieve musical results far beyond the scope of the earlier small combos.

The nature of the sections also evolved with the passage of time. Clarinet trios may have been used before in vaudeville shows and sweet bands, but they took on a new energy when pitted against brass trios in the Henderson band. Yet this innovation proved to be only a starting point. The use of saxophones, less shrill than the clarinets and better suited for articulating rich mid- and lower-range harmonies, gradually emerged as the dominant force in the reed section. Brass trios grew into whole brass sections that could subdivide into separate trumpet and trombone units, each able to work separately or in conjunction with the other. The rhythm instruments also began taking shape as a separate section. Piano, tuba (later replaced by the string bass), drums, banjo (later replaced by guitar)—their roles within the group became more specialized, more focused on linking together, providing rhythmic momentum for the band, and a sonic cushion for section work and solos.

Armstrong's greatest impact may have been on the rhythmic component of Redman's chart writing. A more supple sense of timing begins to appear in his arrangements during this period. They become hotter, more syncopated. Plodding, on-the-beat phrases are replaced by more vibrant excursions, reflecting in the written parts the same dynamism that distinguished Armstrong's ad-lib horn lines. The symphonic jazz aspirations of Whiteman, an early model for Redman, slowly give way to a different standard in which the hot solo provides the raw material for the arrangement. In an odd reversal of the classical tradition, written parts were now made to sound like improvisations, especially in their phrasing and fanciful use of melodic material; the only difference was that these solo-like lines were now fleshed out and given harmonic depth in the full-blown polyphony of the horn section. On this basis, a more fervent dialogue between the brass and reed sections takes root.

With "The Stampede," recorded shortly after Armstrong's departure from the band, this more insistent style of ensemble work is already noticeable. The textures behind the soloists are no longer passive harmonic cushions, but extroverted lines that propel the improvisation with incisive counterrhythms. "The Henderson Stomp," from November 1926, finds Redman experimenting with the structures of Harlem stride—the performance features Fats Waller on piano, who also apparently wrote the composition (although it was copyrighted by Henderson)—and tapping the inherently percussive and orchestral qualities of that idiom. By the time of "Tozo," recorded in January 1927, Redman's style is almost fully formed: the written parts, with their assured command of polyrhythms and instrumental textures, are as compelling as the solos. With "The Whiteman Stomp," from May 1927, Redman even delves into the avant-garde, crafting a highly eccentric orchestration in which fragments of musical shrapnel take flight unpredictably, coalescing into an odd type of jazz, one built on disjunction and entropy. That same year, half a world away, physicist Werner Heisenberg was articulating his famous uncertainty principle, the foundation for quantum physics. Here Redman shows his allegiance to the same zeitgeist, espousing a jagged, pointillistic style in which all continuities are called into question. This piece, commissioned by Paul Whiteman, cannot be called a success. But it is a masterful failure, sounding like the jazz of some alternative universe, while demonstrating the extraordinary command of his medium that Redman had developed over the previous four years.

This period also marks the close of Redman's formal ties with the Henderson band. In 1927, he became musical director of McKinney's Cotton Pickers, an association that continued for the next several years. Although his new group lacked the extraordinary cadre of soloists that had distinguished the Henderson ensemble, it featured two outstanding arrangers in Redman and John Nesbitt. Redman also figured prominently as a saxophone soloist and singer with the band. He left to form his own group in 1931, but during an era marked by a proliferation of big bands, this unit never succeeded in rising above the level of a second-tier ensemble—although it made numerous recordings and broadcasts and stayed together until 1941. Another group that drew heavily on the same personnel, the Chocolate Dandies, was never a working band, but left behind a handful of exciting recordings that marry Redman's arrangements with outstanding solo contributions from Coleman Hawkins, Benny Carter, Fats Waller, and others. These several settings allowed Redman to put together a body of work that firmly established him as a preeminent jazz orchestrator and innovator during the years preceding World War II. In the following two decades, Redman may not have remained at the cutting edge of the jazz world; nonetheless his charts continued to grace the bandstands of many important leaders, ranging from Count Basie to Pearl Bailey. His recorded output was negligible in his last years, but he continued to compose, and left behind a number of extended pieces at his death in 1964 that have yet to be performed in public.

Benny Carter, some seven years younger than Redman, followed a similar career path, one that included affiliations—sometimes overlapping with Redman's but more often following his departure—with Fletcher Henderson, McKinney's Cotton Pickers, and the Chocolate Dandies. And, like Redman, Carter eventually gravitated toward leading his own band. Talented, progressive, eager to learn and assimilate new techniques, Carter represented the best of the new generation of arrangers who were coming into their own at the close of the 1920s. Yet Carter's versatility as an instrumentalist has often served only to obscure his substantial contributions as an orchestrator and composer. This precocious young talent, born in New York on August 8, 1907, appeared to possess a telling knack for mastering each and every instrument in the band. Along with Johnny Hodges, Carter was a key figure in developing the alto saxophone as a major jazz voice, and his finest solos on that instrument are as accomplished and musical as any of the era. But Carter's expertise also extended to the brass section. Hear, for example, his trumpet work on "Once upon a Time" from 1933 or his assurance in trading fours on trumpet against Coleman Hawkins's tenor on "Pardon Me Pretty Baby" from 1937. Nor is that all. The previous year, on "You Understand," Carter fills in as pianist, while other recordings find him singing, playing the clarinet, tenor sax, trombone, or soprano sax. This dazzling array of onstage skills goes a long way toward explaining why Carter's behind-the-scenes efforts as an arranger often escaped the attention of all but the most knowledgeable jazz fans.

Bandleaders, however, took notice almost from the start. Joining Henderson at roughly the same time that Redman departed, the twenty-two-year-old Carter soon found that his writing skills were urgently needed by his new employer. Carter has described how, lacking formal training in orchestration, he learned on the job by analyzing and imitating stock arrangements. "You get down on your knees and study each part," he explained, "and then you start writing the lead trumpet first and the lead saxophone first—which, of course, is the hard way. It was quite some time that I did that before I knew what a score was."[21] Yet Carter had soon not only assimilated the primitive techniques used in 1920s stock arranging, but also began building on the jazz scoring techniques of Bill Challis, Don Redman, Archie Bleyer, and others. As early as his 1930 arrangement of "Keep a Song in Your Soul," Carter revealed a knack for scoring syncopated section work to rival Redman's, and his block chord writing for four saxophones in "Symphony in Riffs," "Lonesome Nights," and "Devil's Holiday" from 1933 foreshadowed a signature sound of the Swing Era.

Carter always retained an instinctive feel for the lyrical possibilities of jazz, in both his compositions and his playing. This sentimental Schubertian strain, more than anything else, stands as the defining element in Carter's musical personality, and goes a long way toward explaining the lasting appeal of his work. Carter has sometimes cited Bill Challis and Frank Trumbauer as key influences, yet one suspects that his early listening not only encompassed jazz-oriented work but extended to the sweet band music of the day. Certainly Carter's own writing displayed, almost from the start, a fascination with pretty sounds, soft nuances, and ruminative melodies. In a steady stream of works from the mid-1930s—"Dream Lullaby," "Nightfall," "Lonesome Nights," "Just a Mood," "Lazy Afternoon," "Once upon a Time"—Carter offered listeners a reflective style of jazz program music, one that contrasted strikingly with the heated swing sound that was on the brink of sweeping the nation. Only one of his compositions from this period, "When Lights Are Low," has become established as a widely played jazz standard, but his body of work from the mid-1930s onward is a rich compendium of ingenious melodies. And singable ones as well. Unlike Duke Ellington, the other great ballad composer of the period, Carter's melodic writing was almost always well suited for the human voice. Even an Ellington masterpiece such as "Sophisticated Lady" remains essentially an instrumental number, employing intervallic gymnastics in the bridge that would defy all but the most determined crooner. Carter's genius, in contrast, lay in crafting horn lines that implicitly retained their connectedness to the vocal art.

This singing quality to Carter's work is also the key to understanding his contributions as a soloist. A lazy elegance marks his finest work, whether on trumpet or saxophone. In his 1940 Chocolate Dandies session, he matches up with Coleman Hawkins and Roy Eldridge in a magisterial front line, but breaks the cardinal rule of improvising by starting with climactic energy then slowly bringing down the temperature until he is gliding softly over the chords in characteristic Carter fashion. Even earlier, on "Nightfall" (1936), Carter showed—on the tenor sax, in this instance—how to play Hawkins's own instrument in a cool, lithe manner; usually Lester Young is credited with this contribution to the evolution of the tenor, but "Nightfall" was recorded a half-year before Young's own debut session. This distilled approach became especially prominent in the postwar period, when Carter resisted the dominant Parker alto sound. On his 1961 recording of "The Midnight Sun Will Never Set," he displays a boplike fluidity, but retains a relaxed sense of phrasing and his deeply personal, sweet—at times almost overripe—tone. Equally noteworthy, however, is the rigorously logical development of Carter's improvisations. In the 1950s Sonny Rollins would be lauded for showing the virtues of "thematic improvisation," for using his saxophone to dissect, analyze, and develop melodic material, much as a classical composer might attempt in the context of sonata form. Yet Carter's work from two decades earlier evinces a comparable mastery of thematic development. Even as an improviser, he thought like a composer.

After disbanding his orchestra in 1946, Carter worked for a period with Norman Granz's various Jazz at the Philharmonic ensembles, and supplemented his income with miscellaneous projects and recordings, some jazz oriented but others showing his fluency in a range of commercial idioms. By the mid-1950s, Carter's performances had taken a back seat to his work as an arranger, primarily for many of the leading singers of the day, including Sarah Vaughan, Ella Fitzgerald, and Ray Charles. In his mid-sixties, at the brink of what might otherwise be his retirement years, Carter resurfaced as an instrumentalist. The last major figure of his generation to remain active in jazz, Carter increasingly garnered accolades, honorary degrees, commissions, and awards—somehow both fitting and ironic given the modest and soft-spoken demeanor with which he had always viewed his own work. Despite his self-effacing comments, Carter put to excellent use the opportunities that this second wind in his career provided, and he stayed active into the new millennium—at his death in 2003, obituaries boasted that this artist had made recordings during nine different decades.

Others have matched or surpassed Carter's longevity as a jazz performer, but few have written so many fine compositions so late in life. In 1987, Carter's extended work *Central City Sketches* was given its premiere in a concert by the American Jazz Orchestra at Cooper Union; later that same year, Carter's *Glasgow Suite* made its debut in Scotland; a 1990 commission by Lincoln Center resulted in "Good Vibes," a work for two vibraphones and orchestra; a grant from the National Endowment for the Arts assisted in the performance and recording of two new suites in 1992, *Tales of the Rising Sun Suite* and *Harlem Renaissance Suite*. Almost eighty-five years old at the time these last pieces made their debut, Carter showed himself still capable of maintaining the high-quality standards he had set in previous decades. The melodic warmth and robust musicality of his early work are, if anything, heightened in these late vintages, but a sensitive channeling of elements drawn from modern jazz can also be heard, albeit in a manner that is never derivative. Somehow Carter reconciles progressivism with the aesthetic dictates and proclivities of the pre-bop tradition. If Carter were of a polemical bent, these later works might have taken on the overtones of a counterrevolution in jazz—an African American pre-Raphaelitism—one built on structure, balance, economy of means, and an aversion to the querulous and self-questioning tone.

For Carter, the jazz idiom provided a set of tools that he could use in setting a mood. Some might chafe at such a description. These days we are inclined to dismiss mood music as a lesser art, as an emaciated form of creativity. Yet, as Carter's vast body of work attests, mood music is by no means equivalent to background music. As practiced by the best, the ability to establish an authentic emotional scenario, to create a sonic environment so compelling as to envelop the audience—this is not a simple or simpleminded task, but perhaps the most time-honored wellspring of art. The willing suspension of disbelief is what such submersion in the artistic vision was called in an earlier day.

Among his contemporaries, Carter was second only to Duke Ellington in this skill. But then again, no figure in jazz history could surpass Ellington in creating a completely satisfying and self-sufficient musical mood. And though it is increasingly fashionable to analyze Duke's work in the jargon of academic musicology, the magic of his artistry cannot be reduced merely to a series of breakthroughs in orchestration or harmony. True, the techniques Ellington employed were impressive. But it was always the ends he achieved, not the means, that distinguished the Ellington band from the rest. This commitment to the mood—an unfashionable artistic pursuit in our postmodern age—eludes our grasp. Yet it draws us again and again to Duke's recordings. And it is why, after listening to them, we inevitably reach for metaphors from other fields to describe Ellington's spell: the painter of musical landscapes, the poet of jazz, the alchemist of the swing band. And as the consummate creator of these settings, Ellington the man was equally elusive. So skilled at putting on the mask of the momentary mood, the man underneath often remained—almost by necessity—hidden from view.

DUKE ELLINGTON'S EARLY CAREER

One of the quaint, if puzzling, eccentricities of jazz lay in its apparent obsession with titles of nobility and statesmanship. Bolden, Keppard, Oliver—all at one time were nicknamed "King," while later leading or lesser lights came to be known, both by their fans and peers, as Duke, Count, Lady, Sir, Prince, and Baron. Before long a panglobal sensibility replaced these Eurocentric trappings, ushering in an era in which anything from President to Pharoah could serve as a suitable jazz alias.

Of all these figures, none lived up to the image of nobility better than Duke Ellington. Elegant, reserved without being stiff, articulate even in his evasions, well mannered to the point of ostentation, elitist despite his populist tendencies, always ready with a compliment, a high-flown phrase, or a measured response to deflect the most pointed inquiry—Edward Kennedy Ellington would have been a striking man even if he had never played a note of music. Yet these selfsame qualities, ones that make Ellington an admirable role model, pose problems for historians and biographers. This middle-class youth who made himself into a duke was equally a master at recrafting his biography to match the dimensions of his aspirations and keeping a close guard over his inner life. Probe as deeply as we can, he remains the "Duke," the private man subsumed by the public persona.

"Once upon a time a beautiful young lady and a very handsome young man fell in love and got married. They were a wonderful, compatible couple, and God blessed their marriage with a fine baby boy." Thus begins Ellington's own account of his life and times, as presented in his autobiography, *Music Is My Mistress*.[22] No doubt Ellington viewed his own life in storybook terms. But the elegance of his childhood was more a matter of the family's self-image than a result of affluence or social position. His father, James Edward Ellington, had been working as a waiter when, two years before his son's birth, he took on a position as a servant in the home of a Washington, DC, doctor. For two decades, throughout his son's formative years, the elder Ellington stayed with this employer, moving up the ranks from coachman to butler. By all accounts, the father's sense of fashion, bearing, and grandiloquent manner of self-expression were the model for his son's later assumption of the high style. Ellington's mother, Daisy Kennedy Ellington, came from a more successful family: her father was a police captain; pretty, cultivated, proper—she represented the establishment ideals to which her husband aspired. Family finances may have been modest, but once again the image was what mattered most. Duke recalled that his father always "acted as though he had money, whether he had it or not."[23] In this unusual household—servants' quarters with the decorum of a feudal manor—a son, Edward Kennedy Ellington, was born on April 29, 1899.

An earlier Ellington child apparently died in infancy, and the mother now focused her undivided attention on Edward, as did much of the extended family. "I was pampered and pampered, and spoiled rotten by all the women in the family," Ellington later remarked. But the coddling of the doting mother was tempered by her focus on providing a moral education and her determined view that her son was destined for special achievements—a view that he too came to adopt. "Do I believe that I am blessed?" he asked rhetorically in his autobiography. "Of course, I do! In the first place, my mother told me so, many, many times, and when she did it was always quietly, confidently."[24] Inculcated almost from the cradle, this sense of self-importance would become a defining element in Ellington's character. Even in his youth, he amazed and irritated his cousins, announcing to them: "I am the grand, noble Duke."[25]

Two pianos graced the Ellington residence, and both parents showed some skill at playing them. Before their son reached his tenth birthday he had received lessons from a local music teacher, aptly named Mrs. Clinkscales. From all indications, this early introduction to the piano made little impression on Ellington, and by his adolescence an interest in the visual arts had taken hold of him. He attended a vocational high school and contemplated a career as a commercial artist. Had he been a more dedicated student, Ellington might never have considered music as anything more than a hobby. Instead, his interest in school waned, and he left before earning his diploma. Despite his limitations as a pianist—by his own admission, he only knew three or four songs at the time—opportunities to perform, first among friends but soon for pay, were starting to come his way.

Although his parents' idea of acceptable music stopped far short of ragtime and blues, the young Ellington had already grown familiar with these new styles. A Washington, DC, poolroom that he frequented was a gathering spot for the local rag pianists, and before long Ellington was learning various tricks of the keyboard trade from the best of them and substituting for the regulars at engagements. Around this same time, a high school music teacher, Henry Grant, invited Ellington to come by his house for private lessons in harmony. Duke's musical education was also furthered by surreptitious visits to burlesque shows, where he learned not only popular music styles but also, one suspects, elements of showmanship.

Ellington's musical education was proceeding on many fronts, but the Harlem stride style of pianism made the deepest impression on the youngster's imagination. He studied the piano rolls of James P. Johnson and learned the stride master's "Carolina Shout" note for note. When Johnson came to Washington, DC, Ellington performed it for him, and earned the older pianist's encouragement. Rote learning, however, played only a limited role in the youngster's musical education. Almost from the start, Ellington preferred writing his own compositions, and his zest for learning about music was never greater than when he could apply the pedagogical models at hand to his own efforts. Ellington's later evolution as a jazz composer followed this same pattern: he preferred to learn by doing rather than by analyzing scores, attending classes, or reading textbooks on composition and harmony. Formal study, to the degree he pursued it, was undertaken to meet his practical needs as a composer, not as a means of assimilating abstract theory. And like all great autodidacts, Ellington may have learned more slowly than he might have with an organized regimen, but he eventually learned with a far deeper grasp of the practicalities of his craft than any textbook could have provided.

Until his late teens, Ellington continued to view music as a sideline. But in 1918 he married Edna Thompson, whom he had known since childhood, and the following year their son Mercer was born. Now the responsibilities of supporting a family forced Ellington to think seriously about the career paths open to him. The goal of working as a commercial artist persisted for a period: Ellington even began a sign-painting business that allowed him to design dance posters and advertising materials. Around this same time he earned an NAACP scholarship to study art at the Pratt Institute in New York. Yet Ellington's activities in music continued to blossom, and not just as a player. He began booking other bands, sometimes sending out several in a night, in addition to taking on his own gigs. By 1923, Ellington had established himself as a leading light of the Washington, DC, dance band scene, and had embarked on musical associations—with drummer Sonny Greer and saxophonist Otto Hardwick, among others—that would play an important role in his future. A less ambitious man might have remained content with this comfortable state of affairs. But Ellington, conscious of being marked for greater accomplishments, set his sights on making his name in New York. Together with Hardwick and Greer, he took a sideman's job with a New York band, aiming to use it as a springboard to bigger things.

Rather than taking Manhattan by storm, Ellington and his friends scuffled for work in their new setting, and before long retreated to Washington. Chastened but not deterred, Ellington returned to sign painting and performing, but within months was drawn again to New York. Now he worked assiduously to advance his career on several fronts: he began auditioning songs for music publishers, expanding his network of New York contacts, and performing with a contingent of fellow musicians from DC who had also made the move to Manhattan. A chance encounter with singer Ada Smith, who would later enliven Paris nightlife under the name Bricktop, led to an engagement backing her at a Harlem nightclub. Within a short while, Ellington's band (working under the name the Washingtonians) had moved to a downtown gig at the Hollywood Club near Times Square. The band would work at this location, which was renamed the Club Kentucky in 1924 (although typically referred to by Ellington and others as the Kentucky Club) for the next four years. At some point during this period, Ellington took over as nominal leader of the band.

Leadership is a relative concept in the often free-form world of jazz, and Ellington's sidemen showed, more than most, a resistance to overt forms of control from above. Even so, Ellington soon began to demonstrate the genius for organizing and supervising that would come to distinguish his band from its peers. How much influence Ellington had on the choice of James "Bubber" Miley to replace the departing trumpeter Arthur Whetsel is unclear.[26] Yet the move has all the marks of Ellington's uncanny knack for finding the right individual to advance his own musical vision. Many other bandleaders would have passed on Miley. His technical facility was, at best, average; his gift for melodic improvisation, as evidenced by his knack for milking one or two notes for all they were worth, would have struck many as limited; his range was far from impressive. Yet Miley's instinct for tonal color, for shaping a melody, for bringing a horn line to life was unsurpassed. As a stand-alone soloist he might have been several notches below an Armstrong or a Beiderbecke, but as the melodic voice for Ellington's compositions, he would set the standard. And in one respect, Miley was superior to these more acclaimed players: in his mastery of the plunger and straight mute he was without peer. This South Carolina native, raised in New York, looked to the New Orleans stylist King Oliver for inspiration. Long after most of his contemporaries had adopted the more modern approaches of Armstrong and Beiderbecke, Miley maintained his allegiance to this early master of the muted cornet.

Ellington's next major personnel move confirmed the new, unusual direction he envisioned for the band. When trombonist Charlie Irvis departed in 1926, Ellington brought in Tricky Sam Nanton. As with Miley, the choice of Nanton would have been far from obvious to most bandleaders. His facility with the slide was limited, and his range was constrained. Yet, again like Miley, Nanton was a master of the dirty tone and could make his horn talk in a language that was almost human. Already the pattern of Ellington's future direction could be seen in embryonic form. At this point in his career, Ellington could not afford to hire star soloists—although he tried, for a while, to keep Sidney Bechet in the band—so he compensated by employing the most distinctive stylists he could find. The end result was a band that may have offered little in the way of virtuosity, as measured in cold metronomic terms, but boasted an excess of character. Ellington's own piano style fit in well with this approach. It may have lacked the polished execution of a Waller, the dazzling speed of a Tatum, the soft swing of a Basie, or the riveting electricity of a Hines; but for sheer variety and exoticism, in its surprising twists and turns, the Duke's pianism was nonpareil. This preference for the unusual would remain a calling card of Ellington's music over the next several decades.

Almost from the start, listeners were drawn by the novelty of these new sounds. The earliest known review of the band, dating from 1923, praises Miley's ability to exact "the eeriest sort of modulations and 'singing' notes heard." Another reviewer cited Miley as "responsible for all that slow, weird music."[27] However, the initial recordings of the band only hint at the originality of Ellington's conception. As early as the spring of 1926, Ellington's ambitions could be seen in his choice to augment his small working band with additional players for record sessions; but the music still primarily reflects influences from other quarters—from Oliver, from Henderson, from the New York sweet bands. But with the November 1926 recording of "East Saint Louis Toodle-oo," a more vibrant and original conception jumps to the fore. A foreboding progression of block chords, voiced for saxophones and tuba, sets up the opening theme, which is played by Miley with magnificent guttural intensity. The emotional level diminishes with the entrance of the second theme, a lighthearted bit of derivative syncopation, but the overall impact of the piece is powerful. True, various conventional devices of the day can still be detected—the shift from an ominous minor melody to a rag-inflected major theme was a stock-in-trade of the stride school; the solos, outside of Miley's, are merely workmanlike—but the sense of a new stylistic direction for the Ellington band can be clearly heard.

"Black and Tan Fantasy," from April of the following year—the first of three Ellington versions of this composition recorded in 1927—represents a second stage in the evolution of this new sound. Once again Miley's trenchant mute work over a minor theme is used to fullest effect, but the contrasting melody in major is a strong lyrical statement, several notches above the tepidly swinging second section of "East Saint Louis Toodle-oo." The atmosphere of this composition is, if anything, darker still than the earlier piece—so much so that the band closes with a fitting allusion to Chopin's "Funeral March." Miley's solo work is superlative, and it is not going too far to suggest that his various performances of this composition represent classic statements in the history of jazz trumpet playing, worthy to stand alongside the more celebrated contributions of Armstrong and Beiderbecke. His mastery of tone remains the defining quality of his artistic vision, and gives a human quality to his music, beyond the scope of written scores to convey; yet this virtue tends to draw attention away from his ingenuity in melodic improvisation. Even when notated, when engraved in the dull medium of black notes on a page, his solos here retain a penetrating vitality despite the absence of the evocative growls and moans of his recorded delivery. His role in most histories of jazz—in essence, playing attendant lord to Ellington's Hamlet—does not do full justice to his achievements.

In "Creole Love Call" from the following year, Ellington displays a more ruminative side of his musical personality, crafting one of the first substantial statements in a long series of meditative tone poems from the prewar years—others include "Mood

Indigo," "Solitude," and "Prelude to a Kiss"—many of which would become permanent staples in the band's repertoire. But even in the subdued atmosphere of "Creole Love Call," Ellington's fascination with exotic sounds takes precedence. Singer Adelaide Hall joins the band and contributes a plaintive wordless vocal that, at moments, takes on a rough edge comparable to (and likely inspired by) Miley's mute work. The scoring, although understated, adds to the melancholy flavor of the piece, and is especially noteworthy for Ellington's varied use of call-and-response exchanges.

The question of Ellington's originality has often been raised with reference to these (and other) works. Certainly, there can be little doubt, given the various accounts that have come down to us, about Duke's willingness to borrow whatever musical materials suited his needs. Even though Ellington's name graces the credits of these early compositions, Miley's contribution may have, at times, matched or even surpassed Duke's own. And appropriations from other sidemen would prove to be an ongoing formula for Ellington throughout his career. Nor were band members his only source of inspiration. "Creole Love Call" is just one instance of his delving into riffs and themes that were already part of the jazz heritage (in this case drawing from an earlier piece credited to King Oliver); even tiny musical flourishes were likely to have antecedents—the reference to Chopin in "Black and Tan Fantasy" mimics Jelly Roll Morton's similar use of the funeral march theme in "Dead Man Blues" just a few months earlier—while Ellington's frequent adoption of the techniques of the Harlem stride players has already been noted. Yet, through it all, Ellington's genius lay in adapting the materials of others to his own ends, in weaving the strands and threads of music that he gathered into what can only be described as the "Ellington sound." And though Miley's contributions may have been great—he remains, perhaps due to his early death before the age of thirty, one of the most taken-for-granted figures of early jazz—Ellington's ability to survive the trumpeter's departure and take the band to an even higher level in the following years remains a telling achievement. It gives needed emphasis to the point that it was Ellington's skill in pulling together the historical sources and passing inspirations into memorable compositions, more than any given raw materials he employed along the way, that distinguished his unique musical aptitude.

The end result was a body of music that not only reflected the character of his players but was perfectly suited to their strengths and weaknesses. "Duke studied his men," Barney Bigard has explained. "He studied their style, how they maneuver with their music, with their playing and everything. And he keeps that in his mind so if he wrote anything for you, it fit you like a glove." "If he'd see where a guy had got some type of talent," added Cootie Williams, "he'd go along with him."[28] "Yes, I am the world's greatest listener," Ellington himself wrote in his 1973 autobiography. "Here I am, fifty years later, still getting cats out of bed to come to work so that I can listen to them." And listen Ellington did, consummately, deeply, and out of the listening extract from each player the essence of his musical personality, out of each section its unique character, out of the whole band, a sound like no other. Competing ensembles may have sometimes had more raw talent on an individual level, but somehow Ellington was able to create, in aggregate, an ensemble that was second to none. Even at this early stage of his musical development, Ellington's work revealed a coherent unity of vision, an overarching design that stood out from the pack. Ellington's attentiveness to this vision appears to have extended even to the technical aspects of recordings: the sonic balance and authenticity are carefully gauged—much more so than one finds with Henderson or the other bands of the day—to create a satisfying, holistic musical experience. One suspects that this was more than happenstance, but another sign of Ellington's working behind the scenes.

In the spring of 1927, Ellington was poised to take the next major step in his career. He had gained a dedicated following at the Club Kentucky, had embarked upon a fertile period of composition and record-making—during the late 1920s, Ellington would take his band into the studio almost every month—and had gone a long way toward forging a style of its own. Around this same time, Irving Mills, whom Ellington had met during his earliest days in New York, began taking a more active role in managing Duke's business affairs. Although the extent of Mills's contributions can be debated (especially with regard to his supposed musical collaborations with Ellington), his instincts for promoting the band would prove to be first rate. The final piece in the puzzle fit into place when, later that year, the Ellington band was selected to fill an opening at the Cotton Club in Harlem. Looking back at this signal event, Ellington liked to point to his luck in winning the spot—according to his account, the club's manager showed up too late to hear the other six bands that had auditioned and selected Duke's by default. But luck would have little to do with the successes he would soon achieve in this new setting. Through the hard work and ceaseless ambition of these apprenticeship years, Duke Ellington had prepared himself for just such a springboard to celebrity and was now determined to make the most of it.

THE COTTON CLUB

The burst of creative energy brought about by the Harlem Renaissance did not long remain a secret to white audiences. The written word was the first to travel below the demarcating line, drawn at 110th Street, which separated black Harlem from white New York. Alain Locke's pathbreaking *The New Negro* spread news of the movement on its appearance in 1925, but even earlier works such as James Weldon Johnson's *The Book of American Negro Poetry* (1922) had already signaled the emergence of a new literary culture. In neo-minstrel fashion, white writers were attracted by the primitivist ethos they perceived in these works and, donning a linguistic equivalent of blackface, concocted a host of derivative efforts. Notable examples of "black" fiction by white writers include Waldo Frank's *Holiday* (1923), Sherwood Anderson's *Dark Laughter* (1924), and Carl Van Vechten's *Nigger Heaven* (1926).

In the world of Harlem nightlife, the consumption of black entertainment by an affluent white clientele came to be known as *slumming*. In earlier years, the white audience had waited until black music came to it. A series of shows—*In Dahomey* (1902), *In Abyssinia* (1906), and *Bandana Land* (1907), among others—had titillated New York whites with glimpses of black entertainment that, for all their stereotypes, were far more authentic than the diluted minstrel efforts of earlier years. The turning point, however, was the highly successful revue *Shuffle Along*, which opened at the Sixty-third Street Music Hall in 1921. *Shuffle Along* drew large audiences with its talent-laden collection of black artists, both on stage and behind the scenes (including Paul Robeson, Florence Mills, William Grant Still, Adelaide Hall, Noble Sissle, and Eubie Blake), and represented a major advance for African Americans in the New York entertainment industry.

But white America was not content to remain passive spectators at black artistry. Especially when they took to the dance floor, they were increasingly drawing on the steps and movements created by African Americans. We have already witnessed the symbiotic relationship between the cutting-edge popular dance styles of Vernon and Irene Castle and the music of James Reese Europe, as well as the assimilation of the cakewalk and turkey trot into the ballrooms of mainstream America. The linkages between black dance, jazz music, and the broader culture were furthered in the 1920s with the popularity of the Charleston, the shimmy, and the Black Bottom. Harlem participated in this process, and in many ways drove it, serving in the late 1920s and 1930s as the epicenter of fervent dance activity that would set the model for the next stage in this evolutionary process.

Opened in 1926, the Savoy Ballroom represented the new ethos at its highest pitch. It boasted a spacious dance floor of 250 by 50 feet, fronted by two bandstands, with a special section—the so-called "Cat's Corner"—where the best dancers could display their moves. As the famous song title asserted, the patrons were truly "stompin' at the Savoy"—so much so that management needed to replace the burnished maple dance floor every three years. From the start, the Savoy was fully integrated. And not only did white dancers make their way to this Harlem nightspot, but the dances of the Savoy also came downtown, and from there eventually spread across the nation. When choreographer Frederick Ashton required dancers for *Four Saints in Three Acts*, the modernist opera by Virgil Thomson and Gertrude Stein, he quickly moved to scout the talent on the Savoy floor. But popular dance styles were even more impacted by these Harlem proceedings. The Lindy hop (named after aviator Charles Lindbergh's famous 1927 solo "hop" across the Atlantic) gained widespread notoriety only after Herbert White, the head bouncer at the Savoy, organized some ballroom regulars into a group known as Whitey's Lindy Hoppers. As the dance gained popularity with young white Americans, it became widely known as the jitterbug, although it underwent a subtle transformation in the process, with the horizontal movements of the Lindy hop taking on a more vertical, jumping motion. With the rise of swing in the late 1930s, and its acceptance by young Americans of all colors, the central role of dance in the music continued unabated. Swing music was inseparable from swing dancing, and the competitions on the floor, judged by a jury of one's peers selected from among the patrons, was as much a main event as the proceedings on the bandstand. Even when Benny Goodman played at Carnegie Hall, the newspapers reported that teenagers were literally "dancing in the aisles."

The financial ramifications of these developments in theater and dance were not lost on promoters and impresarios. The procurement of black entertainment for white audiences soon became, inevitably and fortuitously, a mini-industry, a burgeoning microcosm of New York nightlife as a whole. Their appetites whetted by these dances and shows, white audiences began seeking even greater verisimilitude in their samplings of African American culture. But even when journeying into Harlem to witness them firsthand, these spectators nonetheless demanded venues that protected their position as ruling-class elites. In this context, the grotesque spectacle of the Harlem club for all-white audiences was born, a musical menagerie in which social proximity and distance could coexist.

At the height of the Jazz Age, Harlem featured eleven nightclubs that catered to high-class whites, as well as "five hundred colored cabarets of lower ranks," according to *Variety*.[29] It is easy to condemn the leading Harlem establishments for the patronizing attitudes on which they were built. Nonetheless, they served to mitigate, however clumsily, the currents of racism that were running rampant in other social institutions. In America, music was the first sphere of social interaction in which racial barriers were challenged and overturned. And the challenge went both ways: by the mid-1920s, white bands were playing for all-black audiences at Lincoln Theater and elsewhere. These intermediate steps between segregation and integration represented, for all their problems, progress of sorts. Yet from a purely musical perspective, the contributions of the Harlem clubs were almost wholly laudable. Channeling the financial means of white society into black artistry, they created a staging point for a cultural fermentation that would transform American music for good. Connie's Inn, on the corner of 131st Street and Seventh Avenue, may have been a tawdry bootlegger's showplace, but it was also the birthplace of Fats Waller's *Hot Chocolates* show that brought Louis Armstrong, and a number of memorable songs, to the attention of a wider public. Other nightspots—Ed Small's Paradise, Broadway Jones's Supper Club, Barron's Exclusive Club—for all the faux pearl glamor and underworld connections, also served as spawning grounds for an African American artistic revolution that would prove to be, with the passing of time, every bit as important as the more highbrow literary and dramatic achievements of the Harlem Renaissance.

Among all these venues, the most important—the Carnegie Hall for those who could not perform at Carnegie Hall—was the Cotton Club. But the ambiance here was far removed from concert hall propriety: where the more adventurous New Yorkers went for nightlife in those Prohibition years, they expected alcohol; and where alcohol flowed, organized crime usually ran the tap. Opened in 1923 by Owney Madden and his gang—Owney had recently been released from Sing Sing after serving eight years for murder—the Cotton Club served as the most glamorous distribution outlet for Madden's bootleg beer business. The confluence of mobsters, money, and music may have created opportunities for Ellington, but with it came added pressures. In addition to playing its standard repertoire, the group now took on responsibility for backing up the other Cotton Club acts—a daunting change for a band that had, for all its merits, grown comfortable performing charts written to accentuate the instrumentalists' strengths and avoid their weaknesses. But the demands of the new setting were as much psychological as musical. "When I went to the Cotton Club," Sonny Greer recalls, "they put pressure on. They put pressure on us, and no denying at that time, when the Syndicate say they want something, they got it or you wasn't in the business."[30] Yet Ellington was well suited to thrive in this new environment. His sense of showmanship, his own perfectionist tendencies, his ambitions—these were now given a suitably grand setting for their expression. By the close of his Cotton Club years, Ellington would have parlayed this opportunity into a position of preeminence, establishing his group as the most critically acclaimed African American band of its day.

Although Ellington had previously expanded his group for recordings, the Club Kentucky engagement had supported only a sextet. Now required to front a much larger band, Ellington again displayed his unerring knack for finding the right individual ingredients for the complex new sounds he was in the process of concocting. In this defining moment, when he was on the cusp of stardom, Ellington brought in a core group of players who would stay with him for years—in some instances, for decades—and help him create more than a passing style, but in essence serve as building blocks for their employer's lifelong vocation as a composer and bandleader.

Until this point, Ellington's brass players had taken the lead in the giving the band an original personality, but now Duke's new additions to the reed section would change the group in a similarly decisive manner. Saxophonist Harry Carney had played with Duke on a New England tour before the Cotton Club engagement, but now began a full-time association that would last almost a half century. His rich baritone lines would anchor the Ellington sax section and contribute greatly to the group's overall sound. At times Ellington would assign the higher intervals of a chord to Carney's baritone, a striking effect that brought an ethereal quality to the section work. In other contexts, Carney served as an important solo voice, adding a languorous, weighty character to many of Duke's mood pieces. Carney had grown up in Boston, where he had lived down the street from Johnny Hodges, another saxophonist who joined Ellington around the time of the Cotton Club engagement. Hodges, whose career with Ellington spanned over forty years, may have lacked the versatility of a Benny Carter, the vigor of a Coleman Hawkins, or the fluency of a Frank Trumbauer, yet no other player of his generation forged such a deeply personal approach to the saxophone. Like Miley and Nanton, Hodges produced a tone so rich that even a single note could resonate with a universe of emotion. Nicknamed the Rabbit—one explanation linked it to his preference for lettuce and tomato sandwiches, another to his fast footwork—Hodges was more like the tortoise in his approach to the saxophone: breathy phrases often tarried far behind the beat and at times took on a delicious, liquid quality, especially when Hodges delivered one of his calling cards, a lazy glissando sliding from the low to high register of the horn. It remains to this day one of the most singular sounds in the history of jazz. Hodges was especially effective on slow numbers—indeed, no other soloist in the band played a more important role in defining the character of Ellington's ballads—but also ranked among the finer, although rarely acknowledged, masters of the blues. Clarinetist Barney Bigard, another newcomer to the Ellington band during this time, would boast only a fifteen-year tenure with the band—making him a transient compared to the other lifers in the group, although this would be a lengthy stint by the measure of any other jazz band. Playing the Albert system clarinet favored by so many other New Orleans pioneers (among them his own teacher Lorenzo Tio Jr.), Bigard extracted a rich woody tone from his instrument. In an apt comparison, Ellington suggested that the delicacy of Bigard's melodic lines was akin to the beautiful filigree work in wrought iron so characteristic of the clarinetist's hometown. Bigard's playing never lost its strong ties to the traditional New Orleans style, and though that idiom was somewhat at odds with the direction the band was now taking, Ellington delighted in Bigard's clarinet as one more highly personal sound in an orchestra of distinctive voices.

Performing six nights a week at the Cotton Club, participating in radio broadcasts, and recording prolifically, Ellington now needed to increase his own productivity. These new settings also demanded greater versatility, given the wide range of acts the band was now supporting with its music. Despite these pressures, Ellington flourished in the face of recurrent deadlines, expanding considerably his range of compositional devices and refining his skills in orchestration. "Black Beauty," a piece Ellington recorded several times during this period, indicates the scope of these changes: it opens with an introductory sequence of rich chords, which linger ambiguously over an uncertain harmonic center before finally settling into a wistful melody in the key of B flat, while the jazzier second theme emerges after an uncharacteristic modulation into A flat. This adventurous approach to tonality, unusual in jazz or popular music at the time, would become an Ellington trademark. Especially noteworthy was Ellington's willingness to use dissonance and polytonality (at times crossing the border into atonality). These remarkable passages would sometimes appear only in an introduction, as in "Black Beauty" or, even more magnificently, in opening the second movement of *Black, Brown and Beige* from 1943; occasionally, they linger longer, as in Ellington's inspired vignette "The Clothed Woman" from 1947. But, most often, these surprising interjections would surface for one or two bars in the middle of a piece, before subsiding into the fold of a more conventional harmonic sequence. Majestically, imperiously, Ellington made progressive composition and popular music share the same stage. Duke's approach to the piano amplified this anomalous vision of the future of jazz. On top of a fairly traditional stride style he would add flourishes and asides of the most amazing sort, bursts of dissonant chords, whole-tone scales, unexpected percussive attacks, or querulous arpeggios. Ellington's solo piano versions of "Black Beauty" and "Swampy River" from October 1, 1928, already reveal the foundations of this distinctive school of pianism, one that echoed the stride of Willie "The Lion" Smith and anticipated the astringency of Thelonious Monk and Cecil Taylor.

But Ellington's piano skills were featured all too rarely during these years, with his band now serving more and more as a voice for his musical ambitions. It is especially illuminating to compare Ellington's big band charts from the late 1920s with Don Redman's efforts for Henderson and other bands. Redman's writing is packed full with musical activity—call-and-responses, breaks, dense section work, repeated rhythmic figures, and other devices. Ellington's arrangements are much sparser, more focused, less frenetic. This clarity and balance stood out whether Ellington was writing mood pieces ("Black Beauty," "Misty Morning"), his so-called jungle pieces ("The Mooche"), or even standard blues ("Beggar Blues," "The Blues with a Feeling");

while, with a few exceptions, even the showy up-tempo numbers maintain a cohesive musical identity. An atomistic, stream-of-consciousness compilation of devices, along the lines of what Redman attempted in his "Whiteman Stomp" had no place in Duke's holistic music.

The maturing of Ellington's compositional skills and the influx of new soloists served to buffer the impact of Bubber Miley's departure from the group in 1929. Ellington, who usually preferred to avert his gaze from his band members' various indiscretions, apparently fired Miley after the trumpeter consistently showed up disheveled and intoxicated or missed entire performances. "Every time some big shot come up to listen to the band, there wasn't no Bubber Miley," explained Cootie Williams. "And he had the whole band built around Bubber Miley.... That's the only man [Ellington] ever fired in his life."[31] Williams stepped in as Miley's replacement, and though he had never heard Miley play in person and was given little direction by Duke, he soon developed a growl style of his own. "One night I had the plunger, and I said 'wah, wah.' And I woke everybody up. And they said, 'That's it. That's it. Keep on.'" Williams, like so many others, maintained a career-long partnership with Ellington: this initial stint would continue until 1940, while a second association with the orchestra would last from 1962 until after the bandleader's death in 1974.

Duke's brass section was further reinforced during this period by the addition of trombonists Juan Tizol in 1929 and Lawrence Brown in 1932—initiating an association with Ellington that, for both, would last many years. Tizol was seldom featured in solos with the band, but he contributed "Caravan" and "Perdido," two pieces that would become widely played jazz standards, as well as lesser known gems such as "Moonlight Fiesta" and "Pyramid." Brown's buttery trombone tone—at times reminiscent of the sound of a cello—was highlighted on a number of Ellington pieces, including "The Sheik of Araby," "Ducky Wucky," "Slippery Horn," and "Stompy Jones." But, over and above their musical contributions, these two players also provided a much-needed anchor of stability in a group prone to peccadilloes: Brown was a minister's son who avoided alcohol, smoking, and gambling; Tizol, whose vices were restricted to an occasional drink and a penchant for practical jokes, set a new standard for punctuality in the band. Known to arrive a half-hour or an hour before engagements, Tizol was subjected to his colleagues' ribbing about his conscientiousness—but when Ellington could not attend a rehearsal, he often entrusted the band to Tizol's demanding supervision.

Duke's ascendancy during the Cotton Club years enabled him not only to weather the onset of the Great Depression, but even to flourish at a time when most bandleaders needed to retrench. Ellington's group was one of the most widely recorded jazz ensembles of the period, while regular radio broadcasts further expanded his audience. In 1930, Ellington made the jump to the silver screen, participating in his first Hollywood movie, *Check and Double Check*, and appeared with Maurice Chevalier at New York's Fulton Theater. In 1931, Ellington was invited to meet President Hoover at the White House, a rare honor for a black jazz musician. After leaving the Cotton Club, that same year, Ellington embarked on a series of highly profitable tours. Traveling in their own Pullman car, bringing their own lighting equipment, sporting different uniforms for each show—even if there were

four or five shows in a day: the Ellington band conveyed an aura of slick professionalism that few, if any, African American groups of that era could match. And the
critical accolades also started coming Duke's way. In 1932, R. D. Darrell, a
conservatory-trained musician who served as critic for a number of influential
periodicals, wrote a prescient and detailed study of Ellington's music, rhapsodizing
over the bandleader's "noble, spontaneous, unforced melodies . . . which spring into
being as simply, as naturally as those of Mozart or Schubert."[32] In November 1932,
Percy Grainger, the distinguished composer and chairman of the music department
at New York University, invited Ellington and his orchestra to play for a classroom of
students and distinguished guests. Grainger took the occasion to compare Ellington's
work to that of Bach and Delius.

This high-flung praise from the bastions of classical music did little to quell
Ellington's desire for greater popular success. In the past, he had avoided hiring a
full-time singer for the band, but now brought in Ivie Anderson as a featured vocalist.
It was not lost on Ellington that the public's musical tastes were, more and more,
gravitating toward singers. Indeed, Duke's replacement at the Cotton Club, Cab
Calloway, would never inspire comparisons to Bach or Schubert, but his scat-jive
vocals, epitomized in the "hi-de-ho" call-and-response effects on his hit "Minnie the
Moocher," delighted audiences. Calloway had led the Alabamians in Chicago and,
later, the Missourians in New York, and in 1929 had appeared in the revue *Hot
Chocolates*, before securing the coveted Cotton Club job. Incorporating a heavy dose
of novelty songs and scat vehicles into a more conventional hot jazz sound, Calloway
achieved a celebrity—and record sales—to rival Ellington's at the time. The addition
of Anderson gave a new dimension to Duke's band, and though she may have lacked
the eccentric individualism of a Calloway (or many of the other Ellington sidemen,
for that matter), she was one of the most versatile jazz singers of her era, equally
capable of heartfelt ballads, growling scat singing, or wistful blues.

The presence of a vocalist was just one of several factors that served to crystallize
Ellington's growing interest in popular songs. Irving Mills, in his careful management
of Duke's affairs, was especially sensitive to the commercial potential of the bandleader's skills as a tunesmith. In truth, Mills's role went far beyond the usual promotional activities and apparently extended to creative matters. Although he is listed as
Ellington's collaborator on many pieces, the exact scope of Mills's contribution to
Duke's songwriting is a matter of dispute. However, it is likely that he made sugges-
tions on the types of tunes that might be popular, encouraged Ellington to simplify
the often dense textures of his compositions, and arranged to have lyrics written. For
his own part, Ellington did not shy away from the opportunities presented by the
growing market for popular music. Ellington's compositional output was still meager
compared to the burst of creativity he would experience in the late 1930s—he copyrighted more songs in 1938 and 1939 than in the rest of the decade combined—even
so, these early years of the Depression would see the debut of many of his most
memorable and lasting songs including "Mood Indigo," "It Don't Mean a Thing
(If It Ain't Got That Swing)," "Sophisticated Lady," "Solitude," and "In a Sentimental
Mood." And though he would never challenge a Gershwin or Berlin as a hit maker—
Ellington's melodies were too complex, too rooted in the vertical conception of a

jazz pianist, for that to happen—his body of work as Tin Pan Alley songsmith would be impressive even if he had never led a band or performed as a pianist.

Throughout the decade, these forays into popular music coexisted with Duke's more ambitious attempts to raise jazz to the level of art music. As early as his 1931 work "Creole Rhapsody," Ellington was fighting against the constraints of 78 rpm recordings, tackling a longer form that required the label to use both sides of the disc to contain this single performance. Two versions of the piece were recorded that year, one issued on the Brunswick label that lasted six minutes, while the extended arrangement for Victor took over eight minutes (requiring it to be issued on a twelve-inch record). Although this piece is not wholly satisfying—the melodic material is fairly simpleminded—the structural complexity and effective shifts in mood, especially on the Victor version, clearly revealed Ellington's aspirations to extend the range of jazz music far beyond the conventions of the day. This path-breaking attempt at extended composition would soon be surpassed by Ellington's "Symphony in Black" (1934), not a true symphony but rather a nine-minute suite in four parts that incorporated music from several earlier Ellington pieces, and by his thirteen-minute "Reminiscing in Tempo" (1935), which, in its compositional intricacy and strong melodic and harmonic material, proved to be the most fully realized longer work that Ellington had yet written.

If Ellington felt any doubts about his ability to develop an audience for his more serious works, the band's 1933 trip to Europe certainly put them to rest. Even before Ellington's arrival, Spike Hughes had announced in *Melody Maker* that "America does not honestly know or appreciate the real treasure she possesses in Duke Ellington."[33] A two-week engagement at the Palladium drew fans from all over the country who were anxious to hear Ellington's English debut. Ellington had brought along dancer Bessie Dudley and song-and-dance team Bill Bailey and Derby Wilson in an attempt to recreate a Cotton Club–styled revue in this new setting. Much to his surprise, many of the critics and musicians who had heralded the bandleader as the great new American composer expressed dismay at the show business trappings of these performances. In response to their demands, Duke added a number of his more ambitious pieces to the band's program. "Maybe our music does mean something," was Ellington's characteristically understated comment on his return to America.[34]

Although the serious tone of this response must have been gratifying to Ellington, this was no time for complacency. An exciting swing band led by Jimmie Lunceford had recently arrived in Harlem, ready to challenge Ellington for supremacy on his home turf. Organized in Memphis in the late 1920s, the Lunceford band had polished its approach during summer engagements in Lakeside, Ohio, and then built up a following in Buffalo, New York, before finally coming to Harlem to appear at the Cotton Club. Lacking the depth of soloists and originality of the Ellington band, the Lunceford orchestra compensated with exceptionally fluid ensemble work, a tightly knit rhythm section, and a repertoire of solidly swinging dance charts. Coming of age only a short while before the dawn of the Swing Era—as the second half of this decade would come to be known—Lunceford was anticipating the sound of the future. Streamlined, stylish, and swinging, this was a band well suited to the emerging musical tastes of the American public.

Lunceford had learned several instruments during his youth in Denver, and had formally studied music at Fisk University and the City College of New York. As a bandleader, however, he remained content to delegate much of the direction of the group to others. Will Hudson's 1934 charts "Jazzocracy" and "White Heat," evoking memories of the Casa Loma Orchestra, provided Lunceford with his first recording successes. But it was left to trumpeter and arranger Sy Oliver to develop the mature sound of the group, with its winning interplay of brass, reeds, and rhythm instruments. In a series of memorable charts—such as "Shake Your Head" (1934), "My Blue Heaven" (1935), "Organ Grinder's Swing" (1936), and "For Dancers Only" (1937)—Oliver set out a blueprint for crafting dance hall music of the highest order. This approach would be widely imitated by other swing bands over the following decade, and Oliver himself would resurface in other settings (most notably with Tommy Dorsey's band) to create similar successes.

These carefully structured pieces have given the Lunceford group the reputation of being primarily an arranger's band. However, the Lunceford orchestra was not lacking in talented soloists. Willie Smith, whose sophisticated and sweet-toned saxophone work places him behind only Benny Carter and Johnny Hodges among altoists of the decade, stands out as the most capable of the group's instrumentalists, but the contributions of Trummy Young, Eddie Durham, and Joe Thomas are also worth noting. Even the heralded ensemble sound of the Lunceford band was as much a matter of individual musicianship as of arranging style. The technical facility and relaxed phrasing of the reed section—as seen, for example, in the 1935 performance of "Sleepy Time Gal"—were unsurpassed at the time. And though the brass section may have lacked the unique musical personalities who enlivened the Ellington ensemble, the range and execution of Lunceford's individual players were beyond reproach.

Drummer Chick Webb also made an impact on the Harlem musical landscape during these years. A Baltimore native, Webb came to New York in his mid-teens and before his twentieth birthday was leading a band at Harlem's Savoy Ballroom. Webb demands our respect as one of the most exciting drummers in the history of jazz, but his reputation suffers from four factors: his relatively short career; the limited ability of 1930s recording technology to capture percussion sounds in a big band with any real immediacy; his unprepossessing appearance in an industry that celebrates image and glamor more than it will admit; and finally (and the only one of these obstacles that Webb brought upon himself) his decision to hire a singer whose fame would soon eclipse the achievements of her erstwhile boss. Yet if the history books have been unkind to Chick Webb, jazz fans at the time had no doubts about his preeminence. Relying on the imaginative compositions and charts of Edgar Sampson ("Stompin' at the Savoy," "Blue Lou," "Let's Get Together") and propelled by the leader's forceful drumming, Webb's band developed into a hard-swinging ensemble, primed to compete with Ellington or Henderson at the legendary band battles staged at the Savoy. For a famous matchup with the Goodman band, held at the Savoy in 1937, a record crowd of four thousand packed the hall, while another five thousand were turned away. "Chick Webb Defeats Ben Goodman!" proclaimed the follow-up headline in *Metronome*.

The addition of singer Ella Fitzgerald to the band in 1934 further enhanced the group's jazz credentials and added to its popular appeal, while her vocal on "A-Tisket, A-Tasket" propelled the song to an eighteen-week stint on the Hit Parade in 1938. Fitzgerald had been discovered at age seventeen in a talent contest at Harlem's Apollo Theater and soon gained a reputation for her wide range, impeccable intonation, and sure sense of swing. "A-Tisket, A-Tasket," with its nursery-song quality, proved to be an ideal vehicle for Fitzgerald's childlike vocal style—a style that stood in stark contrast to the sultry sexuality and dark moodiness of a Bessie Smith or a Billie Holiday. Bringing a naive innocence to her interpretation of a lyric, Fitzgerald conveyed a joyous exultation, tinged with a sense of humor, reminiscent of her early model Louis Armstrong (with whom she later collaborated in a memorable pairing). When Webb died from tuberculosis in 1939, Fitzgerald took over as leader and continued in that role for the next three years, until the group disbanded in 1942.

Ellington, Henderson, Lunceford, Calloway, Webb, Fitzgerald—these bandleaders represented a flowering of musical talent in Harlem every bit as vital as the community's much-heralded writers and visual artists. The work of these African American musicians came to exert an influence far beyond the confines of Harlem, playing a critical role in defining the broader cultural tastes of the nation as a whole, and eventually gaining adherents overseas as well. In a very real sense, the rise of the great Harlem bands in the early and mid-1930s was a harbinger of a changing sensibility at hand. During the closing years of the decade, popular music styles would be transformed permanently by the rise of a high-energy dance style, drawing heavily from African American roots, that would come to be known as swing.

To a certain extent, this shift in the musical tastes of the broader American public served to validate Ellington's career to date. After all, had he not already declared that "it don't mean a thing, if it ain't got that swing"? And certainly the aesthetic underpinnings of the swing movement drew on the same roots—especially the music of the Fletcher Henderson band—that Ellington had incorporated into his own efforts.

Even so, the lighter, more propulsive swing of the emerging style reflected a new emphasis in the music, away from the complexities and art music tendencies that had increasingly characterized Ellington's work in the first half of the decade. Swing music was, if nothing else, deeply populist, with few highbrow pretensions. And though Ellington, Henderson, and others had paved the way, it would take a white bandleader of heroic proportions to establish swing music as the dominant popular music style of the era and bring it into the households of middle America. Through this surprising intermediary, the hot jazz of Harlem, intermixed with influences from Chicago and elsewhere, would become the everyday sound of American life.

5 The Swing Era

THE KING OF SWING

The onset of the Great Depression had a chilling effect on the jazz world, as it did on the whole entertainment industry. Record sales in the United States had surpassed one hundred million in 1927, but by 1932 only six million were sold—a staggering decline of over 90 percent. Record labels that had focused on black music—the "race records" of the day—were especially hard hit, but no sector of the music business proved immune to the economic malaise. During the same period, the growing popularity of talking movies led many theaters to halt the elaborate live shows that had previously been a staple of popular entertainment in most cities, further reducing paying jobs for musicians. Thousands of them changed careers—membership in the musicians' union declined by almost one-third between 1928 and 1934—or else remained chronically underemployed. Greater and lesser talents suffered alike. Sidney Bechet, Jelly Roll Morton, King Oliver, Bessie Smith, Bix Beiderbecke—their individual stories are all different, but share at least this one similarity: their careers spiraled downward in tandem with the nation's industrial output.

The end of Prohibition in 1933 transformed many speakeasies into legitimate nightclubs, but the change was hardly a positive one for most jazz players. Not only alcohol but the whole ethos and ambiance of jazz culture were demystified in the process. Both could now be easily consumed at home: alcohol legally purchased at the liquor store, jazz carried into the household over the airwaves. This was progress of sorts. Yet the harsh math of this new equation did not bode well for musicians: a single band could now entertain countless listeners through the magic of radio.

By implication, a few instrumentalists were doing the work that previously required hundreds, maybe thousands, of bands. Thus, the same technology that brought unparalleled fame to a small cadre did irreparable damage to most players, as supply and demand were brought further out of alignment. Perhaps the growth of big bands during this era was as much a result of these economic forces as it was a sign of changing tastes. As wages declined and musician unemployment rose, a dozen players could be hired for relatively little. The big band, formerly a luxury, was now a standard format, as excess workers made labor-intensive activities—in music just as much as in production—more viable, hence more commonplace. Twenty-five years later this trend would reverse, as a growing economy and rising wages helped kill the big band, a bloated relic of a less expensive age.

Although the developments of the 1930s affected most musicians adversely, a handful of performers benefited considerably from the more stratified structure of the entertainment world. The creation of a truly nationwide mass medium in the form of radio catapulted a few jazz players to a level of celebrity that would have been unheard of only a few years before. True, artists had long been accorded fame and favor in the context of modern Western society, but now the concepts of stardom and superstardom began to emerge in their contemporary sense.

Such a step change depended, first and foremost, on a technological shift. In 1920 the first commercial radio station in the United States, KDKA in Pittsburgh, began broadcasting. But, in its early days, this new medium lacked a wide audience. In 1921, only $11 million in radio equipment was sold in the United States; by the close of the decade, annual sales had skyrocketed to over $850 million. The nature of the music business would never be the same. From now on, the twin industries, recording and broadcasting, would exert unprecedented influence over the careers of singers and instrumentalists, arrangers and composers. As finance, technology, and artistic production grew even more intertwined, a new class of entrepreneur grew in importance: the talent agent. Hence, our history is marked by a number of symbiotic relationships—between Louis Armstrong and Joe Glaser, Duke Ellington and Irving Mills, Benny Goodman and John Hammond—in which the creative impulse requires the mediation of the businessman to reach a mass audience. As the stakes grew higher and higher, music became more deeply embedded in "the music business," and the business became more and more consolidated in a few hands.

This transformation did not—and could not—take place overnight. Regional bands continued to flourish in many locales, oblivious to the mass marketing of national figures that would soon deprive them of much of their audience. The vast majority of musicians continued to look after their own finances, or lack thereof, without the aid of agents, publicists, managers, and the like. The "listening public" developed only gradually, as radio evolved from a novelty to a necessity for most American households. But, more than anything, the continuing poor state of the nation's economy was the single most important factor in preventing mass media entertainment from realizing its full potential in the early days of the 1930s. Even so, the American music industry during these years was a tinderbox waiting for the spark that would set it off. The rise of network radio, much more than the earlier spread of record players, transformed the general public into passive receptors of entertainment chosen by a few arbiters of taste. The results were now all but inevitable. The mechanisms of stardom were set in place in the music world. All that was needed was the right star.

Benny Goodman sent this apparatus into motion with a vengeance. In the process, he ignited not only his own amazing career, but set off a craze for "swing music" that would last over a decade. Popular music had never seen the like before. Not with Al Jolson or Russ Columbo. Not with Bing Crosby or Rudy Vallee. Certainly not with the early pioneers of jazz. In a very real way, the phenomenon of Goodman—as distinct from his music—set the blueprint for stardom, with its celebration of an almost religious fervor in "fans" (again, a new concept), one that would repeat cyclically with Frank Sinatra and the bobby-soxers, the cult of Elvis, Beatlemania, and on and on.

It is meant as no criticism of Benny Goodman to point out the benefits he extracted from these economic and technological factors. Unlike so many other targets of mass adulation, Goodman's impeccable musicianship and consummate artistry made him a deserving candidate for such acclaim. Few figures in the history of popular culture have demonstrated such an expansive view of the musical arts. Even a cursory list of Goodman's achievements makes one sit up and take notice: as a soloist he defined the essence of the jazz clarinet as no other performer before or since; as a bandleader, he established standards of technical perfection that were the envy of his peers, while his influence in gaining widespread popularity for swing music was unsurpassed; a decade later he reformed his ensemble to tackle the nascent sounds of bop music—a move that few of his generation would have dared make; in the world of classical music, Goodman not only excelled as a performer, but also commissioned a host of major works—Béla Bartók's *Contrasts*, Aaron Copland's *Concerto for Clarinet*, Paul Hindemith's *Concerto for Clarinet and Orchestra*, and Morton Gould's *Derivations for Clarinet and Band*, among others. At a time when jazz players were often treated as a musical underclass, Goodman used his preeminence to break through the many barriers—of racial prejudice, of class distinctions, of snobbery and close-mindedness—that served only to stultify and compartmentalize the creative spirit.

Goodman's parents had emigrated from Eastern Europe—his father, David Goodman, from Poland, his mother, Dora Rezinsky, from Lithuania—as part of the great wave of Jewish settlement in the United States that took place during the closing years of the nineteenth century. The couple met in Baltimore but moved to Chicago in 1902, where David could ply his trade as a tailor in the local garment industry. In this great melting pot of cultures—some 80 percent of Chicago's population were either first- or second-generation immigrants during those years—Benny Goodman was born, the ninth of twelve children, on May 30, 1909. He was raised in the impoverished and often dangerous Maxwell Street neighborhood, commonly called Bloody Maxwell, where a variety of ethnic gangs held sway over a bleak urban landscape. In such an environment, music was a godsend, not only as a creative outlet or a sign of middle-class refinement, but simply as a way out of the ghetto.

David Goodman, sensing the opportunities for even youngsters to earn a liveli-hood as instrumentalists, prodded his children into musical studies. Along with his brothers Freddy and Harry, Benny was enlisted by his father in a band that rehearsed at the neighborhood synagogue. Only ten years old and the youngest of the three boys, Benny was deemed too small to handle one of the larger horns and was instead assigned a clarinet. In addition to regular rehearsals, Goodman undertook private lessons, first from a local bandleader but later from Franz Schoepp, a former faculty member of the Chicago Musical College whose other students included Jimmie Noone and Buster Bailey, two of the finest jazz clarinetists of their day. Noone's work, in particular, would come to exert a powerful influence over Goodman's conception of the clarinet.

Motivated as much by his own perfectionist tendencies as by his father's ambi-tions, Benny practiced with diligence. Under different circumstances, a symphonic career might have beckoned. But, coming of age during the great period of Chicago jazz, Goodman found himself drawn into the maelstrom of musical activity taking place in the nightclubs, speakeasies, and dance halls of his hometown. During his freshman year in high school, Benny became acquainted with the various members of the Austin High Gang, and some part of their devotion to the jazz art may have rubbed off on him. In the summer of 1923, Goodman met and played with Bix Beiderbecke, and though the cornetist was only nineteen years old, his playing was already distinctive enough to make an impression on the young clarinetist. One hears Bix's influence very clearly on the early Goodman recording of "Blue and Broken-Hearted." Indeed, Goodman's mature style—with its surprising intervallic leaps, its supple yet relaxed swing, on-the-beat phrasing, and sweet tone—would retain a set of musical values similar to Beiderbecke's.

Goodman's professional career, which had started in his early teens, took a major step forward when he joined the Ben Pollack band in 1925, initiating a four-year association that provided him with chances to tour and record, as well as to build his reputation in the context of one of the finest Chicago-style dance bands of the day. Goodman's work from this period is marked by his assured command of the clar-inet, while the influence of various Chicago clarinetists—Noone and Teschemacher, in particular—lurks only slightly below the surface. After leaving Pollack in 1929, Goodman began freelancing as a sideman and occasional leader. "After Awhile" and "Muskrat Ramble," recorded under his own name in August of that year, are still very much in the Chicago/New Orleans vein. But Goodman was also listening care-fully to the more progressive black dance bands of the day. His stint with Pollack in New York had allowed him to hear Fletcher Henderson at the Roseland Ballroom and Duke Ellington at the Cotton Club. The society dance bands, led by Whiteman and others, no doubt also caught his attention during this period.

Certainly Goodman needed to draw on all these sources of inspiration as he strug-gled to make a name for himself during the Great Depression. Studio work, pit-band gigs, and other freelance projects required him to prove his versatility in a wide variety of contexts. The sheer quantity of Goodman's output during these years is staggering: during the early 1930s he recorded hundreds of sides in dozens of ensem-bles. Sometimes these settings were jazz of the highest order—as in a remarkable

1930 date under Hoagy Carmichael's leadership that also featured Bix Beiderbecke, Bubber Miley, Eddie Lang, Joe Venuti, Bud Freeman, Gene Krupa, and Jimmy and Tommy Dorsey (this all-star lineup reportedly received $20 per head for the session)—but more often the music at hand in these freelance gigs was too tepid for a soloist with Goodman's natural instincts for the hot.

The most fruitful collaboration of these years may have been one that Goodman pursued off the bandstand. John Hammond, a Yale dropout and member of the wealthy Vanderbilt family who would come to make a career out of his advocacy for jazz music and civil rights, introduced himself to the clarinetist one evening in the fall of 1933. Hammond announced that he had just returned from England, where he had contracted to produce recordings by Goodman and others for the Columbia and Parlophone labels. This unexpected intervention on his behalf would represent a major turning point in Goodman's career. Under Hammond's guidance, he would record with many of the leading musicians in the jazz world. Sessions conducted under Goodman's leadership during October found Jack Teagarden contributing some of his finest recorded work, including "I Gotta Right to Sing the Blues." The following month, Goodman made an uncharacteristic appearance at a Bessie Smith session, and three days later, he recorded with seventeen-year-old Billie Holiday. Other dates from this period find him working alongside Coleman Hawkins, Teddy Wilson, and other major jazz talents.

The exact degree of Hammond's influence on Goodman's career is open to debate. In time, the pair's relationship would extend well beyond work, growing into friendship and eventually a family tie when Goodman married Hammond's sister Alice. In Goodman's professional career, the impresario was soon handling much more than just the mechanics of setting up recording dates, and his impact made itself felt in the hiring of sidemen, the selection of repertoire, and other important decisions. Above all, Hammond's relentless prodding, his championing of authentic jazz in the face of watered-down imitations, could only serve to reinforce Goodman's better instincts, and may well have precipitated Goodman's final break with the commercial music of his freelance years and the wholehearted plunge into the hotter style that would earn him the sobriquet "the King of Swing."

Contrary to conventional accounts, Goodman's eventual triumph—signaled by his breakthrough performance at the Palomar Ballroom in Los Angeles on August 21, 1935, a date now conventionally cited as the birth of the Swing Era—was anything but an overnight success. The groundwork for this event had been slowly put in place over the preceding months, with many setbacks along the way. Exactly fourteen months prior to the Palomar date, the opening of Billy Rose's Music Hall, at Fifty-second and Broadway, allowed Goodman to leave behind studio work for the more glamorous activity of leading a band in one of New York's most elegant nightspots. But this apparent big break proved to be a blind alley. Rose's venue closed its doors within weeks. The next promising opportunity for Goodman also fell through when a proposed overseas tour failed to materialize. But if high-profile engagements on the bandstand were hit-and-miss in the midst of the Great Depression, the growing radio industry presented an appealing—and possibly even more career-enhancing—alternative. Goodman embraced the new medium wholeheartedly when NBC offered his band the chance to be featured on the new *Let's Dance* program, which showcased three hours of music every Saturday on over fifty affiliate stations across the country. More than anything, this move paved the way for the following year's rags-to-riches tour to the West Coast. Because of the time difference, California audiences heard *Let's Dance* during peak listening hours. The result: a large, enthusiastic audience was waiting for his band when it arrived for the momentous Palomar gig.

Goodman's prickly personality and autocratic approach to bandleading have been the subject of much criticism. But few could doubt his commitment to the highest quality standards in sidemen, in charts, in rehearsals, and in performance. And almost from the start of the *Let's Dance* period, these efforts began to pay off. The addition of Bunny Berigan, the finest of the white disciples of Armstrong among the New York trumpeters, provided Goodman with a world-class brass soloist to match his reed stylings. Berigan's tone conveyed a majestic assurance, at times an audacity, but never lost its emotional pungency. His career would peak with his 1937 recording of "I Can't Get Started," a jazz masterpiece and popular success made with his own band. But, by 1940, this Olympian talent was bankrupt, drinking heavily, and in a precarious state of physical and mental health. Two years later, Berigan, only thirty-three years old, would succumb to cirrhosis and internal bleeding—a tragic ending for an impetuous soloist who, during his stint with the band that set off the Swing Era, seemed destined for greatness. Singer Helen Ward, who joined the band in 1934, may have lacked the deep jazz roots of Goodman and Berigan, but her captivating stage presence and forthright style of singing, with its light swing and supple phrasing, contributed greatly to the ensemble's wide appeal. But just as important as the performers—perhaps even more critical in this instance—were the arrangers. NBC's budget allowed for eight new charts each week, an extraordinary luxury for a bandleader, and Goodman was determined to make the most of this munificence. Goodman's hiring of Fletcher Henderson as an arranger has typically been cited as the major turning point in the evolution of the band's sound. Certainly Henderson's impact was great—perhaps even decisive—in the band's success, but he was only one of a number of outstanding arrangers who contributed to the group's repertoire during the prewar years. Spud Murphy, Jimmy Mundy, Horace Henderson, Eddie Sauter, Mel Powell, Joe Lippman, Deane Kincaide, Gordon Jenkins, Fud Livingston, Benny Carter, Mary Lou Williams, and Edgar Sampson, among others, also made greater or lesser contributions. In aggregate they constituted an impressive roster of composing and arranging talent that no other dance orchestra of the period could match, let alone surpass.

The special nature of Henderson's contribution lay in his access to a gold mine of material compiled during his own lengthy stint as a bandleader, as well as in his deep sensitivity to the swing style that was about to dominate American airwaves. And though Henderson was responsible for somewhat less than half of the band's book, he was the source for many of the most memorable Goodman charts: "King Porter Stomp," "Sometimes I'm Happy," "Blue Skies," and "Christopher Columbus," among others. In the racially charged atmosphere of the day, the symbolic importance of Henderson's role with the Goodman band loomed almost as large as the music itself.

Many jazz enthusiasts rejoiced in Goodman's conscious decision to emulate the hotter music of the Henderson orchestra—a direction that few white bands of the day were then taking—and bring this swinging style to the attention of the mass market. Others were less pleased at this state of affairs, castigating Goodman as one more white musician who managed to build his personal success by exploiting the achievements of black innovators. Yet our concern with the social ramifications of the Goodman-Henderson relationship should not blind us to the influence of personal factors on this important nexus in the history of jazz. Goodman, driven to achieve success no matter what obstacles lay in his course, was prepared to champion swing music to a far greater extent than the more introverted Henderson who, at best, was ambivalent about the commercial aspects of bandleading. In the final analysis, these two jazz pioneers needed each other and together could achieve results that neither, on his own, would reach.

Even so, it is important to acknowledge the advantages enjoyed by Goodman and other white jazz artists during the era. Unlike the black bandleaders, they were more readily accepted by mainstream America. They typically encountered easier working conditions, stayed at better accommodations when on the road, received higher pay, and had more secure careers. They were not forced to suffer the indignities of racism that even the finest black jazz musicians faced on a regular basis. Nor were they quite so likely to find their music borrowed—or sometimes stolen outright—by other performers, a process all too familiar to Henderson and many other African American jazz artists. In aggregate, these were tremendous advantages for a white musician trying to build a career in jazz during this period. Henderson, even if he had been far more ambitious and focused on gaining popular acclaim, could hardly have matched the heights to which Goodman brought swing music, if only for these reasons.

The final building block in Goodman's creation of a premier jazz orchestra lay in his reconfiguration of the band's rhythm section. Jess Stacy, an exciting pianist in the Hines mold, had an immediately positive impact on the ensemble as both an improviser and an accompanist. Guitarist George Van Eps may have lacked Stacy's skill as a soloist, but as a rhythm player he was a world-class talent. His tenure with the Goodman band was all too brief, but when he departed in 1935, he left behind a student, Alan Reuss, who was Van Eps's equal in providing inventive chordal support in a big band setting. But the most celebrated addition to the Goodman band during this period was drummer Gene Krupa. Within a matter of months, Krupa would become the most widely known drummer of his day, and though his influence later waned in the jazz world, his role in bringing the percussionist out of the background and into the limelight has left a permanent stamp on the music. Krupa's approach to the drums, for all its showmanship, was surprisingly unsyncopated and gleefully ignored the two great hooks of jazz rhythm—accenting the backbeat and swinging the downbeat—in favor of a relentless on-the-top groove. Krupa was similarly unconcerned with the other emerging directions in jazz drumming—exploring the melodic possibilities of the drums, or moving the center of the beat to the ride cymbal, or freeing up the instrument from the ground rhythm—trends that would come to define the future of jazz percussion. If anything, Krupa's approach, with its bottom-heavy snare and bass drum pulsations, recalled the earliest roots of jazz drumming, with its evocation of military music and marching bands, or perhaps pointed even further back, to the music's African origins. But, for all these anachronisms, Krupa excelled in swinging a dance band, which he did with the energy of a dynamo. The adulation of Krupa's audience lasted only a few brief years before a 1943 arrest for the possession of marijuana precipitated a backlash. His career would continue for another three decades, but Krupa would never again be so popular, the lasting taint of this scandal combined with changing styles and the critics' indifference (partly a reaction to his earlier fame) ensuring that his activities would be restricted to the margins of the jazz world. But in the years leading up to World War II, Krupa's throbbing attack defined the sound of jazz drums for most listeners. All in all, the Goodman rhythm section was without peer at the time. Not until Count Basie put together the supple foundation for his group—utilizing the skills of Jo Jones, Walter Page, Freddie Green, and Basie himself—would a jazz orchestra boast a more swinging sound.

Let's Dance lasted only twenty-six weeks before being dropped by the network in May 1935. But Goodman had already parlayed the exposure generated by the show into new opportunities. The band's affiliation with the Victor label had begun the previous month, and within a matter of weeks the ensemble had recorded a number of important sides, including "King Porter Stomp," "Sometimes I'm Happy," "Blue Skies," and "The Dixieland Band." Relying primarily on medium and up-tempo numbers, Goodman asserted his commitment to hot jazz, transforming everything from Irving Berlin's saccharine waltz "Always" to the holiday perennial "Jingle Bells" into swinging 4/4 time. Ballads played a modest role in the group's sound, but were not beyond its expertise, as witnessed by Goodman's poignant recording of Gordon Jenkins's "Goodbye," a pensive piece that became a signature song for the band.

As if these multifaceted achievements were not enough, Goodman formed a second unit that summer, a trio with pianist Teddy Wilson and Gene Krupa, and recorded a small body of work with that band that ranks among the finest jazz combo music of the period. The various Goodman splinter bands were not the first racially integrated jazz groups, but they were the most prominent of their day. Here the influence of Hammond, for whom artistic and political issues often coalesced, again made itself felt. Goodman, for his part, was motivated more by his zeal for musical excellence than by any desire to be a social crusader. But in his choice of Wilson (as in his hiring of Lionel Hampton and Charlie Christian for later Goodman combos), the clarinetist could achieve both aims without compromise. In particular, Wilson proved the perfect pianist for the chamber music ambiance that Goodman was refining with his small bands. Boasting a clear, singing piano tone—one as appropriate for a Mozart piano concerto as for a swing combo—and a subtle sense of dynamics, Wilson offered a more delicate variant of jazz piano than that practiced by a Hines or a Waller. The influence of other pianists can be traced in his playing, but Wilson stood above most of his contemporaries in his ability to adapt these influences into something new and distinctive. For example, Wilson had studied Hines carefully, but after an early period of emulation, found a way of assimilating this predecessor's percussive melodicism into a smoother, more legato style—executed with a sense of relaxed control that became a Wilson trademark. This same ability to digest and recast the jazz piano tradition was evident in Wilson's harmonic and rhythmic conception. Here one could detect Wilson's allegiance to the model set by the Harlem stride players, but with one important difference: excess notes were now pruned away, leaving a sparser musical landscape in which much of the swing is felt by implication. In this regard, Wilson represented a halfway point between the florid virtuosity of a Tatum and the minimalistic stylings of a Basie. Wilson's work on the trio version of "Body and Soul" from July 1935 reflects the distinctive virtues of his playing. The swinging tenths played by the left hand provide a firm harmonic foundation for the combo—so much so that the absence of a bass player is hardly noticed—while Wilson's right-hand lines ring out with pristine clarity. If there was a weakness to his playing, it lay in an overuse of ornamental runs—here the Tatum influence predominates—a habit that would be exacerbated in later years, causing much of Wilson's postwar work to sound formulaic. But in the best of his early recordings—solo efforts such as his 1937 renditions of "Between the Devil and the Deep Blue Sea" and "Don't Blame Me," the small-band projects with Goodman, and his sessions with Billie Holiday—Wilson earns respect as one of the finest jazz pianists of his generation.

The association with Wilson and Henderson may have pleased jazz fans, but the general public did not embrace Goodman's big band work until the group's nationwide tour during the summer of 1935. Even then, the Swing Era almost never took wing. Setting out in mid-July, the band played mostly one-nighters, sometimes for as little as $250 per night—by comparison, Goodman's rates would jump to $2,000 after his rise to fame—until the ensemble arrived in Denver for a much-anticipated engagement at a local dance hall. The audience reacted negatively, almost with hostility, to Goodman's swing music—so much so that the ballroom's manager tried to cancel his contract with the band after only one night. To placate the tastes of the local public, Goodman switched to playing tepid stock arrangements and even considered abandoning the hotter approach. After Denver, the group continued to limp along from gig to gig until a surprisingly enthusiastic response to the band's swing numbers in northern California gave Goodman renewed hope. But this reaction was mild compared to the fan response at the Palomar in Los Angeles a few days later. Swarming the bandstand in their excitement, the audience sent a signal, one soon heard all over the nation, that Goodman had tapped into something real.

Within weeks, Goodman's records dominated the charts on the West Coast, with the clamor gradually spreading eastward. For a follow-up engagement in Chicago, Goodman had the band promoted, for the first time, as a "swing band"—a new term, but one quickly picked up by others. The same day the Goodman band opened in Chicago, *Variety* launched a new weekly column titled "Swing Stuff," indicating that the industry power brokers were also paying notice. The Chicago booking, initially slated for one month, was extended to a half-year. By the time of Goodman's triumphant return to New York in the spring of 1936, his band was, without a doubt, the biggest draw in the music industry.

The Swing Era was under way in full force. For over a decade, swing music would remain the paradigm for popular music in America. If jazz ever enjoyed a golden age, this would be it. And through especially fortuitous circumstances, this was equally the golden age of the American popular song. In tandem, these two forces would create a musical revolution unparalleled in modern times, one in which the highest rung in artistry could be achieved without compromising commerciality. Never again would popular music be so jazzy, or jazz music so popular.

THE BIG BANDS

It is tempting to view the Palomar engagement as delineating a sharp break in the history of American popular music, with the new style replacing the old, hot supplanting sweet, in a sudden tectonic shift of sensibility. But long before Goodman's success, a handful of white bandleaders had experimented with a hotter, more jazz-oriented style of dance music, and their efforts helped develop both an audience and the personnel for the later swing bands. Among others, the Whiteman, Goldkette, and Pollack ensembles, as we have seen, attempted—and to a great extent managed—to find a halfway point in which both styles, hot and sweet, could play a role. And though these bandleaders never embraced jazz with the fervor of an Ellington or Henderson, they created a body of ambitious recordings and spawned the next generation of white swing bands—such as the Casa Loma Orchestra and the Dorsey Brothers—that would delve even more deeply into hotter currents.

The Casa Loma band, in particular, cultivated a small but devoted following on college campuses that would help pave the way for Goodman's later success. One of Jean Goldkette's ensembles known as the Orange Blossoms, formed in Detroit in 1927, served as the immediate predecessor of this band. The group re-formed in 1929 as a cooperative, a rare approach to organizing a band, then as now. Taking the democratic structure of the band to heart, the members also set about electing a leader, deciding on Glen Gray, a statuesque and charismatic alto saxophonist, to preside over the group. Gray inherited a band that had already focused on hot jazz, largely under the inspiration of banjoist Gene Gifford's arrangements. In October 1929, this group undertook its first recording session newly christened as the Casa Loma Orchestra. The band explored a wide range of styles, but its up-tempo charts generated the most enthusiasm. Galloping along at around 250 beats per minute, numbers such as "Casa Loma Stomp," "Black Jazz," and "Maniac's Ball" tested the stamina and footwork of the ballroom regulars as few white bands dared to do. But this forward-looking orchestra pushed at more than just the tempos of the tunes. At a time when soloists on recordings were routinely restricted to eight- or sixteen-bar statements, the Casa Loma was willing, for example, to let Clarence Hutchenrider punch out a stirring sixty-eight-bar baritone solo on "I Got Rhythm." Above all, the tight ensemble work of the Casa Loma Orchestra stood out. Even at the fastest tempos, the sections never faltered, never fell out of sync.

All of these elements would come to influence Goodman: the swinging charts, the focus on hot solo work, the emphasis on perfectly executed ensemble passages. Less heralded than the Fletcher Henderson connection, the Casa Loma Orchestra's impact on Goodman—and, through him, on countless other swing bands—may have been just as important. But even more telling, the Casa Loma's ability to build an audience among college students and younger fans also foreshadowed the demographics of the Goodman phenomenon. Setting a pattern that has lasted until the present day, the teenagers and young adults of the late 1930s and early 1940s not only dictated the musical tastes of the nation, but did so in a manner that their parents often could not understand. With its fast tempos, extroverted solos, and unrelenting syncopations, the Casa Loma Orchestra was forging a music distinctly not for the fainthearted. Do we err in describing this as music of *rebellion*—in particular, the rebellion of white youngsters in middle America?

Swing music was taken up by the new generation, searching for its own identity, developing its own way of life. In the new era of mass media and mass marketing of entertainment, the potential for music to symbolize, establish, and communicate one's lifestyle (soon to become an important concept) emerged as one of the defining attributes of popular recordings. Favorite songs, performers and bands, radio stations: all increasingly played an emblematic role in defining each new generation in contrast to the previous one. This supra-musical aspect of jazz, which we first glimpsed in the attitudes of the white Chicago jazz players of the 1920s, now became a broader cultural phenomenon with the epidemic of swing fever afflicting America's youth, circa 1935. Perhaps one goes too far to describe this shift as the Woodstock of the 1930s, but a cultural change was set in motion during this period that set the pattern for many later developments—an initial rupture between the musical tastes of the young and old that would repeat and widen to an enormous chasm some twenty years later with the advent of rock and roll.

The more traditional styles of New Orleans and Chicago also continued to hold sway with a number of white bands during the Swing Era. Bob Crosby's orchestra, formed from the remnants of Ben Pollack's ensemble, offered audiences an appealing big band variant of older styles. Crosby never found much favor with the critics— nor would he ever match the fame of his celebrity brother Bing—but his bands boasted an exceptional crop of soloists, including Eddie Miller, Irving Fazola, Billy Butterfield, Joe Sullivan, Muggsy Spanier, Yank Lawson, Jess Stacy, and Bob Zurke, as well as the inspired and at times unconventional arrangements of Bob Haggart. The Dorsey Brothers also tended toward a more traditional sound during this period, with the lingering influence of Chicago-inflected Dixieland hovering over many of their early efforts. Even in later years, after their abrupt separation, the Dorsey siblings' increasingly overt swing sounds (which both came to embrace, although Tommy more so than his older brother Jimmy) were usually moderated by a heavy dose of sugary ballads, pop vocals, novelty numbers, and an occasional throwback to the two-beat spirit of their Chicago roots.

Born and reared in a Pennsylvania coal mining town, Tommy and Jimmy Dorsey were cut off from the main currents of popular music sweeping the more urbanized areas of America. Music for the Dorseys (much like the Teagardens and Goodmans) was a matter of hearth and home, with the family unit serving as a surrogate center of activity. The elder Mr. Dorsey led a local marching and concert band as well as taught music. Both boys learned multiple instruments, but in time Jimmy gravitated to saxophone and clarinet, while Tommy focused on trombone. The youngsters' isolation from the broader streams of the jazz world left a lasting mark: on the one hand, neither of the Dorseys developed deep jazz roots as soloists; on the other, the focus on solitary practice and the peculiarly pedagogical atmosphere of their home life no doubt contributed to the accomplished technique they both boasted.

First recording together under their own name in 1928, the Dorsey Brothers soon became regulars of the studios, where their skills and versatility held them in good stead. The quality of these early sides is mixed, but the best of them are first-rate jazz performances—for example, the Dorseys' 1933 resurrection of Bill Challis's stirring chart of "Blue Room," written for Goldkette in the 1920s (but never recorded at the time), which still sounded fresh years later. In 1934, the Dorsey Brothers began performing together in a working band, but tensions between the two exploded onstage the following spring, when a disagreement—ostensibly over the tempo of a song—led the mercurial Tommy to walk off the bandstand. They would remain at odds for many years, with Jimmy taking over leadership of the existing band, while Tommy set up his own competing ensemble.

Opportunities for both blossomed during the remainder of the decade and into the 1940s, with the Tommy Dorsey band achieving particular success in a series of big-selling records: "Marie" (1937), with its novelty vocal-and-chant exchanges and a strong solo contribution from Bunny Berigan; "Song of India" (1937), a Rimsky-Korsakov adaptation, also featuring Berigan, which was an influential excursion into the realm of jazz exotica; "Boogie Woogie" (1938), with its clever transfer of the fad-dish piano style to the big band idiom; "Hawaiian War Chant" (1938), echoing Goodman's "Sing, Sing, Sing" (which had caused a sensation at the Carnegie Hall concert a few months earlier) with its assertion of simple riffs over a throbbing drum foundation; and "I'll Never Smile Again" (1940) with a young Frank Sinatra providing a dreamy vocal. The last tune spent twelve weeks on top of the *Billboard* chart—one of seventeen number one singles enjoyed by this immensely popular bandleader. Brother Jimmy offered stiff competition, however, with eleven number one hits of his own. These included the Latin-tinged tunes "Amapola"—which topped the chart for ten weeks in 1941—"The Breeze and I" and "Besame Mucho," but also appealing jazz-pop fare such as "Tangerine" and "Pennies from Heaven," the latter a collaboration with Bing Crosby that was the biggest-selling record of 1936.

In 1939, at the height of the Swing Era, the jazz credentials of the Tommy Dorsey Orchestra were reinforced with the addition of Sy Oliver, whose arrangements had been so influential in shaping the Lunceford sound. As with Henderson's infusion of swing into the Goodman band, Oliver helped make this unit into a hotter, harder-swinging ensemble. Over the next few years, Oliver charts such as "Stomp It Off," "Yes, Indeed!," "Swing High," "Well, Get It!," and "Opus One" provided a more flamboyant and insistent style for Dorsey and made the contrast between his music and that of his more pop-oriented brother all the more noticeable. The move to this hotter style also helped Dorsey secure the services of drummer Buddy Rich, one of the flashiest and most technically accomplished percussionists of the era, and later a prominent bandleader in his own right. Despite a tendency toward bombast, this drummer—born as Bernard Rich in 1917—could fire up the band or, barring that, at least the audience, with a series of celebrated moves: one-hand rolls with either hand, criss-crossing arms-and-drums patterns, whispery passages played at lightning-fast speed, dazzling stick tricks, and other crowd-pleasing trademarks of his craft. Rich had just left Artie Shaw's band and was reluctant to join Dorsey, but when he encountered Oliver's swinging scores during a rehearsal, he changed his mind and signed on with the group. Oliver later penned a feature for Rich, the chart "Quiet Please," a driving piece taken at a breakneck tempo that displays the drummer in top form.

The Dorsey brothers, who had patched up their differences in 1942, increasingly worked in tandem after the end of the big band era. While other jazz stars of the prewar years struggled to hold on to their audience in the 1950s, the Dorseys reinvented themselves as television stars. They even helped usher in the age of rock and roll by featuring Elvis Presley in his first TV appearance—some eight months before the singer's celebrated performance on *The Ed Sullivan Show*. But Tommy's death at age fifty-one in 1956 from suffocation in his sleep, and Jimmy's death from throat cancer the following year at age fifty-three, put an end to the illustrious careers of these Swing Era stars.

The most direct competitor to Goodman during the closing years of the decade was Artie Shaw, a virtuoso clarinetist whose movie star looks and flair (mixed with disdain) for publicity attracted attention and controversy in equal doses. In a shrewd public relations move, Shaw took on the title "the King of the Clarinet," an obvious challenge to Goodman's "King of Swing" epithet. To this day, debate over the relative merits of Goodman and Shaw continues to bedevil swing aficionados, with advocates of one quick to denounce the achievements of the other. Pointless polemics. Both of these clarinetists achieved the highest rung—indeed has any later player on the instrument made such a mark or inspired such passion among listeners as either Shaw or Goodman? The reserved Goodman was the master of hot phrasing, a swing stylist with a concert hall technique. Charismatic, a chameleon in both his music and personality, Shaw offered a fluid, less syncopated approach to melody, but leavened with a sweet tone that is still the envy of other clarinetists so many decades later. His improvised lines were varnished with a haughty elegance, submerging the emotional turbulence far below, which made even the most technically accomplished passages sound like child's play. Compare the two figures, each a puzzling composite: one combined a frigid personality with a hot musical style, while the other evinced a warm-blooded temperament but a sweet and cool approach to the horn. Choosing between them is like discussing the relative merits of ice and fire. Both are forces to contemplate and, as the poet tells us, will suffice.

The distinct odor of public relations permeated more than just Shaw's music. The ups and downs of the bandleader's eight marriages (including conjugal stints with cinema leading ladies Ava Gardner and Lana Turner) and his erratic behavior made him a constant subject of gossip and speculation. Even when Shaw decided to bid adieu to the Swing Era and retire into seclusion—as he did, in grand style, late in 1939—his demands for privacy only heightened public interest. Never one to miss a tearful encore, Shaw was back in the recording studio within weeks, having spent the interim in Mexico, jamming with the locals and garnering a new repertoire of Latin songs. This south-of-the-border sojourn led to Shaw's recording of "Frenesi," one of the clarinetist's most memorable hits.

Breaking up the band would become a Shaw trademark, just as much as the broken marriages, with precipitous dismissals curtailing both the 1941 and 1942 editions of the Shaw orchestra. Even a "final retirement" in 1954 proved temporary, when Shaw resurrected his orchestra some thirty years later, although now serving only as conductor and leader, with his clarinet permanently kept in its case. Burned out by the too-rapid ascendancy of his star, Shaw could not match the staying power of Goodman. But the best of his work ranks among the finest jazz of the era: the popular hits, such as "Begin the Beguine"; "Concerto for Clarinet" and various other demonstrations of Shaw's instinct for grandiloquent gestures; ballad showpieces including "Stardust" and "Deep Purple"; the clarinetist's efforts with the Gramercy Five, such as "Special Delivery Stomp" and "Summit Ridge Drive"; as well as the stellar late-vintage 1954 combo recordings, many of the tracks unreleased for decades, which serve as proof positive that Shaw laid down his horn while still at the top of his game. And, like Goodman, Shaw played a key role in breaking down the racial barriers that stultified the jazz world. His hiring of Billie Holiday in 1938, Hot Lips Page in 1941, and Roy Eldridge in 1944 gave broader visibility to some of the most deserving African American jazz artists of the day.

Roy Eldridge stands out as one of the enigmas of the Swing Era. Recognized by many of his peers as the greatest trumpeter of his generation, Eldridge never enjoyed much financial success as a leader, nor was he capable of staying for very long as a star soloist with a major band. His stint with Fletcher Henderson in the mid-1930s lasted only a few months. A follow-up attempt to lead an octet with his older brother, saxophonist Joe Eldridge, resulted in a number of classic recordings—"After You've Gone," "Wabash Stomp," and "Heckler's Hop" showcase some of the most impressive jazz trumpet work of the late 1930s—but little in the way of sales. For a time, Eldridge's fortune had sunk so low that he studied to be a radio engineer—this at a point when his technical command of the jazz trumpet was unsurpassed.

Eventually Eldridge returned to the bandstand in 1938 with a ten-piece group. This band also soon folded, but Eldridge's skills as a soloist kept him in demand. His 1940 recording of "I Can't Believe That You're in Love with Me" finds the trumpeter, alongside Benny Carter and Coleman Hawkins in the Chocolate Dandies, contributing one of his finest solos. Through his work with the Gene Krupa band in 1941–43 and the Artie Shaw band in 1944–45, Eldridge helped break down the color barrier in the jazz world. In particular, the trumpeter's work with Krupa on "Rockin' Chair" and "Let Me Off Uptown" were as close as Eldridge would come to a hit. After leaving Shaw, Eldridge again attempted to organize a big band of his own, but before long he returned to the small-combo format, where he continued to ply his craft either as leader or in collaboration with many of the marquee names in jazz for another four decades.

The genealogists of jazz often cite Eldridge as a linking figure, whose work represents a halfway point between the styles of Louis Armstrong and Dizzy Gillespie. This reputation as a transitional player in the music's history may ultimately have proven to be more of a curse than a blessing for Eldridge, who soon found himself lost in the shuffle of shifting styles and changing tastes. In particular, the overt modernism of his playing tended to be obscured by the rising star of Gillespie. Although less than seven years older than Dizzy, Eldridge soon came to be seen as part of the older generation, the group of Swing Era veterans whom Gillespie and the other boppers were trying to supplant. In fact, Eldridge had taken part in some of the early bop sessions at Minton's Playhouse and, had he been so motivated, could have adapted to the new style—his mid-1950s Verve recordings with Gillespie clearly reveal that the older trumpeter was more than up to that challenge. But personal inclination kept him in the swing camp, and his later work found him recording or performing with many of the star soloists of the prewar era, such as Benny Carter, Coleman Hawkins, Art Tatum, and Johnny Hodges.

Despite the growing popularity of other big bands, Goodman took the various challenges to his preeminence in stride. Not only did his band win first place in *Downbeat*'s 1936 reader's poll, but it scored a landslide victory, receiving almost three times as many votes as its nearest competitor. Other bandleaders might have grown complacent in response to these accolades, but not Goodman. Always on the lookout for prime talent, he kept the band sounding fresh with a constant influx of new blood. The addition of trumpeters Ziggy Elman in late 1936 and, four months later, Harry James, provided Goodman with two world-class soloists, both of whom were also fine section players. The later overt commercialism of James's work ("Ciribiribin," "Flight of the Bumblebee," "Carnival of Venice") has distracted attention from this trumpeter's exceptional jazz skills. James's brash, energetic style, set apart by his stamina and range, can be heard to good measure on "Peckin'," "Roll 'Em," and "Sugar Foot Stomp" from September of that year, the last in particular revealing the Oliver-Armstrong roots of his trumpet style. Vido Musso, a robust tenor saxophonist in the Hawkins mold, joined the band that same year and contributed impassioned solos on performances such as "Jam Session" (which also includes one of Elman's better solos from this period) and "I Want to Be Happy" during his tenure with the band. Such talent came at a price. Each of these players eventually went on to front his own band—as Berigan had already done and as Krupa would soon do as well—taking advantage of the tremendous exposure granted to them during their Goodman years. Unlike the Ellington band, which could retain key players for decades, Goodman's ensemble constantly needed to replenish its ranks; and though the leader's perfectionist tendencies may have contributed to the turnover—his angry glare at underperforming musicians became so famous, it even got a name: "the Ray"—it is to Goodman's credit that he rarely faltered in finding fitting replacements for his departing stars.

Goodman's next major discovery, Lionel Hampton, was in the rare position of not replacing anyone. Not only was his principal instrument, the vibraphone, new to the Goodman band, but it was relatively unknown in the jazz world as a whole. Hampton stands out as the innovator who took what was a quasi-novelty sound—essentially a high-tech xylophone with added vibrato effect—and transformed it into a mainstream jazz instrument. Adrian Rollini had performed on the vibraphone in earlier years, and Red Norvo had experimented with it, albeit in private, as early as 1928, but Hampton's work in the context of the Goodman combo gave the "vibes" (as it eventually came to be known) a new level of legitimacy. Of course, Hampton's energy, inventiveness, enthusiasm, and sheer sense of swing also had much to do with this. His was a style built on abundance: long loping lines, blistering runs of sixteenth notes, baroque ornamentations, all accompanied by an undercurrent of grunting and humming from above. Few figures of the prebop era, with the obvious exception of Art Tatum (with whom the vibraphonist later jousted in a session of note-filled excesses), could squeeze more into a sixteen-bar solo than Hampton. In the battle of form versus content, the latter always won when this seminal figure was on stage.

During his apprenticeship years in Los Angeles, Hampton adopted various bandstand personas before establishing himself as the vibraphonist par excellence: his first record date, from 1924, finds him on drums, and over the next several years he tried his hand at piano ("Jelly Roll Morton had given me a few lessons and I'd listened to every record Earl Hines ever made") and singing ("I imitate Louis Armstrong. . . . I used to go out on a winter night with no coat on, hoping to get laryngitis so I could sound like Louis"). Armstrong himself stepped in to steer Hampton to the instrument that would bring him lasting fame. During a 1930 Armstrong session conducted at the NBC studio in Los Angeles, the trumpeter suggested that Hampton try his hand at an unusual mallet instrument sitting in the corner of the room. Invented only a few years earlier by the Deagan Company, the vibraphone was the result of an inspired decision to attach rotating fans, powered by an electric motor, in the resonator tubes hung below xylophone-like metal bars, thus creating a modernistic (at least in those halcyon days of acoustic sound) vibrato effect. "It hadn't been used for anything except incidental chime notes—the intermission signals on radio programs," Hampton later explained.[1] This casual encounter led to a new career for the twenty-two-year-old artist, but his big break came when Goodman stopped by, during a visit to Los Angeles in August 1936, to hear Hampton's band at the Paradise Nightclub. Impressed by the proceedings, Goodman took out his clarinet and jammed with the band all night, finally breaking at dawn. The following evening, Goodman returned, this time bringing Teddy Wilson and Gene Krupa. Soon this same foursome would be known as the Benny Goodman Quartet. In November, Hampton joined Goodman full time, initially participating as a member of the clarinetist's combo, and later breaking the color barrier in the big band in March 1938, when Hampton filled in on drums after Krupa's departure. The Goodman relationship would last until 1940 when Hampton, like so many other of the clarinetist's protégés, left to lead his own band.

Goodman's Carnegie Hall concert from 1938 remains the crowning glory of this formative period in the clarinetist's career. With most of his early "discoveries" on hand—Krupa, Wilson, Hampton, James, Stacy, Elman—Goodman was poised to make the most of this highly publicized performance. If that were not enough, many of the leading players from the Ellington and Basie bands were also featured during the marathon concert. The unlikely hero of the affair proved to be Stacy, who contributed a luminous piano solo at the close of "Sing, Sing, Sing." Yet the cultural significance of this concert outweighed any purely musical considerations. A watershed event, the Carnegie Hall concert represented a coming of age for jazz: not only accepted, it was all but venerated under the auspices of this symbolic home of American concert music. This was a new experience—for both jazz fans and the players themselves. "How long do you want for intermission?" Goodman was asked before the performance. "I dunno," he replied. "How much does Toscanini have?"

But just as telling, the concert signaled a newfound fascination with jazz as a historical phenomenon. The program that evening consciously presented a chronology of the music's evolution, reaching back to the ragtime era and offering tributes to Beiderbecke and Armstrong in addition to featuring a selection of swing favorites. Later that year, Hammond would amplify on this same approach in his first "Spirituals to Swing" concert, also presented at Carnegie Hall. Over the next few years, this emerging sense of historical perspective would transform the jazz world, as witnessed by an outpouring of jazz writing and research, a revival of early New Orleans and Chicago styles, and, above all, a new attitude among fans and musicians, one that focused on discerning progressive and regressive trends—a quasi-Darwinian assessment of improvisational idioms—among the panoply of bands and soloists that made up the jazz world.

Given this fascination with the past, who would have expected the forward-looking moves Goodman would make in the months following the Carnegie Hall concert? Then again perhaps Goodman himself was caught up in the emerging view of jazz as a series of progressively more modern conceptions. In any event, Goodman was now at the start of his experimental phase, marked by a new type of talent drawn into the band—Charlie Christian, Mel Powell, Eddie Sauter—a phase that would culminate some years later in Goodman's surprising, if short-lived, attempt to transform his group into a bebop ensemble. This same period saw Goodman make important excursions into contemporary classical music, set off by his decision to commission Béla Bartók's Contrasts in 1940. One of the ironies of jazz history is that, for all these efforts to be at the cutting edge, Goodman (like Eldridge) remained stereotyped as a traditionalist, as the leader of the old regime in jazz, the order toppled by the "real" modernists led by Charlie Parker and Dizzy Gillespie.

Yet the Goodman big band, during the Sauter-Powell years, defies such easy categorization. This was, if anything, a modern jazz ensemble, although brandishing a different type of modern jazz than what the beboppers were creating. Influences from classical music predominate, intermingled with the swing ethos from the Henderson-Mundy-Murphy tradition. In a telling development, Mel Powell, Goodman's premier pianist from this period, would come to abandon jazz for a career as an academic classical composer, studying under Paul Hindemith, teaching at Yale, and eventually earning a Pulitzer Prize in 1990 for Duplicates, a concerto he wrote for two pianos and orchestra—a piece so far afield from Powell's jazz work as to seem the product of a different person entirely. His charts for Goodman ("The Earl," "Mission to Moscow") reflect his sound instincts as a big band arranger, but Powell's piano playing stands out as even more suggestive. Technically accomplished, harmonically daring, endlessly inventive: Powell could easily have established himself as one of the most influential jazz pianists of his generation. Instead, only a handful of recordings testify to his potential. Sauter, in contrast, never made the plunge into full-fledged classical composition but could well have done so. His ambitious charts for Goodman are packed to the brim with activity—his "concerto" for Cootie Williams, recorded by Goodman as "Superman" in 1940, is a case in point: although less well known than Ellington's "Concerto for Cootie," Sauter's feature piece for the trumpeter is an equally impressive effort with its inspired shifts in key, mood, tempo, and texture. In later years, Sauter pursued a range of commercial projects, including work as an orchestrator for Broadway shows, but his best work (such as his 1961 string writing for Stan Getz's *Focus* project) confirms that his personal twist on modern jazz could be breathtaking for all its idiosyncracies.

Who can deny that Sauter and Powell, despite their achievements, represented the way modern jazz did *not* go, the path steadfastly not taken? In contrast, guitarist Charlie Christian, the other forward-looking musician sponsored by Goodman during this period, would prove to be a leader and instigator of the defining modern style: namely bebop, as it soon would be called. This was not a modernism resonant of Bartók and Hindemith, but one driven by hard-swinging monophonic lines, drenched in chromaticism and executed with lightning speed. Christian's credentials in this regard are all the more remarkable when one considers that his major recordings were made in a period of less than two years—and at a point when modern jazz was still in embryo and most listeners had only the sketchiest context within which to grasp the genius of this soft-spoken pioneer of the electric guitar.

To many of his contemporaries, Christian must have seemed more of a novelty act than a harbinger of jazz to come. To this presynthesizer generation, electricity was a practical matter, linked with street lamps and lightning rods, not musical performance. Like Hampton and his vibraphone, Christian may not have actually invented his instrument, but he stood out nonetheless as one of its most visionary pioneers, toying with amplified sound at a time when such ventures had the overtones of a grand experiment. Yet Christian's advocacy of the electric guitar represents only the smallest part of his contribution to jazz. With his daring sense of intervallic high jinks, his dancing triplets and swinging sixteenth notes, his instinct for pouncing on the altered higher notes of the harmony, extracting the maximum amount of emotion from these flatted and sharpened tones—with these weapons at his command, Christian would have been a master at any instrument. His influence on later guitarists can hardly be overestimated. Listen to the small body of performances he left behind—such as "Seven Come Eleven," "Flying Home," "Breakfast Feud," and the amateur recordings of his sessions with the first generation of beboppers—and hear the melodic material that countless later guitarists would imitate, often borrowing whole phrases note for note as though these scattered 78s were a textbook on six-string soloing. The first great electric guitarist in jazz, Christian also demands respect as the most influential.

Born in Dallas and raised in the most impoverished section of Oklahoma City, Christian presented a striking contrast to the other modernists (Powell and Sauter, Bartók and Copland) linked with Goodman. Reserved, laconic, largely self-taught—novelist Ralph Ellison, who grew up with the guitarist, recalled him constructing primitive stringed instruments out of cigar boxes—the willowy Christian would have been easy to ignore if it were not for his stellar musicianship. "An impossible rube" was reportedly Goodman's first reaction to the guitarist. John Hammond, hearing of

Christian through pianist Mary Lou Williams, had flown to Oklahoma City, where he found him playing for $7.50 per week at the Ritz Cafe. Ever the matchmaker, Hammond arranged for Christian to come to California in August 1939 to meet Goodman. The clarinetist's reluctance gave way to rapt admiration after an impromptu jam, lasting almost an hour, on "Rose Room." "He wasn't the most imposing figure in the world," Goodman recalled some forty years later. "But, by gosh, when he sat down to play the guitar he was something. . . . He was way ahead of his time, and a joy to listen to."[2] Goodman immediately enlisted Christian into his small combo, now enlarged to a sextet. Within weeks, Christian had recorded a number of solos that would be widely emulated by other guitarists, and had performed with Goodman at Carnegie Hall. Jazz fans were quick to take notice, naming Christian as *Downbeat* poll winner on guitar for 1939, an honor that would be repeated in 1940 and 1941. But by then his career, though barely begun, was all but over.

In the spring of 1940, Christian was diagnosed with tuberculosis. Although advised to cut back on his activities, Christian found it difficult to turn down the growing number of performance opportunities now available to him. In addition to his small-combo work with Goodman, he also began playing with the big band, while after hours he frequently joined the jam sessions at Minton's Playhouse, a Harlem nightclub where the bebop style was being refined by a group of forward-looking modernists. But the long hours (the sessions would often last until 4 A.M.), combined with the excesses of Christian's lifestyle, served to undermine his already precarious state of health. In July 1941, he was admitted to Seaview Sanitarium on Staten Island, but even there Christian's situation remained precarious. On March 2, 1942, he died from pneumonia.

In the Goodman band, Christian formed part of a powerhouse rhythm section. With pianist Mel Powell, bassist John Simmons, and either Dave Tough or Sid Catlett on drums, Goodman's 1941 band was the most rhythmically exciting unit the clarinetist ever fronted. "There has never been a rhythm section like it in a white band," John Hammond has asserted. "Without question, it was the best Benny ever had."[3] Catlett's tenure with the band lasted only a few months, but a handful of studio sessions and recorded live dates testify to the impact he had. "Big Sid," as he was affectionately known, represented a striking contrast with the Krupa style that had defined the Goodman sound. Supportive, hard swinging without being overbearing, rock solid in keeping a tempo, rarely taking a feature solo but showing remarkable melodicism when he did—Catlett was a musician's musician, avoiding the limelight and working in the trenches to kick the band into action. And with what versatility—his two-decade career included gigs with Louis Armstrong, Sidney Bechet, Fletcher Henderson, Duke Ellington, Benny Goodman, Dizzy Gillespie, and Charlie Parker, a whole history of rhythm encompassed in those seven names.

These were late vintages of the Swing Era. On August 1, 1942, recording of jazz music came to a grinding halt as the result of a standoff between James Petrillo, head of the American Federation of Musicians, and the music industry. Petrillo insisted that the union be reimbursed for the increasing substitution of recorded music—in the form of radios, jukeboxes, and phonographs—for live performances. It wasn't until September 1943 that Decca came to terms with Petrillo, with the Columbia and Victor labels waiting for over another year before capitulating. But even earlier the U.S. government, in an effort to conserve raw materials for the war effort, had instituted a 30 percent reduction in the production of phonograph records. The war impacted the big bands in many other ways: musicians were conscripted; new woodwind, brass, or percussion instruments became almost impossible to find; and the rationing of gasoline made band tours difficult, if not impossible. In their aggregate effects, these causes did more to put an end to the Swing Era than the often-cited onslaught of bebop music.

But swing music also contributed to its own demise. The increasingly formulaic sound of the swing idiom, circa 1942—with only a few exceptional bands maintaining any degree of originality—indicated that this style was at the point of exhaustion as a dominant force in popular music. From this perspective, the rapid rise to prominence of Glenn Miller during these years served as a fitting close to the era. With Miller, the white big band came full circle, back to the ethos of the pre-Goodman period. Relying on catchy melodies, well-crafted if sometimes unambitious charts, and simple dance rhythms, Miller retained only a peripheral attachment to the jazz tradition. Hot solos and expressive soloists—so important to Ellington, Goodman, and Basie—never played a critical role in the Miller style. Miller's frequent reliance on syncopated riff songs, such as "Tuxedo Junction," "Pennsylvania 6-5000," and "In the Mood," marked his one major debt to the Swing Era. And even here, the riffs employed were always the most facile, the syncopations the most stereotyped. Instead of looking backward, Miller mostly anticipated the popular music of the postwar years, with its sweeter, less frenetic ambiance and its growing separation from the African American roots that had inspired Goodman and so many of his contemporaries. A decade would pass before the advent of rock and roll would reenact the Palomar phenomenon, tapping the more impassioned energy of the black R&B idiom and bringing it to a mass audience. In the interim, the pop music ethos of Miller and his heirs would reign supreme.

Between spring 1939 and September 1942, when Miller joined the U.S. Army Air Force, no band exerted a greater impact on the public's imagination. "Moonlight Serenade," a huge hit from 1939, showed how close to the sweet bands Miller was willing to venture. But the singular virtue of Miller's music was its sure instinct for memorable melodic lines. Harkening back to Beethoven's *Moonlight Sonata* and anticipating a host of pop instrumentals from later years (such as "Ebb Tide" and "Theme from *A Summer Place*"), this trademark Miller effort epitomized his knack for paring down the excesses of swing jazz and returning to the basics of tunesmithing. Simple, catchy, unpretentious, more concerned with novelty than originality: these were the traits Miller would bring to bear in a series of hit recordings, "Chattanooga Choo Choo," "Pennsylvania 6-5000," "In the Mood," "I've Got a Gal in Kalamazoo," "At Last," "Tuxedo Junction," and "A String of Pearls," among others. Underpinning Miller's success were a variety of instrumental textures that he had refined over the years, especially a velvety brass sound relying heavily on the use of mutes in the large trumpet and trombone sections, and sonorous reed work with its particularly effective use of clarinet, frequently in the lead role.

Although jazz fans often carp at Miller's popularity, which to their dismay has proven to be remarkably long-lived, this body of work is not so easily dismissed when dealt with on its own terms. As a jazz artist, Miller was a negligible force, but as a maven of popular music, Miller reached the highest rung. And of all the big band leaders, Miller may have been best equipped, in terms of temperament and style, for meeting the musical tastes of postwar America. But this was not in store for him. After the outbreak of World War II, Miller enlisted in the Army Air Corp—even though, at age thirty-eight, he would have been exempted from the draft. On December 15, 1944, the bandleader's plane disappeared while flying over the English Channel. No wreckage or bodies were ever found. In the absence of hard facts, rumors of all sorts circulated and continue to stir debate decades later.

Goodman, for his part, pressed forward with his commitment to modernism in the years following World War II. And though he had made a number of derisive remarks about bebop in the past, he now decided to incorporate many of the elements of the new style into his own music. Did the King of Swing really dare to leave swing behind him? In truth, Goodman's instincts would not allow him to embrace bop wholeheartedly, but he did hire a new crop of artists who managed to adopt progressive mannerisms without veering too far afield from more traditional sounds, such as saxophonists Stan Getz and Wardell Gray, pianists Mary Lou Williams and Jimmy Rowles, and clarinetist Stan Hasselgard. Yet few were surprised when Goodman's interest in matching the progressive sounds of Woody Herman and Stan Kenton proved to be short-lived. By the time of his fortieth birthday, in 1949, Goodman had effectively lost interest in following the trends of the younger generation. With his later bands, Goodman maintained a strict allegiance to the Swing Era style, supplemented by his ongoing second career in classical music. Except for a 1962 State Department–sponsored tour of the Soviet Union, Goodman rarely ventured into the limelight during the final three decades of his life. He seldom fronted a working band during this period, preferring to hire musicians for short tours or special events. Yet Goodman never let go of his perfectionism and his commitment to musical excellence. He continued to play scales every day before breakfast, striving for improvement even in his mid-seventies. On June 13, 1986, Benny Goodman was practicing Mozart when he was felled by a fatal heart attack.

KANSAS CITY JAZZ

The jazz recordings made during the 1920s and early 1930s provide modern listeners with little indication of the rapid and pervasive geographical spread of the music during those formative decades. Our histories tell us of New Orleans, Chicago, and New York—and little else. But no major urban area in the United States was left untouched by this new paradigm of American vernacular music. Piecing together the full history of this transformation would be a Herculean and perhaps impossible task. Our sources are too few, the subject too large. As it stands, a patchwork of information—drawn from hearsay, anecdotes, newspaper accounts, oral histories, and all too few recordings—conveys only the barest outlines, arbitrary and incomplete, of the broader sweep of this movement.

The chance intervention of various record companies saved a few of these regional bands from total obscurity. And even fewer managed to develop national reputations. McKinney's Cotton Pickers was one of these. Formed in Ohio and later enjoying a long residency in Detroit, this band was admired widely for its solid recordings featuring the arrangements of Don Redman. Such notoriety, however, was the exception rather than the rule. Plying their trade in Miami, Alonzo Ross's De Luxe Syncopators caused little stir in the jazz world, but eight mostly forgotten sides recorded for Victor during a tour to the Midwest reveal a polished and swinging band that in its day (1927) would have stood out even in the major centers of jazz. The history of jazz in the Carolinas is typically ignored even by specialists in jazz esoterica, but several ensembles are known to us from scattered recordings: Dave Taylor's Dixie Orchestra, Jimmy Gunn's Dixie Serenaders, the Carolina Cotton Pickers, and the Bob Pope Orchestra, the last leaving behind over three dozen sides to indicate its prescient conception of 4/4 swing. In Los Angeles, the studio work of local bands led by Sonny Clay, Curtis Mosby, Paul Howard, and Les Hite testify to the rapid spread of the New Orleans style and other influences to the West Coast. A number of St. Louis bands made records, including trumpeter Charlie Creath's Jazz-O-Maniacs (which released twelve bluesy sides in the mid-1920s), the Missourians, and the Jeter-Pillars Club Plantation Orchestra. The trumpet tradition was especially vibrant in St. Louis and featured, in addition to Creath, Oliver Cobb, Dewey Jackson, and Harold "Shorty" Baker (and, some years later, Miles Davis and Clark Terry). In Memphis, we find Blue Steele and His Orchestra; in Milwaukee, we encounter Grant Moore and hear word-of-mouth accounts of never-recorded Eli Rice; in Cincinnati, Zack Whyte; in Omaha, Red Perkins and Nat Towles. No major urban area was without its dance orchestras, and smaller communities hosted the many bands that went on the road.

And go on the road they did! Memoirs and biographies of the era are full of accounts of musicians on the move, one-night stands, ephemeral triumphs, and resounding failures in distant cities, or disastrous tours culminating in stranded musicians struggling to earn a fare home. The advent of affordable transportation made such tours possible, while Depression economics made them necessary. As America's infrastructure of asphalt, track, and highway linked up city, town, and village, the nomadic bands of jazz, the modern equivalent of the wandering minstrels of yore, seized the opportunities that this trailblazing offered. Distances of anywhere from several hundred to a thousand miles from gig to gig were not uncommon for these road warriors. From this institutionalized wanderlust comes the term *territory band*, signifying the move beyond city limits to wider geographies of these dance orchestras on wheels.

The Southwest proved an especially fertile area for territory bands. Texas, with its spread-out geography and relatively large population, offered the greatest opportunity, with developed markets for dance music in Dallas–Fort Worth, Houston, San Antonio, El Paso, Austin, Amarillo, and other cities. With homegrown audiences so plentiful, the Texas bands developed to a high degree in relative isolation from outside influences. The black theater circuit, which brought top-quality African

American musical acts to many other cities, did not reach Texas until the middle 1920s. But traditional and down-home musical styles were pervasive—so much so that a distinctive blend of jazz and country emerged under the name of "western swing." Its most famous exponent, Bob Wills, made his name in the 1930s with his Fiddle Boys or Light Crust Doughboys, before settling on the soon-to-be-famous Texas Playboys. As with Goodman, Wills built his reputation over the radio and parlayed local fame into a national audience—most notably on his 1940 hit "New San Antonio Rose," a song that delighted fans with its mixture of big band horns and countrified strings.

The impact of the New Orleans diaspora, so decisive in other parts of the country, was less strongly felt in this region. In contrast, the sound of the blues was pervasive in Texas, building on a local aural tradition that had been shaped by Blind Lemon Jefferson, Leadbelly, and Blind Willie Johnson, among others. So-called "Texas piano," with its evocation of honky-tonk and boogie-woogie, drew heavily from the blues, as did a legion of later Texas guitarists and singers. And with the rise of larger dance bands, this predilection for the blues again stood out. Gradually, the influence of Redman and the Northeast arrangers was also felt and incorporated into this grassroots style, and is especially evident in the work of Alphonso Trent, one of the best of the Texas jazz bandleaders of the day. But, for most ensembles, an informal "head chart" style relying on simple memorized parts was preferred. Many of these same elements would figure prominently in the Kansas City style as it evolved in the 1920s and 1930s. One need not look far to find the reason for this convergence of styles: many of the Texas bands—largely forgotten ensembles such as the Troy Floyd Orchestra, the Deluxe Melody Boys, the Happy Black Aces, and Terrence T. Holder and His Dark Clouds of Joy—served as traveling academies for a number of musicians who would later move to Kansas City.

Again, economic factors played a key role in drawing many of these performers to Kansas City. A wide-open town with a tolerant—albeit corrupt—city hall controlled by political boss Tom Pendergast, Kansas City offered a hospitable environment to most of the social vices. And as the histories of New Orleans and Chicago attest, where leisure and whiskey flourished, so typically did jazz. One newspaper columnist, after visiting the city during the Pendergast years, advised his readers: "If you want to see some sin, forget about Paris and go to Kansas City."[4] At the Reno Club, where Count Basie entertained, beer cost five cents, Scotch ran fifteen cents, marijuana sticks sold three for a quarter, and a "visit upstairs" commanded two dollars. These may seem like small sums, but in aggregate they amounted to big business. A formidable forerunner to Las Vegas, Kansas City boasted gambling revenues of around $100 million per year during this period; in addition, roughly $1 million worth of illicit drugs was sold annually; figure in prostitution and alcohol, and the total impact of the underground economy on the so-called Pendergast prosperity was enormous. As the effects of the Depression ravaged the music communities of other cities in the region, more and more players gravitated to Kansas City to share in the good times. By the middle of the 1930s, Kansas City had emerged as a potential rival to New York and Chicago in its concentration of outstanding jazz talent.

But Kansas City jazz was much more than a matter of favorable supply-and-demand conditions. A distinct style of jazz gradually took root in the city's environs, drawing on disparate elements: the blues tradition of the Southwest, the big band sounds of the Northeast, and the informal jam session ethos of Harlem. Each of these would be transformed in its Kansas City form. The elaborate orchestrations favored by the New York arrangers would be pared down, giving way to simpler riff-based charts. These quasi-minimalist textures of Kansas City jazz imparted a looser feeling to the music, allowing even big band performances to retain the hot-and-ready ethos of the after-hours jam sessions, whose informality of spirit lurked behind—and no doubt inspired—the head charts and written scores. But more than anything, the rhythmic essence of this regional style would set it apart. The two-beat pulse of New Orleans and Chicago would give way to a more modern 4/4 conception of time. Tempos gravitated toward a middle ground. Yet this had little to do, as some have suggested, with lower standards of musicianship among Kaycee players. When the occasion so warranted (hear, for instance, the Moten band on "Toby"), the best of the local ensembles could stoke the fire at a pace well beyond 300 beats per minute, outracing even the fastest jitterbugger on the dance floor. In most settings, however, the ambiance of Kansas City jazz life demanded a relaxed swing, with only a subtle undercurrent of urgency.

This new sense of time was accompanied by a shift in the nature of the rhythm section, a rejuvenescence that reached its fullest realization in the Count Basie band of the mid and late 1930s. Gliding over the powerful 4/4 bass lines of Walter Page, drummer Jo Jones was able to adopt a more open sound, relying less on the insistent pulsations of the bass drum, so prominent in the work of earlier jazz percussionists, instead employing his high hat as the primal heartbeat of the band. The result was a less staccato sound, a more continuous pulse, a shimmering layer of percussion. Time was now a cresting wave, fluid in its motion, rather than the steady, inevitable ticking of a clock. In this context, the role of the piano also changed, *needed* to change. Instead of evoking the ground rhythm with a steady four-to-a-bar stride, the keyboard now offered accents, fills, and asides, became one partner in a conversation, not a long-winded orator declaiming first principles. No one filled this new role—that of the "comping" pianist—better than Count Basie, who stands out as the best-remembered and most beloved of the Kansas City pioneers. In this symbiotic process, Basie, Page, and Jones collectively reengineered the nature of time and space in the context of jazz, not only putting Kansas City on the map as a major jazz center but marking a permanent shift in the rhythmic essence of African American music.

Even before Basie arrived in Kansas City, stranded there in 1927 as a member of a touring show, the incipient sounds of that community's distinctive style of jazz were already in the air. Bennie Moten, a Kansas City native who had studied piano with two of Scott Joplin's pupils, initiated a decade-long recording career in 1923; in fact, Moten fronted one of the first black jazz bands to record anywhere. From the start, the influence of the blues on Moten's work was pronounced—all eight of the numbers recorded at the band's first session in September 1923 were based on the blues form. Over the next decade, this ensemble would undergo a stunning transformation, shedding the last vestiges of the New Orleans tradition—replacing tuba with string bass, banjo with guitar, growing from a combo into a big band—and absorbing influences from other parts of the country, including the Northeast where the band visited on tours after signing with the Victor label in 1926. In time, Moten's soloists proved capable of matching up with the best of the East Coast ensembles, and were especially well served by a strong body of charts, especially those by Eddie Durham, who joined the band in 1929. These captured the loose-and-easy Kansas City ambiance to perfection, mirroring the freewheeling linear movement of the local improvisational style. Moten used these various building blocks to expand the vocabulary of Kansas City jazz, meanwhile serving as mentor to a large group of musicians who would bring this style to greater national attention, most notably Count Basie. By the time of the Moten band's landmark Victor session from 1932, it was playing at a peak level that few jazz ensembles anywhere could match. This December 13, 1932, visit to the studio produced a number of the most exciting big band tracks of the decade, including classic sides such as "Toby," "Prince of Wails," "The Blue Room," and "Moten Swing." Yet these would also be the Moten band's final recordings.

Moten's ensemble had strengthened as he had increasingly attracted talented sidemen from other groups, especially Walter Page's Blue Devils. Originally formed in Kansas City in 1923 as Billy King's Road Show, the group was on the verge of breaking up in Oklahoma City in 1925 when Page took over the band, renaming it and expanding from nine to thirteen players. Having studied music at the University of Kansas, Page brought a rare degree of polish to the rough-and-ready road bands that he graced. With his excellent sight-reading skills and versatility (he also played saxophone), Page had already taken on the role of musical director even before assuming leadership of the Blue Devils. But it was as a bassist that Page made his greatest impact. Cradling the instrument against his massive body frame—Page weighed in at over 250 pounds—he overpowered the bass, drawing out a stronger, more resonant tone than any of his predecessors. True, the shift away from using tuba or bass saxophone as the harmonic foundation for the jazz band was already well under way before the rise of the Blue Devils, but no one did more than Walter Page to legitimize this change, to assert the primacy of the string bass as the most flexible and expressive voice for the "walking line."

The story of Basie's initiation into the Blue Devils has often been recounted, never with more flair than in his autobiography, *Good Morning Blues*. After a late drinking session, Basie made his way back to his Tulsa hotel room, where he fell asleep only to be awakened in late morning by the sounds of a Louis Armstrong record—or so he thought. Groggy and hung over, yet fascinated by the music, Basie made his way downstairs, where the Blue Devils were set up on the back of a truck, performing to a gathered crowd.

I just stood there listening and looking, because I had never heard anything like that band in my life. . . . There was such a team spirit among those guys, and it came out in the music, and as you stood there looking and listening you couldn't help wishing that you were a part of it. Everything about them really got to me, and as things worked out, hearing them that day was probably the most important turning point in my musical career.[5]

The young pianist soon found himself a member of the Blue Devils, a band that was a magnet for great talent—but incapable of holding onto it. Count Basie, Lester Young, Eddie Durham, Jimmy Rushing, Hot Lips Page, Buster Smith: all of them eventually moved from the Blue Devils to the Bennie Moten band. Even leader Page ultimately made the jump to his more successful competitor. And though the Blue Devils lingered on for some time under Buster Smith's leadership, the premier position in the region had already been usurped by Moten. Under different circumstances, Moten's band would have become established in the history of jazz as the paragon representative of the Kansas City sound. Instead, Moten fell ill during a road trip to Denver, and the doctors advised immediate surgery. Moten did not survive the operation. He was forty years old at the time of his death. Most of his sidemen eventually found their way into a successor group led by Count Basie.

Born in Red Bank, New Jersey, on August 21, 1904, William "Count" Basie grew up in a distinctly working-class setting. His father served as coachman and caretaker for a local judge, while his mother took in laundry to supplement the family income. The influence of Harlem stride would predominate in his early musical education, but the youngster's environment exposed him to a wide range of other American vernacular music styles, garnered from player pianos, theater shows, traveling carnivals, and the like. "I just wanted to be on the road with a show so much that I would have gone along just to be a water boy for the elephants if I could."[6] Some time later Basie began doing chores for the local motion picture theater proprietor in exchange for free admission to films and live shows. Before long the adolescent was running the projection booth and filling in for the house pianist. He had already initiated piano studies at home, under his mother's insistence, but drums remained Basie's primary musical outlet for some time—until the precocious skills of his friend Sonny Greer (later to achieve fame as drummer with the Ellington band) convinced him to focus on the keyboard.

Basie's father encouraged his son to work with him, mowing lawns and looking after houses on the local estates. But as his piano skills improved, Basie came to realize that a musical career might offer a way out of the menial jobs his parents and peers pursued. Soon the vibrant nightlife of New York beckoned. Early on, he met James P. Johnson, Willie "The Lion" Smith, and Fats Waller. Waller was the predominant influence and mentor among this group, as Basie himself later acknowledged; the older stride master occasionally allowed the youngster to play the house organ during Waller's stint at Harlem's Lincoln Theater and later helped him get work with a vaudeville act. The impact of the stride style on Basie's music remained a strong undercurrent throughout his career, despite his more minimalist aesthetic—well past his fiftieth birthday the Count recorded an album, *The Kid from Red Bank*, on which the two-handed attack of these early models came surprisingly to the fore. But the blues would prove an even more vital source of inspiration for Basie, although not immediately. "I hadn't ever really paid attention to [the blues] and I hadn't ever played the blues. I hadn't got my first taste of real blues until the burlesque show I first left New York with played in Kansas City."[7] But once transplanted to Kansas City, Basie not only fell increasingly under the sway of the strong local blues piano tradition, exemplified by Pete Johnson and Jay McShann, but in time came to match these masters in articulating an authentic and heartfelt blues style.

Yet there was much in Basie's piano style that refuses to be reduced to a discussion of influences. One of the most singular keyboardists in the history of jazz, Basie refined a sparser, more open-sounding approach than any of his predecessors. It was almost as though jazz piano, under Basie's tutelage, stopped shouting and learned to talk, learned to banter and whisper, at times even to hold its tongue in a silence that said more than the most high-flown eloquence. One of the many delights of his music comes from hearing how he could do so much with so little. Incisive, robust, energized—the ends achieved seem at odds with the meager means employed. Some have been tempted to dismiss Basie as a mere tinkler of the ivories, more noteworthy for his band than for his skills as a player; yet for Basie, a mere tinkle, a simple fill, or the hint of a vamp were rich with implication. These mannerisms became increasingly pronounced late in his career—and at times Basie veered dangerously close to self-parody. But the polish, ingenuity, and veneer of self-deprecating humor that accompanied this music always kept it sounding fresh, even as Basie approached his eightieth birthday. Most of all, the complex note-filled piano attack of the next generation reinforced, if only by contrast, the uniqueness of Count Basie.

But Basie—like Ellington and Goodman—would not have reached such a pinnacle of artistry were he not equally a visionary, were it not for his skills of leadership and his ability to motivate others. Starting with a core group of Moten alumni that included Lester Young, Walter Page, Herschel Evans, Buster Smith, and Hot Lips Page, Basie soon enhanced the rhythm section with the addition of Jo Jones and Freddie Green. This was the most supple, the strongest jazz rhythm section of the era. More than this, it prefigured the advances of the next decade, when modern jazz would build lavish superstructures on the pared-down landscape cleared away by Basie, Page, Jones, and Green. The simplified left-hand voicings of Bud Powell and the pregnant pauses of a Thelonious Monk—these could only come after Basie had blazed the path; just as the pointillistic drumming of a Kenny Clarke or Max Roach would presuppose a Jo Jones. Much has been made of the influence of the Kansas City tradition on the modern jazz of native son Charlie Parker, but that is only one of the many links between these two schools of jazz. Glimpses of the future are everywhere apparent on the Basie recordings from the 1930s.

Even an average soloist would have sounded good with this support. But the Basie band was loaded with talent. Lester Young's genius has been much discussed and analyzed by jazz historians, but he was far from the only star improviser in Basie's horn sections. The contributions of tenor saxophonist Herschel Evans are often obscured by the renown of his celebrated associate, but his powerful sound and rough-hewn phrases—his "Texas moan"—communicated a visceral excitement few of his contemporaries could match. There can be little doubt that his contrasting style both spurred Lester and set off the latter's more delicate improvisations in sharp relief. The complementary nature of their two approaches can be heard to good effect on performances such as "Blue and Sentimental," "Doggin' Around," and "One O'Clock Jump." Had Evans lived longer—he died from heart failure in 1939 shortly before his thirtieth birthday—he would likely have moved out of Young's shadow and established himself as a major tenor voice. Vocalist Jimmy Rushing was primarily a ballad singer when Basie took over the band, but in time he developed a deeply personal approach to the blues. There was a wonderful paradox in Rushing's singing. His resonant voice was a marvel of strength and authority, yet even at his highest energy levels, Rushing somehow retained the clean intonation and heartfelt sensitivity of a balladeer. This happy marriage of the down-home authenticity of the blues with the urbanity of a pop sensibility would set a model for many later Basie singers, such as Helen Humes and Joe Williams. Hot Lips Page's exposure to the blues dated back long before his Moten days, when he had worked with Ma Rainey and Bessie Smith, but the influence of Armstrong also loomed large in his playing (and he eventually left Basie to work with Armstrong's manager Joe Glaser in an ill-fated attempt to become a marquee star). Page was one of the hottest players in the band, and his tone and phrasing revealed a sure instinct for the dramatic. Buck Clayton, who replaced Page, offered a more lyrical style, with a burnished tone that was equally at home in the Basie big band or in small combos alongside Billie Holiday, where Clayton contributed some of his most memorable work. The addition of trumpeter Harry "Sweets" Edison and trombonist Dickie Wells a short time later further enhanced the band's core of soloists, both players distinguished by their direct, conversational approaches to improvisation, set off by impeccable timing. Perhaps the Basie ensemble lacked the arranging and composing genius of an Ellington, or the instrumental virtuosity of a Goodman, but as a "blowing" band it was without peer.

Radio broadcasts and word of mouth soon brought the Basie band to the attention of power brokers in the music industry. A few hardy souls traveled to Kansas City to hear for themselves. In 1936, John Hammond made several visits, his interest excited by a chance hearing of a broadcast performance by the band. Dave Kapp of Decca Records soon followed, as did Joe Glaser, who left town with Hot Lips Page under contract. Finally, Joe Belford, manager of New York's Roseland Ballroom, made the trek. The combined impact of these vistors from the East bearing homage was soon felt. Hammond set up Basie with booking agent Willard Alexander, Kapp signed Basie to the Decca label, and within a few months the band was headlining at Roseland.

Even before arriving in New York, Basie undertook a memorable small-group session under Hammond's direction in Chicago—recording under the name Jones-Smith Incorporated to circumvent the Decca contract. "It was one of the only perfect sessions I ever had," was Hammond's later judgment. And with good reason. Jones, forced to play without a bass drum because of the small size of the studio, reveals his mastery of the high hat and snare drum. Basie's style, with its winning offhand aplomb, comes across as almost fully formed. Page's basslines are executed with metronomic sureness and a tone so full that, on their own, they could swing the whole band. But Lester Young is the real star here. On "Oh, Lady Be Good," he contributes a famous solo, one often memorized and imitated by later generations of jazz players. In its fluidity, clever rhythmic phrasing, and sheer creativity, it stands out as one of the most forward-looking improvisations of the decade.

In New York, the band opened its four-week stint at Roseland to mixed reviews. George Simon, writing in *Metronome*, accused the brass and sax sections of playing out of tune, and even Hammond acknowledged the band's inconsistency in a *Downbeat* review. Growing pains—the result of Basie's quick expansion from nine to thirteen players—may have disrupted the band's cohesion, but the group's problems with staying in tune perhaps owed more to the inferior instruments that many African American horn players relied on during this period. In any event, the first Decca recordings, made the day after the Roseland engagment ended, showcase a swinging, confident ensemble. During his two-year relationship with this label, Basie developed many of the memorable blues-tinged compositions that would help define his contribution to the jazz idiom, including "One O'Clock Jump" and "Good Morning Blues." The addition of Edison, Wells, saxophonist Earle Warren, and trombonist Benny Morton during the Decca years further reinforced the strength of Basie's section and solo work. The contribution of guitarist Freddie Green, another band newcomer, was less noticed by most listeners, but Green's presence served to solidify the already stellar section of Basie-Jones-Page. By the time the Basie orchestra began making its 1939–40 recording sessions under Hammond's supervision—which produced a series of classic sides including "Taxi War Dance," "Clap Hands, Here Comes Charlie," and "Tickle Toe"—it had earned growing respect as one of the very best big bands in jazz.

The departure of the Basie contingent took place toward the close of the great period of Kansas City jazz. City boss Tom Pendergast's conviction on tax evasion charges in 1939, resulting in a year behind bars in Leavenworth, signaled a move away from the fast and loose attitudes that had fueled the local economy during the Great Depression. Even earlier, as the Swing Era took off with full force in other locales, many musicians who had come to Kansas City for the opportunities it provided found ready audiences and gainful employment elsewhere. But even in these late days, world-class jazz could still be heard in the city's environs. Bandleader Andy Kirk, who had assumed leadership of Terrence "T." Holder's Dark Clouds of Joy in 1929, continued to maintain a home base in Kansas City, although his recordings and frequent road trips brought his music to the attention of a wider audience. "Until the Real Thing Comes Along" proved to be a major 1936 hit for the band, and for a while Kirk boasted even greater box office appeal than Basie. With its poised rhythmic flow and strong blues roots, the Twelve Clouds of Joy (as the band was now called under its new leader) was an exemplary exponent of Kansas City jazz, and, though its pool of soloists could not quite match Basie's, Kirk had found in pianist and arranger Mary Lou Williams a major talent.

Williams had studied piano, composition, and harmony during her formative years in Pittsburgh, but her career in music had come to something of a standstill after her marriage in the 1920s to John Williams, a saxophonist who worked in the Kirk band. Since Williams's wife "could play a little piano," she was enlisted as a backup for the band's working keyboardist, Marion Jackson. But, as her 1930 solo piano recording of "Night Life" makes clear, Williams was no amateur, rather a full-fledged keyboard powerhouse with a stirring two-handed attack. Although blessed with perfect pitch, good time, and a sure sense for the blues, Williams was only slowly recognized as a major talent in the male-dominated world of jazz. Women had long been accepted as vocalists, but few had enjoyed successful careers as jazz instrumentalists, and even fewer managed to make records during this period. In 1939, the International Sweethearts of Rhythm, an all-female swing band, would be formed, and after a well-received debut at the Howard Theater would tour the United States and Europe, as well as record for the Victor label. But their example would stand out as a rare exception. Williams, for her part, gradually rose through the ranks of the Kirk organization: for a time she acted as chauffeur for the band (she also worked as a hearse driver during this period), eventually securing a spot as a staff writer and full-time performer. But from 1930 until 1942, Williams served as the main catalyst for the Kirk ensemble. Her charts, such as "Mary's Idea" and "Walkin' and Swingin'," were marked by a happy mixture of experimentalism and rhythmic urgency, while her playing soon earned her star billing as "The Lady Who Swings the Band." In later years, Williams's progressive tendencies became even more pronounced, leading her to adopt much of the bebop vocabulary and inspiring her to compose extended pieces, most notably the *Zodiac Suite* from 1945. Following her conversion to Catholicism in the 1950s, Williams wrote and performed a number of sacred works and continued to expand her musical horizons long after the age when most artists settle comfortably into a familiar style and repertoire, even collaborating with free-jazz titan Cecil Taylor in a controversial meeting of minds. At this Carnegie Hall concert, held four years before Williams's death in 1981, two confident masters of the jazz keyboard confronted each other head on, and neither side blinked. As such daring gestures made clear, none of the Kansas City pioneers brought a broader perspective to their music making than Mary Lou Williams.

But the most influential of the Kansas City players from the 1930s would clearly be Lester Young, who ironically may have been the most introverted, the least focused on inspiring imitators. Redefining the role of the tenor sax was only the first of Young's achievements. In the process, he profoundly changed the essence of melodic improvisation in jazz, offering an alternative to the hot, syncopated style forged by Armstrong and emulated by countless others. The flowering of cool jazz, a supple manner of phrasing across bar lines, a greater sensitivity to intervals such as sixths and ninths not present in the underlying harmonies, the elevation of jazz above hoary clichés borrowed from the New Orleans and Chicago traditions—all these transformations in the music, changes that would gain momentum in later years, owe a great deal to the foresight of Lester Willis Young. In particular, his small combo recordings, especially those with Billie Holiday, revealed a new facet of jazz, one in which the heated syncopations that had given birth to the music were subsumed in a more delicate chamber music style. But this was much more than an expansion in the techniques of jazz improvisation. In espousing a new aesthetic for jazz, Young also broadened the music's emotional vocabulary, broaching an intimacy and subtle gradations of feeling hitherto unknown to the jazz idiom.

JAZZ COMBO STYLE IN THE 1930S

Born in Woodville, Mississippi, on August 27, 1909, and raised in nearby New Orleans, Lester Young came of age in a period marked by an unprecedented blossoming of African American music in this region. Young may have had some contact with the pioneering "hot" jazz players who were virtually at his doorstep during these formative years, yet other sources of inspiration—marching bands, minstrel shows, popular songs—apparently made a stronger impression on the child's imagination. In addition, both parents were strict Baptists, and it is likely that Lester heard far more church music than either jazz or blues during his childhood. In truth, there were all too few leisure hours for the youngster to taste the pleasures of New Orleans jazz: much of Young's early life was spent finding ways to contribute to the family income. Around the age of five, he began working odd jobs—polishing shoes, distributing handbills, selling newspapers. Even Lester's introduction to performing music was driven by household financial needs. In 1919, Lester's father took a job as leader of a circus band. The son, having studied the rudiments of the violin, trumpet, and drums, was soon enlisted as a sideman in the group. He was only ten years old at the time.

Young's relationship with his father, a stern taskmaster, was stormy at best. Sensitive and shy, Lester Young set a pattern early in life of retreating in the face of conflict. Sometimes this retreat was physical, other times merely psychological. Eccentricities, hip jargon, odd mannerisms—the various bric-a-brac of Young's personality, celebrated by the Beat generation, were as much self-defense mechanisms as attempts to set a fashionable tone. Several times Young ran away from home during his teenage years, once disappearing for as long as two months. Around the time of Lester's eighteenth birthday, he left again to join Art Bronson's so-called Bostonians, a misnomer given that this territory band worked primarily in Colorado, the Dakotas, Nebraska, and other nearby areas. In 1929, Young returned to the family band, but left again before the close of the year. By this time he had developed a fair degree of proficiency on the saxophone—he had first started playing the alto sax at age thirteen, and while with Bronson settled on the tenor as his main instrument. Over the next few years, Young bounced from job to job, returning briefly to the family band, working for a period with Walter Page's Blue Devils, rejoining the Bostonians, and playing in Minneapolis, New Mexico, and a host of other locales.

By 1932, Young had settled down with the Blue Devils, but that group was now in its final days. Walter Page had already left, and Buster Smith stepped in as leader. In late 1933, the Blue Devils disbanded, and Young returned to Kansas City, where he played with many of the local ensembles. Already he was developing a reputation as an outstanding young saxophonist. But the arrival in Kansas City of the Fletcher Henderson band in December 1933 gave Lester the rare chance of testing his skills face-to-face with the most prominent tenor saxophonist in jazz. Coleman Hawkins was the featured soloist with the Henderson band, and an after-hours jam session at the Cherry Blossom provided a venue for the visiting celebrity to test his mettle against Kansas City's finest. Mary Lou Williams, who was present that night, later described the scene:

The word went round that Hawkins was in the Cherry Blossom, and within about half an hour there were Lester Young, Ben Webster, Herschel Evans, Herman Walder, and one or two unknown tenors piling in the club to blow. Bean didn't know the Kaycee tenor men were so terrific, and he couldn't get himself together though he played all morning. . . .

Hawkins was in his singlet taking turns with the Kaycee men. It seems he had run into something he didn't expect. Lester's style was light, and, as I said, it took him maybe five choruses to warm up. But then he would really blow; then you couldn't handle him on a cutting session. That was how Hawkins got hung up. . . . Yes, Hawkins was king until he met those crazy Kansas City tenor men.[8]

At the time of this encounter, Hawkins was on the brink of leaving the Henderson band—where his replacement would be Lester Young. Despite his jam session success at the Cherry Blossom, Young's stint with Henderson was short-lived and poorly received. Most of the sidemen had wanted Chu Berry, a Hawkins disciple who would later become a star soloist with Cab Calloway, to take over for the departing tenorist. Young's playing was deemed too light, his tone too thin. While Hawkins (and many of his followers) boasted a vibrato as wide as the lapels on a zoot suit, Young maintained a pellucid tone of almost classical purity. His lines were less rooted to the ground beat, less tied to the underlying harmonies. Such stylistic choices were odd ones in the context of the jazz world of the day, and virtually amounted to heresy in the context of the Fletcher Henderson band. Henderson's wife went so far as to play Hawkins's records for Young, citing them as examples of how the tenor *should* sound. Within a few months, Young left the group, returning to Kansas City. For a time he worked with Andy Kirk, then freelanced with a number of bands, and finally joined Count Basie shortly before the latter's rise to national prominence. Only then, during the closing years of the decade, was Young able to establish his tenor sound as a valid alternative to the Hawkins model.

This was no small achievement. During the late 1920s and early 1930s, Hawkins had forged a powerful full-bodied approach to the tenor saxophone, one that would come to define the mainstream sound of that instrument for years to come. Incorporating elements drawn from Louis Armstrong, Art Tatum, and others, Hawkins constructed a robust, harmonically adept style. The uncertain phrasing and slap tonguing of his earliest recordings had by now been replaced by a smoother legato, a ponderous tone, and a melodic gift enlivened by Hawkins's mastery of passing chords. Only a few weeks after the stock market crash of 1929, Hawkins participated in a pathbreaking interracial session as part of the Mound City Blue Blowers. "One Hour," from this date, is an especially memorable performance, with Hawkins taking the piece at a much slower tempo than any he had attempted previously on record. The result is a rhapsodic mood piece of the kind that would soon become a trademark of the tenorist. Along with Beiderbecke and Trumbauer's work on "Singin' the Blues" (1927) and Louis Armstrong's "I Can't Give You Anything but Love" (1929), "One Hour" represents a key milestone in the early evolution of the jazz ballad style. Over the next few years, Hawkins would build on this distinctive and influential approach to slow tempos, the process culminating in his iconic 1939 recording of "Body and Soul." In contrast to the plaintive style inaugurated by Beiderbecke and Trumbauer (and taken up by Young), Hawkins offered a more expansive approach to the jazz ballad: implying double time with his intricate constructions, the saxophonist would often fill up each beat in the bar with dense, harmonically-charged phrases, employing these baroque arpeggios as cornerstones for a whole solo. Later in his career, Hawkins would typically use fewer notes in such contexts, but these early forays set a standard with their analytical probing of the popular ballads of the day.

In 1932, Fletcher Henderson began advertising his star soloist as the "World's Greatest Tenor Saxophonist." It was a fitting title, and Hawkins was no doubt pleased at the recognition. But morale in the Henderson band was low, work was sporadic, and the leader often ineffective or disorganized. Meanwhile, Hawkins was increasingly active in other settings. In 1933, he undertook his first sessions as leader and also performed on a series of memorable sides with trumpeter Henry "Red" Allen. The following February, Hawkins participated in an interracial session, alongside Benny Goodman, and a few days later made his last recording as a member of the Fletcher Henderson band, ending an eleven-year tenure.

The final break came when Hawkins was offered the opportunity to perform in England by Jack Hylton, an influential British bandleader and booking agent. Hawkins requested a short leave of absence from the Henderson band—in one or two months, he promised, he would be back. In fact, Hawkins would spend most of the decade overseas and would not see Henderson again for six years. From England, Hawkins soon journeyed to the continent, where he played in Holland, Denmark, Switzerland, Norway, and France. Like many American jazz musicians before and since, Hawkins enjoyed the tolerant and receptive attitude of the European audiences. At his arrival in Copenhagen, five thousand fans gathered at the railway station to greet him. A few of them carried Hawkins, who was seated on an ornate chair, to his waiting taxi. A similar entourage awaited his arrival in Oslo, where Hawkins was presented with flowers, and young ladies struggled to get a glimpse of the visiting celebrity. In England, the periodical *Melody Maker*, which had long lavished praise on Hawkins, enlisted him to contribute three articles outlining the secrets of his jazz saxophone method. While working in Switzerland, he learned to ski and toyed with the idea of becoming a vocalist.

Some fifteen years had elapsed since James Reese Europe, Will Marion Cook, and Sidney Bechet had brought the sounds of hot African American music overseas. In the interim, the European audience for jazz had grown more sophisticated, more fanatical. Around the time of Hawkins's arrival, a coterie of ardent supporters—Hugues Panassié, Charles Delaunay, Robert Goffin, and others—were taking the lead on a variety of fronts to promote jazz music on the continent. Their activities extended to founding *Le Jazz Hot*, often cited as the first jazz magazine (although Sweden's *Orkester Journalen* predated it by two years)—which made its debut only a few weeks after Hawkins arrived in Paris; the first issue was printed on the back of a program for Hawkins's concert at Salle Pleyel—as well as to establishing venues for performance, producing recordings, undertaking historical and discographical research, and exhorting their contemporaries to treat jazz seriously as an art form. Their efforts would shape the European taste for jazz and eventually be felt back in the United States.

But European participation in the jazz world was no longer merely as a passive, if receptive, audience. As Hawkins soon saw, European jazz musicians had made enormous strides by the mid-1930s. Although the vast majority were little more than imitators of models from America, a few artists of the highest order were drawing on local traditions and fusing them with jazz to create vibrant new hybrids. Of these pioneers of European jazz, the Quintette du Hot Club de France, featuring guitarist Django Reinhardt and violinist Stéphane Grappelli, had attained an especially rare degree of inspiration, establishing itself as one of the most important jazz groups of the day.

The band's instrumentation revealed a fresh break with the traditions of American jazz. In place of the brass, reed, and percussion elements so prominent in African American music, the Quintette employed a violin, three guitars, and bass. But the distinctive character of this group went beyond its reliance on strings instead of horns. Reinhardt and Grappelli brought a specifically European perspective—drawing on gypsy music, classical composition, and local folk traditions—to bear on their jazz work. The band's repertoire was drawn from disparate sources: a swing version of a Bach concerto movement or a bolero inspired by Ravel might be juxtaposed with pop compositions by George Gershwin or Noel Coward, or coexist alongside a New Orleans warhorse such as "Tiger Rag." This was music that respected no national boundaries, as nomadic as Reinhardt's gypsy forebears. The cross-cultural roots of the Quintette were felt also in the style of improvisation, especially Reinhardt's. With a fresh lyricism, he cut through the clichés of early American jazz guitar, discarding the banjo-inspired syncopations and ponderous rhythms in favor of more a fluid approach, one that was both melodically inventive and rhythmically inspired. Grappelli, for his part, thrived in this context, but this artist demonstrated, in later decades, that his violin could adapt to almost any type of setting, jazz or otherwise. During the course of a career that spanned more than a half-century, Grappelli would create an impressive, diverse body of work that found him in collaboration with modernists (Gary Burton, McCoy Tyner), classicists (Yehudi Menuhin, Yo-Yo Ma), practitioners of roots music (David Grisman, Mark O'Connor), and, of course, traditionalists from his own generation (Earl Hines, Bill Coleman).

Born in Belgium on January 23, 1910, and raised in a gypsy settlement outside Paris, Jean Baptiste "Django" Reinhardt was playing professionally even before his teens. He enjoyed little formal education in music—or in other areas, for that matter: Reinhardt was illiterate and signed his name with an X. But he picked up an odd assortment of skills—in billiards, in fishing, in music—at which he greatly excelled. His musical pursuits began with violin and eventually gravitated to the guitar. In 1928, Django's left hand was severely injured in a caravan fire, essentially depriving him of the use of two fingers. Yet Reinhardt's music would show few signs of compromise with this disability, other than a reliance on chords that use just two or three fingers—emphasizing sixths and ninths in a manner that has been often been imitated by later performers working in this style. Django's supple guitar technique stood out for its speed and assertiveness, and at a time when this instrument was seen more as an accompanist than as a significant solo voice in jazz bands, Reinhardt demonstrated his skill in constructing horn-oriented single-note lines. His rhythmic approach was equally distinctive, and the rapid up-and-down strumming style of accompaniment, known as *la pompe*, has become a trademark of Gypsy jazz—or *jazz manouche*, the French name by which it is often known.

Reinhardt's earliest recordings, accompanying an accordionist and slide whistle player, are far removed from the cosmopolitan jazz of his later years, but by the time of the first Quintette session in 1934, he had come to terms with the African American idiom. On "Dinah" he intermingles bouncy triplets and bluesy asides with forceful octaves, setting a standard for ease of execution and invention that would be amplified in later Quintette recordings such as "Djangology," "Limehouse Blues," "Chicago," and "Minor Swing." In time, the influence of Ravel, Debussy, and Gershwin would impart an impressionist tinge to Reinhardt's jazz, revealed in his exploration of whole-tone scales and in the languorous beauty of his most famous composition, "Nuages."

Reinhardt would not tour overseas until after World War II. But by then he had already played with many of the luminaries of jazz during their European visits and had developed an international reputation. Before the war, Reinhardt had recorded with Benny Carter, Coleman Hawkins, Dickie Wells, and members of the Duke Ellington band. Ellington remained a great admirer of Reinhardt's—Duke lauded him as "among the few great inimitables of our music"[9]—and when the guitarist decided to tour the United States in November 1946 it was in tandem with the Ellington band. Here he adopted an electric guitar and performed in large auditoriums, including Carnegie Hall. Returning to France, Reinhardt continued to play in small clubs and undertake occasional recordings. At his death in 1953, attributed to a cerebral hemorrhage, he was only forty-three years old.

Grappelli and Reinhardt had parted ways at the outbreak of World War II, the violinist staying in England, where the band had been on tour, while Django returned to France. A few weeks earlier, Coleman Hawkins had departed for the United States, arriving stateside only days before Germany's invasion of Poland. The rise of Nazism did not bode well for jazz musicians in Europe. Hawkins himself had been denied the right to perform in Germany because his appearance with white musicians was deemed unsuitable. Reinhardt, for his part, managed to continue his career under the Nazi occupation but was forced to submit his song selections to the local censorship bureau before each performance. Indeed, jazz took on surprising political significance in this charged environment, with W. C. Handy's "St. Louis Blues" getting rechristened as "La Tristesse de Saint Louis"—by musicians who hoped that a French-sounding name might avoid a crackdown by authorities—while Reinhardt's "Nuages" was adopted by some partisans as a defiant alternative anthem after the authorities banned "La Marseillaise."

Hawkins encountered a much different set of challenges back on his native soil. After an absence of five years, he needed to reestablish himself at home in the face of tenorists who had risen to prominence during his European sojourn. Chu Berry, with a rough-and-tumble sound akin to Hawkins's, was among the best of these new aspirants to the throne. Berry had served in the Fletcher Henderson band in the mid-1930s before joining Cab Calloway in 1937, with whom he remained until his death in a car accident in 1941. The Calloway association paid well, but Berry's hard-swinging approach might have been better served in another setting—one wonders what magic might have resulted had Berry accepted Ellington's job offer in the mid-1930s. Ben Webster, who would soon join the Ellington band, also had drawn inspiration from Hawkins, but parted ways from his role model with a breathier, unhurried tone that would become even more languid with the passing years. Webster stepped back from the harmonic acrobatics of Hawkins and the linearity of Young in favor of a celebration of sound. Like a Japanese shakuhachi master, Webster sought the essence of music in texture and timbre, not in well-tempered notes. But the most pressing challenge to Hawkins came again from Lester Young, whose playing had become more confident and distinctive in the intervening years since their Kansas City encounter.

Shortly after his return to New York, Hawkins sought out Young in a jam session at the Famous Door. Their tenor battle was front-page news in *Downbeat*, and the jazz world debated who had emerged the victor. Within days of this engagement, Hawkins matched up with a number of the other top players of his day as part of a Lionel Hampton session that also included Chu Berry, Ben Webster, Benny Carter, Dizzy Gillespie, and Charlie Christian. But the most prominent sign that Hawkins was ready to meet all challengers came on October 11 when he kicked off a series of recordings for RCA's Bluebird label with a version of "Body and Soul" that became an instant hit with both the general public and musicians. "It's the first and only record I ever heard of that all the squares dig as well as the jazz people," Hawkins later remarked. "I don't understand how and why." Certainly Hawkins made no compromises to popular tastes in his whirlwind sixty-four-bar solo. It briefly touches on the melody in the opening seconds before taking off into a marvelously fluid thematic development, rich in harmonic implication and rigidly logical in construction, yet infused with an undercurrent of lush romanticism. Not only was this Hawkins's finest moment, but with "Body and Soul" the tenorist created what is undoubtedly the most celebrated saxophone solo from the first half of the twentieth century.

At the peak of his career, Hawkins remained indecisive in his musical commitments. The next few years found him trying his hand at a wide range of formats: fronting a big band, participating in the Dixieland revival, engaging in small-combo sessions akin to the "Body and Soul" date, and exploring the possibilities of modern jazz. Hawkins's flirtation with bebop stands out as one of the most intriguing chapters in his biography. Among the earliest bandleaders to recognize the importance of the new idiom, Hawkins featured Dizzy Gillespie (as well as Max Roach, Oscar Pettiford, and Don Byas) on a momentous session from February 1944, which is usually acknowledged as the first modern jazz record date. A short while later, Hawkins hired pianist Thelonious Monk, at a time when the latter's eccentricities and modernist leanings made him *persona non grata* on most bandstands. Hawkins's advocacy of modern jazz continued the following year when the tenorist brought the first bebop band to the West Coast, predating the more celebrated Gillespie-Parker Los Angeles engagement by some ten months. During the postwar years, Hawkins further enhanced his progressivist credentials with another first: a jazz recording of unaccompanied saxophone. He first attempted this on a promotional demo disk made for the Selmer company, a leading manufacturer of saxophones—in a two-part variation that includes Hawkins's improvisation over the chord changes of Monk's "'Round Midnight"; he followed this performance with a commercial recording of solo saxophone, released under the title "Picasso." In time, the jazz world would accept that horn players could perform without the support of a band, but though many would follow down this path, few were better suited for this approach than Hawkins, whose harmonically charged manner of improvisation allowed the listener to feel the pull of the chord changes even when no accompanist was on hand to spell them out.

Yet, for all his avant-garde leanings, Hawkins's conception of melodic improvisation never really adapted to the changed musical landscape of modern jazz. His deeply analytical musical mind allowed the tenorist to navigate through intricate bop-oriented charts, but his phrasing and conception remained rooted in the Swing Era. Some have tried to enshrine him as a progenitor of bebop, but Hawkins (much like Benny Goodman) never really mastered the characteristic rebalancing and sub-divisions of the beat that set apart true bop tenorists such as Dexter Gordon, Teddy Edwards, and Sonny Rollins. The idea of modernism often seemed to hold more appeal for Hawkins than its actual execution. To the end, Hawkins enjoyed lingering near the cutting edge—sessions from his last decade find him in the company of Sonny Rollins, Randy Weston, Paul Bley, and Joe Zawinul. But Hawkins was just as quick to retreat to traditional settings, and some of his most satisfying late-career recordings are alongside veterans such as Ben Webster, Roy Eldridge, and Duke Ellington.

Lester Young's relationship to modern jazz stands out as almost the mirror image of Hawkins's. Young had little interest in being perceived as a modernist—his personal listening tastes tended toward popular songs and sentimental ballads—yet his style of playing not only foreshadowed the coming of bebop but to a certain extent inspired it. Of course, the lineage of Kansas City saxophone provides a direct connection between Young and bop progenitor Charlie Parker. But even more than geography, a shared sensibility links the two figures. Both used the higher intervals of the chords—the so-called color tones—as building blocks in their improvisa-tions. But the harmonic content of their music was often implicit—rather than explicit as with Hawkins—for both employed a linear conception in which the augmented fifths, sixths, ninths, elevenths, and such were carefully integrated into taut improvised lines. Chords were never spelled out, merely implied, and even these harmonic hints could be so subtle as to pass notice. But the most significant change signaled by Young, and developed by Parker, came in the rhythmic construction of their phrases. The pronounced syncopations, which had dominated jazz since its New Orleans origins, were used more sparingly in their playing. The dotted eighth note lines, frequently adopted by Young's predecessors, were now replaced by a smoother delivery of notes. Emphasis was less likely to fall on the first beat of the bar. The improvised lines carried a more definite 4/4 feel. One now heard a far greater use of triplets to add vitality to the phrases, perhaps as a substitute for the mostly absent syncopations. All these conceptual elements, propagated by Young, would be taken up and pushed further by Parker. No, Young's music was not modern jazz. He remained, first and foremost, a product of the Swing Era. And even among Young's contemporaries, there were many—Hawkins, Tatum, and Ellington are the most prominent examples—with far more progressive views about jazz as a modern art form. But Young, more than any of these others, set a foundation on which the next generation of modernists could build.

There is a second tradition in jazz that Young revitalized. Cool jazz would not emerge as a major force until the early 1950s. But even in the prewar years, Young was pointing the way to this alternative style. More than any instrumentalist of his generation, Young served as the crucial link between the 1920s cool pioneers (Beiderbecke, Trumbauer) and their Cold War successors (Getz, Mulligan, Davis, Desmond, Baker, Giuffre). In the 1930s, this was a lonely path to travel. Jazz has always been a hot art form—perhaps this is part of its essence—in its celebration of intensity, immediacy, and unbridled energy. The cool aesthetic, championing as it does a different set of virtues, has always been a minority point of view. The wholesale rejection of Young's style at the hands of his peers during his tenure in the Henderson band capsulizes in a telling anecdote this very fact. By the time of Young's mature work, his more relaxed approach was especially out of favor. It was, after all, the *Swing* Era, a time when most jazz bandleaders simply assumed that hotter was invariably better. That Young could rise above these obstacles and gain the admiration (eventually the emulation) of his peers with his cooler musical attitudes testifies to the lasting value of his innovations—and to the determination of this supposedly unassuming protagonist in the history of jazz.

Young's achievements with the Basie band no doubt contributed to this expanding influence, but it is in his small-combo sides that his alternative conception of jazz is most telling. His recordings with the Kansas City Six and Kansas City Seven from the late 1930s are major works. His clarinet playing from this period captures a laconic elegance, galaxies apart from the pyrotechnics of the Benny Goodman/Artie Shaw schools then in fashion, while his tenor efforts produced classic saxophone statements on "Lester Leaps In" and "Dickie's Dream." Young is even more in the spotlight on his stellar trio recordings with pianist Nat King Cole from the early and mid-1940s. But perhaps the most unusual combo performance from this period finds Young and several Basie colleagues joining Goodman for a 1940 session that also featured Charlie Christian. This music, which was not released for many years, adds another valuable perspective on Young's saxophone work, which stands out, even in this elevated company, with its melodic inventiveness and effortless delivery.

Young would continue to record in small-combo settings during the late 1940s and throughout the 1950s, but few of those performances match these early excursions. Many have suggested that Young's disastrous experiences in the U.S. Army during the closing months of World War II precipitated a downward spiral in his playing. Although Young never came close to a battlefield during his fifteen-month tour of duty, almost every other misfortune befell him: he was injured while running an obstacle course, hospitalized, operated on, psychoanalyzed, disciplined, arrested for possession of marijuana and barbiturates, incarcerated, and finally given a dishonorable discharge. The result was that Young, already introverted, became even more withdrawn, even more caught up in the odd mannerisms and jargon of his inner world.

His music also changed during the 1940s. His tone thickened and at times grew coarse; the melodic lines became less sprightly; the phrases sometimes sounded disjointed. But the chronology of this transformation is not as simple as has often been suggested. Some of these stylistic changes were already hinted at before Young's military service, while even after his discharge the saxophonist was capable of performances of merit. Yet, as Young approached his late forties, these exalted moments grew increasingly rare. At times his playing sounded simply tired. Yet these were good years for Young's finances, largely due to impresario and producer Norman Granz, who utilized the saxophonist's talents in a wide range of commercial projects. In the decade leading up to his death in 1959, Young recorded and performed frequently and saw his stature in the jazz world rise in tandem with the growing respect for cool jazz. Beat generation writers would laud him, and hipsters emulated his unusual style of speaking. One 1950s disciple, saxophonist Brew Moore, would go so far as to assert that "anyone who doesn't play like Lester is wrong."

Of all of Young's legacies from his best years, his recordings with singer Billie Holiday hold a special position in the jazz pantheon. Jazz fans admire them for their delicate intimacy, but even audiences blissfully ignorant of most aspects of the Swing Era have come to know and treasure these sides. And rightly so. The marriage of jazz and popular music—which occasionally leads to nuptial bliss, but too often takes on overtones of a shotgun wedding—has never been consummated with greater success than on these combo recordings. Even when weighted down by the most banal pop material, Holiday could transmute the dross of Tin Pan Alley into art song. She left a stamp so personal on many pieces that no later vocalist could attempt "All of Me" or "Foolin' Myself" or "Mean to Me"—and a host of other songs—without inviting comparisons, inevitably unfavorable ones, with her definitive versions. Young's contributions on these sides are small when measured in notes: cooing phrases answering Holiday's vocal line ("Without Your Love"), an eight-bar solo to set off the bridge of a song ("My First Impression of You"), a simple melody statement ("Foolin' Myself"), a snippet of clarinet playing ("I've Got a Date with a Dream"), or just a tantalizing four-bar introduction ("When a Woman Loves a Man"). But in terms of emotional power, these interludes are as persuasive as they come. Was there ever a jazz saxophonist better suited for demonstrating such artistry in four- and eight-bar increments? Given the titanic solos of the modern day, one can safely assume that jazz fans will never again encounter such elegant concision. Above all, there was a magical chemistry between these two elements, Holiday's voice and Lester's sax, leading some to characterize the collaboration between these platonic friends as a musical romance.

Holiday's accomplishments are all the more remarkable when one realizes the limitations within which she worked. Her range, at best, spanned a scant one and a half octaves. Her voice, moreover, did not project strongly—unlike, say, a Bessie Smith, who also had a modest range but could compensate by belting out a song to the back rows. Holiday lacked the scat-singing chops of an Ella Fitzgerald, the tonal purity of a Sarah Vaughan, the exuberance of a Louis Armstrong—but what she had more than made up for these deficiencies. Her mastery was rooted in an incomparable sense of timing, phrasing that was supple yet uncommonly relaxed, and, above all, an ability to infuse a lyric with hitherto unknown depths of meaning. One might say that Billie Holiday was a stylist, not a virtuoso—unless emotional depth is a type of virtuosity. Her interpretations cut to the quick of a song, crafting a music of interiors, not surfaces.

But the limitations that Holiday encountered went far beyond issues of vocal technique and are entangled in the terrible circumstances of her life and times. Holiday's story has been romanticized and dissected by turns. The romanticized version started with Holiday herself, who "wrote" an autobiography (*Lady Sings the Blues*) that mixed large doses of fiction with a smattering of facts. It came as no surprise that Hollywood made this book into a hit movie, further diluting the truth in the process. In later years, an ardent group of researchers—John Chilton, Linda Kuehl, Robert O'Meally, Donald Clarke, Stuart Nicholson, and others—would undertake their own analysis and reconstruction of Holiday's life, while the memoirs of those who knew her (such as John Hammond and Leonard Feather) have provided additional perspectives. Given this outpouring of research and commentary, there is certainly no lack of biographical material at hand. But most commentators have expected too much from Holiday's troubled life: they have wanted to twist it to reveal a moral, or annotate it with a running apology, or infuse it with the grandeur of Shakespearian tragedy. At the end of it all, there remains an enigmatic quality, an aura of mystery that surrounds Holiday's life and refuses to be dismissed. She has become much like the other overanalyzed pop figures of the last century—Marilyn Monroe, Elvis Presley, John Lennon, Michael Jackson—for whom the stacks of biographies, the abundance of "explanations," the ardor of the fans, seem to bring us no closer to their essence. It is the essence we want to understand, and all we are given are an assortment of facts, anecdotes, and hearsay.

In Holiday's case, even the simplest facts—a name, a date, a relationship—can prove stubbornly complex. She typically gave her birth name as Eleanora, but the hospital records show "Eleanor" and the birth certificate states "Elinore." She could borrow one of her mother Sarah's last names, Harris or Fagan, and took on Gough when her mother married Phil Gough, and then changed back to Fagan again after their divorce. At other times her last name was Holiday or Holliday or Halliday. In later years, she adopted the last name of husbands or boyfriends: Monroe, McKay, Guy, Levy. And formal names coexisted from the start with nicknames. At the House of the Good Shepherd in Baltimore, where she was institutionalized briefly during her youth, she was known as Madge or Theresa. Lester Young gave her the lasting nickname of Lady Day (and she responded by christening him Pres). Her father—Clarence Holiday, best known as a guitarist with the Fletcher Henderson band—simply called her Bill. Her ultimate choice of Billie Holiday was deeply suggestive, affirming her ties with her absent father and his world of jazz music and traveling bands.

Few of us get to choose our names, but Holiday went further. She recrafted her life story in articles, interviews, and ultimately her autobiography. As later researchers have come to learn, these excursions into fantasy could take any number of directions: at times Billie would make her life sound more sordid than it actually was; at other moments she would give it an unwarranted varnish of respectability. She tells of being born in Baltimore on April 7, 1915—although jazz writer Stuart Nicholson later showed that the location was Philadelphia—some three years before her parents married. In fact, the relationship between Clarence Holiday and Billie's mother, Sadie Fagan, both in their teens at the time, was a brief affair. No marriage record exists, and the singer's birth certificate lists Frank DeViese as her father. Clarence, for his part, took little heed of his parental responsibilities. He was reluctant to make any public acknowledgment that Billie was his daughter until her career blossomed. In later life, Billie would be attracted to men much like her father: glamorous, fast and loose, irresponsible, tough, worldly—traits that would also characterize the various "no-good" lovers who would populate her songs.

During these years, Billie was often left in the care of relatives, where she was, by turns, abused, neglected, and possibly raped. In January 1925, a juvenile court declared her to be "a minor without proper care and guardianship" and placed her in the House of the Good Shepherd for a year. When she was released, she moved back with her mother, who by now had taken up with Wee Wee Hill, a philandering porter, some eight years her junior. Sadie and Hill soon moved to New York. Sometime in the late 1920s, Holiday followed them to this setting of her first musical triumphs.

Little is known about Holiday's coming of age as a jazz singer. Recordings by Louis Armstrong and Bessie Smith apparently made an impression on her. But the differences between her and these predecessors are as striking as the similarities. Armstrong's carefree jocularity could play no role in Holiday's more doleful worldview and, while she borrowed some material from Smith's repertoire, Holiday was never primarily a blues singer, notwithstanding the title of her autobiography. But Holiday could take command of a lyric like no one else. Her 1936 recording for Brunswick, "I Cried for You"—the first standard she recorded and her biggest hit from the period—finds her wringing the tears from a song that so many other vocalists have delivered in a glib, matter-of-fact manner. Holiday interprets it as a melancholy torch song, even though the band is bouncing along at medium tempo; years later, she would grip audiences by presenting this same song as a ballad.

In 1933, John Hammond heard Holiday singing in a Harlem nightspot and gave her career a boost with a glowing review in *Melody Maker*, heralding her as a "real find" and confiding that the eighteen-year-old vocalist "sings as well as anybody I ever heard." Later that year, Hammond arranged for Holiday to sing with Benny Goodman. Other opportunities followed: a brief film appearance in *Symphony in Black* (alongside Duke Ellington), a booking at the Apollo Theater, and more recordings (this time under Teddy Wilson's leadership) arranged by Hammond. During the remaining years of the decade, Holiday would make dozens of small-combo sides, resulting in many of the finest works of her career. Even before her pairing with Lester Young, Holiday made her mark with classic renditions of "What a Little Moonlight Can Do," "These Foolish Things," "I Cried for You," "Billie's Blues," "A Fine Romance," and "I Can't Give You Anything but Love," among others. The soloists on these performances included some of the finest horn players in jazz (Benny Goodman, Ben Webster, Johnny Hodges, Harry Carney), but with the addition of

Lester Young for a January 1937 session, Holiday found an even more sympathetic partner. Virtually all of the Holiday-Young sides are of lasting value. Even when burdened with a banal tune or awkward lyric—"Now They Call It Swing," "Me, Myself and I Are All in Love with You," "You're Just a No Account," "Sun Showers"—Holiday and Young were still able to create music of near perfection. And when working with stronger material—"All of Me," "Foolin' Myself," "Mean to Me," "He's Funny That Way," and "This Year's Kisses"—they left behind definitive performances that cast a long shadow over later attempts to interpret these songs.

This same period saw Holiday slowly gain a following beyond the inner circle of jazz cognoscenti. Short stints with Count Basie and Artie Shaw broadened her audience, while Holiday's 1939 recording of "Strange Fruit," a disturbing song about a lynching, added to her notoriety and imparted a piquant political quality to her public image. This shift was spurred at the behest of Barney Josephson, a former shoe salesman who had recently opened Cafe Society, a fashionable nightclub in the Village. Josephson had introduced the song to Holiday and encouraged her to close each set with it. Over the next several years, Holiday gradually became less a jazz vocalist and more a torch singer. Her most characteristic works from this period were moody numbers such as "Lover Man," "I Cover the Waterfront," "God Bless the Child," "Good Morning Heartache," "Don't Explain," and the aforementioned "Strange Fruit." Billie's singing still exuded intense emotional commitment but, as the decade progressed, the quality of her sidemen steadily declined, and later her voice followed suit. By the middle of the 1940s, subpar jazz players or maudlin violins had replaced the all-star bands of earlier years.

The travails of Holiday's personal life also became increasingly public during this period. Starting from her Baltimore days, Holiday had veered from the straight and narrow. Before her fifteenth birthday she was smoking tobacco—in time her habit would require fifty cigarettes per day—and marijuana. In her teens she worked in a brothel (and later shocked many readers with a candid account in her 1956 autobiography). Holiday also came to drink heavily. Some years later, her husband Jimmy Monroe introduced Holiday to heroin. Her ensuing addiction led to a series of problems with law enforcement agencies in the late 1940s. In 1947, she was forced to serve ten months at the Federal Reformatory for Women in West Virginia. But even after her release, Holiday continued to pay a heavy price. She could no longer work in New York clubs because of a regulation (eventually repealed in 1967) that denied cabaret cards to convicted felons. Allowed to perform at theaters and auditoriums, Holiday was presented at a successful concert at Carnegie Hall, but a follow-up "Holiday on Broadway" engagement at the Mansfield Theater folded after five days. Barred from nightclubs, Holiday was essentially prevented from earning a living in New York. Even in other locales, Holiday found club owners reluctant to book her, either because of the stigma of her addiction or a reputation for unreliability. In 1949, Holiday was arrested again on drug charges while touring the West Coast but was acquitted when she convinced the jury that she had been set up by her companion John Levy. Sales and airplay of her recordings declined during this period as well, and in 1951 Decca refused to renew Holiday's contract. A *Downbeat* reviewer smugly joked that Lady Day was becoming "Lady Yesterday."

In March 1952, Holiday signed with Norman Granz's Verve label and began the arduous process of rehabilitating her career as a jazz singer. Over the next five years, she would record over a hundred songs for Granz, once again in the company of world-class jazz musicians. These included many of the finest saxophonists in jazz, albeit ones who played in a prebop style—Coleman Hawkins, Ben Webster, Benny Carter, Willie Smith, Flip Phillips, Paul Quinichette—along with such trumpeters as Harry "Sweets" Edison, Charlie Shavers, or Joe Newman. On piano Holiday was supported by Oscar Peterson, Jimmy Rowles, or Wynton Kelly, all top-tier musicians. In sidemen, in material, in style, Granz was attempting to recreate the formula that had worked so well for Holiday during the prewar years. Often she recorded the same songs with which she had made her reputation some two decades earlier.

But Holiday's voice had changed. In the opinion of some it had declined precipitously. The value of Holiday's late recordings remains a matter of debate among jazz fans. Her voice clearly showed the signs of strain, of wear. A darker quality now pervades the music; at times, a sense of despair infuses the performances. A streak of melancholy had always characterized Holiday's singing, but by now the touches of light were all but extinguished. Yet a trade-off was apparent. The deterioration in Holiday's vocal equipment was compensated for by even more nuanced performances. Holiday's phrasing, her timing, her ability to add chiaroscuro shades of meaning to a lyric remain unsurpassed on these late-vintage recordings. And if Holiday could be a subpar vocalist, she was never an indifferent one. Miles Davis, in an oft-quoted assessment offered to Nat Hentoff in 1958, remarked on the greater maturity in Holiday's singing. "You know, she's not thinking now what she was in 1937, and she's probably learned more about different things. And she still has control, probably more control than then. No, I don't think she's in a decline." Altoist Jackie McLean, recalling this period in Holiday's career, explained: "Her voice was just a shadow of what it had been, yet she still put a song over. Her singing voice was gone, leaving emotion her only tool of expression."[10]

Holiday continued to struggle with heroin addiction and bouts of heavy drinking during these final years. In 1956, she was again arrested on a narcotics charge, this time in Philadelphia. But Holiday's self-assertiveness came to the fore that same year with activities on a wide range of fronts: her autobiography was published by Doubleday; she performed to an enthusiastic audience at Carnegie Hall, and extracts from the book were narrated as part of the evening's entertainment; she continued to record and earn large fees for nightclub dates. The next year Holiday appeared on a television show, *The Sound of Jazz*, fronting a superb band that also reunited her with Lester Young, and delivered a finely etched performance of "Fine and Mellow." It is often cited, with justification, as the most moving jazz moment ever captured on film.

Ultimately, physical dissipation, rather than artistic exhaustion, took its toll. Although beset by heart and liver problems, Holiday maintained an extensive touring schedule, including overseas appearances. At a Greenwich Village concert in May 1959, she had to be helped from the stage after singing only two numbers. A week later she fell into a coma. At the hospital Holiday showed signs of recovery, slowly regaining weight and beginning to dictate sections of a new book to her collaborator, Bill Dufty. Her legal problems, however, pursued her even into the hospital ward, with the police claiming that she was in possession of heroin and putting her under house arrest, going so far as to post agents outside the door of her room. Although Holiday responded to treatment for her liver, a kidney infection set in, and on July 17 she died. At the time of her death, Holiday's bank account showed a balance of only 70 cents, but hospital workers who came to take the body found $750 taped to one of her legs—an instinctive gesture of self-preservation by one who, so often betrayed by those closest to her, had come to trust only in herself.

DUKE ELLINGTON: MIDDLE PERIOD AND LATER WORKS

Duke Ellington would eventually benefit from the rising public interest in swing music generated by Goodman's success. Even so, the birth of the Swing Era came at a time when Ellington was increasingly distancing himself from the mass-market demands of the music industry. At a point when jazz was becoming America's popular music, Ellington appeared singularly intent on transforming it into a serious art form. If there was any irony inherent in this situation, Ellington seemed blissfully unaware of it. Perhaps the most remarkable thing about this iconic figure during the heyday of the big bands was that, whatever conflicts there may have been between the demands of commerce and the higher aspirations of his muse, they forced few compromises in his music. Nowhere was Ellington's genius more evident than in this ability—ever so rare in any idiom, but especially in the jazz world—to achieve simultaneously the highest rung of artistic achievement and remain a celebrated mass-market entertainer.

Yet Ellington never made it too easy for his audience. His music was laced with dissonances. His melodies were rarely hummable ditties (and could give even trained singers fits with their odd intervallic leaps). While most bandleaders featured a heavy dose of popular songs in their repertoires, Ellington relied to an extreme on his own pieces. True, Duke could compose hits, but these represented a tiny proportion of the band's output, dwarfed by the extended works, tone poems, ambitious pieces of program music, miniconcertos for his soloists, novelty numbers, blues, reconfigured evocations of stride or New Orleans style, and experimental compositions of various sorts. Sometimes these forays into new territory would produce an unexpected hit—as happened with the Middle Eastern–tinged "Caravan," Juan Tizol's contribution to the band from 1937. But more often, audiences were left to grope as best they could with a "Diminuendo and Crescendo in Blue" or a "Reminiscing in Tempo." And even when Ellington offered a toe-tapping "swing" number, increasingly popular with audiences during this period, he rarely gave them the simple riff-based workhorses that other bands rode to success. Indeed, the riff—in essence, a repeated motif over changing harmonies, sometimes given a syncopated kick through a displacement caused by a contrast between the length of the phrase and the underlying meter—may have been the undisputed musical signature of the era (as witnessed by the success of "Opus One," "In the Mood," "A String of Pearls," "Flying Home," and other like numbers), but apparently no one had told Ellington. Instead, he challenged his fans with complex swing charts such as "Cotton Tail" or "Braggin' in Brass"—clearly two masterpieces of the genre, but the former dauntingly hard to sing along with, the latter impossible. Today, Ellington's conservative works in AABA song form are the best known, the most frequently recorded pieces in his oeuvre, but these represent only one facet of his complex musical personality. Ellington himself was always quick to emphasize his cavalier attitude to these pop song offerings: "Solitude," he claimed, was written in twenty minutes when he needed another number to finish a recording session; "In a Sentimental Mood," he explained, was tossed off to calm down a party veering out of control one night in Durham, North Carolina. Who could doubt that, at the crest of the public's craze for big band music, Ellington remained a reluctant participant in the mainstreaming of hot jazz?

In 1936, with swing sweeping the country, Ellington recorded little and had no hits. That same year, his group fell to fifth place in the *Metronome* poll. Dozens of big bands were being formed around the country, but Ellington responded at the close of the year by initiating a series of combo recordings. Over the next two years, Ellington would be involved in making over sixty small-group sides, but only one—Johnny Hodges's performance on "Jeep's Blues"—became a featured jukebox number. In 1937, Ellington continued to take the high road with his big band work, recording the ambitious "Diminuendo in Blue" and "Crescendo in Blue," companion pieces that filled both sides of a 78. His biggest-selling release of the year, however, was the previously mentioned "Caravan," an exotic piece with modal overtones that few bandleaders would have considered to be hit material.

This apparent lull in the larger band's activity was deceptive. The Ellington orchestra, with its leader now approaching his fortieth birthday, was on the brink of its greatest period, a burst of creativity that would last until the recording ban of the war years. True, Ellington would continue to record outstanding material for the remainder of his life, but the sheer number of masterpieces produced by the band between 1938 and 1942 stands out even in the context of Duke's half-century career. Three additions to the band at the close of the decade—Billy Strayhorn, Ben Webster, and Jimmy Blanton—would contribute greatly to this explosion of artistry. But even before their arrival, Ellington was already increasing his output, both in quantity and quality. The year 1938 saw the band produce a number of classic sides. "Steppin' into Swing Society," the group's first recording of the year, set the tone for Ellington's growing focus on medium-tempo swing charts, another trademark sound of the era. A similar groove is evident on a number of outstanding 1938 tracks, most notably on the two features for Ellington's best brass soloists: "Riding on a Blue Note," a jaunty showpiece for trumpeter Cootie Williams, and "Boy Meets Horn," a memorable Rex Stewart performance that demonstrated Ellington's ability to extract depths of emotion from a simple device, in this instance a half-valve effect on the cornet. Extremely fast virtuoso performances had never played a large role in the Ellington book, but with "Braggin' in Brass" Ellington created a classic of the genre, a breathtaking chart stunningly executed by the band. These ventures into unadulterated swing did not prevent Ellington from continuing to develop his "mood" style. The band achieved especially memorable results on "Blue Light," "Lost in Meditation," "Prelude to a Kiss," and "A Gypsy without a Song." As these performances made clear, Ellington was increasingly able to incorporate a wide array of stylistic devices into his mood pieces—plaintive blues calls, impressionistic harmonies, elements of romantic ballads—without destroying the overall unity of the performance. This ability to cover so much musical ground in a three-minute song (reminiscent of Jelly Roll Morton's best efforts) would stand out as one of the most salient virtues of Ellington's mature work.

One evening toward the close of this fertile year, Ellington was approached after a performance in Pittsburgh by a young composer named Billy Strayhorn, who was intent on showing the bandleader one of his pieces. Sixteen years younger than Ellington, Strayhorn had spent his youth in many locales—Ohio (where he was born in Dayton in 1915), New Jersey, North Carolina, and finally Pennsylvania, where he eventually enrolled at the Pittsburgh Musical Institute. Here he pursued formal study of theory and concert music supplemented by a private passion for jazz and songwriting. Shortly before his decisive encounter with Ellington, Strayhorn had been performing with a trio and studying orchestration, but most of his income came from his day job in a drugstore. This would soon change dramatically. The piece that caught Ellington's attention that night, "Lush Life," stands out as one of the greatest jazz ballads, with its yearning melody line and the haunting poetry of its lyrics, supported by sweeping harmonies more characteristic of classical music than of Tin Pan Alley. Within weeks, Strayhorn was writing arrangements for the band, initiating a relationship with Ellington that would span almost three decades. During this period he would compose or collaborate on over two hundred pieces.

Ellington had long indulged in various musical collaborations with his band members, but previously these relationships were unabashedly one sided. Strayhorn, in contrast, became a true partner, playing a pivotal role in shaping the band's sound. In fact, a Strayhorn song, "Take the A Train," would eventually become the band's trademark theme. But this venture into the hit parade was atypical. Strayhorn's instincts were artistic, not commercial, and Ellington's choice of him as a musical alter ego no doubt reflected the bandleader's own aspirations as a serious composer. Especially in his own mood compositions—songs such as "Chelsea Bridge," "Daydream," "Passion Flower," "Lotus Blossom," "A Flower Is a Lovesome Thing," and "Blood Count"—Strayhorn's mastery rivaled his employer's. Such works remain the closest jazz has ever approached to art song.

In 1939, Ellington continued to expand his efforts on many fronts. The combo sides took a high priority early in the year, but big band activity soon picked up, with the ensemble recording over a dozen numbers in March and June, including the riff-based "Pussy Willow," the mood piece "Subtle Lament," Billy Strayhorn's first major contribution, "Grievin'," and "The Sergeant Was Shy" with its evocation of "Bugle Call Rag." In the spring, the band traveled to Europe for the second time, where Ellington celebrated his fortieth birthday in Sweden. He was feted by a large group of serenading schoolchildren on the occasion and he responded by recording "Serenade to Sweden" on his return to the States. In addition, Ellington also took a higher profile as an instrumentalist during the year, recording as a solo pianist—rare at the time for Duke—and in duet format with bassist Jimmy Blanton after the latter's arrival in the fall of 1939.

The addition of Blanton represented a major turning point for the band. Half Ellington's age, this twenty-year-old prodigy brought a palpable excitement, an incisiveness and momentum, to virtually every performance during his brief tenure with the group. Despite his youth, Blanton's career would span months, not years—at the close of 1941 he would leave Ellington because of poor health and would die from tuberculosis the following July—but in that short time he managed not only to invigorate the Ellington rhythm section but also to revolutionize the role of the string bass in jazz. There had been outstanding players on the instrument before Jimmy Blanton—Pops Foster, Steve Brown, Al Morgan, John Kirby, Wellman Braud, Billy Taylor (with Ellington at the time of Blanton's arrival), Walter Page, and others—but his virtuosity tended to eclipse their accomplishments. For all their virtues, they now seemed mere timekeepers, offering a steady beat and harmonic reinforcement, while Blanton was a complete jazz player. Today, the bass fills multiple roles in most jazz ensembles, propelling the performance, establishing a rhythmic pulse, providing embellishments, crisp walking lines, and countermelodies, and taking its place from time to time as a featured solo voice. Blanton helped define all these responsibilities. He showed that the plucked (pizzicato) bass could be as important as the drums in swinging the band, in pushing an entire jazz orchestra. He, more than anyone else, established the bass as a legitimate solo voice in the jazz idiom. With a resonant tone and a polished execution unsurpassed at the time, he laid the foundation for modern jazz bass technique. One can hear the result not only in Blanton's own recordings but in his pervasive impact on virtually all of the leading jazz bassists of the 1940s and 1950s—including Oscar Pettiford, Ray Brown, Charles Mingus, Red Mitchell, Paul Chambers, and Red Callender. "The most impressive bass player I ever heard was Jimmy Blanton," Callender later recalled. "When I first heard him, I said 'This is the way the bass is supposed to be played.'"[11]

The arrival of Ben Webster, the third important addition to the band during this period, was a major coup for Ellington. A powerful soloist with a deeply personal sound, Webster ranks as the finest tenorist in the history of the Ellington orchestra. His departure left a void that Ellington never adequately filled. At his best, Webster was on a par with the most famous tenor players in jazz, mentioned by fans in the same breath as Hawkins or Young. His mature style revealed a mastery of the sonic possibilities of the tenor saxophone unprecedented in jazz, exhibiting a dazzling range of breathy tones, raspy asides, barks, whimpers, growls, glissandos, cries, and whispers. His playing at times could be aggressive, as could his personality—the pugnacious Webster once claimed to have knocked down heavyweight champion Joe Louis, and who dared challenge the story?—but his music was just as noteworthy for its gentler moments. While emulating the ripeness of Johnny Hodges's sound, Webster added to it a warmer, airy essence. His lingering tones had a delicious, unfocused quality. Eventually he learned how to hint at phrases—a note or two sufficed—rather than state them explicitly, recalling the poet's remark that the unheard melodies are the sweetest of all. Yet Webster was just as adept at declamatory outbursts on the saxophone, leaving behind in his most famous Ellington solo, on "Cotton Tail," a lasting tour de force of improvisational complexity.

Born in Kansas City, Missouri, on March 27, 1909, Webster developed his skills alongside some of the finest saxophonists in jazz, apprenticing in bands led by Bennie Moten and Andy Kirk. After moving to New York in 1934, Webster worked for a time with Fletcher Henderson and Cab Calloway, among others, before joining Ellington on a regular basis in 1940. His tenure with the Duke would be brief: Webster left Ellington in 1943, rejoining the band for a short stint at the close of the decade, but soon departing again to pursue a successful career as a freelance performer and studio player.

Ellington was also making important changes in his business dealings during this period. He parted ways with Irving Mills in 1939 and initiated a new arrangement with the William Morris Agency. Around this same time, Ellington also entered into a long-term relationship with the Victor recording label, signing a contract for five years. One suspects that the security of these new arrangements played some role in the burst of creativity that followed. At a minimum, Ellington must have been given enormous artistic freedom while at Victor. The sides he recorded for the label have only the lightest veneer of commercialism. They are full of subtleties and intricacies—arcane compositional structures, surprising modulations, hints of dissonance—that may have endeared Duke to serious jazz listeners, but probably put off more casual fans.

Ellington's frequent departures from standard song form warrant particular mention. By the time of the Swing Era, the thirty-two-bar form had become entrenched as the dominant structure for both popular song composition and jazz improvisation. The most common variant employed two eight-bar melodies, an A theme and B theme according to standard terminology, which were played in the sequence AABA. A second approach, even simpler in construction, was also frequently used: this was an AA' form, in which both themes spanned sixteen bars, and with only a slightly different ending distinguishing the A melody from the A' version. These two structures, AABA and AA', remain dominant in jazz music to this day. In a typical performance, a jazz band will simply repeat the underlying structure over and over again, in a constant thirty-two-bar loop, with an opening and closing melody statement encapsulating improvisations over the same form. Certainly when the occasion so warranted, Ellington employed these simple thirty-two-bar structures, especially when he was aiming for commercial acceptance. But, just as often, Ellington broke out of this Tin Pan Alley straitjacket, at times squeezing four or more themes into a three-minute song. And instead of restricting himself to eight- or sixteen-bar melodies, Ellington sprinkled his music with occasional sections of other lengths: lasting ten or twenty bars or some even more lopsided duration, not to mention his frequent use of twelve-bar blues structures. These melodies of different length often coexisted alongside each other in a single composition, where they might be further spiced with equally unconventional introductions, codas, or interludes.

Ellington's famous recording of "Jack the Bear" from 1940 is, for the most part, a twelve-bar blues driven by the stunning bass work of Jimmy Blanton. But midway through the piece the song shifts gears into an AABA form. To a seasoned jazz musician, this immediate juxtaposition of blues and pop song form would be like eating spaghetti and pancakes at the same sitting. Yet Ellington not only pulls off this odd mixture without causing indigestion but creates a masterpiece in the process. "Sepia Panorama," also from this period, is another example of Ellington's predilection for arcane forms. Its four-theme structure unfolds ABCDDCBA, with the second half of the song serving as a mirror image of the first. Once again the melodies vary in length, with the A and D themes following a twelve-bar format, while the B and C sections are built on standard eight- and sixteen-bar structures. Moreover, the moods of the various sections are strikingly different, with the pensive B theme separating the more energetic A and C sections, and the two improvised D choruses featuring the outstanding blues work of Ellington, Blanton, and Webster. This represented a level of complexity that swing fans, raised on a diet of simple riffs, may well have found puzzling. But Ellington dared to be different, even using "Sepia Panorama" as the band's theme song during this period.

Sometimes he might simplify matters in performance, just playing the opening sections of the work, but often he treated audiences to a full-blown version. A live recording of the band made in Fargo, North Dakota, on November 7, 1940—a neglected masterpiece on a par with Ellington's more celebrated Carnegie Hall performances or *Sacred Concerts*—captures a vibrant five-minute rendition of "Sepia Panorama" with Blanton and Webster playing at absolute top form. The Fargo tracks, taken as a whole, are important documents of Ellington's 1940 band, showing that the complex and challenging pieces that were a specialty of this ensemble could also serve as spirited, hot jazz for a dancing audience. Indeed, there are few other recordings of the Ellington band, in any setting, that find the group playing with such energy and verve. There was no contradiction in this for Ellington. His artistry was just as much at home in a dance hall in North Dakota as on the stage of Carnegie Hall. Ever so gently and politely, he raised the audience to his level wherever he went. And the band's aficionados invariably learned to expect the most inspired performances in some of the humblest venues.

The Ellington recorded legacy from the beginning of the 1940s is extraordinarily rich. The Victor sides from this period rank with the finest achievements of the jazz idiom, on a par with Armstrong's Hot Fives and Hot Sevens or with the Charlie Parker Savoy and Dial sessions. Where to begin? The ominous "Ko-Ko," with its throbbing pedal tones, evokes Ellington's "jungle music" of earlier years, but now drawing on an even darker palette, almost despairing in its tone. If one didn't know that a world war was in the making, one could almost guess it from this foreboding musical portrait. "Harlem Air Shaft" is poised at the opposite end of the spectrum: jubilant, spirited, carefree. Midway through the piece, Ellington toys with his audience. The rhythm section suddenly drops out, and the horns articulate a more reflective theme in half time. Has the party ended prematurely? Not at all. After a moment of pregnant hesitation, drummer Sonny Greer leads the band back in full force. This cat-and-mouse game is repeated twice, a masterpiece of deferred gratification.

Some of the band's loveliest ballads and mood pieces date from this period, but the surprise is that many of them are written by sidemen. No doubt Ellington's creativity in this vein was still at peak form—as witnessed by "All Too Soon," "Warm Valley," and "Dusk"; but Strayhorn's "Chelsea Bridge," Mercer Ellington's "Blue Serge," and

Juan Tizol's "Bakiff" also stand out as first-class works. Yet this was more than a writers' band. Anyone doubting the improvisational talent of the Ellington orchestra need only hear Cootie Williams on "Concerto for Cootie," Ben Webster on "Cotton Tail," Jimmy Blanton on "Pitter Panther Patter," or Johnny Hodges on "Main Stem." In fact, it is hard to think of any other body of recordings in the jazz idiom that reflect such an ideal balance between composition, orchestration, and improvisation as these Ellington efforts from the early 1940s.

A number of circumstances conspired to put an end to this fertile period in the history of the Ellington band. Cootie Williams decided to join Benny Goodman in November 1940, after eleven years with Ellington. Jimmy Blanton left the band in November 1941 and died from tuberculosis a few months later. In the summer of 1942, Barney Bigard departed, and a month later vocalist Ivie Anderson followed suit. This exodus continued in 1943, with Ben Webster leaving the band. The middle years of the decade also saw the departure of Rex Stewart, Juan Tizol, Tricky Sam Nanton (felled by a stroke), and Otto Hardwick. After years of relying on stable personnel, Ellington now had to cope with an unprecedented level of turnover. Nor was this all. The larger problems of the music industry also served to curtail his activities. A 1941 conflict between ASCAP, which represented composers, and the nation's radio broadcasters effectively limited Ellington's access to airplay (although it did give him a financial incentive to feature songs written by Strayhorn and other band members who were not ASCAP members). Then, for almost two years, Ellington was kept out of the recording studio due to the prolonged strike called by James Petrillo, the hard-headed boss of the American Federation of Musicians. Fans looked on in dismay as the majestic (and prolific) recorded output of 1938–41 was followed mostly—at least for a spell—by silence.

This enforced hiatus and the dramatic turnover in the band did little to stem Ellington's ambitions. His attention increasingly turned to longer works in a jazz vein. Undeterred by the failure of his show *Jump for Joy*, which had been staged for eleven weeks in Los Angeles in 1941, Ellington pushed on with his most daring composition to date, *Black, Brown and Beige*. For over a decade Ellington had talked about his desire to write an extended work that would serve as a musical depiction of African American history. The scope of this project constantly shifted: at one point it was to be a symphony, at another an opera or musical. The end result was none of these. Instead Ellington put together a three-part work, lasting three-quarters of an hour, and scored for jazz band and voice. Given Ellington's stature, this alone would have been a major event in the music world. But his choice of Carnegie Hall for a venue—this was his debut performance in the venerable auditorium—only added to the notoriety surrounding *Black, Brown and Beige*. In the eyes of some, Ellington was doing more than writing an extended work; he was challenging the bastions of serious music.

The critical response to the piece was far from receptive. Paul Bowles, writing in the *New York Herald Tribune*, not only chastised the composer, but made pronouncements about the "proper" scope of jazz. "The whole attempt to fuse jazz as a form with art music should be discouraged"[12]—a judgment with the ominous ring of the plantation owner denouncing his "uppity" slaves. But even listeners who might have been more sympathetic, such as John Hammond, lamented that Duke was "deserting jazz." In truth, *Black, Brown and Beige* was an impressive work, despite minor imperfections. The first movement includes some of the most sophisticated examples of thematic development Ellington would ever write, along with one of his strongest melodies ("Come Sunday") presented in an impassioned saxophone statement by Johnny Hodges. The highlight of the second movement is the unexpected entry of a vocal part, built on an unusual pyramid form of lyric:

The blues
The blues ain't
The blues ain't nothin'
The blues ain't nothin' but a cold, gray day . . .

This section was followed, in the Carnegie Hall performance, by an outstanding tenor solo by Ben Webster. The third movement, *Beige*, is a less structured sequence of disparate themes, each representing Ellington's musical evocation of a specific aspect of African American history or culture. The insertion of a waltz interlude was noteworthy at the time, given the rarity of this meter in jazz settings, but *Beige* as a whole is less cohesive than *Black* and *Brown*. In its entirety, *Black, Brown and Beige* represented a major step forward for Ellington, his boldest attempt to address the demands of longer forms. It suffered, if anything, from an abundance of riches: too much thematic material, too many shifts in tempo, too many moods. Yet, for all its excesses, *Black, Brown and Beige* remains a career milestone for Ellington and deserves consideration as the most important extended work in the history of jazz music.

With encouragement, Ellington might have pushed further in the directions outlined by this massive composition. Instead the mixed reactions of the critics gave him pause. Over the next month he performed the work two more times, then put it on the shelf, never again playing it in its original form. Ellington would continue to debut extended works at Carnegie Hall concerts during the 1940s, but none were as ambitious as *Black, Brown and Beige*. In "New World A' Coming," premiered at Carnegie Hall on December 11, 1943, Ellington offered a more controlled single-movement work, less jazz oriented, and with overtones of nineteenth-century classical music. With *The Perfume Suite*, which made its debut the following year, Ellington (with Strayhorn's participation evident) constructed a longer work out of a sequence of "movements," which were essentially unrelated musical vignettes. Ellington employed the same approach, which allowed him to rely on his skills as a miniaturist, with *The Deep South Suite* from 1946 and *The Liberian Suite* from 1947. During the remainder of his career, this formula would remain Ellington's preferred method of dealing with the challenges of extended form. Over the next quarter of a century, Ellington would compose numerous longer works, but the more thematically probing style of *Black, Brown and Beige* would rarely surface.

Yet as Gunther Schuller has rightly pointed out, "before we judge Ellington too harshly, we might do well to remember that the whole question of large forms in jazz has not been entirely satisfactorily answered by anyone else."[13] A decade after *Black,*

Brown and Beige, the introduction of the long-playing record was heralded as the breakthrough that would liberate jazz from the constraints imposed by 78 rpm records. Once jazz artists were no longer limited by the enforced three-minute duration of a 78, an era of extended jazz composition would blossom—or so it seemed at the time. But the ensuing decades made clear that more than technological problems needed to be solved to effect such a liberation. Why is this so? Schuller points to the challenge of integrating improvisation and composition. Certainly this is an issue. But even more pressing is the question—usually unacknowledged in jazz circles—of what a suitable compositional structure for longer jazz works might look like. In fact, there are only four options. On the one hand, jazz composers can borrow the forms of classical music, creating "jazz operas," "jazz fugues," "jazz sonatas," and the like. Second, jazz composers can continue to use the short forms—twelve-bar blues, thirty-two-bar forms—and simply play them for a long time or string them together in suites. Third, longer works can be created that are essentially formless, or very lax in imposing formal constraints, as with Ellington's many suites. Finally, jazz composers can invent their own compositional structures—not a jazz sonata, but an alternative to sonata form (or fugue, rondo, etc.) for the jazz idiom, whatever that might be. The last option is clearly the most difficult, probably the most promising, and certainly the one least explored to date—not surprisingly so, given the limited concern with (and, at times, antagonism against) formalism that predominates in the jazz world. When commentators lament Ellington's reliance on essentially formless "suites" in his later years, it is not because of their lack of quality—far from it—but because Ellington seemed to be shirking the larger task at hand. More than any other jazz composer of the twentieth century, he possessed the vision, ambition, and genius necessary to create these new structures.

Did Ellington fail in this regard? Not really. At a certain point, he simply decided to direct his energies elsewhere. At times, his most daring musical visions would emerge in brief sketches, as in the four-and-a-half-minute rendition of "The Clothed Woman" from his 1947 Carnegie Hall concert, with its hints of atonality mixed in with elements of stride and blues. The integration of vocal and instrumental lines in "Transblucency," the use of counterpoint on "Fugueaditti" (which also served as part of the longer *Tonal Group*), the canonic interplay and daring reharmonization from the band's 1945 remaking of "Mood Indigo": these too showed Ellington's interest in expanding his musical vocabulary. As the last piece made clear, the reworking of old material often gave rise to some of Duke's most inspired moments. Five years later, Ellington created a fifteen-minute version of "Mood Indigo" for one of his first long-playing records, and the resulting sixteen choruses of variations on this theme must rank as one of the band's greatest, if often overlooked, longer works. This may well have been the closest Ellington ever came to creating an African American equivalent of Bach's *Goldberg Variations* or Beethoven's *Diabelli Variations*.

And the hits continued as well. Even during the recording ban, Ellington continued to enjoy success as a composer of popular songs. Two of Ellington's instrumental numbers were given a makeover, with the addition of lyrics and a new name, and made into hits. "Don't Get Around Much Anymore," based on "Never No Lament," reached the top of the R&B chart in a version by the Ink Spots and spurred Victor to rerelease Ellington's own version, which also sold well. A simplified version of "Concerto for Cootie" enjoyed popularity when rechristened as "Do Nothin' till You Hear from Me." In addition to building his reputation as a songwriter and concert hall composer, Ellington managed somehow to deal with the many other demands on him: the demands of the road, the demands of leading a big band, the demands of celebrity, the demands imposed by commercial interests in the music industry—these continuing for the rest of his life. Time was always in short supply. ("Even the unscheduled work," Billy Strayhorn once quipped, "is behind schedule."[14]) In this context, the marvel is that Ellington succeeded so well on so many different fronts.

The 1950s proved to be a challenging decade for Ellington. The sudden departure of Johnny Hodges, Lawrence Brown, and Sonny Greer in 1951 stands out as the most devastating loss in the history of the band. Ellington regrouped by arranging for the return of Juan Tizol from his gig with Harry James, along with Tizol's cohorts in that band, drummer Louis Bellson and alto saxophonist Willie Smith. The jazz press dubbed the move the "Great James Robbery," but the take on this heist was questionable. There were, clearly, some benefits—Bellson proved to be generally superior to Greer in driving the band on up-tempo charts—but the departure of Hodges left Duke with a gap that simply could not be filled, by Smith (for all his virtues) or anyone else. Hodges would return in 1955, but Ellington never fully adjusted to his absence in the interim. Much of the slack was taken up by saxophonist Paul Gonsalves, whose arrival in 1950 provided Ellington with his strongest tenor soloist of the post-Webster decades. The addition of trumpeter Clark Terry in the following year, however, was clearly a major coup for Duke.

But coping with bandstand turnover was only a small part of Ellington's challenge during this period. At least that could be managed, more or less. The changing musical tastes of the American public was another factor entirely. By 1950, the big band was effectively dead as a major force in American popular music. In the years following World War II, a number of social and economic factors conspired to force the big bands slowly, but inexorably, out of existence. A tax on dance venues, later repealed, may have been the first wedge separating jazz musicians from their mass audience. In the postwar years, the cost of promoting swing music further escalated as the price of transportation, wages, and hotel rooms rose steadily. An increasingly foreboding reputation for jazz as a music for serious listeners only, a legacy of the beboppers, clearly dates from this period as well. In time, the spread of television not only encouraged people to stay at home but distracted the public's attention from radio, which had provided free advertising for jazz music in the previous two decades. But swing music itself was also partly to blame, its vital core enervated by the formulaic gestures of the name bands and the soundalike sameness of the second-tier groups. The public's taste was now shifting to pop singers, such as Frank Sinatra, and soon would embrace the transgressive sounds of rock and roll. Perhaps no single factor was pivotal in killing the big band, but the cumulative impact was enormous. In December 1946, no fewer than eight major swing orchestras disbanded—including those of Goodman, James, Dorsey, and Teagarden. By the close of the decade, only a few surviving units continued to work with any regularity. And in later years, a number of the most prominent exponents of swing were so-called ghost bands—a fitting label for these semimoribund ensembles, boasting the names of now-departed leaders with perhaps only a few holdovers in the orchestra from the glory days. These emblematic ensembles on life support continued to regurgitate the hits of earlier years without even a pretense of novelty or innovation.

The leaders who continued to program new big band music now struggled as never before. The story of Count Basie during these postwar years offers a telling example. Dance hall and hotel engagements steadily declined for his band, forcing Basie into smaller clubs such as Bop City and the Royal Roost. Sales of his recordings for the Victor label were poor, and quality suffered as the label sought desperately for gimmicks to revive the band's popularity. Basie was finally forced to disband in early 1950. His agent of long standing, Willard Alexander, went so far as to issue a statement to the press acknowledging that the Basie big band had been "destroyed as a box office attraction." The Count was left to front a decimated sextet. A less committed bandleader might have given up, but Basie fought back. He soon expanded to a septet, when veteran guitarist Freddie Green unilaterally decided that the band couldn't get by without him. ("He just came in on his own," Basie described Green's return. "One night we were playing somewhere in midtown, and I came to work and there he was with his guitar and everything . . . he's been right there ever since."[15]) When important gigs came up, Basie would add extra players. Slowly he reestablished his big band on an ongoing basis, rebuilding his core of soloists along the way. The so-called New Testament band, described in greater detail in chapter 6, may not have eclipsed listeners' memories of Lester Young and Herschel Evans—who could?—but nonetheless it made a major contribution to the Basie legacy.

Ellington's history during the decade of the 1950s followed a similar course. At one point, his stature had fallen so low that a writer in *Downbeat* urged Duke to retire from bandleading. This was extreme, even given *Downbeat*'s tabloidlike penchant at the time for stirring controversy, yet few could deny that the first half of the 1950s represented a low point in the history of the Ellington band. Ellington was increasingly content to rely on pieces from earlier decades. Only one substantial extended composition was written and recorded during these years, the fourteen-minute tone poem "Harlem," but it is a masterpiece by almost any measure. And with his 1953 recordings of "Satin Doll," Ellington showed himself still capable of writing a radio airplay hit (although this would be his last). Perhaps the most refreshing development of the later Ellington was his higher profile as a pianist and combo performer. His 1953 piano record for Capitol is a major statement for Ellington as both a player and composer ("Reflections in D" and "Melancholia"). In the following years, Ellington would make several other albums in this vein with positive results. His occasional collaborations with leading players of the younger generation—Charles Mingus, Max Roach, John Coltrane—also produced some of his most creative moments as small-combo pianist.

At the same time, a pronounced conservatism is evident in Ellington's big band work from these years. After two decades of continually reinventing his sound, Ellington's musical vocabulary evolved little after the close of the 1940s. The melodic and rhythmic innovations of modern jazz held little fascination for him. Except for token gestures (a gratuitous rock-inflected piece or a passing hint of bop), his efforts focused on reworking the fields he had plowed in earlier decades. And while other bandleaders (Stan Kenton, Gil Evans) sought out exotic instruments to add color to their orchestrations, Ellington appeared content to remain within the confines of the traditional swing band. In this light, it comes as little surprise that the turning point for Ellington in the 1950s was spurred by his revival of a composition almost twenty years old: "Diminuendo and Crescendo in Blue." Ellington's raucous performance of this piece at the 1956 Newport Jazz Festival electrified the audience. "Within an hour, reporters and critics were buzzing about it," Ellington's record company proudly proclaimed. "By next morning, it was generally conceded to have been one of the most exciting performances any of them had ever heard."[16] There was a tinge of irony in this praise. The fans were ecstatic not about Ellington's composition—or his orchestration or even his pianism. Rather, it was tenorist Paul Gonsalves's showboating twenty-seven-chorus solo, filled to the brim with blues clichés and occasional snatches of inspiration, that brought the crowd to its feet.

Ellington's career now had a second wind. Only a few months before Newport, interest in his band had sunk so low that Duke had resorted to playing background music for the Aquacades, a water show staged outside New York City. Better bookings were now coming his way. Ellington's picture graced the cover of *Time* magazine. His band was again recording for a major label. On the heels of Newport, Ellington recorded *Such Sweet Thunder*, an impressive collaboration with Billy Strayhorn, which ranks among their finest moments. Television beckoned, with CBS featuring his 1957 *A Drum Is a Woman*. The film industry was not far behind, commissioning Ellington to compose the score for *Anatomy of a Murder* in 1959 and *Paris Blues* in 1961. And many of the older players were returning to the fold: Johnny Hodges in 1955; Lawrence Brown and Juan Tizol in 1960; Cootie Williams in 1962.

In his final years, Ellington's position as a public figure threatened to overwhelm his purely musical pursuits. He took on the role of elder statesman for the jazz world, traveling to Asia, Australia, North Africa, Latin America, Europe, and Russia. His seventieth birthday was celebrated at the White House. French President Georges Pompidou named him to the Legion of Honor. Haile Selassie of Ethiopia awarded him the Emperor's Star. The Pulitzer Prize was almost presented to him in 1965, but the decision was overruled at the last minute when the Pulitzer board rejected the recommendation of the music jury—a disgraceful move at the time, which looks worse with every passing year. Doubleday paid Ellington a $50,000 advance for an autobiography, unheard of at the time for a jazz book, which eventually resulted in his elegant kiss-and-tell-little memoir *Music Is My Mistress*. Of course, there were always new musical pieces, and they continued to bespeak grand ambitions: suites commemorating Ellington's travels (*Far East Suite*, *Latin American Suite*) or the jazz heritage (*New Orleans Suite*), coexisting alongside hoary classical adaptations (*Peer Gynt*, *The Nutcracker*). Yet the appearance of originality, in a title or dedication, could not disguise the fact that Duke was mostly working over familiar territory. "Mount Harissa" from *The Far East Suite* sounds superficially exotic, but the chord changes are essentially the same as in "Take the A Train"; *Latin American Suite* found Ellington tackling the idiomatic music of that region—but, then again, hadn't he already pioneered this decades earlier with his masterful Latin-tinged works from the 1940s? Ellington's massive and moving *Sacred Concerts* also appeared to break new ground as well, but even here he drew on earlier compositions such as "Come Sunday." Time after time, Ellington's huge ambitions were invariably measured against the even larger proportions of his own past work. These later pieces were not without their virtues—most have held up surprisingly well with the passing years—but Ellington's works were no longer seen as pathbreaking or progressive by most jazz fans and critics. And in the hothouse jazz environment of the 1960s, where being at the cutting edge was lauded as the ultimate virtue, Ellington could no longer demand center stage. Meanwhile, outside the jazz world, only rock and Rolling Stones dotted the desolate landscape of popular music. In this context, few could appreciate the gems that Ellington or Strayhorn still composed: "Isfahan," "Heaven," "Blood Count." Ellington, for his part, increasingly gravitated to settings—overseas or inside the White House—where he could flourish as an unofficial ambassador for jazz, a role for which this Duke was perfectly suited.

But many of the most seasoned veterans of the Ellington band were now passing away or slipping quietly into retirement. Billy Strayhorn's death in 1967 devastated Ellington, depriving him of a close friend and an integral part of his creative life. He responded with a tribute album, . . . *And His Mother Called Him Bill*, which stands out as perhaps his most emotionally charged project of the decade, rivaled only by the *Sacred Concerts*. In 1970, Johnny Hodges died suddenly during a routine dental visit. Jimmy Hamilton left in 1968, Lawrence Brown in 1970, Cat Anderson in 1971. Paul Gonsalves died only a few days before Ellington in 1974. The Ellington band, in its final days, had become faceless—almost unthinkable given its history of strong musical personalities.

In January 1974, Ellington was briefly hospitalized in Los Angeles and diagnosed with lung cancer. Released after eight days, Duke returned to the road and the incessant demands of new musical projects. In March 1974, he left the band in midtour to check into the Columbia Presbyterian Hospital in New York. Here he gave in begrudgingly to his illness, yet insisted on having an electric piano brought to his bedside so he could continue work on his comic opera *Queenie Pie*. On May 24, he died of pneumonia. Ellington's funeral was held three days later, on Memorial Day, with over ten thousand people paying their respects in person, in addition to the numerous eulogies and testimonials from fans and friends around the world. Gunther Schuller compared Ellington to Bach, Beethoven, and Schoenberg. President Nixon praised him as the nation's foremost composer. The *New York Times* concurred, in its front-page obituary, citing him as "America's most important composer."

The passing years have validated this high-flown praise. Ellington's death marked only a brief pause in the expansion of his legacy. On the day of his funeral, Ellington's son Mercer took up his father's baton to lead the band at a Bermuda engagement ("The Duke would have wanted it that way," he explained to a reporter[17]). Mercer Ellington also saw to the completion of Duke's *Queenie Pie* and its premiere in Philadelphia in 1986. But the continuing activity of the band was only a small part of the posthumous explosion of Ellingtonia. Gary Giddins has estimated that, in the decade following Ellington's death, some fifty hours' worth of previously unissued music was commercially released. These works, including virtually complete versions of important Carnegie Hall concerts from the 1940s, only served to reinforce Ellington's glowing and still growing reputation. Certainly in the jazz world, no later composer has matched the breadth, the depth, the inspiration of Ellington's impressive oeuvre. And even when one casts a wider net, searching through the ranks of popular, academic, and classical composers, Ellington still stands among a select handful of masters—Copland, Gershwin, Ives, Joplin, Sousa—whose achievements represent the finest flowering of American music.

6 Modern Jazz

THE BIRTH OF BEBOP

Long before modern jazz emerged as a distinctive style, an ideology of modernism had been implicitly embraced by the music's practitioners. From its earliest days, jazz had been a forward-looking art, continually incorporating new techniques, more expansive harmonies, more complex rhythms, more intricate melodies. Sometimes this ideology of progress was stated explicitly, as in Beiderbecke and the Chicagoans' oft-spoken praise of Stravinsky and other contemporary classical composers; in other instances, no words were necessary, as with the implicit modernism of Armstrong's breakthrough recordings of the 1920s. But whether they expostulated about the future of music or merely announced its arrival through the bells of their horns, the leading musicians of early jazz were modernists in the truest sense of the term. They were admired—or chastised, as the case may be—as daring exponents of the new and bold.

It is easy to lose sight of just how remarkable this modernist bent was, given its context. The concept of progress has played a modest role in most ethnic music traditions. Those who draw connections between jazz and African music miss this important difference. The griots of West Africa, for example, aim to preserve their cultural legacy as it is handed down to them. This is not a mere aesthetic choice, but a cultural imperative: they are the historians of their society and must maintain the integrity of their precious musical heritage. Such an attitude defies casual experimentation. In other preindustrial settings, music partakes of a quasi-sacred efficacy. It may accompany a ritual or initiate a supernatural change. In such charged contexts, any modification in the music is viewed as a risky act, never encouraged and at best tolerated with anxiety and distrust. Of course, musical practices have evolved over time, even in traditional non-Western cultures, but at the slowest of paces. "Performers" raised in such environments have only gradually (and often with great reluctance) accepted the Western concept of music as casual entertainment, with its attendant expectations of novelty (hence change) in the idiom. And it is far from clear whether this ostensibly more "progressive" Western attitude really represents progress for those whom, previously, music had partaken of the divine.

Almost from the start, jazz players embraced a different mandate, accepting their role as entertainers and pursuing experimentation with an ardent zeal. This created a paradoxical foundation for jazz, one that remains to this day: for the jazz musician soon proved to be a restless soul, at one moment fostering the tradition, at another shattering it, mindless of the pieces. Even more striking, this progressive attitude of early jazz players came from members of America's most disempowered underclass. Recall that this music was not only viewed with apprehension by much of the ruling class but was often belittled and derided even within black America's own ranks. In the face of this hostility, simply preserving the African American vernacular music heritage—saving the legacy of a Buddy Bolden or King Oliver from the oblivion that obscures the early history of most traditional forms of music— would have been a major achievement. But advancing the jazz idiom to produce an Ellington or Armstrong was nothing short of miraculous—and all in the span of a single generation. One searches in vain through all the countries of the world to find another example of such a rapid and dramatic transformation from folk music to art music.

Given this feat, the rise of a more overt modernism in the early 1940s should not be viewed as an abrupt shift, as a major discontinuity in the music's history. It was simply an extension of jazz's inherent tendency to mutate, to change, to grow. Jazz had already revealed its ability to swallow other musical idioms—the march, the blues, the spiritual, the American popular song, the rag—and make them a part of itself. To do the same with Stravinsky and Hindemith, Schoenberg and Ravel presented, no doubt, an extraordinary challenge, but also an inevitable one. By the 1930s, the question now was not whether jazz would embrace modernism, but when and how and by whom. As early as 1931, journalists were comparing Ellington to Stravinsky and Ravel. A few years later, Benny Goodman made a more overt attempt to affiliate himself with contemporary classical music, commissioning works from Bartók, Hindemith, and Copland. And these were only the most prominent examples. Who can deny the modernist leanings of an Art Tatum? Or a Coleman Hawkins? Or a Don Redman? Or a Bix Beiderbecke?

The irony is that modern jazz sprang from none of these roots. It came neither from the Carnegie Hall concerts of Ellington and Goodman, nor from the virtuoso pianists of Harlem stride, nor from the other experimental big band sounds of the Swing Era. True, it drew bits and pieces of inspiration from all these sources, but it sounded like none of them. Instead, the leading jazz modernists of the 1940s developed their own unique style, brash and unapologetic, in backrooms and after-hours clubs, at jam sessions and on the road with traveling bands. This music was not for commercial consumption, nor was it meant to be at this embryonic stage. It survived in the interstices of the jazz world. Its comings and goings were not announced in the newspaper of record. Its early stars were, at best, cult figures from beyond the fringe, not household names. Its evolution was not preserved on acetate by record companies—our few glimpses into its early development come mostly from tapes or discs made by amateur engineers, enthusiasts willing to lug bulky equipment to nightclubs or private sessions where the new music was being made. In short, modern jazz was an underground movement, setting the pattern for all the future underground movements of the jazz world, initiating the bunker mentality that survives to this day in the world of progressive jazz. There is irony here, too: at a time when jazz was sweeping the nation, the music's next generation was moving further and further outside the mainstream of popular culture.

What was this new music? Early modern jazz, or bebop as it soon came to be called, rebelled against the populist trappings of swing music. The simple riffs, the accessible vocals, the orientation toward providing accompaniment to social dancing, the thick big band textures built on interlocking brass and reed sections—these trademarks of prewar jazz were set aside in favor of a more streamlined, more insistent style. Some things, of course, did not change. The thirty-two-bar song form and the twelve-bar blues remained cornerstones of the beboppers' repertoire. Frequently bebop composers simply grafted an exotic name and a new (and usually more complex) melody onto the chords of earlier popular standards. For example, Thelonious Monk's "52nd Street Theme" borrowed the harmonies of "I Got Rhythm," while Charlie Parker's "Ornithology" was a similar reworking of "How High the Moon." The instrumentation of modern jazz also stayed true to prewar models. Although the beboppers preferred the small-combo format to the prevalent big band sound, the underlying rhythm section of piano, string bass, drums, and occasionally guitar went unchallenged, as did the use of saxophones, trumpets, and trombones as typical frontline instruments.

Yet how these instruments were played underwent a sea change in the context of modern jazz. Improvised lines grew faster, more complex. The syncopations and dotted eighth note phrasings that had characterized earlier jazz were now far less prominent. Instead, long phrases might stay on the beat for measures at a time, built on a steady stream of eighth or sixteenth notes executed with quasi-mechanical precision, occasionally broken by a triplet, a pregnant pause, an interpolation of dotted eighths or whirlwind thirty-second notes, or a piercing offbeat phrase. The conception of musical time also changed hand in hand with this new way of phrasing; otherwise this less syncopated approach might have sounded rhythmically lifeless, a tepid jazz equivalent to the even sixteenth notes of baroque music. The 2/4 rhythmic feeling of New Orleans and Chicago was now completely replaced by the streamlined 4/4 sound favored by the Kansas City bands. But even more important, phrases often began and ended on the weak beats (two and four) or, increasingly, between beats, with unexpected points of emphasis adding to the querulous, incisive tone of the music. These characteristics imparted an off-balance quality to the proceedings and provided momentum for the solos, which now sometimes stretched on at great length, chorus after chorus. Above all, these crystalline improvisations were made vibrant by the breathless speed with which they were executed. Never before had instrumental technique been so central to the music's sound. Rarely had jazz tempos been so fast. Or, for that matter, so slow—the boppers were not afraid of even the most languid ballad tempos, but even in these instances their solos frequently implied a doubling of the stated time, staying true to the ethos of speed at all costs. The onomatopoeia of its nickname—at first "rebop" or "bebop," eventually shortened further to a simple "bop"—was all too fitting. This was music built out of small jabs and feints, rather than the sucker-punch haymakers, driven by straightforward syncopations, of an Armstrong or Hawkins, a Beiderbecke or Bechet.

The harmonic implications of this music also revealed a newfound complexity. Each of the major modern jazz composers delighted in certain trademark harmonic structures: note Dizzy Gillespie's fondness for patterns that descend in whole or half-steps, for example in "Con Alma" or in his tautly conceived interlude to "A Night in Tunisia," which unfolds with the austere precision of a Bach prelude; or Charlie Parker's predilection for ii–V substitutions in "Confirmation," "Blues for Alice," or the famous bridge to "Ko Ko"; or, most iconoclastic of all, Thelonious Monk's mastery of dissonances and unconventional chord structures, so beyond the mainstream that over a generation would pass before Monk's more outré works became regular parts of the jazz repertoire. True, these devices had been used in jazz before, but never to such a degree. Ellington's keyboard work from the 1930s and 1940s was heavily laced with dissonance, but these avant-garde tendencies were evident only to careful listeners who detected the eccentric piano work that underlay the big band sound. And, of course, the chords of "Ko Ko" were anything but new, having been borrowed wholesale from the swing standard "Cherokee." But before Parker, few dared to solo on this rapid romp through the circle of fifths, and the hearty souls who did would have never tried it at the tempos that the boppers preferred.

But more often, the harmonic complexity of modern jazz was implicit, suggested in the melody lines and improvisations rather than stated outright in the chords of the songs. After all, most bop compositions simply followed, more or less, the conventional progressions of prewar standards. But even when working over the familiar territory of "I Got Rhythm" or the twelve-bar blues, the boppers made heavy use of flatted ninths, sharpened elevenths, and other altered or higher intervals, to a degree unknown in earlier jazz. To gauge the full extent of this change, one need merely study the melody line to "Donna Lee," Charlie Parker's reworking of the standard "Indiana." The melody of "Indiana" is conventional, staying close to chord tones at all times, but Parker's piece immediately moves into deeper waters: almost every bar features one or more altered tones—an augmented fifth, a major seventh played against a minor chord, a flatted ninth leading to a sharpened ninth, and the like. The composition as a whole is nothing less than a textbook example of how bop harmonic thinking revolutionized the flow of the melodic line in jazz. One recalls Parker's alleged statement that an improviser should be able to use any note against any chord—it was simply a matter of placing it in the right context. All in all, the thirty-two bars of "Donna Lee" serve as a compact proof, almost Euclidean in its elegance, of this daring proposal.

Yet there was also a core of simplicity to this music. Arrangements were sparse, almost to an extreme. Renouncing the thick textures of the big band sound, beboppers mostly opted for monophonic melody statements. And even when there were two or more horns in the band—the pairing of saxophone and trumpet was a typical front line for a bop ensemble—they usually played the melody in unison. The quest for extended compositional forms—the holy grail of jazz—held little fascination for modern jazz players. Their compositional forms were mostly ready-to-hand, drawn from the American popular song repertoire.

The boppers were not formalists. Content, not form, was their preoccupation. Instrumental solos were at the heart of each performance, sandwiched between an opening and closing statement of the melody. Deviations from this recipe were rare—occasionally an interlude might be used between solos (as in Dizzy Gillespie's "Salt Peanuts"); introductions or codas might be allowed, but they rarely lasted for more than four bars. The free play of improvisation was the thing. Amateur recordings of the day—such as the famous Charlie Parker tapes and discs made by Dean Benedetti or Ralph Bass's searing account of Dexter Gordon and Wardell Gray battling over "The Hunt"—often leave out the melody statements entirely. The tape is not turned on until the solos start, almost as if the tune itself were inconsequential, like the advertisements and coming attractions that fill time before the feature film begins.

The celebrated histories of Charlie Parker and Dizzy Gillespie might lead one to believe that this musical revolution took place only on the front line, an upheaval among horn players. In fact, much of the changing sensibility of modern jazz was driven by the rhythm sections. In this regard, the rebel streak of modern jazz revealed its ample distance from the New Orleans–Chicago–New York triangle that had defined so much of the music's tradition. The rhythmic pulse of this new music instead traced its lineage to the Midwest and Southwest, and especially to Kansas City. The shimmering high-hat sound of a Jo Jones, the crackling guitar lines of a Charlie Christian, the 4/4 walking lines of a Walter Page or a Jimmy Blanton, the sparse piano comping of a Count Basie—each anticipated crucial elements that would come to define the bebop rhythmic sensibility. Under such influences, each instrument in the jazz rhythm section underwent a transformation during these years. The pulse of the music became less sharply articulated, more pointillistic. Sudden accents—the so-called bass drum bombs dropped by bebop percussionists or the crisp comping chords of pianists and guitarists—now frequently arrived off the beat or on weak beats. The dashing tempos required impeccable timekeeping and unprecedented stamina. After the onslaught of modern jazz, the rhythm section would never be the same.

But musicological analysis only takes us so far. Bebop was defined by its social context as much as by the flats and sharps of its altered chords. Outsiders even within the jazz world, the modern jazz players had the dubious distinction of belonging to an underclass within an underclass. Remember, this was a musical revolution made, first and foremost, by sidemen, not stars. Not by Benny Goodman, but by his guitarist Charlie Christian. Not by Duke Ellington, but by his bassist Jimmy Blanton. Not by Earl Hines, but by his saxophonist Charlie Parker. Not by Cab Calloway, but by his trumpeter Dizzy Gillespie. Not by Coleman Hawkins, but by his pianist Thelonious

Monk. Not by Louis Armstrong, but by his saxophonist Dexter Gordon. Unfettered by the commercial pressures that beset the name bandleaders of the day, these obscure practitioners of an unheralded art were free to pursue the extreme implications of this new sound. These less-than-famous players relished the opportunity to make a statement with "their" music, and the more difficult it was, all the better—little wonder that the resulting bebop style was, in sports parlance, in your face, a twentieth-century African American way of *épater les bourgeoisie*.

The individualism of the beboppers was fired further by their marginal status as black Americans at a critical juncture in U.S. history. In this last generation before the end of segregation and the passage of the Civil Rights Act, African Americans were intent on testing the limits as never before. The first generation of jazz players had succeeded as entertainers, and white America was content to celebrate them on that level. But the black jazz players of the 1940s wanted more. They demanded acceptance as artists, as esteemed practitioners of a serious musical form. Previously only a rare individual—a Scott Joplin or a Duke Ellington—aspired to these heights. But with the advent of bebop, a whole generation of black musicians was asserting itself as coequals with the purveyors of highbrow culture, the classical composers, the dramatists, the poets, the painters, the sculptors. Another generation would pass before jazz musicians began attending music conservatories in large numbers, but already by the 1940s the ethos that would inspire such ambitions was already evident.

Thus, the birth of modern jazz took place at a strange crossroads: drawing, on the one side, from the pungent roots and rhythms of Kansas City jazz, on the other delving into the rarefied atmosphere of high art. If a contradiction existed, it was exemplified most concretely in the music and abbreviated career of Charlie Parker. Parker the highbrow? One could sense it when, calling his sidemen to the bandstand, he summoned them by playing a snippet of Hindemith on the alto; or when he identified Stravinsky's "The Song of the Nightingale" during a blindfold test conducted for *Downbeat* in 1948—"Give that all the stars you've got," he told interviewer Leonard Feather—and went on to discuss Prokofiev, Hindemith, Debussy, and Ravel; or when, at the peak of his career, he announced his intention of taking composition lessons from the visionary classical composer Edgard Varèse. Parker the Kansas City jazz stalwart? This was his other, equally valid lineage. Who could deny it after hearing the bittersweet lament of "Parker's Mood," as deep a statement of the blues as exists in the jazz tradition? Jazz's past and future intersect in the life and times of this seminal figure.

Born in Kansas City, Kansas, on August 29, 1920—and moving across the border to Kansas City, Missouri, at age seven—Parker imbibed this tradition at its source, his formative years coinciding with the Pendergast era of semilegal vice with a jazz accompaniment. Like many of his generation, Parker learned jazz through recordings as well as at first hand—but most of his major influences were linked to his Kansas City environs. Above all, Lester Young—whose recorded solos Parker learned note for note—influenced the youngster with a linear conception of improvisation, one that indirectly set the foundation for modern jazz. But two early employers also left their stamp on Parker's music: saxophonist Buster Smith, a mainstay of Kansas City jazz (who had worked with the Blue Devils and Bennie Moten by the time he hired seventeen-year-old Charlie Parker for his own band in 1937), and Jay McShann, the quintessential Kaycee pianist and master of blues-drenched swing, who helped bring Parker to a national audience a short while later.

Parker's father, Charles Sr., had worked the black theater circuit as a pianist, singer, and dancer before settling in Kansas City. After his son's birth, he was rarely at home, both because of his drinking, which was forbidden in the household, and his second career as a chef on a Pullman line. Before Charlie's tenth birthday, his father had left the household for good. The task of rearing the youngster fell to Parker's mother, Addie, a strong-willed and religious woman who made ends meet through a variety of jobs: taking in boarders, doing laundry, working as a charwoman. Parker was, by all accounts, a mama's boy, coddled and pampered by his doting mother. "That's what I worked for and what I lived for, that boy," she told an interviewer years later, inconsolable after her son's early death.[1]

Parker's first flirtation with music was spurred by an unlikely source. Around the time he entered high school, the youngster heard a radio broadcast featuring the saxophone work of Rudy Vallee, a saccharine crooner more remembered for his stylized vocals than as a horn player. Responding to her son's urgings, Addie Parker purchased a used alto saxophone for $45. The youngster briefly studied music at Lincoln High School—where Walter Page and a host of Kansas City jazzmen had trained before him—but soon became disappointed with the baritone horn he was assigned in the school band ("all I did was play *coop, coop—coop, coop*," he recalled in a 1950 interview). His interest was rekindled when he began associating with older students whose musical interests tended toward jazz.

Parker was no saxophone prodigy. The various accounts of his early musical activities stress enthusiasm rather than depth of talent. A famous anecdote tells of the young altoist's humiliation at a jam session presided over by drummer Jo Jones of the Count Basie band. Struggling with the tempo, Parker faltered on the sax, but continued to press on—until Jones imperiously dismissed the youngster by picking up a cymbal from his kit and lofting it through the air to crash at the altoist's feet. Amid derisive laughter, Parker made his way off the bandstand. Rather than be discouraged by this public failure, Parker practiced with even greater determination. During a summer stint playing and practicing at a resort in the Ozarks, he studied the recordings Lester Young had made with the Count Basie band and deepened his knowledge of music theory. We can only speculate on Parker's progress during this period, but his rapid ascension, after the Ozarks gig, to higher-profile engagements with better-known musicians suggests that the hard work was now paying off. At the close of summer, Parker was hired to play second alto in Buster Smith's band, and the Kansas City veteran now served as a mentor for the teenager. In Smith's group he worked alongside pianist Jay McShann, who would soon be featuring Parker in his own band.

Parker later claimed, in a notorious aside, that he had begun dissipating at age twelve and using heroin by age fifteen. An exaggeration perhaps, but only a slight one. An indifferent student, Parker left Lincoln High School before his sophomore year. By age sixteen, Parker was married, with a pregnant wife, and working as a professional musician. Sometime during the next year, first wife Rebecca Ruffin asserts, he began using intravenous drugs. After leaving Buster Smith, Parker played for a few weeks with Jay McShann before taking to the road, not as a part of a traveling band but merely as a wandering vagabond. In Chicago he caught the attention of Billy Eckstine, as much for his unkempt appearance as for his superlative alto playing—"the raggedest guy you'd want to see," Eckstine recalled years later, "but playing like you never heard." Later, he made his way to New York and he worked as a dishwasher at a Harlem nightspot where Art Tatum played. Like Armstrong and Ellington before him, Parker failed to take New York by storm on his first visit. After gigging sporadically and trying his hand at various local jam sessions, he soon retreated to Kansas City, ostensibly for his father's funeral. Around this same time, he acquired the nickname Yardbird, often shortened to Bird. Accounts of how he earned this sobriquet differ—it may have initially referred to nothing more than an appetite for poultry—but eventually it took on a larger significance, representing to his fans the unprecedented free-flying creativity of his alto sax lines.

The survival of an amateur recording of Parker from this period provides us with the first insight into the pathbreaking approach to improvisation he was in the process of developing. The precise dating of this workout over the changes of "Honeysuckle Rose" and "Body and Soul" has generated much debate. Some have placed it as early as 1937, others as late as 1940. Parker's apparent allusions to a Roy Eldridge and Chu Berry recording of "Body and Soul" from 1938 and to the melody of Jimmy Van Heusen's "I Thought About You," copyrighted and first recorded in 1939, suggest that the document comes from the latter end of this period. Moreover, the maturity of Parker's conception also supports a recording date of around 1940, after his return to Kansas City from his Chicago and Harlem experiences. After all, Parker later claimed that his initial breakthrough—a realization that the higher intervals of the chord could serve as the basic springboard for melodic improvisation—took place during this New York visit. And the "Honeysuckle Rose"/"Body and Soul" performance makes liberal use of this technique. This is no student exercise. No other saxophonist of the day, Hawkins or Young included, was delving this deeply into advanced harmony. The relaxed virtuosity of his later recordings is notably absent, the phrasing is still stiff; but Parker's conceptual understanding is frighteningly mature.

Soon after returning to Kansas City, Parker rejoined McShann, with whom he would stay for most of the next two years. His solos graced a number of McShann recordings from this period, commercial sides as well as amateur transcriptions, and attracted a small cadre of admirers—albeit mostly among other musicians rather than the general public. Especially revealing are performances from November 1940 recorded at a local radio station by several ardent Wichita University jazz fans. On "Lady Be Good," Parker shows that he has mastered the mannerisms of Lester Young (even including a passing allusion to "Mean to Me") in crafting a polished if somewhat derivative solo. But, once again on "Honeysuckle Rose," Parker distinguishes himself with a commanding improvisation, daring in its melodic thrusts and executed with fluidity. Several months later, McShann began recording commercially for Decca, and Parker's solo contributions again stand out. On "The Jumpin' Blues," Parker opens his improvisation with a willowy extended phrase that anticipates the unadulterated bebop of his later composition "Ornithology." This is the saxophonist's strongest recorded work to date, confirmed further by "Sepian Bounce" and "Swingmatism" from the same period.

Although the influence of Lester Young has been frequently highlighted—and no doubt proved crucial in Parker's musical development—the altoist clearly drew inspiration from a variety of other sources during the late 1930s and early 1940s. Parker's early recordings show the wide range of his musical tastes: a hotel room jam session preserved on disk by Bob Redcross in February 1943 finds him quoting Ben Webster's solo on "Cotton Tail"; other amateur sides show Parker alluding to Coleman Hawkins's landmark improvisation on "Body and Soul"; an even more unusual addition to the Parker discography from this period captures the altoist practicing over a recording of the Benny Goodman Trio. At other points, momentary echoes of Willie Smith and Johnny Hodges can be heard in his playing. The lithe phrasing of Young overlays all these sources, providing the basic melodic prism through which the other influences were filtered. A few years later, the jazz press would depict Parker and the other beboppers as rebels who had rejected the swing tradition, but a much different lesson can be drawn from these recordings of bop in transition. The stylistic leap made by Parker (and the other beboppers) would have been impossible without careful study of the earlier pioneers of jazz tradition.

But even the most careful genealogical tracing of Parker's sources fails to explain the unique sound of his alto saxophone. There are no predecessors—neither Lester nor Hawk, Hodges nor Carter—in this regard. A utilitarian philosophy, emphasizing economy of means, appears to be at work here. Each note is articulated with focused energy, each phrase smoothly executed but infused with an acerbic aftertaste. Phrases start and end with crisp precision. No moody rubato timing stretches out the melodic line. There are no lingering breaths, à la Ben Webster, to impart an expansive, velvety quality to the music. Each phrase is attacked with clear intent. All in all, no saxophonist before Parker had such a cutting sound. As such, his influence on later jazz players has been enormous. After Parker, the more warm and rounded tone of a Benny Carter or Johnny Hodges became passé, their diffused romanticism replaced by a surgical sharpness of attack. For all their differences, the testosterone-infused sounds of later jazz saxophonists (Rollins, Coltrane, Coleman) would not have been possible without Parker's pioneering model. This too was part of the bopper's rebellion against the pop music pretensions of Swing Era jazz. The sentimental trappings, the influence of the sweet bands, the various ways the rough edges of jazz music had been softened for consumption by a mass audience—these elements were now to be purged in favor of a purer conception of jazz: an art music with the emotional pungency of a battle cry. Slow dancers seeking a romantic interlude were now advised to keep their distance from the jazz bandstand.

In 1940, the Cab Calloway band came to Kansas City, with a young trumpeter named John Gillespie—already dubbed Dizzy by his colleagues—in the horn section. During an intermission, trumpeter Buddy Anderson told Gillespie about a local saxophonist who was well worth hearing. Gillespie later recalled his low expectations: "'Oh, man,' I said, 'a saxophone player? I'm playing with Chu Berry; and I know Benny Carter and played with Coleman Hawkins, and I know Lester Young.'" Gillespie, despite his youth, was already one of the most harmonically and technically adept trumpeters of the day, and was not prepared to be impressed. However, Anderson persisted, and the following day arranged for the two to engage in an impromptu jam session, with Gillespie comping on piano and Parker playing alto. The meeting would prove to be a major turning point in both careers. "I was astounded by what the guy could do," Gillespie continued the story. "These other guys that I had been playing with weren't my colleagues, really. But the moment I heard Charlie Parker, I said, there is my colleague. . . . Charlie Parker and I were moving in practically the same direction too, but neither of us knew it."[2]

Gillespie had traveled a much different route in reaching this defining moment in his musical development. Unlike Parker, who had been schooled in the midst of a burgeoning jazz scene, Gillespie had come of age in the backwoods of Cheraw, South Carolina. The last of nine children—"only seven of us lived long enough to get a name"[3]—John Birks Gillespie was raised by an indifferent mother and an abusive father. "Every Sunday morning, Papa would whip us. That's mainly how I remember him." The elder Mr. Gillespie was a bricklayer who played piano with a local band on the weekends. He also agreed to store the instruments at his home during the week—to prevent a down-and-out sideman from pawning one in between gigs. The house's front room had the cluttered look of a used instrument shop, its furnishings including a piano, a set of drums, a mandolin, a guitar, and a red one-string bass fiddle. From an early age, John Birks learned about the sound, the feel of these different musical "toys."

Support and encouragement came mostly outside the home, from neighbors and teachers. During fifth grade, Gillespie was enlisted into the school band. The youngest student in the ensemble, he had last choice of the available instruments, and was assigned a slide trombone that was several inches too large for his meager arm span. Undeterred, Gillespie practiced diligently and soon was borrowing a neighbor's trumpet, which he also learned to play. By age twelve he had acquired a rudimentary technique on both horns, but increasingly gravitated toward the trumpet. Opportunities to perform were soon coming his way. In this sheltered environment, the youngster could develop a sense of identity and mastery as a musician that would not have been possible in a Kansas City or New York. Gillespie prided himself on being the "best young trumpeter around Cheraw." In fact, he could only play in one key at the time, and struggled to read music. In an encounter reminiscent of Parker's humiliation at the hands of Jo Jones, Gillespie's pretensions to expertise were shattered when a local trumpeter who had been gigging in Philadelphia came back to Cheraw to visit his family. He "cut me seriously," Gillespie later recalled. "Sonny counted down and started playing in the key of C, but all I could do was fumble around because I couldn't find one note on the trumpet. . . . I felt so crushed, I cried, because I was supposed to be the town's best trumpet player."

A sociology of jazz could glean much from these accounts of jam-session disgraces. Such public embarrassments would stand as a frequent rite of passage for the modern jazz musician. Years later, both Parker and Gillespie would play similar mind games on other, lesser players. At the early 1940s sessions at Minton's and Monroe's, the Harlem clubs where the bebop vocabulary was refined, the cognoscenti used fast tempos and complex melody lines to intimidate outsiders and establish their own credentials. In a setting where conservatory degrees were still unknown, one's curriculum vitae was earned every night on the bandstand. This combative, macho culture is rarely discussed, but remains a core value within the jazz community. In the biographies of Parker and Gillespie—and numerous other players—these painful setbacks take on the luster of defining moments, described with a fervor that recalls the hackneyed adage about "separating the men from the boys." The accepted jazz cliché about "payin' one's dues" puts a more socially acceptable twist on this whole ritual—making it sound, after all, like some sort of economic transaction— but ignores the undercurrent of aggression that infuses this darker side to the jazz mindset. Who knows what modern jazz would have sounded like without this persistent desire for one-upmanship?

In Gillespie's case (as in Parker's before him), the youngster now studied the horn with renewed dedication. Within months he had learned to play with ease in several keys. By the time he was fifteen, Gillespie felt confident enough to sit in with the visiting jazz bands that performed at the Cheraw Elks Hall. But the music that came to Cheraw over the airwaves had an even more profound effect on him. The Gillespie household possessed neither a gramophone nor a radio, but a neighbor who owned both let the teenager stop by to use them. Broadcasts featuring the Teddy Hill Orchestra, captured in performance at Harlem's Savoy Ballroom, would make the strongest impression on Gillespie. The youngster paid particular attention to Hill's trumpeter Roy Eldridge, who would remain the dominant model for Gillespie as he strived to create his own approach to the horn. The solid technique, the rhythmic excitement, the commanding range—these same qualities that he so admired in the elder trumpeter's playing would later infuse Gillespie's own virtuosic conception of the instrument. One measure of how well he succeeded would come several years later when he joined the Teddy Hill band himself, filling the same role that Eldridge had held before him.

In fall 1933, Gillespie entered the Laurinburg Institute in North Carolina, where he pursued the formal study of music. His grasp of harmony was further enriched by his work on the piano, where he tried out chord structures and, in later years, wrote most of his compositions and arrangements. In spring 1935, his family moved to Philadelphia, and the youngster followed a few months later. Here he began working odd jobs as a professional musician and associating with other aspiring young trumpeters—in particular his cousin Charlie Shavers, three months older than Dizzy, who would come to prominence as a soloist with the John Kirby sextet, one of the finer small combos of its day, and later with the Tommy Dorsey big band.

Shavers shared Gillespie's enthusiasm for Roy Eldridge, and they both memorized Eldridge's solos and began playing them note for note on gigs. The Eldridge sound would continue to linger in the background of Gillespie's playing long after he developed his mature style, and would give a veneer of Swing Era traditionalism to even Dizzy's most experimental work. And perhaps it was Eldridge's model that led Gillespie to retain a strong sense of syncopation in his playing while other beboppers—especially Parker—favored more flowing lines. Moreover, Gillespie would often break up the long melodic lines, so favored by modern jazz players, with short, jagged phrases and virtuosic leaps into the higher register of the horn—both mannerisms also reminiscent of Eldridge. These elements of showmanship, which connected Dizzy to the prebop tradition of jazz trumpet—not just Eldridge, but back further to Armstrong—also were appreciated by the general public, who accorded Gillespie a fame and following that no other bebopper enjoyed.

In 1937, Gillespie, only nineteen years old, moved to New York. Here he stayed with his brother and experienced the wide range of music the city had to offer. He frequented the Savoy Ballroom, sat in with Chick Webb, met the great Cuban trumpeter Mario Bauzá—who helped spur an interest in Latin rhythms that would have a lasting influence on Gillespie's music—and began to make a reputation for himself as an up-and-coming trumpeter. A chance encounter with Teddy Hill at the Savoy Ballroom led to Gillespie joining Hill's band for a European tour. His solos on the band's May 1937 recordings of "King Porter Stomp" and "Blue Rhythm Fantasy" make clear that Gillespie was already a skillful imitator of Eldridge's work.

The addition of Kenny Clarke to the Teddy Hill band brought Gillespie into close contact with a drummer who would help transform the rhythmic pulse in modern jazz. A Pittsburgh native who had apprenticed in a wide range of bands in the Midwest and on the East Coast, Clarke had emulated the lighter swinging style of Jo Jones, shifting the underlying beat from the bass drum to the ride cymbal. On top of this Clarke added an array of offbeat accents, percussive asides, and cracking cat-o'-nine-tails interjections designed to propel the soloist. These polyrhythmic explosions came to be called "bombs" by the jazz players of the war years. Clarke's nickname, Klook (sometimes Klook-Mop), may have been an onomatopoeic echo of this technique. He would come to play a prominent role at the Harlem jam sessions where the new modern jazz style was forged. Proficient on several instruments and a skilled composer (he is listed as cowriter of Gillespie's "Salt Peanuts" and Monk's "Epistrophy"), Clarke stood out as one of the most versatile percussionists of his generation.

Gillespie's next major employer, Cab Calloway, was more than a top jazz bandleader but also one of the leading entertainers of the day. His flamboyant wardrobe, his extroverted stage presence, his pseudo-hip scat singing captured the public's imagination—so much so that George Gershwin used him as the model for the flashy Sportin' Life character in *Porgy and Bess*. Calloway and Gillespie had a stormy relationship—the trumpeter was eventually fired after a heated offstage encounter with the bandleader—but Dizzy clearly learned by watching his boss's act. "Playing with Cab, I was always doing my damndest to be hip," Gillespie later acknowledged. Following his stint with the band, Gillespie began sporting the beret and stylish clothes that would become virtual trademarks of the bebop movement. Gillespie would later stand out as the only prominent member of the bebop generation who took the role of entertainer seriously, and he made it a point to charm the audiences who came to see him with his banter as well as with his music. Whether in pursuing hokey onstage routines or simply ad libbing jokes with the audience, he countered and, at times, even parodied the self-serious attitude of his contemporaries. Calloway's influence in this regard has typically been ignored by commentators and critics but may well have been decisive.

Of course, Gillespie's evolution during this period went beyond the superficial veneer of clothing and mannerisms. Section mate Mario Bauzá, who had befriended Gillespie during his early New York days, again took the younger trumpeter under his wing—"Mario was like my father"—as well as nurtured Gillespie's growing interest in Afro-Cuban music. Gillespie's arrangement of "Pickin' the Cabbage" for the Calloway band reflected this new direction in his compositions. His opportunities outside of the Calloway band also began to expand. In 1939, Gillespie was enlisted to participate in the Lionel Hampton recording of "When Lights Are Low" and "Hot Mallets," where he worked alongside a horn section composed of Ben Webster, Coleman Hawkins, Benny Carter, and Chu Berry. Less visible to the public, but even more influential, were the informal sessions Gillespie was attending when the Calloway band resided in New York.

These jam sessions at Minton's and Monroe's Uptown House have frequently been cited as the birthplace of bop, the melting pot where the disparate elements that contributed to this music coalesced into a definable style. Firsthand accounts, supplemented by a few amateur recordings, reinforce the importance of these venues, yet their elevation to mythic status has overshadowed the many innovations that were making headway outside their doors, and glosses over the halting and gradual progress that often took place even on these famous bandstands, where more traditional instrumentalists, vocalists of various stripes, and assorted wannabes often shared the stage with the burgeoning boppers. To a great extent, the historical importance of the Minton's and Monroe's sessions only became clear in retrospect. "I wasn't thinking about trying to change the course of jazz. I was just trying to play something that sounded good," Thelonious Monk later characterized the Minton's gig.[4] Monk and Kenny Clarke were the only prominent modernists on the payroll at the club, but the guests on any given night might include other young progressives such as Gillespie or Parker, Jimmy Blanton or Charlie Christian, as well as seasoned Swing Era veterans Roy Eldridge, Coleman Hawkins, Lester Young, Benny Goodman, or Ben Webster.

Of the younger players involved in the Minton's sessions, pianist Thelonious Monk stood out as one of most adventurous and clearly the least easy to classify. His interest in unconventional harmonies and rhythmic patterns converged to some extent with Gillespie and Parker's, but his overall conception of improvisation and composition remained *sui generis*. As his mature style made clear, the facile virtuosity of the other beboppers held little lasting interest for him, nor was he attracted to the fast tempos and flashy improvisational style that came to characterize most bebop music. Instead, he delved more deeply into textures and dissonances, and pursued a style of improvisation far more compositional in nature. Few other pianists were prepared to follow in this path until the 1950s, and the full extent of his impact would not be felt until after his death in 1982.

Only a few days younger than Gillespie, Monk had been born in Rocky Mountain, North Carolina, on October 10, 1917, but spent most of his youth in the San Juan Hill section of New York. His family's acquisition of a player piano sometime around 1926 inspired the youngster to try his hand at the keyboard, and he began taking lessons at age eleven. In his teens Monk apprenticed in the musical venues of Harlem, which ranged from rent parties to the Apollo Theater, and at sixteen he went on the road with an evangelical troupe. He was a little-known musician, scuffling from gig to gig when, at age twenty-three, he landed the job as house pianist at Minton's.

Monk and the other Minton's players were soon joined by an alto saxophonist who was making a name for himself at after-hours sessions held at nearby Clark Monroe's Uptown House. Charlie Parker, who had crossed paths with Gillespie in Kansas City some months back, was now frequently reunited with the trumpeter onstage at these New York sessions. Now supported by Clarke, Monk, and other talented young players, Parker and Gillespie solidified their experimental leanings into a powerful style. They began recrafting standard songs such as "I Got Rhythm" as well as developing new compositions, pursuing faster and faster tempos, and honing a quicksilver, virtuoso technique that would frighten and astonish, by turns, other instrumentalists. A paper disc recording from the collection of Jerry Newman finds Parker, circa 1942, blowing over the changes of "Cherokee" at a Monroe's session: Bird's rhythm section is stodgy, offering a tepid two-beat support, but Parker's solo is fiery and inventive. Another amateur recording of "Sweet Georgia Brown," from a few months later, finds Parker in more suitable company, with Gillespie joining him on trumpet—the duo's earliest surviving recorded collaboration—and Blanton disciple Oscar Pettiford, a sympathetic accompanist, on bass. This is a raw performance, especially Gillespie's contribution, but there can be no mistaking it for anything other than bebop.

By this time, both Parker and Gillespie were working together in Earl Hines's big band. Despite his prominence as a master of traditional styles, Hines had put together what may well have been the most forward-looking jazz orchestra of its day. From 1928 to 1939, Hines had found a safe haven from the Great Depression, which decimated the careers of so many musicians, as leader of the house band at the Grand Terrace, a posh Chicago nightclub. Hines was almost the antithesis of Ellington, preferring to delegate responsibility for his band's sound rather than take an active role as leader. He prospered by hiring musical talents with different stylistic allegiances from his own and giving them substantial responsibility for shaping the style of the group. This would prove to be a key formula for the 1943 band's success, but even a decade earlier Hines had moved far beyond the "classic" sound of his sides with Louis Armstrong and Jimmie Noone (although he would return to this traditional approach after the twenty-year hiatus that spanned from 1928 to 1948), and was anticipating the advent of the Swing Era. Relying on the strong charts of Jimmy Mundy, Budd Johnson, Quinn Wilson, and others, Hines was fronting one of the hottest dance bands of the day. But almost at the crest of the Swing Era, Hines was already embracing even more modern sounds. The first signs of the Hines band's flirtation with bebop could be seen in 1941, when members Billy Eckstine, Budd Johnson, Freddie Webster, Little Benny Harris, and Shadow Wilson all showed, to a greater or lesser extent, leanings toward a more progressive conception of jazz. These allegiances exploded into full-fledged modernism late in 1942 when Hines hired Gillespie, whose reputation had spread through his work with Calloway, Lucky Millinder, and others. A short while later, Hines brought in Charlie Parker to play tenor sax (in replacement of departing Budd Johnson) as well as vocalist Sarah Vaughan.

In late 1942, Vaughan had won an amateur contest at the Apollo Theater—claiming a prize of ten dollars and a week-long engagement at the famous venue. Hines heard her at the Apollo and, impressed by her vocal skills and range, which spanned almost three octaves, offered her a job with his orchestra. Now, still in her teens, Vaughan was sharing the bandstand with the two greatest talents of the new generation of jazz players. But the young vocalist was singularly well equipped to thrive in this setting. Like the beboppers, who flaunted their virtuosity, Vaughan had unsurpassed technical fluency and a fondness for ornate phrasing. She also shared the beboppers' deep grasp of harmony and, like a growing number of them, could demonstrate it with some facility on the piano. In fact, her original role in the Hines band had her serving as vocalist and backup pianist to Hines. In her range, her skill in navigating difficult interval leaps, her instinct for the grand gesture, her expressive mastery of tones and timbres, Vaughan seemed closer in spirit to Gillespie than to other jazz singers. It comes as little surprise that jazz historians cite Vaughan as evoking an essentially "hornlike" style of vocals. Gillespie, responding to the inspiration of this new addition to the band, began showing an interest in writing parts to back Vaughan's singing. Gillespie's "Night in Tunisia," which would become a bop anthem, dates from this period and was originally recorded (although not until the end of 1944) with a Vaughan vocal under the name "Interlude." In later years, Vaughan, like many jazz vocalists, tempered her bop proclivities in pursuit of a more mainstream pop-oriented style. Drawing heavily on the Tin Pan Alley tradition, she made memorable recordings of various "songbooks" of composers such as Gershwin, Rodgers, and Berlin. In time, her reputation as a jazz diva came to be matched by deserved respect as an interpreter of popular music. But rarely would her later work find her in a jazz setting as inspiring as the Hines band of the war years.

Or so one suspects. Unfortunately, the recording ban prevented this edition of the Hines band from ever entering the studio. Certainly no commercial recordings were made and no taped broadcasts (so common with other bands from this period) have materialized. The 1943 Earl Hines orchestra ranks only slightly below the Buddy Bolden band as the most important unrecorded ensemble in the history of jazz. Nor do later recordings by the band provide much information. Hines was unable to retain this all-star lineup of emerging stars for long, and by the time he returned to the studio the group had lost its key soloists. Little Benny Harris left in July 1943, and Parker departed in August. Soon after, Billy Eckstine quit to form his own band, eventually bringing with him some of Hines's finest talents, including Gillespie and Vaughan.

A powerful singer with a resonant baritone voice, Eckstine had recorded the hit "Jelly, Jelly" while with the Hines band and now was interested in building on that success. As it turned out, his fascination with the cutting-edge sounds of bop may have compromised his success as a pop singer. Under somewhat different circumstances, Eckstine might have approached the popularity of a Nat King Cole, or even a Frank Sinatra, but the broader audience he sought mostly eluded him. This early 1940s Eckstine band, the most important of his career, did little to help his prospects, dividing critics and making little headway with the general public. Yet its solid musicianship and modern jazz ethos established it as a major forerunner to the bop big bands of Gillespie, Woody Herman, and others. But Eckstine, like Hines, found it difficult to retain his star soloists, many of whom were leaving to work in the small-combo format that would come to dominate the bebop idiom.

THE MAINSTREAMING OF BEBOP

The landscape of jazz was now changing in tandem with the music. In the years leading up to World War II, a few small jazz clubs had set up business in the ground floor of the brownstone apartments on Fifty-second Street between Fifth Avenue and Seventh Avenue. As the music's audience shifted from dance aficionados to serious listeners, these clubs gained distinction as the new center of the jazz universe, close enough to Times Square to draw visitors, servicemen on leave, and patrons of New York theater and nightlife. Today this urban landscape is dotted with banks and retail stores—the last jazz club shut its doors in 1968—but while the glory days lasted, this stretch of less than a half-kilometer was the epicenter of hot improvised music in America.

The arrival of bebop on Fifty-second Street marked a signal event, initiated by Dizzy Gillespie's stint with a small combo at the Onyx Club in early 1944. Gillespie had sent a telegram to Kansas City enlisting Charlie Parker's participation, but Bird never replied to—and perhaps never received—the missive. Gillespie had also hoped to have Bud Powell on piano, but eventually settled for George Wallington, a young white player well versed in the new style. But even without Parker and Powell, this band was destined to make a tremendous impact on the jazz scene. To complement Wallington in the rhythm section Gillespie relied on Oscar Pettiford—who, along with Charles Mingus and Ray Brown, would come to rank among the preeminent bassists playing in the Jimmy Blanton tradition of full-toned swing—and drummer Max Roach. In time, Roach would rival Kenny Clarke as the leading exponent of bop drumming. A native of the Carolinas like Gillespie and Monk, Roach had made a name for himself while still in his mid-teens as house drummer for the sessions at Monroe's Uptown House. Now, together with Pettiford, he provided Gillespie with a progressive rhythm section, capable of playing at the fastest tempos without losing the flowing legato that the modern style required. Gillespie eventually expanded the band to a quintet with the addition of Don Byas, a Hawkins-inspired tenor saxo-phonist who stood out as one of the few Swing Era horn players who successfully adapted to the demands of bebop.

The inevitable appearance of Charlie Parker on Fifty-second Street in September 1944, for an engagement at the Three Deuces, built on the interest generated by Gillespie's band. Now elevated from the after-hours clubs and jam sessions of its early days, bebop was legitimized by its presentation in quasi-respectable venues; moreover, the reverberations of modern jazz, already fueled by word of mouth, were now being amplified by commercial recordings and radio broadcasts. In this context, critics and journalists felt compelled to deal with this new music, if only as a fad or phenomenon, although the early reactions of the mainstream media were almost uniformly unfavorable. An article in *Collier's* proclaimed, "You can't sing it. You can't dance it. Maybe you can't even stand it. It's bebop." *Time* magazine, struggling to define bebop for its readers, explained that it was "hot jazz over-heated, with over-done lyrics full of bawdiness, references to narcotics and double-talk."[5] Prominent musicians of the "old school" also chimed in with invective: Cab Calloway and others denounced modern jazz as "Chinese music"; Louis Armstrong lambasted "all them weird chords which don't mean nothing . . . you got no melody to remember and no beat to dance to"; Benny Goodman complained that modern jazz players were "not real musicians," they were "just faking." Traditional cornetist Doc Evans went so far as to hold a mock funeral for bebop. *Downbeat*, which delighted in the controversy, ran a photo commemorating the event.

Before 1945, only a few recordings of this new music had been available to the general public, but now several small record companies, such as Guild and Savoy, began to sense opportunities in promoting the modern jazz idiom. On February 9, Gillespie recorded an impressive performance of "Blue 'n' Boogie" with a band that also included saxophonist Dexter Gordon. Less than three weeks later, Parker and Gillespie recorded several historic sides, including "Dizzy Atmosphere" and "Groovin' High." On "Dizzy Atmosphere," Parker floats over the changes, flirting with polytonality during the second eight bars and executing a stunning rhythmic displacement in the bridge; Gillespie follows with a virtuoso's bag of tricks: dancing leaps into the high register, intricate repeated passages, odd intervals, and choppy change-up phrases. "Groovin' High" (Gillespie's reworking of the song "Whispering") and "All the Things You Are" were more subdued, with Parker contributing supple solos somewhat reminiscent of his Lester Young roots. In May, Parker and Gillespie were reunited at a session that produced "Salt Peanuts," noteworthy for a scalding Gillespie contribution that stands out as one of the most dramatic brass solos in the history of jazz. In November, Gillespie rejoined Parker for a session under the latter's leadership for the Savoy label. Two blues songs from that date—"Billie's Bounce" and "Now's the Time"—would garner respect as classic performances, studied and emulated by many other musicians; but even more impressive was the version of "Ko Ko" recorded that day. This reworking of "Cherokee" opens with an eerie introduction—perhaps the most famous in jazz since Armstrong's clarion call to kick off "West End Blues"—bobbing and weaving phrases played without harmonic support, anticipating the ambiguous tonality employed by Ornette Coleman and Don Cherry some fifteen years later. This is followed by one of Parker's finest solos, two full choruses of driving bebop that few other saxophonists of the day could have played, let alone improvised.

A few days after this session, Gillespie and Parker left New York to bring a bebop band to Southern California for an engagement at Billy Berg's, an upscale nightclub known for its name jazz acts and its (rare at the time) racially integrated audiences. Los Angeles listeners had already enjoyed a small taste of this new music—in the local performances of a bop band led by Coleman Hawkins, as well as through the modern jazz recordings that were making their way out west. Now LA jazz buffs had six weeks to assess the music as played by its greatest innovators. Audiences were intrigued, if not captivated, by the band, but local musicians were clearly paying close attention to the modernistic concepts of Parker and Gillespie.

By this time, Parker's addiction and unstable behavior were increasingly evident to outsiders, the private life of the altoist filtering into the public persona. On any given night, he might skip a performance or arrive late. Finally, at the close of the Los Angeles engagement, Bird missed the flight home. As a result, his planned six-week stay in California would stretch out to over sixty weeks—fifteen tumultuous months that witnessed some of Bird's finest music making but were equally clouded by periods of dissolution. In the first weeks following Gillespie's departure, Parker continued to flourish. Ross Russell, proprietor of a local record store, had attempted to set up a studio session with Parker and Gillespie at the close of the Billy Berg's gig, but Bird never showed up for the date. Undaunted, Russell decided to record Parker as a leader, using local and visiting musicians as sidemen. In exchange for a $100 advance, Parker agreed to record exclusively with the Dial label for the next year. For the first session under Parker's leadership, Russell engaged a band that included trumpeter Miles Davis, only nineteen years old and recently arrived in California with the Benny Carter band, tenorist Lucky Thompson, and a rhythm section composed of pianist Dodo Marmarosa, bassist Vic McMillan, guitarist Arv Garrison, and drummer Roy Porter.

The Dial work, judged as a whole, contains much of Parker's finest music, but this initial date proved especially memorable. Only four compositions were recorded, but each ranks as a bop masterpiece. "Moose the Mooche," named by Parker for his L.A narcotics supplier, features a clever stop-and-start melody over "I Got Rhythm" changes—drummer Porter reports that Parker wrote the lead sheet during the drive to the studio—and stellar alto solos on all the takes. On "Yardbird Suite" and "Ornithology," Parker provides whirlwind thirty-two-bar solos. But the highlight of the session was "Night in Tunisia." This Gillespie composition sets up the first soloist with an interlude leading into a four-bar break. Parker uses this break to execute a mesmerizing double-time jazz cadenza. Few jazz reed players could approach the sheer speed of this passage, but even more impressive is the rhythmic phrasing in which coy accents, oddly placed in crevices between the beats, impart a bobbing, weaving quality to the horn line. Parker follows up with a sleek sixteen-bar solo, which for all its merits is overshadowed by the previous four-bar explosion.

If this session displayed Parker at his best, the next recording date finds him at his nadir. His physical condition had deteriorated markedly in the intervening weeks. In addition to ingesting whatever narcotics he could procure, Parker was drinking heavily. Around this same time he developed a nervous twitch: his arms would shoot up in the air uncontrollably, sometimes in midperformance. His playing, so spontaneous and fresh in his first weeks on the West Coast, now often sounded strained and inconsistent. Those close to him feared that he was at the breaking point. "I thought he was going to die," Miles Davis later recalled. Howard McGhee confided to Russell that he felt Parker was "cracking up."[6]

Despite these warning signs, Russell scheduled a session for July 29. He persevered even when Bird arrived at the studio in an almost comatose state—and despite the warning of Dr. Richard Freeman, a psychiatrist who was the brother of Russell's partner, that Parker was showing symptoms of alcoholism and malnutrition. After all, hadn't Parker played brilliantly in the past despite similar bouts of dissipation? The first number recorded that day went poorly. Dr. Freeman responded by giving Parker six tablets of phenobarbital. To complete the following take of "Lover Man,"

Parker needed to be supported from behind—and even then can be heard to stagger away from the microphone. "He was turning around and around, and his horn was shooting up in the air," Howard McGhee has related.[7] Charles Mingus would later praise this as one of Parker's most powerful solos. McGhee also defended the performance, arguing that, despite Bird's state, the "sound came out fine. There are no wrong notes." Few other commentators have agreed. Parker's tone, usually so taut, sounds flabby, and his phrasing is hesitant, indecisive. The most telling verdict came from Parker himself, who was incensed when "Lover Man" was released by Dial.

Had the fiasco stopped there, the "Lover Man" session would have been merely an unfortunate episode in Parker's career. As it was, events took an even more ominous turn in the hours following the recording. At his hotel that evening, Parker wandered into the lobby naked, and later that night set his room afire, perhaps falling asleep while smoking. When the police arrived, they forcibly subdued him, placed him in handcuffs, and took him to jail. Eventually Russell tracked him down and managed to have Parker transferred to the State Hospital at Camarillo, located seventy miles north of Los Angeles.

The following six months stand out as an unusual interlude in Parker's career. During the first weeks at Camarillo, Bird took little notice of his surroundings, and the doctors talked of applying electroshock treatment. The idea was dropped as Parker became more alert and involved in his day-to-day regimen. By the second month, he was tending vegetables in the hospital garden—and telling visitors it was a "gas." He also laid bricks and talked of becoming a mason. Not that he had forgotten about music—the hospital had its own Saturday night band, and Parker joined in on C melody saxophone. By the time of his release, Parker was no doubt in the best shape of his adult life and (thoughts of masonry left far behind) ready to resume his jazz career.

The first session after Bird's release gives little hint of this renewal. On these sides, Parker insisted on featuring vocalist Earl Coleman, a smooth baritone in the mold of Billy Eckstine, and only a glimmer of Parker's improvisational acumen shines through. A week later, however, Parker undertook a combo recording that found him in the company of a strong bop band that included tenorist Wardell Gray, trumpeter McGhee, and pianist Dodo Marmarosa. "Relaxin' at Camarillo," from this date, is one of Parker's finest compositions, a sinuous blues with a free rhythmic quality to its melody line. On these tracks, and in performances with McGhee at the Hi De Ho Club, Parker made it clear that his playing had reached a new level, as compelling as before, but more pliant, less intense. The coy title of the Camarillo tribute was no false claim. His work increasingly reflected the relaxed command of an established master, rather than the irreverent challenges of a young revolutionary. This new sound would, for a time, coexist with the earlier, more insistent style, finally becoming dominant in Parker's later recordings for Norman Granz. The relative merits of the later and earlier Bird continue to generate debate in jazz circles, with most jazz devotees finding reasons to criticize the eventual "mainstreaming" of Charlie Parker. But few can dispute the underlying truth that this change symbolized: within a few years of its revolutionary arrival on the scene, bebop was no longer a radical underground movement. As surprising as its early disruption of the Swing

Era pieties was the speed with which modern jazz was accepted as part of the mainstream sound of the music.

In April, Parker returned to New York, his reputation only enhanced by the tumultuous events of the previous fifteen months. The New York jazz scene had changed in the intervening period, with bebop in the ascendancy and the Swing Era in its final days. Just the previous December, eight major big bands had broken up—including those led by Goodman, James, and Dorsey—in the face of the changed jazz landscape. Now a cadre of new bebop players was making their presence felt. When Gillespie had returned to New York the previous year, he had hired alto saxophonist Sonny Stitt to take Parker's place in the band. Stitt, who had apprenticed in Billy Eckstine's orchestra, was the only altoist on the scene who could approach Parker in terms of speed and technique. His style may have been derivative—despite his protestations to the contrary, his approach often sounded like a careful imitation of Bird's—but Stitt, at his best, was a spectacular soloist. In jam sessions he could be a devastating opponent, and Stitt delighted in such encounters, with many of his finest performances made in the heat of battle with Gene Ammons, Eddie "Lockjaw" Davis, Stan Getz, Sonny Rollins, and others. In later years, he often played the tenor sax—on which his style was less akin to Parker's—and showed that, in addition to his skill in building elaborate bop superstructures, Stitt also knew how to probe the depths of the blues.

In the Eckstine band, Stitt had worked with trumpeter Fats Navarro, a Florida native who was another up-and-coming master of the bop idiom. Navarro managed to incorporate the intricate improvisational lines of Gillespie into a more controlled style. His was a music of contradictions. His tone was sweeter and smoother than Gillespie's—with greater use of the tongue in articulating notes, in contrast to Dizzy's more slurred attack—but his overall style was still hot and swinging. Much of Navarro's best work was as a sideman: with Bud Powell on "Wail," on "The Squirrel" and "The Chase" with Tadd Dameron, alongside Benny Goodman on "Stealin' Apples," or on "Ornithology" with Charlie Parker. Discographers tell us that the latter performance was recorded at Birdland only a few days before Navarro died from tuberculosis in 1950 at age twenty-six—an assertion almost impossible to believe given the forcefulness and absolute command of Navarro's playing. Under different circumstances, Navarro's reputation might have matched Clifford Brown's or even Miles Davis's. Instead, he left behind just a handful of tracks that leave us musing over what this deeply gifted musician might have achieved with more time.

Navarro's frequent employer, Tadd Dameron, was, for his part, an unlikely modern jazz player. Was Dameron a real bebopper? His compositions are often cited as model bop pieces—but many of the best known were written in the late 1930s before the new movement had crystallized. His early roots straddled musical idioms: as an arranger, he was equally comfortable working for swing bands such as Lunceford's and Basie's or writing for modern jazz ensembles led by Gillespie and Eckstine. Moreover, his approach to the piano had none of the telltale signs of bop: it lacked the insistent linear drive of a Bud Powell as well as the hypermodern harmonic sense of a Thelonious Monk. Instead, Dameron favored a more thoughtful approach, and even his improvisations have a tendency to sound like structured compositions—not surprising, perhaps, given his overriding interest in writing. Almost from the start of the bop movement, Dameron's songs had been favored by the new generation of jazz players, with Sarah Vaughan recording "If You Could See Me Now" and Gillespie relying on "Hot House" (Dameron's reworking of "What Is This Thing Called Love") as a regular feature number. Many of his other pieces—"Good Bait," "Our Delight," and "Lady Bird"—have also become part of the standard jazz repertoire. By temperament, Dameron might have been inclined to focus on composing, but earning a livelihood in the jazz world in the mid-1940s was difficult without toiling nightly as a performer. Hence, Dameron increasingly gravitated toward the club scene. It was a fortuitous decision. A lengthy stint at the Royal Roost found Dameron fronting an outstanding house band, which also included Navarro and drummer Clarke. Later Dameron bands featured Clifford Brown and Miles Davis. By the mid-1950s, Dameron had become inactive, due partly to his reserved personality, but even more to a growing dependence on narcotics, a problem that eventually led to incarceration. Between his release in 1961 and his death in 1965, Dameron attempted to reenter the fray of the jazz world, but never with more than passing success.

But of all the modern jazz players who graced the New York scene at the time of Parker's return, Gillespie still reigned as the only one who not only could approach Bird in terms of raw talent, but also possessed a charismatic stage presence that might bring the new modern sounds to a wider audience. Seizing the opportunity generated by his growing reputation, Gillespie formed a bebop big band in 1946. Larger ensembles would continue to fascinate Gillespie for the rest of his career, despite the economic challenge of maintaining a big band in the postwar years. Yet Gillespie never needed the larger unit—as, say, Ellington did—to define his musical aspirations. Gillespie invariably hired outsiders to write charts and organize the band; the trumpeter was content to front the group and play the role of star soloist. For his postwar band, the role of "musical director" fell to Gil Fuller, who had worked with Dizzy in the Eckstine ensemble. On charts such as "Things to Come," "Manteca," and "Ray's Idea," Fuller provided Gillespie with a suitably modernistic setting to showcase this doyen of the bebop movement.

Gillespie's interest in Afro-Cuban music also continued to develop during this period. As early as 1938, Gillespie had spoken to Mario Bauzá about the potential for using a conga player in a jazz band. Some nine years passed before Gillespie, now fronting his own big band, was ready to make the move. Consulting again with Bauzá, Dizzy was introduced to Chano Pozo, an exciting conga player who spoke little English, read no music, but was a master of Cuban rhythms. Although their collaboration was short-lived—Pozo was killed in a Harlem altercation the following year—it set a precedent rich in implications for both Gillespie and the jazz world as a whole. True, there had been earlier attempts to fuse Latin music with jazz, but none had the symbolic impact of Gillespie's appearance with Pozo on the stage of Carnegie Hall in September 1947.

Jelly Roll Morton is often seen as the originator of this fusion of styles—after all, he had suggested, in an often-quoted remark, that the "Spanish tinge" was the "right seasoning" for jazz, and backed up these words with his own artful compositions and performances ("The Crave," "Mamanita," "Creepy Feeling")—but even earlier rag composers such as Scott Joplin had explored the habañera rhythm, which is the basis for the tango. This rhythm shows up in Joplin's "Solace" and in the second theme of W. C. Handy's "St. Louis Blues." The popularization of dances such as the tango and, later, the rumba also furthered the acceptance of Latin music in the United States. Yet the missing ingredient, a distinctly Afro-Cuban perspective on jazz, did not appear in any meaningful degree until the 1940s, spurred then partly by the growing attention of jazz players to its potential, but even more by the influx of Cuban musicians into the New York music scene. Mario Bauzá left Cuba for New York in 1930 and, as we have seen, furthered Gillespie's interest in this music during their joint tenure in the Cab Calloway band. The Cuban vocalist Machito followed, coming to New York in 1937, where in later years his band, the Afro-Cubans, made pioneering steps in fusing jazz harmonies with Cuban melodies and rhythmic patterns. Around this same time, Duke Ellington found some success with his recording of Juan Tizol's "Caravan," but though this composition is now considered a milestone in the evolution of Latin jazz, most listeners at the time heard more of the Middle East than Tizol's native Puerto Rico in the recording. Even a decade later, when Stan Kenton added Machito and two percussionists from the Afro-Cubans to his band for his 1947 hit recording of "The Peanut Vendor"—made a few weeks after Gillespie and Pozo's Carnegie Hall concert—the mixture of Latin and jazz elements was still considered by big band fans as more a novelty than the sign of the emerging "salsa" style, which would eventually stand out as an important and vibrant musical idiom in its own right. In this context, Gillespie's passionate advocacy of Afro-Cuban styles (or "Cubop" as his hybrid approach came to be known for a time) served as the key turning point, building on earlier forays and giving these new sounds a visibility that no doubt inspired other major jazz artists to explore the Afro-Cuban nexus.

The move from bebop to Cubop did not come easily. Although both Pozo and Gillespie could trace their cultural heritage back to overlapping African roots, the later evolution of their respective musical vocabularies had taken them to far different points. The clave rhythm, central to Cuban music, was antithetical to the more open pulse of modern jazz. And the song structures that permeated jazz felt equally constraining to Pozo, who preferred the freedom of the *montuno* vamps of his native music. Gillespie wanted to draw on Pozo's instincts as a composer, but much of the burden fell on Dizzy and his collaborators Fuller and George Russell to transform Pozo's simple constructs into full-fledged pieces. In the face of these conflicting traditions, a healthy dose of give-and-take proved essential. On "Manteca," Gillespie contributed a contrasting theme to soften the insistence of Pozo's main melody. On "Cubana Be, Cubana Bop," Russell and Gillespie provided Pozo with an unstructured interlude to feature his playing in an open-ended solo. On other pieces the band vacillated between jazz and Cuban rhythms, unsure where to anchor their beat. Did these compromises work? George Russell's description of the crowd's reaction to the premiere of "Cubana Be, Cubana Bop" reflects the upside potential of this meeting of musical minds: "The audience was in a state of shock. They didn't believe that an orchestra could really rise to that level of excitement and innovation."[8]

But with Pozo, as with Parker, Gillespie was dealing with an unstable personality. "Chano was a hoodlum . . . a rough character," bassist Al McKibbon explains. Gillespie in his autobiography describes him as a "roughneck." Pozo carried a long knife with him wherever he went, as well as a bullet permanently lodged in his spine, a carryover from a disagreement over royalties. And like Parker, Pozo did not live to see his thirty-fifth birthday, his lifestyle on the edge eventually exacting its toll. Pozo was shot in a New York barroom in December 1948, only fourteen months after his triumphant Carnegie Hall debut with Dizzy Gillespie.

That same Carnegie Hall performance also featured a much-anticipated reunion of Gillespie with Charlie Parker. These encounters would be rare from now on—Parker was fronting his own group with Miles Davis on trumpet, while Gillespie was preoc-cupied with his larger band. Yet each of the recorded meetings between these two leading lights of modern jazz produced substantial music. At Carnegie Hall, Parker pushed the band relentlessly on "Dizzy Atmosphere," letting loose with a virtuosic solo of the highest order. Who could follow such a solo? Perhaps only Gillespie. Spitting out scorching, jagged phrases, Gillespie played one of the strongest—and almost certainly the fastest—solos of his career. Again at the Clef record date in 1950 and at the Massey Hall concert in 1953, Parker and Gillespie would spur each other to create some of the most memorable performances of the bebop idiom.

For his day-to-day working band, Parker had enlisted a trumpeter who would eventually come to represent the opposite stylistic pole to Gillespie's heated pyro-technics. Miles Davis, the future leader of the cool movement, would seem an unlikely choice to share the front line with the firebrand altoist. Some have suggested this was only part of a long-standing pattern of Parker's. Time and again his musical instincts led him to hire trumpeters who would counterbalance, rather than mimic, his high-powered improvisations. With Davis, with Chet Baker, with Kenny Dorham, with Red Rodney—Parker invariably reached for a more low-key and reflective melodic voice, a tonic to offset his acidic alto lines. But then again, this interpreta-tion may be reading too much into Miles Davis, circa 1947. Davis, at that time, was still under Gillespie's spell, struggling to fit his introverted temperament into the latter's extroverted style. On fast numbers—hear his attempts to follow Parker on "Donna Lee"—Davis is anything but calm and collected. His phrasing is nervous, his articulation suspect. Yet Parker must have seen, if not the future birth of the cool, at least some diamond in the rough in this teenage acolyte, hints of greatness that the surviving recordings from that period do not show. After all, Bird, who could have his pick, more or less, of any trumpeter, opted for unknown and unheralded Miles Dewey Davis.

Davis, even then, was an enigma. Raised in an affluent environment in St. Louis, he exhibited a street-smart toughness that seemed more in tune with life on the wrong side of the tracks. Davis's father was a successful dental surgeon with three degrees, who also owned a two-hundred-acre farm—as late as 1962, when Miles was earning a six-figure income, he could boast that his father was worth more than he was. His uncle was educated at Harvard and had studied in Germany. Yet this scion of a successful family came to be dubbed the "Prince of Darkness" by some—no carefree nickname, Fats or Sonny, for him—and the title matched the moods of this aloof man who associated with prizefighters, filled his autobiography with exple-tives, and left behind a litter of strained relationships. Contradictions run through his entire life story. A fierce critic of established hierarchies, Miles chose Juilliard for his musical education, the ultimate outsider opting for the insider's path—then giving it all away to shadow Parker and the early boppers, again gravitating to the periphery. Once established as a mainstay of the bebop movement, he abandoned that course as well, espousing a radical new style, the cool as it came to be known—then again renouncing this new love to pursue other dalliances—with modal, impressionist, hard bop, and quasi-free styles, and ultimately a controversy-provoking leap into jazz-rock fusion. But most of all, the enigma comes in trying to reconcile the man and his music: one all hard surfaces, the other mostly smooth contours. There are no easy answers, or glib one-paragraph summaries, when one deals with Miles Davis.

Born in Alton, Illinois, on May 26, 1926, Davis moved with his family to East St. Louis when he was still an infant. His father, also named Miles—the trumpeter possessed the elegant formal name of Miles Dewey Davis III—set a tone for achievement that the son strived to match, in his own contrary way, for the rest of his life. The boy's relationship with his mother Cleota Henry Davis was more complex. She viewed his musical pursuits with suspicion, and it wasn't until he was an adult that Miles learned that she was an accomplished pianist. "She sat down one day and played some funky blues," he remembered with astonishment.[9] Davis's parents eventually separated, with mother and son never fully coming to terms. When she died, Davis did not even attend her funeral. Yet her recordings of Tatum and Ellington introduced Miles to the music he would ultimately embrace. But when Cleota planned to give her son a violin for his thirteenth birthday, her husband stepped in to insist that the trumpet was a better choice. Under the tutelage of a local instructor, Miles made some progress, but developed more rapidly when he came under the sway of Elwood Buchanan, a jazz trumpeter who had recently been on the road with the Andy Kirk band. Buchanan directed Davis's attention to jazz players such as Harold Baker and Bobby Hackett—unusual choices, outside of the Oliver-Armstrong-Eldridge orbit, but perhaps stimulating ones given Miles's later gravitation toward the cool. By his mid-teens, other influences and techniques were being assimilated: through additional lessons with the first trumpeter in the St. Louis Symphony ("He said I was the worst trumpet player he ever heard in his life"), as well as through friends who shared his enthusiasm for jazz, such as pianist Duke Brooks and trumpeter Clark Terry, the latter also destined to become a major jazz artist.

By the close of his high school years, Davis seemed poised for a promising musical career. He was playing professional gigs and making some money from music. At home, relations with his mother were strained, and his parents finally separated around the time Miles graduated from high school. His mother, with whom he stayed after the breakup, wanted him to attend Fisk, but Miles protested that he would be better served by studying music at Juilliard. Miles's father intervened in favor of his son's choice. In September 1944, Miles arrived in New York, passed his audition at the conservatory, and enrolled as a student.

As it turned out, Davis acquired a first-rate musical education in New York—but one in which the Juilliard School of Music played little part. Instead, Miles's "classrooms" of choice were Minton's, the Savoy Ballroom, the Three Deuces, the Onyx, the Spotlite, and other centers of jazz activity. But he was mostly drawn to the new generation of bebop players then making a name for themselves on the New York scene. "I spent my first week in New York looking for Bird and Dizzy. Man, I went everywhere looking for those two cats," Davis wrote in his autobiography.[10] Finally he tracked down Parker at a Harlem jam session. Although he was only twenty-four years old at the time—just six years older than Miles—Parker soon took on a fatherly role with the young trumpeter, encouraging him, introducing him to other musicians, and eventually hiring him as a sideman. Davis's approach to the trumpet was now evolving into a streamlined modern jazz style. Here Dizzy was an obvious role model—not just for Miles, but for a whole generation—but perhaps just as influential was the more controlled and sweeter-toned work of Freddie Webster and Fats Navarro. Surrounded by these extraordinary players, Davis soon lost what little interest he retained in studies at Juilliard and eventually dropped out of the conservatory.

These were heady surroundings, and Miles was still in the process of coming to grips with his playing. His lines suffered by comparison with his models, lacking the balance and clarity of a Navarro or Webster, the electricity of a Gillespie. Yet when Parker went into the studio to record for Savoy in November 1945, he brought Miles along on trumpet—an even more telling decision when one considers that Dizzy was also present that day, but enlisted to play piano. This was an extreme vote of confidence in the nineteen-year-old trumpeter. On the blues numbers recorded at the session ("Billie's Bounce," "Now's the Time") Davis contributes thoughtful, if somewhat cautious solos, but when the band came to record "Ko Ko," the fast show-piece based on "Cherokee" changes, Miles simply refused to play. "I wasn't going to get out there and embarrass myself," Davis later explained. "I didn't really think I was ready." The choice was fortuitous: Gillespie stepped in for Davis and played a commanding solo on what was destined to become the most important bebop side to date at the time of its release.

When Parker left for Los Angeles in December 1945, Davis decided to follow him, using a gig with Benny Carter's band as a way of getting to the West Coast. In Los Angeles, Davis played with Bird at the Finale, and again recorded with him for the Dial label. After Parker was committed to Camarillo, Davis went on the road with Billy Eckstine, and then returned to New York where he worked with Gillespie's big band. (Has there ever been a more spectacular trumpet section than the one Dizzy brought to an April 1947 gig in the Bronx with, in addition to Davis and Gillespie, Fats Navarro, Freddie Webster, and Kenny Dorham?) Parker, now back on the scene, occasionally sat in with the band.

But Bird, now at the peak of his career, was no longer content to work regularly as sideman—or even coleader—with Gillespie. In April 1947, Parker opened with his new quintet at the Three Deuces on Fifty-second Street. In forming his new group, Bird again selected Davis, along with Max Roach, bassist Tommy Potter, and pianist Duke Jordan. The following month, Parker brought this band into the studio to record for the Savoy label, the only change being the substitution of Bud Powell for Duke Jordan. The melody line for "Donna Lee," a classic performance recorded that day, has sometimes been attributed to Davis, but the claim is hard to believe. With its rich chromaticism, it comes the closest of any of Parker's themes to matching his style of improvisation. "Chasin' the Bird" from the same session is equally noteworthy, with Parker abandoning the standard unison lines of his melodies in favor of some clever counterpoint. In the closing months of 1947, Parker returned to the studio once each month with his working band to record again for Russell's Dial label, now relocated back East. The most ambitious piece from these three sessions, "The Hymn," attempts to recreate the excitement of "Ko Ko" with a blistering tempo and a melody built, like "Cherokee," mostly on whole and half notes. Parker obliges with a busy solo, impressive but without the edge of its famous predecessor. Parker also contributes several solid medium-tempo originals—"Scrapple from the Apple," "Dewey Square," "Dexterity"—on which he solos with aplomb.

In a surprising twist, however, Parker's most memorable performances from these final Dial sessions are the slowest pieces. This too revealed an important side of the "new" Charlie Parker, more reflective and singularly rhapsodic. "Embraceable You," perhaps Parker's finest ballad recording, is a masterpiece of thematic development, which builds from a simple six-note motif (reminiscent of the "You must remember this" phrase from "As Time Goes By"). "My Old Flame" and "Don't Blame Me," also from this late Dial period, are only a notch below "Embraceable You" in quality. In their own way, these performances constituted a new step forward in the history of the jazz ballad as influential as Beiderbecke and Trumbauer's work on "Singin' the Blues," Armstrong's "I Can't Give You Anything but Love," Young's collaborations with Billie Holiday, and Coleman Hawkins's "One Hour" and "Body and Soul." Here too the rest of the band falls short of Parker, offering a lugubrious four-to-the-bar accompaniment—in a few years, jazz rhythm sections would become much more relaxed in playing these very slow tempos—but Parker's silky improvisations overcome this liability, pointing the way toward a new, more romantic dimension of the bebop idiom and delineating a noteworthy expansion of its musical territory.

For the final Dial session, Parker and Davis were joined in the front line by trombonist J. J. Johnson, who had already impressed listeners with his recordings as a leader for the Savoy label, as well as in sideman stints with Benny Carter, Count Basie, and others. To Johnson fell the unenviable responsibility of translating the advances of modern jazz into the language of the slide trombone. The speed and intricacy of bebop lines made them especially recalcitrant to this transformation, and it is a credit to Johnson's virtuosity and tenacity that he succeeded so well at such a Herculean task. The Parker sides helped to boost an already promising career. They were followed by a series of Johnson collaborations with other leading modern jazz performers—including Dizzy Gillespie, Miles Davis, Clifford Brown, and Stan Getz. Despite the accolades of jazz insiders, Johnson's career dipped for a time in the early 1950s and he was forced to take a day job as a blueprint inspector at a Long Island factory. But, in 1955, Johnson finally won the *Downbeat* poll on his instrument and began enjoying greater success as a leader, often in conjunction with fellow trombonist Kai Winding. In later years, however, Johnson often recoiled from the stresses and strains involved in a leading a jazz band, sometimes focusing instead on arranging and composition (with works ranging from the plaintive ballad "Lament" to highly ambitious pieces such as the six-movement *Perceptions*, recorded in 1961 by Gunther Schuller with Gillespie as featured soloist) and at other times taking on more commercial work in the music industry. After the late 1960s, Johnson's public appearances became increasingly rare, and he retired from the stage in 1996, five years before his death from suicide in the midst of a long illness. Yet, despite the ups and downs of his career, Johnson's legacy is secure and virtually all later jazz trombonists, except only the most traditional, owe a greater or lesser debt to his pioneering efforts.

Four days after his final Dial session, Parker returned to the studio with his working band, this time under the auspices of the Savoy label. Here the compositions are more perfunctory, mere excuses for a blowing date and, as with the late Dial work, the level of intensity is a notch lower than on Parker's pre-Camarillo recordings. Parker's two Savoy sessions from the following year are much stronger, featuring more probing compositions in new styles, such as the Latin-inflected "Barbados" and the counterpoint exercise "Ah-Leu-Cha." But again, the most powerful performance comes on a slow number, this time the stunning blues "Parker's Mood," which marked a surprising return to Parker's Kansas City roots. Renouncing the virtuosity, the arcane chord substitutions, the fast tempos—the very trademarks of the Bird sound—Parker created one of his most gut-wrenching performances, a quasi-vocal horn lament that, in its starkness, is almost the antithesis of the maximalist leanings of his mid-1940s work.

Of course, the more intense side of Parker's music still flourished, but in this later stage of his career it was more evident outside the studio, in the many amateur recordings of his public performances and private jam sessions. This "underground" Parker is extensively documented. The Dean Benedetti tapes and discs alone, which came to light in the late 1980s, include more than four hundred previously unknown Parker solos. But this represents only a small part of the bootleg Bird. In addition, jazz fans are blessed with recorded performances from the Royal Roost, Onyx, the Three Deuces, Birdland, Rockland Palace, Carnegie Hall (with Ella Fitzgerald), the Renaissance Ballroom (with an unknown Latin band)—indeed, at almost every conceivable type of New York venue, from high to low—as well as on the road in Detroit, Los Angeles, Washington, DC, Boston, even Sweden (from Parker's celebrated 1950 visit), among other locales. Then there are even more unusual, more private recordings, the results of informal encounters in apartments, hotel rooms, and the like. The sound quality of this massive unofficial legacy ranges from adequate to nightmarish, but Parker's playing rarely lags. Especially during the final six years of his life, much of Parker's best work—and certainly his most impassioned—comes to us through the surface noise of these tinny-sounding amateur sessions. Such acoustical horrors remind me of a friend's comment about his grandpa's privately distilled whiskey: "If it were any worse, you couldn't stand it; if it were any better, you couldn't get enough." For the most part, only devotees of bop will endure the labor of wading through the buzzes and scratches of this poorly recorded material, but those who are able to tune their ears to the glories of the music are rewarded with some of modern jazz's most intoxicating moments.

In contrast to these uninhibited documents of bop on the fly, Parker's late studio recordings for producer Norman Granz reflect a more homogenized Bird. Here snippets of intense improvisation coexist with overtly commercial attempts to package Parker for the mass market. There was some irony in this turn of events. After all, Granz was one of the best jazz record producers of the period, a stickler for using the finest musicians, both as leaders and sidemen, and putting them in settings where they could play unadulterated jazz. In fact, Granz had been responsible for the inspired 1946 pairing of Parker and Lester Young that produced a classic recording of "Oh, Lady Be Good." But Parker's 1949–54 sessions for Granz rarely approached the level of this one earlier work. Two Granz dates from 1950 are among the best of the lot, notably Parker's June reunion with Gillespie, backed by the fascinating (if unconventional) combination of Buddy Rich and Thelonious Monk in the rhythm section. The low point of this period is the inept mixture of Parker and the Dave Lambert singers, with results that are almost unlistenable. Only slightly more successful are the recordings with a string orchestra, in which saccharine arrangements overwhelm Parker's valiant attempts to make serious music. Parker was reportedly pleased with this effort—especially with his performance of "Just Friends"—and his playing was no doubt poised. Nonetheless, the music has not worn well with the passing years, and jazz fans justifiably lament the missed opportunity to record Parker with other star players associated with Granz (a session planned with Art Tatum never materialized—but what a gem it might have been) or in more sophisticated orchestral settings. Even the work with Latin musicians (marketed as "Charlie Parker Plays South of the Border"), which showed some promise, still failed to match the more exciting Gillespie projects in this vein.

In general, Gillespie's work with Granz was more uniformly successful. This collaboration flourished in the 1950s and was renewed in the 1970s, when Granz formed his Pablo label. Granz tempered Dizzy's tendency to take the easy way out with novelty songs, offbeat vocals, and crowd-pleasing antics, and instead consistently placed him in the midst of other world-class players. A close study of Gillespie's recording career validates the wisdom of this move. With very few exceptions, Dizzy's strongest solos came when he shared the front line with another leading horn player: Parker, Stitt, Eldridge, Getz, Rollins, and other peers. In these settings, Gillespie put aside his affable stage personality and played with fire. By comparison, when Gillespie operated his own record label, Dee Gee, for a time in the early 1950s, the results were uneven. Solid jazz records were interspersed with clumsy offerings such as "Swing Low, Sweet Cadillac," "Umbrella Man," and "School Days." With Granz, however, Gillespie needed to show up at the studio ready for battle. In his 1957 recording of "I Know That You Know," Dizzy must follow a scintillating Sonny Rollins stop-time solo and obliges with a tour de force effort. A 1956 session finds the trumpeter in the middle of a heated saxophone duel between Stan Getz and Sonny Stitt; in song after song, each taken at a furious tempo, Gillespie feeds off the energy of the two combatants. Another successful project from the period matches Gillespie with his early role model Roy Eldridge. Granz, with his passion for the jam session, instinctively understood that Dizzy was at his best when an element of one-upmanship permeated the musical proceedings.

When compared against such spirited outings, Parker's string orchestra efforts, supervised by Granz, are a mixed achievement at best. Certainly the blame here is not solely Granz's. Parker had long been fascinated with contemporary orchestral music. His conversations were laced with references to Prokofiev and Stravinsky. He told a Swedish interviewer that violinist Jascha Heifetz ranked among his favorite musicians ("His phrasing is such that he swings"[11]). At his daughter's funeral, he had a pianist play the music of Bartók. As noted, he discussed taking lessons with modernist composer Edgard Varèse (reportedly offering to cook for Varèse in return), and supposedly sent a letter to Arnold Schoenberg asking for advice. Given these leanings, orchestral settings were an obvious area of exploration for Parker. Yet Bird lacked the patience to oversee the details of such ambitious projects. Unlike an Ellington, for whom composition, arranging, and bandleading were areas of passionate interest, Parker was inclined to delegate these tasks to others and merely show up to play. For the string orchestra projects, arrangements were contracted out—with mediocre results. Rather than Prokofiev or Bartók, the models these charts mostly call to mind are rather the worst examples of Paul Whiteman's concert jazz from the 1920s and 1930s. Alas, they would have been better suited as accompaniment, not to the leading altoist in modern jazz, but at most to an elevator journey of brief duration. Clearly there was a degree of credibility that Parker earned by fronting a string orchestra, an aura of respectability that few jazz artists enjoyed during these years and most craved. Yet, in the final analysis, "Bird with Strings" (as these efforts came to be known) never came close to realizing Parker's aspirations for creating modern jazz on a grander scale. Instead they settled for a petty, hollow refinement, diluting the impact of an artist who was at his best when no strings were attached.

This onstage propriety was increasingly at odds with the travails of Parker's private life. Drug addiction had taken its toll. Rolling up his sleeve and showing the needle marks on his arm, Parker told a friend: "This is my home, this is my portfolio, this is my Cadillac." Bird was barely thirty, yet he looked much older. His once taut figure now took on a bloated aspect, and he tipped the scales at over two hundred pounds. He was bothered by an ulcer and his doctor warned of a possible heart condition. His relationship with Doris Sydnor, who had traveled to California to be lady-in-waiting during his Camarillo internment, was now breaking up, and Parker was renewing his ties with Chan Richardson. Au courant with the ways of jazz musicians and artists, Chan could be a soul mate in a way that Doris was not. But there was a trade-off. Doris, with a doting, almost maternal attitude toward Parker, had shielded him (as best she could) from the seamier side of the jazz milieu. She would wait for him at clubs, carry his saxophone, try to pick up the pieces of his dissipated life. With Chan, Parker made only fleeting attempts to settle down. Such stability ultimately proved too confining. When his daughter Pree died, Parker was on the road, lodging with sculptress Julie MacDonald. Chan had been forced to take Pree to public clinics, because there was no money for a private doctor—this at a time when Parker was at the peak of his fame and earning potential. But even when he wasn't out of town, Parker had little attachment for hearth and home. When he succumbed to his own final illness, Bird was back in New York, but even then he opted to recuperate at the apartment of a lady friend rather than stay with Chan and his son.

The instability could also be seen in Parker's onstage life. True, at any given performance, he was still capable of extraordinary music making. His 1953 Toronto concert at Massey Hall (alongside Gillespie, Mingus, Roach, and Powell) has been marketed as "The Greatest Jazz Concert Ever," and for once the exaggerated hype of the record company is somewhat justified by the level of the music. Other late performances (in 1952 at Rockland Palace; in 1953 with The Orchestra in Washington, DC) show that Parker at his best still had to be considered the preeminent saxophonist in modern jazz, despite his private turmoils. But these moments of glory were far from the norm in Parker's final years. The regular working band of the 1940s had by now given way to less permanent settings. He would play with pickup groups in different cities, or tour with Stan Kenton or Jazz at the Philharmonic. At other times he brought a string orchestra on the road, playing the same warmed-over arrangements night after night, set after set. His behavior onstage could be erratic or rude, and at times he might not show at all, causing club owners to grow wary. One night he fired the entire string orchestra during a performance, then left the empty stage to drink whiskey at the bar. Matters were further complicated by Parker's problems with his cabaret card, which made it difficult for him to work in New York during a period of almost two years. There was heavy symbolism in the fact that Parker even came to be considered *persona non grata* at Birdland, the premier jazz club that had been named in the altoist's honor in 1950. His final club appearance was marred by an embarrassing onstage confrontation with pianist Bud Powell, an unfortunate swan song to cap Bird's volatile career.

His health—both physical and mental—had been precarious for some time. So many rumors circulated, most of them plausible if not true: he had swallowed iodine in an apparent suicide attempt; he had been twice hospitalized at Bellevue; or he made ominous comments about his own impending demise. Friends would tell of Bird arriving unannounced, knocking at doors in the middle of the night, seeking drugs, money, distraction. The inevitable terminal illness came in March 1955. Parker needed to get to Boston for a club engagement but, beset by the pain of his aggravated ulcer, made it no farther than the apartment of his friend, the Baroness Pannonica de Koenigswarter. A doctor was called in, but Parker refused to go to a hospital. Three days later, he finally succumbed; his death was attributed to the combined effects of a bleeding ulcer and pneumonia. But these were only the arbitrary, final causes. Even more telling was the other notation on the death certificate: the doctor's estimate of Parker's age. Not knowing the true dates, he guessed that his patient was between fifty and sixty years old. In fact, Parker was only thirty-four.

"Most of the soloists at Birdland had to wait for Parker's next record in order to find out what to play next. What will they do now?" Charles Mingus queried.[12] There was a touch of exaggeration in Mingus's claim—but only a touch. During his lifetime, Parker exerted a hypnotic influence on the younger generation of jazz musicians, and his mystique not only continued unabated after his death but even intensified. His life now took on the quality of legend. "Bird is not dead," Mingus continued, "he's hiding out somewhere, and he'll be back with some new shit that will scare everyone to death." Picking up on this theme, Parker devotees brandished the phrase "Bird Lives"—anticipating, with their "in-denial" obsession, the postmortem Elvis fascination of a later generation—employing the slogan as a talisman, motto, and enigmatic graffiti all rolled into one.

But when Parker, unlike the King, failed to be spotted at supermarkets (if only on the cover of a checkout counter tabloid), most bop fans turned their energy toward finding the "next Bird," the new hot alto saxophonist who would carry the jazz idiom to another level. Only three months after Parker's death, Julian "Cannonball" Adderley arrived in New York. Within days of sitting in with the band at Cafe Bohemia, he was the talk of the town. True to form, Adderley's record company promoted him as the "new Bird," and though Cannonball's assured technique and flair for improvisation may have reminded many of this famous predecessor, his warmer tone was a marked departure from the Parker model, as was his more rhythmically rooted approach to phrasing. Adderley served a brief but memorable stint with Miles Davis, during which he participated on the seminal *Kind of Blue* session, and in time developed a more controlled style of improvisation, with greater sensitivity to space and a more relaxed delivery. If Adderley failed to become the bebop messiah that fans were seeking, he nonetheless did an admirable job of pleasing both jazz purists and casual audiences, who relished his funk-inflected performances such as "Dis Here," "Work Song," and "Mercy, Mercy, Mercy."

Phil Woods, another much-lauded "disciple of Bird," also made a splash on the New York jazz scene in the mid-1950s, both through his work as a leader and in his extensive sideman efforts. His professionalism, technical facility, and smooth attack enabled Woods to fit in with ease in almost any musical setting, whether the commercial pop music of a Billy Joel (who featured Woods on the hit song "Just the Way You Are") or the much different soundscapes of Benny Goodman or Thelonious Monk. For a time Woods was perhaps too much in demand as a session player. His gigs as a bandleader became less frequent, and his promise as a major jazz star seemed destined to be only partly realized. Between 1958 and 1967, Woods made only four recordings as a leader. But with the formation of his excellent European ensemble in 1968, and his return to bebop roots with his post-1974 American bands, Woods made it clear that he belongs on any short list of leading post-Parker alto saxophonists.

Jackie McLean, a third altoist to come of age in the shadow of Parker during the 1950s, took a different approach to the instrument. While others emulated Parker's virtuosity and borrowed verbatim various licks and ii–V–I cadences, McLean offered a sparser, more jagged approach. It was the spirit of Bird—his intensity, his drive, his raw emotion—not, as with so many other saxophonists, mimicked phrases and patterns, that came through in McLean's music. Unlike Adderley and Woods, he adopted an acerbic tone, one distinctly unsuitable for pop music or pseudo-funk hits. His early work with Miles Davis and as a leader revealed an allegiance to the bop style, but McLean remained open to the influence of other approaches, with elements of John Coltrane's modal excursions, Sonny Rollins's hard bop, and Ornette Coleman's free playing eventually entering into his music. By the time of his vital recordings from the 1960s for the Blue Note label, McLean was brandishing an urgent sax style, one that had largely discarded the formulaic resolutions of bop.

These three players—Adderley, Woods, McLean—in turn came to be revered as influential stylists in their own right, with a host of younger players following in their footsteps. We can trace this influence, for example, in the 1980s work (respectively) of Richie Cole, Vincent Herring, and Bobby Watson. But behind all these figures, the larger influence of Charlie Parker could still be felt, almost as strongly as during his lifetime. Bird's impact extended to the West (Art Pepper, Sonny Criss, Bud Shank) and the East (Charles Mariano, Ernie Henry, Dave Schildkraut), to the baritone (Leo Parker, Serge Chaloff, Cecil Payne) and the tenor (Teddy Edwards, Dexter Gordon, Sonny Rollins)—indeed, almost everywhere one looked on the jazz landscape. For better or worse, the bebop vocabulary refined by Parker and his contemporaries remained either an explicit source of inspiration or, at a minimum, a reference point for virtually all postbop jazz styles during the next half-century. Even the avant-garde musicians who, on the surface, seemed to rebel the most vociferously against the dominance of bop were secret worshippers at its shrine. For it was bebop itself, embodying as it did the spirit of rebellion par excellence within the world of jazz, that stood—yea, still stands!—as the most pertinent role model for all later jazz revolutions.

MODERN JAZZ PIANO

As it is commonly told, the history of jazz piano mirrors the evolution of the music as a whole. Earl Hines is said to have developed a "trumpet style" in response to Armstrong's innovations. The pianism of Ellington is praised for representing a microcosm of his orchestral works. The music of Bud Powell, we are told, translated the advances of Charlie Parker and Dizzy Gillespie to the jazz keyboard. These generalizations, as clumsy as they are—and they are all too easy to criticize—still catch a broad truth. They rightly call our attention to the symbiotic relationship between the harmonic and rhythmic underpinnings of the music, epitomized in the work of jazz pianists, and the evolution of the monophonic improvised lines, best exemplified in the play of the horns. In this regard, jazz music is radically different from painting or literature or other mediums in which individuals work alone, in which the influence of others is felt at a distance, as part of a cultural context. With few exceptions, the nature of jazz performance requires group interaction of the highest level. And much of the irony of jazz is that, for all its celebration of the individual soloist, it remains a music of ensembles. The story of each major innovator in the music's history—Armstrong, Ellington, Parker, Davis, Coleman—repeats this truism. There are no lonely geniuses in the jazz pantheon, for in this medium there is almost always the company of a band.

By the mid-1940s, a distinctively modern jazz piano style had developed. Its historical antecedents were surprising. A decade before, most knowledgeable listeners would have looked toward Art Tatum, or perhaps to Duke Ellington, for an indication of the future of jazz piano. Their music seemed to encompass the most forward-looking thinking in terms of harmony, rhythm, melody. As it turned out, the orchestral approach to the keyboard of a Tatum or Ellington was too thick, too textured to work in the context of a bebop rhythm section. Instead, the new generation of modern jazz pianists looked for a leaner, more streamlined approach. This new style, as it developed, came to emphasize the right hand, which played fast melody lines laced with all the chromatic color tones and rhythmic flurries found in a Parker alto solo. The left hand supported this linear approach with supple comping chords—often simple structures built with only two or three notes—that were almost as important for their rhythmic kick as for their meager harmonic implications. In this regard, the bebop pianists were closer in spirit to Count Basie, the unassuming antivirtuoso of Kansas City jazz, than to the more technically proficient stride and Swing Era players. True, the influence of the stride tradition could not be completely shaken off—in particular, Tatum's triumphant mastery of the keyboard continued to haunt later players. Its influence lurked below the surface of even such committed modernists as Powell and Tristano— and was especially evident when these bebop piano titans played unaccompanied. Hints of the linear styles of Hines and Wilson could also be detected among the boppers (with Monk's modernism looking back even further to the work of James P. Johnson). Yet, for the most part, the bebop players tended to be ruthless in jettisoning the excess baggage of the recent past in their attempts to find a purer, unencumbered voice for the jazz keyboard.

No player realized this ideal better than Earl "Bud" Powell. Other modern jazz pianists might have boasted a more dexterous keyboard technique (Peterson, Newborn), or a cleaner touch (Marmarosa, Tristano, Cole), or more daring harmonies (Monk, Brubeck), or a more ebullient stage demeanor (Shearing, Garner), but none came closer to representing the spirit of the bebop movement than Powell. And none would be more influential during the post–World War II years. Powell's reconfiguration of the jazz piano vocabulary would have a deep and lasting impact on later players on the instrument. As such, he is one of those seminal artists whose influence is so pervasive that it is easy to overlook. When one person steals your stuff, it is robbery; when everybody does it over and over again, your belongings sooner or later become common property.

But even when others imitated the mannerisms of Powell's style—as so many pianists learned to do—they rarely captured the preternatural vibrancy of the original. In the context of a modern jazz culture that celebrated personal commitment to intense and immediate emotional experiences, Powell appeared to have some special relation to the zeitgeist. The irony was that, for Powell, this attitude was no celebration. Perspiration dripping from his brow, his hands slashing at the keyboard, Bud Powell in public performance seemed to be fighting his private demons. And these demons eventually came to dominate him, abbreviating his career, which reached its peak long before Powell's death in 1966 at age forty-one. His most important works were recorded within a decade-long span, from the mid-1940s to the mid-1950s. And even these works of a young man in his prime seem to show a musical mind precariously close to teetering off the edge, as their very titles indicate. "Oblivion," "Un Poco Loco," "Frantic Fancies," "Glass Enclosure," "Wail," "Dance of the Infidels," "So Sorry Please," "Hallucinations"—a casual observer could gather much about Powell simply by glancing at the names of his compositions.

Powell, who was born in New York City on September 27, 1924, was raised in a musical family: his father William played stride piano; his older brother William Jr. learned the trumpet; his younger brother Richie also became a well-known jazz pianist. Bud's early training on the piano emphasized the European classical tradition, but even before his tenth birthday Powell was drawn to the jazz styles of Fats Waller and Art Tatum. By age fifteen, he had left school to work as a professional musician. Before long, the after-hours clubs of Harlem beckoned. Here Powell encountered the nascent sounds of bebop, and met a friend and mentor in Thelonious Monk. Seven years older than Powell, Monk was serving as house pianist at Minton's Playhouse. When veteran players tried to dismiss Powell from the bandstand, Monk came to his defense. Some years later, Powell returned the favor, serving as an undaunted advocate of Monk's music at a time when few others took notice. When Powell embarked on his first major gig with Cootie Williams's band, he was persuasive in convincing Williams to record Monk's composition "'Round Midnight"—the debut recording of this now well-known jazz standard.

It is fascinating to speculate about the nature of the friendship between these two masters of modern jazz keyboard. Each ranks among the most reclusive and enigmatic figures in the history of the music. Both were men of few words, and often even those few words were all but impossible to decipher. Jazz historians would give much to be a fly on the wall at one of their conversations—if indeed they were conversations in the normal sense of the word. In time, both pianists came to be viewed as mentally unbalanced—Powell spent much of his peak period of creativity in institutions of one sort or another, and Monk's reticence eventually reached a pathological extreme—although these tendencies may have seemed mere eccentricities at the time of their meeting. Powell and Monk no doubt shared similarities in background and interests, but even in the area of most common interest—jazz piano—their styles offered more differences than affinities. Monk's vertical keyboard style was almost a polar opposite to the horizontal approach favored by Powell. Yet the two retained a strong mutual admiration and willingness to assist each other, rare among jazz contemporaries who play the same instrument.

In 1944, Powell recorded with Williams, both in big band and combo settings. Here his modern jazz leanings, while already apparent, were tempered by Swing Era conventions. During his stint with Williams, Powell was arrested for disorderly conduct while on a road trip to Philadelphia. In custody, Powell was severely beaten, and even when he was released, his health remained precarious. His mother needed to rent a car to bring him home to Harlem. Some have seen this event as triggering the pianist's chronic psychological instability. Certainly the timing was inauspicious. Ten days after the Philadelphia incident, Powell was placed in a sanatorium for the first time. Other periods of institutionalization followed. In these settings, his medical care ran the gamut from humane to savage, with his various "treatments" including electroshock therapy and beatings.

The miracle is that Powell managed so well for so long in the face of this dual existence as part-time patient, full-time jazz legend. His recordings from the late 1940s—made after his ordeal with electroshock therapy at Creedmoor—include some of the most compelling piano trio music in the history of jazz. His work on fast numbers is especially noteworthy. A session with Max Roach and Ray Brown from February 1949 produced three high-speed masterpieces. On "Tempus Fugit," Powell exudes an almost diabolical level of energy, while on two standards, "Cherokee" and

"All God's Chillun Got Rhythm," Powell anchors his attack with intricate passing chords working in contrary motion to the melody. The effect is surprising and strikingly original. A session from the following year finds Roach replaced by Buddy Rich. Here Powell floors the gas pedal, apparently trying to take the tempo to its limits—it sounds as though the pianist is engaged in a race with the virtuoso drummer—on a thrilling version of "Tea for Two." These tracks possessed an odd, almost paradoxical quality, conveying a sense of mastery, yet also sounding as though they are on the brink of spinning out of control. Much of their appeal comes from this daredevil willingness to push to extremes in performance—a calling card of Powell's finest work.

Powell was equally impressive when playing his own compositions. It is hard to understand why so few of his pieces have been recorded by other musicians. They boast memorable melodies, satisfying harmonic movement, and are generally good vehicles for improvisation. His medium-tempo pieces are especially strong—"The Fruit," "Celia," "Bouncing with Bud," "So Sorry, Please," "Cleopatra's Dream," "Strictly Confidential," "Hallucinations"—and deserve to be as well known as the more frequently played compositions of Parker, Gillespie, Dameron, and Monk. Perhaps Powell himself was partly to blame. Unlike Monk or Gillespie, who frequently recorded the same compositions over and over, and played them often in performance, Powell often left behind only a single studio recording of his finest pieces.

Powell's greatest limitation was as a performer of ballads. But this was also a general weakness of his whole generation of jazz pianists. Not until the late 1950s did modern jazz piano refine an original and authentic approach to ballad playing. Powell had a glimpse of this future, as his impressionistic piece "Parisian Thoroughfare" makes clear. But for the most part, he remained under the shadow of Art Tatum when tackling slower tempos. The pieces are weighed down by ornamentation and cocktail-piano virtuosity. Even a heartfelt composition such as Powell's "I'll Keep Loving You" finally collapses under the burden of these extraneous devices. Jazz piano would eventually break through this stylistic dead end by paring away ruthlessly at the unnecessary notes and ad lib fills—a process propelled by the contributions of Bill Evans and Ahmad Jamal—but this radical pruning, built on a reassessment of the importance of space and silence, was still some years away at the time of Powell's best work. Along with most other pianists who came of age between 1940 and 1950, Powell was at his sharpest when the tempo approached or exceeded two hundred beats per minute.

Almost all of Powell's most important recordings were completed by the time of his thirtieth birthday. His late 1940s and early 1950s sessions for Norman Granz (now reissued on Verve) and Alfred Lion and Francis Wolff's Blue Note label stand out as paragon achievements, defining statement of bebop piano. In fact, Powell's reputation as the leading keyboard voice of the bebop movement would be well established if only on the basis of his extraordinary output from the two-year period stretching from May 1949 to May 1951. These twenty-five months encompassed a lifetime of music: strident trio sessions with Max Roach in May 1949, February 1950, and May 1951; the superb August 1949 combo recordings (under the name Bud Powell's Modernists) for Blue Note, which prefigure the coming hard bop movement; two memorable quartet dates with Sonny Stitt from December 1949 and

January 1950; a brief but notable July 1950 trio session with Buddy Rich; and an outstanding solo piano outing from February 1951.

The quality of Powell's later work has been the subject of much debate, but even its most ardent supporters stop short of comparing it to these early efforts. Clearly the later Powell was capable of occasional stellar performances. The best of these were often in the company of other premier jazz players—with Parker and Gillespie at Massey Hall in 1953; with Coleman Hawkins in 1960; with Dexter Gordon in 1963—or on occasional trio settings where he showed glimpses of greatness, as in his Lausanne recording from 1962. But these were, at best, compelling enough to remind listeners of Powell's early prowess, and never so good as to make them forget it. At its worst, Powell's playing in his later days could be execrable. His touch unsure, the tempo wobbly, his improvisations rarely broaching new ground—Powell, on such evenings, could sound like an automaton, futilely going through the motions of a jazz performance without ever feeling it. His early work had been distinguished by a suppleness and gripping tension; his later work often seemed clouded by malaise.

There were, of course, all too many reasons for this distressing decline. Powell's unstable mental health was increasingly matched by a deteriorating physical condition. Even small doses of alcohol could have a devastating effect, and friends learned to keep him away from the bottle at all costs. The death of his brother Richie in a 1956 auto accident, as well as the passing of Parker and many other of his contemporaries, may also have weighed heavily on Powell. In his early thirties, a period that finds most jazz players in peak playing form, Powell struggled with health problems and hospital stays. "Nobody gave him much longer to live," his companion Altevia Edwards (better known as Buttercup) later told an interviewer, "not even me."[13]

But Powell survived and decided on an ambitious move across the Atlantic. In the spring of 1959, Powell arrived in Paris with Buttercup and her son John. This temporary visit stretched out to five years. The recordings from this period show that Powell was still capable, at times, of playing coherent and moving improvisations, but even Powell's better performances lacked the fire and ice of his earlier keyboard excursions. Despite this inconsistency, work was plentiful and audiences treated the pianist with respect bordering on adulation. In this new setting, Powell was blessed with a supportive phalanx of friends, fans, and acquaintances, who conspired (with mixed results) to shepherd his health and keep him away from alcohol. Francis Paudras, a commercial artist and jazz aficionado, eventually stepped forward as an unofficial guardian, overseer, and financial adviser, as well as vigilant defender of Powell against his critics. "People think Bud is crazy or lost or silent," he told one interviewer, "but he really is in a state of grace."[14] This unusual and troubled relationship provided much of the inspiration for the 1986 film 'Round Midnight.

When Powell returned to the United States for a visit in August 1964, Paudras accompanied him. In New York, however, the pianist could not be controlled as easily as in France, and on at least two occasions he disappeared for days at a time. When Paudras decided to return to France, Powell stayed behind. Even the artist's most devoted fans could take little solace in his pianism during this final stage of his career. An engagement at Birdland received mixed reviews, but Powell's heavy-handed performance at a Charlie Parker memorial concert left few doubts about his diminished capacities at the keyboard. He performed little after this, and his health continued to deteriorate. On July 31, 1966, less than two years after his New York homecoming, Powell died, ostensibly due to the combined effects of tuberculosis, alcoholism, and malnutrition. He was forty-one years old.

During the late 1940s and early 1950s, almost every major or minor keyboardist working in the modern jazz idiom showed, to a greater or lesser extent, the marks of Powell's influence: Lennie Tristano, John Lewis, George Wallington, Dodo Marmarosa, Al Haig, Walter Bishop, Kenny Drew, Joe Albany, and Hampton Hawes, to name just a few. In Detroit, Powell's linear style served as a springboard for a whole school of pianism. This so-called "Detroit style" actually spanned a wide range of sounds, stretching from the refined keyboard mannerisms of Hank Jones and Tommy Flanagan to the harder-driving piano work of Barry Harris, but all of them could trace their lineage back to Powell. By the mid-1950s, other jazz keyboard approaches had emerged, but even the pianists whose work stood out as the most original—Bill Evans, Horace Silver, Ahmad Jamal, Oscar Peterson, Cecil Taylor— still owed an enormous debt to this pioneer of modern jazz.

The career of Powell's mentor and friend Thelonious Monk presents virtually a mirror image of this tale of dissipating creativity and declining fame. When Powell was at the peak of his powers, in the late 1940s and early 1950s, Monk was an all-but-forgotten figure in the jazz world. Around the same time that Powell's most fertile period ended in May 1951, Monk embarked on his own renaissance. In July of that year, Monk returned to the studios to record for Blue Note after a three-year hiatus. This session kicked off a fifteen-year period in which Monk recorded prolifically, setting down classic tracks for Blue Note, Prestige, Riverside, and Columbia. By the 1960s, the reversal of roles was all but complete. At the point when Powell's career was in its final tailspin, Monk was recording for the most powerful label in the music industry, lauded by jazz fans, and even the subject of a 1964 cover story in *Time* magazine.

This was an amazing turn of events for a figure who had been largely dismissed by critics and fans after his early involvement with the birth of modern jazz at Minton's. In 1942 Monk worked with Lucky Millinder, in 1944 he joined Coleman Hawkins, and in 1946 he spent some time with Gillespie's big band. These were solid sideman gigs, but stood out as rare interludes of employment during a difficult time in which chances for Monk to perform and record his music were infrequent at best. For the most part, the 1940s were a lost decade for Monk. In his 1949 book *Inside Bebop*, one of the first critical efforts to come to grips with the new music, author Leonard Feather dismissed Monk out of hand. Monk's reputation, Feather asserted, was "grossly distorted, as a result of some high-powered publicity work. He has written a few attractive tunes, but his lack of technique and continuity prevented him from accomplishing much as a pianist."[15]

It is easy to blame the otherwise astute Feather for his obtuseness with regard to Monk. But Feather was not alone. At the close of the 1940s, Monk's music was per-ceived by most members of the jazz community as too far outside the mainstream to be valued in its own right, and too personal to influence other players. His style, built on disjunction, stood as a puzzling connect-the-dots drawing for which most listeners could not see the overall picture. For a time they called Monk the "high priest of bop," and the nickname revealed how little the jazz world understood him. Despite the Minton's connection, Monk's mature music bore little resemblance to bebop. In contrast to the speed-obsessed work of Parker, Powell, and Gillespie, Monk preferred slow and medium tempos, and his process of improvising had a deliberate, hesitating quality. And though he occasionally tackled the standard songs of the bebop repertoire, Monk preferred to play his own pieces—and played them again and again, often recording the same tune a half-dozen or more times over the course of his career.

Even before Monk's comeback in the 1950s, the pianist gave notice of his singular vision of jazz, although few outside the inner circles of modern jazz were paying attention at the time. The amateur recordings made by Columbia student Jerry Newman at Minton's testify to the pianist's iconoclasm—one would be hard pressed to find a more forward-looking jazz piano performance, circa 1941, than Monk's reconfiguration of George Gershwin's "Nice Work if You Can Get It." In his 1944 sides with Coleman Hawkins, Monk revealed his zeal for experimentation to a wider audience, although he balanced his dissonances here with a judicious dose of more circumspect sounds. Hear, for example, his solo on "Flyin' Hawk," where the first sixteen bars hew close to bebop, but the closing sixteen bars sound the way jazz might be played in another galaxy. Yet the core of Monk's output from this decade came from the four sessions the pianist made for the Blue Note label during 1947 and 1948. Here, in these landmark recordings, Monk revealed his mature style as almost fully formed. In his debut session as a leader for Blue Note, Monk is weighed down by an unsympathetic horn section, and his piano solos are too brief. Yet even in this constrained setting, he showcases many of his characteristic devices: angular phrases and whole-tone scales; the stark repetition of the simplest melodic fragments, serving almost as a parody of traditional thematic development; thick comping chords laced with dissonances, and dropped with the subtlety of a hand grenade.

Monk's second session, held nine days later, dispenses with the horn players. In this piano trio setting, he adopts an even wider range of mannerisms—and not just his futuristic techniques, but snippets of older jazz styles as well. On the alternate take of "Nice Work if You Can Get It," a remnant from Monk's Minton's days still in his repertoire, he slips in several unexpected bars of stride piano. On "Ruby, My Dear" he provides two bars of a figured bass that hint at the left-hand patterns of boogie-woogie. Perhaps Meade Lux Lewis and Albert Ammons were on his mind—after all, they were favorites with Blue Note head Alfred Lion—because on "Well, You Needn't" Monk again adopts elements of boogie-woogie, this time in his right-hand block chords. But all these ingredients—whether old or new, borrowed or blue—manage somehow to cohere. The pianist's personal signature is so strong that everything he touches turns, if not to gold, at least to Monk. This date featured three of Monk's most famous compositions ("Ruby, My Dear," "Well, You Needn't," "Off Minor"), but even the popular standards included end up sounding like his originals. The two remaining Blue Note sessions from this period resulted in milestone performances of a number of other important Monk compositions, including "'Round Midnight," "Epistrophy," "I Mean You," "Misterioso," "In Walked Bud," and

"Monk's Mood." In particular, the July 2, 1948, session, in which Monk plays cat and mouse with vibraphonist Milt Jackson, stood out as the most complete statement to date of his unorthodox musical values.

Yet three years would elapse before Monk returned to the studio as a leader. In a prescient 1948 interview, Orrin Keepnews—who would later become Monk's record producer—cited the pianist as potentially representing "a huge step forward" in modern jazz and noted that his music was further away from the bop idiom than most commentators had realized. But even Keepnews conceded that Monk was a "little known figure" and that "only time and continued playing" would determine his true merit.[16] Most other journalistic accounts from the time preferred to emphasize the bizarre aspects of Monk's demeanor—an oft-repeated anecdote depicted him spending long periods staring at a photo of Billie Holiday taped to his ceiling—while the freshness of his music was usually restricted to a passing mention, a side note to his unconventional lifestyle. And those fans who hoped to make up their own mind about the so-called "high priest of bop" had little chance to do so. Monk played infrequent engagements, with most of his music making taking place at home.

Monk's return to the studio in July 1951 represented progress of sorts. But opportunities to record came at the same time that Monk's cabaret card was revoked due to a narcotics arrest. That event led to a six-year involuntary absence from New York nightclubs. Meanwhile, Monk's recordings during this period document a major burst of creativity and set the foundation for his ascendancy to the top of the jazz world in the late 1950s and early 1960s. In his comeback session for Blue Note, Monk featured some of his most complex compositions. Gunther Schuller has praised "Criss Cross," recorded at this date, for being much more than a "tune" or a "song" but succeeding as a true "composition for instruments" and likened it to the abstract painting in vogue around that time. In fact, all the pieces recorded by Monk at this session reflect the same virtues. The harmonies of "Straight, No Chaser" are built on a standard twelve-bar blues, but the melody is a clever exercise in the rhythmic displacement of a changeable motif, which sometimes ends on a blues note and sometimes resolves into a major third. Even more daring is "Four in One," where Monk employs surprisingly fast, almost glissando-like passages in the melody line, like a painter unexpectedly smearing the canvas with sweeping brushstrokes.

In some respects, these pieces represented a departure from the norm (to the extent that one could discuss a "norm" with regard to this nonconforming keyboardist) for Monk. Throughout his career, Monk had tempered his avant-garde tendencies with simple, repetitive, and almost childlike melodies. Pieces such as "Epistrophy," "Misterioso," "Blue Monk," "Well, You Needn't," "Let's Cool One," "Rhythm-a-ning," "Hornin' In," "Trinkle Tinkle," "Bemsha Swing," and "Off Minor" boasted memorable, rigorously developed themes. These singsong melodies stayed in listeners' ears long after the performance was over, and no doubt served for many as an inviting entry point into musical structures that, viewed from other angles, could be foreboding. Much of Monk's genius lay precisely in this ability to juxtapose the simple and complex, a talent he applied in many other ways: in his dramatic balancing of silence and aural density; his alternating use of thick and thin chords; his manner of incorporating wry humor into the often self-serious atmosphere of modern jazz. But at times Monk would push the limits even further, building elaborate musical mazes such as "Four in One" or "Brilliant Corners," where not only the casual listener but even skilled jazz players risked getting lost in the labyrinth. At the 1957 session that produced "Brilliant Corners"—a maddeningly difficult Monk chart that took twenty-five takes to complete—producer Keepnews interpreted the wry half-smiles of the sidemen (who included Sonny Rollins, Max Roach, and Oscar Pettiford) as signifying a silent lament: "Hard? This is *impossible!*"

At the other end of the spectrum were Monk's ballads. Here his links to the American song tradition were most evident. One could envision compositions such as "'Round Midnight" and "Ruby My Dear" performed by mainstream popular artists, perhaps even appealing to a nonjazz audience—hardly possible for Monk musical koans such as "Epistrophy" or "Well, You Needn't." Of course even these ballads, when played by the composer, could take on all the quirky qualities of Monk's more experimental work, just as he could take pop standards such as "Smoke Gets in Your Eyes" or "The Man I Love" and make them sound like his own creations. But Monk was also capable of more harmonically ambiguous slow numbers, as in his evocative "Crepuscule with Nellie" where his work captures a rarefied sensibility closer to the ambiance of art song than either to jazz or popular music.

The Blue Note relationship was followed by recordings for the Prestige label. These, for all of their musical merits, achieved limited sales and only a tepid response from critics. Prestige eventually released Monk from his contract for the meager sum of $108.27. The pianist now signed with Riverside, a small record company run by Keepnews, who by now had switched hats from journalist to producer—a role at which he would excel. This initiated a six-year relationship during which Monk, under Keepnews's supervision, undertook twenty-eight recording sessions. These were fertile years for Monk, not so much because his music evolved during this period—on the contrary, his style changed very little after the mid-1940s—but because he was finally provided with the chance to express his musical ideas in a wide range of conducive contexts. Monk had always excelled in a trio setting, and his first several Riverside sessions followed that format. But soon Keepnews was planning more elaborate dates featuring larger bands and guest soloists. He was especially intent on creating opportunities for Monk to record alongside name saxophonists. The resulting projects showcased an impressive roster of horn players, including Sonny Rollins, John Coltrane, Coleman Hawkins, Gerry Mulligan, Johnny Griffin, Phil Woods, Harold Land, and Charlie Rouse. The Riverside recordings also found Monk in the company of many of the leading drummers of modern jazz, including Max Roach, Kenny Clarke, Art Blakey, Roy Haynes, Shelly Manne, Art Taylor, and Shadow Wilson. These were ambitious—and almost universally successful—projects, and were especially impressive given that they were undertaken by a small independent jazz label that operated under severe financial constraints (and would go bankrupt in 1964). By comparison, Monk's later recordings for CBS/Columbia, the leading company in the industry with the deepest of pockets, rarely ventured beyond combo recordings with his working band.

But the Riverside recordings were equally notable for their intimate sessions featuring Monk as a solo pianist. This was an ideal setting for him. His playing had always been distinguished by its open, uncluttered landscapes—"It's not the notes you play, it's those you leave out," he had once cryptically explained—but never more so than when working unaccompanied. Here he could expand time and tempo to their limits, as in his solo performance of "I Should Care," where Monk takes a simple statement of the melody and lingers lovingly over these thirty-two bars for a full three minutes. Such performances also captured the full resonance and rich overtones of his harmonics, the distinctive crispness of his piano touch, and the orchestral implications of his keyboard style. Moreover, they represented a type of anti-virtuosity, a refreshing antidote to the elaborate patterns and runs, the florid cocktail piano mannerisms that had permeated the music since the days of Hines and Tatum.

Despite his lengthy absence from the New York nightclub circuit, Monk's reputation was soaring and his records selling in increasing quantities. Infrequent public appearances may have only added to his mystique—a program for a 1955 concert described him, tellingly, as the "Greta Garbo of jazz." The reinstatement of his cabaret card put an end to his apparent reclusiveness but did nothing to hinder his popularity. His booking at the Five Spot during the summer of 1957 showed the breadth and depth of his newfound audience. Drawing full houses night after night, his engagement was extended to eight months, and management brought in a special piano chosen by Monk himself. Even by Monk's standards, this was an exceptional band. "Those of us who heard it will never forget the experience," jazz historian Ira Gitler later recalled. "There were some weeks when I was at the Five Spot two or three times, staying most of the night even when I intended just to catch a set or two."[17]

The attraction of this combo was as much its star saxophonist as it was Monk himself. John Coltrane was on the verge of establishing himself as the leading tenor saxophonist in jazz at the time he joined Monk's band. Coltrane had recently completed a high-profile stint with Miles Davis, following previous sideman gigs with Dizzy Gillespie and Johnny Hodges, and had just recorded his first album as a leader for the Prestige label. Even at this early point in his career, Coltrane stood out from the pack with his explosive improvisations, his technical prowess, and the unprecedented energy of his performances. The following year *Downbeat* would christen him an "angry young tenor"—a misnomer given Coltrane's reflective nature and spiritual leanings, but an appropriate response to his intemperate saxophone playing. More to the point was Gitler's oft-quoted description of Coltrane's style as a relentless spinning forth of "sheets of sound." In this regard, Coltrane took the implications of Bird one step further: the notes are even more densely packed, the traditional jazz syncopations and rhythmic inflections even less prominent. Instead, Coltrane favored cascading waterfalls of notes, scales, arpeggios, figures, sometimes played in short bursts, at other times expanded in breathlessly elongated phrases.

Coltrane's tenure with Monk lasted only a few months and has often been cited as a period of apprenticeship, an important contributor to the tenor player's development as a jazz musician. Coltrane himself frequently expressed his admiration for Monk, praising him as a "musical architect of the highest order." But the recordings made by Monk's band during this period show that the tenorist was anything but overawed by his new employer. Indeed, one is hard pressed to find another Monk sideman who did so little to adapt to the idiosyncracies of the pianist's music. On recordings such as "Trinkle Tinkle" or "Nutty," Coltrane unleashes powerful solos that, rather than emulating Monk's use of space or compositional style of improvisation as so many others did when playing with the pianist, reflect the saxophonist's own emphatic, virtuosic style. (Compare these, for instance, with Sonny Rollins's collaborations with Monk—successful in their own way—which find the horn player constructing incisive thematic solos, challenging the music from "inside," rather than imposing his personality on top of it.) In a surprising turnaround, Monk came to adapt to Coltrane, even going so far as not playing behind some of the sax solos, allowing the tenorist to stretch out with just bass and drum backing (much as the saxophonist would do a few years later with his own band). In the final analysis, this was an extraordinary ensemble, one of the most creative units of its day, *not* because Coltrane served as disciple to Monk, as is so often stated, but because these two masters of the jazz idiom met, for the most part, on equal terms. During their few months together, these two premier stylists—one espousing a music of pregnant pauses and lingering overtones, the other filling each measure to the fullest, to overflowing, in a music of delirious excess—called to mind the physicists' assertion that the creative energy of the universe is founded, ultimately, on the attraction of opposites.

On the crest of the sensation caused by the Five Spot band, Monk was enjoying unprecedented attention and praise, first among jazz insiders, who awarded him first place in the *Downbeat* Critics Poll in both 1958 and 1959, and gradually from the general public. He now toured frequently, both throughout the United States and overseas, and by 1960 was able to demand $1,000 for a one-night stand, substantially more than what he had charged for a full-week booking only two years earlier. For his 1959 Town Hall concert, the pianist was given an ample budget to finance a performance of his music with a large band and cover the cost of suitably "Monkesque" arrangements provided by Hall Overton. The concert was taped and released on Keepnews's Riverside label, which was now recording Monk more freqently than ever, and with constantly improving sales.

But these were also troubling years for the pianist. His odd mannerisms and onstage demeanor may have amused audiences, but the deeper-seated psychological problems they represented were no laughing matter. In 1958, Monk's obsessive pacing in a Delaware hotel lobby, and his steadfast refusal to respond to questions, led to a heated confrontation with local police. The following year, Monk ended a strange performance at Boston's Storyville Club by remaining seated on the piano bench, motionless and impassive, long after his sidemen had left the stage. Later that same night, Monk was arrested at the airport and brought by a state trooper to Grafton State Hospital, where he was placed under observation for a week. During the 1960s, Monk received medical treatment for depression, and his personality grew ever more remote. Sometimes he would remain aloof for days at a time, with even his wife, Nellie, unable to extract more than a word or two from him.

Monk's music seemed largely unaffected by these problems—then again, a certain psychological distance from the mundane and everyday had always been an ingredient of his artistry. Moreover, eccentricity fueled publicity. Indeed, the pianist's fame and following were now great enough to attract the interest of a major label. In 1962, Monk signed with Columbia, and under the aegis of this entertainment industry powerhouse, his reputation continued to grow, even if his music changed little, culminating in a February 28, 1964, *Time* magazine cover story. By the mid-1960s, Monk was as much a legend as a musician. Yet his recordings for Columbia, although solid efforts, broke little new ground. His repertoire drew heavily on material he had recorded in earlier years. The settings were rarely as imaginative as those Keepnews had created for the Riverside recordings—most of the Columbia releases featured Monk in the context of his working band, which now included saxophonist Charlie Rouse. Rouse was a skilled journeyman player, especially sensitive to the nuances of Monk's music, but he did little to make listeners forget the earlier pairings with Coltrane, Rollins, and other saxophone masters. Still, the best of these works served as important additions to Monk's oeuvre.

Despite the travails of his personal life, Monk maintained a fairly hectic recording and performance schedule during his first several years with Columbia, but by the close of the 1960s his activities had tapered off. In the 1970s, Monk's public appearances, like his Delphic utterances, grew even less frequent. As befitted a legend, he remained mostly out of sight. His last official performance came at a Carnegie Hall concert in 1976, but, in an appropriate coda to his career, Monk surprised listeners one night after that by sitting in at Bradley's, a small New York bar where few would have expected this reclusive jazz master to grace the keys. In his final years, the pianist resided with the Baroness de Koenigswarter, who had also befriended Charlie Parker during the altoist's last illness. On February 5, 1982, Monk suffered a stroke, and died twelve days later at Englewood Hospital in New Jersey. He was sixty-four years old.

As early as the mid-1950s, a few jazz pianists were paying close attention to Monk's example. For players such as Herbie Nichols, Richard Twardzik, Randy Weston, Mal Waldron, and Elmo Hope, several elements of Monk's playing proved especially influential. First and foremost, the vertical conception of his music offered a robust alternative to the essentially linear approach of most postwar pianists. Similarly, Monk's textured chords, sinewy melodies, and assertive rhythms served as open marks of rebellion against the "cool school," then in the ascendancy, and its attempts to find a crossover audience for jazz among the general public. In essence, Monk figured as patron saint for those who saw jazz as an underground movement resisting assimilation. His music's prickly exterior was perhaps not intended to make it sound foreboding, but for his admirers the sharp edges were a virtue, a fitting defense mechanism to repel all but an inner clique. But Monk's music was equally admired for its primal insistence, for his vision of the piano as a percussion instrument—a sensibility that shaped the pianist's tone control, phrasing, and sense of rhythm. In many ways, this was merely a return to the earliest jazz keyboard tradition (and, as such, it should come as no surprise that Monk and Nichols had strong ties to the stride idiom); but it was also a link to the later avant-garde players, most notably Cecil Taylor, who would owe much to Monk's celebration of the piano as a giant tuned drum with manifold possibilities.

Following Monk's model, however, was fraught with difficulties in the mid-1950s. Nichols, Twardzik, and Hope have each received far more recognition posthumously than during their abbreviated careers. All were dead before their mid-forties, leaving behind only a handful of recordings to testify to their potent reworkings of the jazz tradition. Herbie Nichols, one of the most brilliant modern jazz composers and pianists of his day, made just three albums as a leader, with most of his working life spent playing in Dixieland bands. Nichols's attack and the basic elements of his musical vocabulary show a great debt to Monk, but his performances are more driving, more densely packed. And in the place of Monk's sly humor, they tend toward a brittle hardness, somber and remote, at times bordering on an academic otherworldliness. Nichols's best recordings—"The Third World," "2300 Skiddoo," "Blue Chopsticks," "Cro-Magnon Nights"—are powerful statements, totally free from cliché, and revealing a poised balance between form and content. Twardzik spent even less time in the recording studio than Nichols, but the few items in his discography reveal a progressive thinker of titanic proportions. His music raises obvious comparisons with Monk's but is also notable for its links to twentieth-century classical music and its anticipation of the later free jazz movement. Twardzik's reputation rests primarily on a single trio session and sideman efforts with Serge Chaloff and Chet Baker. However, these are substantial works by any measure and indicate that had he lived longer—Twardzik was dead of a drug overdose before his twenty-fifth birthday—he might have established himself as one of the leading jazz players of his generation. Hope's visionary style came to the fore on recordings made, as both a leader and sideman, in New York during the mid-1950s, but the revocation of his cabaret card due to drug problems limited his ability to build on these accomplishments. After relocating to California, Hope undertook sessions under his own name, as well as contributed greatly to the success of Harold Land's classic recording *The Fox*. Like Monk, Hope found his music branded as "difficult," and few listeners were willing to make the effort to probe its rich implications. He continued to work and record sporadically after his return to New York in early 1961 until his death six years later, but never gained a following commensurate with the virtues of his steely and multifaceted music.

Lennie Tristano's impact on the development of jazz piano is perhaps even more difficult to gauge than Monk's. During most of his life, Tristano remained an outsider in the jazz world. He recorded little and, as the years passed, increasingly restricted his music making to the confines of his home. His influence was more often exerted indirectly, through the activities of his students and followers, rather than his own efforts. At times this corps of ardent admirers took on the appearance of a cult, of which Tristano stood as high priest and oracle. For members, Tristano was the seer who saw the outlines of the future of jazz, celebrating it as a rugged, cerebral music, unforgiving and uncompromising. For those less favorably inclined, Tristano was a monomaniac whose mark on the jazz scene was a matter of manipulation, rather than a result of superior musical values.

In such a charged atmosphere, it was difficult to find a middle ground in evaluating Tristano. One was either a devotee, or a traitor to the cause—and few could live up to the demands Tristano placed on his devotees. Accordingly, with the passage of time, Tristano's inner circle found fewer and fewer new acolytes. In the last twenty years of his life, his performances were increasingly rare, new recordings all but nonexistent, and older ones mostly out of print. By the time of his death in 1978, Tristano was a largely forgotten figure, relegated to the fringes of the jazz world.

Yet there was some irony to this turn of events. For the evolution of jazz piano was increasingly turning in precisely the direction that Tristano had foretold. His phrasing across the bar lines, his superimposition of elaborate polyrhythms over the ground beat, his biting percussiveness, his splintered harmonic structures: these key elements to Tristano's playing from the 1940s and 1950s were now appearing as defining elements in jazz piano in the years following his death. In many instances, younger players were coming to these same end points *not* because they had listened to Tristano—emphatically, in many instances, they had not (although most had listened deeply to Bill Evans, who had carefully studied Tristano and his school)—but because these developments were logical extensions of the modern jazz idiom. Moreover, a number of Tristano's most daring initiatives from the late 1940s and early 1950s—involving atonality, total improvisation, overdubbing, and other unusual devices—could now be seen as foreshadowing key developments in the later history of jazz. In this regard, Lennie Tristano was something of a Nostradamus of the bop era: when the future of jazz finally arrived, it bore a striking resemblance to his personal vision of how it *should* be.

A flu epidemic left Tristano blind shortly after his birth in Chicago on March 19, 1919. He began piano studies under his mother's supervision and later pursued a more extensive musical education at a school for the blind. By the time he had completed high school, Tristano had learned to play saxophone (tenor, alto, and C melody), clarinet, trumpet, guitar, and drums. Even before his teens, he was working professionally, and only gradually came to focus his energies on the piano. After completing his bachelor's degree at the American Conservatory of Music, Tristano began taking students in addition to performing in and around the Chicago area. By 1945, Tristano had attracted a small coterie of promising pupils, including saxophonist Lee Konitz, guitarist Billy Bauer, and composer/trombonist Bill Russo.

Tristano's first recordings, made around this time, reveal that his style was already fully formed, and that his conception of the keyboard was frighteningly advanced. Gunther Schuller has cited Tristano's 1946 trio performance of "I Can't Get Started" as a landmark in the development of jazz, comparing it to Armstrong's "West End Blues" and Ellington's "Cotton Tail."[18] Again it is the futuristic element of the music that is compelling, its startling harmonic conception, bordering at times on atonality, and its rhythmic complexity leading Schuller to praise the performance as "one of the most prophetic recordings in all jazz history." But in many ways, Schuller concludes, the performance was "too far ahead of its time."

In truth, placing Tristano within the context of a specific period and jazz movement has proven all too difficult. Most commentators and historians have listed him as a member of the cool school that predominated during the 1950s. But this classification captures only a small part of Tristano's legacy. For the most part, his music had little in common with the pared-down melody lines, the warm lyricism, the relaxed tempos and chamber music delicacy that characterized the cool jazz vocabulary. Schuller, for his part, evaluates Tristano as part of his study of *The Swing Era*, and though a case could be made linking the pianist to swing period musicians such as Art Tatum and Mel Powell, this too remains an unsatisfying choice. Finally, one might see Tristano as a precursor of the later free jazz movement. All these supposed genealogies can point to some family likeness to justify their claims. However, to my ears, Tristano's closest allegiance was to none of these schools, but rather to the bebop movement; he shared its fascination with long melodic lines, its celebration of intensity, its refusal to compromise, and its imperative to experiment.

Tristano's activities shortly after his move to New York in 1946 support this contention. His stellar trio sides for the Keynote label find him alternating between a block chord style built on dense harmonic structures and a more driving linear approach in a bop vein. These devices would serve as the bricks and mortar of Tristano's mature piano style, and his skill with them was unsurpassed. Many other pianists of the period—notably Milt Buckner and George Shearing—would be celebrated for their "locked hands" chordal style, but none would take it to the daring extremes that Tristano surveyed. It would be hard to find jazz piano recordings from the mid-1940s more drenched in dissonance, more harmonically "out there" than "Atonement" and "I Can't Get Started," from Tristano's 1946–47 Keynote performances. His way of using elongated phrases was equally pathbreaking. One hears strong hints of Powell and Parker in his melodic constructions, but Tristano was even more radical than his contemporaries in his phrasing across the bar lines. The underlying 4/4 pulse is almost totally obliterated in these linear improvisations, hidden under arcane superstructures of melody and rhythm.

These skills made Tristano an ideal bebop pianist, and on a few occasions he performed and recorded with such key modern jazz figures as Charlie Parker, Dizzy Gillespie, Max Roach, and Fats Navarro. But, for the most part, Tristano preferred to make music in the company of his students and disciples. Two of these, Lee Konitz and Warne Marsh, would come to be major jazz figures in their own right. In time, Konitz, like his teacher, would become associated with the cool school in modern jazz. But with the altoist the connection is far more justified. Konitz participated in the influential Miles Davis *Birth of the Cool* sessions, and for many years affected a sweet tone and lyricism that one never heard in Tristano. The relationship between teacher and pupil was often strained, and after the early 1950s the two players mostly went their separate ways, with Konitz serving for a time with the Stan Kenton band and subsequently leading his own combos. In later years, Konitz's playing took on a rougher edge, and the links with the cool style became less obvious, but his work invariably maintained an integrity and almost ritualistic dedication to the process of improvisation that few of his contemporaries could match. Tenor saxophonist Warne Marsh had already worked as a professional musician for several years before connecting with Tristano around 1947. A technically polished saxophonist with an expansive range, Marsh offered a limpid, smooth tone, at times making his tenor sound like a fraternal twin to Konitz's alto. Marsh's melodic conception, however, lingered closer to Tristano's cerebral remoteness, almost mathematical in its purity, and mostly eschewed the quasi-romanticism with which Konitz briefly flirted. Konitz and Marsh both rank among the most consistently creative improvisers of their generation—and were especially potent when in each other's company. Examples of this musical chemistry can be found not just on the sessions with Tristano but also in other settings, for example, their artful 1955 collaboration for the Atlantic label and their stunning 1959 sessions with Bill Evans at the Half Note.

Tristano's 1949 recordings with Konitz and Marsh include some of the most intriguing jazz performances of the period. His 1949 tracks with Konitz for the Prestige label are especially uncompromising. Charlie Parker once suggested that the essence of modern jazz improvisation came from using the higher intervals of the underlying chords. Tristano and Konitz take Parker at his word here—maybe too much so: it almost sounds as if they are avoiding the lower intervals on these tracks. As a result, this music risks giving listeners a queasy, ungrounded sensation, despite its lissome execution. Tristano's 1949 recordings for Capitol also approach musical vertigo at times, but the playing is more robust, especially in the aptly titled "Wow." "Intuition" and "Digression" from this period are the first recorded examples in the jazz idiom of completely free-form group improvisation. Four years later, Tristano would again anticipate the later evolution of free jazz with his jarringly atonal work "Descent into the Maelstrom"—although this savage assault on the keyboard could exert no direct influence on the late 1950s avant-garde since it remained unreleased for over two decades.

Even when he pursued more mainstream efforts, Tristano seemed doomed to get caught up in controversy and partisan jazz debates. His 1955 recordings of "Line Up" and "Turkish Mambo" for the Atlantic label employed overdubbing and tape manipulation. Critics complained that Tristano "sped up" the tape of "Line Up," and the resulting brouhaha prevented many from hearing the riveting brilliance of the improvisation. Played at any speed, it stands out as one of the finest jazz piano performances of the era. In the aftermath, Tristano retreated even more deeply into seclusion. Seven years would elapse before his next Atlantic release, *The New Tristano*, with the pianist now offering unforgiving, untampered solo piano performances of the highest order, including his virtuosic workout on "C Minor Complex."

One could listen to all of Tristano's commercial recordings in a few hours. Much of his best work was captured on amateur recordings that, like "Descent into the Maelstrom," were not issued for many years. Several of Tristano's outstanding performances with Lee Konitz made in 1955 at the Sing-Song Room of the Confucius Restaurant were issued by Atlantic in 1956, but many other equally compelling tracks from this engagement were kept off the market until the 1970s. Other live sessions—from the Half Note, Birdland, the UJPO Hall in Toronto, or Tristano's 1965 visit to Europe—are seldom heard, but deserve consideration as vital parts of Tristano's legacy. In addition, the pianist made many recordings at home, and these too provide telling glimpses of a major musical mind that often saved its most creative moments for private consumption. All in all, these constitute an important body of work, rich with implications for the future of jazz. However, at the time of Lennie Tristano's death from a heart attack, on November 18, 1978, only one of his records was in print (and that one available only as an import from Japan). The passing years have seen a renewed interest in Tristano's music and a greater availability of his recordings. But the posthumous reverence awarded to many other—and lesser—figures from the past has been granted to him in only the smallest doses.

However, few jazz artists of his day embraced the tenets of modernism with greater fervor, or anticipated the later evolution of the music with greater insight.

These three stylists—Bud Powell, Thelonious Monk, Lennie Tristano—may have redefined the role of the piano in modern jazz, but their music was distinctly unsuitable for the mass market of the 1950s. The listeners who still enjoyed Count Basie or Duke Ellington found little sustenance in the dissonant harmonies of a Monk, the unrelenting energy of a Powell, the serpentine melody lines of a Tristano. It was left to other pianists—Oscar Peterson, Nat Cole, George Shearing, Ahmad Jamal, Dave Brubeck, Erroll Garner—to develop a broader following for contemporary jazz piano. Despite their differences, these six keyboard artists were consummate performers, skilled at smoothing the rough edges of modern jazz piano and extending its appeal. Critics were often ill at ease with the success enjoyed by these crossover artists. But, though occasional compromises may have been necessary to achieve this commercial viability, these pianists retained the respect and admiration of most jazz fans. And with good reason. Except for Cole, who ultimately abandoned the world of jazz piano for an immensely successful career as a popular vocalist, these musicians mostly remained true to their jazz roots. And even their most popular crossover hits—Brubeck's "Take Five," Jamal's "Poinciana," Peterson's *West Side Story*, Garner's *Concert by the Sea*—also merited praise as first-rate creative works.

Throughout his career, Oscar Peterson wore the heavy mantle of being cited as heir and successor to Art Tatum as the greatest virtuoso of modern jazz piano. This is a daunting and dubious honor, akin to being known as the fastest gunslinger in a town of trigger-happy rivals. But Peterson's command of the keyboard was beyond reproach and established him as the most famous among the handful of post-Tatum jazz players—including Phineas Newborn, Dorothy Donegan, Adam Makowicz, Friedrich Gulda, Jessica Williams—who successfully channeled the techniques of the concert hall into a mainstream jazz piano sound. Yet the comparisons with Tatum should stop there. Peterson's music only occasionally betrayed Tatum's thickly textured two-handed style, instead tending toward the forward-driving linear attack associated with Powell. And unlike either Tatum or Powell, Peterson gave highest priority to maintaining the rhythmic momentum of the music, what jazz players simply call "swing." *The Will to Swing* was the name Gene Lees gave to his book on Oscar Peterson, and few titles could have been more apt. Peterson stood out as one of the hardest swinging pianists of his generation, and though his rhythmic phrasing may have lacked the subtlety of a Parker or Tristano, it possessed a visceral appeal that only the stodgiest critics could deny.

Peterson had established a modest reputation in his native Montreal before being discovered by Norman Granz in 1949. That same year, Granz featured Peterson at a much-publicized Carnegie Hall concert, and the impresario continued to play an important role in guiding Peterson's career in later years. Peterson served as an unofficial house pianist for Granz's various record companies and concert promotions, and in that capacity accompanied many of the leading jazz players who were active in the postwar years, including Louis Armstrong, Charlie Parker, Lester Young, Billie Holiday, Count Basie, Dizzy Gillespie, Stan Getz, Ben Webster, Ella Fitzgerald, and Benny Carter. Yet Peterson, unlike Tatum, could be a surprisingly self-effacing accompanist, and his best work typically came when leading his own trio or working as a solo pianist. His *The Trio* recording for Pablo, *Night Train* for Verve, and *My Favorite Instrument* for MPS are excellent, representative recordings of his music. Peterson also occasionally attempted extended works, the best-known of which is his *Canadiana Suite*. Peterson maintained his popularity through the various revolutions and passing fashions of the jazz scene, and though a 1993 stroke compromised the agility of his left hand, he returned to the keyboard after a two-year hiatus and continued performing until shortly before his death in 2007.

Despite the frequent comparisons with Tatum, Peterson's piano style suggests an even greater debt to Nat King Cole. Cole's appealing work as a vocalist eventually came to overshadow his prowess as a jazz pianist, but during the 1940s and 1950s, his keyboard approach was widely admired and emulated on the jazz scene. Like Peterson, Cole embraced a style that represented a middle ground between swing and bop. His intricate improvised lines, rapid-fire runs, and right-hand-oriented attack were in keeping with the dominant piano style of the postwar years, but Cole's sense of phrasing remained rooted in the ground beat, and at times looked back to the earlier style of Earl Hines (to whom Cole had closely listened during his formative years in Chicago). In essence, Cole preferred to dance comfortably over the beat, rather than challenge it head on in the manner of Powell or Monk. This sense of relaxed swing was furthered by Cole's decision to lead a drummerless trio featuring piano, bass, and guitar. In his trio performances, as well as in his memorable recordings with Lester Young and his work with Norman Granz's various Jazz at the Philharmonic touring bands, Cole established himself as one of the most polished jazz pianists of the day. His incomparable singing, promoted almost to the exclusion of his piano work in later years, veered increasingly outside the jazz realm, but still revealed an exemplary sense of phrasing and clarity of expression with roots in Cole's keyboard approach.

London-born George Shearing emigrated to the United States in 1947, at the height of the bebop movement. At his best, Shearing rates praise as an inventive, technically adept pianist with a keen ear and sure sense of swing. However, Shearing's most popular recordings found him leading a quintet where his ambitions were modest. In this setting, he tended to favor a pared-down style employing block chords, reminiscent of Milt Buckner or, at times, of a keyboard translation of the sound of the Glenn Miller saxophone section; vibraphone and guitar were typically used to reinforce the melody line. The resulting "Shearing sound," as it came to be known, was tasteful and inoffensive—but hardly measured the full depth of the pianist's talent. There were, in fact, many Shearing sounds. In time, he proved capable of playing classical concertos with symphony orchestras or of creating his own orchestral sounds as a solo pianist, sometimes letting loose with stunning impromptu variations, for example, reworking his piece "Lullaby of Birdland" first in the style of Rachmaninoff, next à la Waller or Debussy, never flagging as he moved through the paces. Much of Shearing's most creative work was recorded after his sixtieth birthday, when he came across as especially effective in a duo setting, or in collaboration with vocalist Mel Tormé. If musicians were evaluated on native talent and raw potential, rather than on their actual body of recordings, Shearing would undoubtedly rank as one of the finest artists of his generation. As it stands, much of his recorded output only hints at the depth of his musicality.

Shearing's contemporary Erroll Garner also developed a wide following during the 1950s, reaching such heights of fame that in 1958 impresario Sol Hurok, a major force in concert music, made an unprecedented move into the jazz field to represent him. Of all the pianists discussed here, Garner displayed the loosest ties to the bebop idiom (despite having recorded and performed with Charlie Parker during Bird's West Coast period). In fact, it is difficult to pigeonhole Garner as a member of any school. His style was deeply personal, sometimes cranky, never pedestrian. He fought against the constraints of the instrument: at times making the piano sound like a guitar, with his trademark four-to-a-bar strumming chords, or like a drum, employing offbeat bombs in the manner of an Art Blakey, or even like a harp, unleashing Lisztian arpeggios accompanied by a counterpoint of grunts and groans from above. His introductions were pieces in themselves, likely to veer off in any number of directions before honing in on the song in question. His technique was formidable, but so unorthodox that few noticed how difficult his music actually was to perform. His dynamic range was unsurpassed, and nothing delighted him more than moving from a whisper to a roar—then back to a whisper. Just as impressive was his sense of time. In Zeno's paradox, Garner could just as well have been the tortoise as mighty Achilles, given how skillfully he could lag several paces behind the beat with a lazy, catch-as-catch-can swing, or charge ahead with all caution thrown to the wind.

Garner was self-taught—who could have instructed him in this crazy-quilt style?—and unable to read music. This did little to deter him from a career in music. After all, "nobody can hear you read," he was quick to explain. For his hands, Garner needed to make no apologies. They were said to span a thirteenth—hard to believe given his diminutive stature—and he could sign autographs with either the left or the right. Such ambidexterity also showed at the keyboard. "He could play a totally different rhythm in each hand," Sy Johnson once marveled, "and develop equally what he was doing in each hand."[19] And few pianists knew better than Garner how to keep their ten fingers gainfully employed. He is said to be responsible for over one thousand recordings on around seventy labels. Given this massive discography, Garner's consistency, enthusiasm, and freshness of approach are especially impressive. His best-known works include his "Fantasy on Frankie and Johnny," his pop song "Misty" (eventually immortalized in the noir movie *Play Misty for Me*), and his best-selling Columbia recording *Concert by the Sea*. Other Garner projects of note include his *Paris Impressions, Afternoon of an Elf*, and *Magician*. Despite the large audience he attracted during his lifetime, Garner has exerted little influence on players who came of age after his death in 1977—yet this is their loss, since his recorded legacy is rich with implication, unhindered by the prosaic, and could serve as the basis for a sparkling and brazen style even today.

Ahmad Jamal's sparse, ultracool pianism stands as the antithesis of Garner's rocking rococo ruminations at the keyboard. And if Garner was a throwback to an earlier era, with his prebop rhythms and traditional sense of swing, Jamal was a harbinger of the future of jazz. His studied use of space influenced Miles Davis and anticipated the later work of Bill Evans. His understated approach led some to dismiss him as essentially a cocktail pianist with little jazz substance: "Jamal's real instrument is not the piano at all, but his audience," quipped one jazz writer. Such comments reveal more about the state of jazz criticism during these years—deeply suspicious as it was of any musician who developed a wide following among the general public—than about Jamal's streamlined keyboard attack. In this instance, Jamal's cardinal sin was apparently the substantial success of his 1958 live recording at Chicago's Pershing Lounge, *But Not for Me*, which reached number three on the *Billboard* album chart, and remained on the list for over two years. The song "Poinciana," recorded at this engagement, would become Jamal's signature theme, and effectively conveys the trademark virtues of his sparse, vibrant keyboard attack.

This may have been popular music, but its appeal was not achieved through slick commercialism, rather was driven by the singularity of Jamal's vision. Jamal is often praised for his use of silence, but this scarcely conveys the depth of his musicality. After all—the precedent of John Cage notwithstanding—how difficult is it to be silent at the keyboard? The charm of Jamal's music came rather from his ability to maintain the swing, emotional conviction, and mood of his music even when playing the fewest notes. He accomplished this through a mastery of volume and phrasing, outstanding tone control, an orchestral conception of the piano, and an unfailing instinct for how to shape a solo from beginning to end. Yet Jamal's choice of sidemen also figured into this equation. Drummer Vernel Fournier and bassist Israel Crosby were unsurpassed at swinging while retaining the most subdued dynamic level. Together with Jamal they formed one of the most underappreciated rhythm sections of the 1950s. Jamal's later work found him in a variety of settings, sometimes experimenting with electronics or performing with string accompaniment. The quality of these efforts is mixed, but the best of them—typically those finding him at the acoustic piano in a small-combo setting—are on a par with his milestone recordings from the 1950s.

While Jamal's *But Not for Me* was gracing the Billboard charts, Dave Brubeck was achieving even more dramatic popularity with his *Time Out* recording. "Take Five," the Paul Desmond composition included on this album, achieved unprecedented sales for a modern jazz instrumental performance and did much to legitimize unusual time signatures. But this represented no sudden rise to fame for Brubeck. Rather, the building blocks of his success had been slowly put in place during the course of the prior decade. In the late 1940s, Brubeck started drawing attention for his advocacy of the new and unusual, initially through the work of his Octet. This ensemble, which drew on the most progressive strains in both jazz and classical music, was formed during Brubeck's stint at Mills College, where he and many of his colleagues in the Octet were studying with modernist composer Darius Milhaud. Subsequently, Brubeck broadened his following while leading a piano trio that mostly showcased his adventurous reworkings of jazz standards. But Brubeck's greatest popularity came with the formation of his quartet, where his thick harmonies and strident rhythms were set off by the smooth alto work of saxophonist Paul Desmond. The combo recorded a number of outstanding live performances for the Fantasy label, in which the dictates of modernism and melodicism were artfully balanced. In 1954, Brubeck left Fantasy for the Columbia label and, that same year, his photo graced the cover of *Time* magazine. His gradual building of a mass market audience, and the growing polish of the quartet, aided by the addition of the exceptional drummer Joe Morello (in 1956) and journeyman bassist Eugene Wright (in 1958)—to form what many consider the "classic" Brubeck quartet—set the stage for the *Time Out* success.

The fame and enormous record sales that Brubeck enjoyed were all the more remarkable given the uncompromising nature of his piano work. His approach to the keyboard was almost totally purged of the sentimental and romantic trappings or the oh-so-hip funkiness that characterized most crossover hits. His chord voicings were dense and often dissonant. His touch at the piano was heavy and ponderous—anything but the cocktail bar tinkling fancied by the general public. His music tended to be rhythmically complex but seldom broached the finger-popping swing of a Peterson or Garner. Only in his choice of repertoire, which was populist to an extreme with its mix of pop songs, show tunes, traditional music—indeed anything from "Camptown Races" to "The Trolley Song" might show up on a Brubeck album—did he make a deferential gesture to the tastes of the mass audience. But even these familiar songs were apt to take on an unfamiliar guise under Brubeck's hands. He may have put aside the twelve-tone row in favor of "Tea for Two," but by the time he had finished with the Vincent Youmans standard it could sound like Schoenberg had tampered with the sheet music.

Almost all the popularizers of modern jazz piano discussed here felt a degree of hostility from the critics of their day. As previously mentioned, this was very much part of the ethos of the jazz world during the postwar years. Parker and his colleagues had permanently changed jazz into a counterculture movement, suspicious of mass market acclaim, protective of its outsider status. A wide audience was now a sign of having "sold out." The motivations behind this pervasive and persistent attitude among the jazz establishment are complex—no doubt ranging from the personal to the political—and a detailed analysis of its evolution could fill a lengthy monograph. Suffice it to say that, for whatever reasons, the felicitous marriage of popular music and jazz, which reached its apotheosis in the Swing Era, was succeeded by a painful, often acrimonious divorce.

BIG BANDS IN THE MODERN ERA

Nowhere was this new separation more apparent than in the struggles faced by big bands in the postwar years. Working with an instrumentation and vocabulary formed during the period of jazz's greatest popularity, these large ensembles appeared to be distinctly unsuited to lead the jazz idiom into the modern era. By the start of the 1950s, singers—many of them former vocalists with big bands—had taken center stage in the world of popular music. Instead of Ellington, Goodman, Shaw, Basie, and Miller, the pop charts were dominated by Frank Sinatra, Peggy Lee, Nat King Cole, Jo Stafford, Doris Day, and Perry Como. One era had ended, another had begun.

It is not difficult to find reasons to explain this shift. The problems faced by the big band leaders after the late 1940s were legion. The costs of taking a large band on the road had grown prohibitively high. The general public's interest fell to new lows. Even jazz devotees wavered in their loyalty, increasingly showing a preference for smaller combos. An entertainment tax instituted in 1944, which levied a 30 percent surcharge on venues that allowed dancing, led to a decline in ballroom patronage. This created a wedge between jazz music and dance, which widened during the postwar years due, in part, to a shift in performance styles, with medium tempo swing numbers gradually losing favor to a less danceable mix emphasizing very fast or very slow pieces. Meanwhile, a panoply of modern technologies and conveniences—television, high-fidelity sound, various newfangled appliances—seemingly conspired to keep Americans at home in the suburbs. The result was an inexorable decline in the role of dance halls and other big band venues. The contemporary jazz scene of the 1950s was abandoned to the outsiders, the bohemians and beatniks, and the young—those who still frequented the urban clubs late at night. For this crowd, the big band was most often viewed as a dinosaur, the retrograde sound of a generation whose time had already passed.

In the face of these daunting circumstances, a few leaders persisted in their efforts to bring the jazz big band into the modern age, to adapt it to the changed circumstances of the day. The most ambitious of these—a Stan Kenton or Sun Ra—sought nothing less than revitalizing the big band as the creative center of the modern jazz world. A noble but, alas, an almost impossible task—akin to reintroducing sackbuts and lutes into the symphony orchestra. But though these attempts did little to return large ensembles to a position of prominence in the jazz world—that is hardly likely to happen again—they nonetheless spurred the creation of a vital body of work, a music of artistry, which served also as a quixotic protest against the marginalization of the big band sound.

Unlike the dinosaurs, the big bands avoided total extinction—but just barely. Reading press clippings about swing bands from the late 1940s and early 1950s is as uplifting as browsing through a stack of obituaries. There are mostly tombstones and eulogies, few cigars and celebrations. In December 1946 alone, eight major big bands broke up. A host of name leaders, many still in the prime of their lives, took early retirement, changed careers, or retrenched. Artie Shaw, age forty-four, put away his clarinet case for good. Cab Calloway took to the stage to play Sportin' Life in *Porgy and Bess*, the character George Gershwin had based on the Hi-De-Ho man some years before. The Dorsey brothers grew nostalgic, settled their fraternal feud, made a (mostly fictional) movie about their career—*The Fabulous Dorseys* (1947)—and soon took their act to television. Louis Armstrong fired his big band and returned to a small-combo traditional jazz setting—and convinced Earl Hines to do the same. Around the time of his fortieth birthday, Benny Goodman effectively ended his career as a bandleader, restricting himself from that point on to sporadic appearances with ensembles hastily gathered for specific tours or concerts.

Who knows how many big bands were working regularly in America during the peak years of the Swing Era? George Simon's book on the subject refers to several hundred by name—and this is, of course, only a partial roster. A typical issue of *Downbeat*, circa 1940, might list some eight hundred ballrooms, hotels, theaters, and other venues featuring big band music. For a time, big band jazz seemed always within earshot in America's cities. Yet after the painful contraction in swing music, only a handful of major big band leaders from the war years—most notably Ellington, Basie, Herman, Kenton, and James—still kept the flame alive. And even these few survivors struggled.

The challenge, as most bandleaders saw it, was to hold onto the past. But for the most committed ones, the goal was nothing less than to bring the big band into the future. A few daring visionaries looked to the world of contemporary classical music for inspiration. "Serious" composers, such as Igor Stravinsky, were brandished as symbolic figures if not as actual role models by the more progressive big band arrangers. Boyd Raeburn recorded a chart titled "Boyd Meets Stravinsky"—on which, despite the name, Stravinsky did not perform. George Russell responded with his 1949 piece "Bird in Igor's Yard." Shorty Rogers was also, apparently, on a first-name basis with the maestro (after all, the Russian composer reportedly based the horn work in his "Threni" on Rogers's style), penning his song "Igor." In 1948, when jazz writer Leonard Feather gave a "blindfold test" to Charlie Parker, he mixed in Stravinsky's "The Song of the Nightingale" with recordings by Basie, Goodman, and Kenton. Parker immediately identified the composer, adding, "That's music at its best."[20] But Woody Herman had already outdone all of these acolytes—he was actually approached by Stravinsky himself, who offered to write a chart for the band. But the resulting work, the *Ebony Concerto*, should have made it clear that the jazz world, despite all its deference to the more progressive currents in contemporary classical music, had very little in common with such rarefied styles of composition. The *Ebony Concerto* was a turgid work that made little attempt to tap the rhythmic vitality of jazz. Those seeking to bring big band jazz to a higher level would need to look elsewhere for inspiration.

For the most part, they looked to bebop as the magical ingredient that would revitalize the big band. And though this would seem an easy and obvious formula to follow, few did it with any degree of success. As noted before, Earl Hines, Billy Eckstine, and Dizzy Gillespie all led big bands featuring world-class modern jazz players, but none of these celebrated units lasted more than a few years. Boyd Raeburn's ensemble made a similar attempt to marry progressive sounds with traditional Swing Era instrumentation, but was scorned by major labels who thought its music "too weird" for dancers—a verdict all too well borne out by 1946 recordings of George Handy's charts "Dalvatore Sally," which served as the band's theme song, and "Temptation," which, despite its name, fans found all too easy to resist. Critics and musicians were enthusiastic about Raeburn's work, but his big band finally shut down in 1949, without ever having achieved a substantial hit. Benny Goodman also embraced bop, in a famous reversal—only a short while before he had asserted that the beboppers were "not real musicians" and were "just faking"—but by 1948 he was publicly praising the new style and featuring a number of modern jazz players in his band, including Wardell Gray and (for a brief stint) Fats Navarro. Yet the following year, Goodman disbanded his bop unit, and by 1953 he was again bad-mouthing the movement, telling the *New York Times*: "What you hear in bop is a lot of noise."[21]

Among the major white big band leaders, Charlie Barnet was the first to draw on the emerging modern jazz style. The band's 1939 hit "Cherokee" would come to serve as an unofficial anthem of the bebop movement, although at the time Barnet's group stayed fairly close to the model set by Ellington and Basie. But, by 1942, the band had taken on a more modern sound, streamlined and hard-swinging, and incorporating many of the melodic devices of bebop. The arrangements of Andy Gibson and, later, Ralph Burns set a cutting-edge tone for the Barnet band, which was furthered by the addition of pianist Dodo Marmarosa, bassist Oscar Pettiford, trumpeters Neal Hefti and Al Killian, and clarinetist Buddy DeFranco, among others. For a brief period, Barnet even had Dizzy Gillespie in the group. These were bold moves for a white bandleader, and not just from a musical standpoint given the rarity of integration in the ensembles of the day. Yet Barnet had long stood out as a champion of racial tolerance in the jazz world—indeed, rivaling Goodman in this respect—with Roy Eldridge, Benny Carter, Lena Horne, Frankie Newton, and Charlie Shavers, among others, serving stints at various times with his band.

These combined influences gave Barnet's group an authentic bop sound—this coming several months before Gillespie's combo brought modern jazz to Fifty-second Street. In fact, bop had hardly ventured beyond the doors of Minton's and Monroe's at the time that Barnet was presenting it to his audiences. Gunther Schuller, in his masterful study *The Swing Era*, has declared with some justification that with the band's October 1943 recording of "The Moose"—arranged by Burns and featuring seventeen-year-old Marmarosa in top form—"modern big band jazz was born, or at least baptized."[22] Barnet has long been dismissed as a white imitator of the leading black bands, but this ensemble was innovative by almost any measure. Even the old jazz pieces that Barnet revived during this period, such as his 1944 remakes of Ellington's "Drop Me Off in Harlem" and Armstrong's "West End Blues," were presented in new garb, glistening bop-oriented versions as advanced as anything in the swing repertoire of the time. But Barnet, for all his virtues, struggled to retain the talent he discovered. Where his role model Ellington could hold onto key players for years, Barnet often kept them for only a few months. Despite this steady turnover, his bands continued to flourish for the remainder of the decade.

The main beneficiary of Barnet's losses would prove to be Woody Herman, a bandleader with an unfailing knack for continually reinventing his sound. Herman's performing career had passed through virtually every style of popular music by the time he found himself leading a bop big band. Born in Milwaukee in 1913, Herman started performing at age six, singing and dancing in his hometown, and went on the road for the first time at the age of nine. As a youngster he played the vaudeville circuit, where he was billed as the "Boy Wonder of the Saxophone." The next phase of Herman's career found him plying his trade in society and sweet bands, most notably the Isham Jones ensemble that Herman joined in 1934. When Jones disbanded in 1936, Herman drew on its members to form his own group, known for a time as "The Band That Plays the Blues." The group also dabbled in other jazz styles, including Dixieland, and eventually gravitated toward swing numbers, such as the riff-based blues "Woodchopper's Ball," which became Herman's first hit in 1939. Follow-up records such as "Blues in the Night" and "Blue Flame" also sold well, and by 1942 the Herman band had established itself as one of the leading swing orchestras of the day. At this unlikely point in his career, Herman began deviating from the formula that had brought him success and, ever restless, gradually came to embrace the new bop idiom.

Herman's evolution from sweet music to traditional jazz to modern jazz is almost unprecedented in the history of music. Few bandleaders of his generation could consider such a wholesale change, and even fewer would have been capable of it. Yet, when understood properly, this dramatic shift provides a telling insight into Herman's unusual, perhaps unique, relationship to his musical milieu. For Woody Herman is best understood not as a bandleader or even as a musician, but as a catalyst. His talent lay not primarily in what he did, but in what he enabled others to do—spurring those around him to tap their deepest creative currents, inspiring them, letting them "loose," so to speak—so much so that it is easy to lose sight of his own considerable skills as an instrumentalist and vocalist. Hence Phil Wilson's apt quip: "Nobody does what Woody does as well as Woody does. . . . If we could only figure out what it is he does."[23]

With his sure instincts for recognizing talent, Herman quickly sought out the leading lights of the modern jazz movement. In 1942, he hired Dizzy Gillespie to write for the band (some decades later Gillespie introduced Herman to the crowd at the Monterey Jazz Festival as "the first person ever to pay me fifty dollars for an arrangement"), and he brought a large number of enthusiastic young modern jazz players into his ensemble, many of them former members of Barnet's band. The rhythm section was galvanized by the addition of bassist Chubby Jackson, guitarist Billy Bauer, and hard-swinging drummer Dave Tough; and in 1944, two musician-arrangers who had also worked with Barnet, pianist Ralph Burns and trumpeter Neal Hefti, joined the exodus to the Herman band and gave further momentum to its progressive leanings. The trumpet section included Sonny Berman, a masterful soloist who might have established himself as one of the leading brass players of his day had he not died before his twenty-second birthday, as well as Pete Candoli, a fiery instrumentalist with a penchant for high-note dramatics. Two other 1944 additions to the band, trombonist Bill Harris and tenor saxophonist Flip Phillips, were outstanding improvisers and equally at home in either swing or bop settings. Harris's fresh approach to the trombone was so deeply personal that, in the words of pianist Lou Levy, it "circumvented style. ... It wasn't bebop. It wasn't Dixieland. It was his own."[24] Later additions to the First Herd, as this band came to be called, included vibraphonist Red Norvo, trumpeter Shorty Rogers, and pianist Jimmy Rowles.

This was a rare breed of modern jazz ensemble. It drew on the most progressive currents in jazz but did so without taking on the self-serious and aloof, at times pretentious, demeanor that prevented many bop groups from gaining favor with the general public. Here again Herman's savvy and people skills played an important role. Often cited as the name bandleader who was best liked by his musicians, Herman bred a high-spirited enthusiasm among his players, encouraged their (often outré) senses of humor, and added to their emotional commitment through a collective ownership arrangement rare in the music world. The bandleader's tolerant attitude was not without its costs—for one, drug and alcohol problems would bedevil the band for a time—but it also gave the Herman Herds a carefree attitude that audiences found engaging. The initial Herd, in particular, stood out not only as a pioneering band, but also as the most popular and financially profitable ensemble Herman would ever lead.

The First Herman Herd was also one of the most versatile bands of its day. Its exuberance shines through in uptempo recordings such as "Apple Honey" and "Northwest Passage." At other times, the band might take an unabashedly romantic turn with dreamy renditions of "Laura" or "Happiness Is a Thing Called Joe." The group's comic side came to the fore in novelty vocals such as "Caldonia," oddball instrumentals like "Goosey Gander," or surprising midsong twists such as Sonny Berman's bitonal interjections in "Your Father's Moustache." It is hard to believe that this same loose, unrestrained band was the one Stravinsky selected to debut his *Ebony Concerto*—which quickly disappointed any listeners who had expected the Russian composer to embrace Herman's laissez-faire swing. Instead the Herman band was the party that had to adapt the most, doing their best to excite skeptical jazz audiences with Stravinsky's distinctly unswinging piece (surprisingly so, given the rhythmic vitality of many of his other compositions). This was an infelicitous mixture, as even the composer soon learned, discovering that he needed to have the piece rescored so that the players could handle its unusual (for a jazz band) metrics. More idiomatic, and popular with Herman's fans, was Ralph Burns's extended work *Summer Sequence*, a richly melodic piece performed by the band at Carnegie Hall alongside Stravinsky's composition. Other memorable efforts by this edition of the Herman band include Burns's chart "Bijou" (once described by Herman as a "Stone Age bossa nova") with a moving solo by Harris, "Sidewalks of Cuba" with its noteworthy Sonny Berman solo, and Hefti's musical conversation (hear Phillips's give-and-take with the brass) titled "The Good Earth."

The First Herd came to a halt in December 1946. Both personnel and personal problems spurred Herman's decision to disband. Exhausted by a demanding schedule, troubled by his wife's substance addictions, and witnessing the departure of many key band members—only the previous month he had lost the core of his trumpet section when Berman, Candoli, and Rogers all left—Herman saw that the time had come for a hiatus from the road. But just nine months later, he decided to regroup with a new band featuring a largely different crop of soloists. Matching the excitement level of the earlier Herd, one of the most popular bands of the day, would have seemed an almost impossible task, and adding to the challenge was the inhospitable atmosphere for big bands in general during these postwar years. An end-of-an-era ethos permeated the music industry, and though almost a decade would pass before the electrified sounds of rock and roll would drown out the competition, it was clear to many that the old formulas no longer held sway. Herman confronted these obstacle head on, and did so in the grand style, bringing together one of the strongest big bands of the decade, and capturing an entirely new sound in the process.

The heart and soul of the Second Herd, or the "Four Brothers Band" as it is often called, was centered in its sax section. The basic concept of the "Four Brothers" sound was simple enough: its foundation was tight ensemble writing for three tenor saxophones and a baritone sax. But the key to this section work lay in the distinctive approach of the saxophonists in question. Adopting a light, airy tone reminiscent of Lester Young, and combining it with the melodic pyrotechnics of modern jazz, these horns mastered a novel formula, merging the excitement and intricacy of bop with a sweet-toned lyricism. Just a few years later, this mixture of modernism and melodicism would come to be known as cool jazz.

A number of premier saxophonists would play in this section during the Second Herd's existence from 1947 to 1949—including Zoot Sims, Al Cohn, Herbie Steward, Jimmy Giuffre, Serge Chaloff, and Gene Ammons—but the most celebrated soloist of the Four Brothers period would prove to be the youngest member of this group. Tenor saxophonist Stan Getz, barely out of his teens when he joined the Herman band, had already served stints with Jack Teagarden (with whom he recorded when only sixteen years old), Benny Goodman, and Stan Kenton. Born in Philadelphia on February 2, 1927, Getz spent most of his early years in the Bronx, where his father worked as a printer. A precocious talent, Getz dabbled at a variety of instruments—including harmonica, string bass, and bassoon—before settling on saxophone. He finished only one year of high school but already had earned a spot on the coveted All New York City High School Orchestra (as a bassoonist), and his school conductor predicted that a scholarship to Juilliard lay in his future. Instead, Getz ventured on the road at age fifteen with Teagarden, who eventually had to sign guardianship papers to keep his underage saxophonist. Other high-profile gigs followed, but Getz showed little inclination for staying in one place for very long. He left Kenton, after the bandleader made disparaging remarks about Getz's idol Lester Young, then stayed for a brief spell with the Jimmy Dorsey band before joining Goodman, who reportedly fired him—all this while Getz was still a teenager!

The Herman association, although it too ended after only a few months, would prove to be a turning point for Getz. Two other future Herman saxophonists played a central role in setting the stage for Getz's eventual stardom: Herbie Steward encouraged Getz to adopt the lighter, Lester Young–inflected tone and relaxed phrasing that would eventually become his trademark; Jimmy Giuffre would help popularize the "Four Brothers" sound, learned from arranger Gene Roland while he and Getz were working in Tommy DeCarlo's band in Los Angeles. When Herman hired Giuffre (first as an arranger, later as a saxophonist) and Getz, he also brought on board the new sound. Giuffre's "Four Brothers" chart served as a spectacular showpiece for the saxophone section's novel approach. Even more important for Getz was his hauntingly delicate solo on Ralph Burns's "Early Autumn," adapted from "Summer Sequence (Part Four)," the recently added epilogue to the composer's popular *Summer Sequence*. Getz had already left the band by the time this recording was released, but its popularity created a receptive audience for his ensuing work as a small-combo leader.

But Getz, despite his renown, was far from the only major saxophonist in Herman's Second Herd. Another Lester Young disciple, Al Cohn, joined the band shortly after the "Four Brothers" recording. Cohn had little opportunity to solo with the Herman orchestra during this period, but in time would establish himself as an inventive tenor saxophonist and a talented composer. Zoot Sims, who worked with Cohn both in the Herman band and in a later long-lived two-saxophone combo, also showed an allegiance to Young, enriched by Sims's unflagging sense of swing and impeccable taste. Jimmy Giuffre may have been a less distinguished soloist than these peers at the time of the Second Herd, but his later career demonstrated the most pronounced evolution of any member of the group. He worked for a time with the Lighthouse All Stars and Shorty Rogers's Giants in California, where he became a leading exponent of West Coast jazz, later released a series of eclectic, intensely creative recordings for the Atlantic and Verve labels, and, by the close of the 1950s, had embraced atonality—a progression that none of the other Brothers, a conservative fraternity when it came to musical values, could match. Gene Ammons's stint with the Herman band would be brief, but in time he too would come to establish himself as a major player, popularizing the "soul jazz" idiom with a style that drew heavily on blues and gospel roots. Serge Chaloff showed the deepest allegiance to bop among the Herman saxophonists and earned praise for his skill in adapting many of Charlie Parker's innovations to the baritone. Ill health aggravated by drug addiction would sideline Chaloff for much of the 1950s, and at his death in 1957 he was only thirty-three years old, but his work with Herman, as well his various recordings in smaller combos, reveal an expressive, technically accomplished instrumentalist. But this was more than just a band of up-and-coming saxophonists. The Second Herd also benefited from the eventual return of Bill Harris to the band, the maturing of Shorty Rogers, who blossomed into an excellent composer during this period, and the contributions of a number of new composer-arrangers, including Giuffre, Cohn, and Johnny Mandel.

Herman disbanded the Second Herd in late 1949. Although the ensemble had enjoyed great popularity with jazz fans—*Downbeat* readers chose it as their favorite big band that year, with Herman outpolling the second-place Ellington group by a three-to-one margin—it had been a financial disaster. After taking a small combo to Cuba, Herman formed a Third Herd in the spring of 1950. Many earlier Herman associates were hired, along with new faces such as pianist Dave McKenna and drummer Sonny Igoe. Despite the various challenges in his way—including a major reshuffling of the band's personnel at the end of 1955—Herman continued to work steadily throughout the decade. But the jazz world changed dramatically during these years, as did the tastes of the general public. In the context of a transformed music scene—one that included Ornette Coleman, Elvis Presley, Cecil Taylor, Jerry Lee Lewis, John Coltrane, Little Richard, and Muddy Waters—Woody Herman could no longer demand respect as a major force at the cutting edge. By the close of the 1950s, Herman was working frequently with a small combo. He would come to regroup, a Herman trademark, and though some of the Herds of later years made outstanding music—for example, the powerhouse 1962–65 unit, dubbed the "Renaissance Herd" by Herb Wong—they failed to match the renown Herman enjoyed during his glory decade from 1945 to 1955. Herman would stay on the road almost to the end of his life, playing Carnegie Hall and high school assembly halls with equal enthusiasm. With even greater persistence he was pursued by government tax authorities, who claimed violations dating back over twenty years (due to lapses for which Herman's manager, not the bandleader himself, was responsible). In later days, Herman's financial situation was always precarious, with medical expenses adding to the daunting debt owed to the Internal Revenue Service. A few days before his death in October 1987, the ailing Herman was served an eviction notice dismissing him from his Hollywood home. Only a groundswell of grassroots support and donations from friends, fans, and former sidemen—including a bill debated in

Congress to wipe out Herman's tax liabilities—prevented an ignominious end for this important contributor to American music.

For most of this period, Stan Kenton stood out as Herman's greatest rival in creating an unabashedly progressive jazz big band. These two figures are often mentioned in the same breath—and, true, the similarities between the bandleaders are striking. Both were Swing Era veterans from middle America who came of age at the dawn of the Great Depression, and converted to modern jazz at the close of the war years. But these overlapping biographical facts are merely superficial; the contrasts are overwhelming. The affable Herman, genial and permissive, let his bands discover their own musical identity. The strong-willed Kenton, in contrast, forged an orchestra in his own image: as massive as his six-and-a-half-foot-tall frame, as expansive as his personal aspirations, as varied as his moods. Herman had a knack for making modern jazz palatable for the mass market and would not hesitate to record trite novelty songs to capture the public's approval. "I think it's very important to reach that other audience, the larger audience," Herman once explained. "The guys in the band and I put in a good day's work over 300 days a year. We deserve a pay-off sometime."[25] Kenton, in contrast, disdained such compromises—although he was not entirely above them—driven instead by a need to create *important* music, jazz music on a larger scale than anyone had envisioned before. Eventually he established his own corporation and record company, Creative World, to escape the commercial pressures of the music industry. While Herman's modernism drew inspiration from bebop, Kenton avoided the term with a vengeance. Instead, he continually invented new names for modern jazz. He delighted in describing it as "progressive jazz" or in featuring his 1950 band—which included a full string section—under the rubric of *Innovations in Modern Music* or in dubbing the 1952 edition *New Concepts in Artistry in Rhythm*. Eventually he coined his own word: *Neophonic* music, deriving from Greek roots meaning "new sounds." Not that Kenton was against bebop—he simply preferred to pretend that it did not exist. His brand of modern jazz was all that mattered.

Stan Kenton was born in Wichita, Kansas, on December 15, 1911, but spent much of his childhood in California. He dabbled at string, brass, and reed instruments before focusing his energies on arranging and the piano. He apprenticed in a wide range of groups during his twenties, eventually passing up more lucrative opportunities to perform his own music with a Southern California rehearsal band. Through sheer persistence, Kenton managed to secure a few local gigs, and eventually parlayed them into an extended engagement during the summer of 1941 at the Rendezvous Ballroom on Balboa, an island retreat catering to a young clientele. Kenton's band was just as young, perhaps younger—only two sidemen were over the age of twenty-one—and the audience responded with unprecedented fervor to this little-known group of post-adolescents with horns conducted by the statuesque man with a frenzied demeanor, swinging arms, and unceasing motion. The Kenton band soon signed with the Decca label, began performing at the largest ballrooms in the country, and was written up in almost every issue of *Downbeat*.

Kenton had started his orchestra as a way of featuring his own compositions—sweeping themes such as "Artistry in Rhythm," more indebted to Tchaikovsky and Romberg than to any jazz forebears. But in time Kenton realized that his genius lay in creating an environment in which other musical minds could refine and expand the Kenton sound. He had a taste for combining the most disparate ingredients, as in his postwar band, in which the hypermodern compositions of Pete Rugolo were leavened with the bittersweet alto sax of Art Pepper and the conversational, girl-next-door vocal style of June Christy. For a time, Rugolo served as Kenton's alter ego, writing or collaborating on a series of ambitious pieces, some jazzy, others with an Afro-Cuban influence, many of them classically tinged. But before long, Kenton was again broadening his scope, drawing on other composers-in-residence. At the same time he was expanding his musical palette, experimenting with new instruments and different textures.

True, there was a trademark Kenton sound—brassy, extroverted, pseudo-symphonic, grandiloquent. But Kenton also delighted in undermining this very style by hiring writers and soloists with contrasting musical perspectives. Bill Holman's smoothly swinging charts, with echoes of Kansas City jazz, were much beloved by the band's soloists, and he returned the favor by supplying some of the most memorable feature numbers in the band's history: "Cherokee," a chart originally penned for Charlie Parker but taken over with authority by Lennie Niehaus; the more moody "Yesterdays," which evokes a Lester Young strain from tenorist Bill Perkins; "Stella by Starlight," which takes altoist Charles Mariano through ballad and double-time paces. There is little wasted motion in these arrangements, none of the excesses that weigh down many Kenton band charts. But Holman was capable of more daring reworkings of traditional material, as his deconstructions of "What's New," "Stompin' at the Savoy," and "I've Got You under My Skin" make eminently clear. Bill Russo's writing for the band, in contrast, was more firmly rooted in the Kenton/Rugolo tradition. His "Halls of Brass" pushed Kenton's horn obsession to an extreme in a virtuosic exercise that reportedly garnered begrudging admiration from symphony brass sections. But Russo also harbored a more introspective side, betrayed on his finely shaded version of "There's a Small Hotel" or the plaintive romanticism of "Solitaire." Other writers also contributed richly stylized charts, further defying the notion that there was a single Kenton sound: Johnny Richard's *Cuban Fire* arrangements demand respect as among the most powerful and successful explorations of Latin music in a jazz context; Gerry Mulligan's writing for Kenton bespoke a relaxed swing and intimacy in tune with the baritone saxophonist's cool aesthetic. Bob Graettinger's contributions to the band's repertoire were at the other extreme: these dense, dissonant explorations—most notably his magnum opus *City of Glass*—are exquisitely disturbing. No jazz composer of his day anticipated the later advent of free jazz with more gritty determination. Kenton's advocacy of Graettinger's distinctly unpopular music makes it clear how committed this bandleader was to pluralism and staying at the vanguard of big band jazz.

But this was much more than a writer's band. Especially during its glory days of the 1940s and 1950s, the Kenton orchestra was rich in star soloists. Art Pepper graced the band during the earliest days of his career, brandishing a before-the-fall innocence that is most notable on Shorty Rogers's eponymous feature piece for him. He went on to enjoy a substantial career as a leader in his own right, as did trumpeter Maynard Ferguson, who soon drew raves as the most celebrated high-note brass player of his generation. Frank Rosolino was equally admired as a virtuoso on the trombone and demonstrated his facility on such recordings as "I Got It Bad (and That Ain't Good)" and "Frank Speaking." Crediting Rosolino for broadening the technique of the trombone in the 1950s, Bill Russo has recalled: "We were all staggered by what he could do, not only at the speed of his technique and that he played so well in the upper register, but that he had such incredible flexibility."[26] Lee Konitz figured prominently in the Kenton lineup for a brief period in the 1950s and was featured soloist on a number of performances, including an ethereal rendition of "Lover Man" that ranks as one of the altoist's finest recorded moments. Zoot Sims also served a short stint with Kenton and left behind a characteristically hard-swinging performance on Holman's chart "Zoot."

Stan Kenton was not the only 1950s big band leader who attempted to remake modern jazz in his own iconoclastic image. Sun Ra drew on an equally eclectic mixture of forward-looking jazz styles in the various recordings made with his large ensemble, the Arkestra—a band invariably described by the leader with one or more impressive descriptives attached (e.g., the Myth Science Arkestra or the Astro Infinity Arkestra). A certain extravagance permeated almost everything having to do with this artist. Many jazz players are guilty of distorting or exaggerating the facts of their early years, but only Sun Ra went so far as to trace his origins back to the planet Saturn and claim descent from a race of angels. In truth, Sun Ra was apparently born with the more pedestrian name of Herman Blount in Alabama in 1914. He came of age as a pianist and composer during the Swing Era and worked for a time in the late 1940s in the Fletcher Henderson band. His visionary music, however, did not come into its own until the mid-1950s, when he began recording extensively with his large band, first in Chicago and later in New York, Philadelphia, and other environs.

Sun Ra's coterie of fans came to expect the unexpected, and were seldom disappointed. The Arkestra's lineup might include, on a given night, as few as ten musicians or as many as thirty. Dancers, costumes, slide shows, and other "extras" might be included with the price of admission. The Arkestra's music could be equally changeable. Elements of bebop, hard bop, and swing loom large on the band's mid-1950s recordings. But over the next decade, the Arkestra would embrace an even broader palette: swirling layers of percussion, spooky electronic effects, disjointed echoes of rhythm and blues, hints of Asian and African music, dissonance, atonality, at times aural anarchy. Sun Ra's jargon-laden talk of the cosmos and interplanetary music may have sounded like a half-baked script from a Cold War sci-fi movie, but his appetite for the new and anomalous truly spanned a universe, or at least several galaxies, of sounds.

Much confusion has surrounded the dating of Sun Ra's various recordings. When the Impulse label purchased a number of tapes from him in the 1970s, they released old and new works side by side with little attention to chronology. And Sun Ra himself was equally lax: he would often sell his self-financed records (sometimes produced in quantities of less than one hundred copies) at concert intermissions, during which confused fans could browse through boxes of unmarked, unlabeled LPs. But the incompleteness of our discographical information cannot hide the fact that Sun Ra had a knack for being years ahead of the jazz world. The free jazz explorations of *Cosmic Tones for Mental Therapy*, the world music and electronics of *Supersonic Jazz* were pioneering efforts for their time. Sun Ra's anticipation of later trends seems especially prescient when one compares his deconstructive sound collages from the 1950s and 1960s with the Art Ensemble of Chicago and other Association for the Advancement of Creative Musicians (AACM) efforts from the 1960s and 1970s. But by the 1970s, Sun Ra was already looking ahead again, anticipating the return to jazz roots of the 1980s and 1990s with sweeping excursions that spanned the whole history of the music.

Like Ellington, Sun Ra rarely featured his own piano work—although his few solo recordings, especially the magnificent *Monorails and Satellites* session from 1966, showed that he needed no sidemen to weave his richly textured musical tapestries. And though the Arkestra lacked the depth and cohesion of musicianship that characterized a Basie or Ellington, a Herman or Kenton, the band always boasted an inner circle of topflight players. Especially in tenor saxophonist John Gilmore, Sun Ra could draw on a rugged world-class soloist—one who anticipated and, in time, would influence John Coltrane. Gilmore's versatility was well suited for the Arkestra: he could contribute heated hard-bop solos or use the tenor to articulate piercing screams, guttural barks, and mournful cries. His affiliation with Sun Ra spanned some forty years, and he maintained his allegiance to the band even after Sun Ra's death in 1993.

Count Basie's post-1951 work—the New Testament bands, as many have called them—stands as almost the antithesis of Sun Ra and Stan Kenton's experimentalism and pluralistic tendencies. Although Basie stocked his bands of this period with outstanding young talent versed in the bebop idiom, the ethos of this latter-day unit shared many similarities with his various Kansas City and Swing Era ensembles. Basie, old or new, would swing his band to perfection—achieving the comfortable sense of forward motion that jazz musicians describe as "in the pocket." Basie's unsurpassed instinct for the right tempo was never more inspired than on his hit recording of "Li'l Darlin'." Rather than playing this piece at the medium tempo that composer Neal Hefti envisioned, Basie slowed it down to a pace only slightly faster than a ballad but somehow maintaining the finger-snapping momentum of a groove tune. The result was magical.

Basie drew on an outstanding crop of writers, including Hefti, Ernie Wilkins, Frank Foster, Quincy Jones, Thad Jones, and Benny Carter. A wry sense of humor often pervaded these arrangements—as in the Count's postwar warhorse "April in Paris," arranged by Wild Bill Davis, with its fool-the-audience fake ending. The band's charts were more richly textured than in the prewar years but were never so busy as to distract listeners from the talents of Basie's star soloists. These were inevitably quite formidable: even during his bleakest days of the early 1950s, when Basie needed to downsize to a combo, he could still call on the services of Clark Terry, Wardell Gray, Buddy DeFranco, and Serge Chaloff. After resuming his big band, Basie carefully stocked his group with strong musical personalities. Eddie "Lockjaw" Davis was a gripping soloist, a modernist with deep roots in the jazz tradition, whose talents were often underappreciated during the age of Rollins and Coltrane. Brass player Thad Jones—brother of celebrated pianist Hank and drummer Elvin Jones—would later lead an important big band of his own, but in the 1950s and 1960s he provided crisp solos and top-notch charts to the Basie orchestra. Altoist and clarinetist Marshall Royal was also a member of a renowned jazz family—his brother, trumpeter Ernie Royal, had worked with Basie in 1946 and went on to play with Woody Herman, Duke Ellington, Stan Kenton, and Gil Evans. Marshall's playing was enriched by a full and bittersweet alto tone and an understated sense of swing that contrasted with his hard-nosed character; a strict disciplinarian, Royal was given authority by Basie to instill musical order into the band, a role that he filled with zeal. Vocalist Joe Williams worked with Basie from 1954 to 1961, as well as for sporadic periods in later years, and earned particular notice for his 1955 performance of "Every Day I Have the Blues." Blessed with a resonant, full-bodied voice, Williams forged a style built on a fusion of opposites, a heavy dose of blues and gospel roots varnished with an unflappable layer of supper-club elegance. Other stalwart members of postwar Basie bands included Frank Foster, Frank Wess, and the indefatigable Freddie Green, a pioneer of the Old Testament band whose affiliation with Basie would come to span a half-century.

A handful of other leaders pursued a similar vision of the big band in the modern age. Harry James's unfairly neglected work from his later years found him fronting a hard-swinging band in a Basie mold, which he kept viable through Las Vegas appearances and dance engagements, supplemented by occasional forays back East and overseas. Other big bands, such as those led by Les Brown or Doc Severinsen, found stability and a steady paycheck playing for television shows, where they gave viewers an occasional glimpse of the talent hidden in their ranks. But such longevity was rare in an age in which most jazz orchestras lasted weeks or months—or sometimes for a single record date—rather than years. Most of the major figures in modern jazz (Miles, Monk, Gillespie, Parker, Mingus) tried their hand at fronting larger ensembles at some point, but these were sporadic episodes in careers that flourished primarily in small-combo settings. Many prominent arrangers also turned to leading big bands in an effort to have their music heard, with results that were sometimes creative, but rarely financially sound. From 1952 to 1957, Eddie Sauter, who had made his name writing for Norvo, Goodman, and Shaw, teamed up with another big band alumnus, Bill Finegan, who had similarly worked with Dorsey and Miller. Their Sauter-Finegan band garnered recognition for its innovative use of unusual instruments and an expanded rhythm section.

In later years, other big band leaders (Don Ellis, Maynard Ferguson, Buddy Rich) prospered, for greater or longer periods, by tapping into new musical trends: rock, fusion, electronics, odd time signatures, and various popular or novelty forms of music aimed at younger audiences. Other bands survived by staying close to home, where regular or semiregular gigs helped pay the bills. These city bands (as opposed to the territory bands of earlier years) included Herb Pomeroy's Boston-based unit, The Orchestra in Washington, DC, and Rob McConnell's Boss Brass in Toronto. Los Angeles boasted an especially impressive array of hometown big bands that rarely ventured outside Southern California, including ensembles led by Gerald Wilson, Terry Gibbs, Roy Porter, Bob Florence, Marty Paich, Bill Holman, Bill Berry, Clare Fischer, and one co-led by Frank Capp and Nat Pierce. New York also saw a panoply of short-lived big bands, some playing original music, but many also serving as repertory groups focused on recreating jazz sounds from earlier decades.

From the mid-1960s to the late 1970s, the Thad Jones–Mel Lewis band stood out as the most celebrated and polished of the New York big bands. Started in late 1965 as a rehearsal group, the band secured a Monday night gig at the Village Vanguard the following February. The sidemen were paid a meager 17 dollars for their services (increased to 18 dollars after they proved their drawing power)—roughly the same, in absolute dollars, as the major big band leaders had paid their sidemen during the Great Depression. Despite the low wages, Jones and Lewis attracted many of the finest New York players and writers to their band. The reed section featured Joe Farrell and Eddie Daniels and, in later days, Billy Harper and Gregory Herbert, playing alongside seasoned veterans such as Pepper Adams, Jerry Dodgion, and Jerome Richardson. The brass sections could rely on leader Jones, as well as (at various points in the band's history) trombonists Bob Brookmeyer and Jimmy Knepper, and trumpeters Snooky Young, Jon Faddis, Marvin Stamm, and Bill Berry. Drummer Lewis anchored a solid rhythm section that combined the elegant piano stylings of Thad's brother Hank Jones (and, in later days, Roland Hanna, Walter Norris, Harold Danko, and Jim McNeely) with the bass lines of Richard Davis (and, in the early 1970s, George Mraz).

The impeccable musicianship of the band was supported by an outstanding library of arrangements. Leader Jones brought with him a number of charts he had written for Count Basie. His writing spanned a wide range of moods, from the tenderest lullaby waltz "A Child Is Born" to the hardest-edged New York workout "Central Park North." Bob Brookmeyer also contributed a number of major works, including a series of stunning reworkings of some of the oldest jazz standards such as "St. Louis Blues" (composed in 1914), "Willow Tree" (from 1928), and "Willow Weep for Me" (written in 1932). Jones left the band in early 1979 to take on a position as leader of the Danish Radio Orchestra in Copenhagen. For the next decade, Mel Lewis continued to lead a big band on Monday nights at the Vanguard, playing his last gig with the group only a few weeks before his death in February 1990. But the ensemble overcame this blow as well, surviving in the form of the Vanguard Jazz Orchestra, a cooperative effort that maintained the once-a-week tradition at Manhattan's most venerated jazz nightspot.

The only major challenge to the Thad Jones–Mel Lewis Orchestra's preeminence as the leading mainstream large ensemble during the 1970s came from another city band with two leaders: the Toshiko Akiyoshi–Lew Tabackin Big Band, which flourished on the West Coast from 1973 to 1982. Akiyoshi was an unusual presence in the jazz world: an Asian woman, born in China and reared in Japan, who made her reputation in a field previously dominated by American males. A skilled pianist in a Bud Powell vein, Akiyoshi wrote almost the entire book for the band, often drawing on her Japanese heritage in the same manner that Scott Joplin and Duke Ellington extracted art music from their African American roots. Her work was especially skilled in its subtle and versatile use of the reed section. Members doubled on several horns— collectively they were reportedly capable of playing seventeen instruments. On "The First Night," for example, Akiyoshi created harmonies voiced for five flutes, while on "American Ballad" she combined two flutes with two clarinets and bass clarinet. The most formidable member of the section was Akiyoshi's husband and coleader Lew

Tabackin, whose contributions emphasized his classically tinged flute playing and his Rollins-inspired tenor efforts. The band also benefited from the underrated talents of Bobby Shew, a fluid soloist on trumpet and flugelhorn, who combined impeccable technique with a glorious, slightly out-of-focus tone. After moving to New York in 1982, Akiyoshi started another band with new players, although Tabackin continued to be featured as star soloist. Akiyoshi finally disbanded the larger unit in 2003, but the body of work she put together during this thirty-year run stands out both for its artistry and its defiance of the economic constraints that made such longevity the exception rather than the rule for big bands in the modern era.

Akiyoshi's example was not an isolated one. Maria Schneider provides an interesting case study in both the financial and creative ferment of the early twenty-first-century jazz scene. Schneider has persisted in the face of constant challenges, honing her craft and building her audience on a half-dozen leader dates of the highest caliber. Yet, despite Grammy awards and recurring appearances at the top of polls ranking contemporary composers and arrangers, she has never enjoyed a contract with a major label, and in recent years has relied on subsidies from fans, in an innovative cost-sharing arrangement pioneered by the ArtistShare label. What a turnaround from the Swing Era, when the big band was home to the best-paid musicians in America and offered the most secure employment!

Schneider, who was born in Windom, Minnesota in 1960, benefited early in her career from the mentoring of Gil Evans and Bob Brookmeyer, and her own mature work reflects the varied tonal colors and relaxed fluency with the jazz vocabulary of these past masters. She marries her deftly painted soundscapes with sweeping melodies and a heart-on-sleeve emotional immediacy that would have made her a star of Tin Pan Alley in an earlier day. But she also makes bold moves in plotting the structure and texture of her compositions, revealing fresh possibilities in the venerable big band tradition. Perhaps the best comparison point here is not previous jazz orchestra leaders, but classical composers such as Aaron Copland and George Gershwin who managed to be both progressive and popular in their day, pushing ahead with visionary works that didn't require a conservatory degree to appreciate their appeal. On performances such as "Evanescence" (from the 1992 album of the same name), "Three Romances" (from *Concert in the Garden*), and "Cerulean Skies" and "The Pretty Road" (from the 2007 ArtistShare release *Sky Blue*), Schneider has established herself as a modern-day heir of Ellington and Evans, able to put her personal stamp on charts where she somehow balances the intricacies of her often through-composed music with an affable tunefulness that few of her contemporaries can match. Indeed, these pieces would stand out if played on an upright piano in your grandma's parlor, although her rich orchestral palette makes them especially suited for the big band idiom. It is one of the tragedies of jazz in the new millennium that an artist such as Schneider has been forced to scuffle to keep her big band music alive, yet it is also testimony to her persistence and the flexibility allowed by new business models in jazz that she has risen to the top of her field despite an economic and cultural enviroment inhospitable to big band jazz.

Schneider's influence can be detected in the work of other promising bandleaders of the new millennium, such as Darcy James Argue (who adds more rock flavor to his charts) and Joseph C. Phillips Jr. (who incorporates large doses of minimalism). Yet for most jazz musicians and fans in the twenty-first century, the big band is more a tool of historical pedagogy than a means of artistic expression. This is not an entirely new situation—ever since Goodman's Carnegie Hall concert, the idea of using larger groups to tell the history of jazz has found favor. But today this historical approach has become a predominant force in shaping the way musicians and the listening public view big band music. Illustrious institutions—the Smithsonian, Carnegie Hall, and especially Jazz at Lincoln Center—play an ever-expanding role in defining the role of larger ensembles in jazz music. But the single biggest source of big band music in contemporary America is the college campus, where student big bands, some even capable of matching professional ensembles in their standards of musicianship, are an entry point into the art form for a large number of teenagers and young adults. This is one area of growth in a shrinking idiom, but its impact may be felt more as a support in preserving the traditions of the music rather than charting its future course. Perhaps the jazz big band will travel the same path as the symphony orchestra, with bandleaders treating the presentation of older works as their primary function.

But can this situation really be surprising given the changed circumstances in the jazz world? In recent years—for the first time in the history of the music—most of the major pioneers in the development of jazz are mere names in history books and on CD covers; and even those who have firsthand experience of having heard these masters in the flesh are now a dwindling group. In the absence of those who developed and refined the conventions of big band music, the sustainability of the rich tradition created by these innovators depends very much on institutions to promulgate and preserve their legacy. To lament this shift is as pointless as bemoaning the fact that so many jazz big bands today are resident in high schools and colleges. These are signs of jazz's success in entering the mainstream culture, not symptoms of failure. The pedagogy of jazz is not the problem—unless it dominates our attention so much that creative work of the present day is stifled. By the same token, discarding or ignoring the music's history is no solution. The jazz tradition in general, and big band jazz in particular—if they are to survive in any meaningful way as a cultural force—will require a healthy dose of this very same supercharged historical consciousness.

The only danger—and a very real one—is that our respect for the past comes to blind us to the needs of the present. Coming to grips with that second task, one of defining and addressing current needs, for which jazz and the other arts can act as a kind of salve, is beyond the scope of the present historical endeavor. By definition, it comes at the point where any historical project ends. But readers should be advised: this question of present needs and the future history of jazz is never far away from our discussion and will continue to lurk quietly behind the scenes during the concluding sections of this work. For in the jazz world—itself a microcosm of broader artistic trends—the social and aesthetic role of the music has become increasingly uncertain in the modern era, as conflicting visions of the purpose of art clash and styles grow more fragmented. In this charged atmosphere, all agendas become suspect, and even the concept of a history of the music, with the sort of stately chronological unfolding that we associate with such narratives, is not beyond debate.

7 The Fragmentation of Jazz Styles

TRAD JAZZ AND COOL JAZZ

The ascendancy of bebop inevitably invited challenges. A music so radical in its intentions, so open in its defiance of conventions, almost demanded dramatic responses. Perhaps the greatest surprise, though, was that the ripostes came from so many different directions at once. One expected the Swing Era veterans to launch heated counterattacks on the boppers—and this they did, with a vengeance. Less expected was the extraordinary rebirth of traditional jazz in the late 1940s, championed by those who hoped to douse the fires of bop with Lu Watters. Still others sought a tempering effect in "the cool," brandished as nothing less than a new aesthetic for modern jazz. And as the 1950s progressed, a host of other alternative styles emerged on the scene, each with a contingent of devotees: hard bop, West Coast jazz, soul jazz, modal jazz, Third Stream jazz, free jazz.

In the jazz press, interviews and reviews were now interspersed with polemics and philosophical musings on the "validity" of these various forms of improvised music. The most popular rebuttal, a time-honored approach since the advent of bop, was to deny that the opposition's music was "real jazz." During these Cold War years, fans split into factions, and factions subdivided faster than suburban real estate. Of course jazz had always been a source of controversy, since at least the time of Buddy Bolden. Only now the disputes were mostly fratricidal, with few besides jazz fans paying attention. The general public had gone on to other concerns—bobby-soxers and bomb shelters, television and 3-D movies, pop singers backed by string orchestras, and the nascent sounds of rock and roll. In this context, jazz had become a subculture, surviving on the fringes of the entertainment industry.

Meanwhile jazz writers debated the future of jazz. Would it be hot or cool? Would it hail from East or West? Would it maintain allegiance to tonality or demand freedom from the tyranny of the chord? But for the most reactionary fans, this very obsession with the future was castigated, renounced in favor of a return to the past. Under a variety of banners—some calling it traditional or trad jazz, others referring to it as New Orleans or Chicago jazz, still others preferring the term Dixieland—the sounds of older jazz styles grew ever more popular. As early as the late 1930s, the first signs of a traditional jazz revival could be seen, but this movement would not gain momentum for another decade. By then the growing antipathy to bop in certain quarters—certainly among the general public, but also among many jazz fans and musicians—made this return to the roots more than a casual indulgence of nostalgia. It coalesced into a movement, and—irony of ironies—borrowed some of the revolutionary ideology of the boppers. Thus, the trad fans were not just interested in hearing their music, but also wanted to hold it up as a model, assert its primacy, and use it to oppose the "enemy" in the other camps, much like the boppers had done a few years before. The jazz press fueled this antagonism with the tone of its coverage, pitting one faction against the other with the zest of boxing promoters. Booking agents followed suit, staging musical "battles" between boppers and traditional jazz players. A few tried to stay above the fray—Charlie Parker, in his various interviews, had only praise for the exponents of earlier styles—but most fans and players, critics and impresarios, felt compelled to choose sides.

The chronology of this "return to the roots" begins with the resurgent careers of Jelly Roll Morton and Sidney Bechet at the close of the 1930s. Around this same time, jazz historians latched onto the forgotten trumpeter Bunk Johnson, who parlayed his New Orleans connection into a brief period of fame during the 1940s. Johnson's various claims and pronouncements on jazz history later turned out to be largely "bunk," and his trumpet playing made few listeners forget Armstrong and Beiderbecke. But his transformation into a mini-celebrity indicated that the traditional jazz revival was a powerful force, one that could build a substantial following for an aging field worker who had never been more than a second-tier player during his prime. Johnson's lead was followed by many others. George Lewis, who had been making a living as a dockworker, displayed the simple elegance of his clarinet playing on a 1942 session with Johnson, an association that led to a spate of other opportunities to record and perform as a leader. Kid Ory, who had been working on a poultry farm and in a railroad office, returned to active playing in 1942 and delighted audiences for the next quarter of a century—then retired in Hawaii, far from brass bands and second lines, on the proceeds of this unanticipated career turnaround. Like tribal elders in a gerontocracy, these survivors of jazz's earliest days now found themselves venerated and apotheosized in a manner they had never enjoyed in the past. Suddenly they were "historical figures"—formerly they had simply been musicians, often part-time or unemployed.

Almost from the start, the veteran trad jazz players were joined by New Orleans revivalists who brought with them few connections to the Crescent City, merely a zest for the older sounds. On the West Coast, California native Lu Watters founded a traditional jazz group in 1940, the Yerba Buena Jazz Band, that would enjoy a wide following. Turk Murphy, a Watters sideman who formed his own traditional jazz band in 1947, achieved even greater popularity. His group graced the stage of Carnegie Hall, toured extensively overseas, and weathered every changing jazz fad and fancy for almost forty years. In late 1937, Bobby Hackett began leading a band at Nick's, a Greenwich Village nightclub where modern jazz was anathema, and though the trumpeter was a decade younger than most of the New Orleans–Chicago "old timers," he soon distinguished himself through his sure instinct for melodic improvisation and exalted tone. Eddie Condon, who worked with Hackett's band, pursued a similarly successful career as a revivalist—although with more substantial ties to the music's history than many late-to-the-party traditionalists could boast—building a following at Nick's, where he continued to work until 1944, and later at his own nightclub. A number of other seasoned players—Pee Wee Russell, Bud Freeman, Edmond Hall, Miff Mole, Jimmy McPartland, and Max Kaminsky, to name a few—flourished amid the reviving prospects for traditional jazz styles. Much of the revival music, it is true, tended toward banality—it represented the way jazz might have sounded "if it had existed in mid-Victorian times," quipped one critic. But, at its best, this movement was capable of creating fresh, vibrant performances, such as Wild Bill Davison's November 1943 sessions with Russell and George Brunis for the Commodore label; or Muggsy Spanier's illustrious 1939 sides, which inspired comparisons with King Oliver's Creole Jazz Band. Even Bunk Johnson's once-controversial recordings hold up well today, when one simply enjoys them for their verve and free-spirited interplay, and not as evidence submitted in support of a polemic. For those with ears to hear them, such efforts dispelled any notions that jazz needed to progress in order to sound good.

The trad jazz revival quickly spread overseas, in some instances exerting even more influence on local tastes and talents than in the United States. The English scene was especially vibrant, under the impetus of players such as Humphrey Lyttelton, Chris Barber, and Ken Colyer, among others. French clarinetist Claude Luter, who fell under the sway of Bechet after the latter's move to Europe, kept the flame of New Orleans jazz alive on the Continent, as did a host of trad players in Stockholm, Rome, and other locales. By one estimate, around half of the jazz clubs in Europe would eventually come to specialize in traditional jazz styles. But other players on other continents—from Melbourne to Shanghai—would also join in the movement. More than any later jazz styles, the two-step syncopations of New Orleans and Chicago testified to the universal appeal of jazz music.

But the most persuasive sign that early jazz was once again a major force came in 1947. In that year of bop triumphant, Louis Armstrong abandoned the big band format he had pursued for almost two decades and made a much-celebrated return to the traditional New Orleans style. Armstrong no doubt loved this music but, as a savvy artist in tune with changing audience tastes, he would hardly have taken such a step unless he had seen the commercial potential of the revival movement. The following year Earl Hines followed Armstrong's lead. He disbanded his swing orchestra to take a job as pianist in Armstrong's combo. Jack Teagarden, another traditionalist who had made the move to big bands, also retraced his steps. Teagarden joined Armstrong in 1947, and in 1951 formed his own Dixieland combo. Some jazz modernists denigrated these erstwhile pioneers of jazz past and their fans—often alluding to the enthusiasts for bygone styles with the pejorative term "moldy fig." But for Armstrong and Teagarden, Hines and Bechet, this was clearly a misnomer. Their return to the tradition in their middle years signaled a revitalization in their music. Their rollicking sounds had gathered no moss, and one could—should?— view these career moves as a proclamation of core values, and a return to first principles in an age caught up in a sometimes too complacent frenzy of progress, in music as in all other spheres of postwar life.

The most pressing challenge to bop, however, came not from these champions of the past. The "cool" movement, as it soon came to be known, presented an especially promising alternative to the bop paradigm. Spearheaded by members of the younger generation, most of them in their early twenties at the close of the 1940s, cool jazz was—like bop—an overtly modernist music with radical implications. Its exponents shared many of the aesthetic values of the boppers—an allegiance to contemporary trends in music, a predilection for experimentation, a distaste for conformity, and a view of jazz as an underground movement—and many had served as sidemen in prominent bop groups. Miles Davis, who would emerge as the leader of the new cool players, had worked with Parker—even more, had looked up to the altoist as a guide and mentor. The Modern Jazz Quartet, which would earn praise as a quintessential cool combo, got its start as the rhythm section of Dizzy Gillespie's big band. But even those with weaker links to bop—Gerry Mulligan, Stan Getz, Paul Desmond, Art Pepper—could not avoid its pervasive influence. They realized that bop was the defining style of their generation, and that even an attempt to sidestep the idiom would invariably be interpreted as rebellion against it.

Davis had left Parker's band at the close of 1948, disturbed by Bird's increasingly erratic and self-destructive behavior. His new source of inspiration, arranger Gil Evans, was in many ways the antithesis of Parker. A dowdy, introspective country boy from Canada, Evans came to Fifty-second Street clubs wearing a cap and carrying a paper sack full of radishes, munching on them during the performance. "Man, he was something else," Davis would write in his autobiography. "I didn't know *any* white people like him."[1] Evans enjoyed little name recognition at the time, even within jazz circles. His biggest claim to fame, to the extent he enjoyed any, was due to his forward-looking arranging for the Claude Thornhill orchestra.

The Thornhill band was a jumble of contradictions: it was sweet and hot by turns; progressive and nostalgic—both to an extreme; overtly commercial, yet also aspiring to transform jazz into art music. Like Paul Whiteman, Thornhill may have only obscured his place in history by straddling so many different styles. Chroniclers of the music, not knowing what to do with this range of sounds, prefer to relegate Thornhill to a footnote and dismiss him as a popularizer or some sort of Claude Debussy of jazz. True, this band was best known for its shimmering, impressionistic sound, exemplified in Thornhill's theme "Snowfall." But this was only one facet of the Thornhill band. Evans, in particular, brought a harder, bop-oriented edge to the group, contributing solid arrangements of modern jazz pieces such as "Anthropology," "Donna Lee," and "Yardbird Suite." In due course, these songs would become jazz standards, practice-room fodder for legions of musicians, but at the time Evans was one of the few arrangers interested in translating them into a big band format.

Yet Evans was equally skillful in developing the more contemplative side of the Thornhill band. His later work with Davis would draw on many devices—static harmonies, unusual instruments (for jazz) such as French horn and tuba, rich voicings—refined during his time with Thornhill. Gerry Mulligan would also contribute arrangements to the Thornhill band, and later credited the leader with "having taught me the greatest lesson in dynamics, the art of underblowing." He described the Thornhill sound as one of "controlled violence"—perhaps an apt characterization of the cool movement as a whole.[2] Another leading light of the later cool school, Lee Konitz, also participated in the 1947 Thornhill band. Although Miles Davis's work the following year would be dubbed the *Birth of the Cool* (an inspired—and influential—title only added several years after the fact by a savvy marketing mind at Capitol Records), the Thornhill band was its acknowledged model in many respects. By implication, the Thornhill 1946–47 band should be seen as the "incubation" of the cool. In Davis's words: "The *Birth of the Cool* album came from some of the sessions we did trying to sound like Claude Thornhill's band. We wanted that sound, but the difference was that we wanted it as small as possible."[3]

Gil Evans's cramped Fifty-fifth Street basement apartment became an unlikely salon during this period, a gathering place for the emerging "cool school" players as well as unreformed boppers. Miles Davis, Gerry Mulligan, Lee Konitz, John Lewis, and Max Roach were frequently in attendance. Charlie Parker was also a sporadic visitor, but his planned project with Evans never took place—although the two would briefly work together several years later on a subpar recording featuring the altoist in tandem with the Dave Lambert Singers. At the time, Davis took the lead in forming a working band from this coterie of like-minded musicians. Davis, above all, was the visionary and organizer who turned these fledgling concepts into performances and recordings. He scheduled rehearsals, hired halls, and initiated contact with Capitol Records. However, a substantial portion of the band's arrangements were written by Mulligan—whose important role in the proceedings has often been wrongly downplayed in historical accounts, which invariably focus on Davis and Evans—with the efforts of this triumvirate supplemented by occasional charts submitted by other participants.

There was no tenor sax in the *Birth of the Cool* band—almost a heresy in a jazz orchestra—instead the French horn frequently blended with the other saxes and Davis's trumpet. The tuba, a throwback to New Orleans days, was used to support the bottom of the harmonies. This freed Mulligan's baritone to move up in register—sometimes he would double lines with Davis or Konitz. But the conception of the ensemble was as radical as the instrumentation. For a quarter of a century, jazz big bands had been built on the opposition of sections. Reeds, brass, rhythm: these served as separate, quasi-equal forces employed in musical jousting. The interplay between these sections, refined under the guidance of Redman, Carter, Ellington, and others, had come almost to define the sound of larger jazz ensembles. The model for these pioneers of big band jazz was, in some ways, the symphony orchestra, with its similar give-and-take between instrumental groupings. Davis, in contrast, conceived of his band as a single section. The model was not a classical orchestra, but ensemble singing. "I wanted the instruments to sound like human voices, and they did. . . . It had to be the voicing of a quartet, with soprano, alto, baritone and bass voices. . . . I looked at the group like it was a choir."[4] Something of the purified aesthetic of choral music also seeped into the music. Evans's arrangement of "Moon Dreams" captures a sweet languor unknown to the muses of swing or bop; Davis's medium tempo "Boplicity" sounds as if the band is hesitant to swing too hard, preferring instead to linger awhile in the beauty of each passing chord; even the more insistent charts such as Mulligan's "Jeru," Davis's "Deception," or John Carisi's "Israel" come across as similarly chastened.

Was this jazz? Winthrop Sargeant, classical music critic for *The New Yorker*, expressed his doubts. Instead, he staked a claim for the Davis Nonet as an outgrowth of the Western classical tradition. It sounded, to his ears, like the work of an

impressionist composer with a great sense of aural poetry and a very fastidious feeling for tone color. The compositions have beginnings, middles and endings. The music sounds more like that of a new Maurice Ravel than it does like jazz. I, who do not listen to jazz recordings day in and day out, find this music charming and exciting. . . . If Miles Davis were an established "classical" composer, his work would rank high among that of his contemporary colleagues. But it is not really jazz.[5]

Jazz fans apparently agreed with Sargeant's characterization—they virtually ignored the band. In time, the Davis Nonet would be lauded as one of the most innovative groups in the history of jazz, but during its brief tenure, the ensemble drew little attention or praise. Its employment was limited to a few performances at the Royal Roost, and even there the group was billed below the Count Basie band, with whom it shared the stage. After making a few recordings for Capitol Records, the Nonet disbanded.

The cool school may well have benefited from this early failure. The members of the Nonet would have more success as individuals in promoting the cool aesthetic than as part of a single unit. Davis would continue to refine his sound, in a variety of settings, and by the mid-1950s had developed a deeply personal conception of jazz, one that would exert enormous influence on later jazz musicians. Pianist John Lewis would build a major concert hall career as musical director of the Modern Jazz Quartet, a cool band remarkable for its longevity and popularity, as well as its consistently high musical standards. Lee Konitz's later work would secure his reputation as one of the most accomplished altoists of his day and a leading exponent of the cool. Gerry Mulligan would take the lead in developing an audience for cool jazz on the West Coast. Gunther Schuller, who had played French horn with the Nonet, would become a key figure in promoting the "Third Stream"—an ambitious and controversial offshoot of cool jazz that aimed to break down barriers between classical and jazz idioms. Even hardened bopper Max Roach, the drummer on most of the Davis tracks, would bring a measured dose of the cool sensibility to his pathbreaking mid-1950s band with Clifford Brown. All in all, the Davis Nonet was much like a band of disciples, gathered together for a brief time before scattering in their several separate directions, each inspired to proselytize others in turn.

The roots of Lewis's Modern Jazz Quartet actually predated the Davis Nonet. As early as 1946, a predecessor group including Lewis, vibraphonist Milt Jackson, drummer Kenny Clarke, and bassist Ray Brown performed together as the rhythm section in Dizzy Gillespie's big band. This same unit later recorded as the Milt Jackson Quartet in the early 1950s. By 1952, when the band had regrouped as the Modern Jazz Quartet, Percy Heath had taken over for Brown on bass. (After the replacement of Kenny Clarke with Connie Kay in 1955, the quartet would maintain the same personnel for almost four decades—an unprecedented achievement in the jazz world, where a band's longevity is typically measured in weeks or months.) This career-long partnership impacted the music: few ensembles, of any era or style, could play together so fluidly, so effortlessly, so well as the MJQ.

Moreover, no group went further in establishing a valid chamber music style for jazz. This was more than a matter of tuxedos and concert halls. The Modern Jazz Quartet's music captured an intimacy and delicacy, and a sensitivity to dynamics, that was closer in spirit to a top-caliber string quartet than to anything in the world of bop or swing. But unlike their classical world counterparts, the MJQ thrived on the tension—whether conscious or subliminal—between their two lead players. The young Nietzsche made his reputation by untangling the Dionysian and Apollonian tendencies in art—analysts of the MJQ need to do the same. The Bacchic tendency, in this case, is epitomized by Jackson, a freewheeling improviser, at his best when caught up in the heat of the moment. Lewis the Apollonian, in contrast, served as Jackson's collaborator, adversary, and spur, all rolled into one. He constructed elaborate musical structures for Jackson to navigate, embellish, and, at times, subvert. Such tensions between opposites often underpin the greatest art, but rarely make for stable partnerships—and, in fact, Jackson's desire to perform in less structured musical environments led to the Modern Jazz Quartet's breakup in 1974. But a few years later, the group came back together, for the first of many reunion concerts, tours, and recordings.

Milt Jackson's singular efforts also served to bring the vibraphone into the modern age. He pared down the previously dominant style of Lionel Hampton, refining a more distilled approach, swinging but in a softer, more relaxed manner. Commentators have sometimes suggested that Jackson's success came from emulating the saxophone on the vibes. There is some truth to this generalization: Jackson's phrases breathed, unlike the note-filled cadenzas and ornamentation of Hampton's solo outings. His melodic lines had a lighter, airier quality, without the brittle tinniness heard in the work of many previous vibes and xylophone players. Jackson's formative experiences had also included stints with Gillespie, Parker, and Monk, where he had been tested—and found worthy—in the heat of many bop battles and had mastered the intricacies of modern jazz. This background carried over to his work with the MJQ, where Jackson managed to retain a feel for the intensity of bop even in the midst of Lewis's most attenuated compositions.

Lewis, in contrast, brought a distinctly academic flavor to his jazz work. He had studied music and anthropology at the University of New Mexico and had continued his education at the Manhattan School of Music, where he eventually earned a master's degree. He too had worked in major modern jazz bands, including Parker's and Gillespie's, and the influence of Bud Powell could be heard, albeit muted, in his playing. For all this, Lewis was a reluctant bebopper. He lacked Powell's fire, instead favoring a more flowing, at times delicate style, one that remained somewhat at odds with the bop idiom. Yet Lewis's meticulous craftsmanship and formalist tendencies made him an ideal participant in the Davis *Birth of the Cool* project. Still, none of these early associations prepared listeners for the burst of creativity Lewis revealed as musical director of the Modern Jazz Quartet. Although his tastes have often been described as conservative—fueled no doubt by his interest in traditional forms— Lewis showed a voracious appetite for new sounds and experimentation that few jazz artists of his day (or any other) could match. Along with Schuller, he played an key role in furthering Third Stream collaborations between jazz and classical musicians; in addition to his responsibilities with the MJQ, Lewis formed Orchestra USA in the early 1960s, an unfairly forgotten ensemble that straddled a number of musical styles and idioms. Years later he would renew these ambitions, working with Gary Giddins and Roberta Swann to found the American Jazz Orchestra. Lewis was also an early advocate of the jazz avant-garde and was among the first supporters of Ornette Coleman, whom he encouraged to attend the Lenox School of Jazz in 1959, at a time when most jazz players were ridiculing or ignoring Coleman's work. Lewis could find jazz material in traditions few would have thought hospitable to it— everything from fugues to commedia dell'arte—but he was equally successful at penning more recognizably jazz-oriented pieces, such as his wistful ballad "Django" or his riff-driven "The Golden Striker." For want of a better title, he has been claimed as part of the cool jazz movement. Certainly he played a role in the growing popularity of cool jazz during the 1950s, but Lewis's activities were far too varied to be subsumed under any one heading.

Although he never participated in the Davis Nonet, Stan Getz figured as one of the most prominent cool players of the period. On the heels of his ethereal 1948 performance on "Early Autumn" with the Woody Herman band—a late Swing Era vintage that, in retrospect, can be seen as a harbinger of the coming cool school— Getz set out on his own. At first, he settled in New York, where he worked briefly as a staff musician for NBC. The confines of a regular job proved, however, too restrictive for a restless improviser such as Getz. When his recording of "Moonlight in Vermont," made with guitarist Johnny Smith (whom he had met at NBC), showed signs of broadening the popular following he had gained while with Herman, Getz opted to become a full-time combo leader. During the course of the decade, Getz fronted a number of polished ensembles, including a quartet with pianist Horace Silver, a quintet with guitarist Jimmy Rainey, and a West Coast band with valve trombonist Bob Brookmeyer. Getz's lyrical style and strong improvisational skills also made him a frequent choice for all-star recording dates. Noteworthy sessions from this period include a live recording with trombonist J. J. Johnson, a collaboration with Gerry Mulligan, and a heated encounter with Dizzy Gillespie and Sonny

Stitt, with the last session eliciting some of the most assertive tenor work of Getz's career. Despite the quality and quantity of his 1950s work, Getz became an increasingly isolated figure on the jazz scene as the decade progressed. Many factors contributed to his fall from grace: a much-publicized arrest for attempting a drugstore robbery to support his substance-abuse habit; his decision to relocate overseas; his often changeable personality—but, at bottom, it came mostly from factors beyond Getz's control. Jazz tenor sax playing in those years was moving further and further away from Getz's cool stylings. Harder-edged players, such as Sonny Rollins and John Coltrane, were establishing a new model for how the tenor should sound. Getz, who was always a reluctant modernist—his embrace of bop mannerisms had never obscured the more traditional roots in his playing—seemed in danger of sounding old fashioned before his thirty-fifth birthday.

But, in the early 1960s, Getz mounted a major comeback that encompassed both critical success and immense popular acclaim. His 1961 recording *Focus* featured Getz's sleek improvisations darting in and out of Eddie Sauter's acerbic string writing. But the strong reception of this work in the jazz community paled in comparison to the huge public response to Getz's ensuing bossa nova projects. Getz may not have been the first to recognize the jazz potential of this music—Antonio Carlos Jobim's compositions and João Gilberto's vocals had attracted many admirers since their initial Rio de Janeiro recordings from the late 1950s—but no one did more to bring it to the attention of audiences outside Brazil. Getz's 1962 recording of "Desafinado" eventually reached number fifteen on the *Billboard* single charts, and his *Jazz Samba* LP remained on the album charts for over a year, briefly capturing the top position. Quick to capitalize on this success, Getz released several other bossa nova recordings, as did a host of other jazz musicians, anxious to benefit from the Brazilian fad before it faded. In the summer of 1964, just when it seemed as if the public's appetite for the new sound had been sated, Getz achieved an even more celebrated hit single with "The Girl from Ipanema." The *Getz/Gilberto* LP climbed to number two on the charts, kept from the top spot only by the Beatles.

But Getz's tenor work, for all its beauty, was only part of the reason for the public's warm response to the bossa nova. Jobim's compositions, with their mixture of impressionist harmonies, distinctive melodies, and bittersweet lyrics, rank among the finest popular songs of the era. In time "The Girl from Ipanema" became an overplayed cocktail lounge anthem. But Jobim's entire body of work is distinguished by dozens of outstanding pieces, and his name is not out of place alongside those of Gershwin, Berlin, Rodgers, and Porter in the pantheon of those who made art song out of pop tunes. João Gilberto was the perfect performer of this music. His gently stuttering guitar beat epitomized the bossa rhythm, and his whispering vocals pushed the cool aesthetic to its extreme. No singer in any idiom has ever sung with a more relaxed delivery (especially remarkable given his phrasing—seemingly so antithetical to jazz—on top of or ahead of the beat). Even Chet Baker's cooing vocals, reportedly a model for Gilberto, sound sassy by comparison. But, in a surprising twist, João's wife, Astrud Gilberto, provided the most famous vocal on the *Getz/Gilberto* album, launching her own career with her work on "The Girl from Ipanema." Astrud went on to perform with Getz's working band and make her own name as a lead act—a striking turnaround for a woman who had not been a professional singer before her "Ipanema" success. João, in contrast, became increasingly reclusive with the passing years, rarely granting interviews or appearing in public. After the mid-1960s, he made only a handful of records. But his beguiling 1991 release *João* and *João Voz e Violão* from 2000 showed that his style had changed little with the intervening years, despite the fluctuating fashions in pop, jazz, and Brazilian music.

Getz, for his part, would never again sell so many records. But he rarely looked back to the bossa in later years, preferring to return to mainstream jazz with a series of top-notch bands. His quartet with Chick Corea helped pave the way for Corea's own chart-climbing career and produced a major musical statement with the *Sweet Rain* recording. Later bands with Joanne Brackeen, Albert Dailey, Andy LaVerne, Jim McNeely, and Kenny Barron continued in this tradition and maintained a consistently high level of quality, as did Getz's guest recording projects with Jimmy Rowles, Bill Evans, Diane Schuur, and others. In his final years, before his death from liver cancer in 1991, Getz was able to free himself from his long-standing addiction to drugs and alcohol, and find a new career mentoring younger musicians as artist-in-residence at Stanford University.

For a time in the early 1950s, Getz and many other leaders of the cool movement resided on the West Coast. Here cool jazz was in the ascendancy and its leading advocates enjoyed frequent opportunities to perform and record. This marked a stark change from the late 1940s, when a small but talented group of mostly black bebop players, schooled in the clubs and after-hours spots of Central Avenue, had dominated the modern jazz scene in Los Angeles. In many instances, these players maintained their allegiance to bop in later years, but with less financial success than their cool school compatriots—or when compared with the Californians (such as Charles Mingus or Eric Dolphy) who made the smart move to New York. Los Angeles–based saxophonists Dexter Gordon, Teddy Edwards, and Wardell Gray rank among the finest soloists of their generation, and all three played a seldom acknowledged role in defining a distinctive bop sound for the tenor sax, liberated from the Hawkins mannerisms displayed on most early modern jazz tenor outings. Of these three, only Gordon would go on to enjoy widespread fame, albeit after twenty years of relative obscurity. His early recordings for Savoy from the mid-1940s and infrequent releases during the 1950s demonstrate Gordon's freewheeling energy and his bellowing foghorn tone—one of the most distinctive signature sounds in modern jazz—while later sessions for Blue Note present the mature statements of a major soloist. Few were listening, however, and Gordon moved overseas, where he spent most of the 1960s and 1970s. Only upon his return to the United States in 1976 did the tenorist, now in his mid-fifties, begin receiving the accolades and rewards his contributions warranted. Altoist Frank Morgan had an even longer wait before seeing his career blossom. His recordings from the early 1950s reveal a precocious player with formidable technique. But drug problems would sideline him until the late 1970s, and not until the mid-1980s would he enjoy the chance to record extensively and demonstrate the full scope of his abilities. Altoist Sonny Criss and pianist Hampton Hawes had played with Parker during his West Coast sojourn and developed into outstanding bop players in their own right, but both remained mostly local heroes, seldom gigging outside of California and gaining only grudging respect from the mostly East Coast–based critical establishment. Many other gifted players—Harold Land, Curtis Counce, Dupree Bolton, Frank Butler, Carl Perkins, Pony Poindexter, Roy Porter—met similar fates. Often personal problems, mostly drug-related, contributed to the hardships faced by these promising talents. But all of them also suffered from being African American and committed to a harder-edged bop sound at a time when cool jazz played by white musicians was the dominant jazz style on the West Coast.

A number of signal events marked the shift from hot to cool on the Coast. Gerry Mulligan's relocation to California after the completion of the Davis Nonet sessions created a direct link to the fertile East Coast cool movement. In addition, a host of former Stan Kenton sidemen, now settled in Southern California, fueled the progressive tendencies of this music, each with greater or lesser ties to the cool aesthetic. The Lighthouse, a Hermosa Beach jazz club, which had formerly featured some of the more bop-oriented black players, became a regular performance venue for many of these ex-Kentonians. The Lighthouse evolved into a public workshop for emerging jazz trends on the Coast, with a panoply of players (Shorty Rogers, Jimmy Giuffre, Bob Cooper, Bud Shank, Shelly Manne, and many others) pursuing a diverse range of styles, from laid-back to leading-edge. The worst of this music settled for an easy banality, an aural dose of laudanum, but more often the Lighthouse crew tapped into the freewheeling creative currents of the time.

Perhaps even more important than clubs like the Lighthouse were the independent record companies on the West Coast, notably Les Koenig's Contemporary label, Richard Bock's Pacific label, and the Weiss brothers' Fantasy outfit. They recorded and promoted the new music and, in response to their efforts, West Coast jazz gained an international following and emerged as a viable alternative to the hegemony of East Coast models of improvisation and composition. Larger entertainment companies would gradually come to dominate the California music business during this period, with everyone from Walt Disney to MGM seeing recordings as a profitable diversification move. Capitol Records in Hollywood would enter the big leagues with its quasi-monopoly on sophisticated pop, as sung by Frank Sinatra, Peggy Lee, Nat King Cole, Judy Garland, Dean Martin, Nancy Wilson, the Kingston Trio, and other name acts. But the jazz renaissance of the 1950s was promoted primarily by smaller outfits, entrepreneurial businesses built on the growing national reputations of the local jazz players. There is little glamour in the story of these companies— Max and Sol Weiss, for example, started off running a record pressing plant and only got into the music business to maintain the throughput of vinyl and shellac—but without the intervention of such entrepreneurs, West Coast jazz might never have experienced this halcyon era.

Although the movement was never as monolithic as the term suggested, a certain convergence of aesthetic values could be seen in many of the West Coast recordings. The music was often highly structured, rebelling against the simple head charts of East Coast modern jazz and reflecting a formalism that contrasted sharply with the spontaneity of bebop. Counterpoint and other devices of formal composition figured prominently in the music. Larger ensembles—octets, nonets, tentettes—continued to thrive in West Coast jazz circles, long after big horn sections had become an endangered species elsewhere. Unusual instruments were also embraced with enthusiasm, and many of them—such as flute and flugelhorn—eventually came to be widely used in the jazz world. Relaxed tempos and unhurried improvisations were trademarks of the scene, and the music often luxuriated in a warm romanticism and melodic sweetness that was far afield from the bop paradigm. Although the West Coast sound has often been criticized as overly stylized and conventional, the work of many leaders of the movement—Gerry Mulligan, Jimmy Giuffre, Shelly Manne, Shorty Rogers, Dave Brubeck—reveals the exact opposite: a playful curiosity and a desire to experiment and broaden the scope of jazz music were the calling cards of their efforts. It was perhaps this very openness to new sounds that allowed many later leaders of the jazz avant-garde—Eric Dolphy, Ornette Coleman, Don Cherry, Paul Bley—to hone their styles while resident on the Coast.

Gerry Mulligan's stint in California lasted only a few years, but it marked a turning point in the baritone saxophonist's career. He came to Los Angeles as a relatively unheralded player, and left as a major jazz star. Building on his work as composer-arranger with the Davis Nonet, Mulligan wrote charts for the Kenton band and later undertook seminal recordings with his own large ensemble. But Mulligan's most celebrated efforts from this period were in the context of a pared-down quartet. Not only did Mulligan prove that he could write effectively without a full unit of horn players, but he even discarded the piano in this minimalist combo. In a series of memorable performances—"Bernie's Tune," "Line for Lyons," "Lullaby of the Leaves," "My Funny Valentine," and others—Mulligan exploited the potential of this limited instrumentation to the fullest through a variety of techniques: counterpoint between the two horns; use of the bass and drums as melodic voices; *sotto voce* bass lines with the sax or trumpet; and stark variations in pulse and phrasing, ranging from Dixieland two-steps to swinging fours to pointillistic bop beats. The media soon picked up on the novelty of the "pianoless quartet," with a write-up in *Time* magazine exerting particular impact. Before long, patrons were lining up around the block to see the band in performance.

The marriage of the cerebral and the romantic was one of the odd, endearing qualities of West Coast jazz. In the case of the Mulligan quartet, the latter ingredient was provided mostly by trumpeter Chet Baker. There were many limitations to Baker the musician—his range was narrow, his reading skills poor, his technique so-so, his interest in composition almost nil—but as a soloist he deservedly ranks among the finest of his generation. His instinct for melodic development was uncanny, and his improvised lines captured a touching poignancy. Movie-star looks only added to Baker's drawing power, and in time he could challenge Mulligan as a leading jazz star. Unlike the baritonist, Baker had little interest in the more experimental currents of West Coast jazz; most of his career was spent playing and replaying the standards—recording trademark songs, in particular "My Funny Valentine," so often that the estate of Richard Rodgers should put up a statue in the trumpeter's honor.

This conservatism would have served as the death knell for a lesser talent, but Baker proved capable of making even the most threadbare tune sound fresh and new. In time, he branched out as a jazz singer, and though his work in this vein was more stylized than his trumpet playing, it too embodied a heartfelt incisiveness that belied its matter-of-fact conversational delivery. After the breakup of the Mulligan quartet, Baker established himself as a bandleader in his own right. His life and times were always turbulent—drug problems and their legal consequences were constant traveling companions—but his music was a center of stability in the widening gyre. Baker's boyish looks eventually came to be replaced by a grim reaper's visage, haggard and wrinkled, old well before its time. But the trumpeter persisted through it all—even the loss of his teeth in a drug-related beating could only halt his career temporarily—and his last years found him recording prolifically and still capable of moments of greatness. Baker's Tokyo concert captured on film less than twelve months before his death on May 13, 1988—from a mysterious fall from an Amsterdam hotel window—revealed that this musician had lost none of his melodic inventiveness. And, strange to say, the music in those final days captured a sweetness and architectonic order strikingly at odds with Baker's dissolute life.

Alto saxophonist Art Pepper embodied a similar contradiction between the man and his music. But in the case of Pepper, his style eventually came to resemble his personality—honest, imploring, assertive, unapologetic. This marked a major change from the teenage altoist who had joined the Stan Kenton band in 1943, brandishing a soft, almost feminine tone, a relaxed improviser whose shimmering solos danced above the roaring brass of the band. His early work—"Art Pepper" with the Kenton band, "Over the Rainbow" with Shorty Rogers—bespoke a nursery school innocence. But this placid surface could quickly be set into turbulent motion by Pepper's rapid-fire technique and dazzling ear for improvisation. Pepper seemed poised to establish himself as one of the leading jazz soloists of his day and a major protagonist of West Coast jazz, but drug addiction and its resulting complications, both penal and personal, troubled him for the next two decades. By the late 1950s, his playing had taken on a more probing quality, the sugary tone now offering a biting aftertaste. Some of Pepper's finest recordings date from these years: *Art Pepper Meets the Rhythm Section* finds the altoist borrowing Miles Davis's sidemen for a classic encounter; on *Art Pepper Plus Eleven* his lithe sax work propels the bop-oriented Marty Paich arrangements; his sessions with pianist Carl Perkins, little known for many years due to their initial release on tape format, rank among the finest combo sides of the period. But during the 1960s, Pepper almost entirely disappeared from the scene. While in prison he came under the sway of John Coltrane and Ornette Coleman, and engaged in the musical equivalent of psychotherapy, dissecting and reassembling his style with these new influences grafted onto the old. For a time the process was awkward and unsure, but there were few listeners to notice: even when on the outside, Pepper struggled to find an audience in the Age of Aquarius. He took a sideman gig with the Buddy Rich band for a spell and even contemplated retiring from music to pursue a desk job. During his lengthy involvement with Synanon, a drug rehabilitation program, Pepper managed to integrate these new influences into an amazing whole, a predatory alto attack with a soft, vulnerable underbelly. The lyricism of his 1950s work was still evident, but his playing had become much freer, his tonal palette more varied, his creativity less fettered by the chord changes. A series of exceptional albums for the Galaxy and Contemporary labels documented this transformation and enabled Pepper to mount a major comeback after more than a decade of semi-obscurity. On the late ballad "Patricia" he adds a searing coda to the performance that both celebrates and subverts cool jazz with its penetrating cries and whispers. His engagement at the Village Vanguard, with drummer Elvin Jones in the band, found him at such a high level of inspiration that his record company eventually released all of the tapes, hours of performance at a fever pitch. Other late recordings of live performances—in Japan or in the States—reinforced his now-ascendant reputation. Yet the passion of this music seemed at odds with the altoist's advanced years and failing health. Shortly before his death in 1982, Pepper published his autobiography, *Straight Life*, matching in prose the unflinching candor of his playing.

For a time in the 1950s, a West Coast alto style was taking form, a more mellifluous alternative to the astringent Parker-inflected lines of the other coast. Art Pepper, Bud Shank, Lennie Niehaus, and Paul Desmond, among others, exemplified this warm, dulcet-toned approach. In time, the styles of these players diverged. Of this group, Paul Desmond stayed truest to the ultracool aesthetic. He had little interest in adopting a flashier style, jokingly referring to himself as the "world's slowest alto player." On the surface, Desmond's solos appeared to offer a lush romanticism, but only careful listeners were apt to catch their richer implications. Desmond carefully avoided excesses of sentimentality with a range of devices: witty references to other songs and solos, playful call-and-response motives, oblique references to an odd assortment of substitute chords and modes, even quasi-aleatory exercises in translating phone numbers into musical phrases using intervals relating to each digit—a steady stream of melodic surprises linked by Desmond's exceptional skills in thematic improvisation. A single solo from the Dave Brubeck Quartet's twenty-fifth anniversary reunion tour finds Desmond celebrating these old acquaintances with a snippet of "Auld Lang Syne"—followed by allusions to "52nd Street Theme," "The Gypsy," "Taps Miller," "Drum Boogie," and "Organ Grinder's Swing"—all in the context of a complex piece that shifts back and forth between 3/4 and 4/4. The next night, in a different town, Desmond no doubt initiated the process all over again, drawing on still other sources in his artfully constructed saxophone stream of consciousness. Yet these clever asides were never forced, and Desmond somehow made the cerebral and the plaintive coexist in the same solo, even in a single phrase. For much of his career, Desmond served as an appropriate foil for Brubeck. Their collaborations were experimental in the best sense of the term: open to new sounds, but never (as with so many progressive works) in a doctrinaire manner. After the breakup of the Brubeck Quartet, Desmond's music became even more introspective and delicate. His guest pairings with Chet Baker and Jim Hall, and his final quartet recordings with guitarist Ed Bickert, are neglected gems of the improvisational arts, jazz performances that bespeak a *serene* mastery as rare as it is affecting.

By the start of the 1960s, this burst of creative work on the Coast was mostly completed. These were hard years for jazz in any locale—with the audience for improvised music at an all-time low—but several factors were especially damaging to West Coast jazz during this period. The leading exponents disappeared from the scene, some going into studio work (Rogers, Shank), others to prison (Pepper, Hawes, Morgan), a handful gravitating to New York (Dolphy, Coleman, Cherry) or overseas (Baker, Gordon), a few meeting early, tragic deaths (Gray, Counce, Perkins). Each musician's story was somewhat different, but the overall effect was devastating to the local jazz scene. Although some of these players would rebuild their careers in the 1970s and 1980s, the West Coast's relevance as a defining force in the jazz world had now virtually come to an end, the legacy of these glory years mostly forgotten in the midst of a new California youth culture with its surf music, fast cars, longer and longer hair, and shorter and shorter attention spans.

JAZZ IN TRANSITION: MILES, 'TRANE, EVANS, DOLPHY, ROLLINS

In time, Miles Davis would come to personify the cool jazz movement of the 1950s. His demeanor and his trumpet playing were one in this regard, both reflecting the enigmatic mixture of aloofness and emotional immediacy, that odd contradiction that added fire to the cool, invigorating this otherwise subdued, quasi-chamber music. Yet in the early 1950s, all this still lay in the future. At the time, Miles, despite his key role in the Capitol *Birth of the Cool* (as they would come to be called) sessions, maintained only a peripheral relationship to the burgeoning cool jazz scene. While Getz, Brubeck, the Modern Jazz Quartet, Gerry Mulligan, and others generated publicity and built followings, Davis struggled in his attempts to define a personal style on the horn and attract an audience for his music. "The club owners just froze me out," he later reflected. "Wasn't no gigs happening for me."[6]

After the breakup of his Nonet, Davis traveled to Paris with a combo led by Tadd Dameron. In this band, Davis returned to the bop-inflected style promulgated during his stint with Charlie Parker. Recordings show the spirit of Dizzy Gillespie and Fats Navarro hovering over his playing. Yet, though his technique on the trumpet is more proficient than in earlier years, the Dameron collaboration represents, on the whole, a step backward from the more innovative Capitol project. French audiences, however, gave the music an enthusiastic response, and Davis luxuriated in the tolerant, hip attitude of the Parisians who gathered around the visiting jazz players. Kenny Clarke, the drummer with the band, decided to stay on in France, where he remained—enjoying a successful career working with small combos and a large band he co-led with Francy Boland, as well as writing for films—until his death in 1985. Miles also felt the attractions of the European environment and briefly considered a similar move.

Returning to New York in the summer of 1949, Davis fell into a deep depression. He had left behind a promising romance with French actress Juliette Greco ("the first woman that I loved as an equal human being . . . she taught me what it was to love someone other than music"[7]), which now left him emotionally numb. Moreover, the racial divisiveness of postwar America stood in stark contrast to the more open attitudes he had experienced in France. Finally, few opportunities to perform and record were coming his way, while many of Davis's former sidemen were enjoying success in the new cool movement. In the face of these various problems, Miles fell under the sway of heroin. For the next four years, drug addiction would afflict him physically, drain him financially, and limit him artistically.

Davis's recordings of this period provide only the barest hints of the dramatic evolution that would distinguish his post-1954 work. His "Bluing" recording with Sonny Rollins from October 1951 anticipates the classic "Walkin'" performance of 1954, but the lines are less formed, and the solo lacks the continuity of the latter piece. "Yesterdays" from May 1952 indicates Davis's potential as a balladeer, but his tone has yet to show the burnished patina of his mature work. A restless quality permeates these sides, perhaps a reflection of Davis's life during this period. His stay in New York was followed by moves to St. Louis, California, and Detroit, but old problems followed him to these new locales. Finally, after several failed attempts, Davis broke his addiction to heroin and in February 1954 returned to New York. He was healthy, his musical ambitions were revitalized, and, as subsequent events would prove, he was playing better than ever.

Critics would later acknowledge Davis's 1955 performance at the Newport Jazz Festival as the turning point in his career. In fact, Davis in early 1954 was already showing that he had reached a new plateau in his music. His solo on "Walkin'," from April 1954, is a major statement and clearly represents Davis's best playing on record to date. His improvisation is taut; his tone is rich. Moreover, Davis's relaxed swing inspires the whole band. This thirteen-minute track—at the time, an extreme length for a studio recording of a jazz combo—never lags, even when Davis is not playing. Follow-up sessions with Sonny Rollins, Milt Jackson, and Thelonious Monk proved that this performance was no fluke. At age twenty-seven, Miles Davis had blossomed into a major jazz soloist with his style now almost fully formed.

Around this same time, Capitol contributed to the trumpeter's reputation by rereleasing the earlier Nonet recordings on a long-playing album, titling them *Birth of the Cool* for the first time. But it was Davis's unexpected success at the 1955 Newport Jazz Festival that galvanized his following and spurred Columbia, the most powerful record company in the world, to sign the trumpeter to a contract. Davis had not been listed on the festival program, but he was added at the last minute to an all-star jam session. For his feature number, Davis performed Thelonious Monk's composition "'Round Midnight" on muted trumpet. "When I got off the bandstand," Miles later noted, "everybody was looking at me like I was a king."[8] During their drive home, Monk told Davis that he had played the song wrong. But for jazz audiences, Davis's moody interpretation would stand as the definitive version, even more than Monk's own, of this classic jazz ballad. It remained in Miles's repertoire for years to come.

Miles disdained the hubbub following the Newport appearance. "What's the fuss?" he seemed to say. "I always play that way." In truth, Davis had made a remarkable artistic leap, with few counterparts in the history of jazz. Some months earlier, Davis had recorded "'Round Midnight" with the Lighthouse All-Stars, and that rendition, for all its virtues, was a far lesser achievement. Now, almost overnight, Davis had staked out a position as one of the most original ballad players in the history of jazz.

One recalls, to cite a rare point of comparison, Ben Webster's triumphant struggle with the dominant Coleman Hawkins tenor model of the 1930s, which Webster finally distilled into his own personal approach. But doing so required a radical pruning and Webster's inspired shift away from Hawkins's voluptuousness toward a more oblique style. Miles had now made a similar transformation of the dominant Gillespie trumpet model. Hints of the bebop vocabulary remained but were now subsumed into a more minimalist style. A handful of tones sufficed, where the younger Miles would have played baroque phrases. And the notes themselves were only the smallest part of the overall effect, with Miles's toucan tone steadfastly refusing to be reduced to black-and-white notes on a page. As with Webster, timbre and texture, breath and silence were the decisive factors.

With high-profile engagements coming his way, Davis was now able to hire and retain a world-class band. One suspects that the Ahmad Jamal Trio, greatly respected by Davis, served as the main model for the working ensemble he was now putting together—indeed, even the tunes Davis called on gigs would, over the next several years, echo Jamal's own choices. Like Jamal, Davis's pianist Red Garland boasted a delicate touch, a taste for sweet comping chords, and solos that made their point without unnecessary ostentation. Garland was also a consummate swinger, in which regard he was ably supported by bassist Paul Chambers and drummer Philly Joe Jones. Barely out of his teens, Chambers had resided in New York only a few months before he was hired by Davis. Other leaders might have overlooked this Pittsburgh native, whose unassuming style hewed close to the walking-line tradition of Blanton and Pettiford. But with a resonant tone and sure sense of time, Chambers was perfectly suited for Miles's group, now in the process of honing a more understated swing. He would come to serve eight years with Davis. Philly Joe Jones was the old man of the band, in his thirties at the time he joined the Davis combo. He had apprenticed with Parker, Gillespie, and other modern jazz players, and brought a bop-oriented urgency to his work that energized the Davis band. But Jones was also a master of nuances: subtle polyrhythms, delicate brushwork, and crisp cymbal playing were his trademarks. None of these three players were well known at the time Davis hired them, but soon they would garner recognition as one of the finest rhythm sections of their day.

In the summer of 1955, the new Davis band opened at Cafe Bohemia with tenorist Sonny Rollins joining Miles in the front line. Rollins's robust sax sound and linear style made him a perfect counterweight to Davis's more pointillistic approach. Rollins, however, like Miles before him, soon left the New York scene to break himself of his heroin addiction. Seeking a replacement, Davis briefly tried John Gilmore before settling on John Coltrane. In time, Coltrane would be revered as the most influential saxophonist of his generation, but when Miles brought him into the band, Coltrane's reputation in the jazz world was modest, built on a few low-profile sideman stints—with limited chances to solo—most recently as part of Johnny Hodges's band. One of the jazz world's most successful late bloomers—his maturing as a major stylist took place, for the most part, during the last twelve years of his life—Coltrane was a practice-room fanatic, obsessed with constantly improving and expanding his skills. Davis had heard him a few years earlier and had been distinctly unimpressed, but now Coltrane was poised to challenge Rollins and Getz, then established as the leading modern jazz tenor saxophonists. Once again, Davis (like his mentor Charlie Parker) sought a frontline player with a contrasting style to his own. The newcomer filled this role to perfection. Coltrane's elaborate solos conveyed a restless urgency. Hear him follow Miles's plaintive interpretation of "'Round Midnight," on the quintet's celebrated 1956 recording, with a probing examination of the harmonic crevices in the music. Such solos were an odd hybrid: a world of emotion diffused through the analytical perspective of a scientist. This Davis group stayed together only a short while before a falling-out between the trumpeter and tenorist—aggravated by Coltrane's heroin addiction—sent the saxophonist packing to join the Thelonious Monk quartet. However, the Davis unit recorded prolifically before disbanding. Miles needed to fulfill his obligations to the Prestige label, in addition to his Columbia work, and quickly recorded a host of material released in four solid albums (under the names *Steamin'*, *Cookin'*, *Workin'*, and *Relaxin'*).

Only a few weeks after Coltrane's departure, Davis entered the studio to record with a large ensemble under the direction of Gil Evans. Building on the aesthetic leanings and instrumentation the two had developed during the *Birth of the Cool* recordings, Davis and Evans created a series of chiaroscuro pieces joined by linking passages composed by Evans. This project, titled *Miles Ahead*, ranks among the high points of both artists' careers. Davis's playing on flugelhorn represented a novel "anti-virtuosity" that he would refine over the next several years. He rarely challenges the band in the style of a Gillespie or Eldridge, content to float over Evans's impressionistic harmonies. His phrases reach for the essence of the music, for sheltered spaces within the chords. The success of *Miles Ahead* inspired several follow-up projects. Davis and Evans's 1958 recording of compositions from *Porgy and Bess* came close to matching the high quality of the earlier work. A third project, *Sketches of Spain*, was recorded in late 1959 and early 1960 and features an exceptional adaptation of Joaquin Rodrigo's *Concierto de Aranjuez*, originally written for guitar and orchestra, as well as a gripping Davis performance on "Saeta." At his most inspired moments, Davis could now manage to draw a primal cry from the horn, a haunting sound unlike anything else in modern jazz. In such a deeply charged musical flow, even his "mistakes" were effective. They hinted at a depth of feeling that may have been undermined by a more meticulous approach, much as the mourner's sob cuts deeper than the orator's eulogy.

Follow-up Evans-Davis projects, *Quiet Nights* and a live recording from a Carnegie Hall concert, were released in the early 1960s, but were lesser efforts, although not without their moments. Davis's finest music after 1960 was invariably made with smaller bands, and even during the period of studio work with Evans, Davis had maintained his preeminence as a combo leader. For a time, Sonny Rollins had returned as tenor soloist in the band, but Coltrane rejoined the trumpeter at the close of 1957. Coltrane had undergone a dramatic personal rebirth during his time away, and had now foresworn tobacco, alcohol, and narcotics. Moreover, he was now widely acknowledged as a rising star in the jazz world on the strength of his work with Monk and Davis, as well as his first recordings under his own name. In September, Coltrane had recorded his sole leader date for the Blue Note label, *Blue*

Train, a top-flight effort distinguished by the tenorist's strong work on the title blues, and on "Moment's Notice," an intriguing exploration of shifting ii–V chords played at a fast clip. This piece—half composition, half harmonic exercise—anticipated the even more complex "Giant Steps" of 1959. During this same period, Coltrane recorded extensively for the Prestige label, as both leader and sideman. This body of work tends to be obscured by the more adventurous material recorded by Coltrane for Atlantic and Impulse in the 1960s. Yet the Prestige recordings, despite the more conventional repertoire and "blowing date" ambiance, successfully showcased Coltrane's skills as a mainstream jazz soloist in a variety of spirited settings, including memorable frontline battles with other name saxophonists. All in all, the previous eighteen months had marked a major transformation for Coltrane. The man who rejoined the Davis band was a more mature soloist—and person—than the one who had left in the summer of 1957.

The addition of John Coltrane, however, was only one of the steps Davis was taking to rebuild his band into what would prove to be the most celebrated working unit of his illustrious career. When the new Davis combo opened at the Sutherland Lounge in Chicago in December 1957, Coltrane and Davis were supported in the front line by alto saxophonist Julian "Cannonball" Adderley. Adderley's impassioned playing had caused a sensation in the jazz world almost immediately on his arrival in New York in 1955. For a time he had worked with Oscar Pettiford and later with his brother Nat Adderley, but in performing on a regular basis with Coltrane and Davis the altoist was challenged as never before. "The first night in Chicago," Davis would later relate, "we started off playing the blues, and Cannonball was just standing there with his mouth open, listening to 'Trane. . . . He asked me what we were playing and I told him 'the blues.' He says, 'Well I ain't never heard no blues played like that!'"[9] But Adderley, himself a master of the twelve-bar form, came to flourish in this competitive setting, countering Coltrane's baroque explorations with vigorous, hard-swinging solos. The chemistry between the three frontline players was amply demonstrated on the *Milestones* album, recorded for Columbia the following February and March, which consisted entirely of medium-tempo and fast numbers played with almost unrelenting energy. This edition of the Davis band seemed destined to be remembered as one of the most assertive jazz combos of its day, almost the antithesis of the cool sound that Davis had honed in other settings.

This would soon change. The addition of pianist Bill Evans shortly after the *Milestones* date brought, in Davis's words, a "quiet fire" to the group. Soft-spoken and introspective, Evans acted little and looked even less like a jazz musician: hunched over the instrument, with his horn-rimmed glasses and slicked-down hair only inches from his probing fingers, he seemed lost in some private communion with the ivory keys. In time, this unassuming figure would demand respect as the most influential jazz pianist of his generation, forging an innovative style that would permanently alter improvised keyboard music. But in 1958, few jazz fans had heard of this mild-mannered white pianist, whose major sideman credits were low-profile stints with Tony Scott and George Russell. True, Evans's lucid work on Russell's "Concerto for Billy the Kid" and "All About Rosie" had caught the attention of more discerning listeners. Yet his 1956 debut recording as a leader for the Riverside label sold only eight hundred copies in the twelve months following its release. Two years would elapse before Evans, now validated by his role in the Miles Davis band, would record again as a leader.

Born in Plainfield, New Jersey, on August 16, 1929, Evans began learning piano at age six and started his performing career at age twelve. He later studied music at Southeastern Louisiana University, focusing on piano, flute, and music theory. He brought to his jazz playing a deep knowledge of the classics, especially late nineteenth- and early twentieth-century composers such as Ravel, Debussy, Scriabin, Bartók, Prokofiev, and Rachmaninoff, supplemented by a keen appreciation of the jazz work of Powell, Tristano, Konitz, and others. In time, these disparate influences would coalesce into a unique, integrated style of Evans's own creation. Although previous jazz pianists had experimented with chords built on higher intervals, Evans refined a comprehensive and systematic understanding of voicings, derived primarily from the French impressionist composers, which made extensive use of ninth, eleventh, and thirteenth chords. At times, Evans would craft richly layered block-chord solos, as on the Davis recording of "On Green Dolphin Street"—a technique largely abandoned by the pianist in later years but which persuasively set forth the varied and subtle palette of sounds at his disposal, akin to a Maurice Ravel playing cool jazz. These same higher intervals figured prominently in Evans's melody lines, which employed altered ninths and sharp elevenths the way earlier jazz pianists had used blues notes: to add color, tension, and release to the improvised phrases. Evans's touch at the piano was equally noteworthy, tending toward a smooth legato, softening the staccato attack preferred by his bop predecessors. In time, Evans would learn how to construct phrases that broke away almost completely from the gravitational pull of the ground beat—a technique he would master with his later trios and teach by example to the next generation of jazz players—but even on these early recordings with Davis, Evans's attenuated approach to melodic development was evident, furthered by the frequent use of triplets and three-against-two rhythms, as well as the sometimes aeriform, free-floating quality of his solos.

Is it going too far to see this Davis unit as the most impressive working combo in the history of modern jazz? Certainly it not only included some of the greatest individual talents of the era, playing at a peak level, but the band also possessed a rare chemistry. The cooler aesthetic of Davis and Evans tempered and counterbalanced the fire-and-brimstone exhortations of Coltrane and Adderley. Yet only a handful of recordings exist, making a complete evaluation impossible: the ensemble's total oeuvre can be heard in a couple of hours. A late May session for Columbia produced several landmark performances: "Fran Dance," "Love for Sale," "Stella by Starlight," and the aforementioned "On Green Dolphin Street." Other tantalizing extracts of this band in action have also been released—often issued scattershot by Columbia, which, for example, waited eighteen years before making "Love for Sale" available. But, for the most part, the Olympian reputation of this sextet rests on a single recording project, *Kind of Blue*.

Yet what a remarkable recording it is! On the title track of his previous *Milestones* release, Davis had experimented with modal-based improvisation, and he was intent on delving more deeply into this technique on *Kind of Blue*. The essence of modal jazz lay in the use of scales as a springboard for solos, in place of the busy chord progressions that had characterized jazz since the bop era. For example, Davis's composition "So What" may have appeared, at first hearing, to be a traditional thirty-two-bar piece in AABA song form. But there was one critical difference: a seven-note D Dorian scale (equivalent to the white notes on a piano keyboard) served as the basis for improvisations in the first section of the piece, while an E-flat Dorian scale was the foundation for the middle section. The soloists were expected to rely solely on these scales during their improvisations. "Flamenco Sketches" took the modal concept even further. Traditional song form was abandoned in favor of interludes of indeterminate length; each soloist worked through a series of five scales, proceeding at his own pace, lingering on each mode for as long or as short a time as he wished. This approach gave the players unprecedented freedom but also demanded a degree of austerity unknown in bebop. Musicians raised on Parker's precept that a soloist could—indeed, should—"play any note against any chord," felt understandably constrained when limited to predetermined modes. Sometimes they responded by ignoring the "rules" Miles had set for the songs. When Sonny Stitt played "So What" with the Davis band, he treated the modal sections as long vamps on minor chords, spicing them with Parkeresque chromaticism. In time, modal jazz playing would evolve in this very direction—especially in the later works of Coltrane where static harmonies were used as foundations for the most complex melodic superstructures. But Davis's original conception, although more restrictive, bespoke an almost childlike fascination with the basic building blocks of music. In his hands, modal jazz served as a healthy corrective, a minimalist response to the maximalist tendencies of postwar jazz. Bill Evans's impressionist harmonies added to the emotive power of *Kind of Blue* and served to reinforce Davis's Zenlike insistence on simplicity of means. Coltrane and Adderley, who by temperament were much hotter players, responded with some of the crispest solos of their careers.

Evans had already left the band by the time these pieces were recorded, after only eight months with Davis. "I felt exhausted in every way—physically, mentally and spiritually," he later recalled.[10] In September 1959, Cannonball Adderley departed as well, despite Davis's guaranteeing a minimum annual salary of $20,000, which was more than the altoist could hope to earn leading his own band. After reluctantly joining Davis for a European tour in early 1960, John Coltrane also left the fold. These were devastating losses. Davis would eventually regroup with a superb mid-1960s band, but in the interim he struggled to recruit suitable replacements for these unique talents. On saxophone, for example, the early 1960s found Davis using, for greater or shorter periods, Jimmy Heath, Sonny Stitt, Hank Mobley, Frank Strozier, George Coleman, Sam Rivers, and others. Many of his sidemen during this period were outstanding players, and even the lesser lights were solid journeyman soloists; for example, Davis's keyboard accompanists, Wynton Kelly and Victor Feldman, were both top-tier talents and their sound well matched with Davis's needs—yet the resulting ensembles rarely approached the chemistry of the late 1950s and mid-1960s bands.

During his brief stint with the Davis sextet, Bill Evans's playing reached a new peak, and it continued to evolve in his ensuing trio work. Together with bassist Scott

LaFaro and drummer Paul Motian, Evans achieved a degree of interaction and heightened sensitivity rarely heard in the jazz world, and created a body of work that would prove to be vastly influential during the coming decades. Only twenty-three years old at the time he joined Evans, LaFaro had already performed on both coasts with musicians as diverse as Sonny Rollins, Chet Baker, Thelonious Monk, and Benny Goodman. But with the Evans trio, LaFaro took far greater chances, departing markedly from traditional walking lines, instead offering countermelodies and guitar-like phrases. His sense of time was freer, less tied to the ground beat, than any jazz bassist had previously attempted. In this regard, he was ably assisted by drummer Motian, whose subtle percussion work—especially his brush and cymbal playing— added color and texture to the music as much as it did rhythmic drive. For this band, the underlying pulse was implied rather than stated. Evans referred to this approach as the "internalized beat." It is not going too far to see this short-lived trio as redefining the nature of the jazz rhythm section. Almost all the great piano-bass-drums units of later years—perhaps most notably the exceptional Herbie Hancock–Ron Carter–Tony Williams combination that powered Miles's mid-1960s band—would, in some measure, draw on the innovations of this seminal trio.

Studio recordings from December 1959 and February 1961 showcased the band's progress in breaking free from bop-era clichés in an attempt to create a more purified style of trio music. The trio's follow-up recording—which would also prove to be its last—finds these hints of greatness coalescing into a full-fledged mastery. On June 25, 1961, Evans's record company taped the trio's performance at New York's Village Vanguard. The two dozen selections recorded that day achieve a telepathic level of group interplay, one in which the line between soloist and accompanist— isolated and distinct in the swing and bop idioms—often blurs and at times totally disappears. The piano work, the bass line, the percussion part weave together in a marvelous, continuous conversation. Such a description might make it seem that the music is busy, filled with content. Nothing could be further from the truth. The marvel was how this music could say so much while leaving so much unsaid. One would struggle to find a jazz recording from the day with a slower tempo than "My Foolish Heart," yet the performance never lags; indeed, it could serve as a textbook case in how to use space and silence to accentuate the forward momentum of jazz music. Other tracks are equally exemplary: the intimate dialogue between the bass and piano on "Some Other Time"; the shimmering percussion work on "My Man's Gone Now," supporting Evans's poignant solo; the probing across-the-bar-lines phrasing on "Gloria's Step" and "All of You"; the pristine beauty of "Waltz for Debby" and "Alice in Wonderland"; the avant-garde deconstruction of "Milestones." A band might rightly be willing to rest its reputation on the basis of a single day's worth of work when it was a day such as the one the Evans trio enjoyed at the Village Vanguard; alas, as it turned out, that would perforce be the case. Eleven days later, LaFaro died in a car accident. He was only twenty-five years old.

Evans retreated from public performance for a time, but eventually regrouped. He recorded prolifically during the 1960s and 1970s, most often in a trio format, but also occasionally in the company of well-known horn players (such as Stan Getz, Freddie Hubbard, Zoot Sims, Lee Konitz, and Warne Marsh). In an era when many jazz players were outspoken in their embrace of new movements, from free jazz to fusion, Evans continued to rely on the traditional American popular song repertoire and tonal, linear improvisation. Yet a considerable amount of innovation lay hidden behind this apparent conservatism. Evans's chord voicings, with their expressive use of color tones, would became widely imitated, almost serving as a default standard among later pianists. Less obvious to many listeners, but equally important, were the subtleties of Evans's rhythmic phrasing. Even when playing in strict time, he could create the feeling of an effortless rubato. Above all, his music was virtually free of base sentimentality, even when he played the most saccharine pop songs, and never relied on the hackneyed or empty display of technique for its own sake.

Like Davis and Coltrane, Evans struggled with drug addiction. During the 1960s, his heroin habit punished him physically and financially. Yet Evans's music seemed to reflect a different reality, often suggesting a contemplative otherworldliness above the fray of day-to-day concerns. Indeed, these years produced some of the finest work of Evans's career: the glorious solo album *Alone* with its incomparable exposition of "Never Let Me Go"; the memorable live recording at Town Hall; a classic pairing with guitarist Jim Hall; experiments with overdubbing; and various trio and combo dates. During the 1970s, Evans was free for a time from drugs, and his music making took on a smoother sheen, less introspective and more assertive, especially in the pianist's work alongside the accomplished bassist Eddie Gomez. Even more aggressive—at times almost angry—was the music made by his final trio, which featured bassist Marc Johnson and drummer Joe La Barbera. By this time, Evans had turned again to drugs, now primarily cocaine, and those nearest him feared that he was slowly, almost deliberately, killing himself. On his last tour with the trio, he frequently surprised audiences with his strident interpretation of the theme from the TV series *M*A*S*H*, a song also known as "Suicide Is Painless." The irony of the title was disturbing. A bleeding ulcer was the final, official cause of a cumulative process of self-destruction. At the time of his death, on September 15, 1980, Evans was fifty-one years old.

How influential was Bill Evans? A survey of forty-seven jazz pianists conducted by Gene Lees in 1984 found that Evans ranked second to only Art Tatum as the most influential pianist in the history of jazz keyboard music; it is worth adding that Evans ranked first when these same players were asked to choose their personal favorite among jazz pianists.[11] Yet describing the scope of this influence is made difficult by its very pervasiveness—much like trying to determine Johnny Appleseed's impact on a grove of Red Delicious, it seems to blossom wherever one looks. A host of later Davis sidemen also showed Evans's influence, especially Herbie Hancock and Chick Corea. Less well known are Denny Zeitlin's stunning 1960s trio recordings for Columbia, produced by John Hammond, that served as especially powerful examples of how Evans's probing style and concept of trio interaction could serve as the basis for the next generation of jazz pianists. Zeitlin's music displayed a rare skill in mixing quasi-avant-garde techniques with sublime lyricism, as demonstrated on such projects as *Cathexis*, *Live at the Trident*, and *Zeitgeist*. Evans returned the favor by adding Zeitlin's "Quiet Now" to his repertoire, recording it on several occasions. Zeitlin's work from this period, as well as Steve Kuhn's and Paul Bley's, can be rightly described as the "missing links"—rarely noted and insufficiently appreciated—between Evans's pioneering efforts and the classically tinged ECM sound (discussed in chapter 8) that came to the fore during the 1970s. In later years, the Evans influence continued to figure in the work of many of the finest young pianists emerging on the scene, including Michel Petrucciani, Fred Hersch, Andy LaVerne, Jim McNeely, Richie Beirach, Eliane Elias, Alan Broadbent, and Enrico Pieranunzi. Yet the magnetic pull of this singular artist also was felt by nonpianists: its impact is evident, for example, in the vibraphone work of Bobby Hutcherson and Gary Burton, or even more conspicuously in the magisterial guitar stylings of Lenny Breau.

Coltrane's post-Miles career took him in a far different direction from the one Evans pursued. Only a few days after the final *Kind of Blue* session, Coltrane entered the studio as leader for the Atlantic label. The resulting *Giant Steps* release would rank as the tenorist's most commanding recording to date. This music stood at the opposite end of the spectrum from the Davis modal work. In many ways, the title track represented the epitome of chord-based jazz material, with its difficult progressions played at a rapid pace. On this number, pianist Tommy Flanagan falters noticeably—and who can blame him? Unlike Coltrane, he had not had the benefit of practicing in advance for this daedal musical obstacle course. But the tenorist shows no hesitancy, handling the changes with ease. On closer examination, much of Coltrane's work on the solo is based on a simple pattern—employing the first four notes of the pentatonic scale over each chord—and the seemingly novel harmonies are borrowed in large part from the bridge of the old Rodgers and Hart standard "Have You Met Miss Jones?" But Coltrane's adroit execution and relentless energy are impressive. No other saxophonist of his generation could have put his personal stamp so completely on this music. On "Countdown," from the same project, Coltrane runs the gauntlet on an almost equally difficult chord pattern, while the ballad "Naima," played over a shifting pedal point, ranks as one of the tenorist's loveliest compositions.

For another musician, such a record might have been the crowning achievement of a career, but for Coltrane *Giant Steps* served merely as a way station on an unceasing journey. By the following year, Coltrane's fascination with complex chord progressions was tempered by a renewed interest in pieces with a modal flavor. On his June 1960 recording with Don Cherry, backed by Ornette Coleman's rhythm section, Coltrane makes frequent use of modal techniques. "My Favorite Things," recorded a few months later, finds him alternating between conventional chord progressions and simple vamps suitable for modal improvisation. Yet Coltrane's use of modes was moving far beyond Davis's spartan conception. Even when Coltrane's rhythm section was playing a quasi-modal harmonic pattern, based on one or two chords, Coltrane's saxophone lines ranged widely, superimposing a variety of scales, with different degrees of consonance and dissonance. In time, Coltrane would push this technique to its limits. On pieces such as "Spiritual" and "A Love Supreme," he builds Byzantine structures over simple bass lines, paltry foundations that—were one not confronted with the final, unimpeachable results—might otherwise seem incapable of supporting such colossal ambitions.

In this regard, Coltrane was well served by a world-class rhythm section. These static harmonies might have sounded merely banal when played by lesser artists. But in pianist McCoy Tyner and drummer Elvin Jones, Coltrane had found two of the finest musicians of the younger generation, both largely unheralded at the time, but each—like Coltrane himself—boasting a solid technique combined with a desire to develop and expand his musical vocabulary. These three players would mature in tandem over the next several years, feeding off each other's energy, pushing each other deeper and deeper into the music. A member of a prominent jazz family, Elvin Jones was less well known than his siblings Hank and Thad at the time he moved to New York in 1956. But, by the close of his tenure with Coltrane, Elvin Jones had established himself as one of most influential drummers in the history of jazz. His mastery of polyrhythms was unsurpassed, yet even more striking was the unabashed intensity he brought to every performance. More than any other percussionist of his generation, Jones showed that delving into the interstices between the beats was not incompatible with pushing the band forward with unrelenting force. Time and time again, Coltrane's own assertive musical personality seemed to draw its strength from Jones's drum work—so much so that bass and piano would sometimes drop out of the proceedings for extended interludes, allowing these two dynamos to go at it. In these superheated moments, the line between leader and accompanist was replaced by a transcendent and combined will to power. Coltrane himself realized how important Jones was to his musical development. At one point, the drummer borrowed Trane's car and totaled it in an accident. "I walked away with just bruises and scratches," Jones later recalled. "When I told Trane about it, he said, 'I can always get another car, but there's only one Elvin.'"[12]

Pianist McCoy Tyner similarly primed himself for greatness during his time with the Coltrane quartet. Born and raised in Philadelphia, Tyner had studied piano and music theory at the West Philadelphia Music School and Granoff Music School, and at age fifteen began leading his own rhythm and blues band. His early jazz role models included Thelonious Monk and Bud Powell, as well as Richie Powell, Bud's lesser known brother. Like them, he favored a heavier touch at the keyboard and a penchant for percussive effects. At age seventeen, Tyner met John Coltrane and played two gigs with the saxophonist, then between stints with the Davis band. Some four years would elapse before Tyner joined Coltrane's quartet. In the interim, he struggled to make a living at music, and as late as 1959 was working as a shipping clerk during the day while taking occasional evening gigs. That year Tyner's career received a boost when he was asked to join the Benny Golson/Art Farmer Jazztet. Less than a year later, Tyner left to become a member of the Coltrane quartet, where he would stay until 1965. Blessed with a crisp, clean piano attack and a knack for constructing elaborate improvised lines, Tyner could have been a premier hard-bop pianist. But alongside Coltrane, Tyner gradually grew to be much more. Where other pianists would have backed Coltrane's horn phrases with conventional comping chords, Tyner challenged the soloist with vamps and clusters and various percussive effects that, in aggregate, constituted a veritable pianistic tsunami of sound. The band's excessive reliance on songs with simple harmonic structures may have played a role in this evolution, forcing Tyner to exert the utmost creativity in weaving a whole tapestry of harmonic color out of these most meager of threads. Tyner delighted in ambiguous voicings, liberally spiced with suspended fourths that rarely resolved, often played with a thunderous two-handed attack that seemed destined to leave permanent finger marks in the keys. Tyner's solos were, if anything, even more energetic. Single-note lines, leavened with wide, often unpredictable interval leaps, jostled with sweeping arpeggios, cascading runs, reverberating tremolos. His touch at the piano, which originally possessed brittle sharpness, took on volume and depth, eventually emerging as one of the fullest and most easily identifiable keyboard sounds in jazz. Tyner's career continued to flourish long after he left Coltrane, and his work in subsequent decades, especially his 1970s albums for the Milestone label—including vital projects such as *Echoes of a Friend*, *Atlantis*, *Trident*, *Supertrios*, and *Fly with the Wind*—would exert a noticeable influence on the jazz pianists of that era. But though others mimicked Tyner's mannerisms, voicings, and modal runs, these acolytes seldom approached the intensity of the original.

In 1961, Coltrane was among the first musicians to sign with the new Impulse record label. A sizable advance made Coltrane the second highest paid musician in jazz, an honor in which he trailed only his former employer Miles Davis. Given this investment, Impulse was understandably anxious to broaden Coltrane's following and frequently featured him in settings far afield from the increasingly outré approach Trane was pursuing in nightclubs and concert halls. Yet the more mainstream projects were invariably well conceived and almost uniformly successful: the pairing with vocalist Johnny Hartman ranks among the finest collaborations ever between saxophonist and singer and resulted in definitive performances of "Lush Life," "My One and Only Love," and "You Are Too Beautiful"; the *Ballads* release pursued a similar aesthetic, with comparable results; the session with Duke Ellington was a daring move—both parties may have seemed accommodating on the surface, yet each was driven by a tough-as-nails commitment to his personal musical principles—but this odd couple proved that, on occasion, demigods do consent to give-and-take. On "In a Sentimental Mood" Coltrane even elicited a breathtakingly fresh reconfiguration of the standard from Ellington (of a piece Duke had been playing regularly for almost thirty years). Some time later, Johnny Hodges, who had put an indelible stamp on this composition as a member of the Ellington band, told the record's producer, Bob Thiele, that Coltrane's version was "the most beautiful interpretation I've ever heard."[13]

These respectful reworkings of the traditional jazz repertoire coexisted with Coltrane's more emphatic explorations, also recorded extensively by Impulse during these years. One finds a vast range of styles broached in these releases: tour de force blues such as "Chasin' the Trane" and "Bessie's Blues"; elaborate soprano sax excursions in 3/4 time—perhaps consciously aiming to recreate the success of "My Favorite Things"—in which Coltrane deconstructs singsong melodies such as "Chim Chim Cheree," "Afro Blue," and "Greensleeves"; "Alabama," "Crescent," and other epic pieces that find the quartet majestically flowing in and out of tempo; virtuosic modal performances such as "Impressions"; a stunning variety of hypermodern ballad styles, including moody rubato pieces ("Soul Eyes"), volcanic eruptions over standard changes ("I Want to Talk About You," "Nature Boy"), and lilting superimpositions of a waltz feel over a slow 4/4 (the late live recordings of "Naima"); hypnotic mixtures of music and chanting ("Om" and the opening section from *A Love Supreme*) or quasi-vocals ("Kulu Se Mama"); and more tightly structured efforts with a larger ensemble (*Africa/Brass*).

These adventures, however, were merely a preamble to the full experimental zeal of Coltrane's final evolution. Coltrane was increasingly drawn to the liberating possibilities of free jazz—a quest that resulted in uninhibited performances invariably dubbed with names drawn from mystical and religious literature. But even here the range of styles was impressive, with the ethereal "Offerings" from the final quartet with Alice Coltrane and Rashied Ali standing in contrast to the fire and brimstone of "Om," "Ascension," or "The Father and the Son and the Holy Ghost" from *Meditations*. A whole career's worth of music was crammed into these final six years, studio work for Impulse complemented by various live recordings (at the Village Vanguard, Birdland, the Newport Festival, on the road in Europe, Japan, and other locales). "We couldn't possibly put out all the records we were making," later recalled producer Thiele, who persisted in preserving the saxophonist's growing oeuvre, even in the face of opposition from the label's senior management. "I believe his contract called for two albums a year to be recorded and released. Well, hell, I recorded six albums a year. . . . It reached a point where I would record late at night, so at least we'd have peace then, and no one in the company would know where I was." The total extent of these recordings was so great that new material was still being released many years after the saxophonist's death.

These constant changes in Coltrane's music were highly representative of the man, a restless seeker and obsessive autodidact. Continual striving marked virtually all aspects of his life. A voracious reader, Coltrane's interests ranged widely, with everything from Aristotle to Edgar Cayce finding its way to his bookshelves, as well as *The Autobiography of a Yogi* (suggested by Sonny Rollins) and Krishnamurti's *Commentaries on Living* (recommended by Bill Evans). This insatiable appetite for the new and different was equally evident in Coltrane's music. Years before world music was in fashion, Coltrane delved into the aural cultures of India, Africa, Latin America, and other parts of the globe. Classical composers, especially contemporary ones, were studied with similar enthusiasm. For his practice sessions, Coltrane favored Nicolas Slonimsky's *Thesaurus of Scales and Melodic Patterns*. This too was a fitting choice, since both Coltrane and Slonimsky shared the same obsession: to know all the scale patterns possible within the well-tempered tonal system. (Before long, numerous jazz players were "digging" Slonimsky in emulation of Trane, and the publisher of the *Thesaurus* puzzled over the sudden surge in orders for this previously unheralded volume.) At other times Coltrane would use music written for piano or violin or harp as practice-room fodder for his sax technique, knowing that this too would force him to expand his musical horizons. He delighted in new instruments, new mouthpieces, new collections of sheet music—indeed in anything that might add to his arsenal of sounds. He, along with fellow progressive Steve Lacy, played a key role in restoring the soprano sax to prominence as a legitimate jazz horn after years of neglect. In private, Coltrane tried his hand at other instruments, including koto and sitar (both brought back from his Japanese tour), even snubbing the purists with his interest in the electric Varitone sax. Perhaps one could not have predicted that the polished "inside" player of *Giant Steps* would eventually evolve into the daring "outside" exponent of *Ascension*, yet anyone who had experienced Coltrane's unquenchable thirst for personal development lived with the expectation of dramatic changes to come from this restless giant of the jazz world.

Eric Dolphy was Coltrane's sometime partner in these explorations. This too was fitting. Like Coltrane, Dolphy had mastered the jazz art through diligence, an openness to new sounds, and assiduous practice. Both saxophonists came to adopt the most radical techniques of improvisation, but—and this was the marvel—did so in careful, almost methodical steps. What a fancy: that a revolution could be pursued in tiny increments! Yet such was the foundation of their success. Unlike most other practitioners of free jazz, Dolphy (like Coltrane) had first established his prowess in more structured formats. Although he came of age in the heated jazz environment of postwar Southern California, Dolphy had only the most peripheral involvement in the Central Avenue scene of that day. Instead, his early musical tastes tended toward Debussy, Ravel, and Webern. He aspired to study music at the University of Southern California and eventually become a symphony oboe player. Music teacher Lloyd Reese fueled the youngster's interest in jazz—and infuriated Eric's parents—when he suggested that a college degree was not necessary to pursue a career in music.

A precocious talent, Dolphy was nonetheless a late bloomer in the jazz world. His first major gig, with Roy Porter's big band, did not take place until he was twenty, but even then almost a decade would pass before Dolphy began drawing attention through his work with Chico Hamilton. Most of the intervening years were consumed by private study, supplemented by occasional low-profile gigs in the LA area. By the close of the 1950s, Dolphy had developed into a virtuoso saxophonist, in many ways the most fitting heir among his generation to the Parker mantle, not due to any slavish imitation of the master—that Dolphy emphatically did *not* do—but through his insistence on following the implications of Bird to the logical next level. Like Parker, his music was played with urgency, at times explosiveness, daring to linger at the tenuous juncture where the human cry and musical scale meet. But the differences between the two were equally notable. Dolphy's solos were more angular, zigzagging from interval to interval, taking hairpin turns at unexpected junctures, making dramatic leaps from the lower to the upper register, and belting out insistent flurries of notes. And, in time, Dolphy would push his music to an even more pronounced modernism than Parker's, ultimately breaching the conventional limits of tonality and structure.

After moving to New York in 1959, Dolphy soon found himself in the midst of a vortex of radical changes sweeping the jazz landscape. He would only live another five years, but for Dolphy this would be a teeming half-decade of musical achievements. His sideman work with Coltrane found him writing arrangements for an enlarged combo in addition to matching up with the leader as a frontline soloist. Taking on Coltrane nightly on the bandstand was a task few saxophonists would have relished at the time, but Dolphy flourished in such charged settings. His sideman work with Charles Mingus was equally productive, as documented on a handful of projects, including the Candid release *Charles Mingus Presents Charles Mingus* and a memorable concert recording made at Antibes. Dolphy's presence also contributed to a number of high-profile sessions with other leaders, including Ornette Coleman's *Free Jazz*, Andrew Hill's *Point of Departure*, Oliver Nelson's *The Blues and the Abstract Truth*, and George Russell's *Ezz-thetics*—four milestone recordings from the early 1960s, each demanding a different facet of Dolphy's musical personality. He also graced important larger ensembles led by John Lewis, Gil Evans, and Gunther Schuller, as well as performed classical composer Edgard Varèse's challenging solo flute work *Density 21.5* at the 1962 Ojai Festival in California. In many ways, Eric Dolphy was the perfect sideman, boasting exceptional technique, outstanding reading skills, mastery of several instruments, and a flexibility that allowed him to work with equal comfort in a variety of genres, from the most structured to the most free-form, whether inside the chord changes or outside their sway. And these many talents were married to a soft-spoken, sweet disposition that added to his skill in adapting to new bands and different situations. Dolphy would be well known and admired today if only for these sideman stints. But his work as a leader has also left a large mark on the jazz world. His studio projects produced a number of estimable efforts, including *Far Cry* for Prestige and *Out to Lunch* for Blue Note, as well as a compelling set of live performances recorded with the brilliant young trumpeter Booker Little at the Five Spot on July 16, 1961.

The latter collaboration succeeded despite many obstacles: this was the band's first and only extended club engagement, the piano was badly out of tune, the audience noisy and seemingly indifferent, the repertoire a hodgepodge of ballads and disparate originals from group members. Yet the ensemble rises far above these constraints, pushing each number to its limits, and maintaining a fierce energy on pieces such as "The Prophet," "Aggression," and "Fire Waltz." The obvious point of comparison here is with Ornette Coleman and Don Cherry. But while Coleman and Cherry used free tonality as a starting point, with Dolphy and Little it is the opposite: the pieces are tonal and highly structured, with the horn players adopting quarter tones, cries, and dissonance as a way of expanding and stretching the jazz vocabulary from within, rather than reinventing it *de novo*. In comments that are equally representative of Dolphy, Little explained his aesthetic principles: "I have more conventional ideas [than Ornette]. . . . But I can't think in terms of wrong notes—in fact I don't hear any notes as being wrong. It's a matter of knowing how to integrate the notes and, if you must, how to resolve them."[14] These precepts are very much evident in the Five Spot recordings. This was music at the edge. Perhaps these musicians could have taken a further step, fully embracing the "freedom principle" (as it has come to be known), collaborating on even more iconoclastic music. Dolphy, for his part, seemed half ready to make this leap, as witnessed by his *Out to Lunch* recording, made shortly before his death. But even at this late stage, Dolphy evinced, especially through his elaborate compositions, a reluctance to leave structure and tradition behind (as on his *Free Jazz* sideman date with Ornette Coleman). Certainly it is tempting to speculate how Dolphy and Little might have evolved had their partnership lasted another five or ten years. As it turned out, both players would be dead before the middle of the decade: Little felled by uremia in 1961 at age twenty-three, Dolphy succumbing to heart failure spurred by a diabetic condition in 1964 at age thirty-six. It would be left to others, more revolutionary in their ambitions and even less wedded to the bebop and hard-bop tradition, to bring freedom music to its fullest expression: an Ornette Coleman, an Albert Ayler, a Cecil Taylor.

In the late 1950s, however, the chief challenge to Coltrane's preeminence as the leading saxophonist of his day came not from Coleman or Ayler—little known at the time—or even from Dolphy. The most persuasive alternative to his "sheets of sound" approach emanated, rather, from the heart of the jazz tradition, in the person of tenorist Sonny Rollins. More than any of these celebrated peers, Rollins would play the lead role in defining the mainstream sound of the tenor during these transition years. While other saxophonists were exploring the limits of dissonance, free improv and extended forms, Third Stream mergings with classical music, exotic instruments, nonets and octets and other expanded bands, Rollins stayed mostly focused on forging a classic solo style. Much of the history of Adolphe Sax's invention found its way into Rollins's playing. One could hear the connections that tied him to the legacy of a Coleman Hawkins or a Don Byas and other vintage horn players, seamlessly blended with hypermodern elements drawn from the current scene. "I like to think there is a direct link between early jazz and jazz of any time," Rollins told interviewer Bob Blumenthal in 1982. "I like to think that jazz can be played in a way that you can hear the old as well as the new. At least that's how I try to play."[15]

A celebration of improvisation lay at the core of his artistry and served as the organizing principle for his finest recordings and performances. At times his zest for the spontaneous flow of musical ideas would lead Rollins to produce extravagant unaccompanied sax musings. Here his creativity could run freely, with everything mixing together—snippets from operatic arias, movie themes, hoary pop tunes, bebop licks—a Joycean stream of consciousness as viewed through the bell of a horn. These unpredictable excursions came to achieve quasi-mythic status. Indeed, many of Rollins's fans refused to acknowledge that any of his albums, even the best, matched what they had heard in person, especially when the tenorist was unfettered by a rhythm section. But extended *a cappella* inventions were only a small part of Rollins's broad musical vision. Few jazz players of his day could boast of a more extensive repertoire, one that featured the highs and lows of the popular song tradition with equal fervor. And not just the standard American tunes: Kurt Weill, Noel Coward, and other Old World composers were honored alongside Gershwin and Porter. These deferential bows to songs from afar coexisted with the oddities, moldy oldies, and novelty tunes that Rollins somehow transformed into jazz, such as "I'm an Old Cowhand" or "The Tennessee Waltz" or "Toot, Toot, Tootsie."

The scope of his music continued to grow with the passing years: in the early 1980s, it spanned everything from Dolly Parton to Stevie Wonder, tweaking the sensibilities of jazz purists and even occasionally unnerving his sidemen. But Rollins's own hearty compositions played an equally critical role in his success. These were usually simple blowing pieces, favored not for their sophistication or their experimental implications but simply because they were inviting springboards for soloing.

To this day, many of Rollins's tunes ("St. Thomas," "Pent Up House," "Doxy," "Sonnymoon for Two," "Airegin," "Oleo") remain standard fare at jazz jam sessions for this very reason. Especially refreshing are the calypso-inflected pieces, etudes in foot tapping and finger snapping such as "St. Thomas" and "Don't Stop the Carnival," which eventually became Rollins trademarks. But even when Rollins tried his hand, uncharacteristically, at a longer form, as in his *Freedom Suite*, the performance still retained the feel and flow of a spontaneous jam. In an age when jazz was becoming increasingly self-conscious and wedded to various ideologies, Rollins showed that it was still possible to create great works simply by abandoning himself to the flow of the music, immersing himself in the magic of the moment.

Yet one should not minimize the cerebral aspect of his work. In an often-cited essay, Gunther Schuller analyzed Rollins's style of improvisation, calling attention to the tenorist's skill in constructing solos through the manipulation of simple musical motives. Rollins excelled in using these as thematic material—restating them, varying them, elaborating on them—a jazz equivalent of the development section in sonata form. Schuller's observation may have made the spontaneous flow of Rollins's creativity sound like the result of a pseudo-mathematical process. (And Schuller glossed over the fact that a similar claim could be made for many earlier jazz artists. Is there a better example of thematic development than King Oliver's solo on "Dipper Mouth Blues" from 1923?) Still, much truth lay at the heart of these observations. At a time when jazz solos were increasingly sounding like a discontinuous flow of scales and licks, Rollins built his improvisations the old-fashioned way, phrase by phrase. This gave them a solidity, a strength, much like a house built carefully, one brick at a time—alongside these edifices, the work of other, lesser talents, like the fairytale piglet's house, seemed mere palaces of straw, losing their shape after the first huff and puff. Even so, Rollins's reaction to Schuller was equivocal. "When I read that I was sort of taken aback, because I didn't know what I was doing," the tenorist later explained. "It made me self-conscious about playing. It took me a while to get over that."[16] This may well be construed as a disavowal of Schuller's thesis, but just as likely, it reveals how instinctive the whole process of thematic improvisation had become to Rollins.

Perhaps no jazz musician has ever had a more intense upbringing in the heart of the jazz world than Sonny Rollins. Born in New York on September 9, 1930, Rollins was always surrounded by world-class players. While still in his teens, and after only two years playing the sax, he spent idle hours rehearsing with Thelonious Monk. During his high school years, Rollins fronted a band with other like-minded youngsters: Jackie McLean, Art Taylor, and Kenny Drew—no typical student band, this. At age eighteen he participated in the classic Bud Powell's Modernists session for Blue Note, a date that could be pegged as the birth of the hard bop style. Other early performances and recordings find him alongside Charlie Parker, Miles Davis, the Modern Jazz Quartet, J. J. Johnson, and many other stars of the postwar jazz scene. In the mid-1950s, he was a member of the Clifford Brown–Max Roach Quintet, a unit that ranks, by any measure, among the most important working bands of the decade. Right before the breakup of that group, following trumpeter Brown's death, Rollins participated in another classic session: the "Tenor Madness" date where he matched wits with John Coltrane in a historic pairing. By the time Rollins began releasing his many classic recordings as a leader in the late 1950s, he could boast a curriculum vitae unsurpassed by any of his contemporaries in the jazz world.

Flourishing in these settings would, one might think, dispel any self-doubts Rollins might have had. Yet they apparently had the opposite effect, leaving a permanent undercurrent of self-criticism and dissatisfaction below Rollins's calm exterior. Fans have grown familiar with this attitude—few were surprised when Rollins decided not to release the recording of his celebrated 2007 Carnegie Hall concert, which, despite rave reviews, did not live up to his own expectations. This was simply the tenorist's standard *modus operandi*, as demonstrated over the course of a career clouded by retracings, temporary retirements, and disappearances from the scene for practice and self-assessment. A half-century before the nixed Carnegie Hall album, Schuller's essay had caused Rollins even greater anxiety as he tried to live up to its theoretical implications. Similarly, the advent of Ornette Coleman and free jazz helped to spur another period of introspection. However, Rollins's most famous sabbatical from the jazz scene, which lasted from August 1959 to November 1961, has taken on mythic proportions in the artist's biography. This period often found the famous jazz star strolling up and down the Williamsburg Bridge on many evenings, playing his horn for the astonished passersby.

At the time of his departure, Rollins was at the peak of his fame. During the previous four years he had put together a remarkable body of work. A series of tenacious trio and quartet recordings were at the core of his oeuvre. No tenorist has ever played better when accompanied simply by bass and drums, as Rollins's work from this period makes clear: *Way Out West*, featuring him with Ray Brown and Shelly Manne from March 1957; the seminal trio recordings from a November 1957 date at the Village Vanguard; and *Freedom Suite* with Oscar Pettiford and Max Roach from the following February. Among the quartet projects, *Worktime* from December 1955 stands out as a major statement, perhaps Rollins's finest to that point in his career. This was followed by the even more lauded *Saxophone Colossus* from June 1956, and *The Sound of Sonny*, with pianist Sonny Clark, made one year later. These efforts, as well as his various guest appearances with other artists, such as the aforementioned showdown with Coltrane, made it clear that Rollins ranked among the premier improvisers of his generation.

Yet Rollins, as we have noted, was dissatisfied. He went into seclusion for over two years, practicing, refining his craft, reading, thinking. His return was eagerly anticipated by jazz fans—especially given the superheated atmosphere of the jazz world circa 1960. New sounds were in the air. At no time in the history of jazz music had the mandate to progress been felt so pervasively by the leading players. At times it seemed as if progressivism were the only aesthetic measure that really counted for many critics and some fans at this juncture in the music's evolution. Rollins felt these pressures yet ultimately reacted with ambivalence. When he returned, Rollins may have been a changed man—during his sabbatical he had become a Rosicrucian, studied philosophy, exercised, practiced—but his music was strikingly unchanged, disappointing those who felt that Rollins, like Coltrane and Coleman, would create a totally different sound. His comeback album, *The Bridge*, was a solid effort, but found Rollins again playing jazz standards with a fairly traditional combo. The main change here was the addition of guitarist Jim Hall, a subtle accompanist and inspired soloist, but hardly the "new thing" in jazz.

Post-1960, Rollins's career tended to display tentative forays into the latest trend, followed inevitably by a return to more familiar ground. For a time, Rollins hired some musicians associated with Ornette Coleman, but never made the full plunge into "freedom" music. Later recordings found him flirting with jazz-rock fusion but never assimilating it fully either. When interest in acoustic jazz increased in the 1970s, Rollins obliged by joining McCoy Tyner, Ron Carter, and Al Foster for a much-publicized concert tour and recording. But this, too, proved to be a passing phase. In general, latter-day Rollins's finest moments came in mainstream settings of this sort, where he was challenged by formidable peers—a duet with Tyner, a sax battle with Branford Marsalis, a recording with Tommy Flanagan and Jack DeJohnette—or playing without a band, as on *The Solo Album* from 1985, rather than fronting his often merely adequate working combo.

Rollins's various retirements, reclusions, and reconsiderations could stand as symbolic of the whole era. Jazz was in a period of transition, of self-examination, of fragmentation into different schools. The music's modernist tradition, which Rollins epitomized, could no longer simply be taken for granted. Its assumptions—about harmony, melody, rhythm, song structure, instrumentation, and perhaps even more about the social role of jazz music—were constantly being questioned and increasingly found wanting by the more revolutionary musicians of the younger generation. Rollins's self-doubts were in many ways the same anxieties felt by his whole generation as it struggled to clear a path through this seeming pandemonium. Some looked for even more, for a transfiguring movement, the *next* new thing, that would draw these fragments back together into a new coherence. Others, less sanguine, felt that there would be no more towering figures, titans of the caliber of Armstrong, Ellington, Goodman, or Parker, who could define a whole age, give impetus to an entire generation. Instead jazz, it seemed, was condemned to—or was it blessed by?—a pluralism, in which "next new things" would come and go with amazing alacrity.

HARD BOP, POSTBOP, AND SOUL JAZZ

In the fall of 1953, Max Roach moved to California to replace Shelly Manne as drummer with the Lighthouse All-Stars. This sideman stint lasted only a few months before promoter Gene Norman approached Roach about leading his own band at the California Club. Roach had occasionally taken top billing on the marquee in the past, but by his own admission had never pursued bandleading with serious intent. The Norman proposal, however, spurred Roach to form a working quintet, one that not only would signal a turning point in the drummer's career but, even more, would stand out as arguably the most influential jazz unit of the early 1950s.

Roach invited the young trumpeter Clifford Brown to serve as co-leader. Brown had made his first recordings, as a member of a rhythm-and-blues band, only two years before, but was already being heralded by jazz insiders as a major talent. Born in Wilmington, Delaware, on October 30, 1930, Brown had played the bugle as a youngster, and began trumpet lessons at age twelve. His studies, under the guidance of influential Wilmington jazz educator Robert Lowery, emphasized ear training and basic trumpet technique. For a time, Brown attended Delaware State College as a math major, but by his late teens had decided on a career in jazz. A 1950 car accident—eerily foreshadowing his later death—sidelined Brown for almost a year, but in the interim he practiced the piano and expanded his knowledge of harmony.

Brown's musical education, thus described, may seem haphazard, but the end result would have been the pride of Juilliard or Eastman. By the time of his emergence on the jazz scene in the mid-1950s, Brown had developed into a poised virtuoso. Perhaps he lacked Gillespie's range or Miles's inspired moodiness, but Brown's tone control, his "fat" sound (literally and metaphorically, given its source in Brown's chief inspiration, Fats Navarro), and flawless execution stood out even in a jazz world filled with hot young trumpeters. A quarter of a century before Wynton Marsalis straddled the jazz and classical fields, Brown showed a similar precocious talent. Had he been so inclined, Brown could have flourished as an interpreter of the classical repertoire for the trumpet. As it was, he successfully married concert-hall polish with the unbridled energy and creative impetus of modern jazz.

Brown's work with Roach built on this same combination. The rougher edges of bebop were rounded off with finesse. Composition and arrangement were emphasized. Even when playing standards, the band would usually add an interesting twist to their interpretation, as in the shifting meters of "I Get a Kick Out of You," "Love Is a Many-Splendored Thing," and "What Am I Here For." In other instances, the unison heads typical of bop would be replaced with counterpoint or harmonized trumpet and saxophone lines. Increasingly, medium tempos were favored, but when pieces were played very fast, the performances still sounded controlled and collected. Even Roach's most impassioned drum solos reflected a concern with compositional structure and subtle dynamic effects. A lyrical strain was always evident to some degree, but never obscured the prevalent influence of the blues. The music collected these divergent streams into a coherent style, one that still showed an underlying allegiance to the bebop tradition but was tempered by these other currents.

In time, this style would come to be known as hard bop. The Brown-Roach Quintet may not have been the originator of this sound: elements of it can be heard, for example, on the August 1949 Bud Powell combo session for Blue Note, in some of the early 1950s West Coast jazz combos (including the Lighthouse All-Star band Roach had just left), and in the work of two previous Brown employers, Tadd Dameron and Art Blakey. Nor did Brown and Roach explore all the implications of this style of jazz. Yet no group did more to give impetus to the hard-bop idiom than this seminal quintet. Over the next decade, this style would gradually gain acceptance as the dominant mainstream sound of modern jazz.

Even before leaving California, the Brown-Roach Quintet gave notice of its evolving approach to combo playing through a series of recordings made in Hollywood in early August 1954. Two Brown compositions destined to become jazz standards,

"Joy Spring" and "Daahoud," were given definitive performances, graced by exceptional trumpet solos, as was Duke Jordan's "Jordu." "Delilah" and "Parisian Thoroughfare," from the same sessions, further highlighted the thoughtfully arranged, medium-tempo sound that would become widely imitated by later hard-bop ensembles. The following February, the band made additional recordings in New York, producing a number of memorable sides including "Sandu," a gospel-tinged piece that anticipated the later "soul" jazz side of the hard-bop movement. "The Blues Walk," from the same period, showcased the more assertive side of the combo in a fiery performance climaxed by a dazzling series of "chase" choruses that pitted Brown and saxophonist Harold Land against one another. Soon after this recording, Land was replaced by the young Sonny Rollins, who was featured prominently on the band's 1956 recordings at Basin Street in New York. This period also witnessed the growing maturity of the quintet's pianist Richie Powell (brother of Bud Powell), who contributed two compositions to the band's repertoire—"Powell's Prances" and "Time"—built on moody minor key themes (also destined to become a trademark of the hard-bop style).

The Brown-Roach Quintet would last little more than two years. In June 1956, Brown was killed in a late-night automobile accident on the Pennsylvania Turnpike, along with pianist Powell and Powell's wife Nancy. Brown's early demise was an ironic tragedy. He was one of the few major modern jazz musicians of the period who had avoided the indignities of substance abuse, who offered younger musicians a worthwhile role model not only in his musicianship but equally in his mature offstage demeanor. If any artist of this generation seemed destined for a long and productive jazz career, it was Clifford Brown—yet he was dead at age twenty-five.

After a time, Roach regrouped, forming a quintet with trumpeter Kenny Dorham; in the wake of Dorham's departure the drummer employed Booker Little, another trumpeter fated to die in his twenties. Although these were solid units, Roach's musical interests were increasingly taking him further afield from the hard-bop style. For the most part, his strongest later works would look elsewhere for inspiration: some would incorporate elements of free jazz, or explore different aspects of percussion music, or feature vocal work (often provided by Abbey Lincoln, his wife from 1962 to 1970), or even embrace hip-hop. Some fans were shocked when he laid down tracks for rapper Fab 5 Freddy—could this be the same drummer who played with Bird on Fifty-second Street?—but anyone who had followed the career of this forward-looking percussionist knew that Roach took delight in expanding his own musical horizons. In other instances, he would put his rhythmic stamp on symphonic concerts, dance performances, gospel singing, or theater productions. Roach was also an early and ardent supporter of the civil rights movement, an advocacy that influenced his music. "Two theories exist," he told an interviewer in the early 1970s. "One is that art is for the sake of art, which is true. The other theory, which is also true, is that the artist is like a secretary. . . . He keeps a record of his time, so to speak. . . . My music tries to say how I really feel, and I hope it mirrors in some way how black people feel in the United States."[17]

It would be left to another modern jazz drummer to push the hard-bop style to the next level. Born and raised in Pittsburgh, Art Blakey was already working in the local steel mills at age fourteen. Music provided an escape from this grueling day-to-day labor. In the evenings, Blakey would play piano at local venues—he had received a few lessons and showed a ready knack for music. When a young Erroll Garner joined the band, Blakey switched to drums. (Was there a lingering influence? As a percussionist, Blakey came to delight in sudden dynamic shifts and odd interjections, strikingly similar to Garner's idiosyncratic approach to the piano.) In 1939, Blakey joined Fletcher Henderson and later worked with Mary Lou Williams before getting his first taste of modern jazz as drummer with Billy Eckstine's bop-oriented big band. Here Blakey crossed paths with Gillespie, Parker, and a host of other forward-looking young musicians. Blakey revealed his affinity for the new music, forging a crisp, driving drum sound marked by a ferocious cymbal attack and punctuated unpredictably by swelling crescendos, brash rolls, and careening bombs. Blakey would later serve as a sideman on a number of important modern jazz recording sessions, including many of Thelonious Monk's finest early efforts. In the late 1940s, Blakey also led a large band and a smaller combo under the name Jazz Messengers. In the mid-1950s, he revived the name with a co-op quintet that featured pianist Horace Silver and a front line of trumpeter Kenny Dorham and tenor saxophonist Hank Mobley. The Jazz Messengers, in various formats, would remain a major force in the jazz world for the next thirty years. In the process, it served also as a finishing school for up-and-coming jazz stars, many of whom would become important bandleaders in their own right.

Blakey's early efforts with Silver kept faithful to the bebop model. But in early 1955, the Messengers embarked on a new direction with their recording of "The Preacher," a funky blues piece infused with elements of gospel music. This recording was immensely popular and widely imitated by later hard-bop bands. The time was ripe for this return to the roots. Rhythm and blues and the gospel sounds of the sanctified church were starting to exert a powerful influence on American popular music. Singers as ostensibly different as Mahalia Jackson and Ray Charles were drawing on these same traditions in pursuing their sharply contrasting sacred and secular agendas. A new generation of Chicago blues artists, such as Muddy Waters and Howlin' Wolf, was similarly showing that traditional sounds could revitalize contemporary musical styles, and over the next few years rock and roll would incorporate many of these same ingredients into a brusque, clangorous approach whose impact still reverberates. The jazz idiom also benefited from a return to these first principles of African American music—at least for a time. Eventually, these funky and soulful sounds would become stale clichés in the jazz world, but for a period in the 1950s their simpler attitudes—grooving two-steps, guttural backbeats, insistent melody lines drenched with blues notes—offered a healthy alternative to the more cerebral and aggressive strands of modern jazz.

Silver and Blakey parted ways in 1956, with the drummer retaining the Jazz Messengers name for his band, while the pianist continued working with Mobley. Both Blakey and Silver relied on the hard-bop sound in their combos, at times drawing on the "down home" approach exemplified by "The Preacher" but also refusing to be limited by it. Silver is often described as a key exponent of this funk-inflected style, yet his major compositions reveal, in fact, a refreshing diversity. These efforts include explorations of 6/8 rhythms ("Señor Blues"), Caribbean-Latin hybrids ("Song for My Father"), medium-tempo jaunts ("Silver Serenade"), free-spirited romps ("Nutville"), jazz waltzes ("Pretty Eyes"), and serene ballads ("Peace"). The unifying factor in these works is not so much Silver's funkiness, but rather the sharp focus of his musical vision. His sound is uncluttered. His melodies are succinct and memorable. The rhythms are propulsive without being overbearing. The obsession with virtuosity, so characteristic of bebop, is almost entirely absent and never missed.

Art Blakey also worked to broaden the scope of hard bop. But with Blakey, much of the evolution in his music was driven by changes in the personnel of the Jazz Messengers. After separating from Silver, Blakey explored a wide range of possibilities. In 1957 alone, Blakey led sessions for eight different record labels. Around this time he renewed his musical relationship with Thelonious Monk; put together a percussion ensemble; led a fifteen-piece big band; spearheaded small combos that featured, among others, Jackie McLean, Johnny Griffin, and Donald Byrd; and, with the Messengers, even gave the movement a flagship album with his *Hard Bop* release. For a period, he relied heavily on writers outside his band, enlisting the services of Duke Jordan, Mal Waldron, and Jimmy Heath. But in time Blakey realized that his greatest successes came through nurturing the talents around him, as composers as well as players. The band's 1958 Blue Note release *Moanin'* mesmerized listeners with pianist Bobby Timmons's title track—which evoked church music and early African American call-and-response refrains—as well as with "Blues March" and "Along Came Betty" by Messenger saxophonist Benny Golson. *Moanin'* remains one of the defining statements of the hard-bop idiom, largely because of Blakey's willingness to let his sidemen take the lead in crafting the music.

This unit of the Messengers also benefited from the gritty contributions of Lee Morgan, an impassioned improviser and, in many ways, the quintessential hard-bop trumpeter. There was no brass player better able to extract the maximum amount of emotional energy from the bluesy minor-key groove numbers that characterized the new sound. A Philadelphia native, Morgan had honed his skills in the working-class taverns and clubs of his hometown before joining Dizzy Gillespie's big band while still in his teens. Originally under the sway of Clifford Brown, Morgan came to develop a more personal style that mixed pungent short phrases with swinging longer lines and repeated figures. After leaving Blakey in 1961, Morgan recorded extensively as a leader for the Blue Note label and achieved a major success with his 1963 staccato funk outing "The Sidewinder," which eventually reached number twenty-five on the *Billboard* chart. Morgan spent much of the rest of his career trying to recreate this winning formula, although he was also capable of probing, less jukebox-friendly artistic statements, such as *Search for the New Land*, an exquisite release recorded only a few weeks after "The Sidewinder." One of the most spirited improvisers of his generation, Morgan was killed in 1972 between sets at a Lower East Side nightclub, shot with a pistol by a jealous lover.

Benny Golson left the Messengers in 1959—prodded in part by Blakey's expressed distaste for the overly arranged drum parts on his charts—and formed the Jazztet, a combo that he led with Art Farmer. This ensemble, which for a brief period chal-lenged the Messengers as the preeminent hard-bop band of the day, lasted until 1962. Its work, superbly realized on the 1960 release *Meet the Jazztet*, relied heavily on Golson's writing. This music represented a different facet of the hard-bop sound, less funky, more song-oriented, and in many ways modeled on the work of Golson's former employer Tadd Dameron. In this regard, Golson ranks among a handful of jazz composers (among them Jimmy Heath, Gigi Gryce, Oliver Nelson, and Quincy Jones) whose stately and uncluttered style, reflecting firm roots in the Swing Era and stylistic affinities with the West Coast sound, has tended to be overshadowed by the more extroverted efforts that dominated the jazz world during these transition years. In time, many of these players gravitated to work as composer-arrangers, often outside the context of jazz music.

After Golson's departure, Blakey hired tenorist Hank Mobley for a spell, recording a stirring nightclub performance under the title *At the Jazz Corner of the World* during this period. The addition of saxophonist Wayne Shorter later in the year initiated a new expansion in the scope of the band, which was solidified by the arrival of trumpeter Freddie Hubbard and pianist Cedar Walton in 1961. Shorter's elliptical manner of improvising and composing would come to exert a decisive influence on the Messengers, signaling a break with the rhythm-and-blues orienta-tion of the Morgan-Timmons-Golson unit. A Newark, New Jersey, native who studied fine arts during his adolescence and early teens, Shorter did not take up music until age sixteen. The work of his mature years would retain the painter's singular vision and sensitivity to subtle shadings: indeed, many of Shorter's finest pieces could be described as tone poems evoking mental vistas. "I was thinking of misty landscapes with wild flowers and strange, dimly-seen shapes," was Shorter's explanation of his masterful *Speak No Evil* recording,[18] but this description would be equally appropriate in characterizing many of the saxophonist's other works. After high school, Shorter worked for a year in the Singer sewing machine factory, saving the money he needed to attend New York University as a music major. While in the army, Shorter continued to visit Manhattan on weekend passes, where he was befriended by John Coltrane, who would become a role model for the younger player. In time, Shorter would develop a deeply personal take on Coltrane's approach, using more space and adding a languorous, off-centered manner of phrasing wholly his own.

The advent of Freddie Hubbard to the band represented a less radical break with the past. Hubbard shared many similarities with his predecessor Morgan. Like Morgan, his trumpet playing was fiery, propelled by insistent rhythms, but also soft-ened by a warm, full tone. Hubbard made greater use of the lyrical potential of the instrument, developing into a stellar ballad player, and offered a slightly more pol-ished alternative to the sometimes rough-and-tumble Morgan. But he built his rep-utation on his nonpareil mastery of medium and fast tempos, where he stood out as an intimidating player you wouldn't want to battle at a jam session. An outstanding improviser with solid technique, Hubbard was an ideal choice for Blakey. Like many other Indianapolis-born jazz musicians (such as Wes Montgomery, Buddy Montgomery, Carl Perkins, and Leroy Vinnegar), Hubbard showed an uncanny natural feel for the music. How did he learn to play the trumpet? "I just picked it up and started playing," he once explained to an interviewer.[19]

In 1958, Hubbard came to New York, where he gigged with Sonny Rollins, Quincy Jones, Philly Joe Jones, and J. J. Johnson before joining the Messengers. Hubbard fit comfortably into the band's hard-bop approach, but his musical aspirations also took him on productive detours into other styles. Even before joining Blakey, he had participated on Ornette Coleman's *Free Jazz* session, one of the most adventurous recording projects of the period, and he also shows up as sideman on albums by John Coltrane, Eric Dolphy, Randy Weston, and Oliver Nelson. His leader dates for Blue Note from the 1960s, including *Hub-Tones* and *Ready for Freddie*, are outstanding examples of the hard-bop style. His ensuing work for the CTI label tended to be a slicker product, incorporating some elements of the jazz-rock fusion idiom; but the best of these projects, most notably *Red Clay* from 1970 and *First Light* from 1972, were effective vehicles for the trumpeter. The next decade found Hubbard vacillating between mainstream jazz and funk-pop offerings of varying quality (some of them later repudiated by Hubbard himself). He returned to a more straight-ahead style in the 1980s, and although he still commanded respect as a major soloist, his accomplishments tended to be obscured by the rising stars of Woody Shaw, Wynton Marsalis, and Terence Blanchard. An injury to his lip in 1992, complicated by an infection, came close to ending his career. Hubbard continued to record and perform until his death in 2008, and though his late-period work is several steps below the masterful output of his earlier years, his legacy is secure as one of the most formidable trumpeters in the history of the music.

With Hubbard and Shorter fronting the band, Blakey electrified audiences and produced a series of outstanding recordings, including *Caravan*, *Kyoto*, *Three Blind Mice*, and *Ugetsu*. Already a solid soloist, Shorter blossomed as a composer during his Blakey years. "This is for Albert," "Lester Left Town," "Children of the Night," and other Shorter contributions bespoke a far greater sophistication than the rhythm-and-blues-influenced numbers that had dominated Blakey's late 1950s repertoire. Hubbard's extroverted improvisations served as an attractive foil for Shorter's moody lines, while the addition of trombonist Curtis Fuller completed a potent horn triumvirate that gave depth to the Messengers' sound. Until the saxophonist's departure to join the Miles Davis Quintet in September 1964, this edition of the Messengers stood out as the most captivating mainstream jazz combo of its day. Over fifteen years would elapse before a Blakey band, then bolstered by the presence of Wynton and Branford Marsalis, would cause such a stir on the jazz scene.

Horace Silver's mid-1960s combo might have challenged Blakey's supremacy in the hard-bop idiom, if only it had lasted longer. Saxophonist Joe Henderson and trumpeter Woody Shaw, two of the most promising younger jazz talents of the day, fronted this edition of Silver's band, but unfortunately only one studio project, *The Cape Verdean Blues*, captured this lineup in action. Henderson joined the group in 1964, a few months before Shaw's arrival in the band, and participated on Silver's notable *Song for My Father* date. This release marked a critical juncture in Silver's development as a composer, oddly inspired by a return to the Cape Verdean–Portuguese musical roots of his father—a tradition Silver had long dismissed.

"My dad, through the years, had always said to me, 'Why don't you take some of this Portuguese folk music and put it into jazz?' I never could see it. To me it always seemed corny."[20] But a trip to Rio de Janeiro, where the inviting sounds of bossa nova were in the air, inspired Silver to attempt just such a Cape Verdean–jazz fusion. The resulting album became one of the biggest-selling releases in the history of the Blue Note label. Silver's follow-up project, *The Cape Verdean Blues*, built on this same foundation and featured, in addition to Henderson and Shaw, guest artist J. J. Johnson. Shaw had already performed and recorded with Eric Dolphy, whose influence was reflected in the trumpeter's use of wide intervals and his insistence on pushing harmonic structures to their breaking point. Shaw did this through the use of dissonances and melodic patterns that stretched the underlying chord changes and occasionally danced on the dividing line between tonal and atonal improvisation. Saxophonist Henderson was equally adept at this type of deconstructive phraseology. The title of his Blue Note release *In 'n Out* could serve as an apt description of Henderson's approach, in which his sandpaper sax lines insistently rub away at the hard-bop structures undergirding the music.

Shaw's later career was defined by deferred gratification amid many setbacks. The trumpeter did not receive widespread recognition in jazz circles until the late 1970s, when he made a series of celebrated recordings for the CBS label. Here his sinewy melodic lines often superimposed jagged melodic fragments and modal stop-and-start phrases, spiced with a heavy dose of fourths, on top of conventional chord structures. This was an increasingly faddish sound of the period—if intervals were fashions, the perfect fourth would have been the jazz equivalent of the leisure suit during the late 1970s—but no horn player employed this technique with more verve and sheer energy than Shaw. And no jazz trumpeter of the day seemed to have a brighter future. Yet by the early 1980s, Shaw's prominence was abruptly eclipsed by the arrival of Wynton Marsalis, who not only was quickly tagged as the new young lion of the trumpet, but also succeeded Shaw as the major focus of jazz promotion efforts at CBS Records. Still other events conspired to derail Shaw's career: a broken relationship, depression, substance abuse, failing eyesight. A career that looked as though it would take off through the stratosphere now faltered, and finally came crashing down when Shaw lost his arm in a mysterious 1988 fall in the path of a New York subway train. This accident—if it was, in fact, an accident—was followed by a number of setbacks during the ensuing hospitalization, which led to the trumpeter's death from kidney failure ten weeks later.

Henderson's career, in contrast, revealed a gradual ascendancy, a pilgrim's progress marked by a steady accumulation of good works with few lapses. He recorded extensively for Blue Note in the mid-1960s, both as a leader—resulting in major efforts such as *In 'n Out, Inner Urge, Mode for Joe,* and *The Kicker*—and as a sideman. In the late 1960s and early 1970s, Henderson undertook a series of gigs with such high-profile bands as Miles Davis's, Herbie Hancock's, and Blood, Sweat and Tears. During this same period, Henderson continued to evolve as a bandleader, a process documented on a number of solid recordings for the Milestone label. These were laudable achievements, but in retrospect only a preamble to Henderson's widespread beatification, as he approached his fiftieth birthday, as a leading tenor of the times. This second phase in Henderson's career was kicked off by the magisterial *State of the Tenor* releases on Blue Note, recorded live with a trio at the Village Vanguard in 1985. Such an effort demanded—and survived—comparison with Rollins's classic trio project (same label, same club, same instruments, same multivolume format) from 1957. In the 1990s, Henderson enjoyed the greatest critical success—and record sales—of his career, with a series of theme albums celebrating Billy Strayhorn, Miles Davis, and Antonio Carlos Jobim. Possessed of a powerful tenor voice, Henderson skillfully adapted the leading influences of his formative years into a vehement personal style. The Coltrane element is reflected most clearly on early Blue Note recordings where Henderson is accompanied by McCoy Tyner and Elvin Jones; the Rollins influence comes more to the fore in his mid-career works, especially the various trio projects; and at times a wistful Getz-inspired warmth is evident on Henderson's 1990s projects, particularly when the tenorist interprets Strayhorn's "Blood Count" or Jobim's bossa nova compositions.

Although he appeared on some of the biggest-selling recordings in the history of the Blue Note label (*Song for My Father*, *The Sidewinder*), Henderson never became mesmerized, as did many of his contemporaries, by the commercial potential of soul and funk-oriented music. In this regard, Henderson was something of an exception on the Blue Note roster. Alfred Lion, founder and manager of the Blue Note label, had originally objected to the release of Silver's "The Preacher," the piece that established this crossover sound. But skyrocketing sales made Lion a true believer, and in time he was aggressively promoting an assortment of similar recordings. Other labels followed suit, propelling a whole cadre of musicians, of greater and lesser talent, to relative fame (by jazz standards) supported by airplay, jukebox spins, and brisk record sales. Many critics dismissed this "soul jazz" style out of hand, but listeners responded with enthusiasm, boosting the careers of a new crop of jazz stars, including Jimmy Smith, Ramsey Lewis, Cannonball Adderley, Jimmy McGriff, Brother Jack McDuff, Eddie Harris, Ray Bryant, Richard "Groove" Holmes, Wes Montgomery, Les McCann, Lou Donaldson, Stanley Turrentine, and others.

This style drew on a number of historical antecedents. The burgeoning rhythm-and-blues movement of the late 1940s and 1950s profoundly influenced the soul jazz players, as did (tracing the sound even farther back) the blues-drenched Kansas City and Texas tenor traditions. The crowd-pleasing antics of battling sax players, a jazz staple from the 1950s—celebrated by Gordon and Gray, Ammons and Stitt, Cohn and Sims, even Coltrane and Rollins—also anticipated this later idiom. (The successful relaunching of the battling tenors format during the heyday of soul jazz, under the capable hands of Eddie "Lockjaw" Davis and Johnny Griffin, was no coincidence. It demonstrated how close this time-honored approach was to the newer style.) Bits and pieces of other African American idioms were further tributaries flowing into this hybrid music: big band riffs, urban blues, call-and-response forms, and gospel music, among others.

Soul jazz found its own voice most clearly in the electronically produced tones of the Hammond B-3 organ. The B-3's rough-and-ready, distorted sounds—in theory, they were intended to emulate "real" instruments, but in practice were *sui generis*—captured the essence of the jazz sensibility, exciting audiences with their unabashed vigor, much as King Oliver's "dirty" cornet playing had done a generation earlier. Of course, the organ had appeared previously in jazz, mostly at the hands of keyboardists who usually played piano, such as Fats Waller and Count Basie. And it had always figured prominently in African American sacred music. But the secularization of the organ in the jazz world did not gain momentum until the 1950s. Eddie "Lockjaw" Davis's 1951 recording with Bill Doggett was a pioneering effort in popularizing the tenor-and-organ combination. Around this same time, Wild Bill Davis established an organ trio that would also prove influential. But it was not until the arrival of Jimmy Smith on the jazz scene in the mid-1950s that the Hammond organ achieved wide recognition as a legitimate jazz instrument. In time, a legion of other keyboardists followed Smith's example and, by the close of the decade, the Hammond organ was firmly established as a mainstay of soul jazz.

Smith had studied piano as a child and later learned to play the string bass. But around 1953, Wild Bill Davis's work inspired him to devote his energies to the organ. In 1955, Smith, accompanied only by guitar and drums, opened in Atlantic City and soon caused a sensation with his passionate performances: stretching out for forty choruses on "Sweet Georgia Brown," propelling the band with driving bass lines played on the foot pedals of the organ, exploiting the Hammond's full range of wails, buzzes, groans, shouts, honks, and screams. Within months, Smith was gigging in New York, where he caught the attention of Alfred Lion. Over the next several years, Smith would undertake dozens of sessions for Blue Note and establish himself as one of the label's biggest-selling artists. Jukebox singles and radio airplay helped build his career, but Smith frequently ignored the demands of these outlets, recording lengthy works that could never fit on the side of a 45-rpm record. Classic Smith performances, such as "The Champ" and "Back at the Chicken Shack," might last eight minutes or more, while Smith's "The Sermon" clocked in at twenty minutes and eleven seconds of gut-wrenching blues. Yet the records sold despite (or perhaps because of) their length. The unrelenting intensity and powerful drive of the music were hypnotic, a soul jazz anticipation of John Coltrane's marathon performances, which audiences would find similarly compelling a few years later.

By the late 1950s and early 1960s, a host of other jazz organists were plowing this same field, promoting a sound that soon would be in danger of becoming a stale cliché. Before long, sales of tenor-and-organ and organ trio records would plummet, and eventually the Hammond B-3 would be taken off the market, replaced in the public's imagination by the more versatile (but perhaps colder) sounds of "synthesized" music. But during these glory years of the Hammond B-3, audiences could enjoy the work of Jimmy McGriff, Brother Jack McDuff, Shirley Scott, Richard "Groove" Holmes, Johnny "Hammond" Smith, Charles Earland, and other masters of the instrument.

Without the sterling example of Larry Young, one might have thought that the possibilities of the Hammond organ had been exhausted by the mid-1960s. Although Young was well schooled in the soul jazz idiom, he came to reject the narrow funk and blues orientation of most Hammond players. Over the next several years, Young would record a series of important releases for Blue Note that incorporated modal phrasing and denser harmonies, and drew inspiration from John Coltrane, McCoy

Tyner, free jazz, even hard rock. He would later record with Miles Davis on the influential *Bitches Brew* release, as well as with fellow Davis sidemen John McLaughlin and Tony Williams. His 1970s work with them, recorded under the band name Lifetime, was one of the most promising developments of the jazz-rock fusion movement, although it never achieved the commercial success that many lesser fusion bands enjoyed. This most forward-looking exponent of the Hammond organ, perhaps its final major innovator, was only thirty-eight years old when he died in 1978, the victim of an improperly treated stomach ailment.

The jazz organ would never again match the level of popularity it achieved during the soul jazz years, yet—strange to say—the many advances in synthesizer and programming technology failed to make this comparatively primitive instrument obsolete. Even in the new millennium, the organ is the most popular jazz keyboard outside of the piano, attracting a cadre of dedicated fans and world-class exponents. The glory days of the Hammond B-3 were all but over by the time Joey DeFrancesco was born, in 1971, but he has completely assimilated the tradition of Jimmy Smith and other predecessors, and has introduced new generations of fans to its persuasive sounds via relentless touring, amounting to around two hundred nights on the road in any given year, and more than two dozen recordings as a leader. DeFrancesco has done more than anyone to keep the organ in a prominent position in the jazz world during the new millennium, but he is far from a lone evangelist. A talented cohort of performers—including Gary Versace, Sam Yahel, and John Medeski—has expanded the vocabulary and expressive range of the instrument and moved it beyond the soul jazz clichés of the past.

The electric guitar also played a key role in the soul jazz idiom, sometimes working in tandem with the Hammond organ. This too would quickly become a hackneyed sound, although major players such as Kenny Burrell and Grant Green proved capable of important recordings that transcended the form's limitations. Burrell's 1963 *Midnight Blue* is a classic hard-bop release, while his *Guitar Forms* project with Gil Evans, from the following year, less easy to categorize, is a major milestone by almost any measure. Grant Green's *Matador*, recorded in 1964 but not released for fifteen years, finds the bandleader in the inspirational company of Elvin Jones and McCoy Tyner, then anchoring John Coltrane's rhythm section, while Green's collaborations with pianist Sonny Clark from the early 1960s represent one of the most inspired pairings of piano and guitar in the hard-bop oeuvre. Yet of this generation of guitarists, Wes Montgomery stood out as the most skillful in combining commercial appeal with jazz street cred. An incisive soloist with an unsurpassed gift for melodic improvisation, Montgomery was an ideal candidate for crossover success as a pop jazz star. His recordings cover a wide gamut—from straight-ahead to soul jazz to mood music—but his singular talent gave even the most blatantly commercial efforts a stamp of artistry.

Born in Indianapolis in 1923, Wes was a member of a musical family that also included bassist Monk Montgomery and pianist/vibraphonist Buddy Montgomery. Despite a late start—he did not begin playing the guitar until he was almost twenty years old—and a lack of formal training, Wes quickly developed into a distinctive stylist and a quirky but exquisite improviser. He never made much traction in learning to read music, or even chord symbols, but this hardly hindered his progress. Within months, Wes was working on gigs with his brothers and other local musicians. A reluctant traveler, Montgomery went on the road with Lionel Hampton in the late 1940s, but returned to Indianapolis in 1950 where he raised a family, worked by day in a radio factory, and performed at night.

Montgomery's career might well have ended in obscurity in this setting. However, an enthusiastic recommendation by Cannonball Adderley led to the Riverside label's signing Montgomery in 1959. Under the direction of producer Orrin Keepnews, Montgomery recorded extensively over the next several years in jazz combo settings with top-quality sidemen, creating a number of milestone performances, including "Four on Six," "West Coast Blues," and "Besame Mucho." A modest man, with recurring doubts about his self-taught technique, Montgomery ultimately made a virtue out of his unconventional methods of playing the guitar. Whether through necessity or choice, he pared down the guitar vocabulary of the bebop years, replacing the convoluted, note-filled phrases of the post-Christian period with taut, uncluttered solos. Using his thumb instead of a pick, Montgomery produced a vibrant, singing tone on the instrument, reinforced by his frequent use of octave melody lines. Montgomery's later work, produced by Creed Taylor, found his playing increasingly featured in lackluster settings with syrupy strings. By the time of his final projects with the A&M label, Montgomery was relegated to playing cover versions of Beatles songs and other pop/rock tunes. But even these recordings were not without their moments, and they had at least the benefit of broadening Montgomery's audience—indeed, Montgomery's *A Day in the Life* release became the biggest-selling jazz record of 1967. The guitarist did not live long enough to enjoy the full benefits of this success. The following year he succumbed to a heart attack at age forty-five.

As Montgomery's late-career switch to a more pop/rock-oriented format should make clear, the soul jazz idiom was showing its age by the late 1960s. For many years, the soul jazz players had managed to maintain a solid following among the black working class. But other musical styles were now on the rise, usurping this audience. The Motown sound, jazz-rock fusion, and other related idioms reflected a slicker, more contemporary facet of African American music. The 1970s saw the completion of this trend, with the urban market for soul jazz almost completely displaced by funk, disco, reggae, soul, and rock. Jazz devotees sometimes groused that this shift reflected a watering down of standards in black popular music. To some degree, this may have been true. But what these critics missed was that the most talented artists in these new styles—Stevie Wonder, Jimi Hendrix, Bob Marley, James Brown, Marvin Gaye, Sly Stone, Minnie Riperton, Bill Withers, Earth, Wind & Fire, and others—were offering listeners a body of music that was, for the most part, fresher and more creative than the increasingly predictable soul jazz regurgitations of gutbucket blues and organ-and-tenor groove tunes.

On a broader level, the entire hard-bop movement was similarly in danger of running out of steam. By 1960, hard bop, in the opinion of historian James Lincoln Collier, "had come to a dead end." Amiri Baraka, viewing the music from a much different perspective than Collier, reached essentially the same conclusion in his book *Blues People*: hard bop, "sagging under its own weight, had just about destroyed itself" by the close of the 1950s. It had become "a self-conscious celebration of cliché, and an actual debilitation of the most impressive ideas to come out of bebop."[21] The ideological distance between these two critics can be gauged by the fact that Collier follows his denunciation of hard bop by praising the superiority of the Dixieland revival, while Jones's critique is in the context of a paean to free jazz. The fact that they could agree on the degraded state of hard bop, post-1960, is revealing. There may have been debates about the line of succession, but many concurred that the old king was dead.

Yet both critics go too far. As we have seen, Blakey and Silver—the two main protagonists in the birth of hard bop—led some of their finest bands during the 1960s. Blue Note, the label most responsible for promoting the style, refused to be limited by their customers' preconceived notions about the so-called "Blue Note sound": during this decade, the label released iconoclastic projects such as Cecil Taylor's *Unit Structures*, Eric Dolphy's *Out to Lunch*, and Ornette Coleman's *Love Call*. Most listeners would have had trouble linking these projects to the traditional Blakey-Silver approach, but other, less radical Blue Note releases showed that there could be a meeting point between hard bop and the avant-garde. Important projects such as Andrew Hill's *Point of Departure*, Bobby Hutcherson's *Dialogue*, and Jackie McLean's *Let Freedom Ring* were anything but drab repetitions of old hard-bop formulas. A host of other Blue Note projects by Herbie Hancock, Joe Henderson, Lee Morgan, Wayne Shorter, Sam Rivers, and others also made it clear that this idiom was far from exhausted.

Anyone who doubted that hard-bop stylings could adapt and evolve during the 1960s need merely listen to pianist Andrew Hill's 1960s recordings for Blue Note. Few fans did so at the time—and it is testimony to the label's commitment to this artist that Blue Note continued to release new music by the pianist throughout the decade despite his poor sales. Hill, born in Chicago in 1931, drew on a wide range of influences at an early stage in his development, studying with mentors as diverse as Bill Russo and Paul Hindemith, and gigging with beboppers and rhythm-and-blues bands. Hill's mature work was a strange amalgamation, prickly and cerebral by turns, and not targeted at crossover airplay like so many other Blue Note releases from the period. At the time, his music was too "inside" to be embraced by the avant-garde, but too "difficult" to appeal to most soul jazz and hard-bop fans. Yet history has validated his importance: his hybrid of experimentalism and formalism, dissonance and tonality, above all his focus on pushing at the limits of musical structures while still respecting their value, have made Hill an influential role model for many later pianists. At the time of Hill's death in 2007, one could hear echoes of his work in leading younger-generation artists such as Jason Moran, Vijay Iyer, and Matthew Shipp.

Two preeminent jazz bandleaders of the era—Charles Mingus and Miles Davis— also drew inspiration from the hard-bop style, albeit transforming it in the process. Mingus's music during this period is especially interesting when viewed from the perspective of hard bop. He drew heavily on the same ingredients that had proven successful for Blakey and Silver: an appreciation for African American roots music such as gospel and blues; a zest for hard-swinging, often funky playing; a rigorous schooling in the bebop idiom; a renewed emphasis on formalism and the possibilities of jazz composition; and a determination to exploit the full expressive range of the traditional horns-plus-rhythm jazz combo. Despite these similarities, few critics of the period saw Mingus as part of the hard-bop school. Yet his mature musical explorations rarely ventured far afield from this ethos. Had Mingus recorded for Blue Note and drawn on the services of other musicians affiliated with that label, these links would have been more evident. As it stands, he is typically seen as a musician who defies category—more a gadfly, skilled at disrupting hegemonies rather than supporting the current trends in play. Mingus is remembered as a progressive who never really embraced the freedom principle and a traditionalist who constantly tinkered with and subverted the legacies of the past. Yet for all these contradictions, his ouevre has stood the test of time and has grown in influence while others more easy to pigeonhole have faded from view.

This convergence of conflicting influences was a product of Mingus's development as a musician. His early biography is the history of a heterogeneous series of allegiances to a variety of styles. Known as a steadfast advocate of modern jazz, Mingus had actually been late to the party. Under the sway of Ellington, the younger Mingus had denounced bebop, going so far as to claim that his friend Buddy Collette could play as well as Bird. But when he changed his mind, he did so—in typical Mingus fashion—with a vengeance. "Charles Mingus loved Bird, man," Miles Davis later recalled, "almost like I have never seen nobody love."[22] Later Mingus passed through a phase where cool jazz was a predominant influence, and even aligned himself for a time with the Tristano school. His relationship with the free players was even more complex, with Mingus vacillating from disdain to extravagant praise. These various strata were underpinned by Mingus's early study of classical music, diligent practice on the cello, and rapt listening to Bach, Beethoven, Debussy, Ravel, and Strauss, among others. This was an odd musical house of cards, in which Strauss's *Death and Transfiguration* and the Duke's "East St. Louis Toodle-oo" were precariously balanced against one another.

The miracle of Mingus's music was that he could develop a coherent and moving personal style out of this hodgepodge of influences. A generation later, such eclecticism—the "style without a style"—would increasingly become the norm in the jazz world. Jazz players would aspire to be historians, using the bandstand as a lectern, the bells of their horns quoting a series of textbook examples. Alas, only a fine line often separates these histories from mere histrionics: hearing many latter-day players struggle to tie together the various strands, most often serving only awkwardly to regurgitate the past, makes it all the more clear how extraordinary was Mingus's ability to ascend and descend through the various roots and branches of the jazz family tree. Then again, Mingus had the advantage of learning these styles firsthand—he was among a select group who could boast of having worked as sideman for Armstrong, Ellington, and Parker, the three towering giants of the first half-century of jazz, not to mention having served alongside Tatum and Powell, Norvo and Hampton, Dolphy and Getz, Eldridge and Gillespie. This was jazz history of a different sort, imbibed directly and not learned in a school or from a recording. Perhaps because of this training, perhaps merely due to his sheer force of personality, Mingus managed not only to embrace a world of music but to engulf it in an overpowering bear hug. Despite these many linkages to jazz history, his music sounded neither derivative nor imitative. Whether playing a down-home blues, a silky ballad, an abstract tone poem, a New Orleans two-step, or a free-wheeling jam, his work was immediately identifiable, bearing the unique imprimatur of Charles Mingus.

A few months after his birth in Nogales, Arizona, on April 22, 1922, Charles Mingus lost his mother, Harriet, to myocarditis, an inflammation of the heart. The child was raised mostly in the Watts neighborhood of Los Angeles by a prim and devout stepmother who advocated spiritual flagellation, and an abusive father, Sergeant Charles Mingus Sr., who simply handed out earthly whippings. Around the age of six, Mingus began learning to play a Sears, Roebuck trombone. Studies on the cello followed, and for a time Mingus performed with the Los Angeles Junior Philharmonic. Lloyd Reese, who trained two generations of Southern California's finest jazz talent, helped transform the youngster from a classical cellist into a jazz bassist; his efforts were supplemented by other teachers including jazz bassist Red Callender and classical bassist Herman Rheinschagen. With diligent practice and a clear goal—to be the world's greatest on his instrument—Mingus developed quickly into a solid player in a Jimmy Blanton mold.

From the start, composition also fascinated Mingus. While still a teenager he wrote "Half-Mast Inhibition" and "The Chill of Death"—works he proudly revived and recorded decades later. He learned traditional jazz at the source, gigging with Kid Ory in 1942 and Louis Armstrong in 1943. His late initiation into the world of bop came, oddly, when he joined an LA band of white would-be boppers, including Parker's most fanatical disciple, Dean Benedetti (who later gave up performing to trail Parker from gig to gig, a portable recording device in tow, aiming to capture the altoist's solos for posterity). In time, Mingus was jamming with Bird and immersing himself in modern jazz. Yet his early recordings show that other jazz styles continued to be a source of inspiration. Tracing a lineage through these efforts is not easy: the shadow of Ellington looms over many early recordings (and would never entirely be absent from Mingus's music); his trio work with Red Norvo and Tal Farlow from the early 1950s was, in contrast, bop of the highest order; Mingus's ensuing projects for the Debut label also included noteworthy modern jazz sessions, but of a much different flavor, especially on the dazzling Massey Hall concert recording with Parker, Gillespie, Roach, and Powell; these efforts coexisted with a series of involvements with various cool players, ranging from Getz to Tristano. Indeed, the cool style, for a time, seemed like it might become a decisive influence. The bassist's 1954 *Jazzical Moods*, for example, reveals a cerebral and restrained Mingus very much at odds with the hot-blooded extrovert of a few years later.

It was not until the late 1950s that these different allegiances began to be subsumed into a more distinct, personal style. These years constituted a prolific and exceptionally creative period for Mingus, as documented by a number of outstanding projects, including *Pithecanthropus Erectus* from 1956, *Tijuana Moods*, *East Coasting*, and *The Clown* from 1957, and *Blues and Roots* and *Mingus Ah Um* from 1959. Some of Mingus's finest music from this period was not released at the time. As a result, his impact on the jazz world of the late 1950s may have been diluted compared to what it might otherwise have been. Yet, viewed cumulatively, Mingus's efforts from the era represent landmark accomplishments. His mature style had now blossomed into full-fledged artistry, and was evident in the music's exuberance, its excesses, its delight in the combination of opposites. Here, the vulgar rubs shoulders with royalty: a stately melody is bent out of shape by sassy counterpoint lines; a lilting 6/8 rhythm is juxtaposed against a roller-coaster double-time 4/4; the twelve-bar blues degenerates into semi-anarchy; tempos and moods shift, sometimes violently.

As a jazz composer, Mingus is often lauded for his formalist tendencies, for the novel structures of his works. Yet, just as pointedly, these are pieces stuffed to the brim with content. Even the name Jazz Workshop, which Mingus favored for his bands, evokes this image. The impulses of the moment are primary. Compositional structures change and adapt to meet the dictates of the here and now. The rough-edged counterpoint that sometimes takes over Mingus's most characteristic music, a surreal evocation of Dixieland, often makes his approach sound like a subversive type of anti-composition.

Fans had at least one guarantee: Mingus's work never was boring. A visceral excitement radiated from the bandstand at his performances and lives on in his recordings. Pieces such as "Better Git It in Your Soul," "Jelly Roll," and "Wednesday Night Prayer Meeting" may recall the jazz tradition, but do so in a way that is tellingly alive, that could never be reduced to notes on a page—hence it comes as little surprise that Mingus delighted in teaching his pieces by ear. "Wednesday Night Prayer Meeting" bore an all-too-fitting title. Mingus's music was an aural equivalent of the sanctified church, delighting in a loosely structured give-and-take, electrified with evangelical zeal. This was a musical speaking in tongues, accompanied by hand clapping, shouts, exhortations, improvised narrative, and other spontaneous outbursts. Yet these unpredictable elements of a Mingus performance also had their dark side: there were songs cut short in midflow, sidemen fired and rehired on the bandstand, denigrating asides and intemperate outbursts. With Mingus, whether onstage or off, even the moments of gentle introspection often merely marked a deceptive quiet before the storm.

Mingus was increasingly returning to the early roots of jazz music during this period. As with his idol Ellington, Mingus found the twelve-bar blues to be an especially fertile departure point. While most jazz musicians typically treat the blues form as a generic set of blowing changes, Mingus transformed the twelve-bar choruses into true compositions. Only a handful of jazz artists—Ellington, Morton, Monk—were his equal in this regard. Mingus's "Haitian Fight Song" was an early indication of this approach, with "Pussy Cat Dues" and "Goodbye Pork Pie Hat" from *Mingus Ah Um* standing out as especially brilliant examples, the latter following a twelve-bar form that evokes a minor blues while deviating far from the standard progressions. All in all, Mingus's 1959 recordings for Columbia present some of the most fully realized works of his career. But once again, the label hid Mingus's light under a bushel, holding onto much of this material and releasing it in piecemeal fashion over a period of many years.

The early 1960s found Mingus standing on the outside of the free jazz clique, staring at it with a mixture of curiosity, envy, and disdain. Mingus's roots in the jazz tradition and his impulses as a composer prevented him from fully accepting atonality and open structures, yet his fondness for new sounds motivated him to find some common ground with the avant-garde movement. His group with Eric Dolphy from this period was one of the most daring of his career, and the band is in especially fine form on a live recording made at the 1960 Antibes Jazz Festival and on the release *Charles Mingus Presents Charles Mingus.* "What Love," an early Mingus composition revived during this period—in part because Dolphy noted its similarity to Ornette Coleman's work—exhibits the bassist engaging in intricate free-form dialogues with Dolphy's bass clarinet. The piece is loosely based on "What Is This Thing Called Love?" but the deconstruction is so complete that even composer Cole Porter may have failed to recognize the linkage.

The traditional side of Mingus's music resurfaced the following year when his band featured, for three months, multireed player Roland Kirk (later known as Rahsaan Roland Kirk). Kirk was an ideal sideman for Mingus. A stellar soloist, he could play with authenticity and forcefulness in any jazz style, from trad to free, and on a host of instruments—not just conventional saxes and clarinets but pawnshop oddities such as manzello, stritch, siren whistle, and nose flute. Kirk's arsenal of effects was seemingly endless, ranging from circular breathing to playing three horns at once. This versatility came, in time, to be a curse. Had he focused on a single instrument, he would have been acknowledged as a master. Instead he was too often dismissed as little more than a jazz novelty act. While with Mingus, Kirk invigorated the 1961 *Oh Yeah* release with a handful of penetrating solos, including an extraordinary "old-timey" outing on "Eat That Chicken." A dozen years later, Kirk rejoined Mingus for a Carnegie Hall concert and stole the show with his sly maneuvering inside and outside the chord changes. The small body of recordings featuring these two jazz masters in tandem is a cause for much idle speculation as to what might have been had they collaborated more often.

Mingus's recordings for the Impulse label in the early 1960s continued to find him in top form. His 1963 *The Black Saint and the Sinner Lady* stands out as his strongest and most structured extended piece. Mingus apparently composed many of his works in snippets, with some of the bits and pieces (such as the bridge on his early "Eulogy for Rudy Williams") showing up in several different efforts. With *The Black Saint and the Sinner Lady*, Mingus was able to fine-tune the composition after it was recorded, using splices and overdubs, to create a more unified artistic statement. Not all of Mingus's efforts from this period held together so well. His 1962 Town Hall Concert is most often remembered as one of the great fiascos in the history of jazz. Scores were still uncompleted at curtain time, with two copyists continuing to work after the curtain was raised. Years later Gunther Schuller would struggle valiantly to realize Mingus's original vision for the Town Hall concert, but despite his best efforts, the music remained a series of fragments, only loosely tied together.

This is no criticism of Mingus. Fragmentation was a recurring curse as well as a blessing of the twentieth century. After all, this was an age that began with physicists contending that continuity was merely a statistical illusion—a premise that artists of all sorts quickly embraced. "These fragments I have shored against my ruins," Eliot proclaims toward the end of "The Waste Land." "I cannot make it cohere," announces Ezra Pound near the conclusion of his massive *Cantos*. These assertions, with their measured fatalism, could stand as mottos for the modernist agenda in jazz as well. In fact, Mingus was the closest jazz has come to having its own Ezra Pound. And as with Pound, Mingus's life too often mimicked the dissolution of his art. Psychological troubles plagued him throughout his career. In 1958, Mingus even tried to refer himself to the Bellevue mental hospital. In naive fashion, he had knocked on the door. Looking only for counsel, he soon found himself confined.

This was the same man who enlisted his analyst to write liner notes and who named a song "All the Things You Could Be by Now if Sigmund Freud's Wife Was Your Mother." The 1960s were tumultuous years for the bassist. Before the Town Hall concert, Mingus's temper exploded during a meeting with trombonist Jimmy Knepper, who was working as a copyist. Mingus punched Knepper, who eventually took him to court on assault charges. The most memorable moment from the documentary *Mingus*, filmed in 1966, was not of music making, but of the movie's subject being evicted from his apartment for nonpayment of rent. When the *Mingus at Monterey* recording was released a short while later, it included a personal note from the bassist, soliciting donations to compensate for "the misfortunes I have suffered." But such was the instability in Mingus's life that, by the time the record hit the stores, he could no longer be reached at the post office box listed in the liner notes. By the close of the 1960s, Mingus was barely visible in the jazz world, performing rarely, recording not at all.

It comes as little surprise that Mingus had such trouble summing up his chaotic life in a proposed autobiography. When a publisher contracted him to write his life story, Mingus intimated that he was putting together a fifteen-hundred-page manuscript. When *Beneath the Underdog* finally appeared in 1971, it was only a fraction of that length. And those looking for a point-by-point exposition of Mingus's career as a musician were likely to be disappointed by the text. Musical activities play a subsidiary role in the proceedings. Instead, the work is a patchwork of braggadocio, real or fantasized sexual exploits, pop psychology, fanciful dialogue, and odd anecdotes. Mingus the man, like his alter ego the musician, appeared to be an accumulation of the most disparate fragments. All the same, the book makes for compelling reading, brimming with excesses even in its abbreviated state.

On the heels of this literary effort, Mingus saw his musical career rejuvenated. He signed with Columbia, and—in a telling irony—recorded "The Chill of Death," a piece that same label had shelved back in 1947. Mingus's 1970s band with saxophonist George Adams and pianist Don Pullen, joined by longtime Mingus drummer Dannie Richmond, was a powerful unit that could hold up under the inevitable comparisons with earlier Jazz Workshop ensembles. This was also one of the most energized bands Mingus had ever fronted: Pullen's slashing piano style combined dissonant tone clusters, percussive chords, and biting single-note lines; Adams's tenor offered a sheets-of-sound approach analogous to Coltrane's. Both were capable of playing inside or outside of the structural foundations Mingus laid down on the bass. This band is well represented on a series of recordings for the Atlantic label, including *Mingus Moves, Cumbia & Jazz Fusion*, and the two volumes of *Changes*. Mingus's compositional skills continued to shine in diverse works, ranging from the constantly shifting "Sue's Changes" to the unabashedly traditional swing ballad "Duke Ellington's Sound of Love." *Three or Four Shades of Blue* from 1977 found Mingus joined by electric guitar and leaning, ever so coyly, in the direction of jazz-rock fusion. Mingus was reportedly upset at the label for pushing his music in a commercial direction but softened his criticism after the release turned out to be the biggest seller of his career.

Around this time, Mingus sought medical treatment for a recurring pain in his legs. When in public, he could be seen using a cane. Toward the end of 1977, the doctors diagnosed amyotrophic lateral sclerosis—known more commonly as Lou Gehrig's disease—a humbling disorder marked by a gradual loss of coordination and mastery over one's body. Mingus continued to compose, singing into a tape recorder when he no longer had control over his fingers. He initiated projects, including one with pop diva Joni Mitchell, that he did not live long enough to see through to completion. In his final days, Mingus was feted as became a jazz legend: his fifty-sixth birthday was celebrated with a performance of his *Revelations* by the New York Philharmonic; a few weeks later he appeared at the White House as part of an all-star gathering of jazz musicians during the Jimmy Carter administration. His last days were spent pursuing alternative medical therapies in Mexico, where he died in Cuernavaca on January 5, 1979. His music continued to flourish posthumously. The Joni Mitchell tribute recording, *Mingus*, came out a short while after his death, introducing the bassist's music to legions of new fans. A tribute band featuring former sidemen performed under the name Mingus Dynasty, while a similar continuation of the bassist's influence was seen in a combo led by George Adams and Don Pullen. And over a decade after his passing, Mingus's unwieldy two-hour long *Epitaph*—drawn from the music of the 1962 Town Hall concert described above—was pieced together by Gunther Schuller and performed and recorded to much fanfare.

In these transition years for jazz, only Miles Davis challenged Mingus in continually redefining the modern jazz-combo vocabulary while still keeping a distance—often only a small distance—from the more extreme implications of free jazz. Davis, like Mingus, was able to borrow judiciously from Ornette Coleman, but with results that were never merely imitative. On such classic recordings as *E.S.P.*, *Miles Smiles*, and *Nefertiti*, Davis and Wayne Shorter succeeded brilliantly in creating a more tonally centered counterpart to Coleman and Cherry—much as Eric Dolphy had done with Mingus, or alongside Booker Little on the seminal Five Spot performances. Here one finds the same haunting vocal quality to the horns, the free-floating rhythms, the indirect manner of phrasing, lethargic and biting by turns. The sense of freedom is so pervasive that the robust harmonic structures underlying the music pass by almost unnoticed. Many listeners have, no doubt, heard these Davis performances and surmised that there were no set chord changes or patterns dictating the flow of the music.

In fact, this music was much more tightly structured than it sounds at first hearing. The compositions of Davis and Shorter, masterful exercises in subtlety, were a major factor in this achievement. But the essence of this music lay, ultimately, in its multi-layered rhythmic motion—an enlivening and unconfined energy that was just as evident when the band was playing familiar standards as in the more attenuated compositions of the group's members. In this regard, the interaction of pianist Herbie Hancock, bassist Ron Carter, and drummer Tony Williams was critical in defining the band's sound. In time, this unit would demand respect as the premier rhythm section of its day and one of the finest that the jazz world has ever produced. It built on the Bill Evans–Scott LaFaro–Paul Motian trio work from the early 1960s, emulating the latter's celebration of the internalized beat, but with more assertiveness, a harder edge, and a more overt sense of forward momentum.

Behind all this lay Davis's foresight in selecting the three rhythm players, each of them relative newcomers to the New York scene at the time they joined his band. Herbie Hancock had spent his formative years in Chicago, where he was born in 1940. During his teens he served as a sideman with visiting jazz stars and performed with his own groups. After graduating from Grinnell College in 1960, Hancock came to New York as a member of trumpeter Donald Byrd's band. In May 1962, just twelve months before joining Davis, Hancock made his first album as a leader, *Takin' Off* for the Blue Note label. Although this release featured Hancock's funk composition "Watermelon Man," destined to become a crossover hit, the project gave only the barest hints of the flair and cogency the pianist would manifest with the Davis band, as well as on three superb later Blue Note recordings: *Maiden Voyage*, *Empyrean Isles*, and *Speak Like a Child*. Each of these releases broke new ground and showed a different side of this restless visionary at the keyboard. Indeed, few jazz artists would expand their musical horizons during the 1960s with more persistence than Hancock—a path of growth and development in which his stint with Miles was just one more stopping point—yet through it all certain trademark elements of his style stayed constant, notably his creative improv work, clarity of rhythmic expression, and taut compositional structures.

Ron Carter was in his late twenties when he joined Davis, but his résumé in the jazz world was fairly brief at the time, since most of Carter's training had been in classical music. Until his late teens, Carter had focused his energies on the cello. Perceiving that racial prejudice would make it difficult to pursue a symphonic career, Carter switched his emphasis to the double bass, but even then continued to study and perform the classical repertoire. After completing studies at the Eastman School in 1959, Carter worked with Chico Hamilton, Thelonious Monk, and Cannonball Adderley, and recorded with Eric Dolphy, Jaki Byard, Randy Weston, and Don Ellis, among others. These engagements paved the way to Carter's five-year stint with Davis beginning in 1963. A skilled technician, versatile section mate, and solid soloist, Carter would come to be the most in-demand bassist of his generation, eventually appearing as sideman on more than two thousand recordings, as well as leader at more than fifty sessions.

These two recent arrivals on the New York scene were, however, seasoned professionals in comparison with Davis's choice for drummer. Tony Williams was only seventeen years old when he joined Davis in May 1963—just a few months after having moved to New York at Jackie McLean's behest. Williams was so young that Davis faced problems with authorities when he was booked to play in nightclubs where minors were not allowed. But Williams compensated for his lack of professional experience with an abundance of power, passion, and creativity—one could make the case that no other percussionist in the history of jazz ever played so well, so young. In other settings, Williams might have dominated the proceedings, driving the band with his unbridled energy. But this Davis unit demanded different skills. Along with Hancock and Carter, Williams engaged in a complex polyrhythmic dialogue, a cat-and-mouse game in running meter. This was, for the most part, a music of implication, a path half hidden in the underbrush, not a paved two-lane highway. True, at appropriate moments, Williams could and would kick the Davis combo into a steady groove, but these outbursts were especially effective because they came in the context of the more open and unfettered sound typically favored by the quintet.

On the surface, it appeared as if Davis's mid-1960s band led two separate lives. The studio recordings revealed a pioneering unit performing quasi-abstract original compositions, whose musical iconoclasm bordered on the avant-garde. Yet, in concert, Davis continued to program the same ballads and popular standards ("Stella by Starlight," "My Funny Valentine") as well as 1950s jazz originals (often blues-based, such as "Walkin'" or "All Blues") that had been in his repertoire for years—despite his sidemen's desire to play the newer material in front of audiences. But this duality was only superficial: in performance, the Davis band played the old songs with such experimental zeal that no one could have accused the band members of harboring the slightest tinge of nostalgia or conservatism. Any lingering sentimentality was being squeezed out of these pieces, the tempos were getting faster and faster, and the band's interpretations more daring and unpredictable. We are fortunate that this combo was so well documented in performance—its recorded legacy includes memorable concerts in Europe and Japan, and more than seven hours of ardent music making captured at Chicago's Plugged Nickel in December 1965. In total, this body of work encompasses some of the most vital reworkings of the jazz standard repertoire from any era.

The influence of this Davis unit would linger long. Its sound hovers behind the scenes in the music made by Wynton Marsalis early in his career and by other young traditionalists during the closing years of the century and into the new millennium. The release of the complete Plugged Nickel recordings, some three decades after they were taped, reinforced how fresh and contemporary Davis's music still sounded despite a whole generation of passing jazz fads and fashions. Yet Davis himself, at the very moment he had reached the pinnacle of mainstream jazz, was anxious to explore newer approaches. Around this time, the trumpeter began listening to the music of James Brown, Jimi Hendrix, Sly and the Family Stone, Muddy Waters, and other artists with only peripheral ties to the jazz world. His own music was now evolving in response to these new influences. The big break with the past would come with his seminal *Bitches Brew* release of 1969, but even before that seismic shift, the signs of this coming change could be seen in his growing use of electric instruments and vamp forms. Sessions from late 1967 and early 1968 find Davis experimenting with the addition of electric guitar (played by George Benson or Joe Beck). During this same period, Hancock began using an electric piano on some tracks. By the time of *Filles de Kilimanjaro*, recorded during June and September 1968, the multilayered textures of the earlier quintet releases were increasingly replaced by more insistent ground rhythms. With *In a Silent Way* from the following February, the change was all but complete. The band's sound now tended toward uncomplicated patterns reminiscent of the dance and soul music of the day. The harmonies were often static. To cement this change, Davis was enlisting the skills of a wider range of musicians, including keyboardists Joe Zawinul and Chick Corea, guitarist John McLaughlin, and bassist Dave Holland. Within a few months, the last fading elements of the mid-1960s band were purged in favor of the more overtly rock-oriented approach celebrated in *Bitches Brew*. This release, lamented by many of Davis's older fans, would attract a younger audience to his music and earn the trumpeter the first gold record of his career.

In time, this style came to be known as jazz-rock fusion—or more simply fusion. For the next decade this sound would exert a powerful influence on the jazz world with a host of former Davis sidemen using it as a foundation to promote their own careers. But for all its commercial success, fusion failed to establish itself as a dominant style. By the close of these transition years, the jazz idiom had become too fragmented to embrace any one approach as representative of the age, as swing and bop had tended to do in earlier decades. Instead a smorgasbord of sounds, a range of possibilities, prevailed.

The most pressing alternative to the fusion style during this period would come at the opposite end of the spectrum. Free jazz was virtually its mirror image. If the one style was a path to financial success, the other represented economic isolation. If the one style was tied to commerce and the music industry, the other thumbed its nose at these same forces. If the one style reflected a return to simpler dancelike musical structures, akin to what jazz had done during the big band era, the other preferred to subvert structures in whole or in part. One style espoused pragmatism, the other progressivism. The jazz magazines of the day rarely talked about a battle between free and fusion styles—as they had years earlier in the days when traditional and modern forms had engaged in an ongoing war of words and, occasionally, horns— but this may have been only because the chasm between the two styles was too wide to admit any common ground. Then again, perhaps it was only that, by this time, the fragmentation of jazz styles had become so much a part of the musical landscape that it was accepted as an inexorable fact.

And though many of the proponents of free jazz saw their music as a logical development, evolving clearly from the music's history to date, the obvious "next thing" in a history of next things that could be traced back to Buddy Bolden, others remained unconvinced. For them a clear progression to a new dominant style, an unambiguous linear development in the history of the music, the ascendancy of one more advanced and liberated jazz language, was very much in doubt. For still others—as would become clear with the new traditionalism of the 1980s and 1990s—a return to earlier styles of jazz (whether in the guise of New Orleans back-to-basics, Duke Ellington's visionary moods, Miles's mid-1960s aesthetic, or other strands of the music's heritage) would come to emerge as a beguiling option, a comforting way of regaining this lost sense of unity, and even then perhaps only achieving a symbolic wholeness. Yet the true heir to the jazz mantle, as subsequent events proved, would be neither free nor fusion, a return to roots or a celebration of rock and rap. Instead, there was merely an exemplary splintering, a disintegration into isolated modules.

8 Freedom and Fusion

FREE JAZZ

Freedom stood out as a politically charged word in American public discourse during the late 1950s and early 1960s—it would be hard, in fact, to find a term more explosive, more laden with depths of meaning, or proclaimed with more emotion during these tumultuous years. This truism of civics classes and refrain from the nation's founding documents now took on new force, in the process outlining a sharp divide in the country's social and economic structures. The civil rights movement of the day raised it aloft as a battle cry, held it forth as a goal, and asserted it as a first principle on which all else depended. It could no longer be put out of mind as an empty phrase or accepted as a fait accompli in American society. "Freedom" was very much something to live for, or, for a few, even to die for.

The *Brown v. Board of Education* decisions of the mid-1950s, which were critical in reversing a long history of racial segregation in American schools, were not, as some may have suspected at the time, closing chapters of a struggle for racial equality that had raged since before the Emancipation Proclamation. Instead, these moves to integrate public institutions set off a chain of reverberations throughout American society, reenergizing the civil rights movement and setting the stage for a series of confrontations in which the quest for freedom would figure as a repeated motif. "Freedom riders" defied segregation in buses and terminals in the Deep South, often at great personal risk. The "Freedom Vote" of 1963 attracted tens of thousands of participants to mock elections that demonstrated the absence of real representative democracy in the South. The "Freedom Summer" of the following year found activists organizing to register African American voters in large numbers in anticipation of the fall presidential election. The "Freedom Singers" chorus toured the country, giving concerts and raising money for civil rights advocacy. Black leaders sought to form "Freedom Schools" and establish a "Freedom Democratic Party." The word was imprinted on the public's consciousness, dramatized in speeches by Dr. Martin Luther King, sung in hymns, brandished at Little Rock, Birmingham, Selma, and other battlegrounds in the fight for equality.

It is impossible to comprehend the free jazz movement of these same years without understanding how it fed upon this powerful cultural shift in American society. Its practitioners advocated much more than freedom from harmonic structures or compositional forms—although that too was an essential part of their vision of jazz. Many of them saw their music as inherently political. They believed that they could, indeed must, choose between participating in the existing structures—in society, in the entertainment industry, in the jazz world—or rebelling against them. The aesthetic could no longer be isolated from these cultural currents. In the overheated Marxist rhetoric that increasingly found its way into mainstream political debate during those days, even a "pure" art such as music was ultimately part of a super-structure of social institutions and events that was delineated and determined by economic realities and, ultimately, class values. "Pure" music? One was advised that such abstractions were, at best, an idle delusion, at worst a conscious deception.

An undercurrent of political advocacy had always existed in the jazz world, but now it exploded on the surface as never before. Amiri Baraka, then writing under the name LeRoi Jones, declared in his 1963 book *Blues People* that the new music signi-fied "more 'radical' changes and reevaluations of social and emotional attitudes toward the general environment." Critic Frank Kofsky took this view further, assert-ing that the free jazz movement represented nothing less than a vote of "'no confidence' in Western civilization and the American Dream." In the 1964 U.S. election, Kofsky even wrote in John Coltrane's name on his ballot as his choice for Vice President, alongside Malcolm X as his pick for President, a strange ticket only for those unaware of the larger symbolic resonance of progressive jazz currents dur-ing this period. This overt linking of free jazz and sociopolitical criticism went so far that Ekkehard Jost, a historian of the movement, lamented that the "autonomous musical aspects of the evolution of free jazz—i.e., those aspects which escape a purely sociological analysis—often were ignored."[1] The music risked being relegated to a secondary, utilitarian role, valued for what it advocated rather than for how it actually sounded.

In truth, the sociopolitical ramifications of this music remained, in many ways, decisive in distinguishing the new free jazz players from the older generation of experimental jazz performers. From a purely musical point of view, freedom or ato-nality in jazz music had appeared many years before Ornette Coleman and Cecil Taylor raised it to a decisive issue. Lennie Tristano had experimented with free tech-niques in a series of pieces—"Intuition," "Digression," "Descent into the Maelstrom"—some of them dating back to the late 1940s. Bob Graettinger's writ-ings for the Stan Kenton band, most notably his 1948 magnum opus *City of Glass*, were uncompromising works that defied the conventions of existing jazz harmonic and melodic techniques, as was Jimmy Giuffre's 1953 recording of "Fugue." Contemporary classical composers were also attempting to use jazz instrumentation to explore avant-garde techniques, as in Stravinsky's *Ebony Concerto* (1946) or Milton Babbitt's *All Set* (1957). Sensing the potential of these various trends, Gunther Schuller—who had composed *Atonal Studies for Jazz* in 1948 and, at the start of the 1950s, was playing with Miles Davis's nonet and composing twelve-tone-row works—coined the term Third Stream in 1957 to describe a merging of the most promising and progressive currents in jazz and contemporary classical music.

But each of these precursors of free jazz was white, and each was, to a greater or lesser extent, representative of the established order of things. The proponents of free jazz who came into prominence at the close of the 1950s were, in contrast, almost all outsiders: as African Americans they were outsiders from mainstream society; as musical renegades they were outsiders from mainstream jazz. For many years, they lacked access to concert halls, grants, prestigious commissions, and other time-honored measures of artistic achievement. During his formative years in Los Angeles, free jazz pioneer Ornette Coleman worked as an elevator operator in a department store. Pianist Cecil Taylor labored as a dishwasher, even after he achieved notoriety in the jazz world, rather than pursue more overtly commercial musical projects. The Third Stream movement had offered atonality with a smiling face, dressed up in top hat and tails. The major exponents of free jazz, in contrast, tended to represent an outgrowth of the bohemians and "angry young men" of the 1950s. They emerged *despite* the established order, and were all too aware of that fact.

The parallels with the rise of bebop are striking. In the late 1930s, as in the late 1950s, many established jazz stars were pushing the music forward and adopting new concepts in shaping the sound and style of their work. But in both instances, it was *not* the progressives of the older generation who succeeded in transforming the music: instead, it was a group of younger, largely unheralded musicians who rocked the foundations, tore down the existing structures, and built afresh with formidable new materials. In retrospect, we can trace the moves that made free jazz possible—in the 1950s works of Coltrane, Dolphy, Mingus, Tristano, Giuffre, Davis, and others. But it took Ornette Coleman, Cecil Taylor, Albert Ayler, and other new arrivals on the scene to make a musical revolution. In the process, they forced many of the older players to dance to *their* tune. Coltrane and Dolphy were still playing tonal music when Ornette arrived on the New York scene, but before long both were pushing the limits of their music. Sonny Rollins, the other iconic young tenor of the era, also showed his comprehension of the changes afoot in the jazz world—first by choosing to retire from the scene to study and practice, and later, after returning, by hiring several of Coleman's former sidemen. Even Miles Davis, who had derided Coleman in the late 1950s ("Hell, just listen to what he writes and how he plays . . . the man is all screwed up inside"[2]), came to be influenced by the new sound in the mid-1960s, forging a two-horn sound with Wayne Shorter that bore an uncanny resemblance to the Don Cherry–Ornette Coleman collaborations.

Coltrane, Dolphy, Rollins, Miles: to see these masters of mainstream jazz not only acknowledge the new music but strive to emulate it—this marked an extraordinary change in the jazz world. This shift was all the more stunning when one considers how little respect Coleman had received just a short while before his rise to fame. When Ornette had attempted to sit in with name bands—Dexter Gordon's, the Brown-Roach Quintet, and others—he had almost always been subjected to derision and ridicule, sometimes ordered to leave the stage; in other instances, the musicians simply began packing up their instruments while he was still playing. But this response was mild compared to the night in Baton Rouge, some years before, when a Coleman tenor solo had stopped the dancers in their tracks and roused an unruly gang. A half-dozen thugs cornered the saxophonist outside, beat him until he passed out, and threw his saxophone into the street. For almost a decade afterward, Coleman hesitated to play the tenor again—he sensed some potential for bad karma in the horn and decided to focus his energies on the alto instead. Years before, Charlie Parker had suffered a painful initiation into musical maturity, when he was laughed off the bandstand during a Kansas City session, but Coleman's formative years were even more tainted by humiliation and rejection. Indeed, no major figure in the history of jazz has had a less propitious early career.

Coleman was born and raised in Fort Worth, Texas, during the heart of the Great Depression. These were difficult years—Coleman's father scuffled, finding what work he could as a cook, mechanic, and construction worker, among other pursuits; Ornette's mother worked as a clerk in a funeral home and sold Avon-type products on the side. But these were also fecund years for African American music in the Lone Star State: dozens of top-notch bands worked the territory, firing the ambitions and nurturing the talents of numerous future jazz stars; boogie-woogie piano flourished—during this period, some simply called it "Texas piano" or "fast Texas piano." Similarly, a blues-drenched tenor sax style was an ever-present ingredient in the jazz and popular music of the day, in time coming to be known as "Texas tenor." A host of saxophonists either born or raised in Texas—such as Arnett Cobb (1918–1989), Illinois Jacquet (1922–2004), David "Fathead" Newman (1933–2009), and Buddy Tate (1913–2001)—exemplified this sound in their gritty, soulful playing, defining an approach that permeated the local jazz scene during Coleman's formative years. It is unclear how much of this music was heard by Coleman at the time. By his own admission, church songs and big band recordings made a stronger impression on him, at least at first. But the pronounced blues sensibility that recurs in his later work, rooting it in the black tradition even as it broke new ground, suggests that the various indigenous styles eventually found a place in his personal aesthetic vision. Honkin', shoutin', riffin', riding high on a single note or barking out a guttural howl: this Texas saxophone heritage lingers in the background, like the Jungian archetype of a primal jazz style, sometimes rising to the surface at the least expected moments in Coleman's mature oeuvre.

During his early teens, Coleman acquired an alto saxophone but struggled in his attempts to learn the rudiments of the horn. Confusing the alphabet and musical scale, he determined incorrectly that the concert scale began with A, rather than (as it does) with C. Coleman slowly, painstakingly gained a basic education in music, but with many setbacks along the way. Joining a church band, Coleman was ridiculed for his lack of training. A much-anticipated lesson with Walter "Foots" Thomas, a journeyman jazz player, provided little guidance or encouragement: the veteran simply had Coleman play for an hour while looking in the mirror—so that Ornette would quit making "faces" while he blew the horn. A short while later, Coleman was thrown out of his high school marching band, ostensibly for mixing swing and Sousa, an unacceptable combination in the minds of the powers that be. His early professional career was equally marked by ups and downs. One bandleader, Coleman claimed, even got to the point of paying him *not* to play.

In the face of these obstacles, Coleman persevered and continued to develop and grow as a musician. The miracle was that he did this without abandoning his own personal approach to improvisation, despite the constant negative feedback. "He could play the blues," an early employer recalls, "but he didn't want to."[3] In time, Coleman developed an equally complex relationship to the bebop idiom. He listened to bebop, studied it, learned the tunes, performed them: yet the end result retained a certain foreignness, just as his blues work had done during his Texas years. Amateur recordings made of Coleman at the Hillcrest Club in Los Angeles shortly before his rise to fame fortuitously captured this odd hybrid on tape. Playing Charlie Parker's "Klactoveedsedstene," Coleman echoes the composer's astringent sound and phrasing, yet his choice of notes and cadences veers far from the expected path. It almost seems as if Coleman has taken the modern jazz vocabulary and translated into a new tongue, some private Esperanto of his own creation. Certainly the animating force in this music comes not from Parker, but from Coleman's singular take on it.

The Hillcrest engagement also represented a rare occasion for Coleman to work with a group of like-minded musicians. Trumpeter Don Cherry, unlike Coleman, had earned the respect of local Southern California players for his bop prowess. Along with Billy Higgins, the drummer on the Hillcrest gig, Cherry had played in the Jazz Messiahs, an up-and-coming local modern jazz band, and had graced the stage at high-profile clubs such as the Haig and the Lighthouse. Like many others, Cherry was originally put off by the eccentric Coleman—of his first meeting, he recalled: "He had long hair and a beard. It was about 90 degrees, and he had on an overcoat. I was scared of him"[4]—but soon grew fascinated with Coleman's unconventional compositions and improvisations. Cherry would later share Coleman's rise to fame, developing his own range of odd behavior patterns in the process. For a time, he favored performing on a pocket cornet (called a pocket trumpet by Cherry) to complement Coleman's plastic alto—quasi-toy instruments used to fight a musical revolution. Bassist Charlie Haden was an anchor both musically and personally to the horns. Bespectacled, owlish, Haden looked the part of an apprentice clerk in a bank. But his bass lines subverted the image: they captured a piquant meeting ground between consonance and dissonance, powered the band with a rock-solid beat, and softened the hard edge of this freedom music with a sweet, warm tone. Paul Bley, the pianist and nominal leader of the Hillcrest band, would stay with Coleman for only a short while but would make his own mark on free jazz in later years. In a series of seminal recordings—*Footloose, Mr. Joy, The Floater Syndrome, Open, to Love*—Bley demonstrated a masterful conception of solo and combo playing, distinguished by a rare sensitivity to space and time, tone and texture.

Coleman's persistence, aided by a referral from bassist Red Mitchell, led to an audition with Les Koenig of Contemporary Records. Koenig had been alerted that

Coleman's compositions, for all their oddities, might be suitable material for other players to record. At first the audition faltered—Coleman was unable to perform his pieces on the piano—and, in desperation, he resorted to playing them on alto, backed by Cherry's pocket cornet. Koenig was fascinated by the music and set up a trial session with a full band, which in turn led to Coleman's first record date, *Something Else! The Music of Ornette Coleman.* Pianist Walter Norris described to me, in a 1990 interview, the peculiar preparations for the unconventional session: "We rehearsed two or three times a week for about six months leading up to the recording. A number of times we rehearsed at my house. I would take a paper and pen and make notes about the compositions and about what we were supposed to be doing. But the funny thing was that at every rehearsal Ornette would change what we had done the last time. He would change the structure of the song or where the rubato was. And then when we finally showed up for the record date, he changed everything again."[5]

Even before it was released, the jazz grapevine picked up on the coming event, with *Downbeat* promising that it would be "very, very *Avant Garde.*" In retrospect, we can see that *Something Else!* represents a less radical departure from the jazz tradition than both its critics and supporters claimed at the time. Conventional thirty-two-bar and twelve-bar structures are evident, and familiar chord changes, borrowed from standards such as "I Got Rhythm" and "Out of Nowhere," underpin the solos. Moreover, Coleman's improvisations capture a modal flavor and only hint at the atonality of his later work. Yet the freshness of Coleman and Cherry's melodic lines stood out despite these remembrances of jazz past. It was as though the music had undergone an exemplary unburdening; as if all of the clichés and hoary riffs accumulated over a half-century of jazz music were thrown overboard, lightening the load and opening up the horizon.

Coleman's star was clearly in the ascendancy. Influential patrons, including Gunther Schuller and John Lewis, befriended him and helped open doors. Coleman and Cherry were invited to attend the Lenox School of Jazz, ostensibly as students but in fact serving as unacknowledged faculty members. Coleman got a regal welcome at the 1959 Monterey Jazz Festival where, in a program billed as "The Three Saxes," he shared the stage with Coleman Hawkins and Ben Webster. Earlier that same year, two follow-up recordings had been taped by different labels within a few weeks of each other: *Tomorrow Is the Question* (on Contemporary) and *The Shape of Jazz to Come* (on Atlantic). The Atlantic release stood out as an especially important statement of the new music. For the first time, Coleman was able to record using his working quartet of Cherry, Haden, and Higgins. The breadth of their music was striking, ranging from the almost unbearably poignant "Lonely Woman" to the forceful "Congeniality" and the moody "Peace."

But the notoriety of these achievements paled beside the fierce debates ignited by the New York debut of the Ornette Coleman Quartet on the heels of the release of these two records. The band opened at the Five Spot on November 17, 1959, with interest running so high that the club took the rare step of offering a preview for the press and select members of the local jazz establishment. Some listeners walked out, others sat transfixed, and though there was no consensus among the audience, almost every opinion was adamant. Controversy proved good for business and for Coleman's career. His two-week gig was extended by two months. Visiting players clamored to sit in, with everybody from Leonard Bernstein to Lionel Hampton taking the plunge. Mainstream periodicals, including *Newsweek* and *Harper's Bazaar*, covered Coleman's arrival on the scene as a major cultural event, and jazz magazines seethed with heated exchanges. Anxious to capitalize on the Coleman phenomenon, Atlantic released *Change of the Century* the following June, drawing on tracks recorded shortly before the quartet left California. This was another intriguing project by the altoist, showing his skill in slyly referencing other idioms: the blues in "Ramblin," bebop in "Bird Food," and Latin music in "Una Muy Bonita." The subtlety of these allusions was striking, and in each instance Coleman forced the other style into subservience to his freer approach.

In the nine months following the release of *Change of the Century*, Atlantic set up a number of additional recording sessions for their new star jazz artist. These featured several different facets of the altoist's work, including Coleman's follow-up efforts in a quartet setting (with Ed Blackwell replacing Higgins) and in larger ensembles conducted by Gunther Schuller. But the most daring project took place on December 21, 1960, when Coleman gathered together a double quartet at A&R Studios in New York. The resulting record, *Free Jazz*, represented a radical extreme even by the standards of Coleman's previous work. In the past, for all his nonconformism, Coleman had favored performances that retained elements of the jazz tradition: his incisive compositions were, for the most part, highly structured; melody statements encapsulated horn solos backed by rhythm section; a 4/4 sense of time predominated; most pieces lasted around four or five minutes. *Free Jazz*, in contrast, broke all these rules. Instead, it took on overtones of a spectacle, serving as a jazz equivalent of those battles royal favored by television wrestling aficionados, brutish encounters in which a number of well-toned bodies engage in simultaneous, extemporaneous sparring. Clearly the talents gathered by Coleman for this session were heavyweights: two quartets were used, separated into the left and right channels of the stereo recording, with Coleman and Cherry, backed by Higgins and Scott LaFaro, countering the efforts of Eric Dolphy and Freddie Hubbard, supported by Haden and Blackwell. The texture of the music was much thicker than earlier Coleman efforts. Churning and seething, sounds ricocheting between the two quartets, a relentless energy permeating the music, *Free Jazz* fulfilled all the prophecies made about Coleman, both positive and negative. Devotees who had sought a sonic revolution in his work were not likely to be disappointed: this was radical music by any measure, a horn-playing assault that could bring down the walls of Jericho all over again. By the same token, those critics who wished to dismiss Coleman as a purveyor of cacophonous, jarring notes and tones, an exponent of shrill noise, found ample ammunition in *Free Jazz* to justify their attacks, seeing it as fulfillment of Shakespeare's descriptive "sound and fury signifying nothing."

Yet in the final analysis, Coleman's embrace of free-form-energy jazz would prove to be prescient. Over the next several years, the work of Albert Ayler, Cecil Taylor, Pharoah Sanders, even John Coltrane, among others, would increasingly gravitate toward longer, uninhibited, loosely structured, often disturbing performances, explosions of sound that are much closer to *Free Jazz* than to any of Coleman's earlier works. In time this very same approach would become a cliché of free jazz, with even the most impassioned atonal performances tending toward a certain somber sameness. But for at least the next decade, this subversion of the various jazz conventions—chord changes, tempos, song forms, structured solos, and the like—would retain its radical flavor and maintain its credentials as the most progressive strain in jazz. With *Free Jazz*, Coleman not only gave a fitting name to the movement but effectively captured the essence of its sound.

Coleman himself seemed increasingly ambivalent about the path he was now pursuing. Over the next four years, he would enter the recording studio on only a handful of occasions. Four sessions for Atlantic in 1961 resulted in the release of *Ornette!* and *Ornette on Tenor*, but during this period he made just a few public appearances. Coleman's sole recording during the following year documented his December 21, 1962, Town Hall concert, promoted by the altoist himself in response to his growing distrust of booking agents and club owners. This ambitious affair, which featured Coleman's trio along with a string quartet and several rhythm-and-blues players, barely broke even. For the next two years Coleman disappeared almost completely from public view. This represented no resignation on Coleman's part, merely a tactical retreat. In private, the altoist formulated bold, at times grandiose plans. He decided to open his own jazz club and even selected a site. He planned to start his own music publishing company. But, like the Town Hall concert, these attempts to wrest control of the business side of his career met with little or no success. Coleman also aimed to expand his instrumental skills—but instead of embarking on formal saxophone study, he decided to learn trumpet, violin, and guitar. Meanwhile, he turned down offers to work as a bandleader, although around this same time he participated in high-profile jams with Cecil Taylor, Albert Ayler, and John Coltrane.

Finally, in January 1965, Coleman returned to the bandstand, performing at New York's Village Vanguard, an engagement that in retrospect can be seen as initiating a second phase in his career, one that lasted for the next eight years and would culminate in Coleman's collaboration with local musicians in Joujouka, Morocco. In place of the sharply focused altoist of his early work now stood a restless musician running in many directions at once. Ornette the altoist? Ornette the trumpeter? Ornette the violinist? Ornette the serious composer? Ornette the explorer of world music? Ornette the jazz traditionalist? Ornette the theorist of harmolodics? He was all of these, and more. There were passing glances backward: his live recording at the Golden Circle in Stockholm, for example, recalled the focused energy of his work for the Atlantic label. But other efforts broke surprising new ground. He wrote "Forms and Sounds" for woodwind quintet. He was awarded his first Guggenheim fellowship (a rare honor at that time, when jazz players seemed all but blacklisted from this prestigious award), which resulted in his orchestral work *Inventions of Symphonic Poems*. His composition "Emotion Modulation" was performed on trumpet and violin, and found Coleman backed by two bassists, a drummer, and vocalist Yoko Ono. Coleman himself emerged as a vocalist, singing as part of a backup chorus on a Louis Armstrong album. "Sun Suite of San Francisco" was written for trumpet soloist Bobby Bradford backed by Coleman's quartet and a thirty-five-piece orchestra. Other pieces were composed for string quartet. The range of Coleman's new music was documented on a series of recordings, including *The Empty Foxhole*, *New York is Now!*, *Science Fiction*, and *Skies of America*.

In the liner notes to the latter album, an ambitious project featuring the London Symphony Orchestra, Coleman first referred to "harmolodic theory." Harmolodics, Coleman explained, was based on the use of "melody, harmony and the instrumentation of movement of forms."[6] This doctrine would loom large in Coleman's public pronouncements during later years. As a theoretical approach, harmolodics came to represent more a metaphysical doctrine than a musicological tool—a sort of Rosicrucianism for improvisers. And even the loose links with music theory were ultimately subverted by Coleman himself: he eventually came to insist that harmolodics could help in almost any area of creative expression, including fiction and poetry. From the vagueness of Coleman's comments, one suspects that it could equally apply to bricklaying or the culinary arts.

But the ultimate test of Coleman's artistry during this period was not as a theorist, but as a musician. On the heels of his harmolodic philosophizing, Coleman began experimenting with new approaches to combo playing. For years, he had avoided hiring harmony instrument players, such as pianists or guitarists, for his band. But in the early 1970s, Coleman began an association with guitarist James Blood Ulmer. Ulmer brought a radically different texture to Coleman's ensemble, mixing free jazz with elements of funk, rock, and experimental electronic music. Bassist Jamaaladeen Tacuma and drummer Ronald Shannon Jackson also became prominent Coleman sidemen, furthering the altoist's new direction with their hard-grooving, dance-oriented styles. The A&M release *Dancing in Your Head* revealed how far Coleman had come since *Free Jazz*. At the height of the fascination with jazz-rock fusion, Coleman showed that it was possible to use electric music as a springboard for improvisation without resorting to the overtly commercial, slickly streamlined sounds that were now drowning the jazz world in wave after wave of synthesized slush. Follow-up releases such as *Body Meta* and *Of Human Feelings* built on this same approach, presented under the banner of "Prime Time," a name chosen by Coleman to represent this facet of his music. This greater comfort playing with harmony instruments could also be seen in later Coleman projects, such as his *Song X* collaboration with Pat Metheny from 1985, his invitation to Jerry Garcia to join in Coleman's *Virgin Beauty* project from 1988, and his work with pianists Geri Allen and Joachim Kühn in the mid-1990s. Coleman recorded little after this point, but his 2006 release *Sound Grammar* was awarded the Pulitzer Prize in music, only the second time a jazz artist had received that honor.

Cecil Taylor, whose influence on the free jazz movement would come to rival Coleman's, presents a stark contrast to the altoist. Where Coleman was self-taught and struggled to learn the rudiments of music theory, Taylor boasted a blue-ribbon musical education. Where Coleman drew much of his early inspiration from bebop, blues, R&B, and other African American forms of music, Taylor called upon a wider range of influences, including contemporary classical composers such as Stravinsky and Bartók—the latter's use of Hungarian folk music in his compositions was seen by Taylor as a counterpart to his own relationship to the jazz tradition—and his tastes in jazz were notably expansive, ranging far beyond the reigning bop figures of his formative years, and spanning Fats Waller, Jimmie Lunceford, Chick Webb, Cab Calloway, Erroll Garner, Dave Brubeck, Jaki Byard, Dick Twardzik, Horace Silver, and, above all, Duke Ellington. Where Coleman's later works drew on popular dance styles with pronounced funk and rock elements, Taylor gravitated to formal dance, writing and performing original pieces for ballet artists and modern dance companies. Above all, Taylor's music, despite frequently being mentioned in the same breath as Coleman's, is cut from different cloth. It is denser, atomistic, more explosive, more insistently percussive, more thoroughly purged of romantic sentiment. In place of Coleman's human cry on the saxophone, one finds Taylor's fusillade of notes, unforgiving and unapologetic.

Born in Long Island City, New York, in 1929, Taylor was raised in the predominantly white neighborhood of Corona. His father was a cook and servant who worked for a state senator, his mother a housewife with diverse interests: she spoke French and German, played the piano, enjoyed the theater, and counted Ellington drummer Sonny Greer as one of her childhood friends. "Music to me was a way of holding on to Negro culture, because there wasn't very much of it around," Taylor has recalled.[7] At age five he began studying the piano. Lessons were supplemented by instruction from his piano teacher's husband, a tympanist who had played under Toscanini—an especially fitting early association given the extremely percussive nature of Taylor's mature style. In 1952, Taylor entered the New England Conservatory of Music, where he expanded his knowledge of contemporary classical music but grew disenchanted with the academy's indifference to the black musical experience. This same period found Taylor deepening his knowledge of the jazz idiom. Writer Nat Hentoff, who first met Taylor around this time, has recalled that "no one had clearer, firmer and more unexpected opinions about music than Cecil."[8] This confident sense of direction was critical for Taylor, since his music, even at this stage, was increasingly deviating from the then prevailing styles of late bop and cool jazz.

"By 1954 my style of playing was developed," Taylor has noted.[9] A half-decade before free jazz emerged as a controversial new movement, Taylor was already employing arch dissonances, fragmented improvised lines, disjointed rhythms, and the jackhammer piano attack that would characterize his mature work. His 1956 session for the Transition label indicates the scope of these experimental leanings. At first hearing, Taylor's approach reveals a number of connections to the jazz tradition: the repertoire here draws heavily on standards based on conventional song forms, and the instrumentation is a typical jazz combo (Taylor is supported by bassist Buell Neidlinger and drummer Dennis Charles as well as, on some tracks, by saxophonist Steve Lacy). But on a deeper level, the music is unflinchingly subversive. Taylor sometimes follows the chord changes played by Neidlinger, other times imposing his clashing polytonal structures on top of them, elsewhere trying to undermine any assertion of an underlying harmonic roadmap. His piano attack, with its rumbling thick chords and caustic single-note lines, is somewhat reminiscent of Thelonious Monk's. But in place of Monk's sly humor and masterful use of space, we encounter a more treacherous and overgrown aural landscape. Restless, insistent, at times foreboding, this is music that seemingly bypasses the listeners' faculties of judgment and evaluation and instead heads straight for the central nervous system.

During the late 1950s and early 1960s, Taylor recorded and performed on only a handful of occasions, but each of these outings further reinforced his image as the most intransigent of the young jazz modernists. He shook up the audience at the 1957 Newport Jazz Festival, where his performance was recorded and released. A stint at the Five Spot in New York spurred further controversy and attracted an enthusiastic following among artists and bohemians. Follow-up recordings for Contemporary and United Artists (including a session that paired the pianist with John Coltrane) found Taylor playing in a vein similar to the Transition releases, employing ponderous dissonances and an acerbic piano attack in dramatic reworkings of standards, supplemented by probing new compositions.

In 1960 and 1961, Taylor had the opportunity to record for the short-lived Candid label. The Candid work finds Taylor at a new level of musical maturity and reveals a number of stylistic devices that would achieve fuller expression on his mid-1960s recordings for Blue Note: he is less constrained by chord changes and bar lines; his link with the bop tradition of Powell and Monk is less overt; his playing is more tex- tured, more two-fisted; the demarcation between soloing and accompanying, bet- ween comping chord and melody line—vital distinctions in mainstream jazz—are now overridden by oceanic torrents of sound. Taylor still plays the occasional stan- dard such as "Lazy Afternoon" and "This Nearly Was Mine"—performances that border on reconstructive surgery—and engages in stock devices such as trading four-bar phrases with the drummer on "Air." But these last lingering affectations of traditional jazz playing do little to blunt the porcupine quills of this prickly music.

A second Candid session from 1961, ostensibly under the leadership of bassist Neidlinger, found Taylor refining these same techniques. "Cell Walk for Celeste," from this date, underscores the formalist elements often hidden beneath the apparent free-form flow of the pianist's work. This eighty-eight-bar theme captures a number of distinct moods, ranging from brooding melancholy to sardonic exultation. The piece represented Taylor's most successful endeavor to date in blending contemporary classical elements into a distinctly African American style—"almost as though riding in on the morning train from Danbury, Charles Ives got off at 125th Street instead of Grand Central Terminal," is how Neidlinger later described the performance.[10]

Downbeat awarded Taylor its prestigious New Star award in 1962, but this did little to improve his commercial prospects. "Gigs for me have been mostly, like a concert a year, filled in with one or two short nightclub or coffeehouse gigs," Taylor told author A. B. Spellman around this time.[11] To support himself, Taylor took jobs as a dishwasher and short-order cook. But, in 1966, Taylor burst forth with a number of important projects, including two milestone dates for the Blue Note label and a live recording made in France. Unit Structures, recorded for Blue Note in May, stands as a landmark performance for Taylor, a full flowering of the promise shown on "Air" and "Cell Walk for Celeste." Conquistador, from this same period, is less well known, but an equally impressive statement of the pianist's mature style.

The flow of time in Taylor's music was, by this time, completely free of conven- tional jazz metrics. Taylor's collaborations with drummer Sunny Murray during the early 1960s had assisted in this process, one furthered by the pianist's later work with Andrew Cyrille. Cyrille played an important role on *Unit Structures*, varying his attack from the ominous reverberations and asides of "Enter Evening" to the explosive interjections of "Steps" and "Tales (8 Whisps)." Despite the absence of typical swing and bop phrasing, these pieces maintain, for most of their duration, a powerful rhythmic dynamism. The essentially physical nature of the performance comes across, even on record. Single-note runs burst from the piano sounding board; short, acidic phrases crack like a whip; inquisitive chord voicings tremble, stutter, bellow; tone clusters ripple up and down the keyboard. The horns crisscross arrhythmically on top of these layers of sound, entering into haranguing dialogues with the rhythm section and each other. In the final analysis, *Unit Structures* ranks with Coleman's *Free Jazz*, Ayler's *Spiritual Unity*, and Coltrane's *Ascension* as defining statements of the free jazz movement as it matured in the early 1960s. But of these four efforts, Taylor's is the most controlled and multidimensional. No vestiges of sentimentality, no easy resolutions or soothing cadences, deflect the sharp edges in this music. Yet it equally avoids empty emoting and unrelenting sturm-und-drang exhortation. Taylor remained a voluptuary with the heart of an ascetic: even when this music achieved paroxysms of release, an overriding austerity lingered just below the surface.

Taylor's efforts during the 1960s solidified his reputation as the most uncompromising exponent of the jazz avant-garde. With the jazz revival of the early 1970s, Taylor emerged as a respected elder statesman of the music—a surprising twist for this erstwhile revolutionary. But this was an uneasy process at best, and Taylor often found ways of subverting the established institutions that now tried to embrace him. Taylor was invited to teach at a major university—then caused an uproar by failing a large number of students and defying administration pressures to change the grades. Taylor played at the White House but scampered away from the bandstand after his performance—with the President of the United States, who simply wanted to give the pianist a compliment, forced to hustle after him. Taylor agreed to perform in tandem with the swing-to-bop modernist Mary Lou Williams—but rather than meeting Williams halfway, Taylor all but overpowered her playing with an explosive accompaniment of avant-garde piano technique. Yet by the close of the decade Taylor—for all his aloof exterior—had developed an unmatched skill in "working the system." On the back cover of his release *3 Phasis*, Taylor's record company boasts about its many sources of funding: "This disc was made possible through grants from American Broadcast Companies; Armco Inc.; Capital Cities Communication; Dow Jones; Mr. Francis Goelet; Gilman Foundation, Inc.; Occidental Petroleum Corporation; the Rockefeller Foundation; Sony Corporation; Union Pacific Corporation; and the National Endowment for the Arts." In time, Taylor would possess a curriculum vitae that few mainstream jazz players could dream of, with his Guggenheim fellowship, NEA grants, MacArthur "genius grant," and even an honorary doctorate from the New England Conservatory of Music, of which he had been a fierce critic in earlier years. He was voted into the *Downbeat* Jazz Hall of Fame by the critics in 1975, while McCoy Tyner, Keith Jarrett, Herbie Hancock, and others, perhaps more popular but less iconoclastic, had to wait another quarter of a century to join him. The militant outsider, it seems, had become the consummate inside man.

Yet Taylor's music stayed at the outer fringe despite his growing eminence. The 1970s were especially fertile years for Taylor's solo piano work. *Silent Tongues*, from 1974, was a major statement, with Taylor moving deftly from subtle quasi-classical moods to erupting volcanoes of dissonance. Other solo outings—*Air Above Mountains (Buildings Within)*, *Fly, Fly, Fly, Fly, Fly, Indent*—rounded out this picture of the keyboardist as human howitzer. At such times, Taylor almost succeeded in making solo jazz piano into an athletic exhibition: no one in jazz—or any other music—had ever attacked the keyboard so aggressively, had created such *big* sounds, had so overpowered the instrument. One expected strings to break, and bits of ivory and ebony to chip off the keys. The experience of seeing Taylor in such a vein could be riveting, convincing even free jazz nonbelievers of the persuasive power of his muse.

Although Taylor found that he was in most demand now as a solo performer, he resisted pigeonholing, continuing to broaden the range of his activities. His efforts increasingly went beyond the confines of instrumental performance, expanding to include chalk-screeching-on-the-blackboard vocals, ritualistic chanting, stylized body movements, poetry—the oddest fragments of cultural bric-a-brac. But even when seated at the keyboard, Taylor broke new ground. He was commissioned to write and perform a piece for ballet artists Mikhail Baryshnikov and Heather Watts. He composed and played for the Alvin Ailey Dance Company. He wrote for larger ensembles. He also continued to work in smaller combos, sometimes joined by long-time sideman Jimmy Lyons—an associate from the early 1960s until shortly before Lyons's death in 1986—whose full-toned alto work served as a firm anchor in the midst of Taylor's aural tidal wave. Taylor's massive recording project, *Cecil Taylor Berlin '88*, was perhaps his most panoramic venture of the period. This multidisc project—some twelve hours of music—found the pianist in collaboration with a wide range of players, many of them European, in settings spanning solo piano, duos, combos, and large bands.

The pioneering efforts of Taylor and Coleman had blossomed, by the mid-1960s, into a full-fledged movement. Former sidemen of these pioneers now emerged as major performers in their own right. Archie Shepp, who had worked with Taylor in the early 1960s, formed a quartet with Bill Dixon and later participated in the New York Contemporary Five with Don Cherry and John Tchicai. Shepp would also stand out as one of the most articulate publicists for the music, speaking frequently on its links to progressive political movements. Cherry went on to enjoy a successful career following his departure from Coleman's band, initiating a relationship with the Blue Note label that resulted in major works *Complete Communion* and *Symphony for Improvisers*. A series of six concerts at the Cellar Cafe, organized by Bill Dixon, presented under the rubric of the "October Revolution in Jazz," further legitimized the movement and featured Tchicai, Roswell Rudd, Paul Bley, Milford Graves, and Sun Ra, among others—in total, some forty groups graced the bandstand, playing mostly to capacity crowds. The success of this venture led to the formation of the Jazz Composers Guild, an umbrella organization for sponsoring the music of the avant-garde.

John Coltrane's conversion to the free style, around this same time, reinforced the expanding power and scope of the revolution. Only a short time before, Coltrane had been the leading light of mainstream tenor playing. Now in a series of recordings—above all with his orgiastic 1965 release *Ascension*—he emerged as one of the most radical of the new school. This formidable forty-minute performance found Coltrane and his rhythm section supplemented by a half-dozen horn players in a wild free-for-all—a superheated encounter that, for many listeners, served as the fitting, logical, and anarchistic end point of this quest for freedom. Follow-up projects—*Om*, *Kulu Se Mama*, *Meditation*—featured Coltrane in different settings, but equally intent on pushing to the outer limits of tonality and structure. A host of free players gathered around Coltrane, including tenorists Shepp and Pharoah Sanders, joining him on record and in concert.

Audiences reacted with mixed emotions to these demonstrations. When Coltrane performed a duet with Shepp at the Downbeat Jazz Festival in Chicago, the crowd split into factions, half cheering and urging on the musicians, the remainder shuffling restlessly, booing, many leaving. A similar divide was evident among jazz critics. Yet the true believers and caustic dissenters had, perhaps, more in common than they realized. Some listeners no doubt found a soothing catharsis in Coltrane's *Ascension* or Albert Ayler's *Spiritual Unity*, yet it is clear that many delighted precisely in the music's foreboding exterior. This latter group never pretended that shrill overtone squeals and distorted quarter-tone barks sounded mellifluous: it may not be going too far to suggest that the *worse* the music sounded, the better it suited their needs. Herbert Marcuse, the Marxist philosopher whose writings were widely read during this period, had built a theory of aesthetics on such grounds, celebrating art that refused to follow the strict ordering, the bureaucratic control, the confining rules of modern capitalist society. Jacques Attali, in his influential 1977 manifesto *Noise*, proclaimed that music—defined as "the organization of noise"—"symbolically signifies the channeling of violence."[12]

Such views marked a stunning reversal from the ancients—who sought for the sublime, for harmony and beauty, in works of art—instead substituting a fascination with disorder and discord. In practice, these attitudes could lead to surprising end points. One jazz critic, exulting in precisely this harsh exterior of the most progressive music, went so far as to brag that the records he recommended were precisely those that people were *least* likely to enjoy. It is impossible, in the final instance, to understand the full impact of the free movement without gauging this ethos, very much representative of the mid-1960s. Free jazz snubbed its nose at the established order, and in an era in which the "establishment" was increasingly under assault, this alone was a powerful rallying point. As such, the freedom movement shared in the same zeitgeist that gave birth to acid rock, campus demonstrations, and the 1960s counterculture. Both the advocates and detractors of the avant-garde sensed this, to greater and lesser degrees, and though their debates often seemed to focus on the music, a deeper strain of discourse, politicized and ideologically charged, almost always underscored these interchanges. Simply put: what one thought about this body of work had much to do with what one felt about the prevailing state of affairs in society.

Yet alongside this celebration of the anarchic elements in the music, a vague utopianism also emerged. Fans of free jazz hardly blinked when critic John Litweiler predicted that avant-garde music would be "philosophically crucial to humanity as a whole" and "lead to a new consciousness that will deter mankind from its present catastrophic course." In a similar vein, David Such announced, in his book *Avant-Garde Jazz Musicians: Performing "Out There"*, that free jazz helps life "achieve purposefulness" and points the way toward "solving at least a portion of the problems and misunderstandings in the world."[13] This profusion of grand claims and counterclaims was very much part and parcel of the progressive wing of the jazz world. One could probably determine this merely by looking at the album covers, which announced "the shape of jazz to come" or the "change of the century"—claims no jazz player in any other style would dare to make. Even after it became clear that atonality was not the end point of jazz, merely a stopping point in a constantly fluctuating scene, this sharply ideological component in free jazz, and even more in discussions about it, has persisted, almost as if the ways critics conceptualize jazz got frozen sometime around the late 1950s and early 1960s. With the passing years, free jazz has become just another style—but the very ethos of the music hardly allows its fans to settle for anything less than a preeminent position as the Hegelian end point in the history of jazz.

Among the second wave of free jazz players, Albert Ayler would grasp with the greatest clarity the deconstructive phase the movement was now entering. He explained to interviewers that the goal now was to escape from playing notes and enter a new realm in which the saxophone created *sound*. In contrast to Ornette Coleman, many of whose solos could be notated and analyzed for their musicological implications, Ayler defied such assimilation. The well-tempered scales of Western music were incapable of encompassing the bellowing, moaning spasms that fled from the bell of his horn. Ayler was a master of the "dirty" tone, that calling card of the African American musical tradition with a lineage predating Louis Armstrong and Robert Johnson. He was a virtuoso of the coarse and anomalous, with an impressive bag of tricks at his disposal: stomach-churning waverings out of tune; low-register barks and high-pitched squeals; a vibrato so wide that it bordered on parody; darting phrases, hieroglyphics of sound representing some hitherto unknown sublunar mode; tones Adolphe Sax never dreamed of and Selmer never sanctioned.

Yet there was also a traditional side to Ayler's music. His compositions frequently featured unadorned diatonic melodies, which contrasted starkly with his heated free jazz improvisations. Ballads found Ayler's expansive vibrato lingering over simple whole-note and half-note patterns. On faster compositions, Ayler's efforts often sounded like lilting folk songs, evoking quasi-European vernacular music of another place, another century. These influences coexisted with more specific African American sources of inspiration, the residue of Ayler's personal history. In his native Cleveland, where he was born in 1936, Ayler performed saxophone duets in church with his father, who also introduced his son to swing and bebop jazz styles. During Ayler's teens, formal saxophone study was supplemented with work in jazz and rhythm-and-blues bands, as well as summer stints on the road with bluesman Little

Walter. In his early twenties, Ayler served three years in the military, playing in army ensembles, occasionally gracing the bandstands of European jazz clubs while stationed overseas, and listening to the free jazz sounds that were beginning to gain wider exposure.

Ayler's first recordings, made during the early 1960s in Scandinavia, find him fighting against the constraints of the mainstream jazz tradition. By 1964, however, Ayler had developed his mature style, distinguished by an untempered excitability. Ayler had meanwhile found a group of sympathetic fellow travelers to support his explorations: drummer Sunny Murray, a master of free-time percussion; bassist Gary Peacock, who could move with ease between conventional structures and atonality, and was especially skillful at exploring the ambiguous middle ground between the two; Don Cherry, who frequently sat in with Ayler and joined his band on a European tour. *Witches and Devils*, Ayler's February 1964 quartet date, showed how completely the tenorist had broken away from the customary jazz vocabulary. Elements of Ornette Coleman and John Coltrane are more prominent in his playing, but they too are subservient to Ayler's rougher, looser conception. Murray's drum kit is the epicenter of unsettling reverberations hinting at underlying rhythms, but never resolving into conventional time. The ensuing trio recording *Spiritual Unity*, which featured Ayler alongside Murray and Peacock, was a major statement, the most cohesive ensemble project the saxophonist had undertaken to date. Ayler showed that his radical remaking of the jazz saxophone vocabulary was largely self-sufficient, needing no other horns to set it off or support its blistering attack. It encompassed fervent explorations of harmonics, haunting stringlike evocations in the higher register, and Vesuvian explosions of sonic lava. Peacock and Murray hold onto these energized lines with the determination of cowpokes latching onto steers at the rodeo. To their credit, they grapple masterfully with Ayler's unpredictable leaps and turns.

Ayler's brother Donald joined as trumpeter in the band in March 1965 and remained a key colleague for the next three years. The younger sibling contributed uninhibited sound collages that complemented the saxophonist's fractious work. But he suffered from emotional instability and a drinking problem, which precipitated his firing from the band in 1968. In the latter half of the decade, Albert Ayler's music began to incorporate elements of a variety of vernacular styles. These included rock, R&B, blues, gospel, vocal harmonies, even bagpipe music. His 1968 release *New Grass* must rank among the strangest jazz albums of the decade, with its attempt to mix freedom music and formulas from the commercial hits of the day. Here Ayler's untempered saxophony is backed by a hard-grooving rhythm section that includes funkmeister drummer Bernard Purdie, and is overwhelmed by a team of sassy if undistinguished Motown-ish singers. This new direction was mostly lamented by fans of Ayler's earlier work and did little to broaden his appeal among the dominant rock audience of the day. Shortly before his death, the saxophonist showed signs of moving away from these crossover efforts.

In November 1970, Ayler disappeared, and some three weeks later his body was found in the East River. He was thirty-four years old. Death by drowning was the verdict of the New York Medical Examiner's office. Some commentators mused about foul play, with rumors circulating about a mysterious bullet wound in the corpse (although denied by pianist Call Cobbs, who helped to identify the body). Others recalled signs of depression and mental instability that may have led Ayler to take his own life. Under other circumstances, the 1970s jazz revival would have surely given a major boost to Ayler's career, but his early death ensured that the accolades would be posthumous.

Yet this saxophonist's period of peak creativity, for all its brevity, marked an important turning point in the history of jazz. Anthony Braxton has sometimes spoken of a post-Ayler era in the music, setting up this figure as point of demarcation in the evolution of the avant-garde in jazz—a revealing nomenclature that helps us understand why so much later jazz retreated from a full embrace of the freedom imperative rather than try to move "beyond Ayler" into a further stage of liberation from the strictures of Western tonality. In truth, it was hard to conceive what freedom "beyond Ayler" might represent, since the saxophonist's bold leap outside the world of notes into the full flux of sound seemed more a liminal point than a springboard to the next thing. Perhaps, then, it should come as no surprise that, almost at the moment of Ayler's death, the biggest sensation in the jazz world was a rock-inflected album by Miles Davis, called *Bitches Brew*, that rudely countered rather than extended the avant-garde tendencies that had been so powerful during the previous decade.

FUSION AND ELECTRONICA

Jazz has always been a music of fusion. "Nothing from New Orleans is ever pure"—so goes an old throwaway phrase. But even by Crescent City standards, early jazz was an especially complex mélange. The southern mentality that obsessively measured infinitesimal gradations—delineating differences of quadroon from octoroon the way Aquinas demarked archangels from cherubim and seraphim—quickly came to a cul-de-sac in tracing the lineage of this radical new music. Impure at its birth, jazz grew ever more so as it evolved. Its history is marked by a fondness for musical miscegenation, by its desire to couple with other styles and idioms, producing new, radically different progeny. In its earliest form, jazz showed an ability to assimilate the blues, the rag, the march, and other idioms; as it evolved, it transformed a host of even more disparate sounds and styles. It showed no pretensions, mixing as easily with vernacular musics—the American popular song, the Cuban *son*, the Brazilian samba, the Argentinian tango—as with concert hall fare. Jazz in its contemporary form bears traces of all these passages. It is the most glorious of mongrels.

Yet the concept of jazz as music of fusion took on particular relevance at the close of the 1960s. Jazz was on the brink of an especially pronounced period of absorption and expansion. Over the next decade, the music's leading exponents would attempt ambitious fusions with a dizzying array of popular, ethnic, and classical styles. At times, the resulting hybrids would be so far afield from the music's tradition that listeners would ask in puzzlement whether the results could still be called jazz. Such experiments would even call into question the jazz world's most sacred legacy: the syncopated sense of swing. In its place, one now encountered a wide array of alternative rhythms: on-the-beat rock riffs, world-beat drones, smoothly flowing quasi-classical styles, and experiments in free time. The types of fusion would vary widely, from the ethereal concert hall overtones of the ECM sound to the grooving disco beat of jazz-rock, but they shared an increasingly outward-looking focus. By the close of the 1970s, Buddy Bolden's legacy had truly conquered the world, but the New Orleans pioneer would hardly recognize his own progeny. It had become more than a style of music—it was a perspective that seemingly could encompass all musics.

Yet for most listeners during this period, the term *fusion* had a very narrow and specific meaning. It described highly commercial attempts to combine jazz with rock music. Miles Davis's recording of *Bitches Brew* at the close of the 1960s was a signal event in this regard. It legitimized a whole new area of exploration and experimentation for jazz musicians. This emerging rock-tinged sound substantially broadened the jazz audience, and one suspects that it played a decisive role in spurring the improving financial environment for all jazz styles during the 1970s. Fans who were introduced to jazz through fusion soon developed a taste for other styles of improvised music. As a result, the economic base of jazz broadened and stabilized during this period, after years of stagnation and decline. New clubs opened, jazz labels proliferated, and expatriate musicians returned from their overseas exiles.

Sales figures for *Bitches Brew* provide an impressive measure of this change of affairs. A typical Davis mid-1960s release, despite the critical acclaim and lasting significance of this music, would sell fewer than 100,000 units at the time of release. But fans purchased 400,000 copies of *Bitches Brew* within its first year. Davis built on this new audience with a vengeance: he recorded prolifically over the next eighteen months, amazing Columbia executives, who had previously found it difficult to entice him into the studio; he showed up at company publicity functions and played on television shows; he agreed to perform in rock venues, such as Fillmore West and Fillmore East, even when it meant serving as lead-in act for another band. Davis was also now working with a wider range of musicians and sounds—for instance, the *Bitches Brew* sessions found Davis using twelve sidemen, ten of them in the rhythm section. Only Wayne Shorter was a holdover from the mid-1960s quintet.

Some critics accused Davis of selling out. Yet the remarkable thing about *Bitches Brew* was how little Davis attempted to mimic current trends in pop and rock music. All but one of the tracks lasted for over ten minutes—virtually guaranteeing that Davis would receive little radio airplay. The songs studiously avoided slick commercialism. Listeners seeking tight arrangements, melodic hooks, simple dance beats, or memorable lyrics were inevitably disappointed. This was raw, unfiltered music, rambling, discursive, and often unwieldy. The large rhythm section created thick, soupy textures. And the bandleader remained coy, often allowing the sidemen to work over long static vamps before entering on trumpet. Even then, Davis's horn lines were far from solos in any conventional sense. Instead, they seemed just one more layer of sound, placed on top of the churning cauldron underneath. This record may be, as many claim, the father of 1970s fusion. Yet if so, one struggles to see its paternal resemblance to the overly arranged, ever-so-slick Grover Washington and Spyro Gyra releases it supposedly spawned.

Davis built on this aesthetic vision in a series of follow-up projects. Producer Teo Macero took on an increasingly important role at this time, employing radical tape-splicing techniques to sculpt finished performances from the mass of studio and live material that Davis was recording. On the release of Davis's soundtrack music for the film *Jack Johnson*, one of the trumpeter's strongest projects from the period, Macero created a dramatic shift in Davis's piece "Yesternow" by incorporating excerpts from "Shh/Peaceful"—recorded over a year before with a different band. The contrast is unnerving and disjunctive, yet very much in keeping with the helter-skelter sensibility of the new Davis sound. *Live-Evil*, from this same period, offers a similarly bizarre contrast, with the results of Davis's intriguing studio project with the quirky Brazilian instrumentalist-composer Hermeto Pascoal strangely juxtaposed with live performances of Davis's working band. At times it almost seemed as if Davis were defying the rock audiences who were now flocking to see him. Above all, he avoided the onstage recapitulation of hit records—the time-honored formula for popular bands—in favor of a restless linking of sundry fragments, set to a miasma of rhythmic sound.

Yet the rawness of this music, one suspects, accounted for much of its commercial success. It displayed a rebellious streak that was in tune with the counterculture attitudes of the late 1960s, giving Davis credibility with younger listeners who probably would have been "turned off" by a slicker format. The proof of this came with Davis's 1972 *On the Corner*. Here Davis was willing to employ more overtly commercial elements, especially more insistent dance rhythms. Yet critics mostly panned the new sound, and sales failed to meet Davis's expectations. With *Bitches Brew*, Davis had tapped into young and mostly white rock listeners, but with *On the Corner* and its follow-up projects, Davis looked to draw an urban black following. In truth, many of Davis's former sidemen were passing him by in this regard. In 1975, Davis was relegated to touring as warm-up act for Herbie Hancock, whose jazz fusion/funk band Headhunters was reaching the same young black audience to which Davis merely aspired.

The mixed reaction to his music was only one of many problems Davis now faced. An October 1972 car accident left him with two broken ankles. His left hip, which had been operated on years before, was increasingly in pain and often left him immobilized. A bleeding ulcer added to his medical complaints, as did nodes on his larynx that constricted his breathing and left him short-winded when playing the trumpet. His drinking and drug problems further contributed to his deteriorating condition. Despite these aggravations, Davis continued an active schedule, undertaking concert performances in Japan in early 1975 that were recorded and eventually released as *Agharta* and *Pangaea*. But these were parting shots. Soon Davis had retired from the music scene. By his own admission, he did not pick up the horn for over four years and rarely left his home.

Yet the fusion movement, Davis's legacy, was now entrenched as the most commercially viable jazz style of the period. Former members of Davis's various bands were taking the lead in this area, with three ensembles proving especially influential: Chick Corea's Return to Forever, John McLaughlin's Mahavishnu Orchestra, and Weather Report, co-led by Wayne Shorter and Joe Zawinul. But this represented only part of the impact of former Davis sidemen on the new idiom. Hancock's 1973 *Head Hunters* release achieved massive sales and brought many younger listeners into the jazz camp with funk-oriented pieces such as "Chameleon" and an updated version of "Watermelon Man." This album initiated a bifurcated career for Hancock, with his efforts now divided between mainstream jazz, often of the highest quality, and overtly commercial projects with little jazz substance. His 1979 release *Feets Don't Fail Me Now* found him lamely singing (albeit with the aid of a voice synthesizer) and regurgitating a vapid pseudo-disco sound—yet around that same time, Hancock participated in a stunning two-piano concert tour with Chick Corea and an impressive reunion with the VSOP band, essentially a regrouping of the mid-1960s Davis quintet with Freddie Hubbard filling Miles's role. In later years, Hancock would prove to be something of a chameleon himself, with projects that showcased his mainstream jazz skills (*Quartet, Directions in Music*), his world music interests (*The Imagine Project*), his taste for funk and electronica (*Perfect Machine*), and his celebration of diverse songwriters (*Gershwin's World, The New Standard, River: The Joni Letters*—the latter release earning a Grammy as album of the year in 2008, the first time a jazz record had been so honored since *Getz/Gilberto* back in 1965). George Benson, whose guitar work had graced Davis's *Miles in the Sky* release, made a more successful switch to vocal work. His mid-1970s cover version of Leon Russell's "This Masquerade," from the *Breezin'* album, initiated a series of pop hits for Benson—a success that threatened to obscure his talent as a soloist in a Wes Montgomery vein. Tony Williams's Lifetime band, which included organist Larry Young and guitarist John McLaughlin, was not as commercially successful as Hancock's or Benson's fusion efforts, but provided an even more sophisticated blending of rock energy with jazz instrumental prowess. Many lesser-known Davis associates—Airto, Lonnie Liston Smith, Michael Henderson, and others—would never achieve the success of *Head Hunters, Breezin'* or *Bitches Brew*, but also sought, with varying degrees of success, to seize the momentum of the moment in attracting a crossover audience for their own bands.

Chick Corea had already established himself as one of the most prominent jazz pianists of his generation when he founded his Return to Forever fusion group toward the close of 1971. Corea's early professional efforts found him working in both jazz ensembles and Latin bands. His mainstream jazz approach, as it evolved, boasted a clean, sharply articulated piano sound, a mix of modal and impressionist harmonies, and a driving on-top-of-the-beat rhythmic feel. His 1967 sideman work on Stan Getz's *Sweet Rain* project already bespoke a mature piano stylist and composer, and his 1968 leader date *Now He Sings, Now He Sobs* drew much-deserved praise as one of the most creative piano trio projects of the period. Around this same time, Corea joined Davis's group and participated on *Bitches Brew* and several follow-up recordings, but, by the start of the 1970s, Corea had left the trumpeter to explore freer structures in his Circle band. In addition, Corea's exceptional two volumes of piano improvisations for the ECM label from 1971 showed him refining a more song-oriented style, one that became even more prominent in Return to Forever. This ensemble, formed in 1972, found the keyboardist assisted by a strong cast of accompanists, especially bassist Stanley Clarke and later guitarist Al Di Meola, both virtuoso instrumentalists who could match Corea in moving from electric to acoustic settings and creating an appealing blend of jazz, rock-pop, and Brazilian/Latin sounds. Corea was especially adept at incorporating the latter elements into his compositions, as demonstrated by the crossover success of his pieces "La Fiesta" and "Spain."

In the 1980s, Corea increasingly played in a trio format, for a time reuniting with veterans Roy Haynes and Miroslav Vitous (who had participated on the *Now He Sings, Now He Sobs* project), and later forming a dynamic ensemble with bassist John Patitucci and drummer Dave Weckl. Like Hancock, Corea was now alternating between electric and acoustic settings, yet without the sharp disjunction of styles revealed by the former's efforts—indeed the same Corea-Patitucci-Weckl group would perform alternately as the Elektric Band and the Akoustic Band, with the two approaches revealing a marked convergence. Later Corea groups would play variations on these themes and encompass everything from gritty acoustic combos (such as the New Trio with Avishai Cohen and Jeff Ballard, and the beefed-up Origin sextet) to electric supergroups, as demonstrated on the 2008 Return to Forever reunion and the 2009 Five Peace Band collaboration with John McLaughlin. Along the way, Corea has recorded duet projects with everyone from vocalist Bobby McFerrin to banjoist Béla Fleck, performed classical works, and even composed his own piano concerto and string quartet. As with so many of his peers, Corea's embrace of jazz-rock fusion has ultimately proven to be merely one facet of a career that is ultimately more eclectic than electric.

John McLaughlin worked in Tony Williams's Lifetime band, as well as on Davis's early fusion efforts, before branching out on his own with the Mahavishnu Orchestra in 1971. Born in Yorkshire, England, in 1942, McLaughlin was active in the London scene, where he played not only with jazz groups but also alongside rock musicians such as Eric Clapton, Mick Jagger, and Jack Bruce, before moving to the United States in 1969. The Mahavishnu Orchestra's music reflected McLaughlin's deep rock roots—in many ways Hendrix was more of a role model for these efforts than Miles—an orientation that was heightened by the absence of a horn player in the band. Yet McLaughlin's interests also ranged over many genres beyond jazz and rock, as witnessed by his facility in flamenco (demonstrated in his later collaborations with Paco de Lucia), Indian music (highlighted in his late 1970s band Shakti), and the classical/acoustic guitar tradition (increasingly evident in the 1980s and 1990s, for instance, in his guitar concerto, premiered with the Los Angeles Philharmonic Orchestra in 1985). Jazz writer Joachim Berendt seemingly went out on a limb in the early 1970s when he claimed McLaughlin "symbolizes the complete integration of all the elements that have played a role in today's music."[14] Yet McLaughlin's later career has tended to substantiate this high-flown praise.

Like Corea and McLaughlin, Joe Zawinul and Wayne Shorter worked on the *Bitches Brew* sessions, only to leave to form their own fusion band at the start of the 1970s. The resulting supergroup Weather Report would rank as one of the most popular and influential jazz bands of its day. Both Zawinul and Shorter had come of age in the hard-bop era; Shorter apprenticed with Art Blakey while Zawinul had worked with Cannonball Adderley, for whom he wrote the hit "Mercy, Mercy, Mercy." This blues-drenched funk piece must have seemed, to listeners at the time, an incongruous output from the Vienna-born, conservatory-trained Zawinul, yet this same sensitivity to dance rhythms and popular styles assisted Weather Report in its rise to fame. With Weather Report, Zawinul used his many electric keyboards to create orchestral layers of sound and a much more compositionally-oriented style than the other fusion bands of the era were pursuing. The line between soloist and accompanist was blurred; in its place was a flowing, electronic ambiance in which the band would move between different grooves and composed vignettes. The group's biggest hit, Zawinul's piece "Birdland" (from the 1976 release *Heavy Weather*), was a stirring example of this approach at its best. The piece shifts between several contrasting moods, underlined by distinctive pulses and textures, culminating in a simple, catchy melody locked atop a perky harmonic and rhythmic foundation. With its sophistication and tunefulness, and above all in its variety and compression, such an approach can be viewed as the aesthetic of Ellington applied to the dominant electronic pop style of the 1970s.

Yet there were crucial differences between Ellington and Weather Report. Duke's band had been marked by a consistency of personnel, with many players staying for decades, while Weather Report went through frequent changeovers, with only Zawinul and Shorter maintaining the band's continuity. But even more telling, where the Duke had built his compositions around his soloists, Zawinul preferred to submerge the individual musicians into the total atmosphere of his pieces. In time, Wayne Shorter's fans began to grumble that one of the great saxophonists in jazz was being relegated to occasional fills and interludes, and would point to Shorter's mid-1970s work with the VSOP Quintet and his stellar 1974 leader date *Native Dancer* (with Milton Nascimento) as better vehicles for his talents—not to mention his classic Blue Note leader dates and Jazz Messenger efforts from the 1960s. Yet to Zawinul's credit, one must acknowledge that this "negation" of the soloist allowed him to craft an innovative, quasi-conversational approach to composing. Melodic fragments might be stated by any instrument and inspire a response from an equally unpredictable direction. Stitch by stitch, these scraps of sound were woven together into impressive large-scale works.

The arrival of electric bassist Jaco Pastorius in the band during the mid-1970s represented a jarring contrast with this collectivist ethos. Brash and flamboyant, Pastorius defied the stereotype of the bassist as the behind-the-scenes member of a jazz combo who hid out next to the drummer. He was a charismatic figure who dazzled audiences and introduced legions of rock fans to the intricacies of jazz. Who else could have inspired countless teenage bassists to learn Charlie Parker's intricate "Donna Lee" bop line on their instrument? Yet Pastorius's flashy recording of this piece proved to be one of the most admired and emulated fusion outings of the decade. Critics sometimes dismissed his onstage antics as the work of a superficial showman, but Pastorius usually backed up his posturing and pouting with prodigious technique and remarkably pure intonation. His presence energized the *Heavy Weather* recording, as well as many other sideman and leader projects.

One of the most noteworthy of these sideman appearances came on *Bright Size Life*, a 1976 release that represented the debut leader date for guitarist Pat Metheny.

Metheny arrived on the scene at a late stage in the jazz-rock fusion movement, and his career can be seen both as a final culmination of this movement's potential and also as a sign of the jazz world's desire to move beyond the constraining formulas of the genre. Certainly Metheny's music has frequently defied categorization, running counter to the expectations of the fusion audience. One suspects that much of his artistry is intertwined with this very ambivalence about adapting to commercial demands. At the height of his career, Metheny recorded a densely atonal project with Ornette Coleman, almost as a way of distancing himself from the increasingly vapid commercial jazz scene with which he was associated. A few years later, Metheny once again surprised his audience by taking on a sideman gig with young tenor titan Joshua Redman. But even back at the time of *Bright Size Life*, Metheny showed a knack for integrating pop-rock elements into a probing jazz style, while studiously avoiding the clichés of both idioms.

Although Metheny is a masterful technician (teaching guitar at the Berklee jazz conservatory while still in his teens), his playing avoids the empty demonstration of finger facility so common among jazz-rock guitarists. Instead, he has refined a lucid, melodic style that, at its best, merits comparisons with the incisive electric guitar work of Wes Montgomery. The addition of the like-minded keyboard soundscapist Lyle Mays to Metheny's band in 1976 spurred an especially fruitful partnership documented on recordings for the ECM and Geffen labels. Metheny's most impressive achievements in the fusion idiom have been a series of genre-crossing recordings—*Still Life (Talking)* from 1987, *Letter from Home* from 1989, and *Secret Story* from 1992—that incorporate advanced jazz compositional techniques with pop-rock and Brazilian elements. These are highly original projects that sound deceptively simple, yet include some of the most sophisticated jazz writing of the late 1980s and early 1990s. Periodically Metheny has returned to more mainstream settings, most notably in collaborations with Charlie Haden, Brad Mehldau, and Jim Hall, where he reveals a chamber jazz sensibility that contrasts markedly with the loud and boisterous tendencies of the fusion style.

Like Metheny, the Brecker Brothers established themselves as fusion masters without first passing through a period of apprenticeship with Miles Davis. Yet these talented siblings—saxophonist Michael born in 1949 and trumpeter Randy born in 1945—were already journeyman players with deep jazz and rock roots by the time they released *The Brecker Brothers* on the Arista label in 1975. Michael had worked with Horace Silver and Billy Cobham, while Randy had played on the first Blood, Sweat and Tears album as well as with Art Blakey, Horace Silver, and Larry Coryell's The Eleventh House. Even after they had become marquee artists, both brothers continued to supplement their leader dates with frequent sideman appearances and were in great demand as session players—in time their instrumental work would be featured alongside a veritable who's who of late twentieth-century popular music stars, including Bruce Springsteen, Paul Simon, Frank Sinatra, Joni Mitchell, Frank Zappa, and James Taylor. But the Brecker Brothers were jazz musicians first and foremost, and their most characteristic work mixed large doses of hard bop and modal music with rock and funk elements in an appealing hybrid. Michael Brecker would emerge as an especially influential post-Trane stylist. His rapidfire technique and mastery of a seemingly endless array of patterns and licks, married to a hard, cutting tone, made him the perfect saxophonist to survive in an age of guitarists, a flamboyant soloist who could rise to the occasion, whether he was working with an intimate jazz combo or on a festival stage surrounded by mountains of amplification and thousands of fans. While other fusion stars struggled to maintain their audience when the new traditionalists emerged on the scene in the 1980s and 1990s, Michael Brecker didn't miss a beat. His post–Brecker Brothers leader dates often took on a more mainstream guise, with fewer rock-funk elements, yet he was just as prepossessing flying over the changes of the old standards as grooving over a funky backbeat.

Most historical surveys of the fusion movement have focused on bands with deep jazz roots such as Weather Report and Return to Forever. Yet many of the most creative efforts in the fusion idiom came from rock musicians who borrowed and adapted the techniques of jazz. Even before *Bitches Brew*, the rock bands Chicago and Blood, Sweat and Tears had successfully married a jazz horn section to a rock rhythm section. The latter's recording of Billie Holiday's "God Bless the Child" from their second album was as creative as any of the efforts coming from the jazz side of the fence during fusion's heyday. Woody Herman alumnus Bill Chase took a similar approach with his invigorating early 1970s band Chase, which matched four trumpets with a rock rhythm section and vocalist. Rock guitarists were also expanding their use of jazz techniques with great success during this period. Jimi Hendrix's efforts in this regard were so successful that they in turn influenced jazz musicians such as Davis and McLaughlin. The more soul-oriented recordings of Sly Stone and James Brown were also acknowledged as important precedents by many jazz fusion players. During this period, the group Steely Dan was proving that pop-rock could equally benefit from a healthy dose of jazz. On projects such as *Pretzel Logic*, *Katy Lied*, *Aja*, and Steely Dan co-founder Donald Fagen's solo project *The Nightfly*, the results were quirky yet appealing, delighting fans with a new type of electrified art song suitable for FM airplay. The presence of jazz icons as guest artists—Wayne Shorter and Phil Woods made cameo appearances with the band—no doubt raised the level of Steely Dan's sessions, but even the lowliest accompanists on these projects were studio demigods with serious jazz chops. Recordings of this caliber proved that fusion was a two-way street, and that for every hard bopper who went electric, there were creative pop acts raising the level of their music through a judicious borrowing of jazz stylings.

In contrast, Frank Zappa's connections to the jazz idiom were mostly hidden behind an outlandish onstage persona, yet his projects from the late 1960s and early 1970s such as *Hot Rats*, *Uncle Meat*, *Waka/Jawaka*, and *The Grand Wazoo* represent, on the whole, some of that period's most ambitious and effective examples of the integration of jazz (as well as many other) techniques into a rock setting. Zappa always chose to distance himself from jazz—it was, he joked, the "music of unemployment." On other occasions, he would announce: "Jazz is not dead. . . . It just smells funny." Yet his music during the period 1969–72 was so permeated by the jazz fusion vocabulary that it sometimes seemed as if Zappa were on the verge of abandoning his rock roots. His choice of sidemen (including prominent up-and-coming fusion bandleaders George Duke and Jean-Luc Ponty) furthered this stylistic shift, while the demands of his intricate writing ensured that Zappa's groups, perhaps alone among the rock bands of the day, could match many major jazz combos in terms of breadth and depth of musicianship. As the 1970s progressed, Zappa cut back on the jazz trappings of his music—and sold more records as a result. The mass audience clearly preferred Zappa engaging in novelty songs such as "Valley Girl" and "Dancin' Fool" rather than as a competitor to Miles or The Mahavishnu Orchestra, yet his music from this period of flirtation with fusion deserves more respect from the jazz world.

As the 1970s were wrapping up, the golden age of fusion was coming to a mostly unhappy ending. Weather Report continued to record new albums until 1986, but the later installments of the band matched neither the commercial success nor critical esteem it had achieved a decade earlier. The following year Jaco Pastorius, who had left the band in 1981, died as the result of a beating at the hands of a nightclub doorman, but substance abuse problems and mental instability had already effectively ended his brief reign as a fusion star. Return to Forever had split up even earlier, disbanding after the 1977 *Musicmagic* release. Except for a brief get-together in 1983, the group would not reassemble until its 2008 reunion tour. Mahavishnu Orchestra also disbanded in 1976 (although it too attempted a 1980s reunion). Even Miles Davis took an extended break from the scene, all but disappearing from 1975 to 1981. By the time he returned, the fusion movement he had set in motion was clearly in decline.

Did this signal that the integration of electronic sounds into jazz had been a failed experiment? Hardly. If the heroic age of fusion had ended, a new era of electronica had begun. Jazz artists continued to experiment with technological tools after the 1970s, but now they were just as likely to involve a laptop computer or piece of studio equipment as a synthesizer or electric guitar in the center of the stage. Sometime even low-tech devices managed to shake up the proceedings. Herbie Hancock's successful single "Rockit" from his 1983 album *Future Shock* surprised many listeners at the time by featuring Grand Mixer DXT "scratching" records—in essence, moving them back and forth by hand on a turntable to create various patterns of sound, usually highly rhythmic in nature. Even open-minded jazz fans may have had a hard time accepting a turntable as a musical instrument, yet resistance would gradually soften as scratches, loops, and samples, as well as programming tools of various sorts, found their place in the jazz world.

The rise of "acid jazz" a few years later, with its borrowings from soul, jazz, rap, house music, and other sources, made increasingly clear the old roots that often served as fuel for these new sounds. Acid jazz, despite the U.S. origins of its various musical ingredients, was a distinctly international movement from the start. It first gained widespread popularity in London at the close of the 1980s—where Gilles Peterson, credited with coining the term "acid jazz," and other disc jockeys experimented by combining classic jazz recordings with percussion tracks and electronic dance beats. The sound quickly gained an enthusiastic following in Japan, Germany, Brazil, Eastern Europe, and other locales, as well as in the United States. The band Us3, which also came out of the London music scene, followed a similar borrow-from-the-classics formula, underscoring their rap lines with hard-bop elements sampled from the Blue Note catalog. Anyone who had doubts about the potential listener appeal of these mix-and-match styles need only look at the sales figures to understand the commercial potential of sampling jazz recordings. Us3's debut recording quickly became the fastest selling jazz-rap effort to date, attracting many buyers who neither hung out at dance halls nor went to jazz clubs. The band became the first Blue Note recording act to go platinum, selling a million copies in the United States—an ironic turn of events given how much of the creative energy on this CD resulted from appropriating the work of jazz legends who had never enjoyed much financial success.

Around this same time, A Tribe Called Quest borrowed samples from a host of jazz sources—Cannonball Adderley, Art Blakey, Freddie Hubbard, Jack DeJohnette—for its pioneering 1991 release *The Low End Theory*. This disk went platinum and was selected by *Time* magazine in 2006 as one of the one hundred best albums of all time. Yet with A Tribe Called Quest, Us3, and many of the other first-generation bands drawing on jazz material in the rap/acid jazz community, the music stopped short of a true fusion, settling instead for a parasitical relationship in which tasty licks and grooves were plundered from old hard-bop, soul jazz, and fusion records and made subservient to the intentions of their new young masters. Input from the jazz side was usually secondhand, a matter of drawing on the archives as needed. However, by the mid-1990s, more ambitious efforts to combine original jazz and contemporary black popular music were underway, many of them involving respected jazz players, such as Max Roach, Branford Marsalis, Steve Coleman, Greg Osby, and Donald Byrd. Rapper Guru (born Keith Edward Elam in 1966) collaborated with a number of seasoned jazz artists in crafting an appealing hybrid of hip-hop and jazz for a series of albums released under the name *Jazzmatazz*. These projects sold well in the United States and overseas, proving again that a jazz musician could play a role in this music as more than just a source for a sample. One suspects that such participation by first-rate jazz talent—not just through digital borrowings but in the flesh—will prove critical if this hybrid style is to become an influential part of the jazz tradition. Certainly a rapprochement of this sort between hip-hoppers and instrumental improvisers must be seen as a promising development by those who feel that jazz needs periodically to renew its ties to current popular music and dance styles.

Had Miles Davis lived longer, he would no doubt have played a significant role in this process. At the end of his life, he made clear his interest in finding common ground between the two worlds of jazz and hip-hop. Then again, almost every shift in the jazz sensibility during the last half of the twentieth century had involved this mercurial artist, and the trumpeter revealed, if anything, even greater restlessness in seeking after new sounds in the final days of his career. In the 1980s, a new generation of traditionalists were embracing acoustic instruments and the old Tin Pan Alley songs, but Davis was becoming more overtly commercial than ever before. He returned to the recording studio and concert hall, released cover versions of pop songs by Cyndi Lauper and Michael Jackson, and in general worked within tighter, more overtly arranged settings, which often reflected the influence of bassist Marcus

Miller. Davis's death, on September 28, 1991, at age sixty-five, came in the midst of another period of self-invention. The posthumously released *doo-bop* recording gives us an insight into the new direction the trumpeter was taking, relying on rapper Easy Mo Bee as producer and performer. The lyrics adopt various street-smart attitudes, ranging from praise of the trumpeter's musicianship ("Miles Davis style is different, you can't describe it as Pacific / He rip, rage and roar, no time for watchin' Andy Griffith") to even more vehement proclamations of Easy Mo Bee's and the ailing Davis's sexual prowess ("the notes from his horn make ladies get freaky like sex"). Many listeners and critics no doubt cringed at hearing this legendary artist in such a setting, yet Davis was simply following his accustomed script, and trying to anticipate the next stage of jazz fusion.

In an ironic twist, Davis himself would show up on the receiving end of this new mix-and-match sensibility when, after his death, bassist and studio visionary Bill Laswell tinkered with tapes from the trumpeter's electric period to create new versions of the old music. Laswell is credited with "reconstruction & mix translation" on the resulting *Panthalassa: The Music of Miles Davis 1969–1974* release—vague descriptors, but all too indicative of the new state of affairs in jazz in which the roles of musician, producer, and engineer are not nearly as distinct as they once were. Laswell's reconfigurations of Davis were mesmerizing, and many fans no doubt preferred them to the original versions of this music. Yet they raised troubling ethical issues about whether canonical performances from the past should be expropriated in this way. Davis's own practices made these questions all the more pointed, since his late career recordings were heavily dependent on the studio splicing and dicing of his producer Teo Macero, and the hip-hop sensibility he embraced at the end of his life was deeply aligned with the idea that earlier recordings exist to be pilfered, manipulated, and exploited in the interest of doing something new.

While Davis was making cover versions of pop hits, the M-Base Collective, a group of young New York players that included Greg Osby, Steve Coleman, and Cassandra Wilson, was taking a different approach to revitalizing funk-oriented playing in the jazz world. The M-Base crew articulated an ardent defense of the virtues of mixing jazz and popular dance-based idioms, meanwhile concocting a complex type of groove music, with a less stereotyped sense of time and a greater openness to shades of dissonance. Vocalist Wilson soon moved on to a more broad-based style that included jazz standards (most notably on 1988 *Blue Skies* release), traditional blues (including cover versions of Robert Johnson and Muddy Waters songs), unusual pop material (from Hank Williams to the Monkees), and her own compositions. In a series of albums—*Blue Light 'til Dawn* (1993), *Blue Skies* (1988), *Glamoured* (2003), *Thunderbird* (2006)—she has asserted herself as a leading jazz diva. Pianist Geri Allen, another M-Base collaborator, also showed remarkable depth and breadth to her talent when in more mainstream settings, perhaps most notably in her trio work with Paul Motian and Charlie Haden. Steve Coleman's work would stand out for its expansive metrical conception of groove music and its willingness to challenge the conventional—even the word *jazz* is strenuously avoided in his discourses—on both musical and economic fronts. Greg Osby, for his own part, would sign with the Blue Note label in 1991 and, over the course of more than a dozen recordings, showed his ability to integrate disparate influences—free, funky, traditional, inner-city—in a persuasive sax style. The marked affinities that once brought these artists under the same M-Base banner would lessen over time, but each worked to counter the complacency that often accompanied the so-called "new traditionalism" (a topic addressed in chapter 9) of this period.

The trio Medeski Martin and Wood, formed in 1991, may be even more typical of funky jazz in the postfusion age. These musicians adopt technology when it suits them—adding turntables, synthesized sounds, and other plugged-in ingredients as needed—but are also comfortable going "all acoustic" too. The band started out as a conventional jazz piano trio and only gradually came to embrace an electric sound, first as an easier way of taking their music on the road but eventually as a key part of their group identity. Yet the biggest change here versus the heroic age of 1970s fusion is the gritty garage band attitude of their public image. This trio—composed of keyboardist John Medeski, drummer Billy Martin, and bassist Chris Wood—attracts an audience that often has only the vaguest notion of bebop, swing, and other jazz styles, but who are mesmerized by the raw energy and infectious rhythms that are this band's calling cards. Indeed, one can't help but be struck by the contrast with the electric jazz groups of an earlier era. Instead of emulating the slickness and concert hall glamour of these predecessors, this trio takes pride in a back-to-basics, jam band ambiance that is more a rejection than a continuation of the fusion tradition of famous forerunners such as Weather Report, Return to Forever, and the Mahavishnu Orchestra.

Despite these varied and formidable precedents, the most successful—and controversial—form of plugged-in improvisation in the postfusion era has been the style of music known as "smooth jazz." The early roots of this genre can be traced back to the 1960s, when producer Creed Taylor masterminded a series of commercial albums for the Verve, A&M, and CTI labels, presenting leading jazz artists in slick settings well suited for radio airplay and crossover sales to pop and soul music fans. One could see the new sensibility emerging in the Taylor-produced efforts by Wes Montgomery, Freddie Hubbard, George Benson, Stan Getz, Hubert Laws, Chet Baker, Paul Desmond, and other leading performers, in which every detail, from the cover artwork to the arrangements and song selection, reflected the savvy marketing conception at work behind the scenes. Yet the mercantile motivations underpinning these albums did not detract from the music making, and Taylor's efforts have mostly held up well with the passing years, largely due to the high caliber of the creative talents at play and the first-class production values involved. "By 1970, rock had overwhelmed most other genres," Taylor later recalled. "Many other jazz albums from this period looked shabby and sounded slapped together. My strategy was to invest heavily on the talent, sound quality and look of the records."[15] Although some critics carped at the commercial elements that dominated Taylor's approach—string orchestras, cover versions of rock tunes, image-oriented covers that rarely featured the performers—the public embraced these releases with enthusiasm. In the early 1970s, Taylor's CTI was achieving sales of jazz records comparable to those generated by the major labels and inevitably inspiring imitation from entertainment industry players with deeper pockets.

During this same decade, a new wave of smartly packaged crossover jazz acts enjoyed enormous success. Yet their music represented a departure from the Creed Taylor formula, which had been built on taking proven jazz artists who had already made a reputation in straight-ahead jazz and adding a pop or rock twist to their music. The new generation of smooth jazz artists had, for the most part, modest reputations—or in some cases were completely unknown—among serious jazz fans before they became stars. The jazz establishment grumbled at what was perceived as the overnight success of upstarts who hadn't paid their dues. The record labels and concert promoters, however, were in no position to quibble, dazzled as they were by huge sales of albums such as Chuck Mangione's *Feels So Good* (whose title single climbed to number four on the *Billboard* charts), John Klemmer's *Touch*, Spyro Gyra's *Morning Dance*, and other 1970s projects that took in some elements of the fusion movement but married them to pop-oriented melodies and danceable beats. In other instances, former Creed Taylor artists jumped ship to more powerful labels and bigger successes. After moving to Warner Bros., George Benson's career hit the big time with *Breezin'*, which sold more than two million copies. Grover Washington had enjoyed popularity with his recordings for Taylor's Kudu label but reached a far larger audience through his 1981 collaboration with Bill Withers on the hit single "Just the Two of Us."

Yet the term *smooth jazz* did not arrive on the scene until the 1980s. The music industry had toyed with various ways of labeling this style, some preferring to lump it into the fusion or New Age buckets, or coining the cumbersome title "new adult contemporary." In the final result, market research rather than the jazz critical establishment decided the matter. Cody/Leach, a research outfit, undertook a study for WNUA in Chicago that showed positive listener response to the name "smooth jazz." As a result, jazz would be forever linked with a style of easy listening music that many opinion leaders in the art form would prefer not to exist—or at least not inside the gated jazz community—and which, they griped, simply encroached on the livelihoods of legit acts in their field.

Casual listeners were blissfully unaware of the controversy surrounding these pleasant sounds that enlivened their morning commute or served as unobtrusive background music to dinner or a second glass of chardonnay. Headlining acts of the 1980s such as the Rippingtons, Dave Benoit, Acoustic Alchemy, and the Yellow Jackets were especially powerful in generating radio airplay—an achievement all the more impressive given the gradual disappearance of straight-ahead jazz from commercial radio stations during this same period. But the successes of these artists were modest by comparison to the towering giant of smooth jazz—indeed, almost its defining figure—Kenneth Gorelick, who, operating under the name Kenny G, would go on to sell more records than any jazz instrumentalist in history. More than fifteen million copies of his 1992 release *Breathless* were purchased by fans, many of whom had probably never bought a sax album before. This same artist set another breathless mark five years later, putting his name in the *Guinness Book of World Records* by holding an E-flat note for forty-five minutes and forty-seven seconds in an impressive demonstration of the technique known as circular breathing. It is hard to say whether such a feat enhanced Mr. G's reputation among jazz insiders or simply reinforced the view that he was a novelty act outside the scope of serious consideration.

In truth, the jazz component in this music is modest by any measure, yet there is a real issue here that the jazz world can hardly dismiss. At a time when jazz is largely excluded from television and commercial radio, and its most cherished masters can walk unrecognized down the streets of every major city in the land, the word *jazz* still retains a mystique that marketers often try to usurp. A Google search on the term will come up with millions of references that have nothing to do with the music fostered by Louis Armstrong and Duke Ellington: links relating to a car made by Honda, a basketball team in Utah, a technology platform promoted by IBM, or strange hybrids such as Jazzercise, jazz pants, or jazz hands. Usually the lack of connection with the jazz art form is obvious in these instances, but sometimes the matter is more ambiguous. This leads to disturbing innovations, such as the jazz event with no jazz—as fans witnessed at the 2009 Sonoma Jazz Festival, which booked Joe Cocker, Ziggy Marley, Keb' Mo', Shelby Lynne, and Lyle Lovett—all fine acts, but none of them with any ties to the music discussed in this book. As a result of such encroachments, practitioners of the core jazz tradition must learn ways of navigating, and indeed of surviving, in a world that not only marginalizes their contributions but is ready even to usurp their identifying label and confuse the next generation of potential listeners. In recent years, political pundits have made us sensitive to the need to "frame" a viewpoint in the right terms in order to create a space for it in the public sphere. The very concept of jazz now seems in desperate need of this type of framing. Jazz artists themselves must either take the lead in this process or see themselves increasingly squeezed out of the commercial activities that are the sustenance for the practitioners of any art form.

KEITH JARRETT AND CLASSICAL FUSION

A different type of fusion, represented by a mixing of jazz and classical music, also emerged as an important movement during the 1970s. The ECM record label, founded in 1969 by Manfred Eicher, would play a major role in promoting this new and, at times, contentious approach. True, there had been many previous fusings of jazz and classical music—from Gershwin to Third Stream—but none were so influential and far-reaching in their implications. Whereas most of these earlier attempts had emphasized the compositional and formalist aspects of the music, the ECM artists maintained a commitment to the primacy of improvisation. They sought nothing less than a broadening of improvisational techniques to include the full vocabulary of composed music. Instead of the conventional mainstream jazz sounds—syncopations, blues notes, ii–V substitutions—one found a panoply of other devices: drones, ostinatos, vamps, impressionist harmonies, Schubertian melodies, shimmering arpeggios, undulating rhythms, rhapsodic interludes, pristine polyphonic exercises, and jarring expressionist explosions. Yet this was no tepid attempt to recreate the classical improvisation styles of previous centuries. A host of African American and non-Western sounds were also important ingredients in this sonic smorgasbord of influences.

ECM would also stand out as the first major jazz label to rely heavily on non-U.S. talent, and this commitment to broadening the geographical base of the music would prove as important as the distinctive sounds associated with the company's imprimatur. These recordings introduced many jazz fans to the work of Jan Garbarek, Egberto Gismonti, Enrico Rava, Naná Vasconcelos, Tomasz Stańko, Terje Rypdal, Eberhard Weber, John Surman, and Kenny Wheeler, among others, most of them little known on the global jazz stage before Eicher sponsored them. This advocacy, which respected no national or cultural boundaries, enabled ECM to play a major role in the blending of world and ethnic music elements into jazz, and thus added one more ingredient to this new kind of fusion. By any measure, this was an iconoclastic approach at the time, one that challenged the conventional wisdom on many fronts. Even so, Eicher was anything but dogmatic, promoting the works of a range of stylists far afield from the so-called ECM sound, including those more overtly rooted in the African American tradition, such as Jack DeJohnette and the Art Ensemble of Chicago, as well as contemporary classical composers as different from one another as Steve Reich and Arvo Pärt.

No artist better exemplified this powerful synthesis of disparate styles than pianist Keith Jarrett. The influence of classical music is, at times, as pronounced as the jazz ingredients of his playing—hence, it came as little surprise that Jarrett eventually chose to pursue separate, if complementary, careers in the two idioms—while elements of different ethnic musical traditions also figure in his playing and composing. Yet the calling card of Jarrett's achievement is less the breadth and depth of his influences than his ability to blend these various sources of inspiration into a coherent, persuasive whole. Nowhere is this clearer than on his solo concerts, lengthy excursions of completely improvised piano music that refract a kaleidoscope of aural colors through Jarrett's highly individualistic perspective.

Jarrett's far-reaching musical interests were evident from his earliest days: at age five he performed on a televised show hosted by Paul Whiteman and, at seven, he gave a two-hour piano recital to a paying audience, working his way through Beethoven, Mozart, and Saint-Saëns and capping the concert with two of his own compositions. In his teens, Jarrett attended a jazz camp sponsored by the Kenton band and later went on tour with Fred Waring and His Pennsylvanians. Through Waring's intervention, Jarrett was offered the chance of studying with Nadia Boulanger, but the young pianist declined. By the time he entered the Berklee School of Music, the budding Boston jazz conservatory, Jarrett was already a seasoned pianist with solid playing experiences under his belt.

Jarrett only lasted one year at Berklee before being expelled—ostensibly for playing on the strings of a piano. Soon after, Jarrett moved to New York, where he caught the attention of bandleader Art Blakey. Jarrett made only one record with Blakey, the vibrant *Buttercorn Lady* release, but the twenty-year-old pianist's solos on "Secret Love" and "My Romance" were enough to generate excitement in the jazz world. Four months with Blakey were followed by a longer stint with Charles Lloyd, a charismatic saxophonist with a Coltrane-oriented sound, who attracted a young audience via an eclectic mix of acoustic jazz-oriented music. Drummer Jack DeJohnette, a powerful and sophisticated percussionist, also worked with Lloyd during this period and would participate with Jarrett on a number of important later projects. In 1970, both Jarrett and DeJohnette joined Miles Davis and played important roles in what was one of the trumpeter's strongest fusion bands.

Jarrett's career gained rapid momentum after his departure from Davis in 1971. He initiated his ECM relationship with a duet recording with DeJohnette and an extraordinary solo piano release, *Facing You*. The latter marked a compelling departure from the conventions of mainstream jazz piano, delineating an orchestral two-handed approach that revealed Jarrett's novel, integrated concept of harmony, rhythmic momentum, and melodic phrasing, perhaps demonstrated most notably on the ten-minute composition "In Front." Jarrett's 1973 masterpiece *Solo Concerts: Bremen and Lausanne* built on these same elements in two titanic improvised performances, three hours of inspired keyboard music. Jarrett's follow-up *Köln Concert* may have lacked the depth of *Facing You* and *Bremen*, but it attracted a large nonjazz audience with its sparse, simple harmonies and flowing melodic lines. The record quickly sold over one million copies and spurred a rash of imitators. It is only a slight exaggeration to claim that the burgeoning market for New Age music grew out of the influence of the opening twenty minutes of this recording, a mostly diatonic improvisation built primarily over a simple two-chord progression. But Jarrett quickly moved on to other projects, leaving it to other, far lesser talents to build on the commercial potential of this quasi-minimalist approach.

During this period, Jarrett recorded a number of multifaceted, uncompromising projects for the ABC/Impulse label with an acoustic jazz quartet featuring Charlie Haden, Paul Motian, and Dewey Redman. A second "European" quartet, finding Jarrett alongside Jan Garbarek, Jon Christensen, and Palle Danielsson, recorded for ECM and adopted a more pastoral strain, most evident on the 1977 sessions that produced *My Song*. Jarrett returned to the solo piano format for his massive *Sun Bear Concerts*, which included the complete output of five concerts in Japan. These seven hours of keyboard improvisations might have represented a career's worth of music for another artist, but for Jarrett it was one small part of an ever-expanding range of activities that found him also playing soprano sax, writing for strings and other classical ensembles, composing and playing original organ music, recording the piano music of G. I. Gurdjieff, and undertaking a unique 1985 project, *Spirits*, on which he created neoprimitive sound textures by overdubbing his efforts on a variety of unconventional instruments, from glockenspiel to Pakistani flute.

Around the time of *Spirits*, Jarrett's music began taking on more traditional dimensions. As a bandleader, Jarrett had previously focused primarily on playing his own compositions and occasionally those of his sidemen. He now reversed directions, building entire performances and recordings around familiar jazz standards in the context of a trio with DeJohnette and bassist Gary Peacock. These were wholly successful, satisfying efforts: not since Bill Evans had a pianist developed the interpretation of standards in a trio format to such a high pitch. Perhaps the biggest surprise here was the depth of Jarrett's commitment to the old songs. The Standards Trio would continue to be a major focal point for the pianist in later decades, representing a rare anchoring point in a career that, in earlier years, had been mercurial and unpredictable. This embrace of the tradition, however, extended beyond the jazz world, as demonstrated by Jarrett's exploration of the classical music repertoire. While other jazz musicians had dabbled with classical music, few had attempted the range of efforts that Jarrett was now undertaking: he performed Bartók, Barber, Stravinsky; he recorded and released crisp, solid readings of Bach's keyboard music, including the *Well-Tempered Clavier* and the *Goldberg Variations*; he championed the works of deserving contemporary composers such as Lou Harrison, Peggy Glanville-Hicks, and Alan Hovhaness. Other projects found him recording Shostakovich's twenty-four Preludes and Fugues, or performing Handel, Mozart, and other composers from earlier centuries. He also continued to develop his own skills as a quasi-classical composer, and his growing maturity can be traced on a series of recordings: *In the Light* (1973), *Luminessence* (1974), *Arbour Zena* (1975), *The Celestial Hawk* (1980), and *Bridge of Light* (1994).

Despite these impressive endeavors, Jarrett has been far from universally loved in the jazz world. Almost from the start of his career, Jarrett's demanding, often prickly personality led to a backlash, which the artist himself did little to discourage. In interviews, he was likely to answer a question with a question, or offer gnomic responses. On stage, he frequently complained and berated audiences, and even when playing the piano, his odd mannerisms—standing, swaying, grunting, moaning, humming—struck some as unnecessary theatrics. A profanity-laden outburst at the Umbria Jazz Festival in 2007 was so extreme that organizers vowed never to invite him back to the event. Time and again, this artist has offered up an unsolvable puzzle for fans who struggle to reconcile the intemperate man and his poised music, and though the jazz world has known many prima donnas and nettlesome characters over the decades, Jarrett stands out in this regard almost as much as he does for the sublimity of what he achieves at the keyboard.

A number of other musicians were pursuing a similar aesthetic vision during this period, broadening the techniques of improvisation to encompass a panoply of new sounds, yet—unlike the jazz-rock fusion players—emphasizing traditional, acoustic instruments. The group Oregon, formed in 1970 as an offshoot of the Paul Winter Consort, was an early exponent of this emerging style. The band's individual members each played multiple instruments: Paul McCandless was featured on oboe, English horn, and bass clarinet; Collin Walcott's instruments included sitar, tabla, clarinet, and percussion; Glen Moore performed on bass, violin, piano, and flute; Ralph Towner's talents extended to classical guitar, twelve-string guitar, piano, French horn, trumpet, and flugelhorn. In total, the members of Oregon were capable of playing over sixty instruments. Such versatility invites an obvious comparison with the Art Ensemble of Chicago (discussed in the next chapter), which was also creating an eclectic approach featuring dozens of instruments during this period. Yet the similarities, for the most part, stop there. Oregon aimed to forge a unified, holistic sound, almost the exact opposite of the deconstructive techniques fostered by the Chicago postmodernists. In a series of 1970s recordings for the Vanguard label and later for Elektra,

Oregon created a fresh and unconventional body of work, noteworthy for its sensitive and subtle integration of these various strands of earlier musical traditions. As the 1970s progressed, the group's members increasingly focused on projects outside Oregon. Towner's twelve-string work gripped listeners on his guest appearance on the 1971 Weather Report recording of "The Moors" (released on *I Sing the Body Electric*), demonstrating a mastery that is all the more extraordinary when one considers that he did not begin playing the guitar until age twenty-two. Towner also recorded a number of diverse and almost uniformly successful projects for ECM, including solo guitar efforts and collaborations with various other artists affiliated with the label.

Other musicians associated with ECM played a major role in this expansion of the jazz vocabulary. Beyond Jan Garbarek's collaborations with Keith Jarrett, his leader dates for Eicher went a long way toward validating a distinctively European perspective on jazz, one that drew on both American precedents and folkloric elements from outside the United States. Steve Kuhn, a Harvard-educated pianist who had been an early member of the John Coltrane Quartet, recorded exceptional solo and combo projects that demonstrated his compositional skills and mastery of piano dynamics and tone control. Vibraphonist Gary Burton, who had anticipated the jazz-rock fusion movement with his 1967 recording *Duster*, fostered a more pristine, chamber-music ambiance on his ECM projects, which highlighted his adept four-mallet technique and rich harmonic approach on leader dates as well as in tandem with other artists such as Ralph Towner, Chick Corea, and bassist Steve Swallow.

As such instances make clear, the supposedly Eurocentric ECM label proved adept at finding talent that the major U.S. labels were ignoring in their own homeland, both American-born artists (Jarrett, DeJohnette, Burton, Metheny) as well as expats such as bassist Dave Holland, originally from Britain but a U.S. resident for most of his career. Holland's releases stand out for their vital, cliché-free music making, evident whether he was recording as a solo bassist (as on *Emerald Tears* from 1977), serving as a member of a progressive jazz collective (as on his recordings with the Circle quartet from the early 1970s), or leading small combos and big bands. In the combo setting, Holland has compiled an impressive body of work over the course of four decades, as documented on projects such as the *Conference of the Birds* release from 1972, *Jumpin' In* from 1983, *Dream of the Elders* from 1995, and *Prime Directive* from 2000. The core virtues of Holland's music include its tight, metrically advanced arrangements, a transparent contrapuntal sound (typically accentuated by the absence of piano or guitar), and a disavowal of the familiar or hackneyed. Even when trying his hand at leading a big band, as Holland has occasionally attempted in the new millennium, he somehow manages to cut through the weightiness—of both the the format and its attendant tradition—in forging the same pellucid sound and nimbleness associated with his small combo works.

By the close of the 1970s, the collective impact of these various fusion efforts—whether the sources of inspiration were rock, ethnic, or classical music—had succeeded in aggressively expanding the boundaries of jazz. There was virtually no musical tradition that, by now, had not been touched by it. Given this dramatic extension, a period of retrenchment was not unexpected. The publication of Albert Murray's book *Stomping the Blues* in 1976 served as an influential attempt to recall jazz to its origins as African American music. Murray emphasized the decisive role of the blues, which had figured insignificantly in the ECM efforts, and celebrated the sense of swing, so important to the jazz tradition, yet increasingly obscured in contemporary currents of improvisation. Although Murray could hardly have anticipated it at the time, his words would prove strikingly prophetic. A new generation of jazz players, who came to prominence during the next decade, would champion this same cause, initiating a host of historically-conscious efforts that attempted to promote the inherently African American elements of the jazz tradition. The age of forward-looking fusions may not have ended, but practitioners of these hybrid styles now needed to look over their shoulders as the past was trying to overtake them.

9 Traditionalists and Postmodernists

THE NEW AND OLD TRADITIONALISTS

Free jazz may have promised a revolution, and fusion might have offered financial rewards, but anyone seeking controversy in jazz circles during the closing years of the twentieth century would have found it coming from a different—and at first unlikely—direction. After decades of debating the future of jazz, the arguments now focused on the role of the music's past, and especially the resurgence of traditional mainstream acoustic jazz styles under the auspices of Wynton Marsalis.

In truth, these older styles had never really disappeared. During the ascendancy of free and fusion, mainstream artists had continued to follow their muse, although they rarely received the press, airplay, or record sales of the crossover artists. Indeed, the intense compression of jazz history had led to a vertiginous overlap of traditions and styles. At the close of the 1960s, jazz fans could enjoy the contemporary styles of the period; but, just as easily, they might attend concerts by Louis Armstrong, Earl Hines, Duke Ellington, Benny Goodman, Count Basie, Roy Eldridge, Dizzy Gillespie, Art Blakey, Charles Mingus, Dave Brubeck, and Gerry Mulligan, among others. Even in the mid-1990s, many early pioneers of jazz music were still active, such as Stéphane Grappelli, who attracted votes in the first *Downbeat* poll in 1936 and, sixty years later, in the 1996 edition, again placed first in his category; or Benny Carter, who continued to demonstrate his immense talent as a soloist and composer sixty-five years after he built his reputation writing arrangements for Fletcher Henderson and McKinney's Cotton Pickers.

The 1970s mainstream jazz sound continued to draw heavily on the swing and bebop idioms. Major jazz festivals often emphasized these styles, and a number of record labels promoted these once innovative sounds, now transformed into "heritage music." Norman Granz, who had made his mark as a concert promoter and record producer during the postwar years, returned to active involvement in the studio with the founding of his Pablo label in 1973. Granz quickly gathered together a roster of some of the leading traditional stylists in jazz, including Duke Ellington, Ella Fitzgerald, Oscar Peterson, Count Basie, Dizzy Gillespie, Sarah Vaughan, Ray Brown, Milt Jackson, Zoot Sims, and others. The availability of these jazz legends was a telling sign of how little interest major labels were showing in mainstream jazz after the rock-dominated 1960s. However, Granz's belief in the commercial viability of this music proved prescient. The Pablo recordings sold well, and the various artists associated with the label demonstrated that they could still pack nightclubs and concert halls.

Granz placed special emphasis on showcasing Ella Fitzgerald's talent in the finest jazz settings. He had taken over as Fitzgerald's manager in 1953 and soon after secured her release from Decca to feature her on his own label. Fitzgerald was a successful popular singer at the time, having sold over twenty million records since stepping in as surrogate leader of Chick Webb's band in 1939. Now in her late thirties, she was at an age when most pop music stars have already started to lose their audience to younger and more up-to-date performers, yet Granz never paid much attention to keeping current angle, and under his stewardship Fitzgerald's music reached a new pitch of artistry. Her 1956 release *Ella Fitzgerald Sings the Cole Porter Songbook* ranks among the biggest-selling jazz albums of the decade, put Granz's Verve label on a firm financial footing, and even impressed Cole Porter himself, who reportedly remarked: "My, what marvelous diction that girl has." Fitzgerald solidified her preeminence among jazz divas in memorable live recordings in Berlin and Rome, and in other "songbook" releases featuring her interpretations of popular standards by George and Ira Gershwin, Harold Arlen, Duke Ellington, Jerome Kern, Irving Berlin, and Johnny Mercer. Under the Pablo aegis, Fitzgerald continued to record strong material in world-class settings, singing with the Basie band, engaging in duets with Joe Pass, fronting all-star combos, or working with premier accompanists who had supported her in the past, such as pianists Paul Smith and Tommy Flanagan.

Although Granz typically preferred working with major names from previous decades, he also occasionally promoted lesser-known artists and newer talent. For example, virtuoso guitarist Joe Pass had spent much of his early career battling drug addiction, a struggle that found him spending lengthy periods incarcerated, at hospitals, or in halfway houses; even when he was playing music, it often was as an anonymous studio sideman or hidden in Las Vegas hotel bands. Yet in the early 1970s, when the guitarist was in his mid-forties, Granz aggressively promoted Pass in leader dates, prominent sideman gigs (with Oscar Peterson, Ella Fitzgerald, and others), and concert appearances. Pass's 1973 solo recording *Virtuoso* attracted attention for the guitarist's speed of execution and astonishing technical mastery of the instrument. Inspiring comparisons with Art Tatum and Oscar Peterson, *Virtuoso* justifiably ranks among the half-dozen most important recordings of modern jazz guitar music. It was followed by dozens of other Pass recordings, as leader or sideman, on the Pablo label.

Pablo was far from an isolated example. Other labels thrived by focusing on mainstream jazz sounds played by middle-aged artists. Nils Winther founded the Steeplechase label in Copenhagen in 1972 and recorded over two hundred releases during the next fifteen years, including important projects by Dexter Gordon, Jackie McLean, and other American musicians, as well as such rising European stars as bassist Niels-Henning Ørsted Pedersen and pianist Tete Montoliu. The following year, Carl Jefferson started his Concord label in California, which specialized in albums by a wide array of players associated with swing, bop, and West Coast styles of jazz. During the course of the decade, other small labels—including Muse, Chiaroscuro, and Timeless—moved in a similar direction, keeping the flames of earlier jazz styles alive in the face of free and fusion fare. A host of seasoned jazz artists from earlier decades rode this wave, pursuing revitalized careers and proving that traditional sounds were again on the ascendancy. Altoist Phil Woods led several vibrant combos in the 1970s, including his European Rhythm Machine, and in the 1980s was joined for a spell by the stellar trumpeter Tom Harrell. Dexter Gordon returned from overseas, recording his celebrated *Homecoming* release for CBS. Stan Getz renewed his allegiance to straight-ahead jazz after his love affair with bossa nova and briefer flirtation with fusion. Even crossover stars, most notably Herbie Hancock, put away their electric instruments for a time to test the growing market for acoustic jazz. "Jazz Comes Back," *Newsweek* proclaimed in a 1977 cover story focusing on the return of prominent jazz artists to more traditional settings—more than a year before Wynton Marsalis's arrival in New York.

New mainstream artists began gaining notoriety alongside these veterans, with almost every style finding fervent advocates. In 1977, twenty-three-year-old saxophonist Scott Hamilton scandalized the New York scene with his "retro" tenor sound reminiscent of Coleman Hawkins and Ben Webster and reflecting a private universe in which Coltrane or Rollins had never existed. Unlike the postmodernists, who were resurrecting old sounds with a tongue-in-cheek humor, Hamilton was dead serious about what he was doing, fostering these styles because he thought they "sounded good"—the most anachronistic of defenses, it seemed, during this ideologically-charged period of transition. Although some critics belittled or ignored his efforts, those who listened with open ears were forced to acknowledge his rare gift for improvisation. Hamilton might have been an extreme case, yet such historical consciousness-raising would prove a precursor of things to come. By the dawn of the 1980s, every style and sound from the music's past seemed to find a ready audience, each one celebrated, fostered, and marketed alongside the most up-to-date offerings of the current day. Visitors to jazz record stores witnessed fascinating juxtapositions in the racks: George Lewis, the Dixieland clarinetist, sharing a bin with George Lewis, avant-garde trombonist; Woody Shaw lying adjacent to Artie Shaw; Ruby Braff rubbing shoulders with Anthony Braxton; or Sadao Watanabe sidling up to Ethel Waters. The extreme diversity of the traditions that were now acclaimed indicated the tremendous scope of the music's history and the remarkable breadth of Buddy Bolden's progeny.

The mainstream jazz vocal tradition was especially vibrant during this period. Although atonality and other experimental techniques had, at times, made inroads here, most jazz vocalists preferred to work with traditional repertoire and instrumentation. Many major artists who had emerged in earlier decades continued to dominate the world of jazz singing in the 1970s and 1980s. Carmen McRae and Betty Carter, who had first recorded as leaders in the 1950s, made clear that the Billie Holiday tradition could still sound fresh and new decades later. No singer since Holiday had been more adept at singing behind the beat than McRae, or more skilled at shifting from an intimate conversational delivery to hard-edged reconfigurations of melody and lyric. Carter also took extreme rhythmic liberties with her material, sometimes offering such arcane reinterpretations of standards that one is tempted to include her among the jazz avant-garde. Yet this brand of experimentation was one that found inspiration in the traditions of early masters, as disparate as Cole Porter and Charlie Parker, and—once again—Holiday, whose emotionally charged vision of invigorating jazz song with the raw honesty of the confessional also colored Carter's work. Sheila Jordan took a similar tack, avoiding conventional readings of standards in favor of a more deeply personalized approach, best shown in her collaborations with pianist Steve Kuhn. Mel Tormé, who had refined a virtuosic singing style in early years, also found a ready audience for his serious jazz work in this period, which included successful projects with George Shearing, Marty Paich, and others. Tony Bennett, who had expanded his audience as a pop-oriented singer in the 1960s, rediscovered his jazz roots during the following decade, as demonstrated most clearly in two memorable albums of duets with pianist Bill Evans. All in all, the vocal arts stood out as the most tradition-steeped facet of the jazz scene during the 1970s and 1980s. Most of the young singers who initiated their careers during these years reflected this same immersion in the music's history; and though the least inspired of them settled for a superficial supper-club elegance, the best of the new generation—Bobby McFerrin, Diane Schuur, Cassandra Wilson, Dianne Reeves—found ways of revitalizing the tradition.

This nostalgia for the music's past was especially evident among practitioners of vocalese—a style in which lyrics are added to pre-existing jazz melodies and solos. As this idiom gained wider popularity under the influence of such singers as Jon Hendricks and Eddie Jefferson, who had helped create the style some two decades before, or via high-profile projects by pop artists such as Joni Mitchell or the Manhattan Transfer, it became increasingly common practice for the vocalese lyrics to be *about* jazz musicians—hear, for instance, Jefferson singing eloquently about Coleman Hawkins, Miles Davis, and Charlie Parker; or Hendricks's lyrics to "Birdland"; or, in a crossover format, Joni Mitchell focusing on Charles Mingus as the subject of her version of the bassist's "Goodbye Pork Pie Hat." In such settings, the jazz singer became something of a modern-day equivalent of the African griot, using music not just to continue the jazz tradition but also to relate its history.

The concept of preserving the music's heritage through jazz repertory companies, akin to the way symphonies propagate the classical music tradition, also gained momentum during this period. In 1973, Chuck Israels founded his National Jazz Ensemble, and the following year George Wein promoted his New York Jazz

Repertory Company. The Smithsonian Institution began taking an increasingly active role in preserving and promoting the jazz tradition during the 1970s, assisted admirably by jazz critic Martin Williams. Gunther Schuller pursued a wide range of activities during the decade—concerts, recordings, writings—to further the same agenda. Other signs pointed to a revival of interest in the jazz tradition during the 1970s: more reissues of earlier material by record companies; expanding attention to the music's history and heritage at academic institutions; and the publication of a growing numbers of jazz books and journals.

Given these precedents, it would be wrong to claim that the mainstream acoustic jazz tradition was dormant before the arrival of Wynton Marsalis at the start of the 1980s. Rather than being its cause, Marsalis's success was very much a product of this emerging historical consciousness. Even so, Marsalis must be seen as the key figure who, more than anyone else, vehemently asserted the centrality of this tradition in the face of fusion and free styles, and aimed to be its preserver, propagator, promoter, and publicist all rolled into one. His efforts often ignited controversy, yet even the heated disputes that flamed around him can be read as signs of the growing importance of jazz's inheritance from past generations in the way the art form would be conceptualized and commoditized by both insiders and outsiders. At times ideological and aesthetic issues have gotten muddled in these debates, and one suspects that it will take many years before Marsalis the musician can be dispassionately assessed, without being lost in discussions of the personal or political trappings of his art.

Marsalis's rise to fame while barely out of his teens was an unprecedented event in the jazz world. No major jazz figure—not Ellington or Armstrong, Goodman or Gillespie—had become so famous, so fast. The story of his formative experiences in music is compact and impressive. Born in Kenner, Louisiana, on October 18, 1961, Marsalis had the benefit of local teachers and mentors, such as Alvin Batiste and Danny Barker, who were living exponents of the rich New Orleans jazz tradition. Marsalis's home life was equally supportive: his father, Ellis, was a professional jazz pianist, and in time Wynton's siblings Branford, Delfeayo, and Jason would also pursue musical careers of note. At age fourteen, Wynton played the Haydn Trumpet Concerto with the New Orleans Philharmonic. At seventeen, he was allowed to participate in the Tanglewood Festival and, despite being the youngest attendee, won an award as the outstanding brass player. At eighteen, he entered Juilliard. At nineteen, he was performing with jazz masters such as Art Blakey and Herbie Hancock. At twenty, the CBS record label signed Marsalis simultaneously to their classical and jazz artist rosters—an unprecedented move for the world's most powerful recording company.

The wisdom of this step was quickly validated: within two years, Marsalis had won Grammy awards in both fields. Even casual listeners were now aware of his reputation. In the popular imagination, he was to the trumpet what Segovia was to the guitar, Van Cliburn the piano. Marsalis had a deep reservoir of talent to back up this flurry of attention. His recording of the Haydn Trumpet Concerto was impressive, especially in the cadenza, which was a breathtaking exposition of the young trumpeter's rhythmic and melodic imagination. His performances with Blakey had quickly caused a sensation among jazz musicians. Not since the days of Clifford Brown had a young jazz trumpeter shown such tone control or fluid execution. Listening to his featured solo on "How Deep Is the Ocean," recorded with the Jazz Messengers at the Keystone Korner in June 1981, one could easily imagine a spectacular future for this young virtuoso. His warm, fat tone was on exhibit in the slow introduction, and retained lucent clarity even in the fastest runs during the double-time section of the piece. A few months later, Blakey hired Wynton's brother Branford to play saxophone with the Messengers, and a follow-up recording helped to amplify the growing reputations of both.

The two brothers were prominently featured on Wynton's eponymous debut jazz release for CBS. This project was more of a hodgepodge than a unified artistic statement, but many of its individual moments were compelling: "Hesitation" found the Marsalis brothers evoking Ornette Coleman's early style in a playful workout over "I Got Rhythm" changes; the shifting rhythmic moods of Wynton's piece "Father Time" prefigured the trumpeter's later concern with complex compositional structures; on "Sister Cheryl" Branford made his mark with an ingenious soprano sax solo that even outshined his brother's formidable contribution; Wynton's solo on "Who Can I Turn To" was a simple affair, but his trumpet sound was riveting in its depth and purity. His follow-up recordings *Think of One* and *Hot House Flowers* were similarly eclectic, ranging from the varied combo moods of the former to the sweet string orchestra-backed melodicism of the latter.

For another young trumpeter, these would have been laudable achievements. But the intense publicity and attention directed at Marsalis had raised expectations to a fever pitch that such efforts could do little to fulfill. Jazz listeners and critics who had grown accustomed to a history of towering figures—Armstrong, Ellington, Parker, Gillespie, Davis, Coltrane, Coleman—each of whom had remade the music in his own image, expected something more revolutionary from the young trumpeter. His two follow-up recordings, *Black Codes (from the Underground)* and *J Mood*, attempted to break new ground. The ensemble textures were now more interactive than on previous Marsalis recordings, and increasingly the rhythm section was challenging the trumpeter. Marsalis's compositions were also growing much more intricate. "J Mood," for example, is a twelve-bar blues, but the main melody employs twelve very unusual bars: the meter changes with virtually each one, completing a total of thirty-six beats broken down (according to this writer's ears) in the pattern 4/2/1/3/3/4/1/4/4/3/4/3. "Phryzzinian Man" from *Black Codes* takes a similar circuitous route, starting with a bar-length pattern of 4/4/2/4/4/2/3/2/4/4/4/4. The band returns to straight 4/4 during the solos—which is something of a letdown after the intriguing melody statements—however, the ambitions of the compositions showed the direction in which Marsalis was now moving.

The trumpeter's next two recordings, *Marsalis Standard Time, Vol. 1* and *Live at Blues Alley*, delivered on the promises of these previous projects and remain the most impressive examples of modernist combo playing in Marsalis's oeuvre. After them, Marsalis overtly renounced this approach in favor of a traditionalist ethos. In contrast, these two midcareer projects betray little of the hyperconscious historicism that would become the dominant theme of the trumpeter's later work, but are vibrant, forward-looking works. On the first, *Marsalis Standard Time*, the band is at its finest pitch, incorporating the experimental metrics of *J Mood* into the heady motion of jam-session jousting: on "A Foggy Day" Marsalis superimposes 6/8, 12/8, 5/4, and other meters onto the song's basic foundation; during part of "Autumn Leaves" the band changes meter every bar; "Caravan" is masterfully reworked, once again with virtuosic cross-rhythms. Much credit was due to Marsalis's rhythm section for this tour de force. Pianist Marcus Roberts stood out as an advanced structural thinker in the mold of Monk, Tristano, and Hancock and clearly delighted in pushing and prodding Marsalis, who in turn showed how far his phrasing had grown since his first recordings. Jeff "Tain" Watts and Robert Hurst, on drums and bass respectively, also proved to be facile at these games in running time, but equally skilled in maintaining the drive and swing of the music. *Live at Blues Alley* moved in this same direction, but with even greater intensity. This recording features the most aggressive solos of the trumpeter's career. The rhythm section plays at fever pitch for long stretches. The music moves confidently from modal to chordal structures and into different conceptions of time, but with a fiery, unrelenting undercurrent. On the whole, these two releases represent Marsalis's most successful and fully realized attempt to expand the vocabulary of combo playing set out in the Miles Davis, John Coltrane, Bill Evans, and Ornette Coleman recordings from the 1960s.

Yet at the peak of this forward-looking period, Marsalis was increasingly sounding a cautionary note. "I knew that when I did that album at Blues Alley that I wasn't going to make another record in that type of style—all those really complex rhythms, playing fast, wild," he explained. "Now I'm trying to really put together an approach through which I can create a more accurate tonal picture of my experiences, of the world I come out of, of the things in my life that have the deepest meaning to me."[1] For Marsalis, this "world I come out of" meant the sounds of his native New Orleans and the traditional African American roots of jazz. In retrospect, we can see that the resulting album, *The Majesty of the Blues*, initiated a new period in Marsalis's career. In some respects, the new style marked an extension of earlier concerns—one notes the shifting meters of the deceptively simple-sounding "Hickory Dickory Dock"— but in other ways, Marsalis was moving dramatically away from his previous practices. The trumpeter who, as a teenager, had amazed audiences with his pure, clean tone was now exploring the "dirtier" approach favored by prebop jazz musicians, increasingly distorting his sound with a mute. Instead of living up to his early reputation as the "next Clifford Brown" or his midcareer tag as the bandleader who would build on Miles's work from the 1960s, Marsalis now seemed intent on reviving the aesthetic of King Oliver and Bubber Miley. At the same time, Marsalis's melody lines were becoming more compact; as he would later describe it, he was focusing on "clarion" phrases rather than imitating saxophone lines. The ensemble textures were more open and uncluttered.

On the title track of *The Majesty of the Blues* Marsalis adopted a spacious 6/4 meter that gave the underlying blues progression an ambling, unhurried feeling. In place of the restless probing of *Live at Blues Alley*, a more restrained and controlled approach comes to the fore. In the age-old struggle between form and content, Wynton seemingly changed camps overnight, setting himself up now as an architect of sounds rather than the churning, burning soloist heading off into the great unknown. Above all, Marsalis was consciously trying to reconnect with the premodern jazz tradition of his hometown. For some of the music, Marsalis relied on seasoned jazz players flown in from New Orleans, including eighty-year-old Danny Barker. The same return to the roots was evident on Marsalis's *Resolution of Romance*, a follow-up recording of standards, in which the seething polyrhythmic piano of Marcus Roberts was replaced by the more traditional approach of the trumpeter's father, Ellis Marsalis.

The blues was now emerging as a focal concern for Marsalis. One suspects that the influence of critic and mentor Stanley Crouch, who was increasingly playing Boswell to Marsalis's Johnson, was decisive in this regard, as was the aesthetic vision outlined by Albert Murray in his book *Stomping the Blues*. Crouch praised the latter, in his liner notes for *The Majesty of the Blues*, as a work "all musicians of my generation should read." Clearly Marsalis had taken to heart Murray's celebration of the blues tonality as the essence of African American music. Blues progressions had played a very modest role in Marsalis's early works, but now his music was permeated with I, IV, and V chords and bent notes, amply demonstrated on the three volumes of *Soul Gestures in Southern Blues* and the later *Blue Interlude* release. Only a few years earlier, Murray's vision of jazz had seemed an exercise in nostalgia, out of touch with the currents of fusion, free, and European classical strains in the jazz world. But now the most famous young jazz musician of the day was championing the same cause. In the hands of Wynton Marsalis, jazz was coming full circle in a return to the roots that, in its own way, proved as shocking and unexpected as the earlier controversial career shifts of Miles, Coltrane, and the various jazz progressives of the 1960s.

This turnaround was bound to puzzle those who had looked for Marsalis to extend the "advances" of earlier leading jazz figures. Marsalis's new rhythm section was clearly more reverential than his early accompanists, rarely pushing the trumpeter the way Marcus Roberts, Jeff "Tain" Watts, or Kenny Kirkland had in previous bands. Criticism was further spurred by Marsalis's outspoken attitudes. In interviews, the trumpeter had always been uncommonly blunt, not hesitating to ridicule other musicians, even some of the most famous, taking a polemical spin to questions, and frequently showing that he did not need to have a trumpet in hand to blow his own horn. "When I first came to New York in 1979 . . . the established cats who should have been setting an example were bullshittin', wearing dresses and trying to act like rock stars," he had once confided to jazz writer Francis Davis. "So when people heard me, they knew it was time to start takin' care of business again." Marsalis was especially critical of Miles Davis, telling one interviewer that "Bird would roll over in his grave if he knew what was going on."[2] Some time later, when Marsalis tried to sit in with Davis's group at a jazz festival, Miles stopped the band cold in mid-tune and refused to continue until Wynton had left the stage.

Marsalis's music in the 1990s increasingly highlighted his role as composer and section player in settings that often downplayed his skills as a soloist. His band was expanded to a septet, and this spurred an even more pronounced departure from the aggressive and uninhibited attitudes of his earlier quartet and quintet efforts. During the course of *In This House, on This Morning*, which was given its premiere in May

1992 at Avery Fisher Hall in Lincoln Center, a beachcomber's assortment of musical styles is paraded onstage by the seven instrumentalists, who are joined by vocalist Marion Williams: the gospel sounds of the sanctified church; the twelve-bar blues; boisterous New Orleans counterpoint; waltz time and two-beat struts; even a measured dose of atonality in a memorable moment when Marsalis uses his horn to mimic a babbling speaking-in-tongues. Yet this backward glance never collapsed into mere mimicry, and Marsalis, perhaps preeminently among his generation, proved capable of resurrecting the vocabulary of past masters while putting the stamp of his own personality on the proceedings.

In time even this enlarged combo proved too small to realize the trumpeter's growing ambitions. Marsalis at midcareer found his most comfortable setting was the Jazz at Lincoln Center Orchestra—a far cry from his fast-and-loose early bands. Yet bigger ensembles also gave Wynton a chance to flex his muscles as a leading post-Ellington composer, demonstrated most notably on his 1994 piece *Blood on the Fields* (later awarded the Pulitzer Prize) for a fifteen-member jazz orchestra. This impressive and lengthy work, some three and a half hours in duration, seemed determined to swallow whole not only the early jazz tradition but elements of a range of other African American musical styles—gospel, work songs, blues, and other cultural bric-a-brac from a bygone era. This historical eclecticism would constantly reemerge, in ever-differing forms, in Marsalis's later work, whether he was sharing the stage with country artist Willie Nelson, collaborating with Ghanaian drum master Yacub Addy on the trumpeter's composition *Congo Square*, or devoting tribute albums to everyone from Jelly Roll Morton to Thelonious Monk.

Yet Marsalis's successes in funding and promoting such projects did little to stifle the surrounding controversies—so much so that commentators even began talking of a jazz "war" between progressives and traditionalists. When Marsalis took on the role of artistic director of the jazz program at Lincoln Center, harsh economics entered the picture as well. Some critics complained of the exclusionary tone of the Lincoln Center proceedings, carping that those aligned with Marsalis's vision of the jazz tradition were celebrated—and financed with commissions and employment—while players whose aesthetic was too avant-garde or too European were neglected. When Marsalis was awarded the Pulitzer Prize in Music—the first time an artist had earned this honor for a jazz work (although it should be noted that former Benny Goodman sideman Mel Powell had won it in 1990 and Third Stream guru Gunther Schuller did the same in 1994, albeit not for jazz compositions)—an event that should have been celebrated by fans as the end of the unspoken segregation practiced by the judges of America's most cherished music award was instead treated as just one more grievance by a vocal group of Marsalis detractors.

At the height of the hostilities, which appeared to peak around the year 2000, almost anything relating to the trumpeter seemed destined to fuel the flames of contention. In some instances, Marsalis made missteps that contributed to the backlash, yet with the passing years he increasingly grew into the role of global ambassador for jazz that had been thrust upon him when he was scarcely out of his teens. His mentoring of young musicians, his advocacy for the music's importance in the broader culture, his ability to mobilize financial resources, all contributed to the greater good of jazz. At the same time, his critics sometimes conveyed the impression that their resentment was more an anger that jazz history had not gone some other way, more futuristic, more "out there," more whatever. Marsalis was a convenient target for such attacks but, in this instance, even his adversaries may have been giving him too much credit. As we have seen, Marsalis's success was more a result of renewed interest in the jazz heritage than its cause.

Branford Marsalis's evolving career reflected a careless disregard for the rigid hierarchies espoused by his younger brother. If Wynton championed mainstream jazz, Branford played with rock bands; as Wynton's music grew more structured, Branford increasingly delighted in loose, blowing dates; when Wynton frequented Lincoln Center, Branford took a prominent television gig on the *Tonight Show*; while Wynton focused on the traditional sounds of gospel and blues, Branford experimented with the contemporary sounds of funk and hip-hop. But under the superficial laxity of Branford Marsalis lay a musical mind capable of the most rigorous logic. His melodic lines unfolded with a structural elegance at times reminiscent of Sonny Rollins, developing with clarity and precision, but not without incorporating surprising twists and turns along the way. Although his devil-may-care choice of engagements at times raised concerns about whether he most valued artistry or mere fame, Branford Marsalis's talent could not be doubted. At his best, invariably in small-combo jazz settings, he showed that he deserved mention on any short list of the finest saxophonists of his generation.

At times it is hard to separate the personal influence of the Marsalis siblings from the institutional impact of record companies hoping to replicate their success stories. These moves, especially those of the CBS label, often took on a formulaic aspect. Eager to find a "second Wynton," CBS signed Terence Blanchard, a teenage New Orleans trumpeter who had replaced Marsalis in the Blakey band and who frequently collaborated with a fellow Crescent City jazzman, saxophonist Donald Harrison. Pianist and vocalist Harry Connick Jr., another New Orleans native, was also signed by CBS when barely out of his teens. Connick showed very real talent, especially as a singer, and exuded a rare degree of stage presence for a young musician, yet these gifts were hyped beyond recognition when the publicity machine tried to anoint him as the "next Frank Sinatra" on the basis of a few early, albeit promising recordings. Trumpeter Marlon Jordan was also signed to the label while still a teenager—his hometown, few will be surprised to learn, was New Orleans. These artists' recordings were often produced by Delfeayo Marsalis, who also became an important participant in the expanding New Orleans quarter of the CBS jazz empire. Other labels joined the New Orleans craze, with MCA/Impulse promoting Henry Butler, an exciting pianist and vocalist with a dynamic, heartfelt style, Verve signing Nicholas Payton, a sweet-toned trumpeter who was barely out of his teens at the time, and Novus recording the aforementioned Delfeayo Marsalis, who showed his skill in playing the trombone in a manner reminiscent of J. J. Johnson.

This concept-driven campaign, so obsessively focused on the city scrawled on an artist's birth certificate, threatened to collapse under its own weight. CBS Records, acquired by Sony in 1987, eventually parted ways with almost every one of the New Orleans artists it had signed, including Wynton Marsalis. For the most part, the musicians swept up in this Crescent City fever were genuine talents, even if the fame and expectations thrust upon them from the start were new phenomena in the jazz world. As the preceding chapters of this book make clear, many of jazz's greatest figures of previous eras never enjoyed a contract with a major label, and others did so only after mastering their craft the slow way as sidemen in the trenches and on tightly budgeted leader dates for small labels. Some critics feared that the industry's quest for young blood would create a generation of instrumentalists with unripened talent or lacking the deep commitment to a set of musical values that comes only from hard dues paying. Others lamented how many brilliant artists in midcareer, mainstream players born between 1940 and 1955—pianists Jessica Williams, Kenny Barron, Steve Kuhn, and Adam Makowicz; trumpeters Tom Harrell, Valery Ponomarev, and Bobby Shew; saxophonists Bobby Watson, Eric Kloss, Ricky Ford, and Jane Ira Bloom; trombonist Steve Turre (to cite but a few)—seemed part of a lost generation who were mostly forgotten by the power brokers and magazines, seen as too old to be part of the youth movement, but too young to be respected veterans from the early days of jazz.

Yet, as subsequent events would confirm, this flowering of the traditionalist movement in jazz was much more than a passing fad or a short-lived marketing angle pursued by the record labels. The concurrent spread and institutionalization of jazz education during this same period no doubt played a key role in this process. At almost the same moment that Wynton Marsalis was embracing a more traditional musical vocabulary, the National Association of Jazz, a modest organization of music professionals and teachers started in the 1960s, changed its name to the grander International Association for Jazz Education and would build its annual get-together into the single biggest event in the jazz world—a distinction it maintained until the organization's collapse from financial stresses in 2008. Who could have imaged, back in the Swing Era or Jazz Age, that the biggest annual jazz party would coalesce around a collection of educators? Equally surprising to old-timers would be the music's journey from the nightclubs of Fifty-second Street to Lincoln Center. Jazz at Lincoln Center had also started on a small scale, with a budget of less than $1 million when it was established, in 1986, as a department of Lincoln Center for the Performing Arts. But JALC's budget had grown to more than $40 million by 2008—making it the biggest power broker in the jazz world of the new millennium. These are profound changes, yet in an era of codification, institutionalization, and historical consciousness-raising, such shifts should not be surprising.

One can measure this transformation in many ways, but perhaps the most obvious sign of the new state of affairs is the proliferation of tribute bands, tribute recordings, reissues, historic boxed sets, reunion tours, and repertory projects. In the old days, an occasional "ghost band" would work the circuit, usually the result of musicians keeping a group afloat after the death of a prominent leader. But after the return to the roots movements of the 1980s and 1990s, ensembles devoted to the dearly departed seemed to sprout up everywhere, professing allegiances to bygone styles and artists even if none of the musicians on hand had any firsthand contact with the original source of inspiration. Perhaps it is some consolation to readers of this book that, even though they will never get a chance to see the deceased exponents of jazz past in the flesh, they can almost certainly find a tribute band, whether their tastes run to Cannonball Adderley or Lennie Tristano, Bix Beiderbecke or Herbie Nichols, or some other figure from the the the last century.

How sobering it is to consider that the most momentous jazz milestones of 1959 were the release of classic recordings such as *Kind of Blue*, *Time Out*, and *Mingus Ah Um*; but—strange to say—the most publicized jazz events of 2009 were the fiftieth-anniversary reissues of these same albums. The Columbia (now Sony) label that had originally presented this fresh and unapologetic music to the public had by this stage mostly abandoned the idea of promoting any jazz that wasn't a reissue or some marketing-driven concept of minimal substance and credibility. Certainly there are many jazz fans and performers who would prefer a more revolutionary art form with grander aspirations. Yet, like latecomers to a party after all the best food and drink has been consumed, artists of the current day must make do with what scraps are available—and usually those are elements drawn from the music's heritage. To build a revolutionary new style from these bits and pieces may well be too large a task for even the most talented among them, although a few still aspire to such heights—albeit almost invariably without the support of a major label.

Yet should we demand such perennial revolutions? Is it the jazz world that is amiss—or merely our perspective? How valid is our ingrained expectation that the music should always be progressive, always break the mold, always embrace the new-est new thing? Is it not enough simply for music to be enjoyable, intelligent, well played? On the other hand, if young jazz musicians are content to work within the framework of earlier styles, why should we listen to their compact discs rather than to the history-making performances by Armstrong, Parker, Ellington, and other past masters that serve as the blueprints for these latter-day works? Why pay attention to the imitator when the original is—through the miracle of recording technology—almost as accessible? These are deep questions, beyond the scope of this work, and ones that this author hopes to pick up on a later occasion. They are questions, more-over, that are relevant to many arts and genres beyond the world of jazz. It suffices to point out that, after five hundred years as a dominant aesthetic vision, the very notion of an art form following a progressive evolution, quasi-scientific in its con-tinual "breakthroughs," is now tottering at its foundations. Various New Age, mini-malist, and other styles of art, for all their limitations—and though their aesthetic underpinnings are largely unformed—suggest the possibility of a "degree-zero" style (to borrow the terminology of critic Roland Barthes), one that has no relation to the time warp of advancing techniques. In a complementary vein, other aestheticians have spoken of the arrival of the "end" of the history of art—a vision that, to some, represents the glorious advent of a nonlinear age of unconstrained creativity, but, to others, implies a frightening abandonment of our previous assumptions and points of reference.

The history of jazz is at a critical point where such questions become increasingly important. The music's past threatens to dwarf its present and cloud its future. Only in the last few years, visitors to jazz record stores have encountered a novel situation in which most of the music for sale is by artists who are no longer alive. The sur-viving jazz radio stations are moving in a similar direction, celebrating the legacy of past masters and putting fewer and fewer current releases into rotation. The rise of movements to propagate the jazz repertory; the emergence of generation after generation of neotraditionalists; even the interest in jazz historical studies, which validates the work you hold in your hands: these are all symptoms of the same tectonic shift inexorably altering the structure of the jazz world. As a result, any new artist attempting to make a reputation in today's environment must compete not just with other young talents but with the entire history of the music. That is a heavy burden indeed.

Responding to this set of circumstances, an alternative approach to the tradition was espoused by a group of progressive, and often irreverent, postmodernists during the closing decades of the twentieth century. Starting a few years before Wynton Marsalis began his ascent to the pinnacle of jazz fame, these less-heralded artists were attempting a more confrontational approach to the various preexisting styles and vocabularies of jazz. Realizing that the music's weighty tradition could not be avoided completely, these postmodern players nonetheless refused to be mere acolytes celebrating the past. Instead, they applied a deconstructive approach, a willfully manipulative attitude that aimed to transform elements pulled from the jazz (and nonjazz) musical archives into building blocks for new hybrid sounds. These performers grappled with their musical inheritance not to turn jazz into a museum piece—far from it—but rather seeking aural weapons that still might have the capacity to shock and awe.

THE POSTMODERN IMPULSE

"The fox knows many things, but the hedgehog knows one big thing," runs a famous aphorism from the ancient poet Archilochus—a saying that inspired Oxford don Isaiah Berlin to categorize visionary individuals as either foxes or hedgehogs, based on whether their careers emphasize single-minded allegiance to one big concept or constant shifts from idea to idea. The distinction is useful in understanding the postmodern turn in jazz, which aimed to change the art form from the home of heroic hedgehogs into a frenetic free-for-all of fleet foxes.

If jazz was built by big personalities with strongly defined individual styles, in the waning years of the twentieth century it would be inherited by eclectic improvisers who were comfortable with a range of idioms and could mix and match them depending on the setting or their inclination. Starting in the 1970s, the leaders of the jazz world were increasingly those who knew "many things" and delighted in the opportunity to show audiences the full range of their musical learnings. The postmodern jazz musician, a figure who exemplified this turn of events—reflecting tendencies also evident in other art forms during this period—inevitably reminds us of those famous linguists who have mastered several languages and can quickly jump from one to the next. Perhaps even this comparison is too tame, since the jazz postmodernists even dared to superimpose incongruous styles one on top of the other—conversations in multiple tongues happening simultaneously—forcing them together into provocative new combinations. Leading jazz performers had rarely done this in earlier decades. They worked to develop personal styles as unique as a fingerprint, and created their individual sound almost as much by their ruthlessness in excluding certain phrases and structures as by what they included. The postmodern turn in jazz, in contrast, stood out for its vast inclusiveness, its reluctance to abandon any avenue of expression, no matter how far from the mainstream. "Rather than a single notion of 'freedom,' various freedoms were being asserted across a wide spectrum of musical possibilities," George Lewis has written, offering what could easily serve as a definition of the postmodern impulse in jazz.[3]

Even the institutional structures of jazz changed to reflect this new sensibility. Instead of towering individuals who led the jazz world by courageous example, musicians whose very names—Armstrong, Ellington, Parker, Davis, Coltrane—defined and symbolized the evolution of the art form, collectives and associations of various sorts now became the leaders of the progressive wing of the jazz world. The looseness of these confederations reflected the increasingly prevalent open-mindedness to varied methods of musical expression. The formation of the Jazz Composers Guild toward the end of 1964 was an early sign of how this new approach might work. In time, other groups emerged on the scene in different communities, including the Underground Musicians' Association in Los Angeles, the Black Artists' Group in St. Louis, and the Detroit Creative Musicians Association. But the Chicago-based Association for the Advancement of Creative Musicians (AACM) would prove to be the most influential of these collectives.

The AACM began in 1965 with the aim of helping progressive musicians find performing opportunities, rehearsal space, and other career support. Pianist Muhal Richard Abrams served as the organization's first president—his Experimental Band, a large free jazz ensemble established in 1961, had helped lay the groundwork for the AACM, and many of Abrams's later recordings would stand out as important statements of the movement's aesthetic vision. Other early participants included Roscoe Mitchell, Joseph Jarman, Anthony Braxton, and Lester Bowie. In its charter as a non-profit organization, approved on August 5, 1965, the AACM outlined nine purposes, which included the cultivation and training of young musicians, the presentation of concerts and recitals, the creation of employment opportunities for performers, and the fostering of "the tradition of cultured musicians handed down from the past."[4] In time, the group would expand its scope to sponsoring recordings, producing radio shows, helping inner-city students, and many other behind-the-scenes efforts of advocacy and community service.

Important early recordings documenting the AACM's music included Mitchell's *Sound* (1966), Jarman's *Song For* (1967), Bowie's *Numbers 1 & 2* (1967), Abrams's *Levels and Degrees of Light* (1968), Braxton's *Three Compositions of New Jazz* (1968), and the Art Ensemble of Chicago's *People in Sorrow* (1969), *Tutankhamun* (1969), and *A Jackson in Your House* (1969). The title of Mitchell's *Sound*, a project that helped usher in this new Chicago-based movement, gave testimony to an especially vital aspect of this multifaceted music. Like Albert Ayler, these artists often focused on qualities of sound as opposed to conventional delineations of harmony, melody, and rhythm. Standard notation was insufficient to contain these nonscalar explorations—which to some degree are throwbacks to African and early African American systems of organizing music—given the frequency with which the sonic textures moved beyond the twelve standard tones. Yet this was only one part of the Chicago school's approach. Unlike Ayler and other early avant-gardists, the Chicagoans often downplayed the intensity of so-called energy jazz in favor of a comparatively open sound. They were less enamored with "hot" solos (that grand tradition invented a half-century earlier in the Windy City) and embraced instead a more layered and episodic approach to composition and performance. Other trademarks of the emerging Chicago school included diverse borrowings from other genres, aspects of performance art, minimalist and aleatory tendencies, and a pan-African/world music sensibility.

In many ways, the work of the AACM musicians signaled the first stirrings of postmodernism in jazz. Increasingly, the younger progressive players in the jazz world would temper their quest for new, radical sounds in favor of a pronounced eclecticism, one that included the embrace— sometimes the vivisection—of earlier styles and other traditions. In this postmodern sensibility, a two-stepping cakewalk could share the stage with an Aylerian exercise in saxophone glossolalia. This postmodernism was also reflected in a deconstructive attitude toward the music, a desire to break down styles into their constituent elements, sometimes focusing on one isolated aspect, at other times combining the pieces into surprising new wholes. This music was capable of evoking the high seriousness of earlier progressive styles, but postmodernism also experimented with a range of other perspectives including— but not limited to—pastiche, put-on, and parody. In this regard, the jazz world was following a path that other art forms had already trod. Its irreverent and encyclopedic approach to manipulating the materials at hand—largely made up of bits and pieces of past traditions—was comparable to contemporary techniques adopted by practitioners in literature, theater, and the visual arts.

With the benefit of hindsight, we can see the roots of this new perspective in a number of projects from the 1960s and 1970s. Not just the AACM, but artists as diverse as Carla Bley and Frank Zappa were using jazz elements, alongside other fragments of cultural detritus, in a manner that can only be deemed postmodern. Bley's 1971 opera *Escalator over the Hill* was an artful blend of free, jazz rock, and classical influences. A series of later Bley projects amplified on these diverse sources of influence, with a playful, postmodern tinge often present, as in her "Spangled Banner Minor," which scrambles the U.S. national anthem and other patriotic airs into a peculiar jumble of the familiar and strange. Other Bley pieces emulate the sound of a needle skipping on a phonograph record or scales played by a student at a music lesson. Steve Lacy's work from this period also anticipated a number of currents that would crystallize in the work of such later postmodernists as Anthony Braxton, David Murray, and John Zorn, including a blending of a progressive aesthetic with an interest in celebrating past stylists (most notably Thelonious Monk, in Lacy's case), as well as a commitment to frequent recording in diverse settings. Lacy's early career, which found him working in varied idioms from Dixieland to free, made it clear that his artistic vision held few prejudices, and his later efforts cast an even wider net, incorporating electronics, language, vocals, and dance.

The New York loft scene of the 1970s drew on many of these postmodern tendencies and served as an especially fertile meeting ground for the different schools of progressive music trying to establish themselves in the jazz world. A series of recordings from 1976 drawn from performances at Rivbea Studio, the loft home of saxophonist Sam Rivers, and released under the name *Wildflowers*, showcased the tremendous heterogeneity of this hotbed of experimentation. One of the bands highlighted was Air, a trio featuring saxophonist Henry Threadgill, bassist Fred Hopkins, and drummer Steve McCall, whose work was reflective of the emerging aesthetic and as likely to embrace Scott Joplin as Albert Ayler. In addition to his legacy with Air, Threadgill forged a fresh, highly experimental body of work with larger combos drawing on sometimes surprising instruments (accordion, pipa, oud, tuba, French horn, etc.), most notably with his 1990s band Very Very Circus. In these various settings, Threadgill's visionary music implied a rejection of existing jazz hierarchies and an egalitarian openness to a broad range of influences. After the often doctrinaire avant-garde attitudes of the 1960s, many musicians and fans welcomed this approach, one that avoided rigid adherence to any one school and celebrated the possibilities of sound over the rigidity of ideologies.

These new currents would flow far beyond Chicago and New York. The work of Hamiet Bluiett, Julius Hemphill, Oliver Lake, and other musicians associated with the Black Artists' Group in St. Louis revealed a similarly expansive approach to jazz, which encompassed aspects of theater, poetry, and visual arts. On the West Coast, John Carter, who along with Bobby Bradford had formed a Los Angeles splinter group building on the avant-garde principles of Ornette Coleman, created a magnum opus of postmodernism during the 1980s with his five-volume *Roots and Folklore* project, which chronicled in words and music the history of African Americans. In Europe, Dutch reed player and composer Willem Breuker would pursue a similarly eclectic postmodern style with his Kollektief, which was formed in the mid-1970s. In Britain, Mike Westbrook brought everything from circus acts to the poetry of William Blake into his similarly expansive view of jazz performance.

Yet the biggest boost to this deconstructive approach would come from the AACM musicians. The influence of Ayler still predominated on many of the early Chicago school recordings. But it began to coalesce with other postmodern elements in the evolving work of the Art Ensemble of Chicago. The Art Ensemble's motto, "Great Black Music—Ancient to Modern," fittingly denoted their attitude toward the tradition. Fragments of gospel or funk might rub shoulders with dissonance and noise. A stately waltz might disintegrate into musical anarchy. Their fondness for unusual garb and makeup and their borrowings from other genres (theater, dance, pantomime, comedy) validated the performance art elements that had long lurked below the surface of the jazz idiom. Their choices in instruments were equally diverse: banjo, bassoon, bongos, bike horn, bells—and this is just a smattering of the listings under the letter B—and hundreds of other items made their way onto the bandstand along with the standard jazz brass and reed horns.

The Art Ensemble initially featured Roscoe Mitchell, Joseph Jarman, Lester Bowie, Malachi Favors, and, for a brief spell, drummer Phillip Wilson. The band ignored the division of labor traditionally practiced by most jazz combos. Although Mitchell and Jarman periodically stood forth to brandish their saxophones in the front line, they were just as likely to be accompanists as lead soloists, just as inclined to play percussion or unusual wind instruments—conch shells or whistles—as the alto or tenor sax. Lester Bowie could show off his mastery of a wide range of trumpet styles, covering the gamut from pseudo-trad jazz growls and groans to up-to-date funk grooves. But he also might energize an Art Ensemble performance by pounding on the bass drum or engaging in quirky and sometimes humorous onstage antics. Malachi Favors served as bassist for the group, but almost any stringed instrument, from banjo to zither, might show up in his hands, as well as the ever-present percussion instruments that became Art Ensemble trademarks. Indeed, the Ensemble reportedly brought some five hundred music-making implements with them when they moved to France at the close of the 1960s.

The Art Ensemble caught the attention of European audiences in this new setting. Within a few months of arriving, the band had recorded a half-dozen projects, including some of its finest work. The Ensemble was very much in demand, with recording opportunities supplemented by frequent concerts, radio performances, and commissions for movie scores. During this period, percussionist Don Moye joined the band, and though this addition was lamented by some of the group's fans—who saw it as giving a more conventional rhythmic foundation to the Art Ensemble's free-flowing sound collages—Moye's background in free jazz and his wide-ranging collection of percussion instruments fit nicely with the Ensemble's artistic impulses. By the same token, Moye added a more structured and overtly polyrhythmic, often more insistent, undercurrent to the band's sound. By the time of their return to the United States in April 1971, the expanded Art Ensemble had gained a reputation as a powerful exponent of what critic Gary Giddins aptly called "guerrilla jazz." Their variegated approach borrowed from earlier styles while undermining them. No sound, no approach, seemed out of place in the context of an Art Ensemble performance.

Concerts and club appearances conveyed the band's essence in a way that the group's later studio sessions often only approximated. In truth, this band needed to be seen as well as heard. Dressed in African garb, their faces painted or wearing masks, surrounded by their "little instruments"—so many that it sometimes took two hours simply to set up the bandstand—the Art Ensemble presented a striking appearance that had few precedents in the jazz world. The group's various live recordings, such as *Live at Mandel Hall*, *Bap-Tizum*, and *Urban Bushmen*, may stop short of documenting the total experience of the Art Ensemble in performance, but they still manage to convey the band's vitality and unpredictability, as well as its kaleidoscopic range. The Mandel Hall concert, for example, gyrates from fierce energy jazz to strutting backbeats and pensive interludes, interspersed with campy exhortations to the audience.

The postmodernist wave of 1970s jazz found a brilliant exponent and champion in another Chicagoan, saxophonist Anthony Braxton. When viewed in its broadest outlines, Braxton's career bears a superficial resemblance to that of the Art Ensemble. Braxton too was an advocate of free jazz and an early member of AACM and, like the Art Ensemble, he moved to Paris at the close of the 1960s. His recordings have sometimes featured him alongside other AACM musicians; like them, his work crossed stylistic barriers, borrowing from a grab bag of genres. Yet Braxton, if anything, seemed to forage even more widely—could it be possible?—than his Chicago contemporaries. Indeed, no other figure of the period more closely epitomized the postmodernist zeal to rework all earlier traditions, digest every possible style, incorporate each disparate sound into his oeuvre, all under the banner of progressivism. Just a glance at the instrumentation of Braxton's output tells much about his eclectic, and eccentric, approaches. He has written for two pianos, five tubas, even for four amplified shovels. One finds music for solo saxophone; for duo, trio, jazz quartet, string quartet; music for orchestra, for orchestra and four slide projectors, for orchestra and puppet theater, even music for four orchestras.

Braxton succeeded brilliantly in tearing down the artificial barriers that had segregated the avant-garde jazz community—often stirring controversy in the process. In contrast to the Art Ensembles's motto of "Great Black Music," Braxton daringly embraced European as well as African American visions of contemporary music and was not afraid to include Schoenberg, Webern, Cage, and Stockhausen among his influences, alongside Coltrane, Coleman, and Ayler. Further, he broke down the barriers between free and straight-ahead jazz, raising eyebrows by a series of "in the tradition" recordings featuring mainstream renditions of standards. He defied the dichotomies of white and black, still a stubbornly pervasive divide in the jazz world, by frequently lauding the music of Paul Desmond, Lee Konitz, and Warne Marsh and by working in racially diverse ensembles such as the Circle quartet (featuring Braxton, Chick Corea, Barry Altschul, and Dave Holland) or alongside Dave Brubeck, or with various European musicians. He ignored the categorization that separated free players into New York energy jazz advocates and Chicago sound landscapists. Finally, Braxton refused to recognize any conflict between the emotional and cerebral aspects of jazz, even inviting ridicule by his embrace of intellectual mannerisms—playing chess, smoking a pipe, dressing like an Ivy League academic, discoursing on philosophy, using pseudo-scientific diagrams rather than conventional titles for his compositions—a thoughtfulness that also permeated his music. One of the ironies of Braxton's career was that his tearing down of these Berlin Walls within the jazz psyche, this acceptance of any source of inspiration, without prejudice or bias, won him so few friends. "I don't like Braxton," one anonymous elder statesman of jazz told a journalist. "I don't like that sweater. I don't like that pipe. I don't like that hair." Reviewing Braxton's career, critic Greg Tate concludes: "Braxton's talent for inspiring antipathy may be unrivalled by any living jazz creature."[5]

Braxton's diversity is amply represented by his prolific recorded output. His *For Alto* from 1968 legitimized the role of solo saxophone in contemporary jazz and was the most important effort of its kind since Coleman Hawkins's "Picasso" from the late 1940s. His *Paris Concert* recording with the ensemble Circle from 1971 indicated that Braxton's personal brand of abstraction could flourish in a hot-blooded jazz combo, perhaps best demonstrated by the quartet's intense reworking of the standard "There Is No Greater Love." Braxton's recordings for the Arista label in the 1970s gave him unprecedented freedom to realize some of his more ambitious projects, including his *Creative Orchestra Music* (1976), which showcased Braxton the composer in a definitive postmodern effort, almost a compendium of musical Americana. Here Braxton shifts in midpiece from a Sousaesque march to Reich/Glass one-chord minimalism and Aylerian saxophone spasms, elsewhere evoking Ellington or AACM stylings. Other Arista works of note ranged from intimate duos with Muhal Richard Abrams to the massive *For Four Orchestras*. His work with mainstream jazz forms came to the fore in his *In the Tradition* recordings from the 1970s and continued with late 1980s releases focusing on the music of Thelonious Monk and Lennie Tristano. Various combo recordings on Black Saint, Hat Art, and other labels have further documented the incessant probing and roving curiosity of this key figure. His recordings have never found the large audience that tuned into Armstrong or Basie or Coltrane or Davis—those ABCs of jazz popularity—but Braxton would eventually become, like many of the previous "outsiders" of the AACM, a savvy insider, earning a coveted "genius" grant from the MacArthur Foundation in 1994 and becoming a tenured professor at Wesleyan University.

The major heroes of postmodern jazz have tended, like Braxton, to be prodigious in their output and omnivorous in their tastes. Few musicians have exemplified these traits to a greater extent than saxophonist David Murray. Before his fortieth birthday, Murray had some one hundred and fifty recordings, more or less, to his credit. These covered a dizzying range of formats and styles, from solo saxophone to big band, and most stages in between. It is a symptom of postmodern jazz in general, and Murray's career in particular, that attempts to describe this music tend to collapse into a listing of various influences. Certainly, jazz genealogists could spend a long time tracing the predecessors who have left their mark on one Murray recording or another. The title track of his celebrated early recording *Flowers for Albert* was dedicated to Albert Ayler, whose influence on Murray was evident, as was the impact of other avant-garde saxophonists such as Eric Dolphy and Ornette Coleman. But Murray would, in time, also be compared to a host of mainstream saxophone stylists—Sonny Rollins, John Coltrane, Paul Gonsalves, Eddie "Lockjaw" Davis, Ben Webster, even Sidney Bechet—with greater or lesser degrees of plausibility.

Certainly Murray's career, as it evolved, came to reflect the growing distance between progressive jazz and freedom music, a chasm that opened in the 1970s and widened noticeably in the 1980s and 1990s. "The music has to start swinging again," Murray remarked in a 1983 interview. "I think it reflects the sociological aspects of the times—people don't want music they have to suffer through."[6] Both as a composer and an instrumentalist, Murray pursued this ideal. In the process he incorporated the influence of other great jazz composer-players, especially Mingus and Ellington, as is most evident in his larger ensemble work. Murray's octet recordings for the Black Saint label were especially persuasive, recalling Mingus's knack for mixing formalism with a devil-may-care heedlessness. Sideman stints with James Blood Ulmer and Jack DeJohnette amplified on the breadth shown in the saxophonist's leader dates, while his work with the World Saxophone Quartet further testified to Murray's diversity. In later years, Murray increasingly would look outside the jazz world for inspiration, and his midcareer projects include a series of collaborative efforts with traditional Guadeloupian gwo-ka percussionists, a music-meets-poetry partnership with Amiri Baraka, and even the release of a tribute album devoted to the Grateful Dead.

The World Saxophone Quartet (WSQ)—where Murray worked alongside Julius Hemphill, Oliver Lake, and Hamiet Bluiett—was founded in 1976 during the course of a visit to New Orleans to give seminars and concerts when the foursome discovered that audiences responded most favorably to their work without a rhythm section. The concept of four horns interacting without further support invites comparisons with the classical string quartet, yet the WSQ defied any expectations of chamber music snobbishness. They made music that cut across boundaries, that might doff its hat at Ellington one moment, veer into atonality the next, or set a groove drawing on African music, soul, or R&B. A series of releases on the Elektra label—*Plays Duke Ellington*, *Rhythm and Blues*, *Metamorphosis* (with African percussion)—demonstrated the WSQ's expertise in these different genres, while earlier recordings for the Black Saint label, such as *Steppin' with the World Saxophone Quartet*, *Revue*, and *Live in Zurich*, served as effective showcases for the compositional skills of the individual members.

Hemphill had grown up in Fort Worth, Texas, where he had gained familiarity with the city's rhythm-and-blues tradition, as well as with its progressive jazz currents, which Hemphill assimilated firsthand in the course of his studies with John Carter. Lake also boasted deep roots in the free jazz scene, having led the St. Louis–based Black Artists' Group. In the early 1970s, Lake worked in Paris with other BAG musicians before moving to New York. Bluiett had also been associated with the Black Artists' Group before moving to New York in 1969, where he worked with Sam Rivers and Charles Mingus. Each of the four original members of the World Saxophone Quartet was a skilled composer. But much of the magnetism of their playing came from the artful balance between structure and spontaneity, between following the written scores and leaving them behind. Hemphill's health problems, including diabetes and heart surgery, ended this fruitful partnership at the end of the 1980s, but the remaining members maintained the WSQ, with Arthur Blythe, John Purcell, and other saxophonists filling Hemphill's chair in later years.

Postmodern currents in all the arts have typically come to embrace the use of parody and pastiche as the ultimate tools in deconstructing inherited traditions. The deadly seriousness of the first generation of avant-garde pioneers is eventually succeeded by a glib, irreverent hipness, a path that quickly takes us from the steely abstractions of cubism to Campbell's soup cans on canvas. In the jazz world, no artist has been more representative of the Warholian spirit than saxophonist and composer John Zorn. While a student at Webster College in the early 1970s, Zorn had been inspired by the music of the AACM and the Black Artists' Group. But like many of the other new faces of the 1980s and 1990s New York downtown scene—including fellow postmodernists and collaborators such as Tim Berne, Wayne Horvitz, Bill Frisell, and Bobby Previte—Zorn pushed the eclecticism of his models a step beyond, even surpassing a Murray or Threadgill in his unexpected choices for source materials. His tastes wander far beyond the jazz world, and on any given project may include punk rock, aleatory music, klezmer, or spaghetti western film scores, among other genres. Often these styles are juxtaposed in surprising ways—an aural equivalent of channel surfing—inspiring, for instance, Ornette Coleman compositions played with the frantic energy of a heavy-metal band or the theme from a James Bond movie sprinkled with a seasoning of electronic noise.

Zorn's work falls into a number of broad categories. His game pieces provide an alternative to the chord- and meter-based structures of mainstream jazz in favor of more or less complex instructions—in essence, the "rules" of the game—that establish a framework for the composition without specifying any preferred outcome. His release *Cobra* provides a glimpse at the different possible outcomes resulting from a specific game piece for twelve musicians (although the hand signals that direct the flow of the piece are not adequately conveyed by the recording). For all their limitations, such works attempt to rediscover the essential jazz celebration of process over the certainties of a finished product—in the same manner as a Japanese tea ceremony differs from the merely functional cup of diner coffee. A second body of work, including Zorn projects such as *Naked City* and *The Big Gundown* (featuring the music of Ennio Morricone), is driven by Zorn's fascination with cinema, especially genres such as westerns, gangster movies, and film noir. He has written a number of cinematic scores himself, usually for independent filmmakers and often for documentaries, and his music is rich in implied visual corollaries. Other Zorn projects might focus on facets of world music, a specific jazz figure, whether famous (Ornette Coleman) or semiobscure (Sonny Clark), or dip into contemporary classical music ("Forbidden Fruit," written for the Kronos String Quartet).

Trumpeter Dave Douglas first came to the attention of many jazz fans while working with Zorn's Masada group in the early 1990s. This band's blending of klezmer and avant-garde jazz could almost serve as an emblem of the self-conscious postmodern posture. Yet Douglas was also recording works by Igor Stravinsky, Anton Webern, and Duke Ellington on his debut Soul Note leader date *Parallel Worlds* from this same period, and only a few years earlier had been playing hardbop tunes in Horace Silver's band. His later career highlights have included a spirited tribute to Mary Lou Williams, *Soul on Soul* from 2000, but with almost all of the Kansas City jazz elements strangely purged from the music, and Douglas's work with his Tiny Bells trio, which started out focused on Eastern Europe folk material but eventually encompassed a vertiginous array of genres. Douglas's ability to master many vocabularies is striking, yet the range of his work is so wide that he risks comparisons not with Miles or Dizzy, but rather with those crack Hollywood studio players who can play a country music session in the morning, record a commercial jingle in the afternoon, and show up on a reggae date in the evening. In a jazz scene that sometimes seems like a land grab, few artists have staked out more territory than Zorn and Douglas, and where the early postmodernists found eclecticism a means of refreshing their styles, this second wave of adherents has increasingly relied on it as the central value of their careers.

Guitarist Bill Frisell too has exhibited, at times, a taste for genre-hopping and pastiche, but his work more often reflects a singular focus and a rare concern, given his cultural surroundings, with preserving an individual and identifiable style. Even on his most decidedly eclectic project, *Have a Little Faith*—an impressive tour of musical Americana from Sousa, Copland, and Ives to Dylan, Rollins, and Madonna—Frisell's viewpoint avoids reduction into mere satirical distance, and on his *Disfarmer* album from 2009 he achieves a stark and moving unity of purpose that has more in common with roots music than postmodern deconstruction. Although he is quick to praise the many guitarists who have influenced him, from Jim Hall to Jimi Hendrix, his playing retains an unmistakable originality that defies any tracing of guitar licks back to original sources. His undulating lines convey a minimalist aesthetic married to a painter's concern with color, texture, and tone. And though Frisell is enamored with the use of various electronic tools to distort his guitar sound, he typically uses them as means toward deeper artistic expression, not as ends in themselves. For all the superficial diversity of his efforts, Frisell's musical landscapes are mostly painted in washed-out pastels, depicting sparsely populated settings under blanched horizons. The moody ruminative side of this artist is well documented on a number of jazz-oriented leader dates for the ECM and Nonesuch labels; but it also plays a role in his genre-crossing pop culture projects, which range from collaborations with rock icons such as Ginger Baker and Elvis Costello to soundtrack music for everything from television cartoons to Buster Keaton silent movies.

This ragtag postmodernism seemed to lose some steam in the new millennium, as the jazz world took on a more institutional and reverential tone, but a number of provocative examples showed that radical juxtapositions of different genres and traditions could still delight and even—a rarity given the "I've seen it all" attitude of seasoned club hoppers by this time—surprise the audience. The Bad Plus, a collective trio established by pianist Ethan Iverson, bassist Reid Anderson, and drummer Dave King in 2000, tweaked its combined noses at jazz snobs and found a sizable audience of jazz newbies with cover versions of songs by Nirvana, Black Sabbath, The Bee Gees, and similarly outré material. A 2009 video released by the band finds the Bad Plus performing a dauntingly avant-garde work by classical composer Milton Babbitt while sexy dancing girls cavort in the foreground.

Jason Moran has similarly constructed a career that straddles genres and categories. This Houston-born pianist first made his name in the late 1990s as sideman with saxophonist Greg Osby, a relationship that led to Moran signing with the Blue Note label, where his releases have shown a restless urgency in which almost any type of sound—acoustic, electronic, spoken, looped—can serve as an ingredient. On Moran's compact disc *The Bandwagon*, a cover version of Brahms coexists with high-octane free jazz and a musical composition built around a woman speaking on her cell phone in Turkish. His 2009 *In My Mind* project incorporated multimedia effects into a musical tribute to a Thelonious Monk Town Hall concert that took place fifty years earlier. Yet Moran is equally comfortable working sans cell phone and slide projector within the mainstream jazz tradition, and from time to time has shown up in the bands of an impressive if diverse range of bandleaders, including Joe Lovano, Charles Lloyd, Cassandra Wilson, Lee Konitz, and Dave Holland. At his most characteristic moments he builds thick and sometimes overpowering sound textures at the keyboard where the listener seems to be following an aural tropical storm, surging and abating from moment to moment, rather than a conventional solo over chord changes.

Pianist Uri Caine, another champion of postmodern attitudes, has specialized in similarly radical reconfigurations, often of works drawn from the classical repertoire, as demonstrated on *Urlicht/Primal Light* (1997), *The Goldberg Variations* (2000), *Uri Caine Ensemble Plays Mozart* (2006), and *The Othello Syndrome* (2008). Whereas in the past, jazz artists had looked to highbrow role models as ways of uplifting the art form—the Third Stream movement of the 1950s was perhaps the most ambitious program of this nature—the later postmodernists treat the work of "serious" composers as just one more example of cultural bric-a-brac available for manipulation and expropriation. After hearing Caine's version of Bach's *Goldberg Variations*, where if you wait long enough almost every style of music—samba, gospel, klezmer, electronica, etc.—shows up, the listener will find it hard to remember why people got so hot under the collar when Glenn Gould played this work on the piano instead of the harpsichord.

Clarinetist Don Byron has frequently collaborated with Caine, Moran, Frisell, and other jazz postmodernists, and his personal aesthetic vision shows a similar delight in genre bending and juxtaposition. In various projects, he has celebrated klezmer music, updated nineteenth-century classical compositions, championed fringe composers such as Raymond Scott, Junior Walker, and Mickey Katz, and played the standard jazz repertoire from a variety of angles, with perspectives from both inside and outside the changes. One seeks in vain for the defining elements of Byron's style, and would do better to see his work—as well as that of many of his contemporaries—as embracing a jittery anti-style that seeks constantly to redefine its own parameters and limits.

Although the term *postmodernism* might suggest an end point for jazz history, a happily-ever-after where all ingredients combine in ever-fresh recipes, the period of ascendancy of this freewheeling philosophy may have already passed. So much of the power of this music derives from the shock value attendant on its violation of boundaries and transgression of norms, yet this element of surprise is harder to come by with each passing year. The juggling of different jazz vocabularies will never entirely lose its piquancy, but these mash-ups hardly have the same jolt in the new millennium that they did in the 1980s and 1990s. In the aftermath of this age of cut-and-paste, with its aural collages made from snippets of everything from Ayler to Zorn, a more earnest and focused tone seems to be coming to the fore in the art form.

10 Jazz in the New Millennium

VIRTUAL JAZZ

Even back in the 1970s, the jazz world understood that technology would change the music. Yet most performers, if pushed for particulars at that time, would have talked about the spread of synthesizers and keyboards, advances in electric guitars, and the impact of various other plugged-in devices on the bandstand. Who would have thought, back in those heroic days of jazz fusion musicians strutting like rock stars, that the real technological revolution would take place a generation later—but mostly offstage, in the ways music is conceived, recorded, distributed, marketed, and shared? Welcome to the jazz scene of the new millennium, where the music itself is evolving more slowly than everything surrounding it.

As I sit writing, I have two catalogs in front of me, both apparently sent as junk mail to the addresses of musicians and wannabe performers. "You're not dreaming," proclaims the cover of one of them, "1,000 CDs in jewel cases now just $890." Make your own compact discs for less than a dollar each? Who needs a record label? The other brochure quotes slightly higher prices, but offers everything from eco-friendly packaging—with the CD trays made from recycled soda and water bottles—to promotion services that promise to get a compact disc with the musician's songs into the hands of radio DJs, promoters, managers, record labels, and potential licensers.

What a dramatic change from the old days, when an unproven musician who wanted to release an album needed to convince "the man"—and invariably it was a man—at one of a small number of record labels to take a chance on a new artist. Nowadays, anyone and everyone can release a CD with a modest investment, paid for by a few gigs.

And judging by the number of jazz compact discs coming out every month, countless musicians are taking advantage of this opportunity to become their own label. In the last year, I have received more than one thousand jazz CDs in the mail, sent to me in hopes that I would write a review, most of them financed and released by the artist. By my estimate there were probably a couple thousand more that were released but never made it to my mailbox (an oversight for which the postal worker who covers my block is deeply grateful). If one measures the success of the jazz scene by the quantity of product out there, then we are living in the Golden Age. More jazz recordings are released in a single month now than came out in an entire year back in the 1950s.

The irony is that this profusion of compact discs is happening at the very time that the CD is no longer necessary and is under attack from nimbler virtual ways of distributing music. Recordings can now be sent around the world at no cost with the click of a mouse—no disc required and even more eco-friendly than a recycled Pepsi bottle. Millions of tracks are available for purchase on dozens of websites, and even if you don't want to spend any money, plenty is offered for free or accessible from various illegal sources. Musicians can easily find electronic distributors for their songs or (as they are increasingly doing) setting up their own web presence to promote and sell their work. Just as performers in the past needed membership in the musicians' union or a cabaret card to launch their careers, nowadays they require a profile on MySpace, a Twitter account, and a Facebook page. A search for "jazz" on YouTube comes back with more than one million hits.

The ways this technological revolution is impacting jazz are both subtle and profound, with the digital track increasingly usurping the role once held by live performance. At the Punkt Jazz Festival in Norway, audience members can go to the Alpha Room immediately after a concert and experience a "live" remix of the music they just heard—with DJs and guest musicians reworking the songs assisted by a stage full of equipment; indeed the remix is the heart of the festival, and often more exciting than the initial performance. Back in the States, trumpeter Dave Douglas performs in a jazz club, and a few hours later is selling downloads of the music on his website. Crossborder jams are harder, given the time lag in sound traveling long distances, yet in 2007 Dave Brubeck pulled off a "live" performance with the BBC Orchestra during which the pianist was in a studio in Rockefeller Plaza in New York, while the orchestra and conductor were facing the audience in London. Of course, you don't need to be a star to jam over the web these days, and if you aren't ready for the competition, online music lessons are easily available on numerous sites—get some tips from an established pro in New York or Hollywood, without leaving your apartment in Budapest or Bangalore. In North Carolina, a startup company called Zenph Studios is producing jazz recordings without any musicians at all, creating software equivalents of great performers of the past, virtual pianists and virtual bassists that are essentially indistinguishable from the originals. Inexpensive software packages, such as Finale and Sibelius, allow composers the privilege of hearing orchestral realizations of their work without the need to hire a single performer. In short, every aspect of the jazz world from conception to consumption is being transformed by technology.

Not many jazz musicians use the word *disintermediation* in their conversations—it is a term more often heard in corporate boardrooms—but this may well be the most important trend impacting their careers in the coming decades. Disintermediation describes the removal of key participants in an economic process because they no longer add sufficient value to justify their roles. In popular parlance, it is called "cutting out the middleman." Who needs record stores if music is sold over the Internet? Who needs a record distributor, if no stores are left? Who needs a company to make a physical CD, if a download is just as good? Who needs an agent, if an artist can deal directly with club owners and concert promoters via the web and e-mail? Who needs a musician, if software equivalents are just as good, and much less expensive? Of course, you can't dispense with everybody—and especially not with the consumer, increasingly an endangered species in jazz—but now all participants in the jazz value chain need to justify their contribution and defend themselves against the encroachment of others.

In this environment, jazz musicians have been forced to become entrepreneurs and savvy managers of their own careers. Not too long ago, it was a great rarity when a jazz artist such as Marian McPartland or Horace Silver decided to launch a home-grown record label. In the new millennium, this is commonplace, in fact far more typical than the old model of an independent company taking on the risk of promoting an artist. New types of organization are also emerging to empower artists and create support networks in this changed environment. The ArtistShare company, founded by Brian Camelio in 2001, allows musicians to tap their own audience base to fund creative projects. Fans who make contributions get special perks, which might even include an invitation to the recording session or having their name printed in the liner notes to the resulting compact disc. When an ArtistShare's fan-funded project, Maria Schneider's *Concert in the Garden* from 2004, won a Grammy, one of the key donors (listed as executive producer on the project) was invited to join Schneider at the award ceremony. Certainly this "label" (although Camelio is ambivalent about the term when applied to his business model) is no mere vanity outfit for the musician not talented enough to get a "real" record deal. Some of the finest jazz artists on the scene—Jim Hall, Bob Brookmeyer, Chris Potter, Brian Lynch, Kurt Rosenwinkel, Billy Childs and others—have embraced the concept, and (as Schneider's Grammy honors attest) the resulting projects present some of the best jazz on the market. Could it be that this economic model—which bears an uncanny resemblance to the arrangements between composers and patrons that emerged back when the musical arts were first adapting to the dictates of capitalism—is also conducive to great art making? Certainly it represents a realistic response to the economic marginalization of jazz as an art form and the pressures of reconciling creative goals with dollars-and-cents practicalities.

Perhaps the increasingly unstable financial situation of the jazz world explains the greater tone of seriousness that seems to have entered the music in the new millennium. The ironic attitudes that had been so common among the first wave of postmodern players in the 1980s and 1990s have lessened; the playful mixing and matching of genres still takes place but far less often; and above all a new earnestness permeates the scene. Several factors have no doubt contributed to this state of affairs. After 9/11, a number of pundits proclaimed the "death of irony," and the economic malaise of the decade did little to lighten the cultural tone, which even outside of the music industry is increasingly brusque and down-to-earth. But one suspects that a change in attitude in the jazz world would have emerged under any circumstances, just as we have witnessed similar shifts from playful to serious approaches in earlier decades—for example, with the rise of bebop in the mid-1940s and the emergence of the avant-garde fifteen years later.

No artist reflects this earnest attitude more decidedly than pianist Brad Mehldau. It is not just his tendency to quote German philosophers in his liner notes that contributes to this perception. (An academic paper available for download on the pianist's website is titled "Smashing the Framework with a Piano Hammer: An Interpretation of Nietzschean Existentialism in the Music of Brad Mehldau.") Nor is it Mehldau's dour mien on his CD covers, where he seems to have a deep-set aversion to showing even a glimmer of a smile. Rather, the singular gravitas of Mehldau's artistry comes most to the fore on the bandstand, where he combines the cerebral and lyrical in artful reconfigurations of popular songs and his own sharply etched compositions. The vehemence of this music is all the more striking when one considers Mehldau's marked preference for pop and rock material that has only the loosest links to the jazz repertoire. He is just as likely to draw on the Beatles and Paul Simon for his set lists as on Monk and Trane, and Mehldau's example is the key reason why songs by Radiohead and Nick Drake have now become jazz standards. That said, don't expect to hear his versions on rock radio stations anytime soon. By the time Mehldau has refracted these compositions through his own house of musical mirrors, these former hit tunes have been turned into jazz art songs and bear the full weight of the pianist's exploratory tendencies. The song he is playing might be "50 Ways to Leave Your Lover," but when Mehldau's trio performs it in 7/4 meter with dauntingly dense instrumental textures, you will be forgiven for not recognizing Paul Simon's number one hit from 1975.

Born in Jacksonville, Florida, in 1970, Mehldau spent much of his youth in Connecticut and moved to New York in 1988 to study at the New School under Fred Hersch. The pianist's early work inspired critics to make comparisons to Bill Evans, much to Mehldau's displeasure. On one of his CDs he included a lengthy essay asserting his independence from this influential forerunner. "The constant comparison of this trio with the Bill Evans trio by critics has been a thorn in my side. I remember listening to his music only a little, when I was 13 or 14 years old, for several months. . . . Often what I am doing in my solo is basing its melodic content on the initial melody of the song. You won't find the model for this approach in Bill Evans."[1] In truth, Mehldau's earliest recordings are peppered with reminders of Evans's work in the pianist's choice of material, in his approach to phrasing, and in the interactivity between piano, bass, and drums; yet by the time Mehldau was in the midst of his *Art of the Trio* projects in the late 1990s, this artist was increasingly staking out his own territory, creating a vibrant body of work that was more likely to influence others than to show its own sources of inspiration. Mehldau's advanced rhythmic conception and orchestral two-handed technique, his expansion of the repertoire noted above, and his musical rapport with bassist Larry Grenadier and drummer Jorge Rossy (or Jeff Ballard on later recordings) made clear that a jazz performer could continue to work within popular song forms and conventional tonality while still pushing the art form in exciting new directions.

Just as Brad Mehldau has needed to assert his independence in the face of those who would like to pigeonhole him as a Bill Evans clone, pianist Matthew Shipp has often had to deal with those who want to typecast him as an acolyte of Cecil Taylor or enter him as a combatant in the free jazz controversies that began before he was even born. Yet Shipp is too complicated a musician for such simple genealogies, and though he is capable of titanic atonal attacks on the keyboard, as he has demonstrated ever since his apprenticeship days in the band of saxophonist David S. Ware, he can also flex his musical muscles within conventional chord changes or even while handling simple pentatonic-based figures. Indeed, his recordings include astringent versions of the most unlikely songs, such as "Frère Jacques" and "When Johnny Comes Marching Home," that coexist happily with his gritty interpretations of jazz standards and original compositions. Perhaps the best way of conceptualizing Shipp is to see his music as existing "on the edge" rather than (like many so-called free players) "over the edge." In this regard, he is less an extension of Cecil Taylor and perhaps more aligned with the attitudes of predecessors such as Thelonious Monk, Sun Ra, Horace Tapscott, and Andrew Hill, who preferred to grapple at the boundaries of tonal systems rather than completely abandon their Gravitational Pull on the music.

Shipp was born in Wilmington, Delaware, in 1960, and though jazz was heard frequently at his home—his mother had known that other great Wilmington musician, Clifford Brown—he also played in rock bands during high school and listened to artists such as Stevie Wonder and Earth, Wind & Fire. This wide mix of early influences has been occasionally reflected in Shipp's own eclectic approach to bandleading, which has found him sometimes drawing on hip-hop elements, synthesized sounds, loops, and other electronic effects, but also achieving equal success in all-acoustic settings. Certainly no one would mistake Shipp for a crossover or fusion artist, and he looks to music outside of the mainstream jazz tradition not so much for its commercial aspects but rather as part of his search for new sound colors he can incorporate into his uncompromising personal vision of jazz. Here, a ruthless domination of the music somehow coexists with the artist's analytical and almost architectonic mindset, and the unresolved tension between these two approaches is perhaps the most alluring aspect of Shipp's work. Listening to his music, one is reminded of those hard-nosed doctors who can cure the patient, but only by enforcing the most brutal regimen.

Yet this new earnestness in the postmillennial jazz scene is even more marked among the vocalists. The three most commercially successful singers of jazz-oriented material during the opening years of the new century have been Norah Jones, Diana Krall, and the late Eva Cassidy. Yet their vocal work is so cleansed of the skippety-ippety-doo pyrotechnics of the previous generation, so introspective and austere, that some critics would contend that they aren't real jazz singers at all. A tempting verdict—except that the history of jazz teaches us that attempts to exclude whole groups of performers by the application of narrow definitions are usually a sign that something important is underway in the art form. Certainly a different aesthetic sensibility is rising to the fore here. These three singers each operate at a subtle, microtonal level, creating hushed emotional effects through nuances of phrasing and a psychologically attuned performance style that is a world apart from the extroverted stylings of the past.

Diana Krall, born in British Columbia in 1964, is an adroit pianist as well as a star singer, and her early recordings often reminded listeners of another singing pianist, Nat King Cole. As her work evolved, Krall found her sweet spot in moody ballads and gentle bossa novas, and though she drew her repertoire from the most familiar standards, songs that jazz fans have heard countless times, this artist made them feel as raw as a fresh wound. Krall is at her best when she is most emotionally exposed, and few jazz singers are more skilled at turning the old tunes into plausible modern-day testimonies. Sometimes she brings down the tempo below forty beats per minute, a pace at which most vocalists would require a lifeline from the rhythm section to survive from bar to bar, but for Krall these slo-mo renditions give her access to new dimensions of these songs, aspects of George Gershwin or Cole Porter that are both true to the original impetus of the composition at hand yet also so new that it seems as if Krall is singing about a heartache that happened earlier today. Her talent made her a celebrated jazz diva—and her marriage to Elvis Costello boosted her fame further to a paparazzi level of notoriety—yet Krall's popularity is less due to these trappings of grandeur than to a confessional tone to her music that, if anything, lessens the distance between the vocalist and her listeners.

Even Krall's impressive record sales have failed to match the spectacular levels achieved by Norah Jones, whose 2002 debut album *Come Away with Me* sold a staggering twenty-five million copies. For a time, the fan fever for this music, and especially for the hit single "Don't Know Why," ran so high that her album accounted for more than half of the jazz compact discs sold in many retail outlets. Many critics and insiders, uneasy at this disproportionate success compared with *everything else in the art form*, tried to disavow any affiliation between jazz and Norah Jones. But one need merely hear her version of "Nearness of You" on this release, or her acute phrasing on the original compositions that have been her most popular numbers, to realize that Jones is not just one of the biggest-selling artists of her day but also one of the most talented. As with Krall, much of the "action" here could be missed by a fan not sensitive to the subtle microtonal shifts in the melody line that create the potent overall effect. With Jones it is tempting to link this skill to her father, Ravi Shankar, who was a master of the same types of effects on the sitar. But Jones, who was born in Brooklyn in 1979 and raised in Texas, also incorporates a gentle country twang to her singing, and includes Willie Nelson, alongside Billie Holiday and Bill Evans, when listing mentors and influences. Jones's greatest impact, however, may be less in the specifics of her interpretations than in her blending of the jazz vocal tradition with the ethos of the singer-songwriter, especially its emphasis on pro-moting new material and tone of intimate self-expression. In the aftermath of the success of *Come Away with Me*, a host of new young jazz singers with original songs arrived at the doors of record labels. Much of this music proved ephemeral and undistinguished, but this collective decision by singers and industry execs to move beyond the repetition of Tin Pan Alley favorites and consider a broad range of contemporary attitudes has to be a healthy development for the art form.

Eva Cassidy's situation is quite similar to Jones's, both in her mastery of chiaroscuro shades of phrasing and in the jazz establishment's reluctance to embrace her as one of its own. Fans have been unequivocal, however, in their advocacy of this singer, who tragically died from melanoma in 1996 at the age of thirty-three. She was little known during her lifetime, and her posthumous rise to fame ranks as one of the most unexpected and gratifying grassroots movements that the music world has witnessed in recent times. Cassidy thus has the rare distinction of ranking among the biggest-selling singers in a century she didn't survive to see. If she had lived longer, Cassidy herself could have made clearer to what degree she should be considered a jazz singer. Yet her performances of "Autumn Leaves," "Fields of Gold," and "Over the Rainbow" suggest that, whatever label one chooses to apply to her work, Cassidy was one of the most emotionally astute interpretive vocalists of recent decades and very much aligned with the earnest tone that is increasingly on display in jazz clubs and on recordings.

It would be wrong to infer from these three prominent examples that all jazz singers have put their scat singing under lock and key and opted for moody ballads in the new millennium. Jamie Cullum struts and prances on the stage and does handstands on the piano when he is not delivering scintillating versions of both familiar old songs and clever new ones of his own invention. Kurt Elling has kept the bohemian spirit of the Beat Generation alive with his forceful onstage personality, spirited delivery, and smart arrangements of material—performances that are clearly rooted in the jazz tradition yet sound very vital and modern. Patricia Barber can sing the old tunes straight from the heart, deconstruct them like arcane literary texts, or write some of the most poetic and adventurous new songs of the current day. Her live recording in Paris starts with her singing: "Did you ever think a piano could fall on your head," and one would have loved to watch the French audience try to do real-time translations of her outré lyrics. Her music defies easy categorization and is all the more worth hearing for its freedom from the conventional and prosaic. Roberta Gambarini and Jane Monheit, in contrast, are so deeply embedded in the tradition that one might think a time machine has transported them from the 1950s jazz scene and placed them smack dab in the middle of the current day. Yet when it comes to retro, they can hardly match Michael Bublé, Matt Dusk, Peter Cincotti, and Tony DeSare, who channel Frank Sinatra through Harry Connick—without much real jazz sensibility to their music, but with a Rat Pack stage presence that apparently taps into some subliminal desire among audiences to resurrect the glamour of days long gone and entertainers dearly departed.

The younger male singers on the scene could perhaps learn a thing or two from vocalist Bobby McFerrin, who has achieved sales few of them have any hopes of matching, yet has done so by breaking almost every rule of career management. While others of his generation looked to recreate earlier styles, McFerrin pursued *sui generis* projects, ranging from solo voice concerts to the mimicry of horn parts (hear his uncanny trumpet imitation on the soundtrack to the movie *'Round Midnight*)—in addition to his many non-singing activities, which include conducting symphonic orchestras and furthering various music education endeavors. His intonation, range, and improvising skill drew rave notices from the start of his career, but his stage presence and willingness to defy expectations soon proved to be defining trademarks of his oeuvre, almost as much as his vocal pyrotechnics. McFerrin has surprised and at times irritated listeners—yet no doubt delighting others—with the unpredictable zigzags his career has taken. He achieved tremendous success with his 1988 reggae-inflected hit "Don't Worry, Be Happy," although one suspects that few of the radio listeners who pushed it up the charts realized that it was one facet of an ambitious project in which all of the parts were overdubs of McFerrin's voice. McFerrin evinced little interest in capitalizing on his growing renown after this crossover hit, choosing to take a sabbatical just at the moment when he could have packed concert halls and conquered the airwaves with follow-up tunes. His ensuing projects included an intriguing series of duet recordings, each provocative in its own way but hardly destined for the *Billboard* charts: with actor Jack Nicholson on narrative-and-voice versions of Rudyard Kipling stories; with cellist Yo-Yo Ma in renditions of classical pieces; and with Chick Corea in interpretations of familiar jazz material. His body of work, as it has developed, has maintained the highest standards of musicianship and creativity while avoiding allegiances to the passing fads and ideologies of jazz discourse. For this reason, he is often neglected in discussions of various trends and styles in the jazz world—when others jump on bandwagons, McFerrin is invariably missing in action. Yet his life-affirming humanism, his childlike curiosity about the possibilities of sound, and his refusal to be caught in the clichés of another era would be well worth emulating by later generations of jazz performers.

A host of other singers (some discussed elsewhere in this volume) are also creating strong, vibrant work in the new millennium—artists such as Cassandra Wilson, Dianne Reeves, Luciana Souza, John Pizzarelli, Nnenna Freelon, Esperanza Spalding, Ian Shaw, Kevin Mahogany, Diane Schuur, Kate McGarry, Madeleine Peyroux, Gretchen Parlato, Karrin Allyson, Tierney Sutton, Sara Gazarek, and Julia Dollison—individuals who may not have matched the popularity and fan devotion of Krall or Jones or McFerrin, but have demonstrated artistry of the highest rank and are contributing to a jazz vocal scene that is much deeper and richer than most fans realize. The biggest challenge many of these performers face in furthering their careers perhaps comes from the obsessively image-driven approaches of the leading jazz record labels, who seem increasingly fixated on a singer's glamour and looks rather than musical talent—a perspective that inevitably leads to a dilution of standards, a churning of rosters, and an unwillingness to support artists for the long run. These and many other vocalists have the requisite talent, but will the music industry provide them with the platform they need to reach their full potential?

Turning our attention to the state of jazz trumpet in the new millennium, we might be forgiven for seeing this instrument as the main upholder of time-honored traditions in the current environment. When we examined the careers of Wynton Marsalis, and other trumpeters from New Orleans such as Nicholas Payton and Terence Blanchard, we saw how these artists' particular visions were informed by the heritage of their hometown, and that their aspirations for the future of jazz were often married to a celebration of music's past. Yet this historically charged approach to the horn is not restricted to performers raised in Louisiana. Philadelphia-born Wallace Roney is a contemporary of Marsalis's, but he is perhaps best known as an heir to the legacy of Miles Davis. This pigeonholing is not entirely fair: Roney's work with Art Blakey, Chick Corea, Kenny Garrett, and others has shown that he is anything but a one-dimensional acolyte of Mr. Davis. Yet Roney's close affiliation with Miles— capped by his stepping in to play Davis's own parts side-by-side with the master at a historic concert at the 1991 Montreux Jazz Festival shortly before Davis's death—testifies to his close affiliation with this earlier body of work. As we will see in our look at European jazz scene, a number of trumpeters across that continent have found inspiration in the stylings of cool school icon Chet Baker, and there is similarly no shortage of younger players following in the fingerings of Freddie Hubbard, Don Cherry, Dizzy Gillespie, and other past masters of the jazz idiom. If jazz is becoming a museum, the trumpeters have proven to be the most fervent curators.

This return to the roots was controversial in the 1990s but is less so in the new millennium. In fact, the most striking fact about the jazz scene of post-2000 is the gradual lessening of tension between the combative camps that have long dominated the art form. In the 1940s, the battle was between bop and swing; in the 1950s it was East Coast versus West Coast; in the 1960s it was free versus tonal; in the 1970s it was fusion versus acoustic; and in the 1980s and 1990s the the progressives bickered with the new traditionalists. It seems that jazz players (but even more the fans and critics) have rarely been able to celebrate their own personal vision of the music without putting down some other contingent. This contentiousness didn't disappear overnight when the calendar turned to a new century, but the overall trend has been unmistakable. Back in 1960, sociologist Daniel Bell stirred controversy by announcing the "end of ideology" in a famous essay—a prediction that proved to be premature, to say the least. Yet jazz musicians are now showing sociopolitical thinkers what this freedom from cant actually looks like.

Take, for example, trumpeter Tom Harrell, a fluid player and creative improviser, who has served as sideman with artists as diverse as Stan Kenton, Dizzy Gillespie, Joe Lovano, Lionel Hampton, and Bill Evans. Harrell has struggled with schizophrenia, and his productivity and artistry in the face of it serve as eloquent testimony to how little he has let this disability restrict his onstage career. Despite his travails, Harrell made his reputation as a musician's musician, praised by jazz insiders before he became well known among fans; but a talent this large was impossible to keep secret for long. In time Harrell moved beyond serving as a superior sideman and made his mark on numerous leader dates, racking up awards and honors, and sometimes even beating out the famous Mr. Marsalis in the jazz polls. Less clear is what position Harrell occupies in the jazz wars. His music seems to be focused on soloing at a high level no matter what the setting, and one struggles to find an ideological platform undergirding his efforts. And after so many years of ideological skirmishes in the jazz ranks, this emphasis on the music and neglect of slogans must be seen as a refreshing change of pace.

Much the same could be said about Roy Hargrove, another leading trumpeter, who is equally at home leading a big band, fronting an Afro-Cuban ensemble, accompanying singers, working with his hip-hop collective, the RH Factor, or playing the old standards in a small-combo setting. Hargrove was born in Waco, Texas, in 1969, and while still in high school benefited from the mentoring of Wynton Marsalis—who has emerged as a guiding light for many younger players and may eventually prove to be the leading talent scout of his era in addition to everything he has done as a performer-composer. In the early days of Hargrove's career, critics might have been tempted to pigeonhole him as another young traditionalist. Yet the trumpeter has pursued a wide range of projects over the years with little regard for categories and competing camps. His versatility may remind some of the mix-and-match postmodernists, but whereas the latter enjoy the mash-ups that take place when different idioms collide, Hargrove respects each project on its own terms, without need for irony or deconstruction to "frame" it. The most salient quality of his music is his mastery of the horn and his ability to make his presence felt no matter what the setting.

Among the saxophonists, no one has done more to cut across ideological lines than Joe Lovano. On his exceptional double-disc live recording at the Village Vanguard, Lovano offered a stirring tribute to Ornette Coleman on his composition "Fort Worth," yet on his previous release *Rush Hour*, named album of the year by *Downbeat*, the saxophonist collaborated with Third Stream progenitor Gunther Schuller. Then again, on his *52nd Street Themes* album, Lovano showed how comfortable he could be playing bop-oriented songs composed before he was born. In other settings, Lovano is not afraid to take an unabashedly lyrical approach to a ballad, stirring up comparisons to Stan Getz, or to battle other tenor icons in his Saxophone Summit sparring with Michael Brecker, Dave Liebman, and Ravi Coltrane. He has delighted audiences with in-the-tradition duets with veteran pianist Hank Jones, mixed it up with Paul Motian and Bill Frisell in an iconoclastic trio, and put his stamp on theme albums dedicated to Frank Sinatra and Enrico Caruso. Is he a traditionalist or a progressive? Old school or new school? Such questions become meaningless in the face of his expansive body of work. Lovano is a stellar soloist, plain and simple, with big ears and a big heart. His fan base has grown because of how his music sounds, not because of what it signifies.

Tenor saxophonist Joshua Redman, born in Berkeley in 1969, has followed a far different route to get to a similar end point, growing up on the West Coast, thriving in academics—he was valedictorian of his high school class and attended Harvard University, where he graduated summa cum laude—and toying with the idea of becoming a doctor or lawyer before settling on the sax. But like Lovano, Redman stands out as a unifying figure, drawing on many camps without giving full allegiance to any one of them. His father, Dewey Redman—who had come of age with Ornette Coleman and later played in Keith Jarrett's so-called American quartet—was demonstrating a similar flexibility back when the jazz world was far more polarized; but Redman the younger has been, if anything, even more peripatetic in his music making. He dazzled listeners at the 1991 Thelonious Monk competition, captured a recording contract with Warner Brothers, and on his 1993 recording *Wish* seemed to be following in his father's footsteps, covering Ornette on the opening track with a band that featured Coleman alums Charlie Haden and Billy Higgins, as well as guitarist Pat Metheny. Other early releases, such as the exemplary double compact disc release *Spur of the Moment*, recorded at the Village Vanguard in 1995, and the *MoodSwing* project from the same period, were more overtly traditional but hardly conventional. Redman has also grooved in odd time meters with Brad Mehldau, served as sideman with the Japanese blues band the Seatbelts, crafted low-key chamber jazz on his 2009 *Compass* release, and taken on a funk-oriented attitude with his Elastic Band. Yet, whatever the setting, Redman impresses as one of the most consistently inventive soloists of his generation.

James Carter, born in Detroit in 1969 and just four weeks older than Redman, espouses a similar disregard for party lines yet shows his versatility in a still different way.

He plays tenor sax, soprano sax, alto sax, baritone sax, flute, and bass clarinet, and one would be hard pressed to say which of these is his main outlet. His repeated victories in the *Downbeat* poll baritone sax category might suggest that this could be a promising area of specialization for Carter, yet he seems happier switching from horn to horn rather than pursuing a monogamous relationship with any one of them. His knowledge of the jazz tradition runs deep, and his recordings are peppered with cover versions of tunes from decades past that only the cognoscenti would recognize. Yet Carter doesn't fit easily into the traditionalist mold, and his music also borrows from contemporary stylings or moves into avant-garde territory as the situation warrants. With his all-star *Heaven on Earth* project, Carter even adopts a rockish jam band aesthetic, although he finds a place here for a dose of Ayleresque energy jazz. Jazz history is often unkind to musicians who try to cover too much ground, as demonstrated by the careers of Benny Carter, Rahsaan Roland Kirk, Oliver Nelson, Jimmy Giuffre, and others who might have been better known if they had remained faithful to a single instrument and concept throughout their careers. Time will tell whether Carter can overcome this tendency of the jazz world to celebrate that which they can pigeonhole. Certainly his talent is large and could carry him to the highest rung of the art form.

Although few artists match the versatility of James Carter or Joshua Redman, jazz saxophony in the new millennium is represented by a number of performers who impress by their adaptability, their professionalism, and their dedication to their craft. Chris Potter is just as comfortable filling in as sideman with Herbie Hancock or Steely Dan or Dave Holland as on his own leader dates, but he doesn't try to show off how quickly he can change gears; rather his playing is marked by a serious immersion in the gig at hand, and hearing him in any one of these ensembles, the listener might surmise that this particular setting was his entire focus. Kenny Garrett boasts, if anything, an even more wide-ranging résumé, having started with the Duke Ellington Orchestra in 1978 (when the band was led by Mercer Ellington) and gone on to work alongside Art Blakey, Miles Davis, Freddie Hubbard, Chick Corea, McCoy Tyner, and other prominent jazz artists; one suspects that these bandleaders sought him out because he does more than play at different styles but can insert his own strong musical personality into the mix without any sense of gamesmanship or contrivance. As one looks at these artists and other leading reed players of the new millennium—such as Miguel Zenón, Donny McCaslin, Mark Turner, Antonio Hart, and Anat Cohen, among others—one is struck by how these artists can be so effective with so little grandstanding or ostentation. After several generations of heroic jazz horn players who inspired others with their cult of personality—obsessed acolytes even founded a church to honor John Coltrane—as much as their musical methods, this down-to-business earnestness may strike casual fans as a letdown, but the insiders are likely to applaud a new phase in which musicianship and professionalism, pure and simple, have their day.

These emblematic qualities of the current generation of jazz performers—professionalism, versatility, musicianship, earnestness—are accentuated by the expanding influence of jazz education programs and the increasing codification and institutionalization of the art form. Joshua Redman came out of a Berkeley school system that, over a period of several decades, established a substantial jazz program, starting with efforts by Dr. Herb Wong back in 1966 and blossoming when Phil Hardymon became the band director at Berkeley High in 1975. Other alums of this system include David Murray, Benny Green, Peter Apfelbaum, Dave Ellis, Rodney Franklin, Craig Handy, and Michael Wolff. School programs of this sort serve as sources of talent for an expanding roster of colleges and universities where jazz, once excluded from most academic settings, is nurtured and supported. The most prominent of these environments, the Berklee College of Music, has risen from humble roots to become something of a Juilliard of jazz. It boasts four thousand students from more than seventy countries and employs more than five hundred faculty members. Berklee's influence can be seen everywhere in the jazz world—80 percent of its graduates go on to pursue careers in music and its alums have earned hundreds of Grammy awards. Other prominent jazz programs—at the University of North Texas, the Manhattan School of Music, William Paterson University, NYU, USC, CalArts, the New School, and many other places, both in the United States and overseas—have transformed jazz from the domain of the self-taught and those who learned on the job to a schematized body of knowledge disseminated in classrooms and assimilated by students as though it were calculus or accounting. This has influenced everything from the historical consciousness of today's performers to the way they phrase—increasingly with clean, crisp notes hit dead center with no bent edges or murky aftertaste. One is even tempted to divide jazz history into pre-Berklee and post-Berklee eras, a way of conceptualizing the music that is no doubt simplistic yet represents a meaningful divide in the evolution of the art form. Jazz, a music long associated with outsiders and bohemians, has somehow become a respectable insider's game, complete with endowments and scholarships.

What a change from an earlier day! Yet if many listeners wax nostalgic for an era in which the music was less codified and more intuitive and malleable, few would dare deny that the current batch of jazz players tends to be better trained and more technically proficient than its predecessors. In addition to the players cited above and elsewhere in this volume, I would call attention to guitarists Kurt Rosenwinkel, Marc Ribot, Ben Monder, Nels Cline, and Julian Lage; bassists Ben Allison, Esperanza Spalding, Avishai Cohen, and Drew Gress; vibraphonists Stefon Harris, Joe Locke, and Steve Nelson; drummers Brian Blade, Dafnis Prieto, and Nasheet Waits; trombonists Steve Turre, Wycliffe Gordon, and Robin Eubanks; violinist Regina Carter, banjoist Béla Fleck, and accordionist Gary Versace. Not all of them learned their jazz at school, but their skill and professionalism are very much emblematic of the ways and means of the modern-day jazz musician. What this list does not convey, however, is the depth of available talent—for every name mentioned, hundreds are waiting in the wings or already in the process of making their own mark on an art form that, though it has changed much in recent decades, has never had such a large reservoir of talent at its disposal. And this trend is even more evident when we turn our attention outside of the United States.

THE GLOBALIZATION OF JAZZ

Fans and critics often proclaim, with a self-satisfied complaceny, that jazz is "America's classical music." The phrase has a pleasant ring about it, yet close observation of the jazz world shows that many of the most exciting developments in recent years have taken place outside of the music's homeland. And if one were to set betting odds on predictions about the future of the art form, the further globalization of jazz may be the safest wager of them all. In short, America's classical music is now the common property of the whole world.

Perhaps the term "glocalization"—favored by critic Stuart Nicholson[2]—is an even better way of describing this shift. In recent years, the development of jazz outside the United States has been increasingly marked by the assimilation and celebration of national, regional, and local elements. Jazz from New York, Los Angeles, Chicago, New Orleans, and other centers of stateside musical activity is still heard and admired all over the world, but it is now mixed with—or competes against—other influences from afar. As a result, the repertoire of jazz music is broadening, the range of styles expanding, and even the instruments on the bandstand are changing in response to new sounds coming from multiple directions. This state of affairs, which can be traced at least as far back as Django Reinhardt, has existed to some degree for many decades, but has become a pervasive force in the music only in recent years.

This shift is evident whether one focuses on recordings, live performances, or, looking outside the music itself, the insitutions and cultural prestige that surround and support the art form. European jazz labels—such as ECM, ACT, HatHut, and CAM (which acquired the Italian Black Saint/Soul Note labels in 2008)—rank among the most creative and daring forces in the music today, and they increasingly find outstanding talent within the European community itself. The jazz festival circuit is much healthier in Europe than in the United States, with thousands of annual events—more than three hundred in Italy alone—keeping the art form vibrant and in front of the public's eye. These festivals—which typically receive subsidies from national, regional, and municipal funds as well as private sponsors—have long been a major source of income for U.S. jazz players who often find their skills more highly remunerated outside their home country; but the promoters are also now cultivating homegrown artists, and it is not unusual these days to encounter lineups with few, or sometimes no, American bands on the schedule. Yet the most striking measure of the new state of affairs is a harder one to quantify, but no less tangible in its impact: the quality of jazz music outside of the United States has taken a quantum leap over the last quarter century. No longer content to play a passive role as mere consumers or imitators of American jazz, a new generation in Europe and elsewhere on the globe is making fresh and potent music of its own that demands our attention.

In truth, Europe has played a catalytic role in the history of jazz almost from the beginning. The first example of a trained musical mind writing an insightful review of a jazz performance occurred in Europe, back in 1919, when Swiss conductor Ernst-Alexandre Ansermet contributed an article to *Revue Romande* about the London appearance of the Southern Syncopated Orchestra with New Orleans clarinetist Sidney Bechet. Around this same time, the Original Dixieland Jazz Band spent more than a year in Great Britain and received extensive press coverage—they earned as much as $1,800 per week (equivalent to more than $20,000 in current dollars) and frequently drew standing-room-only crowds. Europe continued to lead the way in embracing this music in later years. Jazz festivals were held in Belgium and the

Netherlands in the early 1930s, long before the format became known in the United States. The first great discographer of jazz was Charles Delaunay of France, while Belgian Robert Goffin's *Aux Frontières du Jazz*, from 1932, represents the first serious book-length study of the music. Goffin and London-born Leonard Feather literally invented jazz as an academic discipline, jointly teaching a class at the New School for Social Research in 1942 that was the forerunner of today's plethora of jazz education programs. French jazz critic and producer Hugues Panassié ranks toward the top of any list of important early critics of the music, and in works such as *Hot Jazz: The Guide to Swing Music* (1936) and *The Real Jazz* (1942) showed that he understood the nuances of the music in a way that few, if any, American commentators at the time could match. *Orkester Journalen* began publishing in Sweden in 1933 and the French periodical *Jazz Hot* followed in 1935 and both helped establish jazz journalism as a commercial proposition.

Even at this early stage, Europe had its first major jazz star, Django Reinhardt, who, with Stéphane Grappelli, founded the Quintette du Hot Club de France in 1934. Yet the importance of Reinhardt was not just that Europe could now boast of a jazz artist of the first rank, but even more that his music built on distinctively European ingredients that expanded and enhanced the art form. To this day, *jazz manouche*—the latter word signifying the French branch of the Romani (or Gypsy) people—is a popular performance style, with its own specific techniques, song preferences, and vocabulary. Fast forward to the jazz scene of the twenty-first century and we see this same phenomenon writ large around the world: jazz musicians are finding inspiration in their own local and regional traditions, creating exciting new hybrids that marry the sensibility of African American music to homegrown elements. At a time when many commentators complain that jazz is no longer "advancing," these exciting cross-cultural fusions prove that new sounds still arise on the foundations of America's classical music.

Despite the example of Django, indigenous European jazz styles were slow in emerging from the shadows of American jazz. During the second half of the twentieth century, jazz players outside the United States typically needed to move there, or at a minimum to play in the style of the leading U.S. artists, to make a name for themselves. George Shearing is lauded today as one of the leading jazz pianists of his generation, but this would hardly have been the case if he had not moved to New York in 1947. Around the same time, another UK pianist, Marian McPartland, also settled in the United States, initiating a true American success story that not only encompasses dozens of recordings but also entrepreneurship (McPartland's company Halcyon was one of the first artist-owned record labels in jazz), a sideline writing jazz criticism, and most notably a career in broadcasting destined for even greater fame than what McPartland had already achieved in nightclubs. Her *Piano Jazz* program on National Public Radio, founded in 1978, would eventually become the longest-running cultural broadcast in the history of NPR—an extraordinary achievement considering that McPartland had turned sixty a few weeks before the debut of the show. In 1952 Belgian harmonica player and guitarist Toots Thielemans moved to the United States, where he worked with Shearing, among others. His 1962 recording of "Bluesette," featuring Thielemans whistling and playing the guitar in unison, was a surprise hit, but his most important contribution to the idiom has been his championing of the humble harmonica, which he established as a legitimate solo voice in jazz. This would hardly have been possible had Thielemans stayed in his native Brussels. His countryman, saxophonist and flautist Bobby Jaspar, followed a similar path, marrying vocalist Blossom Dearie and settling in the United States in the mid-1950s, although his death in 1963 at age thirty-six cut short a promising career. The same phenomenon would repeat in later decades. European-born artists such as John McLaughlin, Dave Holland, and Joe Zawinul would come to the United States, play with Miles Davis and other American jazz legends, and become stars themselves. They deserve their reputations at the top of the jazz hierarchy, but would they have arrived there with a London or Vienna address?

Certainly there were great European talents who stayed home during this period, although none reaped the fame of the better-known expats. While Holland and McLaughlin were making their names in the States, Mike Westbrook, John Surman, Michael Garrick, Kenny Wheeler (Canadian-born, but a UK resident since 1952), Norma Winstone, and others were revitalizing the British jazz scene. Niels-Henning Ørsted Pedersen earned a reputation as a world-class jazz bassist without moving from his native Denmark—but primarily through his sideman work with American band leaders. In contrast, Lars Gullin of Sweden deserves inclusion on any list of the finest baritone saxophonists of his generation, and as one of the defining talents of the cool jazz style, but because he never relocated to the United States, his name is still unfamiliar in many jazz circles. By the same token, the biggest-selling jazz album in the history of Sweden is pianist Jan Johansson's *Jazz på Svenska*, a sly reworking of folk melodies that would delight even U.S. jazz fans—that is, if they ever had a chance to hear this music, which is hardly known in America. Even back in the years before World War II, we find significant music linked to unfamiliar artists who simply had the misfortune of pursuing careers as jazz players outside of the United States. Trumpeter Pierre Allier and tenor saxophonist Alix Combelle were playing with a harmonic conception that was quite advanced during these years; British trumpeter Nat Gonella earned the praise of Louis Armstrong; drummer Bill Harty propelled English jazz bands with a swing that would have been the pride of many U.S. orchestras—so much so that when Ray Noble came to New York in 1934 he insisted on bringing Harty along, despite the many experienced American drummers available. Yet today the names of these musicians will draw a blank from even knowledgeable jazz critics.

This situation has changed markedly in the new millennium. Wherever one looks in Europe today, one finds not just interesting jazz but also an elite few who can become global stars without moving to Manhattan. The rise to fame (or at least the jazz equivalent thereof) at the close of the 1990s of pianist Esbjörn Svensson and his trio e.s.t.—featuring fellow Swedes Dan Berglund on bass and drummer Magnus Öström—was a signal event in this regard. European audiences had already embraced the trio's CDs *From Gagarin's Point of View* and *Good Morning Susie Soho* as major statements by a visionary band when the Columbia label decided, in 2001, to release a compilation for U.S. audiences, an event that was followed by a three-week American tour. Although this may have appeared like an overnight success story to new fans stateside, e.s.t. (which had started life as the Esbjörn Svensson Trio) had developed both their preternatural group rapport and devoted following during a long period of arduous performing and touring, mounting up to two hundred gigs per year. When Svensson and company finally decided to focus on building a U.S. audience, e.s.t. was already a proven act with staying power and a stack of awards from across Europe.

The band's music, full of unexpected shifts and turnabouts, was as unconventional as the group's path to acclaim. The trio was capable of constructing complex, maximalist structures rich in harmonic movement; yet with little warning e.s.t. might shift into a loose, open jam or engage in a laconic dialogue between the instruments. Sometimes bass and drums would fall out entirely, and Svensson would perform solo, but with an unabated rhythmic drive that seemed to suggest he continued to hear a supporting cast in his own head; or else the musicians would incorporate electronic effects into their sonic palette, finding a middle path between the supposed dichotomies of plugged-in and unplugged that many players accept as an unbridgeable divide. One could pinpoint the band's more obvious sources of inspiration—which ranged from Keith Jarrett's early ECM recordings, especially *Facing You*, to rock and pop attitudes of various flavors—yet the way these influences were assimilated into a new holistic vision was little short of breathtaking. Svennson's death in a swimming accident in 2008 at age forty-four ended the career of this artist and his trio. But one can be confident that not only his music but his success in breaking down the "made in America" lock on jazz reputations will inspire many future musicians in their own careers.

Although no combo has yet emerged that can fill the place held by e.s.t., a number of promising European ensembles are making fresh, invigorating music. Swiss keyboardist Nik Bärtsch, for example, describes the approach of his band Ronin as "zen funk," and his combination of minimalist stylings and groove music might seem to be a contradictory mixture. Yet this hybrid, which has one foot in the music conservatory and the other tapping its toes at a street party, coheres against all odds and creates a different ambiance for contemporary jazz. This particular approach is very much the creation of Bärtsch and his colleagues, but the general mindset of infusing jazz with nonjazz elements is one of the most pervasive—and appealing—themes of the current European jazz scene. Perhaps the musicians are following the lead of European political and social trends, which are tending toward a unification of previously isolated or even hostile communities. Or an even simpler reason might be at play here: European jazz musicians have never felt they owned this art form the way Americans have, and this sense of sharing in a global phenomenon cannot fail to have some impact on how these players conceptualize and execute their work. Whatever the underlying causes, jazz in Europe today has realized, even more than in the United States, an ideal of a music without boundaries or borders. We find countless bands featuring performers of different nationalities working alongside one another, or artists setting up shop outside their home country, or dealing with musical languages that are not their native birthright, and the results of these dislocations and rapprochements can be heard unmistakably in the music.

This blossoming of an indigenous and increasingly self-directed European jazz scene is visible across the continent. The keyboard tradition is especially vibrant in the new millennium, as demonstrated by the work of artists young and old, such as Stefano Bollani, Enrico Pieranunzi, Franco D'Andrea, and Giorgio Gaslini of Italy; Vassilis

Tsabropoulos of Greece; Marcin Wasilewski and Leszek Możdżer of Poland; Michael Wollny, Joachim Kühn, Florian Ross, and Herbert Nuss of Germany; George Gruntz and Malcolm Braff of Switzerland; Martial Solal, René Urtreger, and Laurent de Wilde of France; Michel Herr, Nathalie Loriers, and Jef Neve of Belgium; Ketil Bjørnstad and Bugge Wesseltoft of Norway; and John Taylor, Django Bates, Gordon Beck, and Robert Mitchell of Britain, among others. A distinctive European trumpet tradition has also emerged in recent years, less beholden to models from hard bop and more aligned with the lyrical tradition of Miles Davis and Chet Baker, or even the quasi-minimalist soundwashes of Jon Hassell. One suspects that Baker's long-term residency in Europe and frequent performing and recording around the continent played a role in this turn of events—an ironic one at that, given the tendency of U.S. critics to dismiss this artist's late career efforts, despite the improvisational creativity Baker retained to the end of his life, in favor of edgier fare. Even so, there is nothing merely derivative about the trumpet work of world-class players such as Tomasz Stanko of Poland, Enrico Rava and Paolo Fresu of Italy, Nils Petter Molvaer, Arve Hendriksen, and Mathias Eick of Norway, Eric Vloeimans of Holland, and Till Brönner of Germany. It is harder to make generalizations about a European saxophone tradition that encompasses the avant-garde sensibilities of Peter Brötzmann of Germany and Evan Parker of Britain, the neotraditionalism of Italian Francesco Cafiso (who earned the praise of Wynton Marsalis while still in his midteens), and the chamber-music-meets-world-fusion attitudes of Jan Garbarek. Yet it seems safe to predict that here as well the scene is in good hands. Among other instrumentalists, clarinetist Gianluigi Trovesi of Italy, trombonists Ilja Reijngoud of Holland, Gianluca Petrella of Italy, and Mark Nightingale of the United Kingdom, drummers Wolfgang Haffner of Germany and Han Bennink of Holland, as well as guitarists Nguyên Lê, Sylvain Luc, and Biréli Lagrène of France, to cite just a few, are standout talents, although their names may not be well known even in jazz circles. The state of the jazz vocal tradition in Europe is less well defined, perhaps because the heritage is so closely linked to the English language, yet UK singers such as Jamie Cullum and Ian Shaw as well as Italian-born Roberta Gambarini, David Linx of Belgium, Savina Yannatou of Greece, and Solveig Slettahjell and Silje Nergaard of Norway are top-rank performers by any measure.

Yet the collectives often seem as important as the individuals here. This is evident in AACM-type organizations, such as the F-ire Collective and Loop Collective in the UK, which take on the role of impresarios, teachers, and even record labels, also in the more collaborative structure of many of the leading bands. Ensembles such as the Italian Instabile Orchestra, the Norrbotten in Sweden, the Jazz Orchestra of the Concertgebouw in Holland, and the Danish Radio Jazz Orchestra also help foster an atmosphere that is less star-driven than the New York club scene. A few decades back, one might well have doubted whether jazz, with its macho and sometimes predatory culture of self-assertion, could ever develop a truly group-oriented culture. Yet if this happens, Europe will have played a key role in showing the way. Starting at the top with substantial government support (at least by American standards), the European jazz culture is far more comfortable with institutional structures and collaborative give-and-take than one would find anywhere in the music's country of origin.

The jazz scenes in Latin America and Asia Pacific are hardly so self-sufficient, and this is perhaps due to the comparative scarcity of institutional funding and support. This does not mean that these regions do not produce great jazz talent, but rather that they have trouble nurturing, retaining, and sustaining it. Hence those strange anomalies in the history of jazz: that Afro-Cuban music has typically found a more secure economic base in New York than in Havana; that bossa nova needed to come to the United States to develop a large global audience; and that the most visible attempts to merge jazz techniques with Indian and South Asian musical traditions, from Bud Shank's 1962 *Improvisations* project with Ravi Shankar to John McLaughlin's Shakti band and John Handy's collaborations with Ali Akbar Khan during the 1970s and onward to the present day, have been promoted by U.S. record labels and supported largely by fans in the West.

The 2008 compact disc *Miles From India*, an exciting meeting ground for jazz icons and leading Indian musicians, could stand as a symbol for this state of affairs, not just in its performances, artfully produced by Bob Belden, but even in its very name, given how exciting currents in South Asian jazz are taking place thousands of miles away from their Indian sources of inspiration. Almost at the same time that Belden was putting together his East meets West project, alto saxophonist Rudresh Mahanthappa was building a following for his own Indian musical roots in projects such as *Kinsmen*, featuring Kadri Gopalnath, and *Apti*, with his band Indo-Pak Coalition. Gopalnath, a pioneer in adapting the saxophone to Carnatic musical traditions, made a stir when he was invited by altoist John Handy to come onstage at the 1980 Jazz Yatra festival in Mumbai. In contrast, Mahanthappa—who was born in Trieste in 1971 and grew up in the United States—is a jazz player first and foremost, yet it is striking how congruent his postbop sax stylings are with the South Asian musical elements he has increasingly assimilated into his work. Mahanthappa's sometime collaborator, pianist Vijay Iyer, has also risen to a place of prominence on the jazz scene, and though he sometimes draws on non-Western traditions in his performances, no one would ever mistake his brisk, angular keyboard stylings for so-called world music. Iyer, educated at Yale and Berkeley, is the American-born son of Indian immigrants, and his personal musical lineage is as likely to link back to Thelonious Monk and Andrew Hill as to precedents from Asia. With advocates such as Mahanthappa and Iyer, India can boast of world-class talents on the jazz scene—albeit second-generation ones—but it is revealing that these creative currents are centered far outside of India's borders.

Elsewhere in Asia, Japan has the most developed jazz scene with the strongest institutional supports. Yet a mere listing of prominent Japanese-born jazz artists—such as pianists Toshiko Akiyoshi, Makoto Ozone, Hiromi Uehara, and Yōsuke Yamashita, guitarist Ryo Kawasaki, saxophonist Sadao Watanabe, trumpeters Terumasa Hino and Tiger Okoshi—fails to convey the importance of this nation as a vital force in the economic well-being of the art form. Japanese audiences have supported the music with an enthusiasm and discernment that is rarely matched elsewhere, and the number of venues offering jazz, whether live in nightclubs and concert halls or via recordings at the country's many jazz cafés, puts most of the rest of the world to shame. It is inevitable that these savvy fans will increasingly devote their attention to nurturing homegrown acts rather than celebrating the achievements of the American masters of the art form—a process that is already well underway, although rarely noticed by U.S.-based observers of the jazz scene. Elsewhere in the Asia-Pacific region the situation is even more embryonic, yet the growing trend toward inner-directedness and self-sufficiency is evident, in varying degrees, almost everywhere. The evolution of the local and regional jazz scenes in these countries will be exciting to watch in the coming years, and though one would be foolhardy to try to predict specific developments, one can safely anticipate that the nations of the Asia Pacific will increasingly influence, rather than merely follow, trends in the jazz world.

This same dislocation has been even more visible in the world of Latin jazz. Although Jelly Roll Morton long ago spoke about a "Spanish tinge" that was an essential ingredient in jazz, the overt development of a distinct Latin jazz idiom took place only in fits and starts. Machito, born Francisco Raúl Gutiérrez Grillo in Havana, set an influential example with his 1940s bands, and his mambo hit "Tanga," composed by his brother-in-law Mario Bauzá, was a major milestone, as was Machito's 1957 album *Kenya*, which stands as one of the defining statements of the genre. Dizzy Gillespie's work with Luciano "Chano" Pozo, discussed earlier in this book, was also a signal event, and in time almost every major jazz bandleader was featuring Latin jazz material or pursuing entire Latin theme albums. But New York, not Havana, would prove to be the center of the Afro-Cuban musical revolution, where—adding to the complexity of the geographic lineage—Puerto Rican musicians often played the central role in this process of migration and definition. The career of Tito Puente, New York–born of Puerto Rican descent, is a case in point. While with Machito's band, Puente brought the timbales to the front of the bandstand and played them while standing up—a move both symbolic and viscerally attuned to the central role of rhythm in this music. In later bands under his own leadership, Puente did much to introduce Latin rhythms into the mainstream of American music. As Latin music played by Latin musicians found economic support and a fan base in the jazz world, its growth was invariably accompanied by the relocation of leading players to the United States—a trend we see, for example, in the careers of percussionist Mongo Santamaría (born in Cuba in 1917 but relocated to New York in 1950), pianist Eddie Palmieri (whose parents moved from Puerto Rico to New York in 1925, where Eddie was born ten years later), saxophonist Paquito D'Rivera (born in Havana in the 1948, but seeking asylum in the United States in 1981), and pianist Danilo Pérez (born in Panama in 1965 but moving to the United States in 1984), among others.

Brazil has long enjoyed the most stable homegrown jazz scene of any South American country. True, it has also lost talent to the United States, starting with guitarist Laurindo Almeida's move to join the Stan Kenton band in 1947 and accelerating during the bossa nova craze of the 1960s. But many of the leading Brazilian jazz figures either returned home or never left. In addition to their role as global ambassadors for bossa nova, Antonio Carlos Jobim and João Gilberto gave Brazilian jazz a sense of self-directedness and independence that it retains to this day. Even though the leading Brazilian jazz artists of more recent decades—Egberto Gismonti, Hermeto Pascoal, Eliane Elias, Luciana Souza, Airto Moreira, Flora Purim, and others—often show only the loosest ties to the bossa and samba traditions, they have inherited a confident sense of national musical identity that persists even while various styles go in and out of fashion. Yet just as important is the distinctively Brazilian tradition of sophisticated pop music, which has allowed figures as diverse as Milton Nascimento, Elis Regina, Ivan Lins, Gilberto Gil, Caetano Veloso, Djavan, Gal Costa, and others to exert an influence over the jazz world even though they themselves are not jazz musicians by any conventional definition of the term.

And finally, what of Africa? This continent, which provided the building blocks from which jazz was constructed in the United States, has often been forgotten by the jazz world. Widespread poverty makes it an unlikely place for a major jazz act to tour, and the challenges of building a substantial jazz career from an African base are almost insurmountable except for the most driven and determined of individuals. Even back in the 1950s, the "township jazz" sound of southern Africa, with its strong rhythm-and-blues elements and absence of modern jazz mannerisms—think of it as hard bop without the bop—showed that fresh sounds could arise from this part of the world, although few overseas were paying attention at the time. A handful of African-born talents have managed to come to the attention of jazz audiences since the 1960s. Duke Ellington's championing of pianist Abdullah Ibrahim (then known as Dollar Brand) was an important moment in the validation of African jazz. Yet it is striking how few later artists—with the notable exception of the musicians who came out of two influential South African jazz bands, the Blue Notes and the Jazz Epistles, such as trumpeter Hugh Masekela, saxophonist Kippie Moeketsi and pianist Chris McGregor—have been able to gain the attention of global fans. It is all too telling that when an artist overcomes these obstacles, as guitarist Lionel Loueke has recently done, it was only because the musician came to America and not because America noticed what was happening in Africa.

But even these few precedents indicate that African jazz is a distinctive idiom and not just a mirror of trends from abroad. Who can doubt that major jazz talents will rise from this continent, a birthplace for so many musical styles, and a land that may perhaps be economically poor but is so rich in its sonic traditions? And what a grand moment that will be—when the continent whose diaspora made jazz possible becomes a vital partner in shaping the art form's future evolution. Our story then will almost have come full circle.

Yet the genealogies of the players themselves will almost certainly be less crucial to the future history of jazz than the intermingling of the panglobal sounds they have inherited. When it first appeared as a commercial phenomenon, jazz may have stood out as a specific local style, a certain way of playing instruments and combining aural textures, with a lineage traced back to New Orleans. But with the passing years, jazz has become more an attitude than a static body of practices, more an openness to the possible than a slavish devotion to the time honored, and no single city or country or region can contain its omnivorous appetite. Looking back at the first century of jazz's history, its most identifiable trademark may simply be this unwillingness to sit still, this mandate to absorb other sounds and influences, this destiny as a music of flux and fusion. As such, all addresses are its home, but none are likely to be its resting place.

Notes

CHAPTER 1: THE PREHISTORY OF JAZZ

1. Ned Sublette, *The World That Made New Orleans: From Spanish Silver to Congo Square* (Chicago: Lawrence Hill, 2008), p. 282.
2. Sterling Stuckey, *Slave Culture: Nationalist Theory and the Foundations of Black America* (New York: Oxford University Press, 1987), p. 16.
3. See Henry Kmen, "The Roots of Jazz and Dance in Place Congo: A Reappraisal," in *Yearbook for Inter-American Musical Research*, vol. 8 (Austin: University of Texas, Institute of Latin American Studies, 1972), pp. 5–16; Jerah Johnson, "New Orleans's Congo Square: An Urban Setting for Early Afro-American Culture Formation," *Louisiana History*, Spring 1991, pp. 117–157; and Sublette, *The World That Made New Orleans*, pp. 120–121, 274–277, 280–282.
4. Samuel A. Floyd Jr., "Ring Shout! Literary Studies, Historical Studies, and Black Music Inquiry," *Black Music Research Journal*, vol. 11, no. 2 (1991), pp. 265–287.
5. Sidney Bechet, *Treat It Gentle* (New York: Hill & Wang, 1960), p. 6.
6. Edward Gibbon, *The Decline and Fall of the Roman Empire*, vol. 6 (London: Methuen and Co., 1912), p. 16.
7. Alan Lomax, *Mr. Jelly Roll* (New York: Duell Sloan & Pearce, 1950), p. 62. See also John Storm Roberts, *The Latin Tinge* (New York: Oxford University Press, 1979), esp. pp. 34–39.
8. See Gwendolyn Midlo Hall, *Africans in Colonial Louisiana: The Development of Afro-Creole Culture in the Eighteenth Century* (Baton Rouge: Louisiana State University Press, 1992), esp. pp. 28–55.
9. John W. Blassingame, *The Slave Community: Plantation Life in the Ante-bellum South* (New York: Oxford University Press, 1972), p. 39.
10. Alan Lomax, *The Land Where the Blues Began* (New York: Pantheon, 1993), p. 81.
11. Bill C. Malone, *Southern Music, American Music* (Lexington: University Press of Kentucky), pp. 18–22. See also Ken Emerson, *Doo-Dah: Stephen Foster and the Rise of American Popular Culture* (New York: Simon & Schuster, 1997); Robert C. Toll, *Blacking Up: The Minstrel Show in Nineteenth Century America* (New York: Oxford University Press, 1974); and Dale Cockrell, *Demons of Disorder: Early Blackface Minstrels and Their World* (New York: Cambridge University Press, 1997).
12. See Ted Gioia, *Work Songs* (Durham: Duke University Press, 2006).
13. John Miller Chernoff, *African Rhythm and African Sensibility* (Chicago: University of Chicago Press, 1979), pp. 23, 50.
14. This and below from Henry Edward Krehbiel, *Afro-American Folk Songs* (New York, 1914; reprinted, New York: Frederick Ungar, 1962), pp. 64–65.
15. John Storm Roberts, *Black Music of Two Worlds* (New York: Praeger, 1972), p. 10.
16. Included in Julius Lester's compilation of slave memoirs, drawn primarily from the Library of Congress collection, *To Be a Slave* (New York: Dial Press, 1968), pp. 112–113.

17. Johan Huizinga, *The Waning of the Middle Ages*, trans. F. Hopman (New York: St. Martin's, 1984), p. 88.

18. Eugene D. Genovese, *Roll, Jordan, Roll: The World the Slaves Made* (New York: Pantheon, 1974), pp. 311–312.

19. For more on Robert Johnson, Son House, Charley Patton, and the Delta blues tradition, see Ted Gioia, *Delta Blues* (New York: W.W. Norton, 2008).

20. Samuel Charters, *The Roots of the Blues: An African Search* (New York: Perigee, 1982), p. 127.

21. Sandra Lieb, *Mother of the Blues: A Study of Ma Rainey* (Amherst: University of Massachusetts Press, 1981), p. xiii.

22. Quoted in Daphne Duval Harrison, *Black Pearls: Blues Queens of the 1920s* (New Brunswick, NJ: Rutgers University Press, 1993), p. 43.

23. For much of this information I am indebted to Robert Dixon and John Godrich's *Recording the Blues* (New York: Stein and Day, 1970), pp. 20–43.

24. This and the following quote from Rudi Blesh and Harriet Janis, *They All Played Ragtime* (New York: Knopf, 1950), pp. 134–135.

25. See Craig H. Roell, *The Piano in America, 1890–1940* (Chapel Hill: University of North Carolina Press, 1989), esp. pp. 32–36. See also John Edward Hasse, "Ragtime: From the Top," in *Ragtime: Its History, Composers and Music*, ed. John Edward Hasse (New York: Schirmer, 1985), pp. 11–16.

26. From the *St. Louis Globe-Democrat* of June 7, 1903, cited in Blesh and Janis, *They All Played Ragtime*, p. 68.

CHAPTER 2: NEW ORLEANS JAZZ

1. See James P. Baugham, "Gateway to the Americas," in *The Past as Prelude: New Orleans 1718–1968*, ed. Hodding Carter (New Orleans: Tulane University Press, 1968), pp. 280–281.

2. Leonard V. Huber, *New Orleans: A Pictorial History* (Gretna, LA: Pelican Publishing, 1991), p. 9.

3. Pops Foster and Tom Stoddard, *The Autobiography of Pops Foster, New Orleans Jazzman* (Berkeley: University of California Press, 1971), p. 13. For further information on epidemics in New Orleans, see John Duffy's essay "Pestilence in New Orleans," in Carter, *The Past as Prelude*, pp. 88–115. See also Huber, *New Orleans*, p. 12.

4. Ned Sublette, *The World That Made New Orleans: From Spanish Silver to Congo Square* (Chicago: Lawrence Hill, 2008), p. 11.

5. For an especially extreme characterization of the link between vice and the origins of jazz, see Stephen Longstreet, *Sportin' House: A History of New Orleans Sinners and the Birth of Jazz* (Los Angeles: Sherbourne Press, 1965).

6. Donald Marquis, *In Search of Buddy Bolden, First Man of Jazz* (Baton Rouge: Louisiana State University Press, 1978), p. 58.

7. Foster and Stoddard, *The Autobiography of Pops Foster*, pp. 29, 37.

8. Bill Russell, "New Orleans Music," in *Jazzmen*, ed. Frederic Ramsey Jr. and Charles Edward Smith (New York: Harcourt, Brace, 1959), p. 35. For more information on Storyville, see also Al Rose, *Storyville, New Orleans* (Tuscaloosa: University of Alabama Press, 1974); Leroy Ostransky, *Jazz City: The Impact of Our Cities on the Development of Jazz* (Englewood Cliffs, NJ: Prentice-Hall, 1978), esp. pp. 32–44; and Samuel Charters, *A Trumpet Around the Corner: The Story of New Orleans Jazz* (Jackson: University of Mississippi Press, 2008), pp. 158–161.

9. These comments by Paul Barbarin, Johnny St. Cyr, and Kid Ory are from interviews conducted by the noted New Orleans jazz scholar Bill Russell and published posthumously

in his *New Orleans Style*, comp. and ed. Barry Martyn and Mike Hazeldine (New Orleans: Jazzology Press, 1994), pp. 60, 63, 175.

10. Alan Lomax, *Mister Jelly Roll* (New York: Duell, Sloan & Pearce, 1950), p. 61.

11. Baby Dodds and Larry Gara, *The Baby Dodds Story*, rev. ed. (Baton Rouge: Louisiana State University Press, 1992), p. 16. See also William J. Schafer, *Brass Bands and New Orleans Jazz* (Baton Rouge: Louisiana State University Press, 1977).

12. Marquis, *In Search of Buddy Bolden*. See also Donald Marquis, *Finding Buddy Bolden: The Journal of a Search for the First Man of Jazz* (Goshen, IN: Pinchpenny Press, 1978; rev., 1990). For an alternative account of Bolden's career, see Danny Barker, *Buddy Bolden and the Last Days of Storyville*, ed. Alyn Shipton (London: Continuum, 1998); this version is entertaining and typical of jazz myth making at its most colorful, but unfortunately draws heavily on a single source, notably an "oral history" conducted with non-musician "Dude Bottley," who is in turn a fictionalized composite of other unnamed informants.

13. Louis Armstrong quoted in Bill Russell, *New Orleans Style*, ed. Barry Martyn and Mike Hazeldine (New Orleans: Jazzology Press, 1994), p. 136. For Bolden's band as "routineers," see Lomax, *Mister Jelly Roll*, pp. 58–60.

14. Matthews and Bocage quoted in Marquis, *In Search of Buddy Bolden*, pp. 100, 105.

15. Quoted in ibid., p. 111.

16. See H. O. Brunn, *The Story of the Original Dixieland Jazz Band* (Baton Rouge: Louisiana State University Press, 1960).

17. Lomax, *Mister Jelly Roll*, p. 3, emphasis mine.

18. This story was recounted by Nesuhi Ertegun to Whitney Balliett. Ertegun had heard it originally from Kid Ory. See Whitney Balliett, *American Musicians: 56 Portraits in Jazz* (New York: Oxford University Press, 1986), p. 25.

19. This letter is reprinted in Ralph de Toledano, ed., *Frontiers of Jazz* (New York: Frederick Ungar, 1947), pp. 104–107.

20. Nat Shapiro and Nat Hentoff, *Hear Me Talkin' to Ya* (New York: Rinehart, 1955), p. 123.

21. Ibid., pp. 40, 45, 22.

22. Beiderbecke quote from George Hoefer, "Bix Beiderbecke," in *The Jazz Makers*, ed. Nat Hentoff and Nat Shapiro (New York: Rinehart, 1957), p. 94.

23. Gary Giddins, "Happy Birthday, Pops," *Village Voice*, August 23, 1988, p. 101. See also Gary Giddins, *Satchmo* (New York: Doubleday, 1988), esp. pp. 42–47.

24. See James Lincoln Collier, *Louis Armstrong: An American Genius* (New York: Oxford University Press, 1983), pp. 18–33, for an especially hard-nosed account of this period of Armstrong's life.

25. Giddins, *Satchmo*, p. 64. Terry Teachout, *Pops: A Life of Louis Armstrong* (Boston: Houghton Mifflin Harcourt, 2009), pp. 36–37.

26. Quoted in Whitney Balliett's essay "Le Grand Bechet," in *Jelly Roll, Jabbo and Fats: 19 Portraits in Jazz* (New York: Oxford University Press, 1983), pp. 37–38.

27. Teachout, *Pops*, p. 71.

28. Martin Williams, *King Oliver* (New York: A. S. Barnes, 1960), p. 4. For texts of the letters, see Frederick Ramsey Jr.'s essay "King Oliver and His Creole Jazz Band," in *Jazzmen*, ed. Frederick Ramsey Jr. and Charles Edward Smith (New York: Harvest Books, 1939), esp. pp. 87–91.

CHAPTER 3: THE JAZZ AGE

1. John Chilton in the liner notes to *Louis Armstrong: The Hot Fives Volume One* (Columbia CK 44049).

2. From a radio interview, cited in James Lincoln Collier, *Louis Armstrong: An American Genius* (New York: Oxford University Press, 1983), p. 133.

3. Gary Giddins, *Satchmo* (New York: Doubleday, 1988), p. 82.

4. Ansermet's comments have been translated and reprinted in a number of anthologies. See, for instance, "Bechet and Jazz Visit Europe, 1919," in *Frontiers of Jazz*, ed. Ralph de Toledano (New York: Frederick Ungar, 1947), pp. 115–120.

5. Richard Hadlock, *Jazz Masters of the Twenties* (New York: Macmillan, 1965), p. 18. Emphasis is Hadlock's.

6. Quoted in Bob Doerschuk, "A Visit with Earl Hines," *Keyboard*, April 1982, p. 39.

7. Max Kaminsky with V. E. Hughes, *My Life in Jazz* (New York: Harper & Row, 1963), p. 40.

8. For example, compare Collier, *Louis Armstrong*, p. 287, with Giddins, *Satchmo*, p. 225.

9. Russell Sanjek and David Sanjek, *American Popular Music Business in the 20th Century* (New York: Oxford University Press, 1991), pp. 12, 20.

10. Quoted in Ralph Berton, *Remembering Bix* (New York: Harper & Row, 1974), p. 13.

11. George Johnson, "The Wolverines and Bix," in Toledano, *Frontiers of Jazz*, pp. 126–127.

12. Eddie Condon with Thomas Sugrue, *We Called It Music* (New York: H. Holt, 1947), p. 80; Hoagy Carmichael and Louis Armstrong quoted in Nat Hentoff and Nat Shapiro, *Hear Me Talkin' to Ya* (New York: Rinehart, 1955), pp. 142–143, 158; Mezz Mezzrow, from his autobiography, written with Bernard Wolfe, *Really the Blues* (New York: Random House, 1946), p. 68.

13. Hentoff and Shapiro, *Hear Me Talkin' to Ya*, p. 153.

14. William Howland Kenney, *Chicago Jazz: A Cultural History, 1904–1930* (New York: Oxford University Press, 1993), p. 12.

15. Ibid., p. 13.

16. For these and other witticisms and commnetaries by Eddie Condon, see Condon with Sugrue, *We Called It Music*, and Eddie Condon and Hank O'Neal, *The Eddie Codon Scrapbook of Jazz* (New York: St. Martin's, 1973).

17. Condon with Sugrue, *We Called It Music*, p. 107.

18. Bud Freeman, *Crazeology: The Autobiography of a Chicago Jazzman* (Urbana, IL: University of Chicago Press, 1989), p. 4.

19. Hentoff and Shapiro, *Hear Me Talkin' to Ya*, p. 119.

20. Quoted in Burt Korall, *Drummin' Men: The Heartbeat of Jazz: The Swing Years* (New York: Schirmer, 1990), p. 54.

21. Robert Hilbert, *Pee Wee Russell: The Life of a Jazzman* (New York: Oxford University Press, 1993), p. 17.

22. Leonard Feather, *The Book of Jazz from Then Till Now* (New York: Bonanza Books, 1965), p. 88; Nat Hentoff, "A White Jazz Original," *Inquiry*, June 26, 1978, p. 31; Gunther Schuller, *The Swing Era: The Development of Jazz, 1930–1945* (New York: Oxford University Press, 1989), p. 610. Bud Freeman comments here and below from Hilbert, *Pee Wee Russell*, p. 67.

23. For a fuller discussion of Teagarden's unusual techniques see Schuller, *The Swing Era*, pp. 591–593.

24. Joe Darensbourg and Peter Vacher, *Jazz Odyssey: The Autobiography of Joe Darensbourg* (Baton Rouge: Louisiana State University Press, 1987), p. 76. Michael Brooks quote from accompanying notes to *Bix Beiderbecke, Volume 1: Singin' the Blues* (Columbia CK45450).

25. Budd Johnson, as told to Michael Zwerin, "Dues Paid," *Downbeat*, February 8, 1968, p. 19.

26. This interview, originally published in *Downbeat* (March 7, 1956, pp. 9–11) is reprinted in Lewis Porter, ed., *A Lester Young Reader* (Washington, DC: Smithsonian Institution Press, 1991), pp. 157–164.

27. Rex Stewart, *Jazz Masters of the 30s* (New York: Macmillan, 1972), pp. 11–12. Sonny Greer comments from an oral history conducted by Stanley Crouch in January 1979, on file at the Rutgers Institute of Jazz Studies.

28. Robert Goffin, *Jazz: From the Congo to the Metropolitan*, trans. Walter Schaap and Leonard Feather (New York: Doubleday, 1944), p. 145.

29. Berton, *Remembering Bix*, p. 353.

CHAPTER 4: HARLEM

1. David Levering Lewis, *When Harlem Was in Vogue* (New York: Vintage, 1982), p. 108.

2. Willie "The Lion" Smith with George Hoefer, *Music on My Mind* (New York: Doubleday, 1964), p. 156.

3. Lewis, *When Harlem Was in Vogue*, p. 107.

4. Many early studies of the Harlem Renaissance downplayed the role of jazz, but in the final years of the twentieth century a more nuanced appreciation came to the fore. See, for example, *Black Music in the Harlem Renaissance*, ed. Samuel A. Floyd Jr. (Westport, CT: Greenwood Press, 1990); and Steven Watson, *The Harlem Renaissance: Hub of African-American Culture, 1920–1930* (New York: Pantheon, 1995).

5. Cab Calloway and Bryant Rollins, *Of Minnie the Moocher and Me* (New York: Thomas Crowell, 1976), p. 105.

6. Quoted in Ed Berger's liner notes to Benny Carter's recording, *Harlem Renaissance* (MusicMasters 65080).

7. See John Howland, *Ellington Uptown: Duke Ellington, James P. Johnson and the Birth of Concert Jazz* (Ann Arbor: University of Michigan Press, 2009), pp. 202–211.

8. Smith with Hoefer, *Music on My Mind*, p. 101.

9. W. O. Smith, *Sideman: A Memoir* (Nashville, TN: Rutledge Hill Press, 1991), p. 77.

10. Tom Davin, "Conversations with James P. Johnson," reprinted in *Ragtime: Its History, Composers and Music*, ed. John Edward Hasse (New York: Schirmer, 1985), p. 170.

11. Gunnar Askland, "Interpretations in Jazz: A Conference with Duke Ellington," *Etude*, March 1947, reprinted in *The Duke Ellington Reader*, ed. Mark Tucker (New York: Oxford University Press, 1993), pp. 255–258.

12. Davin, "Conversations with James P. Johnson," p. 170.

13. From Duke Ellington's foreword to Smith with Hoefer, *Music on My Mind*, p. x.

14. Duke Ellington's comments come from his foreword to ibid., pp. x–xi. James P. Johnson quote is from Davin, "Conversations with James P. Johnson," p. 177. Nat Hentoff's remark is from his liner notes to *Luckey & the Lion: Harlem Piano* (Goodtime Jazz 10035).

15. Count Basie, as told to Albert Murray, *Good Morning Blues: The Autobiography of Count Basie* (New York: Random House, 1985), p. 9.

16. Ethan Iverson, "The Dozens: Ethan Iverson on Stride Piano," ed. Ted Panken, January 12, 2009, Jazz.com (http://www.jazz.com/dozens/the-dozens-ethan-iverson-on-stride-piano).

17. See Maurice Waller's account of this legendary session in his biography of his father, Maurice Waller and Anthony Calabrese, *Fats Waller* (New York: Schirmer Books, 1977), pp. 96–98.

18. André Hodeir, "Art Tatum: A French Jazz Critic Evaluates the Music of a Great Pianist," *Downbeat*, August 10, 1955, p. 9 (see also Billy Taylor's rebuttal to Hodeir in *Downbeat*, September 21, 1955, p. 19); Gunther Schuller, *The Swing Era: The Development of Jazz, 1930–1945* (New York: Oxford University Press, 1989), pp. 478–479.

19. As reported by Noble Sissle. See Reid Badger, *A Life in Ragtime: A Biography of James Reese Europe* (New York: Oxford University Press, 1995), p. 65.

20. See James Lincoln Collier, *Jazz: The American Theme Song* (New York: Oxford University Press, 1993), pp. 165–172, for a revisionist account of the development of the jazz band, which stresses the contributions of Ferde Grofé, Art Hickman, and several other unsung musicians.

21. From the interview with Gary Giddins included in the liner notes to Benny Carter, *Central City Sketches* (MusicMasters 5030).

22. Duke Ellington, *Music Is My Mistress* (New York: Doubleday, 1973), p. x.

23. Ibid., p. 10.

24. Ibid., pp. 6, 15.

25. See James Lincoln Collier, *Duke Ellington* (New York: Oxford University Press, 1987), p. 12.

26. The trumpeter's name is usually spelled Whetsol, yet the preponderance of evidence—including his own signatures, copyright documents, etc.—indicate that the correct spelling is Whetsel.

27. These and other early reviews are reprinted, in their entirety, in Tucker, *The Duke Ellington Reader*. See pp. 21–32.

28. Comments from Barney Bigard and Cootie Williams are from oral histories on file at the Rutgers Institute of Jazz Studies. Quote from Ellington from Ellington, *Music Is My Mistress*, p. 446.

29. Quoted in Chad Heap, *Slumming: Sexual and Racial Encounters in American Nightlife, 1885–1940* (Chicago: University of Chicago Press, 2009), p. 82.

30. From Sonny Greer's oral history on file at the Rutgers Institute of Jazz Studies.

31. This and below from Cootie Williams's oral history on file at the Rutgers Institute of Jazz Studies. Note that, although Williams claimed that Ellington never fired anyone except Miley, Charles Mingus later recounted his own dismissal from the Ellington band. Yet Mingus adds that Ellington was protective of his reputation for not firing musicians—so he merely insisted that the bassist offer his immediate resignation (which Mingus did).

32. R. D. Darrell, "Black Beauty," originally from *disques*, June 1932, pp. 152–161, reprinted in Tucker, *The Duke Ellington Reader*, pp. 57–65.

33. Spike Hughes, "The Duke—in Person," *Melody Maker*, May 1933, reprinted in Tucker, *The Duke Ellington Reader*, pp. 69–72.

34. Barry Ulanov, *Duke Ellington* (New York: Creative Age Press, 1946), p. 151.

CHAPTER 5: THE SWING ERA

1. This and above from Lionel Hampton with James Haskins, *Hamp* (New York: Warner Books, 1989), pp. 31, 37.

2. Jas Obrecht, "On Charlie Christian: Benny Goodman," *Guitar Player*, March 1982, p. 61.

3. John Hammond with Irving Townsend, *John Hammond on Record* (New York: Ridge Press/Summit Books, 1977), p. 232.

4. For this and the figures below, see Ross Russell, *Jazz Style in Kansas City and the Southwest* (Berkeley: University of California Press, 1971), pp. 8–9.

5. Count Basie, as told to Albert Murray, *Good Morning Blues: The Autobiography of Count Basie* (New York: Random House, 1984), pp. 4–5.

6. Ibid., p. 29.

7. Ibid., pp. 7–8.

8. Mary Lou Williams's full account of this evening is included in Nat Shapiro and Nat Hentoff, *Hear Me Talkin' to Ya* (New York: Rinehart, 1955), pp. 292–293 (and originally appeared in *Melody Maker*, May 1, 1954, p. 11).

9. Duke Ellington, *Music Is My Mistress* (New York: Doubleday, 1973), p. 141.

10. Jackie McLean quote from liner notes to *Let Freedom Ring* (Blue Note 46527).

11. Red Callender and Elaine Cohen, *Unfinished Dream: The Musical World of Red Callender* (London: Quartet Books, 1985), p. 45.

12. Paul Bowles, "Duke Ellington in Recital for Russian War Relief," *New York Herald Tribune*, January 25, 1943, reprinted in *The Duke Ellington Reader*, ed. Mark Tucker (New York: Oxford University Press, 1993), pp. 165–166.

13. Gunther Schuller, *The Swing Era: The Development of Jazz, 1930–1945* (New York: Oxford University Press, 1989), p. 150.

14. Quoted in Nat Hentoff, "This Cat Needs No Pulitzer Prize," *New York Times Magazine*, September 12, 1965, reprinted in Tucker, *The Duke Ellington Reader*, pp. 362–368.

15. Basie, as told to Murray, *Good Morning Blues*, p. 283.

16. From George Avakian's liner notes to *Ellington at Newport* (Columbia CL 934).

17. See, for example, Radcliffe Joe, "Thank You, Duke: Thousands Say Farewell to Ellington, a Prince Who Loved People Madly," *Billboard*, June 8, 1974, p. 3.

CHAPTER 6: MODERN JAZZ

1. Robert Reisner, ed., *Bird: The Legend of Charlie Parker* (New York: Citadel, 1962), p. 167.

2. Dizzy Gillespie with Al Fraser, *To Be or Not . . . to Bop* (New York: Doubleday, 1979), pp. 116–117.

3. This and below from Gillespie with Fraser, *To Be or Not . . . to Bop*, pp. 1–2, 27–28.

4. Valerie Wilmer, "Monk on Monk," *Downbeat*, June 3, 1965, p. 20.

5. *Collier's*, March 20, 1948, cited—with other early putdowns of modern jazz—in Lewis Porter and Michael Ullman, *Jazz: From Its Origins to the Present* (Englewood Cliffs, NJ: Prentice-Hall, 1993), p. 207. Armstrong quote from "Bop Will Kill Business Unless It Kills Itself First," *Downbeat*, April 7, 1948, p. 2. For the *Time* magazine quotation, presented in the context of an excellent discussion of the tensions between traditional and modern jazz players, see David W. Stowe, *Swing Changes: Big Band Jazz in New Deal America* (Cambridge, MA: Harvard University Press, 1994), p. 207.

6. Miles Davis quote from Miles Davis with Quincy Troupe, *Miles: The Autobiography* (New York: Simon & Schuster, 1989), p. 93. Howard McGhee quote from Scott DeVeaux, "Conversation with Howard McGhee: Jazz in the Forties," *Black Perspectives in Music*, Spring 1987, p. 75.

7. From Robert Reisner, ed., *Bird: The Legend of Charlie Parker* (New York: Citadel, 1962), p. 144.

8. Quoted in Gillespie with Fraser, *To Be or Not . . . to Bop*, pp. 324–325. McKibbon quotes below from ibid., pp. 320, 325.

9. Quoted in Nat Hentoff, *The Jazz Life* (New York: Da Capo, 1978), p. 214.

10. Davis with Troupe, *Miles: The Autobiography*, p. 52.

11. Quoted in Reisner, *Bird: The Legend of Charlie Parker*, p. 293.

12. Ibid., p. 152.

13. Quoted in Robert Perlongo, "Bud Powell in Paris: A Situation Report," *Metronome*, November 1961, p. 16.

14. Quoted in Alan Morrison, "Jazz Great Bud Powell Dies," *Jet*, August 18, 1966, pp. 58–62.

15. Leonard Feather, *Inside Bebop* (New York: J.J. Robbins, 1949), p. 10. See also, Robin D. G. Kelley, *Thelonious Monk: The Life and Times of an American Original* (New York: Free Press, 2009), pp. 149–150.

16. Keepnews's original 1948 interview (along with his later reflections on Monk) are included in Orrin Keepnews, *The View from Within: Jazz Writings 1948–87* (New York: Oxford University Press, 1988), pp. 110–111.

17. From Ira Gitler's liner notes to *Thelonious Monk with John Coltrane* (Jazzland JLP-46).

18. Gunther Schuller, *The Swing Era: The Development of Jazz, 1930–1945* (New York: Oxford University Press, 1989), p. 840.

19. Quoted in Whitney Balliett, *Jelly Roll, Jabbo and Fats: 19 Portraits in Jazz* (New York: Oxford University Press, 1983), p. 151.

20. Leonard Feather, "A Bird's-Ear View of Music," *Metronome*, August, 1948, pp. 14, 21–22.

21. Cited in Ross Firestone, *Swing, Swing, Swing: The Life and Times of Benny Goodman* (New York: W.W. Norton, 1993), p. 354.

22. Schuller, *The Swing Era*, p. 719.

23. Quoted in Steve Voce, *Woody Herman* (London: Apollo Press, 1986), p. 8.

24. Quoted in William D. Clancy and Audree Coke Kenton, *Woody Herman: Chronicles of the Herds* (New York: Schirmer, 1995), p. 146.

25. Nat Hentoff, "Pop Record Hit for Woody Could Help Whole Band Biz," *Downbeat*, July 27, 1955, p. 11.

26. From Will Friedwald's liner notes to *Stan Kenton: The Complete Capitol Records of the Holman and Russo Charts* (Mosaic MD4–136).

CHAPTER 7: THE FRAGMENTATION OF JAZZ STYLES

1. Miles Davis and Quincy Troupe, *Miles: The Autobiography* (New York: Simon & Schuster, 1989), p. 122.

2. Quoted in George Simon's liner notes to *The Uncollected Claude Thornhill: 1947* (Hindsight 108).

3. Davis and Troupe, *Miles: The Autobiography*, pp. 117–118.

4. Ibid., p. 118.

5. Winthrop Sargeant, *Jazz, Hot and Hybrid*, 3rd ed. (New York: Da Capo Press, 1975), p. 257.

6. Davis and Troupe, *Miles: The Autobiography*, p. 140.

7. Ibid., p. 127.

8. Ibid., p. 191.

9. Ibid., p. 221.

10. Quoted in Don Nelsen, "Bill Evans," *Downbeat*, December 8, 1960, p. 17.

11. *Gene Lees Jazzletter*, January 1985, p. 3.

12. Quoted in J. C. Thomas, *Chasin' the Trane* (New York: Doubleday, 1975), p. 132.

13. This and below from Bob Thiele and Bob Golden, *What a Wonderful World: A Lifetime of Recordings* (New York: Oxford University Press, 1995), pp. 127, 123.

14. These comments, originally from an interview conducted for *Metronome* in the spring of 1961, are included in Robert Levin's liner notes to *Eric Dolphy at the Five Spot, Volume 2* (Prestige P-7294).

15. Sonny Rollins, interview by Bob Blumenthal, *Downbeat*, May 1982, p. 18.

16. Juan Rodriguez, "Sonny Rollins: Improvisational Virtuoso," *Montreal Gazette*, June 27, 2010.

17. Arthur Taylor, *Notes and Tones: Musician-to-Musician Interviews* (New York: Perigee, 1982), p. 112, originally printed in Belgium in 1977.

18. From the liner notes to Wayne Shorter, *Speak No Evil* (Blue Note 46509).

19. Ira Gitler, "Focus on Freddie Hubbard," *Downbeat*, January 18, 1962, p. 22.

20. Quoted in Michael Ullman, *Jazz Lives* (Washington, DC: New Republic Books, 1980), p. 82.

21. James Lincoln Collier, *The Making of Jazz: A Comprehensive History* (New York: Houghton-Mifflin, 1978), p. 453; Baraka's quotes from LeRoi Jones, *Blues People* (New York: William Morrow, 1963), pp. 223, 217.

22. Davis and Troupe, *Miles: The Autobiography*, p. 86.

CHAPTER 8: FREEDOM AND FUSION

1. LeRoi Jones, *Blues People* (New York: William Morrow, 1963), p. 235; Frank Kofsky, *Black Nationalism and the Revolution in Music* (New York: Pantheon, 1970), p. 131; Ekkehard Jost, *Free Jazz* (Graz, Austria: Universal Edition, 1974), p. 9.

2. Joe Goldberg, *Jazz Masters of the '50s* (New York: Macmillan, 1965), p. 231.

3. Valerie Wilmer, *As Serious as Your Life*, rev. ed. (Westport, CT: Lawrence Hill, 1980), p. 68. It is worth noting that the bandleader in question, Pee Wee Crayton, later denied asking Coleman not to play on gigs.

4. Quoted in Nat Hentoff's liner notes to Coleman's *Tomorrow Is the Question* (Contemporary 7569).

5. Ted Gioia, *West Coast Jazz* (Berkeley: University of California Press, 1998), p. 353.

6. From liner notes to Ornette Coleman, *Skies of America* (Columbia 31562).

7. Quoted in A. B. Spellman, *Black Music: Four Lives* (New York: Schocken, 1970), originally published as *Four Lives in the Bebop Business* (New York: Pantheon, 1966), p. 49.

8. From Nat Hentoff's accompanying essay to *The Complete Candid Recordings of Cecil Taylor and Buell Neidlinger* (Mosaic MD4-127).

9. Spellman, *Black Music: Four Lives*, p. 53.

10. From Buell Neidlinger's liner notes to *The Complete Candid Recordings of Cecil Taylor and Buell Neidlinger* (Mosaic MD4-127).

11. Spellman, *Black Music: Four Lives*, p. 75.

12. Jacques Attali, *Noise: The Political Economy of Music*, trans. Brian Massumi (Minneapolis: University of Minnesota Press, 1985), p. 25.

13. John Litweiler, *The Freedom Principle: Jazz after 1958* (New York: William Morrow, 1984), p. 299; David G. Such, *Avant-Garde Jazz Musicians: Performing Out There* (Iowa City: University of Iowa Press, 1993), p. 161.

14. Joachim Berendt, *The Jazz Book: From New Orleans to Rock and Free Jazz*, trans. Dan Morgenstern (New York: Lawrence Hill, 1975), p. 399.

15. This quote from part 15 (of nineteen installments) of Marc Myers's extensive interview with Creed Taylor, published on April 27, 2009, on the JazzWax blog (www.jazzwax.com/2009/04/interview-creed-taylor-part-15.html).

CHAPTER 9: TRADITIONALISTS AND POSTMODERNISTS

1. Wynton Marsalis quote from the liner notes to *The Majesty of the Blues* (Columbia CK 45091).

2. Francis Davis, *In the Moment: Jazz in the 1980s* (New York: Oxford University Press, 1986), p. 32; quote on Miles Davis from Hollie West, "Wynton Marsalis: Blowing His Own Horn, Speaking His Own Mind," *Jazz Times*, July 1983, p. 10.

3. George Lewis, *A Power Stronger Than Itself: The AACM and American Experimental Music* (Chicago: University of Chicago Press, 2008), p. 37.

4. Ibid., p. 116.

5. Quoted in Greg Tate, "Grooves of Academe," *Village Voice Literary Supplement*, November 1989, p. 26.

6. Quoted in Davis, *In the Moment*, p. 42.

CHAPTER 10: JAZZ IN THE NEW MILLENNIUM

1. Brad Mehldau quote from his liner notes to *Art of the Trio 4: Back at the Vanguard* (Warner 4763).

2. Stuart Nicholson, "Jazz in a Global Village," presentation at the Association Européenne des Conservatoires, Académies de Musique et Musikhochschulen meeting in Amsterdam, February 13, 2009.

Further Reading

Balliett, Whitney. *American Musicians: 56 Portraits in Jazz*. New York: Oxford University Press, 1986.

Basie, Count, and Albert Murray. *Good Morning Blues: The Autobiography of Count Basie*. New York: Random House, 1986.

Bechet, Sidney. *Treat It Gentle: An Autobiography*. London: Cassell & Co., 1960.

Berlin, Edward A. *King of Ragtime: Scott Joplin and His Era*. New York: Oxford University Press, 1994.

Blesh, Rudi, and Harriet Janis. *They All Played Ragtime*. New York: Knopf, 1950.

Brothers, Thomas. *Louis Armstrong's New Orleans*. New York: W.W. Norton, 2006.

Charters, Samuel. *A Trumpet Around the Corner: The Story of New Orleans Jazz*. Jackson: University of Mississippi Press, 2008.

Chernoff, John Miller. *African Rhythm and African Sensibility*. Chicago: University of Chicago Press, 1979.

Chilton, John. *The Song of the Hawk: The Life and Recordings of Coleman Hawkins*. Ann Arbor: University of Michigan Press, 1990.

Cohen, Harvey G. *Duke Ellington's America*. Chicago: University of Chicago Press, 2010.

Collier, James Lincoln. *Benny Goodman and the Swing Era*. New York: Oxford University Press, 1989.

———. *Jazz: The American Theme Song*. New York: Oxford University Press, 1993.

Crouch, Stanley. *Considering Genius: Writings on Jazz*. New York: Basic Books, 2006.

Dahl, Linda. *Stormy Weather: The Music and Lives of a Century of Jazzwomen*. New York: Pantheon, 1984.

Davis, Francis. *The History of the Blues*. New York: Hyperion, 1995.

———. *In the Moment*. New York: Oxford University Press, 1986.

Davis, Miles, and Quincy Troupe. *Miles: The Autobiography*. New York: Simon & Schuster, 1989.

DeVeaux, Scott. *The Birth of Bebop: A Social and Musical History*. Berkeley: University of California Press, 1997.

Ellington, Duke. *Music Is My Mistress*. Garden City, NY: Doubleday, 1973.

Firestone, Ross. *Swing, Swing, Swing: The Life and Times of Benny Goodman*. New York: W.W. Norton, 1993.

Friedwald, Will. *Jazz Singing*. New York: Scribner's, 1990.

Giddins, Gary. *Celebrating Bird: The Triumph of Charlie Parker*. New York: William Morrow, 1987.

———. *Rhythm-a-ning*. New York: Oxford University Press, 1985.

———. *Riding on a Blue Note*. New York: Oxford University Press, 1981.

———. *Satchmo*. New York: Doubleday, 1988.

———. *Visions of Jazz: The First Century*. New York: Oxford University Press, 1998.

Giddins, Gary, and Scott DeVeaux. *Jazz*. New York: W.W. Norton, 2009.

Gillespie, Dizzy, and Al Frazer. *To Be or Not . . . to Bop*. Garden City, NY: Doubleday, 1979.

Gioia, Ted. *Delta Blues*. New York: W.W. Norton, 2008.

——. *The Imperfect Art: Reflections on Jazz and Modern Culture*. New York: Oxford University Press, 1988.

——. *West Coast Jazz: Modern Jazz in California, 1945–1960*. New York: Oxford University Press, 1992.

Gitler, Ira. *Jazz Masters of the Forties*. New York: Macmillan, 1966.

——. *Swing to Bop: An Oral History of the Transition in Jazz in the 1940s*. New York: Oxford University Press, 1985.

Gourse, Leslie. *Louis' Children: American Jazz Singers*. New York: William Morrow, 1984.

Gridley, Mark. *Jazz Styles*, 10th ed. Englewood Cliffs, NJ: Prentice-Hall, 2008.

Gushee, Lawrence. *Pioneers of Jazz: The Story of the Creole Band*. New York: Oxford University Press, 2005.

Hadlock, Richard. *Jazz Masters of the Twenties*. New York: Macmillan, 1965.

Hajdu, David. *Lush Life: A Biography of Billy Strayhorn*. New York: Farrar, Strauss and Giroux, 1996.

Hasse, John Edward. *Beyond Category: The Life and Genius of Duke Ellington*. New York: Simon & Schuster, 1993.

——, ed. *Ragtime: Its History, Composers and Music*. New York: Schirmer, 1985.

Hentoff, Nat, and Nat Shapiro. *Hear Me Talkin' to Ya: An Oral History of Jazz*. New York: Dover, 1966.

Hodeir, André. *Jazz: Its Evolution and Essence*. New York: Grove Press, 1956.

Kahn, Ashley. *The House That Trane Built: The Story of Impulse Records*. New York: W.W. Norton, 2006.

Kelley, Robin D. G. *Thelonious Monk: The Life and Times of an American Original*. New York: Free Press, 2009.

Kirchner, Bill, ed. *The Oxford Companion to Jazz. New York*. New York: Oxford University Press, 2000.

Korall, Burt. *Drummin' Men: The Heartbeat of Jazz: The Bebop Years*. New York: Oxford University Press, 2002.

——. *Drummin' Men: The Heartbeat of Jazz: The Swing Years*. New York: Schirmer, 1990.

Lees, Gene. *Leader of the Band: The Life of Woody Herman*. New York: Oxford University Press, 1995.

——. *Meet Me at Jim and Andy's: Jazz Musicians and Their World*. New York: Oxford University Press, 1988.

——. *Waiting for Dizzy*. New York: Oxford University Press, 1991.

Lewis, George. *A Power Stronger Than Itself: The AACM and American Experimental Music*. Chicago: University of Chicago Press, 2008.

Litweiler, John. *The Freedom Principle: Jazz after 1958*. New York: William Morrow, 1984.

——. *Ornette Coleman: A Harmolodic Life*. New York: William Morrow, 1992.

Lomax, Alan. *The Land Where the Blues Began*. New York: Pantheon, 1993.

——. *Mister Jelly Roll*. New York: Duell, Sloan & Pearce, 1950.

Mandel, Howard. *Future Jazz*. New York: Oxford University Press, 2000.

Marquis, Donald. *In Search of Buddy Bolden, First Man of Jazz*. Baton Rouge: Louisiana State University Press, 1978.

Mingus, Charles. *Beneath the Underdog*. New York: Knopf, 1971.

Morgenstern, Dan. *Living with Jazz*. Edited by Sheldon Meyer. New York: Pantheon, 2004.

Murray, Albert. *Stompin' the Blues*. New York: McGraw-Hill, 1976.

Nicholson, Stuart. *Ella Fitzgerald: A Biography of the First Lady of Jazz*. New York: Scribners, 1994.

———. *Jazz: The Modern Resurgence*. London: Simon & Schuster, 1990.

———. *Jazz-Rock: A History*. Edinburgh: Canongate Books, 1998.

Owens, Thomas. *Bebop: The Music and Its Players*. New York: Oxford University Press, 1995.

Pearson, Nathan W., Jr. *Goin' to Kansas City*. Urbana: University of Illinois Press, 1987.

Pepper, Art, and Laurie Pepper. *Straight Life: The Story of Art Pepper*. New York: Schirmer, 1979.

Pettinger, Peter. *Bill Evans: How My Heart Sings*. New Haven: Yale University Press, 1998.

Porter, Lewis. *John Coltrane: His Life and Music*. Ann Arbor: University of Michigan Press, 1999.

———, ed. *A Lester Young Reader*. Washington, DC: Smithsonian Institution Press, 1991.

Ramsey, Frederick, Jr., and Charles Edward Smith. *Jazzmen*. New York: Harcourt Brace Jovanovich, 1939.

Ratliff, Ben. *Coltrane: The Story of a Sound*. New York: Farrar, Straus and Giroux, 2007.

Roberts, John Storm. *Black Music of Two Worlds*. New York: Praeger, 1972.

———. *The Latin Tinge: The Impact of Latin American Music on the United States*. New York: Oxford University Press, 1979.

Rockwell, John. *All American Music: Composition in the Late Twentieth Century*. New York: Knopf, 1983.

Rosenthal, David H. *Hard Bop: Jazz and Black Music 1955–1965*. New York: Oxford University Press, 1992.

Russell, Bill. *New Orleans Style*. Compiled and edited by Barry Martyn and Mike Hazeldine. New Orleans: Jazzology Press, 1994.

Russell, Ross. *Bird Lives! The High Life and Hard Times of Charlie (Yardbird) Parker*. New York: Charterhouse, 1973.

———. *Jazz in Kansas City and the Southwest*. Berkeley: University of California Press, 1971.

Sales, Grover. *Jazz: America's Classical Music*. Englewood Cliffs, NJ: Prentice-Hall, 1984.

Santoro, Gene. *Dancing in Your Head: Jazz, Blues, Rock and Beyond*. New York: Oxford University Press, 1994.

Schuller, Gunther. *Early Jazz*. New York: Oxford University Press, 1968.

———. *The Swing Era: The Development of Jazz, 1930–1945*. New York: Oxford University Press, 1989.

Shipton, Alyn. *A New History of Jazz*. London: Continuum, 2001.

Simon, George T. *The Big Bands*. New York: Macmillan, 1967.

Southern, Eileen. *The Music of Black Americans: A History*, 3rd ed. New York: W.W. Norton, 1997.

Spellman, A. B. *Black Music: Four Lives*. New York: Schocken, 1970.

Sublette, Ned. *The World That Made New Orleans: From Spanish Silver to Congo Square*. Chicago: Lawrence Hill, 2008.

Sudhalter, Richard, and Philip R. Evans. *Bix: Man and Legend*. New York: Arlington House, 1974.

Sudhalter, Richard. *Lost Chords: White Musicians and Their Contribution to Jazz, 1915–1945*. New York: Oxford University Press, 1999.

Taylor, Art. *Notes and Tones: Musician-to-Musician Interviews*. New York: Perigee Books, 1977.

Taylor, Yuval, ed. *The Future of Jazz*. Chicago: A Cappella Books, 2002.

Teachout, Terry. *Pops: A Life of Louis Armstrong*. Boston: Houghton Mifflin Harcourt, 2009.

Travis, Dempsey J. *An Autobiography of Black Jazz*. Chicago: Urban Research Institute, 1983.

Tucker, Mark, ed. *A Duke Ellington Reader*. New York: Oxford University Press, 1993.

Ward, Geoffrey C. *Jazz: A History of America's Music*. New York: Alfred A. Knopf, 2000.

Wilder, Alec. *American Popular Song: The Great Innovators*. New York: Oxford University Press, 1972.

Williams, Martin. *Jazz Masters of New Orleans*. New York: Macmillan, 1967.

———. *The Jazz Tradition*, rev. ed. New York: Oxford University Press, 1983.

Wilmer, Valerie. *As Serious as Your Life*. London: Quartet, 1977.

Woideck, Carl. *Charlie Parker: His Music and Life*. Ann Arbor: University of Michigan Press, 1998.

Recommended Listening

Unlike most lists of recommended recordings, this one focuses on specific tracks rather than on complete albums. This approach is, I believe, preferable for two reasons. First, by narrowing the focus, it aims to increase the intensity of the listening process. In almost every case, the careful study of a few performances is more illuminating than the casual apprehension of lengthy recordings. The second reason for listing only individual performances is a practical one. In recent years, the number of reissues, compilations, and repackagings of old material has grown at an extraordinary rate, as has the range of options for purchasing music online. While these changes have increased the availability of many previously rare or little-known works, they have also made it increasingly difficult for a newcomer to track down specific albums. A compilation available one year may be out of print the next. At the same time, music buyers have increasingly opted to purchase individual songs rather than entire compact discs. In such an environment, a listing of tracks offers a more convenient guide for the listener as well as a more permanent one, unaffected by the decisions of record companies to make cosmetic changes to their catalogs, to repackage, rename, and render obsolete their various releases.

I have provided recording dates, in most cases, to assist in identifying the performance in question, rather than refer to the name of a compact disc. However, in instances in which a piece is closely identified with a specific album (e.g., Miles Davis's "So What" with *Kind of Blue*), I have provided the title of the original project to help readers locate the music. Also, in some instances I have taken liberties in listing titles under the artist most closely associated with a performance instead of under the original group leader—for instance, "Singin' the Blues" is included under Bix Beiderbecke, although Frank Trumbauer was the ostensible bandleader of the date. I have occasionally (but not exhaustively) added cross-references to indicate other recordings where a specific artist appears.

I should say, in conclusion, that this list is intended to be a mere starting point, an indicative selection of the tremendous scope of jazz music. Listeners are encouraged to explore widely, moving beyond its boundaries, although retaining (I would hope) the careful listening habits encouraged above.

Artist	Performance	Date/Other Comments
Abrams, Muhal Richard	Levels and Degrees of Light	December 21, 1967
	The Hearinga Suite	January 17–18, 1989
Adderley, Cannonball	Autumn Leaves	March 9, 1958 (w. M. Davis)
Akiyoshi, Toshiko, and Lew Tabackin	American Ballad	April 3, 1974
Allen, Henry "Red"	I Cover the Waterfront	March 27, 1957 (w. C. Hawkins)
Argue, Darcy James	Phobos	December 15–17, 2008 (from *Infernal Machines*)
Armstrong, Louis	West End Blues	June 28, 1928 (w. E. Hines)
(see also *King Oliver, Jack Teagarden, and Ella Fitzgerald*)	Potato Head Blues	May 10, 1927
	Struttin' with Some Barbecue	December 9, 1927
	Weather Bird	December 5, 1928 (w. E. Hines)
	I Can't Give You Anything but Love	March 5, 1929
	Sweethearts on Parade	December 23, 1930
	Shine	March 9, 1931
Art Ensemble of Chicago	Tutankhamun	June 26, 1969
Ayler, Albert	Ja	May 1978 (from *Nice Guys*)
The Bad Plus	Spirits	July 10, 1964 (from *Spiritual Unity*)
	Smells Like Teen Spirit	September 30–October 5, 2002 (from *These Are the Vistas*)
Baker, Chet	I Fall in Love Too Easily	October 27, 1953
(see also *Gerry Mulligan*)	My Funny Valentine	February 15, 1954
Barnet, Charlie	The Moose	October 21, 1943
Bärtsch, Nik	Modul 35	May 5–7, 2005 (from *Stoa*)

Artist	Title	Date
Basie, Count *(see also Lester Young, Bennie Moten)*	One O'Clock Jump	July 7, 1937
	Taxi War Dance	March 19, 1939
	Dickie's Dream	September 5, 1939 (w. D. Wells and L. Young)
	April in Paris	July 26, 1955
	Li'l Darlin'	May 26–27, 1958
Bechet, Sidney	I Found a New Baby	September 15, 1932
	Maple Leaf Rag	September 15, 1932
	Summertime	June 8, 1939
	Blue Horizon	December 20, 1944
Beiderbecke, Bix	Riverboat Shuffle	May 9, 1927
	I'm Comin' Virginia	May 13, 1927
	Singin' the Blues	February 4, 1927
	In a Mist	September 9, 1927?
Berigan, Bunny *(see also Benny Goodman, Tommy Dorsey)*	I Can't Get Started	August 7, 1937
Berry, Chu	Ghost of a Chance	June 27, 1940
Blakey, Art	Moanin'	October 30, 1958 (w. L. Morgan)
	Lester Left Town	March 6, 1960 (w. W. Shorter)
	How Deep Is the Ocean	June 1981 (w. W. Marsalis)
Bley, Paul	Syndrome	September 12, 1963 (from *Footloose*)
Blood, Sweat and Tears	God Bless the Child	January 1969 (from *Blood, Sweat and Tears*)
Braxton, Anthony	For John Cage	October 1968 (from *For Alto*)
	Composition 57	February 1976 (from *Creative Orchestra Music*)

continued

Artist	Performance	Date/Other Comments
Brown, Clifford, and Max Roach	The Blues Walk	February 24, 1955
Brubeck, Dave	Joy Spring	August 6, 1954
	Daahoud	August 6, 1954
	You Go to My Head	October 1952 (w. P. Desmond)
	Blue Rondo à la Turk	July 1, 1959 (from *Time Out*)
	Take Five	July 1, 1959 (from *Time Out*)
Burton, Gary	Crystal Silence	November 6, 1972 (w. C. Corea)
Byron, Don	I Want to Be Happy	May 23–24, 2004 (w. J. Moran)
Caine, Uri	Symphony no. 5, Adagietto	June 1996 (from *Primal Light*)
Calloway, Cab	Minnie the Moocher	March 3, 1931
Carter, Benny	When Lights Are Low	June 20, 1936
(*see also Chocolate Dandies*)	The Midnight Sun Will Never Set	November 13, 1961
Carter, James	'Round Midnight	October–November, 1994 (from *The Real Quietstorm*)
Casa Loma Orchestra	Casa Loma Stomp	December 6, 1930
Chocolate Dandies	I Can't Believe That You're in Love with Me	May 25, 1940
(w. R. Eldridge, C. Hawkins, and B. Carter)		
Christian, Charlie	Breakfast Feud	January 15, 1941
	Solo Flight	March 4, 1941
Coleman, Ornette	Lonely Woman	May 22, 1959
	Ramblin'	October 9, 1959
	Embraceable You	July 26, 1959
	Free Jazz	December 21, 1960
	Theme from a Symphony (Variation 1)	December 1976

Coltrane, John	Giant Steps	May 4, 1959
	My Favorite Things	October 21, 1960
	In a Sentimental Mood	September 26, 1962 (w. D. Ellington)
	My One and Only Love	March 7, 1963 (w. J. Hartman)
	Acknowledgement	December 9, 1964 (from *A Love Supreme*)
	Ascension	June 28, 1965
Corea, Chick	Steps-What Was	March 14, 19, 27, 1968
(see also Gary Burton)	Spain	October 1972
Crosby, Bob	South Rampart Street Parade	November 16, 1937
Davis, Miles	Boplicity	April 22, 1949
	Round Midnight	September 10, 1956
	Blues for Pablo	May 23, 1957 (from *Miles Ahead*)
	All Blues	April 22, 1959 (from *Kind of Blue*)
	So What	March 2, 1959 (from *Kind of Blue*)
	Footprints	October 25, 1966
	Spanish Key	August 20, 1969 (from *Bitches Brew*)
Dolphy, Eric	Fire Waltz	July 16, 1961 (w. Booker Little)
(see also Charles Mingus, Oliver Nelson, and Andrew Hill)	The Prophet	July 16, 1961 (w. Booker Little)
	Out to Lunch	February 25, 1964
Dorsey, Tommy	Song of India	January 29, 1937 (w. B. Berigan)
	Opus #1	November 14, 1944
Eldridge, Roy	Heckler's Hop	January 23, 1937
(see also Chocolate Dandies)	After You've Gone	January 28, 1937

continued

Artist	Performance	Date/Other Comments
Ellington, Duke	East St. Louis Toodle-oo	November 29, 1926
	Black and Tan Fantasy	April 7, 1927
	Braggin' in Brass	March 3, 1938
	Ko-Ko	March 6, 1940
	Cotton Tail	May 4, 1940
	Harlem Air Shaft	July 22, 1940
	Sepia Panorama	November 7, 1940 (live in Fargo, ND)
	Black, Brown and Beige	January 23, 1943 (live at Carnegie Hall)
	The Clothed Woman	December 27, 1947 (live at Carnegie Hall)
	Mood Indigo	December 18, 1950
	The Harlem Suite	December 7, 1951
	The Star-Crossed Lovers	May 3, 1957
Europe, James Reese	Memphis Blues	March 7, 1919
Evans, Bill	My Man's Gone Now	June 25, 1961
	Gloria's Step	June 25, 1961
	My Foolish Heart	June 25, 1961
	Solo—in Memory of His Father	February 21, 1966
	Never Let Me Go	September–October 1968
Fitzgerald, Ella	Sing Me a Swing Song	June 2, 1936 (w. C. Webb)
	Lady Be Good	March 19, 1947
	I Won't Dance	April 13, 1957 (with L. Armstrong)

Frisell, Bill	Billy the Kid	March 1992 (from *Have a Little Faith*)
Garbarek, Jan	Disfarmer Theme	February–May 2008 (from *Disfarmer*)
Garner, Erroll	Folk Song	November 1979
Garrett, Kenny	I'll Remember April	September 19, 1955 (from *Concert by the Sea*)
Getz, Stan	Sing a Song of Song	January 7–8, 1997 (from *Songbook*)
	I'm Late, I'm Late	July 28, 1961 (from *Focus*)
	The Girl from Ipanema	March 18–19, 1953
Gillespie, Dizzy	The Peacocks	October, 1975 (with J. Rowles)
(*see also Charlie Parker*)	Salt Peanuts	May 11, 1945 (w. C. Parker)
	Hot House	May 11, 1945 (w. C. Parker)
	Anthropology	February 22, 1946
	Dizzy Atmosphere	September 29, 1947 (w. C. Parker at Carnegie Hall)
	Manteca	December 30, 1947
	A Night in Tunisia	June 3, 1954
Goodman, Benny	King Porter Stomp	July 1, 1935 (w. B. Berigan)
(*see also Charlie Christian*)	Sometimes I'm Happy	July 1, 1935 (w. B. Berigan)
	After You've Gone	July 13, 1935 (with the Trio)
	Body and Soul	July 13, 1935 (with the Trio)
	Avalon	July 30, 1937 (with the Quartet)
	Sing, Sing, Sing (with a Swing)	January 16, 1938 (live at Carnegie Hall)
Gordon, Dexter, and Wardell Gray	The Chase	February 2, 1952
Hampton, Lionel	Flyin' Home	May 26, 1942
Hancock, Herbie	Cantaloupe Island	June 17, 1964

continued

Artist	Performance	Date/Other Comments
	Maiden Voyage	March 17, 1965 (w. F. Hubbard)
	Chameleon	1973 (from *Head Hunters*)
Hawkins, Coleman	One Hour	November 14, 1929 (w. P. W. Russell)
(see also F. Henderson, Henry "Red" Allen, and Chocolate Dandies)	Body and Soul	October 11, 1939
	The Man I Love	December 23, 1943
	Picasso	1948
Henderson, Fletcher	The Stampede	May 14, 1926 (w. C. Hawkins)
	Whiteman Stomp	May 11, 1927
	Hop Off	November 4, 1927
	Queer Notions	August 18, 1933
Henderson, Joe	Inner Urge	November 30, 1964
(see also Andrew Hill)	Beatrice	November 14–16, 1985
Herman, Woody	Blue Flame	February 13, 1941
	Apple Honey	February 19, 1945
	Four Brothers	December 27, 1947
Hill, Andrew	Refuge	March 21, 1964 (w. E. Dolphy, J. Henderson)
Hines, Earl	A Monday Date	December 1928
(see also Louis Armstrong, Jimmie Noone)	Cavernism	February 13, 1933
Holiday, Billie	Mean to Me	May 11, 1937 (w. L. Young)
	He's Funny That Way	September 13, 1937 (w. L. Young)
	Strange Fruit	April 20, 1939
	All of Me	March 21, 1941
	Lover Man	October 4, 1944

Holland, Dave	Four Winds	November 30, 1972 (from *Conference of the Birds*)
Hubbard, Freddie	Birdlike (aka Byrdlike)	August 21, 1961
(*see also Herbie Hancock, Oliver Nelson*)	Red Clay	January 27–29, 1970
Jamal, Ahmad	Poinciana	October 25, 1955
Jarman, Joseph	Song For	December 16, 1966
Jarrett, Keith	In Front	November 10, 1971
	Bremen	July 12, 1973
	The Journey Home	November 1, 1977 (from *My Song*)
	The Song Is You	July 13, 1986 (with J. DeJohnette, G. Peacock)
Jazztet	Killer Joe	February 6–10, 1960
Johnson, James P.	Carolina Shout	October 18, 1921
Johnson, J. J.	Turnpike	June 22, 1953
Johnson, Robert	Hellhound on My Trail	June 20, 1937
	Love in Vain	June 20, 1937
Jones, Norah	Don't Know Why	Circa 2002 (from *Come Away with Me*)
Jones, Thad, and Mel Lewis	St. Louis Blues	October 17, 1968
Joplin, Scott	The Maple Leaf Rag	April, 1916 (piano roll)
Kenton, Stan	Artistry in Rhythm	November 19, 1943
	City of Glass	December 5, 1951
	Recuerdos	May 2, 1956
Kirk, Andy	Walkin' and Swingin'	March 2, 1936 (w. M. L. Williams)
Kirk, Rahsaan Roland	Bright Moments	June 8–9, 1973

continued

Artist	Performance	Date/Other Comments
Konitz, Lee	Subconscious-Lee	January 11, 1949 (w. L. Tristano)
Krall, Diana	'S Wonderful	June 3–4, 2001 (from *The Look of Love*)
Lewis, Meade Lux	Honky Tonk Train Blues	December 1927
Lovano, Joe	Fort Worth	March 12, 1994
	Rush Hour on 23rd Street	April–June 1994 (w. G. Schuller)
Lunceford, Jimmie	White Heat	May 15, 1933
	Organ Grinder's Swing	August 31, 1936
	For Dancers Only	June 15, 1937
Mahanthappa, Rudresh	Ganesha	November 13–14, 2007 (from *Kinsmen*)
Mahavishnu Orchestra	The Noonward Race	August 14, 1971
Marsalis, Branford	Just One of Those Things	January 26–28, 1987
Marsalis, Wynton	A Foggy Day	May–September, 1986 (from *Marsalis Standard Time, Vol. 1*)
(see also Art Blakey)	Knozz-Moe-King	December 19–20, 1986 (from *Live at Blues Alley*)
	The Majesty of the Blues (The Puheeman Strut)	October 27–28, 1988
	Blood on the Fields	January 22–25, 1995
McFerrin, Bobby	Peace	1982 (from *Bobby McFerrin*)
McKenzie and Condon's Chicagoans	China Boy	December 8, 1927
	Nobody's Sweetheart	December 16, 1927
McLean, Jackie	Melody for Melonae	March 19, 1962
Mehldau, Brad	Exit Music (for a Film)	May 27–28, 1998
	All the Things You Are	January 5–10, 1999

Metheny, Pat	Song X	December 1985 (with O. Coleman)
	So May It Secretly Begin	March–April 1987
Miller, Glenn	Moonlight Serenade	August 1, 1939
Mingus, Charles	Haitian Fight Song	March 12, 1957
	Goodbye Pork Pie Hat	May 12, 1959
	What Love	July 13, 1960 (w. E. Dolphy)
	Original Faubus Fables	October 20, 1960 (w. E. Dolphy)
	The Black Saint and the Sinner Lady	January 20, 1963
Modern Jazz Quartet	Django	December 23, 1954
	Concorde	July 2, 1955
Mole, Miff	Shim-me-sha-wabble	June 7, 1928
Monk, Thelonious	Misterioso	July 2, 1948
	Brilliant Corners	October 15, 1956 (w. S. Rollins)
	I Should Care	April 12, 1957
	Round Midnight	April 1957
	Well, You Needn't	June 26, 1957 (w. J. Coltrane, C. Hawkins)
Montgomery, Wes	Besame Mucho	April 22, 1963
	If You Could See Me Now	June 24, 1965
Moran, Jason	Out Front	November 29–30, 2002 (from *The Bandwagon*)
(*see also Don Byron*)	Blue Blocks	Circa 2010 (from *Ten*)
Morgan, Lee	The Sidewinder	December 21, 1963
Morton, Jelly Roll	Sidewalk Blues	September 21, 1926
	Dead Man Blues	September 21, 1926

continued

Artist	Performance	Date/Other Comments
	Grandpa's Spells	December 16, 1926
	The Crave	December 14, 1939
Moten, Bennie	Moten Swing	December 13, 1932 (w. C. Basie)
	Prince of Wails	December 13, 1932 (w. C. Basie)
Mulligan, Gerry	Bernie's Tune	August 16, 1952 (w. C. Baker)
	Line for Lyons	September 2, 1952 (w. C. Baker)
Murray, David	Flowers for Albert	June 26, 1976
	Murray's Steps	July 14–19, 1982
Navarro, Fats	Wail	August 9, 1949 (w. B. Powell)
Nelson, Oliver	Stolen Moments	February 23, 1961 (w. B. Evans, E. Dolphy, F. Hubbard)
New Orleans Rhythm Kings	Weary Blues	March 12, 1923
Nichols, Herbie	The Third World	May 6, 1955
Noone, Jimmie	Four or Five Times	May 16, 1928 (w. E. Hines)
Norvo, Red	Dance of the Octopus	November 21, 1933
Oliver, King	Froggie Moore	April 6, 1923 (w. L. Armstrong)
	Dipper Mouth Blues	April 6, 1923
	Tears	October 25, 1923
Original Dixieland Jazz Band	Livery Stable Blues	February 26, 1917
Oregon	Icarus	November 1979
Parker, Charlie	Ko Ko	November 26, 1945 (w. D. Gillespie)
(see also Dizzy Gillespie)	A Night in Tunisia	March 28, 1946

	Relaxin' at Camarillo	February 26, 1947
	Embraceable You	October 28, 1947
	Parker's Mood	September 18, 1948
	Just Friends	November 30, 1949
	Salt Peanuts	May 15, 1953 (w. D. Gillespie at Massey Hall)
Pass, Joe	Cherokee	November 1973 (from *Virtuoso*)
Patton, Charley	Pony Blues	June 14, 1929
Pepper, Art	Patricia	December 1–2, 1978 (from *Art Pepper Today*)
Peterson, Oscar	Blues Etude	March 16–19, 1973
Powell, Bud	Dance of the Infidels	August 8, 1949
(*see also Fats Navarro*)	Tea for Two	July 1, 1950
	Un Poco Loco	May 1, 1951
Rainey, Ma	See See Rider Blues	October 1924 (w. L. Armstrong)
Redman, Joshua	Jig-a-Jug	March 21–26, 1995
Reinhardt, Django	Minor Swing	November 25, 1937
	Nuages	December 13, 1940
Rollins, Sonny	Tenor Madness	May 24, 1956 (w. J. Coltrane)
(*see also Thelonious Monk*)	Blue 7	June 22, 1956
	The Freedom Suite	February 1958
Russell, Pee Wee	Basin Street Blues	June 11, 1929
(*see also Coleman Hawkins*)		
Schneider, Maria	Evanescence	September 1992 (from *Evanescence*)
	Cerulean Skies	January 6–9, 2007 (from *Sky Blue*)

continued

Artist	Performance	Date/Other Comments
Shaw, Artie	Begin the Beguine	July 24, 1938
	Stardust	October 7, 1940
Shaw, Woody	Rosewood	December 15, 1977
Shipp, Matthew	Space Shipp	August 9, 2001 (from *Nu Bop*)
	Galaxy 105	February 20–21, 2004 (from *Harmony and Abyss*)
Shorter, Wayne	Infant Eyes	December 24, 1964
(*see also Art Blakey, Weather Report*)	Ponta de Areia	September 12, 1974 (w. M. Nascimento)
Silver, Horace	The Preacher	February 6, 1955
	Song for My Father	October 26, 1954
	Nutville	October 2, 1965
Smith, Bessie	St. Louis Blues	January 14, 1925 (w. L. Armstrong)
	Empty Bed Blues	March 20, 1928
Smith, Jimmy	The Sermon	February 25, 1958
Spanier, Muggsy	Big Butter and Egg Man	July 7, 1939
Sun Ra	A Call for All Demons	Circa 1956 (from *Angels and Demons at Play*)
Svensson, Esbjörn	Dating	May–November 1998
Tatum, Art	Humoresque	February 22, 1940
(*see also Ben Webster*)	Sweet Georgia Brown	September 16, 1941 (live at Monroe's Uptown House)
	I Know That You Know	April 2, 1949 (live at Shrine Auditorium)
	Willow Weep for Me	July 13–25, 1949
Taylor, Cecil	Cell Walk for Celeste	January 9, 1961
	Enter Evening	May 19, 1966 (from *Unit Structures*)
	Abyss	July 2, 1974 (from *Silent Tongues*)

Teagarden, Jack	I Gotta Right to Sing the Blues	October 18, 1933
	Knockin' a Jug	March 5, 1929 (w. L. Armstrong)
Towner, Ralph	Spirit Lake	October 1979
Tristano, Lennie	I Can't Get Started	October 8, 1946
(see also Lee Konitz)	Line Up	Spring–summer 1955
	C Minor Complex	Autumn 1961
Vaughan, Sarah	Shulie a Bop	April 2, 1954
	Lullaby of Birdland	December 16, 1954
Venuti, Joe	Stringin' the Blues	November 8, 1926 (w. E. Lang)
Waller, Fats	African Ripples	November 16, 1934
	Viper's Drag	November 16, 1934
	The Joint Is Jumpin'	October 7, 1937
Weather Report	Birdland	1977 (from Heavy Weather)
Webster, Ben	My Ideal	September 11, 1956 (w. A. Tatum)
(see also Duke Ellington, Mary Lou Williams)		
Whiteman, Paul	Changes	November 23, 1927
Williams, Mary Lou	Night Life	April 24, 1930
(see also Andy Kirk)	The Zodiac Suite	December 31, 1945 (w. B. Webster)
Wilson, Cassandra	I've Grown Accustomed to His Face	February 1988 (from Blue Skies)
Wilson, Teddy	Don't Blame Me	November 12, 1937
(see also Benny Goodman, Billie Holiday)		
Woods, Phil	Get Happy	November 25, 1955

continued

Artist	Performance	Date/Other Comments
World Saxophone Quartet	Steppin'	November 6, 1981
Young, Lester	Oh, Lady Be Good	October 9, 1936 (w. C. Basie)
(see also Count Basie, Billie Holiday)	Lester Leaps In	September 5, 1939 (w. C. Basie)
	I Got Rhythm	December 21, 1943
	After Theater Jump	March 22, 1944
Zappa, Frank	Peaches en Regalia	July 18–August 30, 1969 (from Hot Rats)
Zeitlin, Denny	Blue Phoenix	March 6, 1964
Zenón, Miguel	Camarón	April 2–4, 2007 (from Awake)
Zorn, John	The Sicilian Clan	1989 (from Naked City)

Acknowledgments

This book would not have been possible without the help of many individuals. I would like to extend my thanks first to a talented group of people who read parts of this work and gave me invaluable feedback. For the revised edition, I am indebted to Rob Bamberger, Bob Blumenthal, Peter Gerler, Todd Jenkins, Alan Kurtz, Steven Lasker, Stuart Nicholson, Peter Pullman, Thierry Quénum, Charles A. Sengstock Jr., and Jeff Sultanof for their guidance and advice. For the first edition of this book, I relied on the input of Donald Marquis, Richard Hadlock, Richard Sudhalter, Grover Sales, Bill Kirchner, John Litweiler, Nathan Pearson, Dr. Herb Wong, John O'Neill, Dana Gioia, Larry Kart, and Chris Sheridan. Although I benefited enormously from the assistance of these individuals, I must absolve them from blame for any of the limitations of the final work. I also need to express my gratitude to Dan Morgenstern and the staff at the Rutgers Institute of Jazz Studies, and to Dr. Bruce Boyd Raeburn of the Hogan Jazz Archive at Tulane University, as well as to Barbara Sawka of the Stanford University Archive of Recorded Sound. Additional thanks are due to Joseph Mailander and Greg Gioia, for their input and encouragement, and to Joellyn Ausanka, of Oxford University Press, for her assistance in shepherding the first edition of this work through various stages of production. I owe a tremendous debt to the late Sheldon Meyer of Oxford University Press, who encouraged me to write the first edition of this book and served as the best of editors and a constant source of valued advice. I also must thank Suzanne Ryan of Oxford University Press, who made it possible for me to update and revise this book for a new generation of readers. Finally, I need to offer my deepest thanks to my wife, Tara, to whom this book is lovingly dedicated, for her unflagging support and help during the course of writing it.

T.G.

Index

AACM. *See* Association for the
    Advancement of Creative
    Musicians (AACM)
Abrams, Muhal Richard, 358, 363
Academy of Music, 32
acid jazz, 333
Adams, George, 302
Adderley, Julian "Cannonball," 215,
    273, 356
Addy, Yacub, 353
African American culture, 101
African Americans, modern jazz
    and, 190
Africanization of American
    music, 3–12
African music
    features, 9–10
    jazz and, 185
    traditional elements, 9–10
Afro-Cubans, 206
"After Awhile," 130
Afternoon of an Elf, 234
"After You've Gone," 140
Agharta, 327
"Ah-Leu-Cha," 211
"Ain't Misbehavin'," 64, 95
Air, 360
"Air," 319
Akiyoshi, Toshiko, 249, 386
Albany, Joe, 221
Albert, Mary, 46
Alexander, Willard, 180
"Alice in Wonderland," 274
"All About Rosie," 271
Allen, Henry "Red," 64, 102,
    159, 374
"All God's Chillun Got Rhythm," 219
"Alligator Crawl," 60

Allison, Ben, 380
"All of Me," 165, 168
"All of You," 274
All Set, 311
"All the Things You Are," 201
"All Too Soon," 175
Allyson, Karrin, 376
Almeida, Laurindo, 387
Alone, 275
"Along Came Betty," 289
"Amapola," 138
"American Ballad," 249
American Conservatory
    of Music, 229
American Federation of Musicians,
    21, 145, 176
American Jazz Orchestra,
    109, 260
American music, Africanization
    of, 3–12
American Symphonic Suite, 93
American Theatre, 31
Ammons, Albert, 96, 222
Ammons, Gene, 204, 242, 243
Anatomy of a Murder, 181
Anderson, Bernard "Buddy," 193
Anderson, Ivie, 122, 176
Anderson, Sherwood, 116
Anderson, William "Cat," 182
And His Mother Called Him Bill, 182
Andrews Sisters, 96
Angelus cabinet player piano, 21
Antibes Jazz Festival, 301
Apex Club, 62
Apfelbaum, Peter, 380
"Apple Honey," 241
Arbour Zena, 341
Arlen, Harold, 99, 346

Armstrong, Louis, 16, 18, 33, 35, 41, 43–51, 70, 71, 79, 82, 92, 102, 105, 106, 114, 118, 128, 140, 142, 143, 158, 165, 167, 190, 198, 201, 210, 229, 237, 239, 255, 299, 338, 345
  Age of the Soloist, 53–56
  Hot Five and Hot Sevens, 57–66
  "Weather Bird," 62–63
  "West End Blues," 62
Art Ensemble of Chicago, 360–61
"Artistry in Rhythm," 244
ArtistShare company, 371
Art of the Trio, The, 372
Art Pepper Meets the Rhythm Section, 265
Art Pepper Plus Eleven, 265
Ascension, 322
Ashton, Frederick, 117
Association for the Advancement of Creative Musicians (AACM), 247, 358–61
"A-Tisket, A-Tasket," 125
"At Last," 146
Attali, Jacques, 322*n*12
"At the Jazz Band Ball," 77
"Auld Lang Syne," 266
Austin High School Gang, 74, 75, 130
Autobiography of a Yogi, The, 279
"Autumn Leaves," 351, 375
Aux Frontières du Jazz, 382
Ayler, Albert, 282, 315, 323–25, 360, 363

Babbitt, Milton, 311
Bad Plus, The, 366
Bailey, Bill, 123
Bailey, Buster, 130
Bailey, Mildred, 64, 80
Bailey, Pearl, 107
Baker, Chet, 207, 228, 264–65, 274, 377
  Tokyo concert, 265
Baker, Harold "Shorty," 148
"Bakiff," 176
Balliett, Whitney, 76, 234*n*19
Bamboula, 6
Bandana Land, 116
Bandwagon, The, 366
banjo, 22, 106, 360
Baquet, George, 55
Baraka, Amiri, 296, 310, 310*n*1
"Barbados," 211
Barbarin, Paul, 29–30

Barber, Patricia, 375
Barbera, Joe La, 275
Barès, Basile, 6
Barker, Danny, 349, 352
Barnet, Charlie, 238–39
Barron, Kenny, 355
Barthes, Roland, 356
Bartók, Béla, 129, 143
Baryshnikov, Mikhail, 321
Basie, William "Count," 94, 96, 107, 146, 150–53, 158, 168, 189, 232, 246, 294, 345–46
  early life, 152–53
  piano style, 150, 153
  professional career, 153
"Basie Boogie," 96
"Basin Street Blues," 65, 77, 79
bass, 151, 173, 274, 330
Bass, Ralph, 189
bassoon, 360
Batiste, Alvin, 349
Bauer, Billy, 229, 240
Bauzá, Mario, 196, 197, 206
Bayersdorffer, Johnny, 35
"Beale Street Blues," 18, 79
"Beatin' the Dog," 77
bebop, 144
  arrival of, on Fifty-second Street, 200
  ascendancy of, 253
  big bands in, 236–51
  birth of, 185–200
  harmonic complexity of, 188
  harmonic implications of, 188
  Hines band and, 198
  instrumentation of, 187–88
  piano, 216–36
Bechet, Sidney, 5, 34–35, 43–44, 48, 54–57, 65, 82, 104, 113, 127, 159, 254
"Begin the Beguine," 140
Beiderbecke, Leon Bix, 45, 73, 75, 77–78, 103, 127, 131, 143, 158
  Frank Trumbauer and, 81–87
  Jazz Age and, 66–71
Beirach, Richie, 276
Belden, Bob, 386
Belford, Joe, 154
Bell, Daniel, 377
bells, 360
Beneath the Underdog, 302

Benedetti, Dean, 189, 211, 299
Bennett, Tony, 348
Benson, George, 328
Berendt, Joachim, 329, 329n14
Berigan, Bunny, 80, 132
Berlin, Irving, 23, 99, 134, 346
Berlin, Isaiah, 357
Berman, Sonny, 240, 241
"Bernie's Tune," 264
Bernstein, Leonard, 66, 315
Berry, Leon "Chu," 80, 102, 158, 161, 162, 197
Berton, Ralph, 86
"Besame Mucho," 138, 296
"Bethena," 23
"Better Git It in Your Soul," 300
"Between the Devil and the Deep Blue Sea," 63, 135
Bigard, Barney, 115, 119–20, 176
big bands
    emergence of, 100–110
    in modern jazz, 236–51
    Swing Era, 136–47
Big Gundown, The, 365
"Bijou," 241
bike horn, 360
Billboard, 138
"Billie's Blues," 167
"Billie's Bounce," 201
Billy Rose's Music Hall, 131
"Bird in Igor's Yard," 238
"Birdland," 330, 348
Birth of the Cool, 230, 257–260, 263, 267, 270
Bishop, Walter, 221
Bitches Brew, 295, 305, 326–27, 329
Black, Brown and Beige, 176–78
"Black and Blue," 95
"Black and Tan Fantasy," 64, 114, 115
Black Artists' Group, 358, 364
"Black Beauty," 120
"Black Bottom Stomp," 40
Black Code of 1724. See Code Noir
Black Codes (From the Underground), 350
black Creoles, 32
"Black Jazz," 136
Black Saint and the Sinner Lady The, 301
Black Swan (record label), 102
Blade, Brian, 380
Blake, Eubie, 24, 94

Blakey, Art, 224, 234, 286, 288–89, 345, 349, 376
Blanchard, Terence, 291, 354, 376
Blanton, Jimmy, 171–76, 189, 200
Blesh, Rudi, 25
Bley, Carla, 359
Bley, Paul, 163, 313
Bleyer, Archie, 108
"Blood Count," 172, 182, 293
Blood on the Fields, 353
Bloom, Jane Ira, 355
"Blue and Broken-Hearted," 130
"Blue and Sentimental," 153
"Blue Chopsticks," 228
Blue Devils, 151–52, 157
Blue Friars, 75
Blue Interlude, 352
"Blue Light," 171
Blue Light 'til Dawn, 335
"Blue 'n' Boogie," 201
Blue Note, 219, 221–24, 262, 286, 289, 291, 297
blue notes, 12–13
"Blue Rhythm Fantasy," 196
"Blue Room, The," 138, 151
Blues and Roots, 299
Blues and the Abstract Truth The, 281
"Blue Serge," 175
"Blues for Alice," 188
"Blues in E Flat," 80
"Blue Skies," 132, 134, 335
"Blues March," 289
blues music
    Bolden, Buddy, 34
    characteristic component, 12–13
    classic blues, 15–19
    country blues, 13–15
    "dues paying," 19
    emergence of, 12
    guitar use, 15
    mythology of, 14
    style of, 13
    transformation by female vocalists, 16
Blues People, 310, 310n1
"Blues Walk, The," 287
Blue Train, 270–71
Bluiett, Hamiet, 360, 364
"Bluing," 268
Blumenthal, Bob, 282
Bocage, Peter, 34

"Body and Soul," 63, 158, 162, 192, 193, 210
Bogart, Humphrey, 73
Boland, Francy, 267
Bolden, Buddy, 5, 29, 45, 53, 55, 110, 186, 199, 326
   as the father of jazz, 33–37
Bolton, Dupree, 263
Bonano, Sharkey, 35
bongos, 360
"Boogie Woogie" 96, 138
"Boogie Woogie Bugle Boy," 96
Book of American Negro Poetry, The, 116
"Boplicity," 258
Boss Brass, in Toronto, 248
Bostonians, 157
"Bouncing with Bud," 219
"Bouncin' in Rhythm," 77
Bowie, Lester, 358, 360, 361
Bowles, Paul, 176
"Boyd Meets Stravinsky," 238
"Boy Meets Horn," 171
Bradford, Bobby, 316, 360
Braff, Ruby, 347
"Braggin' in Brass," 171
Brand, Dollar. See Ibrahim, Abdullah
Brando, Marlon, 73
brass bands, 31
Braud, Wellman, 173
Braxton, Anthony, 347, 358, 359, 361–62
Brazilian jazz, 387
"Breakfast Feud," 144
Breathless, 337
Brecker, Michael, 331–32, 378
Brecker Brothers, The, 331
"Breeze and I, The," 138
Breezin, 337
Breuker, Willem, 347
Bridge, The, 284
Bridge of Light, 341
Briggs, Pete, 60
Bright Size Life, 330–31
"Brilliant Corners," 224
Broadbent, Alan, 276
Brookmeyer, Bob, 249, 260, 371
Brooks, Duke, 208
Brooks, Michael, 82
Brown, Clifford, 205, 259, 285–87, 350, 373
Brown, Lawrence, 121, 179, 181

Brown, Les, 248
Brown, Ray, 173, 200, 218, 259, 284, 346
Brown, Steve, 83, 85, 173
Brown v. Board of Education, 309
Brown-Roach Quintet, 286–87
Brubeck, Dave, 232, 235, 345, 362
Bublé, Michael, 375
Buckner, Milt, 233
"Bugle Call Rag," 172
Burns, Ralph, 239, 240, 242
Burton, Gary, 276
Busse, Henry, 85
Butler, Frank, 263
Butler, Henry, 354
But Not for Me, 235
Buttercorn Lady, 339
Butterfield, Billy, 137
Byas, Don, 282
Byrd, Donald, 289
Byron, Don, 367

Caine, Uri, 366–67
"Caldonia," 241
Caldwell, Happy, 104
Callender, Red, 173
Calloway, Cab, 90, 125, 158, 161, 174, 189, 193, 196, 201, 206, 237
"Camptown Races," 236
Candoli, Pete, 240
Cantos, The, 302
Cape Verdean Blues, The, 291, 292
"Caravan," 170, 171, 206, 351
Carey, Thomas "Mutt," 35, 44–45
Carisi, John, 258
Carmichael, Hoagy, 63–64, 69, 131
Carnegie Hall
   Benny Goodman concert, 251
   Davis Miles concert, 270
   Norman Granz concert, 232
   performance of Charlie Parker, 207
   Sonny Rollins concert, 284
   Thelonious Monk concert, 227
Carney, Harry, 119
Carolina Cotton Pickers, the, 148
"Carolina Shout," 92, 98
"Carolina Stomp," 105
Carter, Benny, 80, 90–91, 100, 102, 107–10, 118, 124, 132, 140–41, 161–62, 169, 193, 197, 202, 285, 345
Carter, Betty, 64, 348

Carter, James, 378–79

Carter, John, 360

Carter, Regina, 380

Carter, Ron, 304

Casa Loma Orchestra, 124, 136–37

Cash, Johnny, 66

Cassidy, Eva, 374–75

Cathexis, 275

Catlett, Sid, 145

"Cat's Corner," 117

CBS (record label), 354 (*see also* Columbia *and* Sony)

Cecil Taylor Berlin '88, 321

Celestial Hawk, The, 341

Celestin, Oscar "Papa," 47

"Celia," 219

"Cell Walk for Celeste," 319

Central City Sketches, 109

"Cerulean Skies," 250

Challis, Bill, 83, 85, 86, 100, 105, 108, 138

Chaloff, Serge, 228, 242, 243

Chambers, Paul, 173, 269

Change of the Century, 315

"Chant, The," 40

Chaplin, Charlie, 50

Charles, Ray, 109, 288

Charters, Samuel, 15

"Chase, The," 204

"Chasin' the Bird," 210

"Chattanooga Choo Choo," 146

Chauvin, Louis, 22

Check and Double Check, 121

"Chelsea Bridge," 172, 175

Chernoff, John Miller, 9

"Cherokee," 188, 218, 238–39, 245

Cherry, Don, 201, 276, 281, 313, 324, 377

Chevalier, Maurice, 121

Chiaroscuro (record label), 347

Chicago

  AACM, 358–361

  Jazz Age, the, 71–80

  jazz players, Swing Era, 137

"Chicago," 161

"A Child Is Born," 249

"Children of the Night," 291

Childs, Billy, 371

"Chill of Death, The," 299, 302

Chilton, John, 166

"Chimes Blues," 49

"China Boy," 75

Chocolate Dandies, the, 107, 109, 140

Christensen, Sigfre, 35

Christian, Charlie, 143, 144, 162, 164, 189

"Christopher Columbus," 132

Christy, June, 245

Churchill, Winston, 50

Cincotti, Peter, 375

City of Glass, 310

Civil Rights Act, 190

Clancy, William D., 240*n*24

"Clap Hands, Here Comes Charlie," 155

"Clarinetitis," 72

Clark, Sonny, 284, 295

Clarke, Donald, 166

Clarke, Kenny, 153, 196, 197, 200, 224, 259, 267

Clarke, Stanley, 328

classic blues, 15–19 (*see also* blues music)

clave rhythm, 206

Clay, Sonny, 148

Clayton, Buck, 154

"Cleopatra's Dream," 219

Cline, Nels, 380

"Clothed Woman, The," 178

Clown, The, 299

Club Kentucky, 113, 116

C melody saxophone, 104

Cobb, Arnett, 312

Cobb, Oliver, 148

Code Noir, 32

Cohen, Avishai, 380

Cohn, Al, 242

Cole, Nat King, 164, 232, 233, 374

Cole, Richie, 216

Coleman, Earl, 203

Coleman, Ornette, 201, 260, 281, 282, 284, 285, 291, 303, 310–23, 316, 317*n*6, 350, 351, 378

Collier, James Lincoln, 201*n*5, 296–97, 297*n*21

color tones, 163

Coltrane, John, 97, 180, 225–26, 246, 261, 269–71, 273, 276–80, 322, 351, 363, 379

Coltrane, Ravi, 378

Columbia Graphophone, 67

Columbia (record label), 356 (*see also* CBS *and* Sony)

Combelle, Alix, 383

Come Away with Me, 374

"Come Sunday," 182

Commentaries on Living, 279
"Con Alma," 188
Concert by the Sea, 232, 234
"Concerto for Billy the Kid," 271
Concerto for Clarinet, 129, 140
Concerto for Clarinet and Orchestra, 129
"Concerto for Cootie," 144, 176, 179
Concerto Jazz a Mine, 93
Concierto de Aranjuez, 270
Concord (record label), 347
Condon, Eddie, 69, 74, 255
"Confirmation," 188
Congo Square, 3–5
    dances in, 4
Congo Square, 353
Connick, Harry, Jr., 64, 354
Conquistador, 319
"Construction Gang," 58
Contrasts, 129, 143
Cook, Will Marion, 54, 101, 159
Cooke, Doc, 62
cool jazz, 242, 253–67
    Miles Davis and, 256–58
"Copenhagen," 54
Copland, Aaron, 129
Corea, Chick, 275, 306, 328–29, 376
"Cornet Chop Suey," 59
Cosmic Tones for Mental Therapy, 246
Cotton Club, the, 116–25
"Cotton Tail," 171, 176, 193, 229
Counce, Curtis, 263
"Countdown," 276
country blues, 13–15 (*see also* blues
    music)
Coward, Noel, 160
"Crazy Blues," 16, 103
Creath, Charlie, 148
Creole Jazz Band, 44, 46–49, 53, 58–59, 67
"Creole Love Call," 75, 114
"Creole Rhapsody," 123
Creoles of color. *See* black Creoles
"Crescendo in Blue," 171
Criss, Sonny, 262
"Criss Cross," 223
"Cro-Magnon Nights," 228
Crosby, Bing, 64, 66, 79, 85
Crosby, Bob, 137
Crouch, Stanley, 352
"Cubana Be, Cubana Bop," 206
Cuban Fire, 245

Cullum, Jamie, 375
culture
    African American, 101
    Harlem, 91
    Latin-Catholic, 6
    mixture of, 5–7
    West Africa, 9
Cumbia & Jazz Fusion, 303
Cyr, Johnny St., 30, 40, 41, 58
Cyrille, Andrew, 320

"Daahoud," 287
"Dalvatore Sally," 238
Dameron, Tadd, 204, 205, 267, 286, 290
"Dance of the Octopus," 80
"Dancin' Fool," 333
Dancing in Your Head, 317
Darensbourg, Joe, 82
Dark Laughter, 116
Darrell, R. D., 122
"Davenport Blues," 78
Davenport Chronicle, 68
Davis, Eddie "Lockjaw," 204, 247, 293
Davis, Francis, 352
Davis, Miles, 57, 169, 202, 202n6, 205,
    207–9, 209n10, 215, 225, 230, 234, 270,
    273, 293, 297, 298, 298n22, 303, 305–6,
    326–28, 334–35, 348, 351, 352
    cool jazz and, 256–58, 256n1, 257n3,
        267–72, 267n6
    performance at Newport Jazz
        Festival, 268
"Daydream," 172
A Day in the Life, 296
"Dead Man Blues," 40
Dean, James, 73
Death and Transfiguration, 298
"Deception," 258
Dee Gee (record label), 212
"Deep Purple," 140
DeFranco, Buddy, 239
DeJohnette, Jack, 285, 339
de Koenigswarter, Baroness Pannonica,
    214, 227
Delaunay, Charles, 159
"Delilah," 287
Delta blues, 13, 14
Deluxe Melody Boys, the, 149
Derivations for Clarinet and Band, 129
"Desafinado," 261

DeSare, Tony, 375
"Descent into the Maelstrom," 231, 310
Desmond, Paul, 235, 256, 266, 362
Detroit Creative Musicians Association, the, 358
"Detroit style," 221
"Devil's Holiday," 108
"Dewey Square," 210
"Dexterity," 210
Dial (record label), 202–203, 210
Dialogue, 297
Dickerson, Carroll, 61–62
"Dickie's Dream," 164
"Dicty Blues," 106
"Digression," 310
"Diminuendo and Crescendo in Blue," 170–71, 181
"Dipper Mouth Blues," 48–49
disintermediation, 370–71
Dixieland, 254
"Dixieland Band, The," 134
Dixie Syncopators, 50
"Dizzy Atmosphere," 201, 207
"Django," 260
"Djangology," 161
Dodds, Warren "Baby," 31, 41, 43
Dodds, Charles, 14
Dodds, Johnny, 41, 43, 46, 58, 60
Dodds, Julia Major, 14
Doggett, Bill, 294
"Doggin' Around," 153
Dollison, Julia, 376
Dolphy, Eric, 280–82, 292, 301
"Donna Lee," 188, 207, 209, 330
"Do Nothin' till You Hear from Me," 179
"Don't Blame Me," 135
"Don't Explain," 168
"Don't Get Around Much Anymore," 178
"Don't Know Why," 374
"Don't Worry, Be Happy," 376
Dorham, Kenny, 207, 287–88
Dorsey, Jimmy, 83, 131, 137–39
Dorsey, Tommy, 83, 96, 131, 137–39, 195
dotted eighth note, 187
Douglas, Dave, 365, 370
Downbeat, 42, 145, 162, 190, 201, 225–26, 237, 243–44, 314, 319, 345
"Down Hearted Blues," 17
"Dream Lullaby," 108
Drew, Kenny, 221

"Drop Me Off in Harlem," 239
Drum(s), 11, 106, 133, 150, 196, 277
"Drum Boogie," 266
A Drum Is a Woman, 181
"Ducky Wucky," 121
Dudley, Bessie, 123
Dufty, Bill, 170
Duplicates, 143
Durham, Eddie, 124, 151–52
"Dusk," 175
Dusk, Matt, 375
Duster, 342
Dutrey, Honore, 46, 49
Dutrey, Sam, 47

"Early Autumn," 242, 260
"Early Every Morn," 55
Early to Bed, 96
East Coasting, 299
"East Saint Louis Toodle-oo," 114
"Eat That Chicken," 301
Ebony Concerto, 238, 241, 311
Eckstine, Billy, 64, 192, 198–99, 203, 238, 288
ECM (record label), 338–39, 342
Eddie "Lockjaw" Davis, 363
Edison, Harry "Sweets," 154, 169
Ed Sullivan Show, The, 139
Edwards, Altevia, 220
Edwards, Eddie, 36
Edwards, Teddy, 163, 262
Eicher, Manfred, 338
Eldridge, Roy, 64, 99, 102, 105, 109, 140, 163, 195–97, 212, 345
Elektra (record label), 364
Elias, Eliane, 276
Ella Fitzgerald Sings the Cole Porter Songbook, 346
Elling, Kurt, 375
Ellington, Daisy Kennedy, 111
Ellington, Duke, 25, 40, 56, 66, 84, 90, 92, 93, 95, 99–100, 102, 119–21, 123, 125, 128, 130, 146, 163, 189, 206, 216, 229, 232, 239, 278, 338, 345, 346 (see also Swing Era)
  early career, 110–16
  famous recordings, 174–75
  health problems, 182–83
  middle period and later works, 170–83
  performances, 171–72

Ellington, James Edward, 111
"Ellington sound," 115
Ellis, Dave, 380
Ellison, Ralph, 63, 144
Elman, Ziggy, 141
"Embraceable You," 210
"Emotion Modulation," 316
Empty Foxhole, The, 317
Empyrean Isles, 304
Encyclopedia of Jazz, 100
"end of ideology," 377
"Epistrophy," 224
Eps, George Van, 133
Escalator over the Hill, 359
Eubanks, Robin, 380
Europe, James Reese, 36, 101, 117, 159
European jazz record labels, 381
"Evanescence," 250
Evans, Bill, 219, 221, 271–76, 348, 351,
   372, 377
Evans, Doc, 201
Evans, Gil, 256, 257, 270, 281, 295
Evans, Herschel, 153, 180
Evans, Stump, 104
"Every Day I Have the Blues," 248
Excelsior Brass Band, 31
Ezz-thetics, 281

Fabulous Dorseys, The, 237
Facebook, 370
Facing You, 340, 384
Fagan, Sadie, 167
"Fantasy on Frankie and Johnny," 234
Farlow, Tal, 80, 299
"Father Time," 350
Favors, Malachi, 360–61
Fazola, Irving, 137
Feather, Leonard, 76, 100, 190,
   221*n*15, 238, 238*n*20
"Feelin' No Pain," 77
Feels So Good, 337
Feets Don't Fail Me Now, 328
Feldman, Victor, 273
Ferguson, Maynard, 65
"Fields of Gold," 375
50 Hot Choruses for the Cornet, 58
Fifty-second Street, 200
"52nd Street Theme," 187, 266, 378
"50 Ways to Leave Your Lover," 372
Filles de Kilimanjaro, 306

Fillmore, John Comfort, 10
Finale, 370
"Fine and Mellow," 169
Finegan, Bill, 248
"A Fine Romance," 167
"Finger Buster," 40
Firestone, Ross, 238*n*21
First Herd, 241
First Light, 291
"First Night, The," 249
Fitzgerald, Ella, 64, 66, 109, 125, 165, 346
Fitzgerald, F. Scott, 38
Five Peace Band, 329
"Flamenco Sketches," 273
Flanagan, Tommy, 221, 276, 285, 346
Fleck, Béla, 380
"A Flower Is a Lovesome Thing," 172
Floyd, Samuel, 4
Floyd, Troy, 149
"Flying Home," 144
"Flyin' Hawk," 222
"A Foggy Day," 351
"Foolin' Myself," 165, 168
For Alto, 362
Ford, Ricky, 355
"For Dancers Only," 124
"Fort Worth," 378
Foster, Al, 285
Foster, George "Pops," 28, 29, 173
Foster, Stephen, 8
"Four in One," 223
Fournier, Vernel, 235
"Four on Six," 296
Four Saints in Three Acts, 117
Fox, The, 228
"Fran Dance," 272
Frank, Waldo, 116
Franklin, Rodney, 380
"Frank Speaking," 246
Fraser, Al, 194*nn*2,3, 206*n*8
Freedom Suite, 283, 284
free jazz, 309–25
Free Jazz, 281, 291
Freelon, Nnenna, 376
Freeman, Bud, 74–77, 131, 255
Freeman, Richard, 202
French Opera House, 32
"Frenesi," 139
"Frère Jacques," 373
Friedwald, Will, 246*n*26

Frisell, Bill, 365
"Froggie Moore," 40, 49
"Fruit, The," 219
"Fugue," 311
"Fugueaditti," 178
Fuller, Curtis, 291
Fuller, Gil, 205
"Funeral March," 114
"Funky Butt"
fusion, 325–38
   classical, Keith Jarrett and, 338–43
   types of, 326
Future Shock, 333

Gable, Clark, 73
Gambarini, Roberta, 375
Garland, Red, 269
Garner, Erroll, 232, 234, 288
Garrett, Kenny, 376, 379
Garrison, Arv, 202
Gazarek, Sara, 376
Gee, Jack, 19
Gelpi, Rene, 35
Gene Lees Jazzletter, 275n11
Genovese, Eugene, 11
genres of music, 8
Gershwin, George, 85, 99, 160,
   196, 222, 237
Gershwin, Ira, 346
Getz, Stan, 147, 204, 212, 242, 256,
   260–62, 347
Getz/Gilberto, 261
ghost bands, 180, 355
Giant Steps, 271, 276, 280
Gibson, Andy, 239
Giddins, Gary, 46, 54, 182, 260, 361
Gifford, Gene, 136
Gil, Gilberto, 388
Gilberto, João, 261–62
Gillespie, John Birks "Dizzy," 64, 80,
   140–41, 143, 162, 188, 189,
   193–207, 194nn2,3, 206n8, 212,
   225, 238, 259, 345, 346, 377
Gilmore, John, 247, 269
"Gimme a Pigfoot," 19
Gioia, Ted, 314n5
"Girl from Ipanema, The," 261
Gitler, Ira, 225, 225n17, 291n19
Giuffre, Jimmy, 242, 311
Glamoured, 335

Glaser, Joe, 65, 66, 128, 154
Glasgow Suite, 109
globalization of jazz, 380–88
"Gloria's Step," 274
"God Bless the Child," 168
Goffin, Robert, 84, 159, 382
Goldberg, Joe, 311n2
Goldberg Variations, The, 341, 367
Golden, Bob, 278n13
"Golden Striker, The," 260
Goldkette, Jean, 81, 83–84, 136, 138
"Go 'Long Mule," 105
Golson, Benny, 289–90
Gomez, Eddie, 275
Gonsalves, Paul, 179, 181, 182, 363
"Goodbye," 134
"Goodbye Pork Pie Hat," 300, 348
"Good Earth, The," 241
Goodman, Benny, 18, 25, 37, 41, 62, 72–73,
   75, 77, 79–80, 100, 102, 117, 128–33,
   186, 189, 197, 201, 237–238, 242, 274,
   345 (see also Swing Era)
   Carnegie Hall concert, 251
   early life, 129–30
   Fletcher Henderson relationship to,
     132–33, 135
   professional career, 130–32
Goodman, David, 129, 130
Good Morning Blues, 151, 155
"Good Morning Heartache," 168
"Good Vibes," 109
Gordon, Dexter, 163, 189–90, 201, 220,
   262, 347
Gordon, Wycliffe, 380
Gorelick, Kenneth, 337
Gott, Tommy, 85
Gottschalk, Louis Moreau, 6
Gough, Phil, 166
Gould, Morton, 129
Gourse, Leslie, 64
Grainger, Percy, 122
Grammy awards. 349
Grand Opera House, 32
"Grandpa's Spells," 40
Grand Terrace, 198
Grant, Henry, 112
Granz, Norman, 98, 109, 165, 169, 203,
   211–12, 219, 346
   Carnegie Hall concert, 232
   Pablo label, 346

Grappelli, Stéphane, 160–61, 345, 382
Gray, Glen, 136
Gray, Wardell, 147, 189, 203, 238, 262
"Great Black Music—Ancient
    to Modern," 360
Great Depression, 67
    effects on jazz, 127
"Greatest Jazz Concert Ever, The," 214
"Great James Robbery," 179
Green, Benny, 380
Green, Freddie, 155, 180
Green, Grant, 295
Greer, Sonny, 83, 112, 152, 175, 179
Grenadier, Larry, 372
Gress, Drew, 380
"Grievin,'" 172
Griffin, Johnny, 289, 293
griots, 185
Grofé, Ferde, 85–86, 100, 105
"Groovin' High," 201
A Guest of Honor, 24
Guitar Forms, 295
guitar, 144, 160, 385
Gullin, Lars, 383
Gunn, Jimmy, 148
"Gut Bucket Blues," 59
"Gypsy, The," 266
Gypsy jazz, 160
"A Gypsy without a Song," 171

habañera rhythm, 206
Hackett, Bobby, 65, 255
Hadlock, Richard, 48, 58
Haig, Al, 221
"Haitian Fight Song," 300
"Half-Mast Inhibition," 299
Hall, Adelaide, 115
Hall, Edmond, 255
Hall, Jim, 275, 285, 366, 371
"Halls of Brass," 245
"Hallucinations," 219
Hamilton, Chico, 280
Hamilton, Jimmy, 182
Hammond, John, 75, 128, 131, 142,
    144–45, 154, 167, 177, 275, 294
Hampton, Lionel, 141, 197, 259, 315, 377
Hancock, Herbie, 275, 304, 328, 347,
    349, 379
"Handful of Keys," 98
Handy, Craig, 380

Handy, George, 238
Handy, W. C., 12, 13, 18, 34, 161
    as father of the blues, 18
Happy Black Aces, the, 149
hard bop, 285–307
"Hard Hearted Hannah," 85
Hardin, Lil, 49, 57, 58
Hardwick, Otto, 112, 176
Hardy, Emmett, 35, 45
Hardymon, Phil, 380
Hargrove, Roy, 377–78
Harlem
    birth of the big band, 100–110
    boogie-woogie, 91, 96–97
    Cotton Club, the, 116–25
    cultures, 91
    Duke Ellington's early career, 110–16
    Harlem Renaissance, 89–91
    low wages in, 90
    second Harlem, 90
    stride piano, 91–93, 96–97
    Waller, Fats, 94–96
"Harlem Air Shaft," 175
"Harlem Rag," 20–21
Harlem Renaissance, 89–90, 116
Harlem Symphony, 92–93
"harmolodic theory," 317
Harney, Ben, 21
Harrell, Tom, 347, 355, 377
Harris, Barry, 221
Harris, Bill, 240, 243
Harris, Benny, 198, 199
Harris, Stefon, 380
Harrison, Donald, 354
Harrison, Jimmy, 102
Hartman, Johnny, 278
Hartwell, Jimmy, 69
Hasselgard, Stan, 147
"Have You Met Miss Jones?," 276
"Hawaiian War Chant," 138
Hawes, Hampton, 221, 262
Hawkins, Coleman, 16, 18, 54, 55, 77, 82,
    84, 102, 104, 107–9, 118, 131, 140, 141,
    157–63, 169, 189, 193, 197, 201, 210,
    220, 222, 269, 282, 347, 348, 362
Hayden, Scott, 22
Haydn Trumpet Concerto, 349
Hayes, Rutherford, 33
Haynes, Roy, 224
Head Hunters, 328

"Heaven," 182

Heavy Weather, 330

"Heckler's Hop," 140

"Heebie Jeebies," 59

Hefti, Neal, 239, 240

Heifetz, Jascha, 213

Heisenberg, Werner, 107

"Hello Dolly," 66

"Hello Lola," 77

Hemphill, Julius, 360, 364

Henderson, Fletcher, 18, 41, 54, 57, 83,
    100–103, 105–8, 125, 130, 132–33,
    135, 140, 159, 161, 174, 246, 288,
    292–93, 345

Henderson, Horace, 132

Henderson, Joe, 291

Hendricks, Jon, 348

Hendrix, Jimi, 14

Hentoff, Nat, 76, 82, 208*n*9, 244*n*25,
    313*n*4, 318, 318*n*8

Herbert, Victor, 85

Herds, Herman, 240–44

Herman, Woody, 80, 147, 238, 239–40

Herring, Vincent, 216

Hersch, Fred, 276

"He's Funny That Way," 168

"Hesitation," 350

Hickman, Art, 100, 105

Hi De Ho Club, 203

Higginbotham, J. C., 102

Higgins, Billy, 313

"High Society," 46, 55

Hilaire, Andrew, 41

Hill, Andrew, 281, 297, 373

Hill, Teddy, 195, 196

Hillcrest band, 313

Hindemith, Paul, 129, 143

Hines, Earl Kenneth, 61–62, 66, 71, 92,
    189, 198, 199, 216, 237, 238, 255, 345
    orchestra, 199
    "Weather Bird," 62–63

Hite, Les, 148

Hodeir, André, 99

Hodges, Johnny, 107, 119, 124, 141, 171,
    173, 176, 179, 181, 193, 225, 269, 278

Holiday, 116

Holiday, Billie, 64, 80, 140, 154, 165–70,
    210, 348
    early life, 166–67
    health problems, 169–70

as jazz singer, 169
    professional career, 167–68
    work of, 168

Holland, Dave, 366, 379

Holman, Bill, 245

Homecoming, 347

"Honeysuckle Rose," 95, 192

"Honky Tonk Train Blues," 96

Hopkins, Fred, 360

Hot Chocolates, 63, 118, 122

Hot Fives and Hot Sevens, 53–54,
    57–66, 175

"Hot House," 205

Hot House Flowers, 350

Hot Jazz: The Guide to Swing Music, 362

"Hot Mallets," 197

Hot Sevens, 57–66

"Hotter Than That," 60

House, Son, 18, 49

Howard, Paul, 148

"How Come You Do Me Like
    You Do?," 105

"How Deep Is the Ocean," 350

"How High the Moon," 187

Hubbard, Freddie, 290–91, 377

Hub-Tones, 291

Hudson, Will, 124

Huizinga, Johan, 11

Humes, Helen, 154

"Hunt, The," 189

Hunter, Alberta, 56

Hurok, Sol, 234

Hurst, Robert, 351

Hutcherson, Bobby, 276

Hylton, Jack, 159

"Hymn, The," 210

Ibrahim, Abdullah, 388

"I Can't Believe That You're in Love with
    Me," 140

"I Can't Get Started," 132, 229

"I Can't Give You Anything but Love," 63,
    158, 167, 210

"I Cover the Waterfront," 168

"I Cried for You," 167

"I Found a New Baby," 56

"If You Could See Me Now," 205

"I Get a Kick Out of You," 286

Igoe, Sonny, 243

"Igor," 238

"I Got It Bad (and That Ain't Good)," 246
"I Got Rhythm," 136, 187, 188, 198, 202, 314, 350
"I Gotta Right to Sing the Blues," 79, 131
"I Know That You Know," 99, 212
"I'll Build a Stairway to Paradise," 85
"I'll Keep Loving You," 219
"I'll Never Miss the Sunshine," 82
"I'll Never Smile Again," 138
"I'll See You in My Dreams," 54
"I'm Comin' Virginia," 81, 82
In Abyssinia, 116
"In a Mist," 80, 86
"In a Sentimental Mood," 122, 171, 278
In a Silent Way, 306
In Dahomey, 116
"Indiana," 188
"In Front," 340
In Search of Buddy Bolden, First Man of Jazz, 33
Inside Bebop, 221
instrument, defined, 10
instrumentation of bebop, 187–88
International Association for Jazz Education, 355
International Sweethearts of Rhythm, 156
In the Light, 341
"In the Mood," 146
In This House, on This Morning, 352
"Intuition," 310
Irvis, Charlie, 113
"Isfahan," 182
"I Should Care," 225
"Israel," 258
Israels, Chuck, 348
"It Don't Mean a Thing (If It Ain't Got That Swing)," 122
"I Thought About You," 192
"I've Got a Gal in Kalamazoo," 146
Iverson, Ethan, 94
"I Want to Be Happy," 141

Jack Johnson, 327
Jackson, Dewey, 148
Jackson, Greig "Chubby," 240
Jackson, Mahalia, 288
Jackson, Marion, 155
Jackson, Michael, 166
Jackson, Milt, 259, 268, 346

Jackson, Preston, 44
Jackson, Ronald Shannon, 317
"Jack the Bear," 174
Jacquet, Illinois, 312
Jamal, Ahmad, 219, 221, 232, 234–35
James, Harry, 79, 141, 179
"Jam Session," 141
Janis, Harriet, 25
"Japanese Sandman," 85
Jarman, Joseph, 358, 360
Jarrett, Keith, 338–43
jazz
  acid, 333
  and African music, 185
  contemporary, 237
  cool, 242, 253–67
  as forward-looking art, 185
  free, 309–25
  fusion, 325–38
  globalization of, 380–88
  landscape of, 200
  modern (*see* bebop)
  paradoxical foundation for, 186
  with popular music, 165
  vs. ragtime, 20
  soul, 285–307
  styles, fragmentation of, 253–307
  technological revolution and, 370
  tempos, 188
  trad, 253–67
  in transition, 267–85
  virtual, 369–80
  West Coast, 263–64
Jazz Age, 39, 53–57, 100, 118, 355
  Bix Beiderbecke and, 66–71
  Chicago and New York, 71–80
"jazz fugues," 178
Jazzical Moods, 299
jazz manouche, 160
Jazz Masters of the '50s, 311n2
Jazzmatazz, 334
Jazz Messengers, 288–90, 350
"Jazzocracy," 124
Jazzola Novelty Orchestra, 35
"jazz operas," 178
Jazz Singer, The, 73
Jazz Yatra festival, 386
"Jeep's Blues," 171
Jefferson, Blind Lemon, 13, 15, 149
Jefferson, Carl, 347

Jefferson, Eddie, 348
"Jelly Jelly," 199
"Jelly Roll," 300
Jelly's Last Jam, 43
Jenkins, Freddy, 77
Jenkins, Gordon, 132, 134
"Jeru," 258
jitterbug, 117
"Jitterbug Waltz," 95
J Mood, 350, 351
Jobim, Antonio Carlos, 261, 293
Johansson, Jan, 383
Johnson, Blind Willie, 149
Johnson, Budd, 82, 198
Johnson, George, 69
Johnson, J. J., 210, 260, 354
Johnson, James P., 18, 25, 61, 91–94,
    98, 112, 152
Johnson, James Weldon, 91, 116
Johnson, Marc, 275
Johnson, Pete, 96, 153
Johnson, Robert, 14–15, 18, 50
Johnson, Willie "Bunk," 35, 36, 254, 255
Jolson, Al, 50, 59, 129
Jones, Elvin, 266, 277, 293, 295
Jones, Hank, 221
Jones, Isham, 239
Jones, Jo, 150, 153, 189, 191
Jones, LeRoi. *See* Baraka, Amiri
Jones, Norah, 373, 374
Jones, Philly Joe, 269
Jones, Tad, 46
Jones, Thad, 247, 249
Joplin, Florence Givens, 22
Joplin, Jiles, 22
Joplin, Scott, 73, 91, 92, 150, 190,
    206, 360
    awards, 25
    compositional techniques, 23–24
    controversies, 24
    death of, 24–25
    history and background, 22–23
    "Maple Leaf Rag" by, 23
    as a pianist, 23
    and ragtime music, 20–25
    Treemonisha, 24
Jordan, Duke, 209, 287
Jordan, Marlon, 354
Jordan, Sheila, 348
"Jordu," 287

Josephson, Barney, 168
Jost, Ekkehard, 310
"Joy Spring," 287
Jump for Joy, 176
"Jumpin' Blues, The," 192
"Just a Mood," 108
"Just Friends," 212
"Just the Two of Us," 337

kalangu, 9
Kaminsky, Max, 62, 255
Kansas city jazz, 147–56 (*see also*
    Swing Era)
Katz, Mickey, 367
"Keep a Song in Your Soul," 108
Keepnews, Orrin, 223, 223*n*16, 227
Kelley, Peck, 79
Kelly, Wynton, 169, 273
Kenney, William Howland, 71
Kenton, Audree Coke, 240*n*24
Kenton, Stan, 25, 147, 214, 237, 242,
    244–46, 246*n*26, 310, 377
Keppard, Freddie, 35, 36, 43, 45, 53, 55,
    71, 100, 110
Kern, Jerome, 346
"Kerry Dance, The," 99
Khan, Ali Akbar, 386
"Kickin' the Cat," 77
Kid from Red Bank, The, 152
Killian, Al, 239
Kincaide, Deane, 132
Kind of Blue, 272, 273, 276, 356
King, Billy, 151
"King of Jazz," 73
"King of Swing, the," 127–36
"King of the Clarinet, the," 139
"King Porter Stomp," 41, 62, 132, 134, 196
Kirby, John, 173, 195
Kirk, Andy, 155, 158, 174
Kirk, Rahsaan Roland, 301
Kirkland, Kenny, 352
"Klactoveedsedstene," 313
Kloss, Eric, 355
"Knockin' a Jug," 79
Koenig, Les, 313–14
Kofsky, Frank, 310
"Ko Ko," 188, 201, 209, 210
Köln Concert, 340
Konitz, Lee, 229–31, 246, 257, 362, 366
koto, 280

Krall, Diana, 373, 374
Krehbiel, Henry Edward, 10
Krell, William, 20
Krupa, Gene, 73, 75, 80, 131, 133–34, 140, 142
Kuehl, Linda, 166
Kuhn, Steve, 342, 348, 355
Kulu Se Mama, 322

Labba, Abba, 94
Lacy, Steve, 279, 359
Ladnier, Tommy, 56, 102
Lady Sings the Blues, 166
LaFaro, Scott, 273–74
"La Fiesta," 329
Lage, Julian, 380
Laine, Papa Jack, 35
Lake, Oliver, 360, 364
Lake Forest Academy, 68–69
Lamb, Joseph, 22, 24, 92
Lambert, Donald, 94
Land, Harold, 228, 263, 287
Lang, Eddie, 72, 81, 83–85, 131
LaRocca, Nick, 35–37, 68
Laswell, Bill, 335
Latin-Catholic culture, 6
"La Tristesse de Saint Louis," 161
Latrobe, Benjamin, 3
LaVerne, Andy, 276
Lawson, John "Yank," 137
"Lazy Afternoon," 108, 319
LeBlanc, Dan, 35
Lees, Gene, 100, 232, 275
Le Jazz Hot, 159
Lennon, John, 166
"Lester Leaps In," 164
"Lester Left Town," 291
Let Freedom Ring, 297
"Let Me Off Uptown," 140
Let's Dance, 132, 134
Levin, Robert, 281n14
Levy, John, 168
Lewis, David Levering, 90
Lewis, George, 254, 347, 358
Lewis, John, 221, 257, 258, 260, 281
Lewis, Meade Lux, 96, 222
Lieb, Sandra, 16
"Liebestraum," 85
Liebman, Dave, 378
Lighthouse, The, 263

Lighthouse All Stars, 243, 285
"Li'l Darlin'," 247
"Limehouse Blues," 161
Lincoln Center Orchestra, 353
Lincoln Gardens, 71
Lind, Jenny, 31
Lindsay, John, 41
"Line for Lyons," 264
"Line Up," 231
Lins, Ivan, 388
Lion, Alfred, 219, 222
Lippman, Joe, 132
Litweiler, John, 323, 323n13
Live at Blues Alley, 350, 351
Live at the Trident, 275
Live-Evil, 327
"Livery Stable Blues," 36
Livingston, Fud, 132
Lloyd, Charles, 366
"Loch Lomond," 96
Locke, Alain, 116
Locke, Joe, 380
Lomax, Alan, 4, 8, 37, 42
Lomax, John, 4
"London Suite," 96
London Symphony Orchestra, 317
"Lonesome Nights," 108
Lopez, Vincent, 105
"Lost in Meditation," 171
"Lotus Blossom," 172
Louis Armstrong Park, 3
Louis' Children, 64
"Louisiana Swing," 64
Lovano, Joe, 366, 377, 378
Love Call, 297
"Love for Sale," 272
"Love Is a Many-Splendored Thing," 286
"Lover Man," 168, 202–3
Low End Theory, The, 334
Lowery, Robert, 286
"Lullaby of Birdland," 233
"Lullaby of the Leaves," 264
Luminessence, 341
Lunceford, Jimmie, 123–25
"Lush Life," 172, 278
Luter, Claude, 255
Lynch, Brian, 371

MacDonald, Julie, 213
Madden, Owney, 118

Magician, 234
"Magnetic Rag," 23
Mahavishnu Orchestra, 329, 336
Mahogany, Kevin, 376
Maiden Voyage, 304
"Main Stem," 176
Majesty of the Blues, The, 351, 352
Makowicz, Adam, 355
Malneck, Matty, 86, 105
"Mandy Make Up Your Mind," 54
Mangione, Chuck, 337
Manhattan Transfer, 348
"Maniac's Ball," 136
"Man I Love, The," 224
Manne, Shelly, 224, 284, 285
"Manteca," 206
"Maple Leaf Rag," 20, 23, 56, 92
Marable, Fate, 41, 47
Marcuse, Herbert, 322
Mares, Paul, 44
Mariano, Charles, 245
"Marie," 138
Marinoff, Fania, 19
Marmarosa, Michael "Dodo," 202, 203, 221, 239
Marquis, Donald, 33, 39
Marsalis, Branford, 285, 350, 354
Marsalis, Delfeayo, 354
Marsalis, Ellis, 352
Marsalis, Wynton, 25, 291, 345, 347, 349–54, 355, 357, 376
    Grammy awards, 349
    Pulitzer Prize, 353
Marsalis Standard Time, Vol. 1, 350, 351
Marsh, Warne, 230, 362
Marshall, Arthur, 22
Martel, Charles, 5
Martin, Billy, 336
"Mary's Idea," 156
Masekela, Hugh, 388
"Masque of the Red Death, The," 28
Matador, 295
Matthews, Artie, 22
Matthews, Bill, 34
M-Base Collective, 335
McCall, Steve, 360
McCandless, Paul, 341
McCulloch, Bill, 14
McFerrin, Bobby, 348, 375–76
McGarry, Kate, 376

McGregor, Chris, 388
McGriff, Jimmy, 294
McKenna, Dave, 243
McKibbon, Al, 206
McKinney's Cotton Pickers, 107, 148, 345
McLaughlin, John, 329, 386
McLean, Jackie, 169, 215, 289, 347
McMillan, Vic, 202
McNeely, Jim, 276
McPartland, Jimmy, 74, 75, 255
McPartland, Marian, 371, 382
McRae, Carmen, 348
McShann, Jay, 153, 191, 192
"Me, Myself and I Are All in Love with You," 168
"Mean to Me," 165, 168
Medeski, John, 295, 336
Meditation, 279, 322
Meet the Jazztet, 290
Mehldau, Brad, 372–73
Melody Maker, 123, 159, 167
"Memphis Blues," 18
Meola, Al Di, 328
Mercer, Johnny, 346
"Mercy, Mercy, Mercy," 329
"Merry Widow Waltz," 85
Metheny, Pat, 330–31
Metronome, 16, 21, 154, 281n14
"Metropolis," 85
Mezzrow, Mezz, 70
Midnight Blue, 295
Miles Ahead, 270
Miles From India, 386
Miles in the Sky, 328
Milestones, 271, 272, 274, 278
Miley, James "Bubber," 113–14, 121, 131, 351
Milhaud, Darius, 235
Miller, Annette, 64
Miller, Eddie, 137
Miller, Glenn, 79, 145–47
Mills, Irving, 128
Mingus, Charles, 25, 80, 173, 180, 200, 203, 214, 214n12, 281, 297–303, 345, 348, 364
Mingus Ah Um, 299, 300, 356
Mingus at Monterey, 302
Mingus Moves, 303
"Minnie the Moocher," 122
"Minor Drag," 74

"Minor Swing," 161

Minton's Playhouse, 218

"Mississippi Rag," 20

"Mississippi Suite," 85

"Misty," 234

Mitchell, George, 40, 41

Mitchell, Joni, 348

Mitchell, Red, 173, 313

Mitchell, Roscoe, 358, 360

MJQ. *See* Modern Jazz Quartet (MJQ)

Moanin', 289

Mobley, Hank, 288

modern jazz. *See* bebop

Modern Jazz Quartet (MJQ), 256, 259–60

Moeketsi, Kippie, 388

moldy fig, 256

Mole, Miff, 77–78, 83, 255

"Moment's Notice," 271

Monder, Ben, 380

"Money Blues," 105

Monheit, Jane, 375

Monk, Thelonious, 77, 153, 162,
  187–90, 197–98, 212, 218,
  221–28, 232, 268, 270, 274, 277,
  288–89, 363, 366, 373

Monroe, Clark, 198

Monroe, Jimmy, 168

Monroe, Marilyn, 166

Monroe's Uptown House, 198, 200

Monterey Jazz Festival, 314

Montgomery, Buddy, 295–96

Montgomery, Monk, 295–96

Montgomery, Wes, 295

Montoliu, Tete, 347

"Mood Indigo," 114–15, 122, 178

MoodSwing, 378

"Moon Dreams," 258

"Moonlight Fiesta," 121

"Moonlight in Vermont," 260

"Moonlight Serenade," 146

Moonlight Sonata, 146

Moore, Brew, 165

Moore, Glen, 341

"Moors, The," 342

"Moose, The," 239

"Moose the Mooche," 202

Moran, Jason, 366

Morello, Joe, 236

Morgan, Al, 173

Morgan, Frank, 262

Morgan, Sam, 43

Morrison, Alan, 220n14

Morton, Benny, 102

Morton, Jelly Roll, 6, 20, 30, 34–44, 59, 61,
  62, 71, 92, 115, 127, 205, 254, 387

Mosby, Curtis, 148

Moten, Bennie, 150, 152, 174

"Moten Swing," 151

Motian, Paul, 274

"Mount Harissa," 181

Moye, Don, 361

Mulligan, Gerry, 77, 245, 256–58, 263,
  264, 345

Mundy, Jimmy, 132, 198

Murphy, Melvin "Turk," 255

Murphy, Spud, 132

Murray, Albert, 352

Murray, David, 359, 363–64, 380

Murray, Don, 83

Murray, James "Sunny," 319, 324, 343

Muse (record label), 347

Music Is My Mistress, 111, 181

"Muskrat Ramble," 130

Musso, Vido, 141

"My Blue Heaven," 124

Myers, Marc, 336n115

"My Favorite Things," 276, 278

"My Foolish Heart," 274

"My Funny Valentine," 264

"My Heart," 59

"My Man's Gone Now," 274

"My One and Only Love," 278

"My Romance," 339

MySpace, 370

"Naima," 276

Naked City, 365

Nanton, Tricky Sam, 113, 176

Nascimento, Milton, 388

National Association of Jazz, 355

National Jazz Ensemble, 348

Native Dancer, 330

"Native or long time Harlemites," 91

Navarro, Theodore "Fats," 204, 238

Neidlinger, Buell, 319n10

Nelsen, Don, 273n10

Nelson, Louis, 55

Nelson, Oliver, 281

Nelson, Willie, 353, 374

Nelson Steve, 380

Nesbitt, John, 107
Netto, Frank, 35
"Never Let Me Go," 275
"Never No Lament," 178
New Grass, 324
Newman, David "Fathead," 312
Newman, Jerry, 99, 198, 222
Newman, Joe, 169
New Negro, The, 116
New Orleans, 254–55
New Orleans, 66
New Orleans jazz
    Armstrong, Louis, 46–51
    black Creole culture, 32
    Bolden, Buddy, 33–37
    brass bands, 31
    city in decline, 27–32
    diaspora, 43–46
    mortality rates, 28
    Morton, Jelly Roll, 37–43
    Oliver, King, 45–51
    opening of theaters, 31–32
    spasm bands, 30
    Storyville, as birthplace of jazz music,
        29–30
    Swing Era, 137
"New Orleans Memories," 42
New Orleans Owls, 35
New Orleans Philharmonic, 349
New Orleans Rhythm Kings, 41,
    44–45, 55, 69, 74, 75, 79
Newport Jazz Festival, 319
"New San Antonio Rose," 149
New Testament band, 180
"new traditionalism," 336
New Tristano, The, 231
"New World A' Coming," 177
New York 71–80, 200
New York Herald Tribune, 176
New York is Now!, 317
New York Jazz Repertory
    Company, 348–49
New York Times, The, 63, 182
"Nice Work if You Can Get It," 222
Nichols, Ernest "Red," 77, 83
Nichols, Herbie, 228, 356
Nicholson, Jack, 376
Nicholson, Stuart, 166, 167
Nigger Heaven, 116
"Nightfall," 108, 109

"A Night in Tunisia," 188, 199, 202
"Night Life," 155
Noone, Jimmie, 43, 62, 71, 130, 198
Norman, Gene, 285
Norris, Walter, 314
"Northwest Passage," 241
Norvo, Red, 80, 141, 299
Now He Sings, Now He Sobs, 328
"Now's the Time," 201
"Now They Call It Swing," 168
"Nuages," 161
"Nutty," 226

O'Day, Anita, 64
ODJB. *See* Original Dixieland Jazz Band
    (ODJB)
"Oh, Lady Be Good," 154, 192, 212
Oliver, Joe "King," 35, 41, 43–55, 58–59,
    62, 67, 71, 82, 105, 110, 113, 127, 186,
    294, 351
    Age of the Soloist, 53–54, 55
Oliver, Sy, 124, 138–39
Om, 322
O'Meally, Robert, 166
"Once upon a Time," 108
"One Hour," 77, 158, 210
"One O'Clock Jump," 153, 155
"On Green Dolphin Street," 272
On the Corner, 327
Onward Brass Band, 31, 45
Onyx Club, 200
"Opus One," 138
Orange Blossoms, 136
Orchestra, The, 248
"Organ Grinder's Swing," 124, 266
"Oriental Strut," 59
Original Creole Orchestra, 71, 100
Original Dixieland Jazz Band (ODJB),
    36–37, 44, 68, 101
Orkester Journalen, 382
Ornette!, 316
Ornette on Tenor, 316
"Ornithology," 187, 192, 202
Ory, Edward "Kid," 30, 35, 41, 43, 47, 58,
    78, 254, 299
Osby, Greg, 335, 366
"Out of Nowhere," 314
Out to Lunch, 281, 297
"Over the Rainbow," 375
Ozone, Makoto, 386

Pablo (record label), 212, 346, 347
Pace, Harry, 102
Pace-Handy Music Company, 102
Page, Oran "Hot Lips," 140, 152–54
Page, Walter, 150, 153, 157, 173, 189, 191
Paich, Marty, 348
Paige, Billy, 103
"Panama," 44
Panassié, Hugues, 159
Pangaea, 327
Panthalassa: The Music of Miles Davis 1969–1974, 335
Papalia, Russ, 35
"Pardon Me Pretty Baby," 108
Paris Blues, 151
"Parisian Thoroughfare," 287
Paris Impressions, 234
Paris jazz festival, 56
Parker, Addie, 191
Parker, Charlie, 54, 80, 97, 143, 163, 187–89, 191–94, 198, 200–3, 207, 210–14, 220, 238, 254, 257, 330, 348
Parker, Charles, Sr., 191
"Parker's Mood," 190, 211
Parlato, Gretchen, 376
Pascoal, Hermeto, 327
Pass, Joe, 346
"Passion Flower," 172
Pastorius, Jaco, 330
"Patricia," 266
Patton, Charley, 13–14, 15
Paudras, Francis, 220
Payton, Nicholas, 354, 376
Peacock, Gary, 324, 340
"Peanut Vendor, The," 206
Pearson, Barry Lee, 14
"Peckin'," 141
Pedersen, Niels-Henning Ørsted, 347, 383
Pendergast, Tom, 149, 155
"Pennies from Heaven," 138
"Pennsylvania 6–5000," 146
Pepper, Art, 245, 256, 265–66
Perez, Manuel, 45
Perfume Suite, The, 177
Perkins, Carl, 263, 265
Perlongo, Robert, 220n13
Peterson, Oscar, 66, 169, 221, 232–33, 346
Petit, Buddy, 45
Petrillo, James, 145–46
Petrucciani, Michel, 276

Pettiford, Oscar, 173, 198, 200, 239, 271
Peyroux, Madeleine, 376
Phillips, Flip, 169, 240
"Phryzzinian Man," 350
piano, 20, 61, 106, 134
    Harlem stride piano, 91–93, 96–97
    manufacture of, 21
    modern jazz, 216–36
    use in ragtime, 21
"Picasso," 163
Picasso, Pablo, 50
"Pickin' the Cabbage," 197
Pieranunzi, Enrico, 276
"Pine Apple Rag," 23
Pithecanthropus Erectus, 299
"Pitter Panther Patter," 176
Pizzarelli, John, 376
Poe, Edgar Allan, 28
"Poinciana," 232, 235
Poindexter, Norwood "Pony," 263
Point of Departure, 281, 297
Pollack, Ben, 79, 130, 137
Pompidou, Georges, 181
Ponomarev, Valery, 355
Pope, Bob, 148
Porgy and Bess, 196, 237, 270
Porter, Cole, 99, 348
Porter, Roy, 202, 263, 280
postmodernism, 367
postmodernists, 357–67
"Potato Head Blues," 60
Potter, Chris, 371, 379
Potter, Tommy, 209
Pound, Ezra, 302
Powell, Bud, 200, 204, 214, 216–20, 232, 277, 286
Powell, Mel, 132, 143–45
Powell, Richie, 277, 287
Pozo, Chano, 205, 206–7
"Preacher, The," 288
"Prelude to a Kiss," 115, 171
Presley, Elvis, 139, 166
"Pretty Road, The," 250
Prieto, Dafnis, 380
Prima, Louis, 64
"Prince of Wails," 151
Pullen, Don, 302
Punkt Jazz Festival, 370
Purdie, Bernard, 324
"Pussy Cat Dues," 300

"Pussy Willow," 172
"Pyramid," 121

Quiet Nights, 270
"Quiet Now," 275
"Quiet Please," 139
Quinichette, Paul, 169

Raeburn, Boyd, 238
Ragas, Henry, 36
"Ragtime Dance, The," 23
Rag Time Instructor, 21
ragtime music (see also blues music)
   compositional structure, 21
   vs. jazz, 20
   pianos use, 21
   publishing of, 91–92
   Scott Joplin and, 20–25
Rainey, Jimmy, 260
Rainey, Ma, 16–17, 19, 154
Rainey, Overton, 98
Rainey, Pa, 16
Ravel, Maurice, 272
"Ray, the," 141
Ready for Freddie, 291
Real Jazz, The, 382
"Reckless Blues," 18
Red Clay, 291
Redcross, Bob, 193
Red Hot Peppers, 39–41, 45
Redman, Dewey, 378
Redman, Don, 54, 64, 100, 102–8, 148
Redman, Joshua, 378–80
Reese, Lloyd, 280
Reeves, Dianne, 348, 376
Regina, Elis, 388
Reinhardt, Jean Baptiste "Django,"
   160–61, 382
Reisner, Robert, 191n1, 203n7, 213n11
"Relaxin' at Camarillo," 203
"Reminiscing in Tempo," 123, 170
Resolution of Romance, 352
Reuss, Alan, 133
Revue Romande, 54
Rezinsky, Dora, 129
Rhapsody in Blue, 85
Ribot, Marc, 380
Rich, Bernard "Buddy," 138–39, 212,
   219, 220
Richard, Johnny, 245

"Riding on a Blue Note," 171
ring shout, 4
"Riverboat Shuffle," 69
Rivers, Sam, 360, 364
Riverside (record label), 224, 226
Roach, Max, 153, 180, 200, 209, 218, 219,
   224, 257, 285–87
Roberts, John Storm, 10
Roberts, Luckey, 61
Roberts, Marcus, 352
Robertson, Alvin "Zue," 39
Robichaux, John, 32, 33
Robinson, Prince, 104
"Rockin' Chair," 140
Rodgers, Richard, 99, 264
Rodney, Red, 207
Rodrigo, Joaquin, 270
Rodriguez, Juan, 283n16
Rogers, Milton "Shorty," 238, 243
Roland, Gene, 242
"Roll 'Em," 141
Rollini, Adrian, 77, 81, 141
Rollins, Theodore "Sonny," 109, 163, 204,
   212, 261, 268, 274, 282–85, 282n15,
   287, 363
Roney, Wallace, 376
Roppolo, Leon, 44, 55
Rosenwinkel, Kurt, 371, 380
"Rose Room," 145
Ross, Alonzo, 148
Rossy, Jorge, 372
"Round Midnight," 162, 220, 224, 268
Rouse, Charlie, 227
Rowles, Jimmy, 147, 169
Royal, Ernie, 248
Royal, Marshall, 247
"Ruby My Dear," 222, 224
Rugolo, Pete, 245
rumba, 206
"Running Ragged," 84
Runyon, Damon, 94
Rush Hour, 378
Rushing, Jimmy, 152, 154
Russell, Bill, 29
Russell, Charles "Pee Wee," 70, 75–77, 79, 255
Russell, George, 206, 238, 271, 281
Russell, Luis, 64
Russell, Ross, 202
Russo, Bill, 229, 245, 246
Ruth, Babe, 50

"Saeta," 270
"Salt Peanuts," 196, 201
Sampson, Edgar, 124, 132
Sanders, Pharoah, 315
"Sandu," 287
Sargeant, Winthrop, 258, 258n5
"Satin Doll," 180
Satterfield, Tom, 86, 105
Sauter, Eddie, 80, 132, 143–44
Sauter-Finegan band, 248
Savoy (record label), 210, 211
Savoy Ballroom, 195, 196
Sax, Antoine-Joseph "Adolphe," 104
saxophone, 103–4, 106
Saxophone Colossus, 284
Sbarbaro, Tony, 36
Schneider, Maria, 250–51, 371
Schoepp, Franz, 130
"School Days," 212
Schuller, Gunther, 76, 99, 177–78,
    223, 229, 229n18, 239, 239n22,
    258, 281, 311, 315, 349
Schuur, Diane, 348, 376
Science Fiction, 317
Scott, James, 92
Scott, Raymond, 367
Scott, Tony, 271
"Scrapple from the Apple," 210
Second Herd, 241, 242, 243
"Secret Love," 339
"Sepian Bounce," 193
"Sepia Panorama," 175
"Serenade to Sweden," 172
"Sergeant Was Shy, The," 172
"Sermon, The," 294
"Seven Come Eleven," 144
Severinsen, Carl "Doc,," 248
"Shake Your Head," 124
"Shakin' the African," 64
"Shanghai Shuffle," 54
Shankar, Ravi, 386
Shape of Jazz to Come, The, 314
Sharpe, Eddie, 86
Shavers, Charlie, 169
Shaw, Artie, 139–40, 168, 237, 347
Shaw, Ian, 376
Shaw, Woody, 291, 292, 347
Shearing, George, 232–34, 348
"Sheik of Araby, The," 121
Shepp, Archie, 321–322

Shew, Bobby, 250, 355
"Shh/Peaceful," 327
Shields, Larry, 36, 37
"Shine," 63
Shipp, Matthew, 373
Shorter, Wayne, 290n18, 326, 329
"Shout for Joy," 96
Shuffle Along, 117
Sibelius, 370
"Sidewalk Blues," 39, 40
"Sidewalks of Cuba," 241
"Sidewinder, The," 289
Silver, Horace, 221, 260, 288, 291–92, 371
Silver Leaf Band, 47
Simeon, Omer, 41
Simmons, John, 145
Simon, George, 257n2
Simon, Paul, 372
Sims, Joe, 59
Sims, John "Zoot," 242, 346
Sinatra, Frank, 64, 80, 129, 179
"Sing, Sing, Sing," 138, 142
"Singin' the Blues," 81–83, 158, 210
Sissle, Noble, 56
"Sister Cheryl," 350
sitar, 280
Sketches of Spain, 270
Skies of America, 317
slave/slavery, 7
"Sleepy Time Gal," 124
"Slippery Horn," 121
Slonimsky, Nicolas, 279
slumming, 116
Smith, Ada, 113
Smith, Bessie, 17–19, 127, 154, 165, 167
Smith, Cladys "Jabbo," 64
Smith, Henry "Buster," 152, 153, 157,
    190, 191
Smith, Joe, 54, 102
Smith, Mamie, 16, 103
Smith, Paul, 346
Smith, W. O., 91
Smith, Willie "The Lion," 90, 91, 93–94, 98,
    120, 124, 152, 169, 179, 193
Smithsonian Institution, 349
"Smoke Gets in Your Eyes," 224
"Smokehouse Blues," 40
smooth jazz, 336, 337
"Snake Rag," 46
"Snowfall," 256

"Solace," 23, 206
"Solitude," 115, 122, 171
Solo Album, The, 285
*Solo Concerts: Bremen and
    Lausanne,* 340
"Some Other Time," 274
*Something Else! The Music of Ornette
    Coleman,* 314
"Sometimes I'm Happy," 132, 134
Song for My Father, 291
"Song of India," 138
"Song of the Nightingale, The," 190, 238
Sonoma Jazz Festival, 338
Sony (record label), 356 (*see also*
    Columbia *and* CBS)
"Sophisticated Lady," 108, 122
"So Sorry, Please," 219
Soul Gestures in Southern Blues, 352
soul jazz, 285–307
Sound, 358
Sound Grammar, 317
Sound of Jazz, The, 169
Sound of Sonny, The, 284
Southern Syncopated Orchestra, 54
Souza, Luciana, 376
"So What," 273
"Spain," 329
Spalding, Esperanza, 376, 380
"Spangled Banner Minor," 359
Spanier, Francis Joseph "Muggsy," 73,
    78, 137
Spanish law for slaves, 6
"Spanish tinge," 205
spasm bands, 30
Speak Like a Child, 304
Speak No Evil, 290
Specht, Paul, 3
"Special Delivery Stomp," 140
Spellman, A. B., 318nn7,9, 319n11
Spirits, 340
"Spirituals to Swing" concert, 143
Spiritual Unity, 322, 324
Spur of the Moment, 378
"Squeeze Me," 95
"Squirrel, The," 204
St. Charles Theatre, 31
"St. Louis Blues," 12, 18, 19, 37, 65, 161
St. Louis Symphony, 208
Stacy, Jess, 137
"Stampede, The," 105, 106

"Stardust," 63, 140
Stark, John, 22–24
Starr, Milton, 17
"Stars Fell on Alabama," 79
State of the Tenor, 293
"Stealin' Apples," 204
Stearns, Marshall, 4
Steely Dan, 379
Steeplechase (record label), 347
Stein, Gertrude, 117
"Stella by Starlight," 245, 272
"Steppin' into Swing Society," 171
Steward, Herbie, 242
Stewart, Rex, 83, 102, 176
Still Life (Talking), 331
Stitt, Edward "Sonny," 204, 212, 219, 273
Stomping the Blues, 352
"Stomp It Off," 138
"Stompy Jones," 121
"Stoptime Rag," 23
Stormy Weather, 96
Storyville, 29–30
Storyville Club, 226
"Straight, No Chaser," 223
"Strange Fruit," 168
Stravinsky, Igor, 238, 365
Strayhorn, Billy, 171, 172, 181, 182, 293
Streisand, Barbra, 66
"Strictly Confidential," 219
stride piano, 91–93, 96–97
"Stringing the Blues," 84
"A String of Pearls," 146
"Struttin' with Some Barbecue," 60, 65
Stuckey, Sterling, 4
Sublette, Ned, 4, 28
"Subtle Lament," 172
Such Sweet Thunder, 181
"Sugar Foot Stomp," 141
"Suicide Is Painless," 275
Sullivan, Joe, 75, 137
Summer Sequence, 241, 242
"Summertime," 56
"Summit Ridge Drive," 140
Sun Ra, 237, 246–47, 373
"Sun Showers," 168
"Sun Suite of San Francisco," 316
"Superman," 144
Supersonic Jazz, 246–47
Sutton, Tierney, 376
"Swampy River," 120

Swann, Roberta, 260
Sweatman, Wilbur, 25
"Sweet Georgia Brown," 198
"Sweethearts on Parade," 63
Sweet Rain, 262, 328
Swing Era, 67, 71, 72, 195, 197, 198,
    203–4, 238, 246, 261, 355
    big bands, 136–47
    Duke Ellington (middle period
        and later works), 170–83
    jazz combo style in 1930s, 156–70
    Kansas city jazz, 147–56
    "King of Swing, the," 127–36
Swing Era, The, 99, 239
"Swing High," 138
"Swing Low, Sweet Cadillac," 212
"Swingmatism," 193
Sydnor, Doris, 213
Symphony in Black, 123, 167
"Symphony in Riffs," 108
syncopations, 187

Tabackin, Lew, 249–50
Tacuma, Jamaaladeen, 317
"Take Five," 232, 235
"Take the A Train," 172, 181
Takin' Off, 304
"Tanga," 387
"Tangerine," 138
Tanglewood Festival, 349
tango, 206
Tapscott, Horace, 373
"Taps Miller," 266
Tate, George "Buddy," 312
Tatum, Art, 20, 25, 94, 96–99, 141, 158, 163,
    192, 216, 218, 219, 232, 275, 346
"Taxi War Dance," 155
Taylor, Arthur, 224, 287n17
Taylor, Billy, 173
Taylor, Cecil, 221, 227, 282, 310, 315,
    317–21
Taylor, Creed, 296, 336–37
Taylor, Dave, 148
"Tea for Two," 219, 236
Teagarden, Jack, 18, 64, 66, 78–79, 242, 255
"Tears," 49
technological revolution and jazz, 370
Temple, Shirley, 50
"Temptation," 238
"Tempus Fugit," 218

"Tenor Madness," 283
territory band, 148
Terry, Clark, 179, 208
Teschemacher, Frank, 72, 75
"Texas Moaner Blues," 56
"Texas piano," 149, 312
"Texas tenor," 312
"That Da Da Strain," 76
"That Haunting Melody," 59
"That's a Plenty," 72
Théâtre d'Orléans, 31
Theatre Owner's Booking Agency
    (TOBA), 17
*Thesaurus of Scales and Melodic
    Patterns*, 279
"These Foolish Things," 167
They All Played Ragtime, 25
Thiele, Bob, 278n13
Think of One, 350
"Third World, The," 228
"This is for Albert," 291
"This Nearly Was Mine," 319
"This Year's Kisses," 168
Thomas, J. C., 277n12
Thomas, Joe, 124
Thomas, Walter "Foots," 312
Thompson, Edna, 112
Thompson, Eli "Lucky," 202
Thomson, Virgil, 117
Thornhill, Claude, 256–57
Threadgill, Henry, 360
"Three Blind Mice," 77
Three or Four Shades of Blue, 303
3 Phasis, 320
"Three Romances," 250
Thunderbird, 335
"Tickle Toe," 155
"Tiger Rag," 98, 160
Tijuana Moods, 299
Timeless (record label), 347
Time, 181
Time Out, 356
Timmons, Bobby, 289
Tio, Lorenzo, 55
Tizol, Juan, 121, 170, 176, 179, 181, 206
TOBA. *See* Theatre Owner's Booking
    Agency (TOBA)
"Toby," 151
Tomorrow Is the Question, 314
Tonight Show, The, 353

Tormé, Mel, 233, 348
Tough, Dave, 75, 145, 240
Towner, Ralph, 341
"township jazz," 388
"Tozo," 107
traditionalists, 345–57
trad jazz, 253–67
"Transblucency," 178
Treat It Gentle, 5, 57
Treemonisha, 24, 91
Trent, Alphonso, 149
A Tribe Called Quest, 334
"Trinkle Tinkle," 226
Tristano, Lennie, 221, 228–32, 310, 356, 363
"Trolley Song, The," 236
Troupe, Quincy, 256n1, 257n3, 267n6,
    298n22
Trumbauer, Frank, 77, 104, 108, 118
  Bix Beiderbecke and, 81–87
trumpet, 64, 140,148
tuba, 106, 257
"Turkish Mambo," 231
Turpin, Tom, 20, 22
"Harlem Rag," 20–21
Turre, Steve, 355, 380
Tuxedo Brass Band, 47
"Tuxedo Junction," 146
Twitter, 370
"2300 Skiddoo," 228
Tyner, McCoy, 277–78, 285, 293, 295

Uehara, Hiromi, 386
Ullman, Michael, 292n20
Ulmer, James Blood, 317
"Umbrella Man," 212
Umbria Jazz Festival, 341
Underground Musicians' Association, 358
Unit Structures, 297, 320
"Until the Real Thing Comes Along," 155
Urlicht/Primal Light, 367
Us3, 333–34

Vallee, Rudy, 191
"Valley Girl," 333
Van Heusen, Jimmy, 192
Varèse, Edgard, 190, 213
Varieties Theatre, 31–32
Variety, 118, 135
Vaughan, Sarah, 109, 165, 198–99, 346
Vaughan, Stevie Ray, 14

Vechten, Carl Van, 116
Veloso, Caetano, 388
Venuti, Joe, 72, 77, 81, 83–85, 131
Versace, Gary, 295, 380
Very Very Circus, 360
vibraphone, 142, 259
Vidacovich, Pinky, 35
Village Vanguard, 266, 274, 284
violin, 72, 83–84,160
"Viper's Drag," 95
Virgin Beauty, 317
virtual jazz, 369–80
Virtuoso, 346
Voce, Steve, 240n23

"Wabash Stomp," 140
"Wail," 204
Waits, Nasheet, 380
Walcott, Collin, 341
Wald, Elijah, 14
Walker, Junior, 367
"Walkin' and Swingin'," 156
Waller, Thomas "Fats," 20, 64, 74, 79, 90,
    92, 94–96, 98, 106–7, 118, 152, 218,
    294
Wallington, George, 200, 221
Walton, Cedar, 290
"Waltz for Debby," 274
Ward, Helen, 132
Ware, David S., 373
Waring, Fred, 339
"Warm Valley," 175
Warren, Earle, 155
Watanabe, Sadao, 347
"Watermelon Man," 304
Waters, Ethel, 102, 347
Waters, Muddy, 14
Watson, Bobby, 216, 355
Watters, Lu, 253, 254
Watts, Heather, 321
Watts, Isaac, 8
Watts, Jeff "Tain," 351
Way Out West, 284
"Weather Bird," 62–63
Webb, Chick, 124, 125, 346
Webern, Anton, 365
Webster, Ben, 99, 102, 162, 169, 171,
    173–77, 193, 197, 269, 314, 347
Webster, Freddie, 198
"Wednesday Night Prayer Meeting," 300

Wein, George, 348
"Well, Get It!," 138
Wells, Dickie, 102, 154, 161
Well-Tempered Clavier, The, 341
"Well, You Needn't," 222, 224
West Africa, culture in, 9
Westbrook, Mike, 347
"West Coast Blues," 296
West Coast jazz, 263–64
"West End Blues," 62, 201, 229, 239
Weston, Randy, 163
West Side Story, 232
"What a Little Moonlight Can Do," 167
"What Am I Here For," 286
"What a Wonderful World," 66
"What Is This Thing Called Love," 301
"What Love," 301
"When Johnny Comes Marching Home," 373
"When Lights Are Low," 108, 197
"Whispering," 85
White, Herbert, 117
"White Heat," 124
Whiteman, Paul, 73, 79, 80, 81, 83,
    85, 100, 105, 107, 213, 256
"Whiteman Stomp, The," 107
Whitey's Lindy Hoppers, 117
"Who Can I Turn To," 350
Whyte, Zack, 148
Wiedoeft, Rudy, 82, 104
"Wild Dog, The," 84
Wildflowers, 360
"Wild Man Blues," 60
William Morris Agency, 174
Williams, Clarence, 19, 50, 54
Williams, Charles "Cootie," 115, 121,
    171, 176, 218
Williams, Jessica, 355
Williams, Joe, 154, 248
Williams, Marion, 353
Williams, Martin, 50, 349
Williams, Mary Lou, 132, 145, 147,
    155–157, 288
Williams, Tony, 304–5
"Willie the Weeper," 60
Willis, Dusty, 14
Wills, Bob, 149
Will to Swing, The, 232
Wilmer, Valerie, 197n4, 313n3
Wilson, Cassandra, 348, 366, 376
Wilson, Derby, 123
Wilson, Phil, 240

Wilson, Phillip, 360
Wilson, Quinn, 198
Wilson, Shadow, 198, 224
Wilson, Teddy, 61, 62, 80, 131, 134–35, 142
Wilson, Wash, 11
Winter, Paul, 341
Winther, Nils, 347
Witches and Devils, 324
Wolff, Francis, 219
Wolff, Michael, 380
"Wolverine Blues," 44
Women in jazz, 15–16, 155–56
Wong, Herb, 243, 380
Wood, Chris, 336
"Woodchopper's Ball," 239
Woods, Phil, 215, 347
World Saxophone Quartet (WSQ), 364
World's Columbian Exposition in
    Chicago, 23
Wright, Eugene, 236
WSQ. *See* World Saxophone Quartet (WSQ)

Yahel, Sam, 295
Yamashita, Yōsuke, 386
"Yardbird Suite," 202
Yerba Buena Jazz Band, 254
"Yes, Indeed!," 138
"Yesternow," 327
"Yonder Come the Blues," 17
"You Are Too Beautiful," 278
Youmans, Vincent, 236
Young, Lester, 82, 102, 152–54, 156–58,
    168, 180, 190, 197, 212, 233, 241
    achievements, 164
    early life, 157
    modern jazz and, 163–64
    professional career, 157–58
Young, James "Trummy," 124
"You're Just a No Account," 168
"Your Father's Moustache," 241
YouTube, 370
"You Understand," 108

Zappa, Frank, 359
Zawinul, Joe, 163, 306, 329–30
Zeitgeist, 275
Zenph Studios, 370
Zodiac Suite, 156
Zorn, John, 359, 364–65
Zurke, Bob, 137
Zwerin, Michael, 82